AN APPLIED COURSE IN REAL OPTIONS VALUATION

Richard L. Shockley, Jr.

*Associate Professor of Finance and
CenterPoint Faculty Fellow*

*Kelley School of Business
Indiana University*

THOMSON

SOUTH-WESTERN

Australia · Brazil · Canada · Mexico · Singapore · Spain · United Kingdom · United States

THOMSON

SOUTH-WESTERN

An Applied Course in Real Options Valuation
Richard L. Shockley, Jr.

VP/Editorial Director:
Jack W. Calhoun

VP/Editor-in-Chief:
Alex von Rosenberg

Publisher:
Steve Momper

Executive Editor:
Mike Reynolds

Sr. Developmental Editor:
Patricia Taylor

Marketing Manager:
Jason Krall

Assoc. Content Project Manager:
Jean Buttrom

Manager of Technology, Editorial:
Vicky True

Technology Project Manager:
Matt McKinney

Manufacturing Coordinator:
Sandee Milewski

Production House:
International Typesetting and
Composition

Art Director:
Bethany Casey

Internal Designer:
Design Matters

Cover Designer:
Design Matters

Cover Images:
© Getty Images, Inc.

Manager Image Acquisition:
Linda Ellis

Printer:
RR Donnelley
Crawfordsville, IN

Library of Congress Control
Number: 2006906379

For more information about our
products, contact us at:

Thomson Learning Academic
Resource Center
1-800-423-0563

Thomson Higher Education
5191 Natorp Boulevard
Mason, OH 45040
USA

THOMSON SOUTH-WESTERN
Finance Series

THOMSON

SOUTH-WESTERN ™

Introductory Courses

Personal Finance
Boone/Kurtz/Hearth: *Planning Your Financial Future*, 4e
Gitman/Joehnk: *Personal Financial Planning*, 10e

Survey of Finance
Besley/Brigham: *Principles of Finance*, 3e
Mayo: *Basic Finance: An Introduction to Financial Institutions, Investments, and Management*, 9e

Entrepreneurial Finance
Leach/Melicher: *Entrepreneurial Finance*, 2e
Stancill: *Entrepreneurial Finance for New and Emerging Businesses*

Corporate Finance

Corporate Finance/Financial Management— Undergraduate
Besley/Brigham: *Essentials of Managerial Finance*, 13e
Brigham/Houston: *Fundamentals of Financial Management, Concise* 5e
Brigham/Houston: *Fundamentals of Financial Management*, 11e
Lasher: *Practical Financial Management*, 4e
Megginson/Smart: *Introduction to Corporate Finance*
Moyer/McGuigan/Kretlow: *Contemporary Financial Management*, 10e
Moyer/McGuigan/Rao: *Fundamentals of Contemporary Financial Management*, 2e

International Finance
Butler: *Multinational Finance*, 3e
Crum/Brigham/Houston: *Fundamentals of International Finance*
Madura: *International Financial Management*, 8e
Madura: *International Financial Management, Abridged* 8e

Intermediate/Advanced Undergraduate Corporate Finance
Brigham/Daves: *Intermediate Financial Management*, 9e

Capital Budgeting/Long-Term Capital Budgeting
Seitz/Ellison: *Capital Budgeting and Long-Term Financing Decisions*, 4e

Working Capital Management/Short-Term Financial Management
Maness/Zietlow: *Short-Term Financial Management*, 3e

Valuation
Daves/Ehrhardt/Shrieves: *Corporate Valuation: A Guide for Managers and Investors*

Financial Analysis & Planning
Harrington: *Corporate Financial Analysis in a Global Environment*, 7e

MBA/Graduate Corporate Finance
Brigham/Ehrhardt: *Financial Management: Theory and Practice*, 11e
Ehrhardt/Brigham: *Corporate Finance: A Focused Approach*, 2e
Hawawini/Viallet: *Finance for Executives: Managing for Value Creation*, 3e
Smart/Megginson/Gitman: *Corporate Finance*, 2e

Corporate Finance—Supplemental Products
Klein/Brigham: *Finance Online Case Library*
Mayes/Shank: *Financial Analysis with Microsoft® Excel*, 4e

Investments Courses

Investments—Undergraduate
Hearth/Zaima: *Contemporary Investments: Security and Portfolio Analysis*, 4e
Mayo: *Basic Investments*
Mayo: *Investments: An Introduction*, 8e
Reilly/Norton: *Investments*, 7e
Strong: *Practical Investment Management*, 4e

Derivatives/Futures and Options
Chance/Brooks: *An Introduction to Derivatives and Risk Management*, 7e
Strong: *Derivatives: An Introduction*, 2e
Stulz: *Risk Management and Derivatives*

Fixed Income
Grieves/Griffiths: *A Fixed Income Internship: Introduction to Fixed Income Analytics, Volume 1*

Real Options
Shockley: *An Applied Course in Real Options Valuation*

MBA/Graduate Investments
Reilly/Brown: *Investment Analysis and Portfolio Management*, 8e
Strong: *Portfolio Construction, Management, and Protection*, 4e

Financial Institutions Courses

Financial Institutions and Markets
Madura: *Financial Markets and Institutions*, 7e
Madura: *Financial Markets and Institutions, Abridged* 7e

Financial Institutions Management
Gardner/Mills/Cooperman: *Managing Financial Institutions*, 5e

Money & Capital Markets
Liaw: *Capital Markets*

Commercial Banking/Bank Management
Koch/MacDonald: *Bank Management*, 6e

Insurance

Risk Management and Insurance/Introduction to Insurance
Trieschmann/Hoyt/Sommer: *Risk Management and Insurance*, 12e

ABOUT THE AUTHOR

Richard L. Shockley, Jr. holds a Ph.D. in Finance from Indiana University and a B.S. in Commerce from the University of Virginia. His research has appeared in both scholarly and applied journals, and he has received numerous teaching honors including the Indiana University Trustees Teaching Award and the Rice University Phi Beta Kappa Teaching Prize. Professor Shockley speaks frequently with large and mid-size firms about how they might adopt the real options paradigm into their capital budgeting systems.

In memory of my dad,

Richard L. Shockley (1925 – 2005)

and of my father-in-law,

James L. Sisco (1938 – 2006)

ACKNOWLEDGMENTS

This project has taken quite a few years and a lot of effort, and it would not have become what you see without the help of many people. I'd like to publicly acknowledge several individuals and groups who made particularly noteworthy contributions.

My first words of thanks must definitely go to Bob Jennings, my department chair in the Kelley School of Business at Indiana University. In 1998, Bob suggested that I construct a new MBA-level elective on real options. I agreed not because I knew anything about the subject, but instead because I was curious to learn something about it. Bob is a terrific scholar and a great administrator, and without his foresight I never would have gone down this path.

Mike Mercier, formerly the Senior Acquisitions Editor for finance at South-Western, was the first to see a potential market for this material. He courted me for several years until I became ready to turn the course into a text. Mike has moved on to other things now, but his early bullishness about the book was critical. He was succeeded by yet another Mike, Mike Reynolds, who expertly managed the production and graciously put up with my delays.

Tom Arnold (University of Richmond) and Mike Ferguson (University of Cincinnati) stand out for their extraordinary help. These two guys spent many hours reading each iteration of the manuscript and then proffering extremely valuable comments and suggestions on both material and pedagogy. More important to the outcome, however, was their enthusiasm. I thought about abandoning the project out of frustration on several occasions, and the only thing that kept me going was their encouragement and unconditional support. Tom even agreed to write the end-of-chapter problems and their solutions. I'm a lucky man to have *two* friends like Tom and Mike.

Domingo Castelo Joaquin (Illinois State University) used the manuscript in his own real options course and provided some excellent technical suggestions and corrections on several of the chapters. Yihong Xia (late of University of Pennsylvania) made an important contribution to Chapter 11 before her untimely death; I think of her every time I look at that material. Chapters 1, 2, and 8 improved substantially due to the input of Raul Guerrero (Decision Dynamics), who supplied the eye of a well-versed practitioner. I am especially grateful to Richard Simonds (Michigan State University), Luke Sparvero (University of Texas at Arlington), and Luiz Brandão (formerly of the University of Texas at Austin, now at Catholic University of Rio de Janeiro and IAG Business School) for their very detailed and helpful reviews of the manuscript.

Guofu Zhou (Washington University in St. Louis), David Nachman (Georgia State University), and Connie Lütolf-Carrol also used early versions of the book in their courses. I thank them and their students for their feedback.

My colleagues at Indiana University were uniformly patient and understanding with me throughout the process. Turning a course into a text is a lot harder and more time consuming than I ever imagined, and this project has surely taken away from my ability to contribute to my department and my school. George Hettenhouse, Bob Klemkosky, Wayne Winston, Scott Smart,

Robert Hauswald, Dirk Hackbarth, and Andrey Ukhov deserve particular thanks for their guidance, insights, and assistance.

I also want to note the very special role played by my excellent students at the Kelley School of Business at Indiana University, at the Olin School of Business at Washington University in St. Louis, and at Sungkyunkwan University's Graduate School of Business (Seoul, Republic of Korea). One of the most enjoyable parts of my job as an academic is that I get to interact with, and learn from, a large number of very interesting and clever students. As you can see in the text, most of my case examples were inspired by student term papers. I have a file cabinet full of great student-generated ideas that didn't make this text but nevertheless helped me understand better both the subject matter and how to teach it.

Finally, and most importantly, I want to publicly thank my lovely wife Denise, who put up with my distracted state and general grumpiness while I struggled to make all this work. I could not have done it without you, sweetheart.

TABLE OF CONTENTS

Part 3   The Binomial Model

Part 4

European-Style Real Options

Part 5 — American-Style Real Options

Part 6   Conclusion

PREFACE AND USER'S GUIDE

This book sprouted from a curriculum innovation in the MBA program at Indiana University's Kelley School of Business. In 1998, we decided to create a point of differentiation by developing a unique set of advanced corporate finance electives. My department chairman thought that a real options course would be value-creating for our students as well as eye-catching to our outside constituents. I didn't know much about the subject, but I had more than a passing interest in learning about it, so I agreed to create the new course as an experiment. I reckoned that I could pull together a half-semester's worth of material from existing articles, published cases, and the like.

When I started planning the actual course, however, I realized that I faced a problem. The existing literature looked like a barbell: On the one end was a large set of very general articles that explained *why* managers should think about optionality in corporate assets, and on the other was a burgeoning group of scholarly papers that generated very precise answers to very precise real options questions in the language of academia. What was missing was the middle piece—the bridge that would take managers from the point of understanding *why* they should use option pricing in their capital budgeting processes to the point of knowing *how* to actually go about doing it.

The goal of this book is to fill that gap. I've strived to create a set of learning experiences like we have for teaching standard capital budgeting: a series of canonical examples and case studies that walk the student through the most basic problems and then into increasingly more complex and difficult situations.

Target Audience

My target audience consists of MBA students, advanced undergraduates, and practicing managers. I've taught the course at all three levels, and I've found that the only necessary differences in approach involve pace and attention to background material. To remain faithful to my target market, I've done several things to limit the technical sophistication required. If you are comfortable with algebra and basic probability, if you understand continuous compounding of interest, and if you can use a calculator to take a logarithm and raise e to a power (i.e., calculate an antilogarithm), then you can make it through the math in this book. No calculus is necessary.

Be that as it may, I've worked very hard to avoid taking too many intellectual shortcuts. When at all possible, I try to present the intuition behind *why* our models work the way they do as well as the assumptions that provide the foundation. There are a few places where I've had to compromise, but I've made every effort to be upfront about these.

Necessary Prerequisites/Background

I designed this text to be used in a finance elective. Before starting this book, the student/reader needs to be familiar with the basics of corporate capital budgeting (identification of incremental free cash flows, the CAPM, risk-adjusted discounting, the effect of leverage, etc.), the basics of options (definitions of calls and puts, standard payoff diagrams, the Black-Scholes model, etc.), and rudimentary probability and statistics. The book also assumes that the reader has had some exposure to the idea that many corporate investments have option-like features. The good introductory corporate finance texts cover all of these topics in sufficient detail.

Outline of the Book

The real options paradigm presents a marriage of basic asset pricing and corporate finance. This is nothing new, as all of the rules of corporate investment trace back to the individual's portfolio problem. Unfortunately, over the last 30 years the pedagogy of corporate finance has not kept up with the modern developments in asset pricing. Just about every major corporate finance textbook presents the foundations of finance in a world of certainty. This makes it easy to motivate things like discounted cash flow, but makes it hard to introduce options in a consistent framework—in a world of certainty, there can be no options. Additionally, it creates the appearance of a huge difference between traditionally taught valuation techniques (such as DCF) and option pricing, even though both are just valuation by arbitrage. This apparent (but nonexistent) disconnect between "old-fashioned" valuation techniques and option-pricing techniques has led to a tremendous amount of misunderstanding about how option pricing fits into the corporate finance toolkit.

Because of this, I've devoted the first part of the book to a rather lengthy review of valuation. The first chapter is introductory in nature: It presents some motivating examples, a normative presentation of how managers should evaluate investment decisions using financial market prices and linear pricing, a brief statement of how DCF follows that prescription, and an attempt at an explanation for why DCF doesn't always work. The second chapter provides a more detailed presentation of the basic idea of arbitrage valuation in financial markets when future cash flows are *risky.* The third chapter then summarizes how and why the principles of valuation from the financial markets should be applied to corporate investments in real assets. In the fourth chapter, I turn to a review of derivatives pricing in which I develop the binomial model in more detail than you'll find elsewhere. That all sets the stage for the real-world applications.

What my academic readers will notice through all of this is that I develop things using what is called a *state price* approach. The notion of macroeconomic states, the priced value of consumption in each possible future state, and the covariance of a financial or real asset's conditional mean payoffs with priced consumption across states together constitute the single principle of risk and return. All arbitrage valuation techniques reflect equilibrium state prices, and recognition of this helps tremendously in describing many subtle but important things (like risk-neutral probabilities, why options are risky, how option pricing captures risk, etc.).

Ultimately, though, the book is about corporate investment, and the majority of the text concerns actual problems. In the early examples, I've simplified things so as to make certain teaching points; later examples become more and more complex. Some caveats are in order. First, I will assume throughout the book that the yield curve is flat and that there is no interest rate risk. Second, I will work in a world where there's only one source of uncertainty; we'll follow the standard assumption that random future asset prices are described by a lognormal probability distribution (i.e., log changes are described by a normal distribution).

Suggested Course Structures

My MBA-level elective has only 13 sessions, so I have to be careful to identify the crucial learning objectives for the course and use my time wisely. I spend one day introducing the course and motivating the material (Chapter 1), and I then launch into a four-day development of derivatives valuation in the binomial model (Chapter 4). In those four days, I spend one day on the basic binomial model (Section 4.2), one entire day on state pricing (Section 4.3), one day on the first two of the three simplified real-world problems (Section 4:4), and one day on extending things to a multiperiod framework (Sections 4.1, 4.5, 4.6, and 4.7). I then devote one day to Chapter 5, one day to Chapter 6, one day to Chapter 7, one day to Chapter 8, one day to Chapter 9, one day to Chapters 10 and 11 combined, one day to Chapters 12 and 13 combined, and then one day to either Chapter 14 or Chapter 15 (or some other material, depending on the color of my mood ring at the time).

I have the luxury of getting a full 90 minutes for each class session, and I use every bit of the time. What might surprise you, though, is that once I get into the real-world cases (Chapter 5 and beyond), I spend the vast majority of class time just framing the problems and setting them up. The mechanics of valuation are quite simple once you've mastered Chapter 4. The hard part of real options valuation is actually identifying the optionality and framing the question correctly. If you are teaching this as a course, don't get lost in the technique—spend sufficient time setting up the problem and working through the *whys*.

Because of the brevity of our term at IU, I have to skip Chapters 2 and 3. I believe the material is important, and I require that students read it and study some additional material I provide. If I had more time, however, I would cover this.

If your term lasts longer than mine, then you might first consider including a refresher on capital budgeting and the basics of options (particularly if you are working with undergraduates or are unsure of your students' backgrounds). You might also include some of the excellent introductory articles on real options referenced in the bibliography to Chapter 1. You could add Chapters 2 and 3, if you like, as well as topics mentioned in Chapter 16 (Monte Carlo simulation, or path dependent options, or rainbows, for example). Finally, you might spend a little time discussing the managerial implications of real options and how the real options paradigm can help managers think about strategy; that topic is covered in other sources, and I don't have anything new to contribute, so I've omitted it from this book.

A Note on Rounding

To keep the exhibits clean (and make them fit the page), I've had to round up or down. I've allowed Microsoft Excel to do this for me, and I've always tried to link calculations in my spreadsheets (as opposed to manually truncating an output of a calculation and then using that *truncated* number as an input somewhere else).

Hence, you won't be able to reconstruct my spreadsheets exactly if you use truncated numbers (i.e., if you use the numbers I present in the text). For example, in Chapter 7, my underlying value is actually $8,647,189,602.87 (rounded to the nearest cent), but I've presented it in the text in the more simple form $8,647 million. If you were to try to reconstruct my binomial tree of that asset's value by working in millions and entering your underlying value as *exactly* $8,467, your tree will look different from mine. A similar statement holds for all of the other inputs.

1

MOTIVATION

Chapter 1   Introduction

INTRODUCTION

If you crack open just about any introductory corporate finance text, you'll learn from one of its early chapters that a corporate financial manager faces three essential decisions: the investment decision, the financial structure decision, and the dividend decision. Even though there are three important decisions, a typical introductory course in corporate finance devotes most of its time to the first. The investment decision involves the use of investor capital, and it focuses on the following question:

> *Suppose that your company is contemplating investment in a new project. The project is financially risky: It requires a substantial commitment of capital upfront, but its future cash returns are uncertain. How should you, a financial analyst within the firm, decide whether or not to recommend investment in the new project?*

I'm sure you remember the prescription. If the role of a manager is to maximize shareholder value, then the manager should evaluate the project by calculating its *net present value* (or *NPV*). Most students I've run across remember NPV like this

Project NPV = Present value of project's cash flows − Cost of investment   (1.1)

or something similar. This, then, gives us the *NPV rule for investment:* Accept the project if its NPV is greater than or equal to zero, and reject it otherwise; if you must choose between mutually exclusive projects that all have positive NPV, take the one with the highest NPV; if capital is constrained, allocate capital so that you maximize the total NPV of projects accepted.

The NPV concept is the workhorse of corporate finance, because NPV tells us how much value would be *created or destroyed* by a corporate use of investor capital. The reason that NPV measures value creation or destruction is because, when estimated correctly, it gives the manager a sharp comparison between the firm's investment opportunity on the one hand and the investor's similar-risk opportunity in the financial markets on the other. If the project displays positive NPV, then the manager expects it to earn a higher rate of return than a similar-risk financial market portfolio. By investing in this project, the manager does something for the investors that the investors cannot do for themselves—hence the project creates value.

1.1 Theory Versus Practice

Unfortunately, it is not always easy to move ideas from the classroom to the executive suite. Estimation of a project's NPV is straightforward in some situations but difficult in others. For certain types of projects, a good estimate of NPV requires some advanced tools—tools that most managers don't yet have. In these situations, managers have learned to either (1) make ad hoc adjustments to their NPV estimates based on prior experience and judgment or (2) ignore NPV entirely and base the investment decision on either intuition or some rule of thumb.

We have evidence of this. In a very nice survey of executives of large American corporations,[1] John Graham and Cam Harvey of Duke University document that only about 75% of CFOs use NPV *always* or *almost always* in their capital budgeting processes. What this means, then, is that roughly 25% of CFOs *never, rarely,* or only *sometimes* use NPV to support investment decisions. Why would managers *sometimes* use NPV? I'm sure there are a variety of reasons, but I'm willing to bet that many of these managers have encountered situations where their standard approaches to the NPV estimate give nonsensical results.

What makes the Graham and Harvey data particularly interesting is the suggestion of an association between firm characteristics and capital budgeting practices: NPV is less pervasive in firms that have low leverage, firms with low dividend payout ratios, and private firms. Even though academics still don't have much to say about how firms *should* choose capital structures, dividend policies, and corporate architectures, we do know a few things about what types of firms make different selections. And, you know what? Low-leverage, low-dividend, and private firms share one important characteristic: They tend to have substantial growth opportunities. These sorts of firms tend to create value by creating options on new opportunities and optimally exploiting these flexibilities over time. As we'll see in the rest of this chapter, application of the NPV rule to investments that create flexibilities (or options) requires an advanced set of tools—tools that most managers don't yet have.

My goal in writing this book is to help managers develop the tools necessary for extending the NPV concept to evaluation of investment opportunities that create, maintain, or alter future flexibilities. I'm not out to change the way managers think, but rather to put some science onto the intuition and judgment that they are currently using. Before I show you some examples of the situations that I'm talking about, I need to make sure you understand two things.

1.2 Two Important Concepts

First, I need to stress to you that NPV is *not* a measure of a project's value—rather, NPV is a measure of *value creation* (if positive) or *value destruction* (if negative). NPV is a relative measure only. If you look hard at Equation (1.1), you'll see that NPV is actually a comparison between the present value of a project and the cost of actually investing in or buying that project. The reason that this is the appropriate comparison for measuring value creation or destruction—and something you may not have completely grasped when you took your first finance course—is that when we say *present value of the project,* we actually mean *financial market value of the project.* The present value of a project is actually the price that the investor would have to pay in the financial markets to create a portfolio that gives the same future cash flows (with same timing and risk) as the firm's

---

[1] See Graham and Harvey (2001).

project. If this is higher than the manager's cost of investing in the project and buying those same future cash flows in the *real asset* market, then the project has positive NPV, because the manager can buy the future cash flows for the investor more cheaply than the investor can.

This concept of the *present value* of a project actually being its financial market value is extremely important for the purpose of this book. It is so important, in fact, that I want to restate the NPV rule to accurately reflect it. The following is the definition of a project's *true NPV* that we will use from this point forward:

$$\text{\textit{True} project NPV} = \begin{array}{c} \text{\textit{True} financial market value of project's} \\ \text{incremental future cash flows} \end{array} - \begin{array}{c} \text{Capital investment required} \\ \text{for project} \end{array} \qquad (1.2)$$

If this is slightly unfamiliar or uncomfortable to you, don't worry. I'll get to a more detailed explanation later in this chapter. For now, I'd like for you to just expand your mind a bit and keep Equation (1.2) in your thoughts.

Equation (1.2) leads me to the second issue we must be very careful about. What Equation (1.2) clearly shows is that to *evaluate* a project using the NPV rule, we must *value* the project first. In other words, we have to come up with a way to estimate a project's true financial market value *before* applying the NPV rule. So we need a valuation technique, and I'm willing to bet that you covered several valuation techniques in your introductory class. The one on which I'm sure you spent the most time was discounted cash flow (DCF) analysis.

DCF is a way of *approximating* the financial market value of a project, and we usually teach the following steps:

1. Estimate the future *incremental free cash flows* that the firm anticipates harvesting from the project. Since the project's cash flows are risky, you should estimate the project's expected (or mean) incremental free cash flows. Make sure you are using incrementals—the difference between the firm's overall free cash flows *with* the project versus the firm's overall free cash flows *without* the project (the base case).
2. Using some asset pricing model like the *capital asset pricing model* (CAPM), estimate the required rate of return that is commensurate with the systematic risk of the project's cash flows. You may have called this the *risk-adjusted rate of return,* the *hurdle rate,* the *opportunity cost of funds,* the *cost of capital,* or perhaps even something else.
3. Discount the expected incremental free cash flow at each future date by the required rate of return, using the following formula:

$$\text{Discounted value of a cash flow in } t \text{ years} = \frac{\text{Expected cash flow in } t \text{ years}}{(1 + r)^t} \qquad (1.3)$$

where r is the annual required rate of return identified in Step 2.
4. Sum up the discounted values of all future risky cash flows thrown off by the project to get the DCF approximation of the project's financial market value.

You probably call the discounted values present values, and I'll bet you usually refer to the DCF value of a project as the project's present value. I have no problem with that, because that usage is ubiquitous. What I want to warn you against, however, is the widespread misperception that DCF and NPV go hand in hand. They do not. As we saw in Equation (1.2), NPV requires a valuation as an input. DCF is one of many valuation tools, and you probably are familiar with some of the others (like option pricing models or valuation by multiples). All of the textbook valuation tools are variations on a single theoretical theme, and each is designed to work in a specific situation. The key to effective application of the NPV rule is to use the right valuation tool in the right situation.

You can actually make a very serious mistake in your NPV calculation if you use a valuation technique that is inappropriate for your situation. DCF is sometimes appropriate, but other times not, and one of my teaching objectives is to help you understand the situations where exclusive use of DCF as an input to your NPV analysis might lead you to make bad decisions. For me to describe exactly *why* you might need to work through this book on real options, I'll have to show you the potential shortcomings of calculating a project's NPV using a DCF approach to valuation. And given that the concepts of DCF and NPV are hopelessly intertwined in some peoples' brains, I'll use very careful language. Hence, here is one very important definition: From now on, I'll use the term *static NPV* to mean "NPV calculated using discounted cash flow (DCF)."

$$\text{Static project NPV} = \frac{DCF \text{ approximation of true financial market}}{\text{value of project's incremental future cash flows}} - \frac{\text{Capital investment required for}}{\text{project}} \quad (1.4)$$

Why *static* NPV? You'll have to wait and see. At this point, I want to show you several examples of situations where managers are aware that static NPV (which is the only NPV they know) can lead to incorrect decisions. After the examples, we'll explore why.

There are two broad circumstances where managers rationally use some non-NPV decision criteria to make value-creating decisions: In one, managers seem to be appropriately investing even though the static NPV is negative; and in the other, managers seem to be appropriately not investing even though the static NPV is positive.[2] We'll look at examples of the former phenomenon first.

1.3 Examples of Managers Investing When the Static NPV Is Negative

Example 1.1 (Home Depot)

The Home Depot, Inc., pioneered the "big box" store concept in the do-it-yourself retail home-improvement sector. Beginning with only three stores and a great business plan in 1979, the company grew to more than 1,800 stores (and an equity market capitalization of nearly $100 billion) by 2005.

Home Depot's strategy for value creation was to consolidate the fragmented home improvement supply industry by building very large storefronts that combined the low prices of warehouse retailing with the knowledgeable customer service of hardware stores. A key to the company's success was its ability to purchase inventory in very large quantities and thus command rock-bottom prices from its suppliers. American do-it-yourselfers (including your author) quickly learned to like Home Depot's concept.

It should come as no surprise to you that this sort of explosive growth required large amounts of external capital. Between 1991 and 1995 the company issued $805 million in convertible debt and $420 million in equity to grow from 145 stores to 340. What may startle you, however, is that in 1991—right at the time that the company had huge cash needs to add Home Depot stores, and right when each new Home Depot store was clearly a value-creating proposition—Home Depot's managers invested around $17 million in a new project that everyone knew had a negative static NPV.

---

[2] The key terms here are *rational* and *value creating*. I freely accept that there are other situations where managers are rationally ignoring the NPV rule because they have skewed incentives that lead them to make value-destroying decisions, and further situations where managers may be acting irrationally. Here, I'm focusing on settings where managers are doing the *right thing* by avoiding the textbook NPV rule based on a DCF approach to valuation.

The new project was a single storefront in San Diego that the firm called Expo Design Center. The Expo store was built to be a "one-stop interior-design wonderland," in which a customer could purchase literally everything needed to furnish and decorate a living space "from inspiration to installation."[3] Instead of targeting Home Depot's do-it-yourself market, management tailored the Expo Design Center to cater to the "do-it-for-me" crowd. The store offered expensive fixtures along with interior design and installation services. A notable feature of the store was that it included dozens of full-size walk-through kitchens and bathrooms, which showcased the high-end products on offer (as well as the store's design expertise and project management skills).

As I mentioned, the investment in this store had a negative static NPV—and management knew it. The biggest problem with the single Expo store was that its turnover would not be large enough to give management any purchasing power over suppliers. As a one-off investment, the single Expo store was nothing more than 10 individual specialty stores (bath, kitchen, outdoor, lighting & lamps, carpets & rugs, appliances, solid flooring, fabrics & drapes, custom closets, and decorative accessories) combined under one very large roof. Figure 1.1 gives my estimation of the static NPV of Home Depot's 1991 investment in the Expo concept store.

Let's make sure we've got the interpretation right. Figure 1.1 shows us that the static NPV of the Expo investment was −$3.221 million. The major input for this was the DCF approximation of the financial market value of the new store, which was $13.779 million. In other words, Home Depot's investors could have recreated the single Expo store's expected cash flows via a financial market portfolio at an estimated cost of only $13.779 million. It "cost" the firm $17 million to buy those same cash flows, so the investment destroyed value from a static NPV perspective.

Why would Home Depot's managers invest very precious capital in a store with negative static NPV when the money could have been used for growth in the value-creating segment?

Figure 1.1	Static NPV Analysis of Expo Design Center Concept Store[4]

	1991	1992	1993	1994	1995
Real cost of capital	10.7%				
Real perpetual growth at maturity	0%				
			Figures (in thousands)		
Free cash flows from open Expo store		−$4,634	−$3,201	−$488	$3,039
Continuation value of mature Expo store					$28,402
Total		−$4,634	−$3,201	−$488	$31,441
Discounted value of incremental cash flows from open Expo store	$13,779				
Investment required to open store	$17,000				
Static NPV of Expo store investment	−$3,221				

This is the *DCF approximation* of the true market value of the Expo project.

[3] *Source:* The Home Depot Inc. website, www.homedepot.com, June 1, 2005.

[4] *Source:* Author's assumptions. I assumed a 90,000 square-foot store that would mature in four years time. In 1991, 1992, 1993, and 1994 (and beyond), sales per square-feet would be $138, $197, $296, and $394, respectively; gross margin would be 32.9%, 37.8%, 43.5% and 50% of sales, respectively; and operating expenses would be 6.1%, 5.8%, 5.5%, and 5.3% of sales, respectively. I calculated taxes at 39%, and used straight-line depreciation. The investment requirement includes land, building, and initial net working capital.

Example 1.2 (Boeing)

In the early 1990s, managers at Boeing thought about the possibility of offering a super-jumbo jet—a jet that could carry up to 800 passengers—around the turn of the new century. To do so, the company would have to spend at least $500 million on preliminary design, over five years time, before the product could be offered to the airlines (and obviously before production could begin). If Boeing were to do the preliminary design, which would involve all R&D efforts required to actually quote performance characteristics, operating costs, and sales price to the potential customers, then the company could solicit orders starting in 2001; then, if orders turned out to be sufficiently strong, Boeing could commence building planes.

After a substantial amount of analysis, the executives determined that Boeing could not expect to sell enough of these behemoths to justify the enormous cost of actually building the first one (I give more details about this example in Chapter 5). To be more specific, Boeing estimated that the cost of actually "bending metal" for the new plane (i.e., the cost of turning a completed preliminary design into the first production plane) would be $20 billion in 2001 dollars, while the 2001 present value of the expected incremental free cash flows from selling planes on a go-forward basis would be only $18.5 billion.

In other words, the super-jumbo-jet product was expected to be value-destroying: In 1996, the *expected* 2001 static NPV was $18.5 billion − $20 billion = −$1.5 billion; discounted back five years to 1996 at the company's 13% cost of capital gives a 1996 static NPV of −$814 million. And this does not even consider the cost of preliminary design!

What this means, then, is that in 1996 the expected future free cash flows to Boeing that would result from the investment in preliminary design would be exactly *zero,* because Boeing's expectation was that the company would not end up in the super-jumbo-jet business. Nevertheless, even though Boeing management thought that they would never build a single super-jumbo jet, they invested approximately $500 million into preliminary design of it anyway. Of course, since the $500 million preliminary design investment created no expected cash flow, the static NPV of the preliminary design investment was −$500 million, as shown in Figure 1.2.

Figure 1.2	Static NPV Analysis of Boeing's 1996 Investment in Preliminary Design of a Super-Jumbo Jet Airliner[5]						
Cost of capital	13%				Figures (in millions)		
		1996	1997	1998	1999	2000	2001
Expected 2001 present value of free cash flows from producing and selling planes							$0
Expected 2001 cost of building production facility and prototype plane							$0
Total							$0
1996 Discounted value of incremental cash flows from investment in preliminary design		$0					
1996 Cost of investment in preliminary design		−$500					
Static NPV of investment in preliminary design		−$500					

> This is the *DCF approximation* of the true market value of the preliminary design investment.

[5]*Source:* Author's estimates.

Again, let's get the interpretation right. DCF approximates the financial market value of the preliminary R&D investment to be $0, because (in expectation) the preliminary R&D investment creates no future incremental cash flows at all. Why would Boeing knowingly invest a large sum of money into preliminary design of a plane that they thought they would never build? Isn't this just out-and-out value destruction?

Example 1.3 (Pharmaceuticals R&D)

The classic example of managers investing when the static NPV is negative occurs in the pharmaceuticals industry. Just about every financial manager at a pharma company will tell you that R&D expenditures appear to be value-destroying from a static NPV perspective. Why? For several reasons. First, successful completion of an R&D program, from initial investigation through marketing of the new compound, is enormously expensive. Second, successful R&D takes many years, so the potential free cash flows from a new drug will be discounted heavily for time value. Third, the likelihood that a new drug makes it through all phases of clinical trials and then is approved by the Food and Drug Administration (FDA) is rather small. Finally, even if the drug goes to market, it probably won't generate lots of free cash flows. It turns out that the distribution of cash flows of approved drugs is heavily skewed—the median new drug does not generate enough cash flow to cover a drug company's average R&D costs.[6]

Let's examine the typical development of a new drug at a pharmaceuticals company. The earliest stages of development are often called *discovery* and *preclinical*, and they involve turning a scientific idea into a molecular compound and the testing of that compound on animals. *Clinical* (or human) testing then usually requires three phases. In Phase I, a small number of healthy humans take the drug so that the drug company can learn about safe dosages, absorption rates, toxicity, and so forth. In Phase II, the company learns about safety and efficacy by giving the new drug to a larger number of humans (sometimes into the hundreds) who suffer from the targeted disease. Finally, Phase III is a double-blind, large-scale trial (often using thousands of subjects) in which the company gains a firm understanding of efficacy and learns about the drug's potential side effects. Only after successful completion of Phase III does the company seek final FDA approval.

The idea for a specific drug targeting a specific disease really does not come about until after the discovery and preclinical stages are over, so we'll investigate the typical decision to start the Phase I clinical trials of a new drug. Figure 1.3 presents historical data concerning the average cost of each phase (if undertaken), the average success rate in each phase (if entered), and the average length of time that each phase takes.

Figure 1.3	Historical Data Concerning the Average Cost, Success Rate, and Time Required For Clinical Trials at Large U.S. Pharmaceuticals Companies[7]			
	Historical Average Cost	Historical Average Success Rate	Historical Average Probability of Entering	Historical Average Length
Phase I	$15.2 *mm*	71%		1 year
Phase II	$23.5 *mm*	44.2%	71%	2 years
Phase III and FDA approval	$91.5 *mm*	68.5%	71% × 44.2% = 31.4%	5 years

---

[6] Of all the new drugs brought to market in the United States in 2000, the top decile accounted for more than half of the cash flow. *Source:* Grabowski, Vernon, and DiMasi (2002).

[7] *Source:* DiMasi, Hansen, and Grabowski (2003). Costs are given in year 2000 constant dollars.

From Figure 1.3, we can see that the expected overall success rate of a drug that enters clinical testing (that is, the probability of actually going to market as an approved drug) is only 21.5% (71% × 44.2% × 68.5% = 21.5%); moreover, success requires eight years of time (on average) between initiation of Phase I and launch of the new drug. And what does a pharmaceutical company expect to get back if a drug is successful? According to Grabowski, Vernon, and DiMasi (2002), the average present value of the net revenues from all new drugs launched in the year 2000, calculated as of launch date using an 11% cost of capital, was $525 million.

Using these data (which I have *not* made up), we can calculate the static NPV of an investment in the Phase I clinical trials of a typical new drug using a DCF approach with an 11% cost of capital:

$$\text{Static NPV} = -\$15.2 \; mm + \frac{(0.71)(-\$23.5 \; mm)}{(1.11)^1} + \frac{(0.314)(-\$91.5 \; mm)}{(1.11)^3} + \frac{(0.215)(\$525 \; mm)}{(1.11)^8}$$

$$= -\$2.25 \; mm$$

This simple calculation shows the conundrum that CFOs of pharmaceutical companies must face: The usual investment in clinical Phase I displays negative static NPV. In other words, application of the NPV rule to a DCF-based valuation would imply that investment in clinical trials of new drugs destroys value on average. But intuition tells these managers otherwise—that their companies exist to create value by developing new drugs, and that their comparative advantages lay in their scientific abilities. Furthermore, the financial markets seem to think that pharmaceutical R&D actually creates value: When pharmaceuticals announce unexpected increases in their R&D budgets, their stock prices typically go up. How can we explain this disconnect between the static NPV and the financial market's wisdom?

Before we turn to examples of managers foregoing projects that have positive static NPV, I'd like to go ahead and give a partial explanation for why the projects in Examples 1.1, 1.2, and 1.3 could be value-creating even though their static NPVs are negative.

What Went Wrong in Examples 1.1, 1.2, and 1.3

Remember the definition of the *true* NPV of a project from Equation (1.2):

$$\textit{True} \text{ project NPV} = \frac{\text{True financial market value of project's}}{\text{incremental future cash flows}} - \text{Capital investment required for project}$$

Now let's compare this to the definition of the static NPV (which is the NPV that we calculated in each previous example) from equation (1.4):

$$\textit{Static} \text{ project NPV} = \frac{\textit{DCF approximation of } \text{true financial market}}{\text{value of project's incremental future cash flow}} - \frac{\text{Capital investment required}}{\text{for project}}$$

I argue that in Examples 1.1, 1.2, and 1.3 the managers believed that the *true* project NPVs were positive even though the *static* project NPVs they calculated were negative. Comparing Equations (1.2) and (1.4) should remind you that the only difference between the true and static NPV is that *static* NPV uses DCF to approximate the true financial market value of a project. So the managers must have believed that there was a flaw in the valuations they got via DCF. As it turns out, these beliefs were justifiable.

To illustrate the flaw, I'll focus on our example of Boeing's investment in the preliminary design of a super-jumbo-jet airplane (Example 1.2). Go back and read it again now, and pay particular attention to the thought process we went through to construct the incremental cash flows in our static NPV analysis in Figure 1.2.

In the Boeing example, we explicitly recognized that the 1996 investment of $500 million in preliminary design would allow Boeing to make another decision in 2001: whether or not to actually spend an additional $20 billion, bend metal, and enter the super-jumbo-jet business.[8] In other words, the 1996 investment in preliminary R&D would create some future *flexibility* for Boeing. We can capture that flexibility in a diagram like I've drawn in Figure 1.4.

Figure 1.4 displays something very important: Boeing's investment in preliminary design creates a *strategy*, and the really big decision in this strategy is not in 1996 but rather is off in the distant future. If Boeing invests in the preliminary design in 1996, it makes no commitment whatsoever to actually enter the super-jumbo-jet business in 2001—but it makes no commitment to stay out of the business, either. That decision will only be made when the preliminary design is complete, and in 1996 we cannot be 100% sure of what that decision will actually be (because we cannot be 100% sure of what Boeing will learn between now and then). The *only* thing we can be sure of is that Boeing's managers will make the *right* decision in 2001 *based on what they learn* between now (1996) and then (2001).

However, the DCF approach to valuation (and hence the static NPV approach to evaluation) does not accommodate the strategic feature of the investment. Rather, DCF forces us to treat this important future flexibility in a very peculiar way. Instead of recognizing that Boeing will *learn and respond*, the DCF approach requires us to *commit to the expected future decision*. The following series of questions illustrate how DCF forces us to substitute a hard-wired decision in place of future flexibility:

> Question 1: If Boeing makes the investment in preliminary design today (i.e., 1996), what future flexibility will arise?
>
> *Answer 1: The investment in preliminary design will allow Boeing to actually market the plane to airlines, learn demand, and then in 2001 decide whether or not to spend $20 billion and enter the super-jumbo-jet business.*
>
> Question 2: Based on what we know today (i.e., 1996), how do we expect Boeing to act in 2001 when the final decision must be made?
>
> *Answer 2: Based on what we know today (i.e., 1996), we expect that Boeing will not enter the super-jumbo-jet business in 2001.*

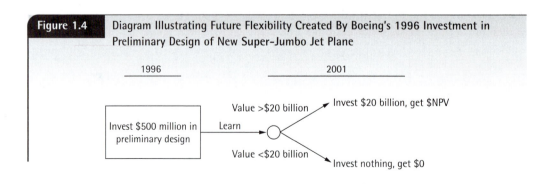

Figure 1.4   Diagram Illustrating Future Flexibility Created By Boeing's 1996 Investment in Preliminary Design of New Super-Jumbo Jet Plane

---

[8] Recall that Boeing could not present the plane to potential customers without doing the preliminary R&D first.

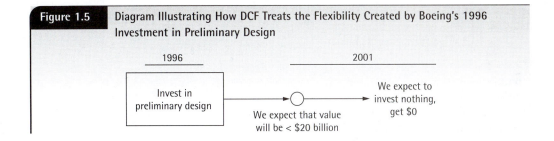

Figure 1.5 Diagram Illustrating How DCF Treats the Flexibility Created by Boeing's 1996 Investment in Preliminary Design

> Question 3: What are the incremental free cash flow implications of that specific course of action (i.e., to not enter the super-jumbo-jet business in 2001)?
>
> *Answer 3: If Boeing does not enter the super-jumbo-jet business in 2001, then there will be no incremental free cash inflows or outflows once preliminary design is complete.*

Do you see what happened here? The key is in Question 2. The DCF approach to valuation forces Boeing to commit in 1996 to a specific course of action in 2001, and to accept the cash flow consequences of that commitment as the expected incremental free cash flows in 2001 and beyond. Figure 1.5 shows how DCF forces us to treat the future flexibility in this case. Before you go any further, make sure you understand the relationship between the diagram in Figure 1.5 and our DCF valuation (and static NPV analysis) in Figure 1.2.

This simple example illustrates the single most important shortcoming of the DCF approach to valuation. DCF is a *no-flexibility* model: It requires that you replace any future flexibility with a hard-wired commitment to a certain course of action and accept the expected cash flow consequences of that commitment, even though you know you are going to learn and respond. This, in turn, can lead to a valuation error, which in the Boeing example is easy to explain. (I'll explain *why* DCF suffers this limitation later in this chapter; for now, I focus on the general intuition.)

Suppose that Boeing does go ahead with the preliminary R&D investment in 1996. When Boeing actually gets to 2001, one of two things will happen: either Boeing will learn (as expected) that the super-jumbo-jet business is a dog, or Boeing will be surprised to learn that the super-jumbo-jet business creates value. If the business is a dog, Boeing will not invest the $20 billion, and the incremental free cash flows from that point on will be zero, as expected and as the DCF valuation model reflected. But if Boeing is surprised to find that the super-jumbo-jet business creates value, the company will invest the $20 billion and receive the free cash flows; that is, Boeing will capture the positive true NPV (whatever it turns out to be at that time). Figure 1.6 presents a graph of the 2001 payoff to the 1996 investment in preliminary R&D *based on what Boeing learns about the true value of the super-jumbo-jet business in the meantime.*

Make sure you understand the graph in Figure 1.6. On the *x*-axis are all of the possible true values of a super-jumbo-jet business that Boeing could learn in 2001 when it markets the plane. The 2001 investment required is $20 billion to enter the super-jumbo-jet business, so if Boeing learns in 2001 that the true value of that business is less than $20 billion, then the 2001 true NPV will be negative, and Boeing will simply do nothing. This is why the 2001 payoff due to the flexibility (which we plot on the *y*-axis) is $0 for all 2001 business values below $20 billion. But suppose that in 2001 Boeing learns that the value of the super-jumbo-jet business is something greater

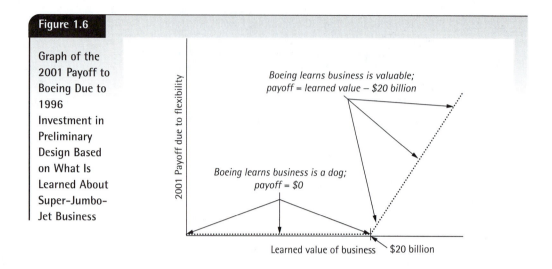

Figure 1.6

Graph of the 2001 Payoff to Boeing Due to 1996 Investment in Preliminary Design Based on What Is Learned About Super-Jumbo-Jet Business

than $20 billion—say, $24 billion. In this case, Boeing would have a positive NPV project: It could invest $20 billion, get back a business worth $24 billion, and thus create value to the tune of $4 billion.

The picture in Figure 1.6 is obviously the payoff diagram of a call option, and one thing I expect you to know before reading this book is that all calls like this have strictly positive value. Even if you don't recall that lesson, you can grasp the intuition from Figure 1.6. If Boeing makes the preliminary R&D investment in 1996, then the worst thing that can happen in 2001 is the expected outcome: Boeing walks away from the super-jumbo-jet business and gets exactly $0. But the 1996 preliminary R&D investment also creates a slim possibility of a strictly good outcome in which Boeing makes a positive NPV investment in 2001 by entering a valuable business line. That slim possibility has positive value in 1996.

In Boeing's situation, investment in preliminary R&D creates a valuable call option, and yet the DCF approach to valuation assigns this flexibility a value of $0. Why? Because the appropriate hard-wired commitment (based only on what was known in 1996) was the worst case: That the 2001 learned value of the business would be less than $20 billion, so the expected payoff to the preliminary R&D investment would be $0. DCF does not reflect the chance (however slim) that the super-jumbo-jet business could be valuable.

Warning: Just because an option has positive value does not mean that a firm should invest in it. The option's value must be at least as great as its cost; in this case, Boeing could only justify investment in preliminary R&D if the managers could conclude that the flexibility (or option) it creates has a true financial market value of at least $500 million.

DCF Works for Straight Investment-Grade Bonds

I argue in this chapter and the next that DCF is a shortcut approach to a more general valuation principle known as *linear pricing*. And like most other shortcuts, it only works in certain situations. As it turns out, the original purpose of DCF was to value straight bonds and corporate investments that look like straight bonds.

Think of how a straight bond investment works: You buy the bond, and then you sit back and submissively accept whatever cash flows actually come to you. You have no ability to alter the cash flows yourself—you are a purely passive investor. To apply DCF to an investment-grade straight bond, you forecast out the cash flows you expect to receive from the bond and then discount at the risk-adjusted discount rate. Future decisions are never an issue.

DCF works extremely well in valuing investment-grade straight bonds (and corporate investments that look like investment-grade straight bonds), and it is no coincidence that bond valuation is the very first application of DCF that we usually teach. But have you ever tried to value a convertible or callable bond using DCF? You can't. A convertible or callable bond has two pieces of value: cash flow value (expected principal and interest payments as if the bond had no embedded options), and flexibility value (i.e., the value of the embedded option).

$$\begin{array}{c}\text{True financial market value of} \\ \text{convertible/callable bond}\end{array} = \begin{array}{c}\text{Static (no flexibility or option-} \\ \text{free) value of bond's cash flows}\end{array} + \begin{array}{c}\text{Value of bond's flexibility} \\ \text{(embedded options)}\end{array} \quad (1.5)$$

DCF works perfectly well to value the straight cash flow component, but it cannot handle the flexibility component. It is not designed to.

We can use this logic to understand why Boeing management felt that the static NPV of its investment in preliminary design (−$500 million, Figure 1.2) was misleading. The preliminary design investment is like a bond with an embedded option but with no straight cash flows (that is, no interest or principal); the DCF approach to valuation correctly assigned a $0 value to its straight (no flexibility) cash flows (Figure 1.2), but incorrectly assigned a $0 value to its incremental flexibility (as discussed earlier). Boeing management knew that the incremental flexibility was valuable.

True financial market value of preliminary R&D	=	Static (i.e., no flexibility) value of preliminary R&D cash flows	+	Value of flexibility created by preliminary R&D
DCF approximation	= $0		+ $0	
Management's intuition	= $0		+ Something >$500 mm	

For the *true* NPV of the investment to have been positive, Boeing management would have had to believe that the flexibility created by the preliminary design was worth at least $500 million. If the flexibility created by the preliminary design investment was worth exactly $500 million, then the preliminary R&D investment had a true NPV of zero; if it was worth anything more than $500 million, then the preliminary R&D investment actually *created value* for shareholders in 1996—even though Boeing's managers did not believe the company would ever enter the super-jumbo-jet business.

Perhaps now you can see what I'm after in this textbook. I'm not out to replace business judgment, and I cannot help managers get around the problem of making good estimates of future incremental free cash flows. My hope is that this book will help managers approach decisions like Boeing's in a more scientific way. Once we recognize that Boeing's investment in preliminary R&D looks suspiciously like an investment in a call option, we can put some structure on the problem so that we can make a more careful analysis of it. Instead of arguing over vague and elusive things like strategic value, managers can distill the debate down into arguments about economic assumptions. I've worked with a lot of companies on this, and they almost unanimously agree that the value of *real options analysis* is not in the numbers that come out of the models, but rather in the discipline that it forces on their thinking.

I owe you a postscript. Boeing invested in the preliminary R&D, but ultimately decided against offering the product. This does not mean that they made the wrong decision, however. Boeing's managers should be judged on what they knew in 1996, not what they learned in 2001. If the option was worth more in 1996 than its cost at that time, then Boeing's managers did the right thing. Not all options will be exercised, but if you repeatedly buy them for less than their true financial market value, you will eventually hit winners and *on average* create value.

What Went Wrong in the Home Depot Example

With that model in mind, let's revisit Example 1.1 (Home Depot's investment in a single new Expo store). If you go back and look at our static NPV analysis in Figure 1.1, you'll see that we treated the new Expo store just as we would treat a straight bond: We forecast the future incremental cash flows we would expect to harvest from the store, and then we discounted those cash flows at a risk-adjusted discount rate. And if this were the way that Home Depot intended to handle the new Expo store (just build it, see if people come, and take the good with the bad) then DCF would have provided a good approximation of the store's financial market value and the static NPV analysis in Figure 1.1 would have given the right recommendation.

But this is *not* the way that Home Depot intended to act. In building the single Expo Design Center store in San Diego, Home Depot's intention was not to simply harvest the cash flows from that one store like it would passively collect the cash flows from a bond. Rather, Home Depot's intention was to use that store as a test—to see if do-it-for-me remodelers would like the store enough to generate a certain level of sales. If the sales of the San Diego store turned out to be sufficiently high, Home Depot would then build out an entire chain of Expo stores, gain purchasing power over suppliers, and create value in exactly the way the company did in the do-it-yourself segment. However, if the single Expo store in San Diego turned out to be uninteresting to the target market, Home Depot would ignore this idea and move on to something else.[9] The investment in a single new Expo store put into place a learn-and-respond strategy, just as Boeing's investment in preliminary design did. Figure 1.7 presents a diagram of the strategy.

So Home Depot's investment in the single Expo store had two key pieces of value: (1) the incremental free cash flows that would be generated by that store and (2) the flexibility created

---

Figure 1.7	Diagram Illustrating Future Flexibility Created by Home Depot's 1991 Investment in Single New Expo Concept Store

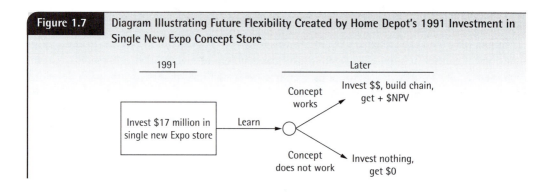

---

[9] Home Depot has tested several other concepts like this, some of which (like Villagers Hardware) have worked out, while others (like Crossroads) have not.

by the new store investment.

True financial market value of Expo concept store	=	Static (i.e., No flexibility) value of test store's FCF	+	Value of flexibility created by test store
DCF approximation	=	$13.779 mm	+	$0
Management's intuition	=	$13.799 mm	+	Something > $3.221 mm

In this case, investment in the test store created the ability to learn about the demand for the concept, and to respond with either a positive NPV investment (build a chain of Expos) or a zero NPV investment (don't build a chain of Expos). The flexibility here has a payoff diagram that looks exactly like the payoff to Boeing's investment in preliminary R&D (Figure 1.6), which makes perfect sense: The Expo test store allowed Home Depot to learn and respond, just as the preliminary R&D allowed Boeing to learn and respond. I've drawn Home Depot's payoff diagram for you in Figure 1.8.

Again, you see the classic "hockey stick" payoff on a call option. When Home Depot's managers invested in the single Expo store in San Diego, they purchased not only the cash flows that store would generate but also this valuable call option: The option to build out a complete chain of Expo Design Center stores if it were to become valuable to do so. Once again, DCF will work quite well for valuing the cash flow component, but it is not designed to capture the flexibility component.

If we look back at our static NPV analysis of the single Expo store in Figure 1.1, we can now understand that the $13.779 million DCF value of the open Expo store captures the financial market value of that store's cash flows but not the value of the flexibility the new store investment creates. Since management invested even though the static NPV was −$3.221 million, they must have believed that the flexibility gained by the investment in the concept store (i.e., the option value created by the new concept store) was more than $3.221 million. If this flexibility was worth anything more than $3.221 million, then investment in the single Expo store in 1991 created value for Home Depot shareholders at that time (even though its static NPV was negative).

In contrast to the Boeing outcome, the Expo test store revealed to Home Depot that the Expo Design Center concept was valuable. But instead of immediately building a nationwide chain of stores, in 1994 Home Depot built a second test store in Atlanta. Home Depot used the second test store to learn more about its ability to manage this business and only later decided to build

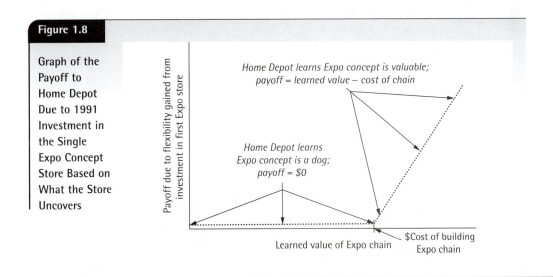

Figure 1.8

Graph of the Payoff to Home Depot Due to 1991 Investment in the Single Expo Concept Store Based on What the Store Uncovers

Payoff due to flexibility gained from investment in first Expo store

Home Depot learns Expo concept is valuable; payoff = learned value − cost of chain

Home Depot learns Expo concept is a dog; payoff = $0

Learned value of Expo chain

$Cost of building Expo chain

more stores. This was all a part of the grand plan back in 1991: Set up a series of *tollgates*, learn from each stage of investment, and only invest at the next tollgate if uncertainty becomes resolved in a favorable way.[10]

You see this sort of staging in a lot of different areas. In fact, the third example (the investment in Phase I clinical trials by a pharmaceutical company) describes this feature.

What About the Pharmaceuticals Example?

We can think about the pharmaceutical investment (Example 1.3) using the model we've deduced from the Boeing and Home Depot examples. If you look back at the static NPV calculation, you'll see that it did not build in any flexibility. Remember that the DCF approximation to valuation is *all or nothing,* and it requires the replacement of any future decisions with a hard-wired commitment to a specific course of action. In the pharmaceuticals case, we tacitly committed to continue at each stage as long as the drug actually passed the technical tests in the trials.

Technical risk is the risk that the new drug passes the scientific hurdles in each phase of the clinical trials. Technical risk is often considered to be purely idiosyncratic (but in Chapter 8 I'll show that this is not entirely true), and purely idiosyncratic risks can be handled with a decision tree. In this example, we accounted for technical risk by probability-weighting the cost of Phase II and III trials by the cumulative probability of *technical* success in all prior stages, and then probability-weighting the expected value of a marketed drug (based only on what we knew at the beginning of Phase I trials) by the cumulative probability of *technical* success in all clinical trial phases.

To reiterate, we built into our static NPV analysis the assumption that we would continue into Phase II trials as long as Phase I was technically successful, and then into Phase III as long as Phase II was technically successful, and so on. But this is not exactly the way a sophisticated pharmaceutical company proceeds through the process. During each phase of the clinical trials, the pharmaceutical company also learns about the ultimate market potential for the new drug; even if a drug successfully completes Phase I of the clinical trials, the pharmaceutical company may choose not to continue into Phase II trials if the profit potential for the drug no longer looks promising. So, the investment in Phase I clinical trials puts into place a strategy, which I've sketched out in Figure 1.9.

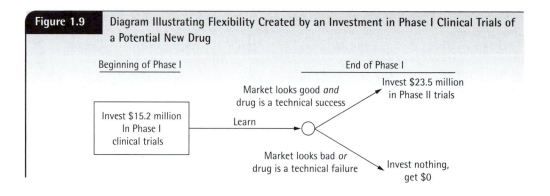

| Figure 1.9 | Diagram Illustrating Flexibility Created by an Investment in Phase I Clinical Trials of a Potential New Drug |

Beginning of Phase I — End of Phase I

Invest $15.2 million In Phase I clinical trials

Learn

Market looks good *and* drug is a technical success → Invest $23.5 million in Phase II trials

Market looks bad *or* drug is a technical failure → Invest nothing, get $0

This is starting to look familiar, isn't it? Investment in Phase I clinical trials creates future flexibility for the pharmaceuticals company: The flexibility to learn more about the demand and potential value-added pricing of the new drug along with the technical results of the Phase I trials, and then to spend $23.5 million on Phase II trials only if the market for the drug looks good *and* Phase I is successful. And what would the $23.5 million investment in Phase II trials purchase? The flexibility to learn even more about the market potential for the new drug, and then to spend $91.5 million only if the market continues to look good *and* Phase II is successful. At every subsequent tollgate before the final decision to go to market, an investment creates future flexibility.[11]

How should we evaluate the investment in Phase I clinical trials? We must recognize, once again, that a corporate investment can have two pieces of value: (1) the incremental cash flows that the investment directly throws off and (2) the incremental flexibility the investment generates. The $15.2 million investment in Phase I clinical trials generates no incremental cash flow on its own, but it does create valuable flexibility. Pharmaceuticals managers must believe that the future flexibility generated by investment in Phase I trials is worth at least $15.2 million.

What We've Learned So Far

There are two important lessons to take from this section. First, we can decompose the true financial market value of a corporate project into two pieces: (1) the financial market value of the incremental cash flows that directly result from investment in the project and (2) the financial market value of any incremental flexibility that results from the investment.

Second, we must recognize that the discounted cash flow (DCF) approach to valuation is a *no-flexibility* model. Because it can't handle future decisions, the DCF approach to valuation supposes that we replace any future flexibilities with a commitment to act a certain way. Therefore, DCF cannot capture the second component of a new project's market value (i.e., the flexibility component).

What this means, then, is that when we apply the static NPV rule (i.e., NPV using DCF as our valuation tool), we are implicitly applying an all-or-nothing rule: If static NPV $\geq$ 0, make the investment with all of its specified future commitments; otherwise, don't ever make the investment at all.

When managers really face all-or-nothing decisions, then DCF and the static NPV rule will work well. These will be situations where the cash flow component of an investment dominates the flexibility component. Examples are investments in cost-saving systems (such as inventory management systems) and brick-and-mortar investments that cannot be reconfigured or redeployed to different uses.

When managers are specifically investing to create flexibility, however, DCF can lead to a poor approximation of the project's financial market value, and the static NPV rule may give the wrong recommendation. These will be *learn-and-respond* situations, and the flexibility component of the project's value may dominate the direct cash flow component. Examples 1.1, 1.2, and 1.3 illustrate this particular sort of situation.

---

[11] Culling the pipeline of drugs with poor market potential before the expensive Phase III clinical trials is an extremely important issue in managing a pharmaceutical R&D program due to the enormous skewness in the cash flows of launched drugs. Grabowski, Vernon, and DiMasi (2002) document that the top decile of marketed drugs make up about half of the cash flows of pharmaceutical companies in the United States, and that the *median* launched drug does not generate sufficient cash flows to cover its fully allocated average cost of R&D. By abandoning just a few more market poor drugs before the expensive Phase III clinical trials, the companies could create a lot more value. I'm well aware, however, that several well-known pharmaceutical companies ignore new information about market potential when making their decision to continue into Phase III.

What we need, then, is a valuation technique that can give good approximations of the financial market value of flexibility. What we saw in the three examples is that the payoff to flexibility created by a corporate project looks exactly like the payoff to a financial option in many situations. This is the point of this book: To show you how to recognize the situations in which corporate flexibility can be thought of as an option and then how to use option pricing techniques to value the flexibility. Since the corporate flexibilities are options on real assets, we call the approach *real options*.

Some readers may wonder why we need a more complex tool for valuing flexibility when managers seem to be able to handle the problem intuitively. My response is that while managers know that flexibility is valuable, they don't always know *how* valuable it is. Thinking about investments in flexibility as investments in options helps managers put science onto their intuition. I'm not really out to change the way managers think—my motivation is simply to make their thinking sharper.

This is important because it is quite common for managers to *overspend* on flexibility. In many organizations, managers appeal to so-called strategic value or option value to justify their otherwise unjustifiable projects. But just because Boeing's investment in preliminary design created some flexibility does not mean that it created value—it would only have created value if the flexibility was actually worth more than the cost ($500 million). The same goes for Home Depot's investment in the Expo test store and the pharmaceutical investment in Phase I clinical trials. We can't really evaluate these investments from the shareholder's perspective unless we have a sharper valuation model.

Now that we have a better idea of why managers might rationally invest even though the static NPV of a project is negative, we need to turn the coin and look at situations where managers are not acting even though the static NPV of an opportunity is positive. This set of situations illustrates another important shortcoming of DCF-based valuation and static NPV analysis.

1.4   Examples of Managers Doing Nothing When the Static NPV Is Positive

Example 1.4 (Mead Johnson)

Mead Johnson is one of the world's largest marketers of formulas for infants, babies, and toddlers. In the mid-1990s, Mead Johnson began selling its formula products in Argentina. This was initially profitable, but the December 2001 lifting of the one-to-one currency peg between the Argentine Peso (ARS) and the U.S. dollar (US$) turned the business completely upside down. The problem was that Mead Johnson did not produce formula in Argentina but rather in Mexico, while the company's Argentine competitors produced locally.

You can think of this issue in two different ways. One way is to think about Mead Johnson's cash flows translated back into US$. The fall in the ARS from a value of $1.00 to a value of $0.285 did nothing to the US$ cost of producing formula, but it cut the company's US$ revenues by over 70%. Mead Johnson could not respond by raising prices because their local competitors did not have to.

Equivalently, you can think in terms of ARS as the local managers would have. The weakening of the ARS from 1 per US$ to 3.5 per US$ did nothing to the Argentine division's ARS-denominated revenues, but it more than tripled its ARS-denominated cost of goods sold. I'll explain the rest of this example in this way.

Since the weakening of the ARS raised costs so drastically, the business quickly turned from one of positive free cash flow generation (in ARS) to one of negative free cash flow generation.

In other words, corporate headquarters was having to subsidize the Argentine division. By January 2003, the Argentine division was bleeding about ARS 100,000 per month. If you treat this as a perpetuity, and discount at a 10% annual required rate of return, then a very quick DCF valuation will tell you that the Argentine subsidiary was worth ARS -12 million:

$$\text{DCF Value} = \frac{-\text{ARS}100{,}000 \times 12}{.10} = -\text{ARS}12{,}000{,}000 \qquad (1.6)$$

Naturally, some managers at Mead Johnson headquarters felt that the right thing to do was to exit the business. As long as exit would cost less than ARS 12 million, the decision to exit the business would actually display a *positive* static NPV: The DCF value of the incremental free cash flows from closing the subsidiary would be positive ARS 12 million, and the cost of exit less than that, giving a positive static NPV. (Remember, the base case here is leaving the business open).

Nevertheless, Mead Johnson's senior management decided to keep the Argentine division open. Notice what this meant. Every month that the Argentine division stayed open, Mead Johnson lost ARS 100,000. Why would Mead Johnson executives agree to lose money on a monthly basis in order to keep open a cash-bleeding business? Why would they ignore the static NPV rule? Isn't this value destruction at its worst?

Example 1.5 (Silicon Valley Real Estate)

In the spring of 2000, I spent a day discussing real options with the financial managers of Palm Computing (now called palmOne) at their comfortable campus in Santa Clara, California. The company's spin-off from 3Comm was in progress, and the financial press couldn't write enough about the upcoming Palm IPO.

Of course, these were heady times for most technology companies (the Nasdaq did not peak until March 10, 2000). And the boom in the tech sector led to a boom in Silicon Valley real estate prices. Even before the big tech run-up, this area's prices for homes and condominiums as well as rental rates for apartments and commercial space were extremely high; by the turn of the century, prices and rents were through the roof.

So you might understand how surprised I was that morning when I looked out a window and saw a huge plot of undeveloped real estate right next door. Here were 39 acres of unused land in the middle of some of the most valuable real estate in the country. Surely it would have been positive NPV to build condominiums or apartments or Internet hotels or strip malls or tattoo parlors or whatever on that land. And yet the land just sat there.

Why would the owner of the real estate not develop the land, even though the static NPVs of many different development alternatives were positive and large?

What Was Going On at Mead Johnson

When you read about Mead Johnson in Example 1.4, you might have thought to yourself that the company would keep the Argentine division open because of the chance that the ARS might strengthen and the business would turn around. This is exactly what management was thinking. Even though their expectation was that the business would not turn around, management recognized the possibility that it *might* so they adopted a wait-and-see attitude.

Once again, we have a case where management's intuition about the value implications of a decision were at odds with their static NPV analysis. In this case, management felt that the true NPV of closing the business was negative (that is, closing the business would actually destroy value), even though the static NPV was positive (in other words, that the company could create value by closing it). And once again, we can look to the difference between true NPV in Equation (1.2) and static NPV in Equation (1.4) to explain the disconnect. The static NPV analysis was based on a DCF valuation of the Argentine division, and the DCF approximation to the market value of an open Argentine division was wrong.

To see why, we need to think about what the wait-and-see strategy actually means. In this case, to wait and see means to accept the fact that the business will lose ARS 100,000 for the next month, consider that ARS 100,000 to be the cost of waiting, and then reevaluate the decision after a month has passed. Diagrammatically, the decision to wait and see looks like Figure 1.10.

Wow! Figure 1.10 looks exactly like the diagrams that illustrate the flexibility created in the Boeing, Home Depot, and pharmaceutical R&D examples. If Mead Johnson spends ARS 100,000 to keep the subsidiary open for one more month, the company in effect purchases the ability to learn and respond. The ARS 100,000 is actually an investment in flexibility: The flexibility to decide *next month* whether to close the business or to keep it open.

What this means, then, is that the true value of the Argentine subsidiary (i.e., the value if it is left open) has two pieces: The value of its expected cash flows over the coming month and the value of the flexibility to either close it and stop the bleeding at the end of the month or to continue to wait and see a bit longer. But just as in the earlier problems, DCF cannot handle the future flexibility.

Remember that DCF forces you to replace any future flexibility with a hard-wired commitment to a specific action and then to consider the cash flow consequences of that decision. This is precisely what happened in Mead Johnson's valuation of the Argentine subsidiary. The ARS −12 million DCF value of the subsidiary is built on the implicit assumption that the business stays open *forever*. To determine the incremental cash flows from a decision, you compare the project's cash flows *with* the decision (in this case, the cash flows from a closed business, which are zero) against the project's cash flows *without* the decision (the base case, which in this case is an open business). Since DCF does not allow for future flexibilities, then the base case is a business that is kept open *forever*.

This flaw in the DCF valuation model translates directly back into the static NPV. Since the base case in the DCF valuation is a business kept open forever, then the static NPV compares the value of closing the business *immediately* with the value of keeping the business open *forever*.

In other words, the static NPV rule is a *now or never again* decision criterion: It compares the value of taking an action now against the value of never taking that action at all. In the Mead Johnson case, the static NPV of ARS −12 million tells us that if Mead Johnson must commit

---

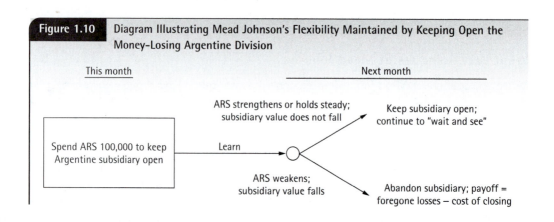

Figure 1.10 Diagram Illustrating Mead Johnson's Flexibility Maintained by Keeping Open the Money-Losing Argentine Division

today to either closing the Argentine subsidiary or keeping it open forever, then the best thing for the company is to close the division at once.

We know, however, that there was a third alternative: Wait. Instead of facing a now or never decision, Mead Johnson's managers faced a *now or maybe later* decision. The alternative to closing the Argentine division in January 2003 was to leave it open a little longer and postpone an irreversible decision. Leaving the division open cost money (ARS 100,000 per month), and spending this amount of money purchased and maintained the flexibility to put off the decision until later. DCF cannot appropriately value the flexibility that this investment of ARS 100,000 created, so it was impossible to use static NPV analysis to pick the best course of action.

To summarize, Mead Johnson's managers intuitively believed that the true value of the Argentine subsidiary was the cost of keeping it open for one more month (−100K) plus the value of the flexibility (the option) to close it at the end of that month, and that this flexibility was worth more than ARS 100,000. Thus, they believed that the true NPV of closing the division was negative, even though their static NPV analysis told them it was positive.

And do you know what happened? The Argentine peso strengthened over the first half of 2003, and Mead Johnson's Argentine subsidiary is still open!

Undeveloped Property in the Silicon Valley

The same logic applies to the Silicon Valley real estate owner's decision to do nothing with the parcel in spite of the fact that several alternative developments had positive static NPV. Suppose that the static NPV of a new condo complex was positive at the time. This would have meant that immediately building a condo complex on the land was more valuable than never developing the land at all. Now versus never again, remember? If the real estate owner had calculated the static NPV of all of the alternatives and compared them to find the highest one, the owner would have been picking the most valuable *immediate* action.

What the property owner must have been thinking was that doing nothing—that is, waiting to decide—was actually more valuable than any of the immediate opportunities. Waiting was probably costly, because the owner suffered an opportunity loss from not immediately developing (e.g., by not developing the owner loses the immediate cash flow that could be earned from renting space or managing a condo complex). This opportunity loss, however, generated the flexibility to put off the development decision until the owner had a better idea of which alternative would be the most valuable. I've drawn our very familiar diagram one more time in Figure 1.11.

Doing nothing in 2000 was a legitimate alternative for the real estate owner, and as Figure 1.11 reminds us, the true value of the do-nothing alternative had two pieces: (1) the value of any cash costs as well as opportunity losses that arose due to waiting and (2) the value of the flexibility that waiting created (or maintained, whichever way you look at it). So the real estate owner must have intuitively believed that the value of this flexibility, net of the opportunity costs of creating it, was

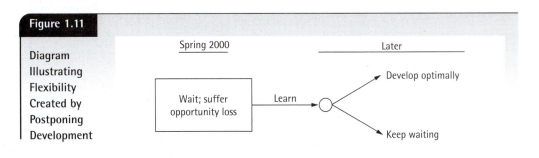

Figure 1.11

Diagram Illustrating Flexibility Created by Postponing Development actually greater than the static NPV of the best immediate alternative. This makes a lot of sense, particularly when you think of how uncertain the owner might have been about which development alternative would be the most profitable.

That land still sits undeveloped, though it is worth much less than it was in 2000. Will the real estate owner ever develop? Perhaps. The owner will optimally develop the land when the benefits of the best immediate development alternative outweigh the benefits of waiting. The owner can use DCF and static NPV analysis to understand the benefits of the best immediate development alternative, but she'll need a different valuation model in order to understand the benefits of waiting.

What We Learned in Examples 1.4 and 1.5

Steve Ross puts it very elegantly: "Every project competes with itself in time." What Steve means by this is that one alternative to doing a project now is to wait and perhaps do it later. Unfortunately, static NPV analysis does not allow you to compare the value of doing a project now with the value of waiting to make a commitment. Static NPV is a *now or never* decision criterion, and it only allows you to compare the value of making an immediate commitment to the project with a commitment to never do the project at all. This flaw of static NPV arises because DCF is not appropriate for valuing the flexibility that accompanies the *perhaps do it later* alternative.

Once again, I think that managers need a sharper tool for understanding when the right time to invest might be. It is easy to fall into one of two traps: Either to think that it is always valuable to wait, or to ignore the value of waiting altogether. A better valuation tool will help managers gain a sharper understanding of the investment issues they face.

Before moving on, I'd like to reiterate the warning concerning the overvaluation of flexibility and the danger in loose appeals to option value. On the day I visited Palm Computing, the company's equity market capitalization went over $20 billion (that's right—20 times *sales*). There were many other stocks that were as richly valued, and there were quite a few people who were willing to attribute the valuations to some mystical "option value" without ever explaining what the specific flexibilities (or options) actually were. Valuation requires discipline, and a big benefit to thinking about flexibilities in a more scientific way (through careful application of option pricing models) is that it forces practitioners to put a lot of discipline into their thinking. Whenever someone tells me that a project has strategic value or option value, I always respond with the same words: Show me. If they can't sketch it out for me fairly quickly, I know that they have not thought about it with any discipline at all.

To understand exactly why DCF is a static, no-flexibility approach to project valuation, you have to understand the general principles of valuation as well as the theoretical foundations of corporate finance. I treat those topics in considerable depth in Chapters 2 and 3, respectively. However, I recognize that many readers will opt to skip those chapters to get to the actual applications, which start in Chapter 5. So, before closing this chapter, I provide a very general outline of the theory of valuation and evaluation at the corporate level. Though this simplified presentation will gloss over some extremely important issues, it will provide enough context to explain DCF's shortcomings.

1.5   A 50,000-Foot Flyover of Chapters 2 and 3

If you recall, the investment decision focuses on the following question:

> *Suppose that your company is contemplating investment in a new project.*
> *The project is financially risky: It requires a substantial commitment of*

Figure 1.12

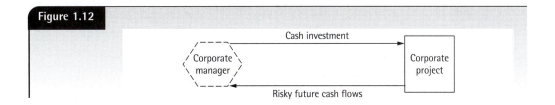

capital upfront, but its future cash returns are uncertain. How should you, a financial analyst within the firm, decide whether or not to recommend investment in the new project?

A lot of teachers begin the discussion by stating that a corporate investment is an action in which a manager gives up cash today in exchange for a risky stream of cash in the future. Many people use a diagram like Figure 1.12 to illustrate the problem, then immediately dive right into DCF analysis.

But to really get a full understanding of the problem, we have to recognize that the diagram in Figure 1.12 is only part of a larger picture. We can't just focus on a project in isolation; rather, we must accept the fact that the manager is a player in a larger network of interactions. Specifically, the manager is an intermediary who takes funds from investors and invests those funds on the behalf of the investor (as in Figure 1.13).

What I'm trying to get at in Figure 1.13 is that the corporate manager is essentially a pass-through for funds: All the funds that the corporate manager uses belong to the investor, and all the cash flows that a project creates belong to the investor. The late Roberto Goizueta, who created a lot of value as chairman of The Coca-Cola Company, put it quite simply: "We raise cash from our investors to make syrup. When we sell the syrup for more than it cost to create, we return the excess cash to our investors."

This is a very important point that is still lost on more than a few corporate managers. Whenever a manager uses corporate resources, the manager is using the investor's money whether or not the firm actually raises cash through a debt or equity offering. Cash that's not immediately returned to an investor still belongs to the investor, and you can interpret recycling of excess cash flow into new projects as actually returning the excess cash to investors and forcing them to give it right back to you.

The gist of Figure 1.13 is that the role of the manager is to *invest for the investor*. When should the manager do so? To answer this question, we have to recognize one more very important fact: *Investors have other opportunities*. Specifically, investors can take their money and buy a diversified portfolio of financial assets—a portfolio that can contain corporate bonds, stocks, government bonds, and even derivatives. Figure 1.14 illustrates.

Now, within this larger picture, how should a manager evaluate a potential corporate use of cash for a new project? Before the manager can evaluate the opportunity (that is, decide whether

Figure 1.13

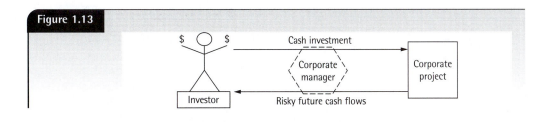

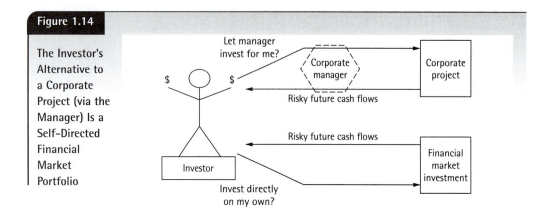

Figure 1.14

The Investor's Alternative to a Corporate Project (via the Manager) Is a Self-Directed Financial Market Portfolio

or not to actually invest in it for the investor), the manager must value the project. In other words, the manager's first order of business is to ascertain how much the project is worth *to the investor*. Valuation is really the central issue of the field of finance, and our method (which is the underpinning of everything we teach to undergrads and MBAs) is called *valuation by close substitutes*. Briefly, the manager finds something of known value, which, in the eyes of the investor, is a very close substitute for the corporate project. If the investor is truly indifferent between the two, then the value of the corporate project to the investor must be the same as the value of the close substitute. Where does the manager find something of known value that the investor considers a close substitute? In the financial market.

Suppose a firm encounters a new project opportunity that would require a capital investment of C. In the first step of valuation by close substitutes, the manager must estimate the future cash flows that the project will throw off, the timing of those cash flows, and the *risk profile* of those cash flows (see Chapters 2 and 3). This stream of cash flows, with a particular timing and risk profile, is what the manager seeks to value. I illustrate Step 1 in Figure 1.15.

Step 2 of valuing the project by close substitutes is to actually create the close substitute. The idea here is that the manager constructs a portfolio in the financial market that provides the same future cash flows, with the same timing and risk profile, as the project does (Figure 1.16). The financial market portfolio can contain anything: Stocks, bonds, derivatives, hybrid securities, whatever. The only restriction is that the price of each security must be observable and void of any "free-lunch" opportunities. (Chapter 2 covers this in considerable detail.)

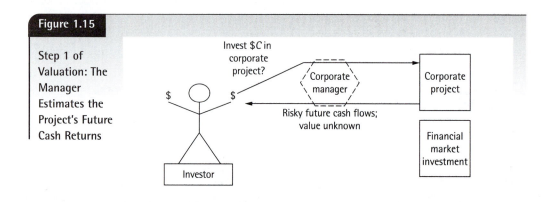

Figure 1.15

Step 1 of Valuation: The Manager Estimates the Project's Future Cash Returns

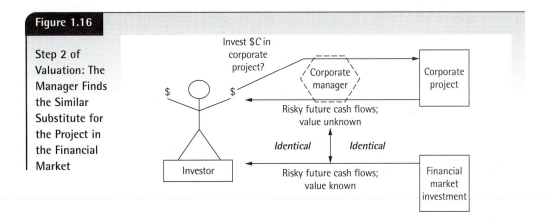

Figure 1.16

Step 2 of Valuation: The Manager Finds the Similar Substitute for the Project in the Financial Market

Step 3 of valuing the project is easy. Since the manager can readily observe the market prices of the securities that make up the similar substitute financial market portfolio, the manager can add up the total value of those securities to learn the financial market value of the similar substitute. This is known as *linear pricing:* If the similar substitute portfolio contains, say, 10 shares of a stock mutual fund, 7 government bonds, and 2 index options, then the portfolio must be worth 10 × the current price of a share in the mutual fund, plus 7 × the current price of the government bond, plus 2 × the current price of the index option. Duh. Let's just say that the total financial market value of the similar substitute portfolio is $ *TFMV*. I've put the result in Figure 1.17.

Step 4 gets us to the value of the corporate project. Since the similar-substitute financial market portfolio is worth $ *TFMV*, and since the investor is absolutely indifferent between owning the corporate project and the financial market portfolio, then the value of the corporate project in the investor's eyes must be $ *TFMV* as well. Therefore, $ *TFMV* is the true financial market value of the corporate project. We say this because $ *TFMV* is the true financial market value of the cash flows that the project throws off. See Figure 1.18.

I know you may be thinking that this is not the way you were taught project valuation because no risk-adjusted discounting went on. Don't give up on me yet—this is exactly what you've been

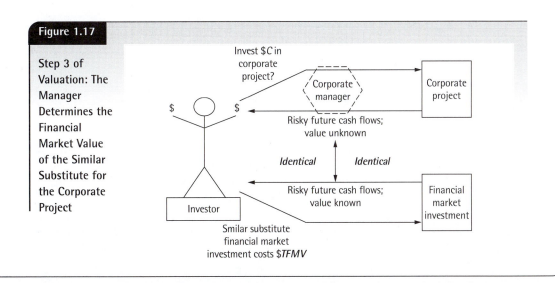

Figure 1.17

Step 3 of Valuation: The Manager Determines the Financial Market Value of the Similar Substitute for the Corporate Project

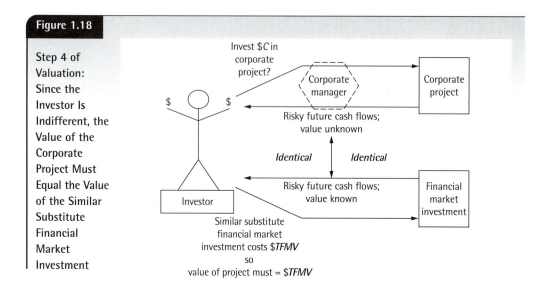

Figure 1.18

Step 4 of Valuation: Since the Investor Is Indifferent, the Value of the Corporate Project Must Equal the Value of the Similar Substitute Financial Market Investment

doing when you've used DCF, and I'll show you why just a few paragraphs down. Now, though, I want to go straight to project evaluation and the true foundation of the NPV rule.

The best way to demonstrate the basis of the NPV rule is to put you in the position of the investor in Figure 1.18, and ask you a very simple question. Which would you rather do: Invest your hard-earned C in the corporate project, or invest your hard-earned $TFMV$ in the similar-substitute financial market portfolio? Whichever one is cheaper, right? Right. If both investments give identical future cash flows (i.e., identical on all grounds that you care about, which I'm assuming are quantity, timing, and risk), then you would rather buy the cheap one. So would I. If the cost of the corporate project C is less than the cost of the financial market substitute $TFMV$, then you save $TFMV - C$ by investing in the corporate project (and you can use that savings to buy something else that makes you happy). In other words, the corporate project makes you $TFMV - C$ wealthier than you would be if the corporate project were not available and your only choice was the financial market portfolio.

We've seen this before. Recall our definition of the true project NPV from Equation (1.2):

$$\text{True project NPV} = \frac{\text{True financial market value of project's}}{\text{incremental future cash flows}} - \text{Capital investment required for project}$$

Or, in the context of Figure 1.18,

$$\text{True project NPV} = \$TFMV - \$C$$

This is why I said at the very beginning of the chapter that the NPV rule, *when correctly applied*, gives the manager a very sharp comparison between the firm's investment opportunity on the one hand and the investor's similar-risk opportunity in the financial markets on the other. The financial market similar substitute is the investor's similar-risk opportunity, and the NPV compares the costs of the two. It is no wonder that finance professors talk about opportunity cost so much!

If the true NPV of the project is positive, then its true financial market value is higher than its investment cost (i.e., $TFMV > \$C$). Let's suppose the investor has $TFMV$ to invest, and let's examine her alternatives. If she invests directly in the financial market alternative, she gives up her $TFMV$ and gets the future cash flows. On the other hand, if she allows the manager to invest for her, she only gives $C to the manager but still gets the same future cash flows, so she ends up with the same future cash flows *plus* an extra $TFMV − $C in her pocket. This shows why NPV rule measures value creation. NPV tells you exactly how much wealthier the investor is if the manager invests for her.

What about value destruction? Well, suppose that the firm has $C of excess cash just lying around, and the managers are considering investing in a project even though the true project NPV is negative (so, $TFMV < $C). If the managers invest, they spend the investor's $C (remember, it is the investor's cash), and they get back for the investor the project's future cash flows. On the other hand, if they just declare a dividend and give $C back to the investor, the investor could buy the similar substitute financial market portfolio at a cost $TFMV, get back cash flows identical to the project's, and have an extra $C − $TFMV in her pocket. In this case, the corporate investment hurts the investor, as she would be better off without it. How much poorer is the investor if the managers invest for her in this case? The negative NPV tells you exactly.

You can restate this intuition in a variety of ways, and your professors probably have their own favorite ways of going through this. All are equally valid and insightful. One way I like is to think of the firm as securitizing the future cash flows from a positive NPV project to generate the capital investment required. In this description, the firm receives $TFMV from the securitization issuance but only spends $C on the project so the equityholders make the difference ($TFMV − $C, which is the positive NPV) either through capital gain or dividend. Viewed this way, the manager appears to be an arbitrageur who buys cash flows in the real asset market (corporate projects), then sells them in the financial markets. NPV measures the arbitrage profit. Why should we expect managers to have access to such arbitrage opportunities in the real asset market? Strategic advantages, cost advantages, skills, patents, monopolies, and the like—all those things you study in a typical business school curriculum.

1.6 Why DCF Is Static

With that being said, it is finally time for me to try to explain why DCF provides a shortcut to the valuation described earlier, and why the shortcut is not always applicable. You'll then see why I use the term *static* NPV to refer to an NPV that relies on a DCF for valuation, and you'll have a better idea of why static NPV can mislead a manager. I'll make my point by way of example, and I'll use the four-step valuation framework presented earlier (see Figures 1.15 through 1.18).

Example 1.6

Suppose that a corporate manager is considering a risky project that will require an immediate investment of $21. The manager begins with Step 1 (Figure 1.15) and determines that the project will generate risky incremental cash flows with expected values of $10 in one year and $20 in two years (and nothing after that). Figure 1.19 summarizes these data.

In Step 2 of the valuation process, the manager creates a portfolio of financial market securities that generates the same future expected cash flows as the project, with the same timing and (importantly) the same risk. We'll be precise about the term *risk* in Chapter 2, but for now let's just suppose that the similar substitute financial market portfolio contains the following: one share of stock that has current market price of $6 and expected cash flows of $0 in one year and

Figure 1.19   Step 1 of the Valuation: Specification of the Incremental Cash Flows

	Cost Today	Future Expected Value of Risky Cash Flows	
	0	1	2
Project	−$21	$10	$20

$10 in two years, and one risk-free bond that has a current market price of $18 and future cash flows of $10 in one year and $10 in two years. This leads directly to Step 3: Sum up the value of the financial market's similar-substitute portfolio (that is, the cost to form it). In this case, since the stock costs $6 and the bond costs $18, the investor's financial market opportunity that is equivalent to the new corporate project is worth $24. Figure 1.20 puts this all together for you.

Step 4 is the appeal to indifference: Since the investor considers the financial market opportunity to be exactly the same as the corporate opportunity, then the two choices must have the same *value* today. The value of the similar substitute in the financial market is $24, so the true market value of the project must also be $24.

With the valuation complete, the manager can apply the NPV rule. Remember, the true NPV of the corporate opportunity is the true financial market value of the opportunity minus the cost of investing in the opportunity. In this particular example, the NPV of the corporate investment is $24 − $21 = $3. It is a good deal for the firm's investors, and management should exploit it.

The DCF approach to valuation does the very same thing. First, notice that the similar-risk financial market portfolio has an expected return of 14.5% per year. You solve for this just by solving for the portfolio's *internal rate of return* (IRR), which is the single discount rate r that equates the DCF value of the portfolios future expected cash flows with its current price in Equation (1.7)

$$\$24 = \frac{\$0 + \$10}{(1 + r)} + \frac{\$10 + \$10}{(1 + r)^2} \tag{1.7}$$

Figure 1.20   Steps 2 and 3 of the Valuation: Construction of Similar-Substitute Financial Market Portfolio

	Cost Today	Future Expected Value of Risky Cash Flows	
	0	1	2
Risky Project	−$21	$10	$20
Financial Market Portfolio with Same Risk as Project			
1 Share Stock	−$6	$0	$10
1 Risk-Free Bond	−$18	$10	$10
Total	−$24	$10	$20

I'll leave it to you to verify that $r = 14.5\%$ is the solution. Now, this is the rate of return that the investor could earn on a similar-risk investment in the capital markets (heard that one before, haven't you?), and we use it as the discount rate in a DCF valuation of the corporate investment. Look what happens when I do this in Equation (1.8):

$$\text{DCF value of project} = \frac{\$10}{(1.145)} + \frac{\$20}{(1.145)^2} = \$24 \tag{1.8}$$

Yes, the DCF value of the inflows, which is the DCF approximation to the financial market value of the project, is $24. So the static NPV of the project is the DCF approximation to the market value of the project ($24) minus the cost of actually investing in the project ($21), or $3 ($24 − $21 = $3). In this case, the static NPV gives us the same answer as the true NPV, and it does so because DCF gives us the correct market value of the project.

What we've just done is what actually goes on every time you use DCF for valuation and then the static NPV rule for evaluation. The one thing you don't usually do, however, is explicitly form the financial market's similar substitute portfolio and then calculate its priced return (IRR) for use as your "hurdle rate" or "cost of capital" or "opportunity cost of funds" (or whatever you call your risk-adjusted discount rate). Instead, you usually use an *asset pricing model* that approximates the cost of capital for you. The one that I'm sure you've used is the capital asset pricing model (CAPM), and the beauty of the CAPM and other asset pricing models like it is that it gives you a way of estimating the expected rate of return on the similar-substitute financial market portfolio without explicitly forming the portfolio. I discuss this in more depth in Chapters 2 and 3.

For now, let's suppose the manager in our example has a model (like the CAPM) that says that *the* risk-adjusted rate of return on the project is 14.5%, and the manager goes to apply it in the DCF valuation of the project, as we did in Equation (1.8). Notice what is going on here. This approach implicitly states that the investor's opportunity cost of funds stays constant at 14.5%.[12] What this means, in turn, is that the risk of the project's similar substitute portfolio is not changing as time goes by, and so the similar substitute portfolio is actually static (which means that its composition does not change). This is why DCF is a static approach to valuation: It is based on the assumption that the investor's equivalent financial market investment is a static portfolio—a portfolio that is formed at the time of investment and then held passively. This will work fine with the asset being valued is also held passively (like an investment-grade straight bond, remember?).

But as I tried to convince you with Examples 1.1 through 1.5 in the first part of this chapter, many corporate investments are *not* held passively like straight bonds, but rather include flexibilities that allow the manager to change the nature of the investment (in particular, the project's cash flows and risk) through learning and responding. When the corporate project involves flexibilities that allow the manager to learn something about the world and then respond by changing the quantity, risk, and timing of the project's cash flows, then the investor's similar-risk financial market opportunity must contain the same flexibility.

For example, let's change Example 1.6 just a little. Suppose that if the managers invest today, they expect the same cash flows with the same risks in Years 1 and 2 as before. But now suppose further that if the firm invests in the project today, it also buys some flexibility that arises at Year 2. If the economy booms in Year 2, the managers can scale up the investment by investing more, and in return they get an additional expected cash flow of $40 at Year 3 (with the same risk as the

---

[12] In a DCF valuation, all cash flows are assumed to be reinvested at the hurdle rate.

earlier cash flows). But if the economy tanks in Year 2, the managers can do nothing—which will make the cash flow in Year 3 absolutely zero for certain. These scenarios are shown in Figure 1.21.

An important aspect to focus on is that the risk of the project in Year 3 will depend on the action the managers take at Year 2, which in turn will depend on the outcome of some macroeconomic uncertainty. When valuing and evaluating the project today, we don't know what the managers will do in Year 2—we only know that they will make the right decision at that time based on what they learn.

So to value this project, we must recognize that the investor's similar substitute financial market opportunity must also change at Year 2: Its risk must change to reflect what the manager does. Moreover, the strategy must be based on learning the same things that the manager learns (i.e., the change in the portfolio must be conditioned on the state of the macroeconomy).

What is important here is that as time passes, the manager will learn about how the economy is developing and thus about the likelihood that the flexibility will be exploited at Year 2. As the economy strengthens, it becomes more likely that the manager will invest in the growth option, and so the financial market's similar-substitute portfolio must look more like $40 with risk in Year 3; as the economy weakens, the similar-substitute must look more like $0 with no risk in Year 3.

What we need, then, is a valuation approach that not only allows the risk of the project to change but also is set up to handle that change easily. This valuation approach must be based on a financial market portfolio strategy that is *dynamic,* meaning that the contents of the similar-substitute portfolio change as the world changes. But the valuation approach must also be consistent with the first principles of finance. Do you know what? We already have such a tool. Our option pricing models are designed specifically to handle this sort of situation.

1.7   Chapter Summary

A potential corporate project's net present value (NPV) measures the amount of investor wealth that would be created or destroyed if the firm were to adopt the opportunity. True NPV is the difference between the true financial market value of the project's future incremental cash flows and the firm's cost of investing in the project.

The true financial market value of the project's future incremental cash flows is equal to the value of a financial market portfolio, which, in the eyes of the investor, represents an equivalent opportunity. The investor only cares about cash flows, and the financial market portfolio's cash flows must be close substitutes for the project's incremental free cash flows in terms of timing and risk profile.

One way to estimate the true financial market value of a potential corporate project is by discounted cash flow (DCF). However, DCF is a shortcut approach to valuation, and it is based on

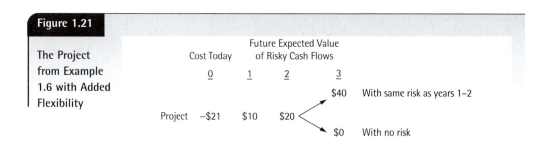

Figure 1.21

The Project from Example 1.6 with Added Flexibility

	Cost Today	Future Expected Value of Risky Cash Flows		
	0	1	2	3
				$40 With same risk as years 1–2
Project	−$21	$10	$20	
				$0 With no risk

an assumption that the financial market's similar-substitute portfolio is static (i.e., its holdings do not change over time). Therefore, we use the term *static NPV* to mean an NPV that is estimated using a DCF valuation of the project. The static NPV will be a good approximation of a project's true NPV when the financial market's similar substitute for the project is a static portfolio. This will be the case when the opportunity in question creates *no new future flexibilities* and is *now or never*.

On the other hand, DCF (and hence static NPV) can be very misleading when the potential corporate use of funds creates or maintains important future flexibilities, or when the investment may be delayed. In these situations, DCF forces the analyst to hard-wire a specific commitment to a future course of action based only on what is known at the time of the analysis. This can lead to serious errors when the project creates the ability to *learn and respond*, or when management may *wait and see*.

Options appear in many, many corporate investments, and they are a lot easier to spot once you know what you are looking for. The exercises at the end of this chapter provide a rather long list of examples, with questions to help guide you through.

1.8 Bibliography

DiMasi, Joseph A., Ronald W. Hansen, and Henry G. Grabowski, 2003. "The Price of Innovation: New Estimates of Drug Development Costs," *Journal of Health Economics* 22, 151–185.

Grabowski, Henry, John Vernon, and Joseph A. DiMasi, 2002. "Returns on Research and Development for 1990s New Drug Introductions," *Pharmacoeconomics* 20 supp. 3, 11–29.

Graham, John R., and Campbell R. Harvey, 2001. "The Theory and Practice of Corporate Finance: Evidence from the Field," *Journal of Financial Economics* 60, 187–243.

Other Suggested Reading

Arnold, Tom, and Richard L. Shockley, 2003. "Value Creation at Anheuser-Busch: A Real Options Example," *Journal of Applied Corporate Finance* 15 (Winter), 52–61.

Chew, Don (ed.), 2003. "University of Maryland Roundtable on Real Options and Corporate Practice," *Journal of Applied Corporate Finance* 15, Number 2, 8–23.

Copeland, Thomas E., and Philip T. Keenan, 1998. "Making Real Options Real," *The McKinsey Quarterly* 3, 128–141.

Copeland, Tom, and Peter Tufano, 2004. "A Real-World Way to Manage Real Options," *Harvard Business Review* (March), 90–99.

Coyne, Kevin, and Sumu Subramaniam, 1996. "Bringing Discipline to Strategy," *The McKinsey Quarterly* 4, 14–25.

Dixit, A. and R. Pindyck, 1995. "The Options Approach to Capital Investment," *Harvard Business Review* (May–June), 105–115.

Kester, W. Carl, 1984. "Today's Options for Tomorrow's Growth," *Harvard Business Review* (March-April), 153–160.

Leslie, Keith J., and Max P. Michaels, 1997. "The Real Power of Real Options," *The McKinsey Quarterly* 3, 4–22.

Luehrman, T., 1998. "Investment Opportunities as Real Options: Getting Started on the Numbers," *Harvard Business Review* (July-August).

Luehrman, T., 1998. "Strategy as a Portfolio of Real Options," *Harvard Business Review* (September-October), 89–99.

Van Putten, Alexander B., and Ian C. MacMillan, 2004. "Making Real Options Really Work," *Harvard Business Review* (December).

PROBLEMS

1. The price of a unit to be manufactured can follow one of three potential paths with equal probability:

Path	Period 0	Period 1	Period 2
Path A	$35.00	$40.00	$45.00
Path B	$35.00	$40.00	$40.00
Path C	$35.00	$35.00	$35.00
Path D	$35.00	$30.00	$25.00

a. What is the NPV of a project that will allow the firm to manufacture 200 units each year for Periods 1 and 2, assuming a cost of $12,800.00 and a discount rate of 10%?

b. Assuming that half the cost ($6,400.00) can be spent now and the rest after Period 1, what is the NPV now?

c. Suppose that after Period 1 the price is $35.00 or $30.00, then what is the NPV of investing the second half of the $12,800.00?

d. Suppose that after Period 1 the price is $40.00, then what is the NPV of investing the second half of the $12,800.00? Is the 10% discount rate appropriate here?

2. In 1998, General Mills looked at an opportunity to expand its headquarters in Golden Valley, Minnesota. At the time, the company's employees were spread over its main campus plus two leased facilities outside its main campus. Even though there was sufficient space to construct an adequately large building on the General Mills campus, the company decided to buy some additional land and build the building *off* (but near) the campus, closer to the freeway.

a. Other than the fact that the company has to buy more land, what is the difference between constructing the new building on the General Mills campus and constructing it off campus?

b. Under what conditions might General Mills want to move out of the new building and sell it in the future?

c. In this case, the static NPV of building on campus was positive, whereas the static NPV of building off campus was negative (simply because the off-campus building required an additional purchase of land). What must explain the disconnect between the static NPV analysis and management's intuition?

d. Can the increasing value of the off-campus building actually make the value of the potentially building on-campus more valuable?

3. A chemical company needed to build a captive power plant. One alternative was to invest in a plant that could produce power by burning either natural gas or naphtha. The other alternative was to invest in a plant that could only use coal as fuel. The gas/naphtha plant cost 30% more to construct than the coal-fired plant.

    a. What is the potential pitfall in using static NPV analysis to evaluate the two competing alternatives?

    b. What are the benefits to having a flexible plant?

    c. If the price of coal, natural gas, and naphtha are expected to be very stable over the foreseeable future, and the static NPV of the coal plant is higher than the static NPV for the flexible plant, is it better to build the flexible plant? Why or why not?

4. A paper products company needed a new production line to make tabletop products and other wiping material. These types of paper products require a production process known as *latex bonding*. Instead of building a dedicated latex bonding line, however, the company spent about 50% more to install a facility that could run either as a latex bonding line or as a *thermal bonding* line. Thermal bonding is used in the production of feminine hygiene products and baby diapers. At the time, the company already had sufficient capacity in their thermal bonding lines.

    a. If the market for thermal bonding products has great expansion potential, does the 50% additional expense to allow flexibility justifiable? Why?

    b. If the thermal bonding product market is at capacity and even shows signs of being at over capacity, does the 50% additional expense to allow flexibility justifiable? Why?

    c. Suppose some products can use thermal or latex bonding, and it is only matter of using the process that is least expensive at a given time, then is there value in having flexibility in the production line? Explain?

    d. Suppose demographic trends indicate that birthrates are decreasing, then would this increase or decrease the value of flexibility within the production line?

5. In 1981, the Japanese car maker Suzuki thought about selling small cars in India. At the time, the Indian auto industry was nascent, and there were only two established manufacturers (Ambassador and Fiat). Suzuki thought that their hatchback would cater to an underserved market niche, but they were unsure whether Indian customers would demand the smaller, lighter-weight, and lower-chassis car in sufficient numbers to provide an appropriate return on the capital investment required to build a new plant.

One alternative was to build a new plant in India right away. The other was to build cars in their existing plants in Japan and then ship them to India as imports. The latter choice generated losses on each car sold, as the cost of shipping and paying import taxes eliminated the profit margin at the company's desired price point. However, this strategy gave Suzuki the ability to learn demand before committing the capital required to build a new factory.

    a. On which alternative will static NPV (based on a DCF analysis) give a good approximation of true value creation or destruction? On which alternative would you be less comfortable with static NPV analysis?

    b. Suppose you were to determine that the static NPV of building a plant immediately was positive, while the static NPV of importing was negative. Under what general circumstance would it be appropriate to conclude that building a plant immediately is the correct thing to do?

c. Suppose Suzuki chooses to import for one year. At the end of that year, it has three alternatives: Build an Indian factory and switch to local production, continue to import, or stop importing and walk away. What is the cost of continuing to import for, say, one more year? Under what circumstances would it turn out to be better to stop importing and build a factory? Under what circumstances would it turn out to be better to walk away from the business?

6. Many electric utilities own what are called *peaking* electricity production units (or *peakers*). A peaker is just a very expensive way to generate electricity. In one form, it is a jet engine that burns jet fuel to turn a turbine and create electricity at a cost of about $100 per megawatt-hour. At first blush, a peaker would appear to be a waste of capital: Even in the summer, when demand is highest, the typical price of electric power is less than $70 per megawatt-hour, and utilities can freely buy electricity from each other to meet local demand.

    a. Suppose you are the manager of a utility that owns a peaker. When would you ever turn it on?

    b. Draw an *x-y* graph that plots the market price of power on the *x*-axis and the payoff from employing the best strategy with the peaker (either turn it on or off) on the *y*-axis. What do you get?

    c. Why does this make it difficult to value a peaker using DCF?

    d. In what parts of North America will a high-cost peaker like this one have the highest true value?

7. *Stainless steel* is a low-carbon-steel product that contains at least 10.5% chromium (sometimes with other metals like nickel and molybdenum, depending on the application). Thus, a mill producing stainless steel takes pig iron, chromium, and energy as inputs and creates stainless steel as an output.

    a. Suppose the break-even price for producing stainless steel is $4.50 per unit. If the current market price for stainless steel is $4.25, should the plant shut down immediately? Consider the cost of closing the plant and the volatility of price in your answer.

    b. Assume the plant is currently shut down and the market price of stainless steel is $4.65 per unit, should the plant reopen immediately? Consider the cost of reopening the plant and the volatility of price in your answer.

    c. Given your answers above, why would a plant that is losing money stay open and a plant that could potentially be profitable stay closed?

8. Grupo Editorio Norma (GEN), a Colombia-based company, is one of the major book publishers in Latin America. In 1997, GEN established a subsidiary that would publish magazines. After careful research, Norma Magazines settled on three opportunities: A DirecTV guide for Colombian customers and two magazines that would be targeted at frequent travelers (*Destinos Colombia* and *Destinos Venezuela*). However, senior managers at GEN were very worried about their ability to generate a profit in this segment. There were three key uncertainties: (1) how well the company's telemarketers could penetrate the target market, (2) how many people would actually demand these products (which would be a function of Norma's editorial skill as well as the strength of the local economies), and (3) the renewal rates (which also were related to the company's skill as well as economic conditions).

The company had two alternatives for investment. In one, it could roll out all three magazines simultaneously. In the other, it could stage its investment by first launching the Colombian DirecTV guide, then *Destinos Colombia* if things were going well, and later *Destinos Venezuela* if the first two were successful.

    a. If gasoline prices are expected to become unstable (which would affect travel), does the value of the staged strategy increase or decrease? Why?

    b. Suppose the company's sales force loses key individuals, which could hurt magazine demand and renewal rates. How does this affect the value of the two strategies for publishing the three magazines, and would one strategy be more affected than the other?

    c. Assume the Colombian DirecTV guide publication performs marginally well but not well enough for GEN to launch *Destinos Colombia*. At the same time, the Venezuelan economy begins to boom. Provide an argument for exercising the option to publish *Destinos Venezuela* and for not exercising the option because *Destinos Colombia* has not been launched first.

9. Citibank Thailand was considering a new operations procedure that would move certain transactions from a paper-based environment to an electronic environment. This was an expensive proposition because it would require a substantial investment in technology, in employee training, and in client education/service/support. However, the new procedure had the potential to create value in two ways: (1) by lowering the cost of doing business and (2) by creating a strategic advantage for the company.

    Instead of making one giant switch, Citibank Thailand decided to implement the new procedure with only large clients. This required investing in a part of the technology as well as overtime pay and a few additional employees, but it gave the company the ability to see whether or not the new system would work.

    a. Assuming that testing the new system with large clients is a success, should Citibank launch the new system or perform further testing? Answer this question based on how representative large clients are relative to the entire client base.

    b. Suppose that testing the new system with large clients was unsuccessful. Based on issues discussed in part a, should the new system not be implemented? Why or why not?

    c. Suppose that years later the new system has been implemented with great success. You are at a meeting in which a colleague is criticizing management for being so slow in implementing the system. How do you defend the decision of taking the time to test the system prior to full scale implementation?

10. Windwood National Corporation is a truck manufacturing company in Lafayette, Indiana. In the 1990s, Windwood developed a new way of making truck trailer sidewalls by sandwiching plastic inside of galvanized steel. The new *DuraSide* sidewalls would be much lighter, stronger, easier to repair, and easier to paint than the existing standard aluminum sidewalls. Nevertheless, DuraSide sidewalls were also more expensive to produce.

    In 1999, Windwood decided to build a factory to produce the new *DuraSide* trailers. Because demand was uncertain, Windwood's executives were not sure what size factory they needed. Expected demand was 2,400 units per year, but the executives realized that this could be as low as 1,600 units in the worst-case scenario or as high as 3,200 units per year in the best-case scenario. A one-line plant would cost $15 million and could produce 1,500 trailers per year. A two-line plant would cost $30 million and could produce 3,000 trailers per year. A third alternative would be an *expandable* one-line plant, which would cost $16.5 million to build but could be scaled up to two lines rather quickly at an additional cost of $14 million.

  a. Assume the plant has an effective life of 30 years and each trailer generates a cash flow of $1200.00. What is the NPV of a one-line plant versus a two-line plant assuming either plant is able to sell all of its capacity (assume a 10% APR discount rate)? What are the NPVs based on the expected demand of 2400 units?

  b. Based on static NPV with a 10% discount rate, which is better if demand is found to be 2800 units per year with certainty: (1) the expandable plant, which will be able to produce 2800 units in its second year (assume that $14 million is spent at the end of the first year and both lines can produce product for a full 30 years after expansion) or (2) a second one-line plant that could begin production in the third year with the $15 million investment made at the end of the first year? Is 10% the appropriate discount rate? Why or why not?

11. In the summer of 2003, a large producer of custom industrial machinery received a somewhat unique bid request from DaimlerChrysler. At the time, DaimlerChrysler wanted to construct additional production capacity for their new pseudo-SUV called the Pacifica. DaimlerChrysler had sufficient existing capacity to meet *expected* demand, but their problem was that they were not sure whether the product would be a hit or a bust. If the Pacifica was a hit, the company would need the extra production capacity so that they would not miss out on demand; but if it was a bust, they would not want an idle production line burning capital. So DaimlerChrysler asked the machinery company to bid for enough machines to construct the entire plant, but to supply them in stages and only if necessary. In other words, DaimlerChrysler wanted a firm commitment for the price of all of the machines, but they only wanted to commit to actually buying the first X% of them upon delivery in T months; at that time, DaimlerChrysler would tell the vendor whether or not the next X% of the machines would be purchased.

  a. As the vendor, should you simply price the staged machinery purchase the same as if all of the machinery is purchased at once (including large purchase discounts)?

  b. As the vendor, why might you counter DaimlerChrysler's offer by providing a discount to the purchase of the machinery if DaimlerChrysler commits to buying all of the machinery now?

  c. If the DaimlerChrysler plan is implemented, who is writing the option, the vendor or DaimlerChrysler? Who should be compensated for providing the optionality?

12. Why is it that the true NPV of *real asset* investments can be positive or negative, while the true NPV of *financial market* investments is assumed to be zero?

2

THE THEORY OF VALUE

2 VALUATION OF FINANCIAL ASSETS

As I discussed in Chapter 1, a corporate manager must estimate the true financial market value of a new project to evaluate whether the firm should invest in it. This is why a typical corporate finance course devotes so much time to topics from the field of investments (like the investor's portfolio decision, diversification, and the risk-return trade-off)—corporate financial managers cannot do their job without understanding what *value* means in the financial markets, and these investments topics provide the foundation.

In a typical corporate finance course, students learn two techniques for attaching a value to a financial market security (one being our old friend discounted cash flow, or DCF, and the other being the Black-Scholes option pricing model) and how to use those tools to value and evaluate new corporate projects. Since finance professors usually don't have the time (and patience) to present a unified framework, many students come away believing that these two valuation tools are unrelated and are based on very different theoretical foundations.

My goal in this chapter is to show you that all valuation techniques in finance (be they DCF or option pricing models) are variations on one common theme—pricing by an arbitrage argument—and are based on a single critical assumption (that the financial market admits no arbitrage opportunities).

Chapter Plan

This chapter starts with some basic definitions and illustrations of what we mean by *arbitrage* and *valuation by an arbitrage argument*. I'll then show that when we value a security by an arbitrage argument, we are employing a very general technique known as *linear pricing*.

The idea behind linear pricing is really simple: If you can decompose a financial asset into a set of simpler *building block securities,* then the value of the financial asset must equal the sum total value of its building blocks (or else there's an arbitrage opportunity). By the end of this chapter you should realize that you've been doing linear pricing every time you've done a DCF calculation, just as you've been doing linear pricing every time you've applied an option pricing model. The theoretical foundation is the same either way: Absence of arbitrage (an assumption) makes it all possible.

The concept of decomposing a complex security's cash flows into a set of simpler building blocks is the motif I'll use throughout this chapter and the next two. In this chapter, as well as in Chapter 3, our building blocks will be basic financial market securities, including a risk-free bond and a market index mutual fund. It will be useful for you to think of these securities as "molecular" building blocks, because in Chapter 4 we'll see that these molecules can be further decomposed into a set of "atomic" building blocks (which my advanced readers will know as *state securities*). The *fundamental theorem of asset pricing* will tie all of this together.

To drive home my point, I'll set up a simplified economy so that we can get a deeper understanding of arbitrage valuation. The economy will present risk in a way that may be different from what you've seen in the past: There will be only one future point in time (i.e., the economy will last only one period), but there will be many possible aggregate outcomes (or *states of nature*). Don't be turned off by this simplification—this is the foundation of the notion of risk in finance, and it is easy to extend it to a world where time marches on.

We'll place ourselves in the model economy and value some securities. An important point will be that all of these securities will be *existing* securities; we'll postpone to Chapter 3 the issue of introducing *new* securities into the financial market. In the first example, I'll show you what purely *idiosyncratic risk* really is, and why we don't care about it (something you already know, but need to see in a different way). We'll then look at a security that has firm-specific risk but no *market risk* (or *common risk*), and I'll show you why the financial market treats this just like a risk-free security. We'll then value a stock that carries both firm-specific and market risk, and finally we'll value an option on the stock.

The one common theme behind all of the examples is arbitrage, and we'll do each valuation using a no-arbitrage argument (i.e., by linear pricing). After each arbitrage valuation, I'll show you that *if* the capital asset pricing model (CAPM) holds, then using it to get a risk-adjusted discount rate for a DCF approach to linear pricing is actually just a shortcut way of doing the arbitrage valuation. Finally, I'll show you *why* the CAPM won't work in all situations (in particular, when you are looking at options). I'll close the chapter by discussing how *trading* in the financial market makes it possible for us to decompose any existing security into a very small number of molecular building-block securities.

2.1 Arbitrage and Arbitrage Opportunities

An arbitrage is a financial market activity that creates a "free lunch"—a profit with no investment. It involves taking a long position in some asset or portfolio and a simultaneous short position in some other asset or portfolio such that one of two things occurs:

1. There is an immediate cash *inflow* from the activity but no future cash *outflow*. This is "money lying on the street," and we eat the free lunch today. It happens when the future cash flows on the long and short positions cancel each other out, but the proceeds from the short sale exceed the cost of the long position.
2. There is no immediate cash inflow or outflow from the activity, but there is a strictly positive cash inflow in some future scenario (without the chance of a cash outflow). This is a free lunch to be eaten tomorrow. This occurs when the current prices of the long and short positions are equal but should be different.

The first situation is the standard definition of an arbitrage, and we will focus our discussions around it. I should point out that if you find yourself in the second situation, you can most likely convert it into the first situation (and cash it in immediately) through some other financial market transactions.

Figure 2.1		Cash Flow Today	Cash Flow in One Year
The Simple Arbitrage	Buy Low: Buy Bond 2	−$925	+$1,000
	Sell High: Sell Bond 1	+$950	−$1,000
	Arbitrage Profit	+$25	$0

The key to finding an arbitrage opportunity is to find two portfolios that have the same future cash flows but different current prices. Once you've located them, simply follow the old saw "buy low and sell high": Short-sell the expensive one, buy the cheap one, and eat your free lunch.[1]

For an absurdly simple illustration, suppose you find two government bonds that each promise $1000 for sure in one year's time. The current price of Bond 1 is $950, while the price of Bond 2 is $925. What do you do? Buy low and sell high—purchase Bond 2 and short-sell Bond 1—and eat a free lunch, as I show in Figure 2.1.

True arbitrageurs do exactly this, and they eat their free lunches without taking any risk at all. And there are a few arbitrageurs who dine very well. But this is an extremely competitive game, and the successful player needs to have huge investments in information and trading technologies along with an enormous amount of skill. Competition for arbitrage profits is so intense, in fact, that the opportunities to capture them only last for brief amounts of time. In Figure 2.1 the arbitrageurs would try to short-sell huge quantities of Bond 1 and simultaneously purchase as many units of Bond 2 as possible. That is, their orders would increase the supply of Bond 1 (which would drive down its market price) and at the same time increase the demand for Bond 2 (which would drive up its market price). The first ones to place the orders would get a free lunch, but the market prices of the two bonds would converge quickly.

What I'm trying to say here is that the existence of sophisticated and powerful arbitrageurs makes it impossible for you, me, or a corporate financial manager to eat free lunches with any frequency at all. For our purposes, we can view the financial market as offering no arbitrage opportunities. This assumption (which is an approximation but a very small one) allows us to value securities by comparing them with very close substitutes—what we call *arbitrage valuation* or *linear pricing*.

Valuation by Arbitrage in the Financial Markets

Valuation of financial market securities is an extremely important area of academic study, and we refer to the many issues involved using the umbrella term *asset pricing*. Modern asset pricing theory provides the foundation of everything finance professors teach (although we show precious little of the theory to undergrads and MBAs), and there's one particular result that is so

---

[1] Short-selling is a very common activity in securities markets. To do it, you borrow the security or portfolio from a securities lender (with the promise to give it back later) and immediately sell it on the market at the market price. When the loan comes due, you have to go to the market and buy the security back at its new market price (whatever it may be) so that you can make good on the loan. You must overcollateralize your securities loan with either cash or Treasury bills, and the interest rate you pay on the loan is determined by the demand for loans of that security (as well as the supply of the security to lend). Also, you must recompensate the lender for any dividends or interest payments that they missed receiving while the loan was outstanding. The major securities lenders are the financial institutions who provide custodial services for mutual funds and large pension funds, and the portfolios of their clients provide the inventory of securities to lend.

Figure 2.2			CF Today	CF in 1 Year
Arbitrage Valuation of the Young Bond	Buy low: Buy two old bonds		−$1,904.76	+$2,000
	Sell high: Sell young bond		+$P_{young}	−$2,000
	No arbitrage assumption		$0	$0

fundamental to our current understanding of the world that we call it the *fundamental theorem of asset pricing*. For our purposes, we can interpret the fundamental theorem as telling us the following: If we are willing to assume that the financial markets are free of arbitrage opportunities, then we can value any existing security by decomposing it into a set of building block securities and adding up the value of the building blocks.[2] The portfolio of building blocks will generate the *similar substitute* (see Chapter 1), and since an investor will be indifferent between the existing security and the portfolio of building blocks, the two must have the same price.

Arbitrage valuation, or valuation by close substitutes, is the method of finance. In fact, it is the single central theme that ties together everything we teach at undergraduate and MBA levels. Here's how we do it. To value a security, we first estimate its future cash flows. We then look into the financial market and form a *tracking portfolio* that has the same future cash flow characteristics. (I'll get to what the terms *future cash flow characteristics* and *same* mean shortly.) If there are no arbitrage opportunities, we can conclude that the price of the security must be equal to the current market value of the tracking portfolio.

For another absurdly simple illustration, suppose the government just issued a new one-year zero-coupon bond with a $2000 face value. We look to the financial markets and find that there also exists an older zero-coupon government bond with one year left to maturity and with face value $1000, and the current price of this old bond is $952.38. Since the old bond promises half as much future cash flow as the young bond, our tracking portfolio must contain *two* of the old bonds to be a similar substitute for the cash flows on the young bond. Now calculate what would happen if you buy two old bonds, short-sell the young bond, and assume that there are no arbitrage opportunities. Figure 2.2 shows the result.

In absence of arbitrage, it must be that $-\$1904.76 + \$P_{young} = \$0$, or $\$P_{young} = \$1904.76$. The current price of the tracking portfolio equals the price of the young bond *given no arbitrage*.

Why do we also call this linear pricing? Because what we've done is decompose the young bond into a linear combination of existing building blocks (the tracking portfolio). In this example, our building block is the old bond, and it is easy to see that the new bond's future cash flows are linear in the future cash flows of the older bond:

$$y = mx + b$$
New bond cash flow $= 2 \times$ Old bond cash flow $+ 0$

---

[2] The *fundamental theorem of asset pricing* tells us that the following conditions are equivalent: (1) absence of arbitrage, (2) existence of a consistent positive linear pricing rule, and (3) existence of some agent with strictly increasing preferences that has an optimum portfolio. The *pricing rule representation theorem* tells us that we can express the positive linear pricing rule in several different ways: As state prices, risk-neutral probabilities, state-price densities, or an abstract linear functional. See Dybvig and Ross (2003) for an elegant proof as well as a very nice discussion.

Since an investor would be indifferent between the new bond and two of the old ones, the price of the new bond must be 2 times the price of the old bond (else there's an arbitrage opportunity):

$$\text{Price of new bond} = 2 \times \text{Price of old bond} + 0$$
$$= 2 \times \$952.38$$
$$= \$1904.76$$

If the future cash flows on a security are equivalent to a linear combination of the future cash flows on a set of building block securities, then the price of the first security must be the same linear combination of the prices of the building blocks. That's linear pricing.

You'll see a lot of different names used for the tracking portfolio. Some people use the term *arbitrage portfolio*. Others call it the *hedge portfolio*. Regardless of what you call it, the tracking portfolio tells us the price of the new security.

Notice that we could have gone about the arbitrage valuation (that is, the linear pricing) in a slightly different way. The price of the $1,000 bond (i.e., the old bond) is $952.38, so its rate of return is 5%:

$$\frac{\$1,000.00}{\$952.38} - 1 = 5\%$$

If we had then discounted the $2,000 future value of the young bond by 5%, we would have arrived at the same answer:

$$\frac{\$2,000}{1.05} = \$1,904.76$$

which illustrates a point that I'll reiterate several times in this chapter: When you value by DCF, you are actually doing an arbitrage valuation. The discount rate you use in the DCF approach is actually the equilibrium rate of return on the tracking portfolio, and the DCF value is actually the market price of the tracking portfolio. This is still linear pricing, just transformed into a percentage return relationship.

The critical issue in arbitrage valuation is obviously the identification of an appropriate tracking portfolio. This is fairly simple when your future cash flows are absolutely certain, as in the earlier examples. The task is more complex, however, when the future is uncertain. Before I can show you the general principles of valuation in a risky world, I have to explain the concept of *risk*. To do this, I need to set up a model economy and generate some molecular building blocks.

2.2   Our Model Economy

Let's think about a world with a large number of firms whose financial securities trade in a securities market. The future cash flows on the securities are risky. The financial market assigns current values (prices) to the existing securities through some equilibrium process that describes the consumption/investment decision of the individuals in the economy (through their current and future endowments, their preferences including their attitudes towards risk, their information and beliefs about the future, and their range of investment opportunities).

We divide the risks of the future cash flows into two broad classes: Risks due to common factors and risks due to firm-specific outcomes. While we don't really need to specify the equilibrium process, I would like to work in a world with which you are probably familiar. So I will assume that the securities in our world share only one source of *common* risk: The overall strength of the macroeconomy.

Common Risk

Economic strength is not entirely predictable, and unexpected changes in economic activity can lead directly to changes in the values of corporate assets and corporate securities. For example, think about firms that produce and/or sell luxury goods like yachts, private jets, expensive watches, and the like. These firms tend to do very well in boom economies, as their sales increase with increasing consumer wealth. On the flip side, the recent recession provides ample proof that these sorts of firms do very poorly when the economy weakens. Of course, current prices of the stocks and bonds of these companies reflect the *expected* future state of the economy—but *unexpected* economic changes (good or bad) will lead to changes in the values of these securities. The risk that a security's value will change because of shocks to the macroeconomy is called *systematic risk,* and you can picture this with the help of an "economic thermometer" as shown in Figure 2.3.

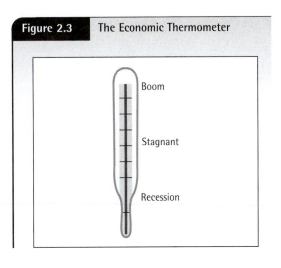

Figure 2.3   The Economic Thermometer

We call the possible levels of future economic activity *macroeconomic states of nature,* or simply *states.* In the economic thermometer, in Figure 2.3, we can think of every possible economic temperature reading as a possible state of nature. A security is exposed to systematic risk to the extent that the resolution of the macroeconomic state (i.e., the economic temperature reading) affects the firm's cash flows.

Of course, temperatures on the economic thermometer lie in a continuous range, and the scaling is quite arbitrary (just as in the physical world, where temperatures can be expressed on many different scales). To understand the world, we will work as if there are only three possible macroeconomic states at the end of one year: *Boom, stagnant,* and *recession* (just as I've labeled on the economic thermometer in Figure 2.3). Suppose further that the generally accepted *subjective* belief is that the economy will boom with probability 0.36, that it will be stagnant with probability 0.48, and that it will go into recession with probability 0.16. Figure 2.4 provides a visual representation of how our economy will evolve over the year:

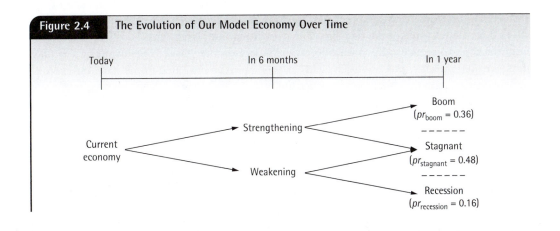

Figure 2.4   The Evolution of Our Model Economy Over Time

The abstraction to only three possible macroeconomic states is not an issue—everything that I'll show you can be generalized to a world with a continuum of states. The essential issues I need to have in my *model* of the world are that the state of the macroeconomy at the end of the year is unknown today (hence there is risk in the world), and that the state of the economy is changing continuously through the year (as opposed to simply lurching into one of the three states). Keep this notion of continuous change in mind. For the time being, we will ignore what happens during the year and simply focus our attention on the three possible outcomes.

Firm-Specific Risks

While the overall health of the macroeconomy is the only source of *common* risk, the securities in our market can also change value because of the outcomes of *firm-specific* risks. There are many, many of these firm-specific risks, and I need to provide only a small number of examples to illustrate the concept:

- Unanticipated success or failure of a pharmaceuticals clinical trial (e.g., Imclone)
- Incapacity of (or bad publicity about) a key executive (e.g., Martha Stewart Living Omnimedia, Inc.)
- Unanticipated technological breakthrough (e.g., DuPont's development of synthetic fibers)
- Unanticipated product defect that triggers product liability (e.g., Bausch & Lomb and *ReNu with MoistureLoc*)
- Fire in a factory, or flood damage to property
- Unexpected windfalls (e.g., a consumer fad, like the craze for the George Foreman Grill)

There are two important features of these firm-specific outcomes. First, they are *independent of the macroeconomic state of nature.* For example, the probability of a fire in a company's warehouse does not depend on the health of the macroeconomy—a fire is just as likely (or unlikely) if the economy is booming or the economy is in recession.[3] Second, they are *independent of each other.* For example, the likelihood that Hasbro discovers another monster hit toy (like Cabbage Patch Dolls) does not depend on the outcome of Lilly's current clinical trial.[4]

In other words, each firm-specific risk is its own random event—like a coin-flip. If I flip two coins next year, their outcomes (heads or tails) will not be affected by the overall state of the economy at that time. Furthermore, the outcome of the second flip will not in any way be affected by the outcome of the first flip. The coins need not be fair (that is, the probability of heads need not be equal to the probability of tails), nor do they need to be identical. The only thing we need is for the probability of heads on any flip to be unrelated to the state of the economy and unrelated to the result of the other flip.

---

[3] I'm ignoring moral hazard here. If you want, you can consider the individual acts of arson that are driven by economic conditions to be macroeconomic risks and the remainder of all warehouse fires to be firm-specific.

[4] OK, I admit that the Imclone and Martha Stewart examples are related, and that a flood can hurt more than one business. We just need these sorts of coincidental outcomes to be isolated among a rather small number of firms in the overall economy.

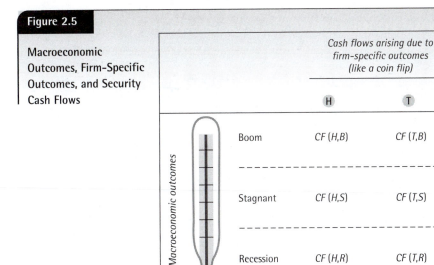

Figure 2.5

Macroeconomic
Outcomes, Firm-Specific
Outcomes, and Security
Cash Flows

	Cash flows arising due to firm-specific outcomes (like a coin flip)	
Macroeconomic outcomes	H	T
Boom	CF (H,B)	CF (T,B)
Stagnant	CF (H,S)	CF (T,S)
Recession	CF (H,R)	CF (T,R)

We can combine our economic thermometer with our coin-flip, as I've done in Figure 2.5, to illustrate the sources of risk in a security.

In Figure 2.5, variations in a security's cash flow *across* states (up and down) are due to systematic risk, while variations in a security's cash flow *within* states (left to right) are due to firm-specific risk. The notation I'm using in the picture is that of joint outcomes. CF(H,B) is the cash flow on the security when the coin turns up heads and the boom economic state occurs.

Example 2.1. The Coin–Flip Security

Thinking of firm-specific risk as being like a coin-flip helps us illustrate a very, very important result in finance—the idea of idiosyncratic risk.

Suppose that someone in our economy offers an interesting new security. At the end of the year, an independent party will flip a fair coin. The coin-flip result and the resolution of the macroeconomic state jointly determine the cash flows on the security. If the economy booms and the coin-flip turns up heads, then the holder of the security receives $500 from the issuer (or the *counterparty*); however, if the economy booms, but the coin-flip turns up tails, then the holder of the security must pay the counterparty $500. If the economy is stagnant, and the coin-flip results in heads, the holder of the security receives $250; however, if the economy is stagnant, and the coin-flip results in tails, the holder of the security must pay the counterparty $250. If the economy is in recession, no cash changes hands, and the coin-flip is irrelevant. What is the market value of this weird coin-flip security?

Figure 2.6 puts the security's end-of-year cash flows in a diagram like that in Figure 2.5. Figure 2.6 includes an important result (which is the key issue in this long but critical example): The *conditional mean cash flow* is $0 given each possible state of nature. I use the term

Figure 2.6	Conditional Mean Cash Flows of Coin-Flip Security		
		Cash Flows Arising Due to Coin-Flip Outcomes		Conditional Mean
		Heads $pr_{heads} = 0.5$	Tails $pr_{tails} = 0.5$	Cash Flow (expected CF given state)
Macroeconomic Outcomes	Boom $pr_{boom} = 0.36$	$CF(H,B) = \$500$	$CF(T,B) = -\$500$	$E\{CF|boom\} = \$0$
	Stagnant $pr_{stagnant} = 0.48$	$CF(H,S) = \$250$	$CF(T,S) = -\$250$	$E\{CF|stagnant\} = \$0$
	Recession $pr_{recession} = 0.16$	$CF(H,R) = \$0$	$CF(T,R) = \$0$	$E\{CF|recession\} = \$0$

conditional mean cash flow to refer to the expected cash flow *given* a possible macroeconomic state of nature. Since the probabilities of heads or tails is independent of the state of nature, we can calculate the conditional mean cash flows as follows:

$$E\{CF|boom\} = pr_{heads} \times CF(H,B) + pr_{tails} \times CF(T,B)$$
$$= 0.5 \times \$500 + 0.5 \times -\$500 = \$0$$
$$E\{CF|stagnant\} = pr_{heads} \times CF(H,S) + pr_{tails} \times CF(T,S)$$
$$= 0.5 \times \$250 + 0.5 \times -\$250 = \$0$$
$$E\{CF|recession\} = pr_{heads} \times CF(H,R) + pr_{tails} \times CF(T,R)$$
$$= 0.5 \times \$0 + 0.5 \times -\$0 = \$0$$

In a situation like this, where the expected payoff on a security is zero given (or within) each possible macroeconomic state, we often say that the security displays *conditional mean-zero cash flows*. The value of a security with conditional mean-zero cash flows turns out to have profound implications for all of our valuation problems, so it is essential that you understand this example.

It should be no surprise that the overall expected cash flow on the coin-flip security is zero:

$$E\{CF^{coin-flip}\} = pr_{boom} \times E\{CF|boom\} + pr_{stagnant} \times E\{CF|stagnant\} + pr_{recession} \times E\{CF|recession\}$$
$$= 0.36 \times \$0 + 0.48 \times \$0 + 0.16 \times \$0$$
$$= \$0$$

What is the variance in the cash flows on the coin-flip security? This is easy if you recall the formula for the variance of a random variable x:

$$var(x) = E\{x^2\} - (E\{x\})^2 \qquad (2.1)$$

Using Equation (2.1), the variance of the cash flows on the coin-flip security is

$$var(CF^{coin-flip}) = E\{(CF^{coin-flip})^2\} - (E\{CF^{coin-flip}\})^2 \qquad (2.2)$$

We've already calculated that $E\{CF^{\text{coin-flip}}\} = \$0$, so we know that $(E\{CF^{\text{coin-flip}}\})^2 = \$0$. To calculate the cash flow variance of the coin-flip security, all we need to do is evaluate the first term in Equation (2.2):

$$
\begin{aligned}
E\{(CF^{\text{coin-flip}})^2\} = & \; pr_{\text{boom}} \times [pr_{\text{heads}} \times CF(H,B)^2 + pr_{\text{tails}} \times CF(T,B)^2] \\
& + pr_{\text{stagnant}} \times [pr_{\text{heads}} \times CF(H,S)^2 + pr_{\text{tails}} \times CF(T,S)^2] \\
& + pr_{\text{recession}} \times [pr_{\text{heads}} \times CF(H,R)^2 + pr_{\text{tails}} \times CF(T,R)^2] \\
= & \; 0.36 \times [0.5 \times (\$500)^2 + 0.5 \times (-\$500)^2] \\
& + 0.48 \times [0.5 \times (\$250)^2 + 0.5 \times (-\$250)^2] \\
& + 0.16 \times [0.5 \times (\$0)^2 + 0.5 \times (-\$0)^2] \\
= & \; (\$346.41)^2
\end{aligned}
$$

(which is denominated in squared dollars). Therefore, filling in Equation (2.2), the variance of the cash flows on the coin-flip security is

$$
\begin{aligned}
var(CF^{\text{coin-flip}}) &= E\{(CF^{\text{coin-flip}})^2\} - (E\{CF^{\text{coin-flip}}\})^2 \\
&= (\$346.41)^2 - (\$0)^2 \\
&= (\$346.41)^2
\end{aligned}
$$

and the standard deviation of the cash flows on the coin-flip security is $346.41.

The coin-flip security is indeed risky—its future payoff is uncertain. Moreover, the amount of cash at risk depends on the state of nature: If the economy booms, the holder faces a large gamble; if the economy is in recession, the holder faces no gamble at all. Does the current market price of the security reflect these risks?

The answer is no, because the coin-flip risk is completely diversifiable. If the security were to carry a reward for this risk, the holder could shed the risk completely and costlessly (through simple portfolio diversification) and keep the reward. This would be a free lunch. Let me demonstrate the diversification.

The way we eliminate the coin-flip risk (which is conditional mean zero, or mean zero in every macroeconomic state of nature) is by combining it with other (unrelated) conditional mean-zero risks into a portfolio. To keep things simple, let's suppose that there's another coin-flip security with the same expected value ($0) and standard deviation ($346.41) as our original coin-flip security. The only thing we need is for the second coin-flip security to be independent of the first—that is, its payoff relies on a completely different coin-flip.

If we form a portfolio with $\frac{1}{2}$ of its value invested in the first coin-flip security and the other $\frac{1}{2}$ invested in the second, the portfolio's expected cash flow will obviously be zero:

$$
\begin{aligned}
E\{CF_{\text{portfolio}}\} &= \frac{1}{2} \times E\{CF_{\text{coin-flip security 1}}\} + \frac{1}{2} \times E\{CF_{\text{coin-flip security 2}}\} \\
&= \frac{1}{2} \times \$0 + \frac{1}{2} \times \$0 \\
&= \$0
\end{aligned}
$$

That is, the expected cash flow on the portfolio of two independent coin-flip securities is identical to the expected cash flow on a single coin-flip security. But will the cash flow risk of the portfolio equal the cash flow risk of each individual coin-flip security? *No.*

If you have N assets in a portfolio, numbered $1, \ldots, N$, you calculate the variance of the portfolio's cash flows as follows:

$$\sigma^2_{\text{portfolio } CF} = \sum_{i=1}^{N}\sum_{j=1}^{N}(\text{fraction invested in asset } i)(\text{fraction invested in asset } j)\,cov(CF_i, CF_j) \quad (2.3)$$

Keep in mind that for any random variable x, $cov(x, x) = var(x)$. In our simple portfolio of two coin-flip securities, the portfolio variance will be

$$\begin{aligned}
\sigma^2_{\text{coin-flip portfolio } CF} = {} & (\% \text{ invested in coin-flip security 1})^2 \times var(CF_{\text{coin-flip security 1}}) \\
& + 2 \times (\% \text{ invested in coin-flip security 1}) \times (\% \text{ invested in coin-flip security 2}) \\
& \times cov(CF_{\text{coin-flip security 1}}, CF_{\text{coin-flip security 2}}) \\
& + (\% \text{ invested in coin-flip security 2})^2 \times var(CF_{\text{coin-flip security 2}}) \quad (2.4)
\end{aligned}$$

We know that the fractions invested in each coin-flip security are $\frac{1}{2}$, and we know that the cash flow variance of each coin-flip security is $(\$346.41)^2$, so to fill out Equation (2.4) we need to calculate the covariance between the cash flows of coin-flip security 1 and coin-flip security 2 (the third line on the right-hand side). The covariance between random variables x and y is defined as

$$cov(x, y) = E\{xy\} - E\{x\}E\{y\} \quad (2.5)$$

Knowing this, the covariance between the cash flows of the two coin-flip securities is

$$cov(CF_{\text{coin-flip 1}}, CF_{\text{coin-flip 2}}) = E\{(CF_{\text{coin-flip 1}} \times CF_{\text{coin-flip 2}})\} - E\{CF_{\text{coin-flip 1}}\} \times E\{CF_{\text{coin-flip 2}}\} \quad (2.6)$$

Since we know that $E\{CF_{\text{coin-flip 1}}\} = E\{CF_{\text{coin-flip 2}}\} = \$0$, we only need to evaluate the first term on the right-hand side of Equation (2.6):

$$\begin{aligned}
E\{(CF_{\text{coin-flip 1}} \times CF_{\text{coin-flip 2}})\} = {} & pr_{\text{boom}} \times [E\{CF_{\text{coin-flip 1}}|\text{boom}\} \times E\{CF_{\text{coin-flip 2}}|\text{boom}\}] \\
& + pr_{\text{stagnant}} \times [E\{CF_{\text{coin-flip 1}}|\text{stagnant}\} \times E\{CF_{\text{coin-flip 2}}|\text{stagnant}\}] \quad (2.7) \\
& + pr_{\text{recession}} \times [E\{CF_{\text{coin-flip 1}}|\text{recession}\} \times E\{CF_{\text{coin-flip 2}}|\text{recession}\}]
\end{aligned}$$

Since the expected cash flow on each coin-flip security is zero given every state of nature, each term on the right-hand side of Equation (2.7) is zero. So $E\{(CF_{\text{coin-flip 1}} \times CF_{\text{coin-flip 2}})\} = 0$ as well; by filling in the right hand side of Equation (2.6), we can conclude that the covariance between the cash flows on coin-flip security 1 and coin-flip security 2 is zero.

The fact that the cash flow covariance between the two coin-flips is zero has significant import for the variance of the cash flows of our portfolio of coin-flips, because the entire second part of Equation (2.4) (the part that depends on the covariance between the two coin-flips) disappears. Plugging what we know into Equation (2.4),

$$\begin{aligned}
\sigma^2_{\text{coin-flip portfolio } CF} &= \left(\frac{1}{2}\right)^2 \times (\$346.41)^2 + 2 \times \left(\frac{1}{2}\right) \times \left(\frac{1}{2}\right) \times (\$0) + \left(\frac{1}{2}\right)^2 \times (\$346.41)^2 \\
&= 2 \times \frac{1}{4} \times (\$346.41)^2 \\
&= \frac{1}{2}(\$346.41)^2
\end{aligned}$$

Notice what happened here—by spreading our wealth equally across a portfolio of two independent coin-flip securities, the variance of the portfolio's cash flows dropped by *one-half*, and yet the expected cash flow remained constant. What happens if we add a third identical but independent coin-flip security to our portfolio and equally weight the three?

$$\sigma^2_{\text{coin-flip portfolio } CF} = \frac{1}{3}(\$346.41)^2$$

What if we put four identical and independent coin-flip securities into an equally weighted portfolio?

$$\sigma^2_{\text{coin-flip portfolio } CF} = \frac{1}{4}(\$346.41)^2$$

I'm sure that you can see the general result by now. If we hold N identical but uncorrelated coin-flip securities in a portfolio with equal weight in each, the cash flow variance of the portfolio will be

$$\sigma^2_{\text{coin-flip portfolio } CF} = \frac{1}{N}(\$346.41)^2 \tag{2.8}$$

and as the portfolio gets large,

$$\lim_{N\to\infty} \sigma^2_{\text{coin-flip portfolio } CF} = \lim_{N\to\infty} \frac{1}{N}(\$346.41)^2 = 0$$

So a portfolio strategy of spreading one's wealth across a large number of independent coin-flip securities has the same expected future cash flow as any individual coin-flip security ($0), but with vanishing variance (i.e., vanishing risk). This does not require each coin-flip security to have the same variance. I used this simplification just to make the point—as long as the coin-flip securities have zero covariance, the portfolio's cash flow variance will be (approximately) inversely proportional to the number of coin-flip securities in the portfolio.

The fact that all of the risk of a coin-flip security can be shed through diversification has a direct effect on its value. If the market value of the coin-flip security is anything other than zero, there's an arbitrage opportunity.

To see this, suppose that the market price of a coin-flip security is $1. An alert market participant could engineer an immediate risk-free profit by getting together N friends and forming a mutual fund (with equal fractional ownership) that short-sells N independent coin-flip securities. The immediate cash inflow is $N \times \$1 = \$N$ (so everyone makes a dollar), the expected future cash flow on the portfolio is $0 (so everyone expects no future cash inflow or outflow), and the standard deviation of cash flows on each individual's claim on the portfolio is $\$346.41/\sqrt{N}$ (so as we add more friends and short more securities, each participant's risk falls).[5] For example, if we find 100 participants and short-sell 100 independent but identical coin-flip securities, the immediate cash flow from forming the portfolio is $100 (so everyone makes $1),

---

[5] Since the coin-flip securities are independent, then each additional security sold short increases the entire fund's expected cash flow by $0 and its cash flow variance by $(\$346.41)^2$. However, each individual participant is spreading their fixed wealth over a larger and larger number of independent securities. We just showed in Equation (2.8) that the cash flow variance of an equally weighted portfolio of coin-flip securities is $\frac{1}{N}(\$346.41)^2$, so the cash flow standard deviation is $\sqrt{\frac{1}{N}(\$346.41)^2} = \$346.41/\sqrt{N}$. Note that each individual's cash flow variance is the variance of the portfolio's *average* cash flows. The more you short-sell, the bigger the fund and the bigger the potential loss if, say, every security turns up heads in the boom state. However, every additional coin-flip security that you short-sell reduces the probability that this extreme event occurs and reduces the fraction of each individual's wealth that is invested in each individual security.

the expected future cash flow on the portfolio is $0, and the standard deviation of each participant's future cash flow is $34.64. If we can short-sell 10,000 independent but identical coin-flip securities, the fund's immediate profit increases to $10,000 (everyone still makes $1), the portfolio's expected future cash flow is still zero, but the standard deviation of each owner's future cash flow falls to $3.46. No matter how big the fund gets, each participant makes $1 today—but as the fund gets bigger, each owner's risk falls.

Of course, if this were to happen, then I would be out on the street short-selling coin-flip securities, and so would just about everyone else I know. Supply of these coin-flip risk securities would be great, and demand would be small, and the market price would surely drop to zero.[6]

On the other hand, suppose you see the market price of the coin-flip being less than zero— say $-\$1$. In other words, some market participants are paying other participants to take the coin-flip risk. Again, there's an arbitrage opportunity, and it would behoove you to find friends, form a fund, and take on as many of these as possible.

The critical feature of the coin-flip security in this section is that its conditional mean cash flow (i.e., its expected cash flow within every possible macroeconomic state of nature) is zero. Whenever you encounter a risky asset with conditional mean-zero cash flow like this, you must conclude that it is worth nothing today (even if the cash flows *within* states are risky).

> Major Result 1: If a security has conditional mean-zero cash flows (i.e., if its expected cash flow given every possible macroeconomic state of nature is zero), the security is worth zero today. A risk that has zero mean given every future state is called an *idiosyncratic risk.*

Why Example 2.1 Is Important

This result is extremely important because we can apply it in almost every situation. Any cash flow risk can be broken into two parts: (1) its risk *across* states (i.e., the expected cash flow conditional on each state occurring) and (2) an idiosyncratic component *within* each state (i.e., a component that has expected value of zero conditional upon any state of nature occurring). Since the conditional mean-zero (or idiosyncratic) component is worthless, we only care about the expected value given each state and the distribution of this expected value *across* the macroeconomic states.

As an illustration, suppose you own a $1000 face value government bond that matures in one year. At the end of the year, you get your $1000 principal for sure. However, interest is not sure but rather is paid by lottery: A number will be drawn from a hat, and if that number matches the serial number of your bond, then you get $5,000 in interest, but if the number doesn't match you get no interest.[7] If there are 500 bonds outstanding, then you have a 1-in-500 chance of receiving interest, and your cash flow diagram looks like Figure 2.7:

---

[6] This is precisely how casinos make money—by short-selling large numbers of independent idiosyncratic risks at positive prices. However, the fact that casinos can sell these risks at positive prices does *not* contradict my message. Gambling laws prevent you and me from opening casinos, and hence prevent competition from eroding to zero the prices at which casinos sell their idiosyncratic gambles. We frequently observe casinos changing the odds on their games in order to increase sales. The point here is that the conditional mean-zero component of a security's risk is diversified away by the conditional mean-zero components of other securities and hence has no value.

[7] Bonds like this actually exist, and I'll say more about them in Example 2.3.

Figure 2.7			Cash Flows Arising Due to Lottery Risk Outcomes	
The Lottery Bond			No Match $pr = 499/500$	Match $pr = 1/500$
	Boom $pr_{boom} = 0.36$		$1000	$6000
	Stagnant $pr_{stagnant} = 0.48$		$1000	$6000
	Recession $pr_{recession} = 0.16$		$1000	$6000

(leftmost label: Macroeconomic Outcomes)

The first step in breaking apart the risks of the bond is to calculate the conditional mean cash flow in each macroeconomic state of nature, which I've done for you in Figure 2.8.

Next, we take the conditional mean cash flows from the right-hand column of Figure 2.8 and calculate the "surprise" or "shock" to those values that will come about when the lottery result becomes known (again, conditional upon each macroeconomic state of nature). The surprise or shock is simply the actual cash flow received minus the conditional mean cash flow in that macroeconomic state. I've detailed this calculation for you in Figure 2.9.

The cash flow risk of the surprise or shock has an expected value of exactly zero in each macroeconomic state of nature (as I show in Figure 2.10). What we've done here is divide and conquer, and we're left with an easy valuation problem. We've cut the strange lottery bond into two securities that we know how to value: (1) a security that promises $1010 no matter what state of nature occurs (in other words, a risk-free bond) and (2) a security whose cash flows have zero expected value in all states of nature (in other words, a coin-flip security). Figure 2.10 summarizes this concept.

Since we *know* that the conditional mean-zero (or idiosyncratic) component has no value, the only thing we need to worry about is the *expected cash flow in each state*! To value the bond, we form

Figure 2.8	Calculating the Conditional Mean Cash Flows on the Lottery Bond			
		Cash Flows Arising Due to Lottery Risk Outcomes		
		No Match $pr = 499/500$	Match $pr = 1/500$	Conditional Mean Cash Flow
	Boom $pr_{boom} = 0.36$	$1000	$6000	(499/500) × $1000 + (1/500) × $6000 = $1010
	Stagnant $pr_{stagnant} = 0.48$	$1000	$6000	(499/500) × $1000 + (1/500) × $6000 = $1010
	Recession $pr_{recession} = 0.16$	$1000	$6000	(499/500) × $1000 + (1/500) × $6000 = $1010

(leftmost label: Macroeconomic Outcomes)

Figure 2.9 Calculating the "Shocks" to the Conditional Mean Cash Flows on the Lottery Bond Due to the Outcomes of the Lottery

		Conditional Mean Component	Cash Flows Arising Due to Lottery Risk Outcomes	
			Surprise or Shock to Conditional Mean (Actual CF − Conditional Mean CF)	
			No Match $pr = 499/500$	Match $pr = 1/500$
Macroeconomic Outcomes	Boom $pr_{boom} = 0.36$	$1010	$1000 − $1010 = −$10	$6000 − $1010 = +$4990
	Stagnant $pr_{stagnant} = 0.48$	$1010	$1000 − $1010 = −$10	$6000 − $1010 = +$4990
	Recession $pr_{recession} = 0.16$	$1010	$1000 − $1010 = −$10	$6000 − $1010 = +$4990

a tracking portfolio with expected cash flows of $1010 in each macroeconomic state. We do *not* need the tracking portfolio to exactly match the cash flows on the lottery bond given the different lottery risk outcomes, because we've transformed the problem in a way that leaves this cash flow gamble worthless (because of diversification). This is a completely general result, and it is why you'll hear finance professors say that "idiosyncratic risk is not priced." A truly idiosyncratic risk has

Figure 2.10 Calculating the Conditional Mean of the Lottery Bond's Cash Flow Shocks

		Conditional Mean Component	Cash Flows Arising Due to Lottery Risk Outcomes		
			Conditional Mean-Zero Idiosyncratic Component		Conditional Mean of Idiosyncratic Component
			No Match $pr = 499/500$	Match $pr = 1/500$	
Macroeconomic Outcomes	Boom $pr_{boom} = 0.36$	$1010	−$10	+$4990	$(499/500) \times (-\$10)$ $+ (1/500) \times \$4990$ $= \$0$
	Stagnant $pr_{stagnant} = 0.48$	$1010	−$10	+$4990	$(499/500) \times (-\$10)$ $+ (1/500) \times \$4990$ $= \$0$
	Recession $pr_{recession} = 0.16$	$1010	−$10	+$4990	$(499/500) \times (-\$10)$ $+ (1/500) \times \$4990$ $= \$0$

We only need to value this part! It is a risk-free bond!

This part is just like a coin-flip security! It has no value!

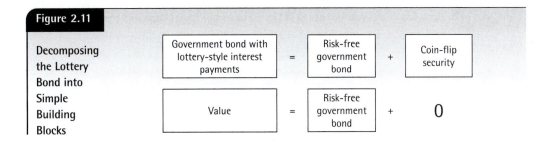

Figure 2.11

Decomposing the Lottery Bond into Simple Building Blocks

an expected value of zero given any possible outcome of the economy, and thus has no value. We can break out the idiosyncratic component of a security's cash flow risk like this because it is diversified away by the idiosyncratic components of the cash flow risk of the other securities in the financial market. Figure 2.11 provides a visual representation of how we can decompose the complex problem of valuing the lottery bond into a set of simple valuation exercises. We'll use this building block visual throughout the rest of the chapter.

To put it another way, we don't need for our tracking portfolio to exhibit *perfect tracking*. A tracking portfolio that only tracks the conditional mean cash flow component of a security has exactly the same value as a tracking portfolio that tracks perfectly, simply because the *tracking error* has conditional mean-zero cash flows, and hence has no value.[8]

> Major Result 2: In arbitrage valuations, tracking portfolios need not be *perfect hedges* for the security being valued. That is, they don't have to match the security's cash flow exactly. Rather, they only must match the *conditional mean* cash flow of the security in every possible state of nature. In other words, the only requirement for arbitrage valuation is that the tracking portfolio has conditional mean-zero error.

We can now get back to our model economy and my illustration of arbitrage valuation in securities markets. Our economy needs just a little more setup.

The Molecular Building Block Securities in Our Model Economy

Our financial market includes three very important securities that may be purchased or sold short in any quantity. The first of these is a risk-free government bond. The government bond is a zero-coupon security, with a face value of $1000 which is paid for sure at the end of the year. Let's suppose that the current market price of the government bond, which is determined in equilibrium, is $951.81. In other words, the risk-free rate of interest is approximately 5.06%:

$$\frac{\$1000.00}{\$951.81} - 1 = 5.06\%.$$

---

[8] A lot of people get tripped up here, because everything they know about option pricing is based on construction of a hedge portfolio that tracks perfectly. The perfect tracking feature of the Black-Scholes hedge is not at all necessary—a hedge portfolio that tracks with conditional mean-zero error would have exactly the same value. If it didn't, there would be an arbitrage opportunity: Buy the cheap one, sell the expensive one, and diversify away the conditional mean-zero tracking error.

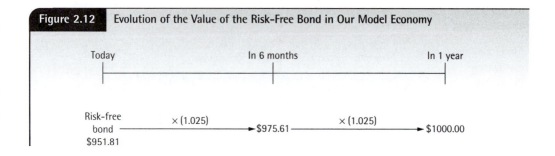

Figure 2.12   Evolution of the Value of the Risk-Free Bond in Our Model Economy

Today   In 6 months   In 1 year

Risk-free bond $951.81 — $\times (1.025)$ → $975.61 — $\times (1.025)$ → $1000.00

Bonds like this accrue interest every six months, so the six-month interest rate is 2.5%. The bond's value will evolve as in Figure 2.12.

Our economy also has a market portfolio. Since our economy is large, and since we've assumed that there's only one source of common risk, then the market portfolio in our economy (defined as the sum total of all securities in the financial market) contains no idiosyncratic risk. The current value of the market portfolio is simply the total value of all securities in the market today, and the possible values of the market portfolio in the future boom, stagnant, and recession macroeconomic states are simply the sum of the conditional mean values of all securities in each of those states. Knowing this, we can create a *market index* that reflects the changing value of all investments in aggregate.

Let's scale the market index so that its current value is 100.00. The value of the market index in the future will depend on the sum total values of all the securities in the economy. By definition, a boom economy is one in which total wealth is increasing, and a recession economy is one in which total wealth is decreasing, so the future value of the market index will correspond to (and reflect) the state of nature. Keeping with our abstract construction, let's suppose that the market index of risky assets will be 144.00 in one year if the economy booms, 102.00 in one year if the economy is stagnant, and 72.25 if the economy goes into recession.

Finally, let's suppose you can purchase an investment in the market portfolio (such as an indexed mutual fund) for $1 per index point. The value of one share of the market index fund will evolve according to Figure 2.13.

What are the characteristics of our market? Let's calculate some summary statistics. In our world, the market index fund returns +44% if the economy booms ($144.00/$100.00 − 1 = 44%), +2%

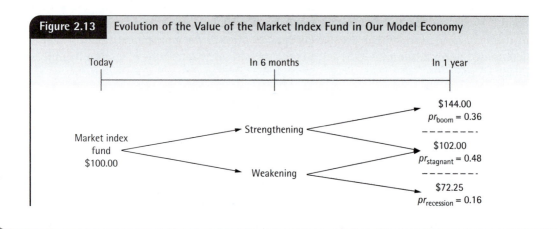

Figure 2.13   Evolution of the Value of the Market Index Fund in Our Model Economy

Today   In 6 months   In 1 year

Market index fund $100.00

Strengthening → $144.00 $pr_{boom} = 0.36$

$102.00 $pr_{stagnant} = 0.48$

Weakening → $72.25 $pr_{recession} = 0.16$

if the economy is stagnant ($102.00/$100.00 − 1 = 2%), and −27.75% if the economy goes into recession ($72.25/$100.00 − 1 = −27.75%).

State	Return on Market	Probability
Boom	$r_{\text{Mkt boom}}$ = 44.00%	pr_{boom} = 0.36
Stagnant	$r_{\text{Mkt stagnant}}$ = 2.00%	pr_{stagnant} = 0.48
Recession	$r_{\text{Mkt recession}}$ = −27.75%	$pr_{\text{recession}}$ = 0.16

Therefore, the expected return on the market portfolio is

$$E\{r_{\text{market}}\} = pr_{\text{boom}} \times r_{\text{Mkt boom}} + pr_{\text{stagnant}} \times r_{\text{Mkt stagnant}} + pr_{\text{recession}} \times r_{\text{Mkt recession}}$$
$$= 0.36 \times 44.00\% + 0.48 \times 2.00\% + 0.16 \times (−27.75\%)$$
$$= 12.36\%$$

The risk-free rate of return is r = 5.06%, so the market risk premium is $[E\{r_{\text{Mkt}}\} − r]$ = 7.3%.

The third building block security we'll need is a one-year European call option on the market index fund with strike price equal to $100. The payoff on the European call will be *max*(index fund value − $100, 0). Let's assume that the current price of this call is $11.42 (I'll demonstrate where this comes from later). The index option's value will evolve as shown in Figure 2.14.

If we enter the boom economy, the return on the index option will be $44/$11.42 − 1 = 285.29%. If we enter the stagnant economy, the return on the index option will be $2/$11.42 − 1 = −82.49%. The return on the index option will be −100% if the recession occurs. So the expected return on the index option is 47.11%:

$$E\{r_{\text{index option}}\} = pr_{\text{boom}} \times r_{\text{ind opt boom}} + pr_{\text{stagnant}} \times r_{\text{ind opt stagnant}} + pr_{\text{recession}} \times r_{\text{ind opt recession}}$$
$$= 0.36 \times 285.29\% + 0.48 \times (−82.49\%) + 0.16 \times (−100\%)$$
$$= 47.11\%$$

The index option is extremely risky. If you invest in the index fund, you can lose some of your money—but if you invest in the index option, you can lose *all* of your money.

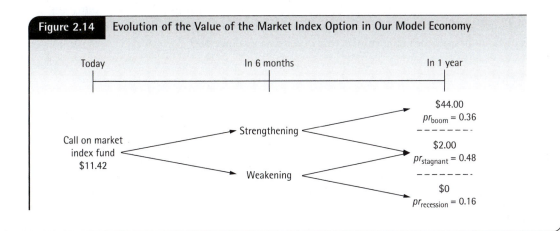

Figure 2.14 Evolution of the Value of the Market Index Option in Our Model Economy

2.3 Valuation by Arbitrage in Our Model Economy

We'll now turn to some valuation problems. In each problem below, we will assume that a security exists in our financial market and that we want to verify its market price. In every case, we will do so via an arbitrage argument. Valuation by arbitrage requires four steps:

1. Determine the *expected* cash flow on the security *given each future macroeconomic state of nature* (i.e., the conditional mean cash flows on the security).
2. Form a tracking portfolio of existing financial market claims (with known prices) in such a way that given each possible future state of nature, the expected cash flow on the tracking portfolio equals the *conditional mean* cash flow on the security.
3. Add up the market value of the tracking portfolio.
4. Assume no arbitrage opportunities, and conclude that the value of the security must be equal to the value of the tracking portfolio.

We'll build our tracking portfolios with only three things: the risk-free bond, the market index fund, and the $100 call option on the market index fund. If our tracking portfolio contains H_{Mkt} units of the market index fund, H_O index options, and H_{RF} risk-free bonds, then at the end of the year the macroeconomic state will determine the value of the tracking portfolio:

End-of-year value of tracking portfolio:

$$= \begin{cases} H_{Mkt} \times \$144.00 + H_O \times \$44 + H_{RF} \times \$1000.00 & \text{in the boom economy} \\ H_{Mkt} \times \$102.00 + H_O \times \$2 + H_{RF} \times \$1000.00 & \text{in the stagnant economy} \\ H_{MktT} \times \$72.25 + H_O \times \$0 + H_{RF} \times \$1000.00 & \text{in the recession economy} \end{cases} \quad (2.9)$$

The current value of a tracking portfolio containing H_{Mkt} units of the market index fund, H_O options on the market index fund and H_{RF} risk-free bonds will be

$$\text{Current value of tracking portfolio} = H_{Mkt} \times \$100 + H_O \times \$11.42 + H_{RF} \times \$951.81 \quad (2.10)$$

The trick behind valuation is finding the holdings H_{Mkt}, H_O, and H_{RF} so that the state-dependent payoffs in the three lines of Equation (2.9) above match the state-dependent *expected* payoffs on the security being valued. If you can accomplish this, then the current value of the security will be equal to the current value of the arbitrage portfolio—which you find by using Equation (2.10). This is linear pricing at work.

After I do each arbitrage valuation, I'll demonstrate that the expected return on the tracking portfolio provides the appropriate discount rate for a DCF valuation. In a DCF valuation, we discount the overall expected future cash flow on a security by a risk-adjusted rate of return that represents an investor's opportunity cost in the financial market:

$$\text{DCF Value} = \frac{E\{CF\}}{1 + r^*}$$

$$= \frac{pr_{boom} \times E\{CF \,|\, boom\} + pr_{stagnant} \times E\{CF \,|\, stagnant\} + pr_{recession} \times E\{CF \,|\, recession\}}{1 + r^*}$$

Example 2.2. Valuation of a Risk–Free Zero–Coupon Bond (the Easiest Problem)

Let's suppose that there exists a risk-free government bond that pays off $150 for sure at the end of the year. How do we value this bond?

Figure 2.15

Cash Flows on
the Risk-Free
Zero-Coupon
Bond

Macroeconomic Outcomes

	Conditional Mean Cash Flows
Boom $pr_{boom} = 0.36$	$E\{CF|boom\} = \$150$
Stagnant $pr_{stagnant} = 0.48$	$E\{CF|stagnant\} = \$150$
Recession $pr_{recession} = 0.16$	$E\{CF|recession\} = \$150$

Step 1. Determine the expected cash flow on the security given each future macroeconomic state of nature (i.e., the conditional mean cash flows on the security).

I do this for you in Figure 2.15.

Step 2. Form a tracking portfolio of existing financial market claims (with known prices) in such a way that given each possible future state of nature, the expected cash flow on the tracking portfolio equals the conditional mean cash flow on the security we're valuing.

What this means is that we have to find H_{Mkt}, H_O, and H_{RF} such that the three equations in (2.9) equal the three possible conditional mean values of the risk-free bond (given in the right-hand column of Figure 2.15).

End-of-year value of tracking portfolio:

$$= \begin{cases} H_{Mkt} \times \$144.00 + H_O \times \$44 + H_{RF} \times \$1000.00 = \$150 & \text{(boom)} \\ H_{Mkt} \times \$102.00 + H_O \times \$2 + H_{RF} \times \$1000.00 = \$150 & \text{(stagnant)} \\ H_{Mkt} \times \$72.25 + H_O \times \$0 + H_{RF} \times \$1000.00 = \$150 & \text{(recession)} \end{cases}$$

Finding the holdings H_{Mkt}, H_O, and H_{RF} that make this work involves solving the three equations simultaneously. The answer here is $H_{Mkt} = 0$, $H_O = 0$, and $H_{RF} = 0.15$:

End-of-year value of tracking portfolio:

$$= \begin{cases} 0 \times \$144.00 + 0 \times \$44 + 0.15 \times \$1000.00 = \$150 & \text{(boom)} \\ 0 \times \$102.00 + 0 \times \$2 + 0.15 \times \$1000.00 = \$150 & \text{(stagnant)} \\ 0 \times \$72.25 + 0 \times \$0 + 0.15 \times \$1000.00 = \$150 & \text{(recession)} \end{cases}$$

(I show how to solve the simultaneous equations in Appendix 2.1).

Step 3. Add up the current market value of the tracking portfolio.

Using Equation (2.10):

$$\text{Current value of tracking portfolio} = 0 \times \$100 + 0 \times \$11.42 + 0.15 \times \$951.81$$
$$= \$142.77$$

And this takes us to the last step:

Step 4: Assume no arbitrage opportunities, and conclude that the value of the security must be equal to the value of the tracking portfolio.

In other words, the market value of the government bond must be $142.77. Notice that the bond's yield is 5.06% ($150.00/$142.77 − 1). This should not be surprising at all—an easy arbitrage opportunity would arise if the second risk-free bond's yield were anything different from the yield on the first risk-free bond.

The following four points are not coincidental.

1. The tracking portfolio weights are $0 \times \$100/\$142.77 = 0\%$ invested in the market index fund, $0 \times \$11.42/\$142.77 = 0\%$ invested in the index option, and $0.15 \times \$951.81/\$142.77 = 100\%$ invested in the risk free bond. Since the expected return on the market index fund is 12.36%, the expected return on the index option is 47.11%, and the expected return on the risk-free bond is 5.06%, the expected *return* on the tracking portfolio is 5.06%:

$$E\{r^{\text{tracking portfolio}}\} = \% \text{ market index} \times 12.36\% + \% \text{ index option} \times 47.11\%$$
$$+ \% \text{ Risk-free bond} \times 5.06\%$$
$$= 0 \times 12.36\% + 0 \times 47.11\% + 1.00 \times 5.06\%$$
$$= 5.06\%$$

2. The tracking portfolio with $H_{\text{Mkt}} = 0$, $H_O = 0$, and $H_{\text{RF}} = 0.15$ represents a *similar sub-stitute* opportunity for an investor in the financial market, and hence the expected return on this tracking portfolio is the investor's *opportunity cost of funds*. Therefore, the required rate of return on the bond being valued is 5.06%.

3. Had we discounted the expected cash flow on the bond we're valuing by this opportunity cost of funds in a DCF calculation, we would have arrived at the same answer.

$$\text{DCF value} = \frac{E\{CF\}}{1 + r^*}$$
$$= \frac{\$150}{1 + .0506} = \$142.77$$

In other words, the DCF value of the bond is equal to the value of the tracking portfolio. If it were not, there would be an arbitrage opportunity. To put it another way, the correct discount rate to use in a DCF valuation is the expected return on the tracking portfolio.

4. Since the arbitrage-free value of the bond is $142.77, the arbitrage-free expected return on the bond is 5.06%.

$$E\{r^{\text{bond}}\} = \frac{E\{CF^{\text{bond}}\}}{P_0} - 1$$
$$= \frac{\$150.00}{\$142.77} - 1$$
$$= 5.06\%$$

That is, the arbitrage-free price of the bond implies that its expected return is identical to the expected return on the tracking portfolio. If it weren't, there would be an arbitrage opportunity.

5. *If* the static CAPM holds, then the beta of the bond we're valuing is 0 (see Appendix 2.2 for the calculation). So in a DCF valuation using the static CAPM:

$$\text{DCF value using CAPM} = \frac{E\{CF\}}{1 + r + \beta[E\{r_{Mkt}\} - r]}$$

$$= \frac{\$150}{1 + 0.0506 + 0[0.1236 - 0.0506]}$$

$$= \frac{\$150}{1.0506} = \$142.77$$

DCF using the static CAPM gives us the same value because the static CAPM gives the same discount rate. Why did the static CAPM give the same discount rate? If we take our static CAPM equation

$$E\{r_i\} = r + \beta_i[E\{r_{Mkt}\} - r]$$

and rearrange it slightly, we get

$$E\{r_i\} = \beta_i E\{r_{Mkt}\} + (1 - \beta)r$$

Filling in the blanks

$$E\{r_i\} = 0 \times 12.36\% + 1.00 \times 5.06\% = 5.06\%$$

The static CAPM return equation is nothing more than the equation for the expected return on a tracking portfolio that has β% of its money invested in the market portfolio and $1-\beta$% invested in the risk-free bond. When the beta of an asset (financial or real) is estimated, it is a shortcut to finding the tracking portfolio that exactly mimics the conditional mean cash flows on the asset. Of course, this only works when a security can be followed by a tracking portfolio containing only the market index and the risk-free bond. There's no place for the return on the index option in the static CAPM equation, and this highlights a shortcoming of the static CAPM (which we'll get to momentarily).

Figure 2.16 represents my attempt to visually illustrate the relationships among the points listed previously. Valuation by arbitrage begins with the identification of the proper tracking portfolio. From there, you can actually take two paths. Traditional DCF analysis moves in a clockwise fashion: You first calculate the expected return on the tracking portfolio, then you recognize that expected return is the investor's opportunity cost of funds and thus is the right discount rate to use in a DCF calculation. The static CAPM, when it works, provides a shortcut to finding this discount rate. When we teach derivatives pricing, however, we simply move in the counterclockwise direction: once we've identified the correct tracking portfolio, we add up its values and assign that sum as the value of our new security.

Example 2.3. Bonds with Random Interest Payments—Rain–Day Bonds

The government of the United Kingdom offers a very interesting investment opportunity called a *Premium Bond.*[9] These bonds cost £1 (the face value), and the UK government promises to buy back any bond at its face value upon demand of the bondholder. These bonds are like floating-rate

[9] Don't confuse a "Premium Bond" (a brand name chosen by the UK government) with a "bond sold at a premium" (a generic description of a bond whose market price is greater than its face value).

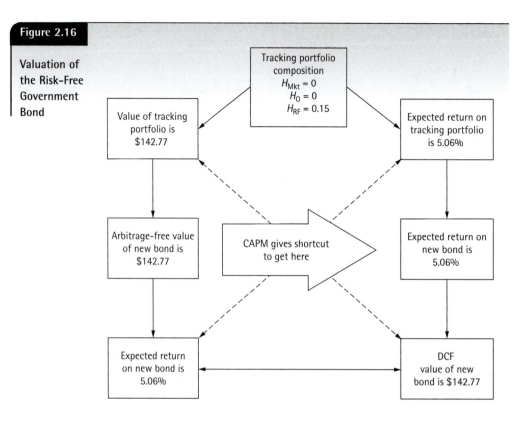

Figure 2.16

Valuation of the Risk-Free Government Bond

securities, in that every month the total interest paid to the bondholders changes to reflect market interest rates. What makes these Premium Bonds interesting, however, is that the UK government distributes the aggregate interest payments to the bondholders via a lottery in which each bond has a small chance of winning a cash prize ranging from £50 to £1,000,000. The *expected* winning (per £1 invested) is equal to the risk-free rate of interest, and the government's *total* interest liability is certain and is equal to the risk-free rate times the total face value of all bonds outstanding, but most bondholders receive nothing. The chance of winning *any* prize in a monthly drawing is only 1 in 24,000.[10]

Clearly, there is some risk involved in holding these Premium Bonds. But how would you go about valuing the bonds? Is there a risk premium associated with the random aspect of the interest payments? To answer this question, let's simplify things.

Let's muse about what would happen if the U.S. Treasury were to issue one-year *Rain-Day Bonds*. Each bond will have a face value of $500. Unlike standard government bonds, however, the interest paid would be determined randomly (like the UK Premium Bonds), but with a twist. Over the next year, the National Oceanographic and Atmospheric Administration (NOAA) would count the number of days in which the accumulated rainfall in Central Park, New York, exceeded 0.01 inch. If, by the end of the year, there were 121 or more *rain days* in Central Park, all bondholders would receive the $500 face value of the bond plus $25.30 of

---

[10] As of June 2003, the UK government had raised over £19.5 billion through the sale of Premium Bonds. Prior to September 2004, the odds of winning any prize were 1 in 30,000.

Figure 2.17

Cash Flows on the Rain-Day Bond

		Cash Flows Arising Due to Rain-Day Risk Outcomes	
		Rain ≤ 120 Days $pr = 1/2$	Rain > 120 Days $pr = 1/2$
Macroeconomic Outcomes	Boom $pr_{boom} = 0.36$	$500	$525.30
	Stagnant $pr_{stagnant} = 0.48$	$500	$525.30
	Recession $pr_{recession} = 0.16$	$500	$525.30

tax-free interest. On the other hand, if there were 120 or fewer rain days in Central Park over the next year, bondholders would receive the $500 face value but zero interest.

The NOAA has operated a meteorological station in Central Park since 1869, and over the 132-year period between 1869 and 2002 there were 66 years with 120 or fewer rain days and 66 years with 121 or more rain days. This pattern is remarkably stable: Over virtually every 30-year or longer period within that time frame, the median number of rain days in Central Park is 120.5. So we will operate with the subjective belief that the bond pays interest with 50% probability (just like a coin-flip). I've summarized the cash flows on the rain-day bond in Figure 2.17.

This looks a lot like the coin-flip security, in that a purely idiosyncratic event determines the payoff on the bond.[11] The difference here is that the coin-flip bond had zero expected cash flow in all states, whereas these rain-day bonds have strictly positive conditional mean cash flows (which I calculate for you in Figure 2.18).

Figure 2.18   **Calculation of Conditional Mean Cash Flows on Rain-Day Bond**

		Cash Flows Arising Due to Rain-Day Risk Outcomes		
		Rain ≤ 120 Days $pr = 1/2$	Rain > 120 Days $pr = 1/2$	Conditional Mean Cash Flow
Macroeconomic Outcomes	Boom $pr_{boom} = 0.36$	$500	$525.30	$(1/2) \times (\$500 + \$525.30)$ = $512.65
	Stagnant $pr_{stagnant} = 0.48$	$500	$525.30	$(1/2) \times (\$500 + \$525.30)$ = $512.65
	Recession $pr_{recession} = 0.16$	$500	$525.30	$(1/2) \times (\$500 + \$525.30)$ = $512.65

[11] I'm assuming here that the weather in New York City and the health of the macroeconomy are uncorrelated. Hirshleifer and Shumway (2003) document that stock markets perform better on sunny days than on cloudy days; after controlling for sunshine, however, rain and snow are not related to market returns.

Figure 2.19	Calculation of Idiosyncratic Component to the Cash Flow Risk of the Rain-Day Bond

		Conditional Mean Component	Cash Flows Arising Due to Rain-Day Risk Outcomes		Conditional Mean of Idiosyncratic Component
			Idiosyncratic Shock to Conditional Mean (actual CF − conditional mean CF)		
			Rain ≤ 120 Days $pr = 1/2$	Rain > 120 Days $pr = 1/2$	
Macroeconomic Outcomes	Boom $pr_{boom} = 0.36$	$512.65	$500 − $512.65 = −$12.65	$525.30 − $512.65 = +$12.65	$0
	Stagnant $pr_{stagnant} = 0.48$	$512.65	$500 − $512.65 = −$12.65	$525.30 − $512.65 = +$12.65	$0
	Recession $pr_{recession} = 0.16$	$512.65	$500 − $512.65 = −$12.65	$525.30 − $512.65 = +$12.65	$0

This part has no value!

We approach this valuation problem by breaking the rain-day bond's cash flow in each state into its *conditional mean* component and a conditional mean-zero *(idiosyncratic) shock* component. If I purchase the bond, I expect to get $512.65 in every state—but a random and idiosyncratic shock will change things. If there are 121 or more rain days between now and the end of the year, the expected value of $512.65 will receive a positive shock of $12.65, giving me a total payoff of $525.30. On the other hand, if there are 120 or fewer rain days between now and the the end of the year, the expected value of $512.65 will receive a negative shock of $12.65—leaving me with a total payoff of $500. Figure 2.19 shows the calculations.

Notice that the expected value of the shock, given any individual state of nature, is zero.

$$E\{CF_{random\,shock}\} = pr_{>120\,rain\,days} \times CF_{positive\,shock} + pr_{\leq 120\,rain\,days} \times CF_{negative\,shock}$$
$$= 0.5 \times \$12.65 + 0.5 \times (-\$12.65)$$
$$= \$0$$

So the shock component of the rain-day bond looks just like the coin-flip security. In other words, the random shock we've created is a purely idiosyncratic risk—and we know that purely idiosyncratic, conditional mean-zero cash flow risks have zero value. So

$$P_{rain-day\,bond} = P_{conditional\,mean\,component} + P_{idiosyncratic\,shock\,component}$$
$$= P_{conditional\,mean\,component} + 0$$
$$= P_{conditional\,mean\,component}$$

What that leaves us, then, is the conditional mean component, which looks just like our original government bond in Example 2.2. In fact, we value the conditional mean component in precisely the same way—by arbitrage.

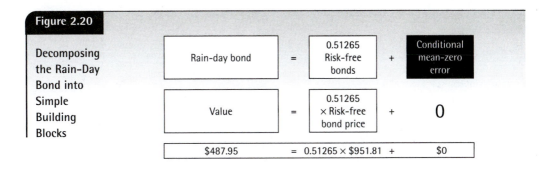

Figure 2.20

Decomposing the Rain-Day Bond into Simple Building Blocks

The answer here is trivial: The tracking portfolio that mimics the conditional mean cash flows on the rain-day bond contains 0.51265 units of the risk-free bond and 0 units of everything else. The current value of the tracking portfolio is thus $0.51265 \times \$951.81 = \$487.95$, and in absence of arbitrage, the market price of the rain-day bond must also be $487.95.

Any other possible market price would create an arbitrage opportunity. For example, if we see a market price on the rain-day bond of $480, I would buy one at that price, short-sell the tracking portfolio, *diversify away the idiosyncratic component,* and keep the $7.95 profit. I would have no risk in the future because I can diversify away the idiosyncratic component, and my tracking portfolio correctly matches the expected cash flow in each and every future macroeconomic state of nature.

So, the rain-day bond is priced to yield $512.65/$487.95 − 1 = 5.06%, and 5.06% would be the correct discount rate to apply if you want to price the rain-day bonds by DCF. Note what this means. Even though the rain-day bonds are risky (i.e., their future cash flows are uncertain), they are priced to yield the risk-free rate of return in expectation. They command no risk premium in excess of the risk-free rate because their expected payoffs are constant across all macroeconomic states of nature. The uncertainty that is added by the rain-day feature can be diversified away in a large portfolio that has many independent idiosyncratic risks, and thus carries no value even if the holder of the bond chooses not to diversify. We can decompose the rain-day bond into two pieces: 0.51265 risk-free bonds and conditional mean-zero error (like a coin-flip security), as I show in Figure 2.20.

> **Major Result 3:** If the *conditional mean cash flows* on a security are the same in all possible states of nature, the security will be priced to yield the risk-free rate of return. A security whose conditional mean cash flows are constant across all future macroeconomic states has no systematic risk; because of costless diversification, the holder receives no risk premium for bearing any idiosyncratic risks associated with it.

Example 2.4. A Risky Stock

Now let's value something with systematic risk. A consumer products company makes a high-end, luxury item with sales that are tightly related to the state of the macroeconomy: At the end of the next year, the stock will be worth $400 if the economy booms, $224 if the economy is stagnant, and $100 if the economy goes into recession. However, the firm also

Figure 2.21

End-of-Year Value of the Luxury Goods Company Stock

Macroeconomic Outcomes	Value Arising Due to Litigation Risk Outcomes: Lose Lawsuit $pr = 1/4$	Win Lawsuit $pr = 3/4$
Boom $pr_{boom} = 0.36$	\$304	\$400
Stagnant $pr_{stagnant} = 0.48$	\$160	\$224
Recession $pr_{recession} = 0.16$	\$56	\$100

faces a patent infringement lawsuit, and if the firm is found in violation it will have to terminate a significant part of its business. The generally accepted belief is that there is a 25% chance that the firm will lose the suit, and if so the stock value will drop to \$304 in the boom state, \$160 in the stagnant state, and \$56 in the recession state. Figure 2.21 summarizes the situation.

What is the current value of this stock? To answer this question, we first have to separate each state-contingent payoff into its conditional mean (or systematic) component and its conditional mean-zero (or idiosyncratic) component. This is simple: Just calculate the expected value of the stock in each state; the lawsuit risk will then represent a mean-zero idiosyncratic shock around this expected value. Figure 2.22 presents the calculation of the conditional mean values on the stock.

Figure 2.23 calculates the shock away from the conditional mean value arising from the outcome of the litigation risk.

Finally, Figure 2.24 shows that the idiosyncratic shock arising from the litigation risk outcome is mean zero in every macroeconomic state of nature.

Figure 2.22 **Calculation of the Conditional Mean Values of the Luxury Goods Company Stock**

Macroeconomic Outcomes	Values Arising Due to Litigation Risk Outcomes: Lose Lawsuit $pr = 1/4$	Win Lawsuit $pr = 3/4$	Conditional Mean Value
Boom $pr_{boom} = 0.36$	\$304	\$400	$(1/4) \times (\$304) + (3/4) \times (\$400) = \$376$
Stagnant $pr_{stagnant} = 0.48$	\$160	\$224	$(1/4) \times (\$160) + (3/4) \times (\$224) = \$208$
Recession $pr_{recession} = 0.16$	\$56	\$100	$(1/4) \times (\$56) + (3/4) \times (\$100) = \$89$

Figure 2.23 Calculations of the Shocks to the Conditional Mean Values of the Luxury Goods Stock Arising Due to Outcomes of the Litigation Risk

		Conditional Mean	Values Arising Due to Litigation Risk Outcomes	
			Surprise or Shock to Conditional Mean (actual − conditional mean)	
			Lose Lawsuit $pr = 1/4$	Win Lawsuit $pr = 3/4$
Macroeconomic Outcomes	Boom $pr_{boom} = 0.36$	$376	$304 − $376 = −$72	$400 − $376 = +$24
	Stagnant $pr_{stagnant} = 0.48$	$208	$160 − $208 = −$48	$224 − $208 = +$16
	Recession $pr_{recession} = 0.16$	$89	$56 − $89 = −$33	$100 − $89 = +$11

Once again, the idiosyncratic component is just like a coin-flip security and has no value today—so we can ignore it and simply value the conditional mean component. What makes this example different from the last is that the stock's conditional mean cash flows differ *across* states of nature. In other words, the stock is risky even after taking out the idiosyncratic component of its cash flows. For this company, the conditional mean cash flow rises quickly as the economy

Figure 2.24 Calculation of the Conditional Means of the Idiosyncratic Component of Luxury Goods Company Stock End-of-Year Values

		Conditional Mean	Values Arising Due to Litigation Risk Outcomes		Conditional Mean of Idiosyncratic Component
			Conditional Mean-Zero Idiosyncratic Component		
			Lose Lawsuit $pr = 1/4$	Win Lawsuit $pr = 3/4$	
Macroeconomic Outcomes	Boom $pr_{boom} = 0.36$	$376	−$72	+$24	$(1/4) \times (-\$72) + (3/4) \times (\$24) = \$0$
	Stagnant $pr_{stagnant} = 0.48$	$208	−$48	+$16	$(1/4) \times (-\$48) + (3/4) \times (\$16) = \$0$
	Recession $pr_{recession} = 0.16$	$89	−$33	+$11	$(1/4) \times (-\$33) + (3/4) \times (\$11) = \$0$

This part has no value

heats up and falls if the economy goes into recession. This is the risk we care about—the systematic risk, or the risk that changes in the macroeconomy will lead to changes in our stock price.

To value the stock, we again must create a tracking portfolio that matches the conditional mean value of the stock given each future state of nature:

End-of-year value of tracking portfolio:

$$= \begin{cases} H_{Mkt} \times \$144.00 + H_O \times \$44 + H_{RF} \times \$1000.00 = \$376 & \text{(boom)} \\ H_{Mkt} \times \$102.00 + H_O \times \$2 + H_{RF} \times \$1000.00 = \$208 & \text{(stagnant)} \\ H_{Mkt} \times \$72.25 + H_O \times \$0 + H_{RF} \times \$1000.00 = \$89 & \text{(recession)} \end{cases}$$

In this case, the correct holdings are $H_{Mkt} = 4$, $H_O = 0$, and $H_{RF} = -0.2$ (see Appendix 2.1 for the calculation). You can check for yourself that all three equations hold:

End-of-year value of tracking portfolio:

$$= \begin{cases} 4 \times \$144.00 + (-0.2) \times \$1000.00 = \$376 & \text{boom} \\ 4 \times \$102.00 + (-0.2) \times \$1000.00 = \$208 & \text{stagnant} \\ 4 \times \$72.25 + (-0.2) \times \$1000.00 = \$89 & \text{recession} \end{cases}$$

The current value of this tracking portfolio is $209.63:

$$\text{Current value of tracking portfolio} = 4 \times \$100 + 0 \times \$11.42 + (-0.2) \times \$951.81$$
$$= \$209.63$$

so the value of the company's stock must also be $209.63. Any other price would provide a quick arbitrage opportunity.

You should be getting the hang of this by now: To value a security, break the security's cash flows into building blocks. Then add up the values of the building blocks, and the result is the security's value. Here, as shown in Figure 2.25, there are three building blocks that together create a share of the luxury goods company stock: 4 shares of the market index fund, -0.2 risk-free bonds, and conditional mean-zero error (like a coin-flip security).

Again, we've got several points that are not merely coincidental:

1. The tracking portfolio has $(4 \times \$100)/\$209.63 = 190.8\%$ of its total invested in the market index fund and $(-0.2 \times \$951.81)/\$209.63 = -90.8\%$ invested in the risk-free

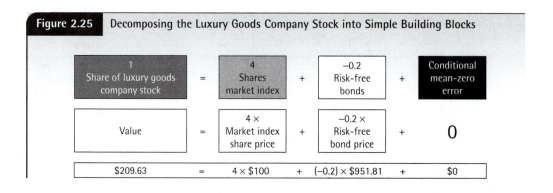

Figure 2.25   Decomposing the Luxury Goods Company Stock into Simple Building Blocks

bond (and nothing invested in the index option), so the expected return on the tracking portfolio is

$$E\{r^{\text{tracking portfolio}}\} = 1.908 \times 12.36\% + (-.908) \times 5.06\%$$
$$= 18.99\%$$

2. The tracking portfolio with $H_{\text{Mkt}} = 4$ and $H_{\text{RF}} = -0.2$ represents an investor's similar substitute (i.e., equivalent risk) opportunity in the financial market, and the expected return on this tracking portfolio, 18.99%, is the investors *opportunity cost of funds.*
3. The expected value of the stock at the end of the year is

$$E\{CF^{\text{stock}}\} = 0.36 \times \$376 + 0.48 \times \$208 + 0.16 \times \$89$$
$$= \$249.44$$

Had we discounted the expected value of the stock by the opportunity cost of funds in a DCF calculation, we would have arrived at the same answer:

$$\text{DCF Value} = \frac{E\{CF\}}{1 + r^*}$$

$$= \frac{\$249.44}{1 + 0.1899} = \$209.63$$

In other words, the DCF value of the stock is equal to the value of the tracking portfolio. If it were not, there would be an arbitrage opportunity. To put it another way, the correct discount rate to use in a DCF valuation is the expected return on the tracking portfolio.
4. Since the expected value of the stock at the end of the year is $249.44 and its current arbitrage-free price is $209.63, the expected return on the stock is

$$E\{r^{\text{stock}}\} = \frac{\$249.44}{\$209.63} - 1 = 18.99\%$$

That is, the price of the stock implies that its expected return is identical to the expected return on the tracking portfolio. If it weren't, there would be an arbitrage opportunity.
5. *If* the CAPM holds, then the beta of the stock is 1.908 (see Appendix 2.2 for the calculation). So in a CAPM valuation:

$$\text{DCF value using CAPM} = \frac{E\{CF\}}{1 + r + \beta[E\{r_{\text{Mkt}}\} - r]}$$

$$= \frac{\$249.44}{1 + 0.0506 + 1.908[0.1236 - 0.0506]}$$

$$= \frac{\$249.44}{1.1899} = \$209.63$$

Again, the CAPM return equation is nothing more than the equation for the expected return on a portfolio that has $\beta\%$ of its money invested in the market portfolio and $1 - \beta\%$ invested in the risk-free bond. When you calculate (or estimate) the beta of a security, you are taking a shortcut to finding the tracking portfolio that mimics the conditional mean cash flows on the security. Make sure you see this: The beta of the stock is 1.908, and the tracking portfolio has $(4 \times \$100)/\$209.63 = 190.8\%$ of its value invested in the market index.

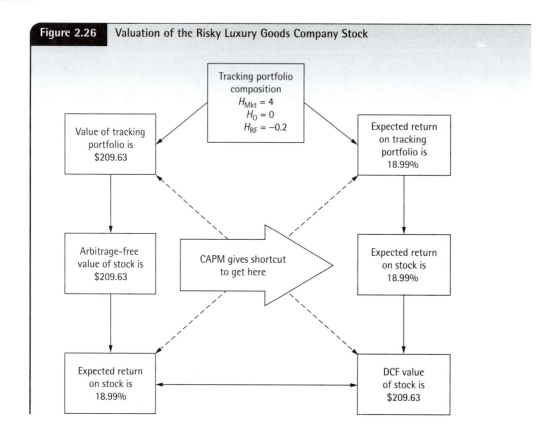

Figure 2.26   Valuation of the Risky Luxury Goods Company Stock

Figure 2.26 demonstrates the tight interrelationship among all of these observations. There are two very important learning points to take away from this example.

Major Result 4: If the conditional mean cash flows on a security are not the same in all states, then the security is exposed to systematic risk in some way. This is the risk we care about.

Major Result 5: When you correctly use the static CAPM to arrive at a discount rate for a DCF valuation of an asset, you are actually determining the expected rate of return on the tracking portfolio that mimics the conditional mean cash flows on the asset in each future state of nature. β tells you how much of the tracking portfolio should be invested in the market index, and the rest $(1-\beta)$ should be invested in the risk-free asset.

Warning: Major Result 5 does *not* say that the static CAPM will always provide the expected return on the tracking portfolio that mimics the conditional mean cash flows on the asset. The static CAPM (like all asset-pricing models) is a convenient shortcut that only works in certain situations. In the next section, I describe the situations in which the static CAPM works—and those in which it will not.

> **Figure 2.27** **Linear Relationships Between Two-Asset Tracking Portfolios and the Market Index**

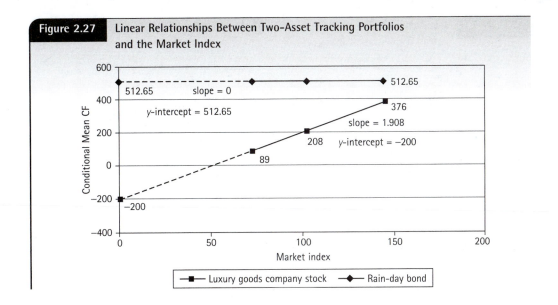

A Digression About the Static CAPM

In our examples up to this point, we've been able to construct tracking portfolios using only the market index fund and the risk-free bond. Moreover, our tracking portfolios have been *static*—we've not considered the possibility that they might change over the year. These two features are required for our tracking portfolio approach to be consistent with the traditional (static) CAPM (although the CAPM requires additional assumptions).[12]

At this point, you might be wondering why I introduced the index option at all. It turns out that there are assets that we cannot track *statically* with only the market portfolio and the risk-free asset. By introducing the option on the market index, we expand the set of possible tracking portfolios and therefore expand the set of assets that we can value by arbitrage with static tracking portfolios.

To see what I mean, let's try to figure out the characteristics of risky assets in our world that we *can* track using only the market index fund and the risk-free bond. If we build our tracking portfolio with Δ units of the market index fund and Ψ units of the risk-free bond, then the end-of-period value of the tracking portfolio will be

$$\text{End-of-period value of tracking portfolio} = \Delta \times \tilde{M} + \Psi \times B$$

where $\tilde{M}$ is the random end-of-period value of the market index, and B is the known end-of-period value of the risk-free bond. In our examples, the bond is worth $1000 at the end of the year, so the end-of-period value of the tracking portfolio will be

$$\text{End-of-period value of tracking portfolio} = \Delta \times \tilde{M} + \Psi \times \$1000$$

for any choice of Δ and Ψ. What you should notice here is that there is only one random variable—the end of period value of the market index. The equation for the end-of-period value of the tracking portfolio is therefore the equation of a line in two dimensional space. Figure 2.27 shows

---

[12] So far, we've been working in a world that exhibits what is known as two-fund separation. The static CAPM describes the equilibrium in this economy only if we assume that individuals share homogeneous expectations about means, variances, and covariances of the returns on the securities in the economy. Moreover, further restrictions on preferences and/or the distributions of returns on the economy's assets are necessary for the static CAPM to hold.

Figure 2.28   A Security with Conditional Mean Cash Flows That Are Not Linear in the Market Index

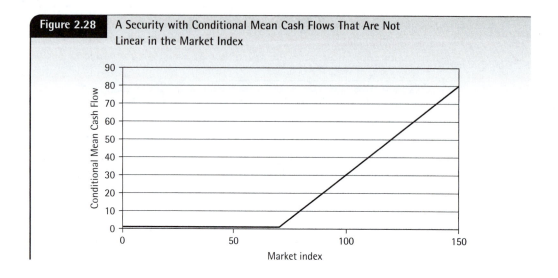

the plot of the conditional mean values of one rain-day bond and one share of the luxury goods company stock against the value of the market index. Check it out.

The general result is simple: Tracking portfolios that contain only the market index and the risk-free bond are *linear in the market index*. What this means is that these kinds of tracking portfolios only work when the conditional mean cash flows of the asset being valued are linearly linked to the value of the market portfolio. More specifically, the conditional mean payoff on the asset being valued must be a linear function of the value of the market portfolio across all macroeconomic states of nature.

This matches up exactly with the notion of risk in a CAPM world: Beta (which is the slope of the line in the graph) is a measure of how sensitive the asset's *expected* payoffs are to the state of the macroeconomy.

But this also points out a weakness of the static CAPM: It can only price cash flows that are *linear* in the market index. In other words, the static CAPM only gives the correct discount rate for DCF valuation when the cash flows on the asset in question take the form

$$\text{Conditional mean cash flow on asset being valued} = a + b \times \tilde{M}$$

where $\tilde{M}$ is the state-dependent value of the market index. What kind of asset has a payoff that does not take this linear form? Take a look at Figure 2.28 to see one.

This is obviously the terminal cash payoff on a call option, and there's no way to match it with a *static* tracking portfolio that contains only the market index and the risk-free bond simply because its conditional-mean payoffs cannot be written as a linear function of the market index. But it is *piecewise* linear, and we can do two different things to get its value by arbitrage in our equilibrium world: (1) use more assets in our tracking portfolio, or (2) allow for dynamic changes in the two-asset tracking portfolio over time.[13]

---

[13] It turns out that (2) implies (1): If we have dynamic trading in the market index and the risk-free bond, we can create a sufficient number of new assets to do the arbitrage valuation. Options on the market portfolio complete the market, and trading in the market index and the risk-free bond makes options on the market redundant securities and hence priced by arbitrage arguments themselves.

Please keep in mind a point I've been suggesting throughout this chapter: When you use the CAPM (or *any* asset pricing model, for that matter) in a DCF valuation, you are taking a short-cut to an arbitrage valuation. Specifically, the asset pricing model tells you the expected return on the static tracking portfolio without you having to identify the tracking portfolio explicitly; when you use the expected return on the static tracking portfolio in a DCF calculation, you are actually determining the value of the static tracking portfolio itself (which, by force of the arbitrage argument, must also be the price of the asset being valued).

A lot of people get confused by this, because they hear the phrase "the static CAPM can't price options," and they immediately conclude that valuation by *discounted cash flow* (DCF) is fundamentally different from valuation with an option pricing model. This logic is not quite right. Absence of arbitrage opportunities in the financial markets guarantees the appropriateness of valuation by linear pricing (i.e., by an arbitrage argument using a comparison to a tracking portfolio). Option pricing models and DCF are the same in that they are both applications of linear pricing. The difference, as I hinted at in Chapter 1, is that DCF is a shortcut that works only when the tracking portfolio is static. The static CAPM provides a way to estimate the risk-adjusted discount rate when DCF is appropriate, but the CAPM is itself a shortcut that only works when the static tracking portfolio can be formed with merely two securities (the market portfolio and the risk-free bond) plus conditional mean-zero error. This is why the static CAPM can't price options—in a purely static world, option payoffs *cannot* be described by two funds plus conditional mean-zero error because their payoffs are nonlinear.[14]

Now to be quite honest, you *can* price options with a static tracking portfolio (and thus by DCF) *if* you can put enough *nonlinear* claims in the tracking portfolio. You'll see that in the next example, and it is actually why I included the index option in our set of building block securities. Our practical problem with this approach is that there's no known asset pricing model shortcut (like the CAPM) that can tell us the correct discount rate without actually forming the tracking portfolio first—and once you've formed the tracking portfolio, you've got the option's value so there's no real point in going back and doing a DCF.

With that being said, let's value an option. Let's consider a call option on the stock from Example 2.4. First, I'll value the call using a tracking portfolio consisting of the market index, the call on the market index, and the risk-free bond. Then, in a couple of advanced sections, I'll show why this works and discuss how the option on the market index gets its value.

Take a deep breath before continuing. You may have never seen a presentation of option pricing like this. Most likely, you've been taught that the only way to value options is with a tracking portfolio that contains the underlying asset and the risk-free bond, and that this tracking portfolio must exhibit *perfect tracking* (i.e., it has absolutely zero error in all future states of nature). Perfect tracking provides *one* way to value options, but it is not the *only* way. Read on.

Example 2.5. A Call Option on the Luxury Goods Company Stock

Let's go back to our consumer products company that is facing litigation risk as well as market risk (Example 2.4). Figure 2.29 restates the possible end-of-year values of its stock.

---

[14] In a dynamic world, on the other hand, options *are* equivalent to a combination of the market index and the risk-free bond plus conditional mean-zero noise over short intervals (as long as the "underlying asset" itself is also a combination of the market index and the risk-free bond) simply because things become linear over very small time horizons. Under an additional restriction on preferences, the single-beta *intertermporal* CAPM does work for options.

Figure 2.29

End-of-Year
Values of the
Luxury Goods
Company Stock

		Values Arising Due to Litigation Risk Outcomes	
		Lose Lawsuit	Win Lawsuit
		$pr = 1/4$	$pr = 3/4$
Macroeconomic Outcomes	Boom $pr_{boom} = 0.36$	$304	$400
	Stagnant $pr_{stagnant} = 0.48$	$160	$224
	Recession $pr_{recession} = 0.16$	$56	$100

If you recall, the arbitrage-free current value of the stock is $209.63, because the stock is equivalent to a portfolio that is long 4 units of the market index fund and short 0.2 risk-free bonds (plus conditional mean-zero error).

The question we want to consider now concerns the valuation of a European call option on this stock, with strike price equal to $340. The terminal payoff on a European call on the stock is *max*(Stock value–strike, 0), so a call like this will only pay off if *two* things happen: If the economy booms *and* if the company wins the lawsuit. The payoffs on the call look as shown in Figure 2.30.

Once again, we want to break the asset into conditional mean cash flows and conditional mean-zero error. The expected cash flow of the call given the boom economy is $45:

$$E\{value\ of\ call\ |\ boom\} = 0.25 \times \$0 + 0.75 \times \$60 = \$45$$

while the expected cash flow on the call in the other two states is $0, because the call is never exercised in the stagnant or recession economies. Figure 2.31 presents the complete set of conditional mean cash flows on the stock option.

Figure 2.30

Calculation of
Cash Flows of the
$340 Call Option
on the Luxury
Goods Company
Stock

		Cash Flows on Call Option Arising Due to Litigation Risk Outcomes	
		Lose Lawsuit	Win Lawsuit
		$pr = 1/4$	$pr = 3/4$
Macroeconomic Outcomes	Boom $pr_{boom} = 0.36$	*max* ($304 − $340, $0) = $0	*max* ($400 − $340, $0) = $60
	Stagnant $pr_{stagnant} = 0.48$	*max* ($160 − $340, $0) = $0	*max* ($224 − $340, $0) = $0
	Recession $pr_{recession} = 0.16$	*max* ($56 − $340, $0) = $0	*max* ($100 − $340, $0) = $0

| Figure 2.31 | Conditional Mean Cash Flows of the $340 Call Option on the Luxury Goods Company Stock |

		Cash Flows on Call Option Arising Due to Litigation Risk Outcomes		Conditional Mean Cash Flow on Call Option
		Lose Lawsuit $pr = 1/4$	Win Lawsuit $pr = 3/4$	
Macroeconomic Outcomes	Boom $pr_{boom} = 0.36$	$0	$60	$45
	Stagnant $pr_{stagnant} = 0.48$	$0	$0	$0
	Recession $pr_{recession} = 0.16$	$0	$0	$0

The outcome of the litigation risk causes a shock to the conditional mean cash flow on the call option in the boom state. The expected cash flow on the option in the boom economy is $45; if the company loses the litigation, the stock price drop causes the option to expire worthless (implying a shock of $-$45$), but if the company wins the litigation the option will expire in the money and bring a cash flow of $60 (implying a shock of $+$15$). So the error or shock around the expected value *conditional* upon the boom state occurring is mean-zero:

$$E\{error \mid boom\} = 0.25 \times (-\$45) + 0.75 \times \$15 = \$0$$

Since the option is worthless in the other two states regardless of the litigation outcome, there is no shock in either case. So with this breakdown, the cash flow from the call option on the stock looks like Figure 2.32.

Just as before, the idiosyncratic risk (the conditional mean-zero component of the litigation risk) is just like a coin-flip security and has no value, because we can eliminate it through cost-less diversification. All we care about is the expected cash flow on the option conditional upon each state of nature. If we can form a tracking portfolio that has the same distribution of conditional mean cash flows across states, we can value the option by arbitrage.

We have to form our tracking portfolio so that it pays off $45 in the boom economy and nothing otherwise. So we have to pick H_{Mkt}, H_O, and H_{RF} such that
End-of-year value of tracking portfolio:

$$= \begin{cases} H_{Mkt} \times \$144.00 + H_O \times \$44 + H_{RF} \times \$1000.00 = \$45 & \text{(boom)} \\ H_{Mkt} \times \$102.00 + H_O \times \$2 + H_{RF} \times \$1000.00 = \$0 & \text{(stagnant)} \\ H_{Mkt} \times \$72.25 + H_O \times \$0 + H_{RF} \times \$1000.00 = \$0 & \text{(recession)} \end{cases}$$

If you solve the simultaneous equations (which I've done for you in Appendix 2.1), you will find that the appropriate tracking portfolio is *short* 0.0772 units of the market index ($H_{Mkt} = -0.0772$), *long*

Figure 2.32 Systematic and Idiosyncratic Components of the Cash Flows of the $340 Call Option on the Luxury Goods Company Stock

		Conditional mean component	Cash Flows on Call Option Arising Due to Litigation Risk Outcomes		
			Surprise or Shock to Conditional Mean (actual CF − conditional mean CF)		Conditional Mean of Idiosyncratic Component
Macroeconomic Outcomes			Lose Lawsuit $pr = 1/4$	Win Lawsuit $pr = 3/4$	
	Boom $pr_{boom} = 0.36$	$45	$0 − $45 = −$45	$60 − $45 = +$15	$(1/4) \times (−\$45) + (3/4) \times \$15$ = $0
	Stagnant $pr_{stagnant} = 0.48$	$0	−$0	+$0	$0
	Recession $pr_{recession} = 0.16$	$0	−$0	+$0	$0

This part has no value!

1.1482 units of the index option ($H_O = 1.1482$), and *long* 0.00558 units of the risk-free bond ($H_{RF} = 0.00558$). You can check for yourself that these equations hold:

End-of-year value of tracking portfolio:

$$= \begin{cases} -0.0772 \times \$144.00 + 1.1482 \times \$44 + 0.00558 \times \$1000.00 = \$45 & \text{(boom)} \\ -0.0772 \times \$102.00 + 1.1482 \times \$2 + 0.00558 \times \$1000.00 = \$0 & \text{(stagnant)} \\ -0.0772 \times \$72.25 + 1.1482 \times \$0 + 0.00558 \times \$1000.00 = \$0 & \text{(recession)} \end{cases}$$

That is, this tracking portfolio exactly matches the expected value of the call option conditional upon every possible state of nature. Since the conditional mean-zero idiosyncratic risk is worthless (because of costless diversification), the value of the call must equal the value of the tracking portfolio. The value of this tracking portfolio is $10.70:

$$\text{Current value of tracking portfolio} = -0.0772 \times \$100 + 1.1482 \times \$11.42 + 0.00558 \times \$951.81$$
$$= \$10.70$$

and, given our assumption of no arbitrage, $10.70 must also be the value of the call on the consumer products company stock. Figure 2.33 provides our building-block interpretation. Notice now that the call on the stock decomposes into four simple parts: the market index, the market index option, the risk-free bond, and conditional mean-zero error (like the coin-flip security).

I want to reiterate the arbitrage here. If the call on the stock has a price greater than $10.70, then I can make a riskless profit by short-selling it (writing a call at $340), buying the tracking portfolio outlined previously, and diversifying away the idiosyncratic risk. If the call value is

Figure 2.33 Decomposition of the $340 Call on the Luxury Goods Company Stock into Simple Building Blocks

1 $340 Call on luxury goods company stock	=	−0.0772 Shares market index	+	1.1482 Index options	+	0.00558 Risk-free bonds	+	Conditional mean-zero error
Value	=	−0.0772 × Market index share price	+	1.1482 × Index option price	+	0.00558 × Risk-free bond price	+	0
$10.70	=	(−0.0772) × $100	+	1.1482 × $11.42	+	0.00558 × $951.81	+	$0

anything less than $10.70, I make a free lunch by buying the call, short-selling the tracking portfolio, and diversifying.

Again, we've got several points that are not merely coincidental:

1. The tracking portfolio has $(-0.0772 \times \$100)/\$10.70 = -72.13\%$ of its total invested in the market index fund, $(1.1482 \times \$11.42)/\$10.70 = 122.51\%$ of its total invested in the index option, $(0.00558 \times \$951.81)/\$10.70 = 49.62\%$ invested in the risk-free bond, so the expected return on the tracking portfolio is

$$E\{r^{\text{tracking portfolio}}\} = -0.7213 \times 12.36\% + 1.2251 \times 47.11\% + 0.4962 \times 5.06\%$$
$$= 51.3\%$$

2. The tracking portfolio with $H_{\text{Mkt}} = -0.0772$, $H_O = 1.1482$, and $H_{\text{RF}} = 0.00558$ represents the investor's equivalent opportunity in the financial market, and hence its expected return (51.3%) is the investors *opportunity cost of funds.*

3. The expected payoff on the call at the end of the year is

$$E\{CF^{\text{call}}\} = 0.36 \times \$45 + 0.48 \times \$0 + 0.16 \times \$0$$
$$= \$16.20$$

Had we discounted the expected cash flow on the option by the opportunity cost of funds in a DCF calculation, we would have arrived at the same answer:

$$\text{DCF value} = \frac{E\{CF\}}{1 + r^*}$$
$$= \frac{\$16.20}{1 + 0.513} = \$10.70$$

In other words, the DCF value of the call is identical to the value of the tracking portfolio that mimics the conditional mean cash flows on the call. If it were not, there would be an arbitrage opportunity. I want to stress this point: The proper discount rate for valuing the call is the expected return on the tracking portfolio that replicates its conditional mean cash flows. Exact replication of the idiosyncratic component is unnecessary—it has no value. DCF worked in this case because we were able to build a very complex static tracking portfolio that included a nonlinear claim (the market index option). However, there's no known shortcut to get us to this discount rate without explicitly forming the tracking portfolio first.

4. Since the expected cash flow on the call at the end of the year is $16.20 and the arbitrage-free price of the call is $10.70 right now, the expected return from holding the call over the year is

$$E\{r^{call}\} = \frac{\$16.20}{\$10.70} - 1 = 51.3\%$$

That is, the call's price implies that its expected return is identical to the expected return on its tracking portfolio. If it weren't, there would be an arbitrage opportunity.

5. *The static CAPM will not work here.* If you were to try to calculate the beta of the call, you would get 7.59 (which I show in Appendix 2.2). This would then imply that the DCF value of the call is

$$
\begin{aligned}
\text{DCF value using CAPM} &= \frac{E\{CF\}}{1 + r + \beta[E\{r_{Mkt}\} - r]} \\
&= \frac{\$16.20}{1 + 0.0506 + 7.59[0.1236 - 0.0506]} \\
&= \frac{\$16.20}{1.6049} = \$10.09
\end{aligned}
$$

Trying to use the static CAPM here is like putting a square peg in a round hole. If you naively try to use it here, you get a discount rate of 60.49% (which is not even close to the appropriate risk-adjusted return). The conditional mean cash flows on the call are not linear in the market index, so the static CAPM shortcut is not appropriate.

Figure 2.34 shows the relationships among these points.

I imagine that right about now, many readers are yelling "nonsense!" (or more likely something much more colorful). In fact, the invective may have begun before you ever got to this point. If it has, calm down and think about things for a second. As I said before, there are many very sophisticated people (including more than a few finance PhDs) who believe that the only way to price an option is through the Black-Scholes "perfect risk-free hedge." The tracking portfolio we constructed above does not provide a perfect hedge—it loses $45 in the boom state if the firm loses the lawsuit (with probability $\frac{1}{4}$) and makes $15 in the boom state if the firm wins the lawsuit (with probability $\frac{3}{4}$). But this error is conditional mean-zero noise ($\frac{1}{4} \times -\$45 + \frac{3}{4} \times \$15 = \$0$) in the boom state (and $0 with probability 1 in the stagnant and recession states), so it is diversifiable and has no value (see Major Result 1). A perfect hedge would track the idiosyncratic component of the option, but the idiosyncratic component has no value. So any tracking portfolio that matches the option's conditional mean payoffs with conditional mean-zero error is just as good as one that provides a perfect hedge and gives the exact same answer.

It all boils down to this. Even though option pricing is *preference-free,* the price of an option must be consistent with the asset pricing equilibrium (since no securities market equilibrium can admit an arbitrage opportunity). And just about every asset pricing equilibrium we've ever studied has two additional features: (1) Mean-zero shocks *within* states are valueless because of costless diversification, and (2) the priced rate of return on *any* asset (primary or derivative) is driven by the covariance between marginal utility of consumption and the asset's conditional mean cash flows *across states of nature.*

I'd like to make one more important observation before moving on. The stock option's conditional mean cash flow in the boom state ($45) is *not* the difference between the conditional mean

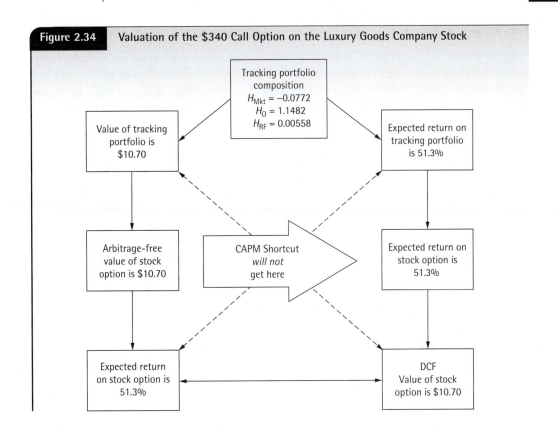

Figure 2.34 Valuation of the $340 Call Option on the Luxury Goods Company Stock

Tracking portfolio composition
$H_{Mkt} = -0.0772$
$H_0 = 1.1482$
$H_{RF} = 0.00558$

Value of tracking portfolio is $10.70

Expected return on tracking portfolio is 51.3%

Arbitrage-free value of stock option is $10.70

CAPM Shortcut
will not
get here

Expected return on stock option is 51.3%

Expected return on stock option is 51.3%

DCF
Value of stock option is $10.70

value of the stock in the boom state ($376) and the strike price ($340). If we change the magnitude of the mean-zero litigation risk in a symmetric way, we won't change the conditional mean value of the *stock* given the boom state, but we *will* change the conditional mean value of the $340 *call on the stock* given the boom state.

For example, suppose that we change the luxury goods company's stock price in the boom state to $432 if it wins the lawsuit but only $208 if it loses. The expected value of the stock conditional upon being in the boom state remains at $376 ($\frac{1}{4} \times \$208 + \frac{3}{4} \times \$432 = \$376$), so the price of the stock will not change since the conditional mean cash flows stay the same. However, the option's value changes because it becomes more valuable in the boom state if the company wins the lawsuit (in which case, its payoff will go up to $92). So the expected payoff on the option given the boom state increases from $45 to $69 ($\frac{1}{4} \times \$0 + \frac{3}{4} \times \$92 = \$69$) and the option becomes more valuable.

This is why the total volatility parameter is necessary in option pricing—it affects the conditional mean payoffs on the option. But please, please, please do not interpret this as saying that the idiosyncratic risk in an option is somehow priced. Because an option's payoff is not symmetric, changing the total volatility of a stock's return alters the option's conditional mean cash flows (in some states) as well as the option's systematic risk. But the conditional mean-zero (idiosyncratic risk) component of an option is worthless, just as the idiosyncratic component of the underlying stock is worthless. If it were not, there would be an arbitrage opportunity (buy low, sell high, and diversify).

The Role of the Index Option

There is no way we could have valued the stock option by *static* arbitrage without the index option. Why? Because without the index option there is no way to build a *static* tracking portfolio that pays off $45 in the boom state and $0 in the other two states (i.e., a tracking portfolio with a nonlinear payoff). As we'll see in section 2.4 (which is for advanced readers), the index option *will not* be necessary if we can build *dynamic* tracking portfolios.[15] But let's leave that issue aside for the moment.

Once again, some readers may object—you may believe that you can price the stock option with a static tracking portfolio that includes the stock itself (the underlying asset) plus the risk-free bond, or even the stock plus the market index plus the risk-free bond. If you think this is true, try it. You have to solve a system of three equations with only two unknowns (since the stock and the market index are collinear).[16]

If there's no index option (or dynamic trading), there's no tracking portfolio that replicates the conditional mean payoff of the stock option. In this situation, we would say that the financial market is *incomplete*. So in absence of the index option (or dynamic trading), introduction of the stock option would provide investors in the economy with a new investment opportunity. This new opportunity, in turn, would change the optimum portfolio of all of the investors in the economy, and it would change the equilibrium demand for every risky asset in the economy and therefore the *price* of every financial asset in the economy. In other words, if there were no index option (or dynamic trading), then anyone who introduces the stock option would not be a price taker, and hence valuation of the stock option by arbitrage would be impossible. The only way to value the stock option would be to crank through the equilibrium analysis.

And so this is why I introduced the index option—It completes our financial market. With the market index option (along with the market index fund and the risk-free bond), we can form tracking portfolios that mimic *any* other existing primary security in our simple, three-state economy as well as any other derivative securities we might construct.

I can make an even more general statement. No matter how many states of nature there are, you can always complete the market by creating options on the market index with varying strike prices. Complete markets don't require large numbers of primitive securities—derivatives do the trick (at a much lower expense of creation). This result, which was given to us in Ross (1976), is perhaps the most underappreciated theorem in the history of financial theory.

> Major Result 6: One way to complete a financial market is to introduce options on the market portfolio with varying strike prices.

The rest of the chapter is somewhat advanced. If you've never seen the binomial option pricing model before, I suggest you skip ahead to Chapter 3 and only come back to the remainder of this chapter after you've worked through Chapter 4.

If, on the other hand, you have some background with derivatives pricing, then I strongly encourage you to work through these last few pages. I'm going to introduce an intermediate time point after six months where financial market participants can trade the market index, the risk free bond, and the luxury goods company stock.

---

[15] If intermediate trading is allowed, the index option itself will be redundant.

[16] The conditional mean cash flow on the stock is equal to $4\tilde{M} - \$200$ regardless of the macroeconomic state of nature.

I'll first show that when we allow intermediate trading like this, we can form a *dynamically changing* portfolio of the market index and the risk-free bond that exactly tracks the market index option. The important message of this result is that dynamic trading serves to complete the market.

I'll then show that we can form a dynamically changing portfolio that tracks the option on the luxury-goods company stock in two very different (but equivalent) ways. The first way is to build a dynamic tracking portfolio that consists only of the market index fund and the risk-free bond. The second way is to build a dynamic tracking portfolio that consists only of the company stock itself and the risk-free bond. The important message of this exercise is that the two ways give absolutely identical valuation results.

Finally, I'll complete the circle and demonstrate *why* you get the same result from the two different approaches to the tracking portfolio.

2.4 Valuation of the Index Option (Advanced)

We now come to a very interesting question. The index option's end-of-year cash flow is not linear in the market index, so we cannot value the index option using a static tracking portfolio that only contains the market index fund and the risk-free bond. How does the market value the index option? The answer is "it depends"—it depends on whether trading in the index fund occurs between now and the end of the year.

If there's no trading between now and the end of the year, then all tracking portfolios are static, and the index option provides a payoff pattern that we cannot track. In this case, the index option will *not* be priced by *any* arbitrage argument (Black-Scholes included). Instead, it will be priced in equilibrium—just like everything else. This highlights one of the great paradoxes of derivatives: They are desirable at least in part because they serve to complete the market, but they can't be priced by arbitrage arguments unless the market is already complete!

But frequent trading in the financial market index changes things. If market participants can trade the market index fund and the risk-free bond between now and the end of the year (when the market index option expires), then we *can* track the index option with a *dynamically changing* tracking portfolio which only contains the market index and the risk-free bond.

This requires more than just frequent trading—the uncertainty about the end-of-period value of the market index has to be resolved in a smooth way (more about that later in the book). But imagine, if you will, that our world evolves as shown in Figure 2.35. Notice that the risk-free bond earns 2.5% per six months, or 5.06% per year. [17] What happens if our market participants can rebalance tracking portfolios at the six-month point? A lot!

If we can trade the market index fund and the bond at the six-month mark, then we can track the index option by a *dynamic* tracking portfolio that contains only the market index fund and the risk-free bond. When I say *dynamic,* what I mean is that the contents of the tracking portfolio change after six months depending on what happens to the economy over that time.

The reasoning is really quite simple. Suppose the economy strengthens over the first six months of the year, and the market index fund is worth $120 at that time. If you get to that state,

---

[17] I constructed the binomial tree of market index values using the discrete compounding method (which I detail in Appendix 4.2), with risk-free rate = 2.5% per six months and standard deviation of 17.5% per six months. The risk-neutral probabilities of the up and down steps are 0.5 each in this model. The subjective probabilities of the up and down steps, which come from the assumption that the expected return on the index is 6% per six months, are 0.6 (up) and 0.4 (down).

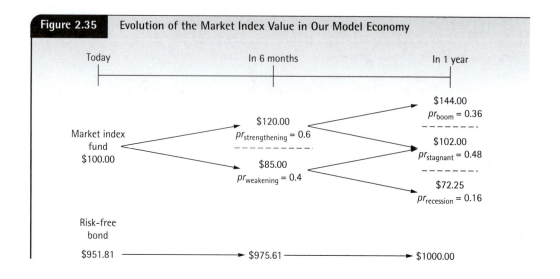

Figure 2.35   Evolution of the Market Index Value in Our Model Economy

Today   In 6 months   In 1 year

Market index
fund
$100.00

$120.00
$pr_{strengthening} = 0.6$

$85.00
$pr_{weakening} = 0.4$

$144.00
$pr_{boom} = 0.36$

$102.00
$pr_{stagnant} = 0.48$

$72.25
$pr_{recession} = 0.16$

Risk-free
bond

$951.81 ———————————→ $975.61 ———————————→ $1000.00

you *know* that only *two* states are possible at the end of the year—the boom economy and the stagnant economy. The index option pays off $44 in the boom economy and $2 in the stagnant economy, and therefore the index option is linear in the value of the market index *over the last six months*. The same thing holds if you are in the weakening state after six months. You know that there are only two possible states of nature—the stagnant economy and the recession economy—and you have two securities to use in your tracking portfolio (the market index and the risk-free bond).[18,19]

So there are only two possible future values of the index option after six months have passed, and you can price the index option at both of the six-month states by an arbitrage argument. But if you know that the index option can take one of only two values at the end of the first six months, and you've got two securities (the market index fund and the risk-free bond), then you can build a tracking portfolio today that correctly tracks the index option over the first six months.

The intuition that there are only two possible states over a short time period (so everything is linear over that time period) is very powerful, and it underlies why the binomial pricing model approximates the Black-Scholes model so nicely. I don't want to get ahead of myself here, so we'll put that off until slightly later. But for those of you that have seen derivatives pricing before, you can verify that the dynamic tracking portfolio which exactly replicates the index option evolves as I show in Figure 2.36.

When we can rebalance our tracking portfolios after six months have passed, the correct tracking portfolio that mimics the index option begins with a long position of 0.613 shares of

---

[18] At any point, $H_{Mkt} = \dfrac{IO_{Up} - IO_{Down}}{M_{Up} - M_{Down}}$ and $H_{RF} = \dfrac{1}{(1 + r^{6-mo})B}[IO_{Up} - H_{Mkt} \times M_{Up}]$, where IO_{Up} and M_{Up} are the values or cash flows on the index option and the market, respectively, if the market goes up over the next six months; IO_{Down} and M_{Down} are the values or cash flows on the index option and the market if the market goes down over the next six months; r^{6-mo} is the six-month risk-free rate of return; and B is the current price of the risk-free bond. We'll derive these in Chapter 4.

[19] Duffie and Huang (1985) provided a rigorous proof that trading in a very small number of securities completes a financial market. In particular, if returns on the market portfolio follow a geometric Brownian motion, then the market is complete with continuous trading in only two securities—the market index and the risk-free bond.

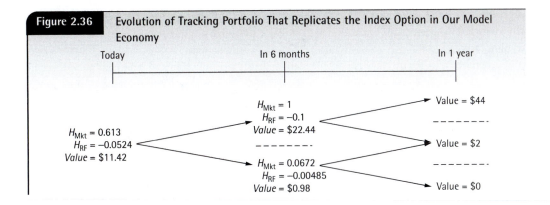

Figure 2.36 Evolution of Tracking Portfolio That Replicates the Index Option in Our Model Economy

the market index fund and a short position of -0.0524 risk-free bonds. The total value of this tracking portfolio is $0.613 \times \$100 - 0.0524 \times \$951.81 = \$11.42$. The composition of this tracking portfolio changes after six months, but the changes cost nothing and yield no cash inflows (check for yourself). Figure 2.37 shows how we break the index option into only two primitive building blocks: The market index and the risk-free bond.

Since trading is possible, the market is complete to the introduction of the index option. Given the no-arbitrage assumption, we can conclude that the index option is worth $\$11.42$.[20]

> Major Result 7: Another way to complete a market is to allow continuous trading in the underlying sources of common risk. If there is only one source of common risk (and if information is revealed smoothly), then only *two traded securities* (the market portfolio and a risk-free bond) complete the market.

A Deeper Understanding of Asset Pricing (Advanced)

Major Result 7 tells us that no matter how many macroeconomic states of nature we have in our model economy, we will have a complete market as long as we have continuous trading in the market index fund and the risk-free bond. With continuous trading in just these two

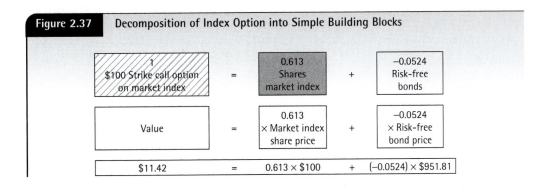

Figure 2.37 Decomposition of Index Option into Simple Building Blocks

[20] $11.42 is the value of the index option if the market is complete *before* the index option is introduced. If the market is not complete before the index option is introduced, the index option's value will depend on the general equilibrium in the economy.

securities, we can create as many different options on the market index as we need to make the market complete, and each of them will be priced by an arbitrage argument (albeit a dynamic one).

Remember that if a market is complete then there's no possibility of financially engineering anything really new—every possible new security will be nothing more than a combination of the existing securities plus conditional mean-zero noise. So what this means, then, is that as long as we can trade continuously in the market index fund, we can price derivatives on *individual stocks* with tracking portfolios that contain only the market index fund and the risk-free bond.

In other words, portfolios created to track options on individual securities (such as stocks) don't need to contain the underlying securities (stocks) themselves. In the preceding example, market participants cannot trade in the stock of the consumer products company between now and the end of the year, and yet we were able to value an option on the stock via an arbitrage with a tracking portfolio.

The reason is really quite simple. In a market where you can trade claims on the sources of common risk (which are building blocks), every individual security is nothing more than a portfolio of those claims on those common risks plus conditional mean-zero errors.

> Major Result 8: If a financial market is complete to the introduction of a new derivative on an existing security, then the tracking portfolio that values the new derivative need not contain the underlying risky security itself.

If we allow the stock in the consumer products company to trade after six months, then its value at the end of six months will be forced by arbitrage. If you recall, the tracking portfolio that arbitrages the stock in the consumer products company is long 4 units of the market index fund and short -0.2 unit of the risk-free bond. So if the economy strengthens after six months, the value of the *stock* at that time will have to be $4 \times \$120 - 0.2 \times \$975.61 = \$284.88$ or else there will be an arbitrage opportunity. Similarly, if the economy weakens over the first six months, the value of the stock at that time will have to be $4 \times \$85 - 0.2 \times \$975.61 = \$144.88$. So if the stock trades at the six month period, the stock's value must evolve like I show in Figure 2.38:

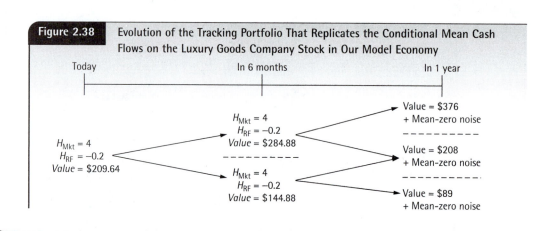

Figure 2.38   **Evolution of the Tracking Portfolio That Replicates the Conditional Mean Cash Flows on the Luxury Goods Company Stock in Our Model Economy**

Today   In 6 months   In 1 year

$H_{Mkt} = 4$
$H_{RF} = -0.2$
Value = $209.64

$H_{Mkt} = 4$
$H_{RF} = -0.2$
Value = $284.88

$H_{Mkt} = 4$
$H_{RF} = -0.2$
Value = $144.88

Value = $376
+ Mean-zero noise

Value = $208
+ Mean-zero noise

Value = $89
+ Mean-zero noise

Figure 2.39 Evolution of The Tracking Portfolio of Stock and Risk-Free Bond That Replicates the Conditional Mean Cash Flows on the Stock Option in Our Model Economy

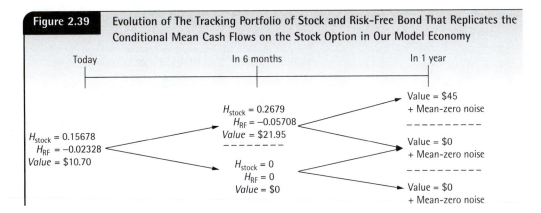

Now *if* the stock trades after six months, then we *can* price an option on the stock using a tracking portfolio that contains only the *stock* and the risk-free bond. I'll show you how to do this in Chapter 4, but trust me on this: The tracking portfolio will evolve as I show in Figure 2.39.

Using this method of dynamically tracking the stock option using the stock and the riskfree bond, we find that the value of the stock option is $10.70—exactly the same as when we formed a *static* tracking portfolio with the market index fund, the option on the market index fund, and the risk-free bond. In this approach, we've broken the stock option into a different set of building blocks: The underlying stock and the risk-free bond (as shown in Figure 2.40).

Why do we get the same answer? *Because the absence of arbitrage forces everything to line up this way.* This is the power of linear pricing.

Approach 1: If you will recall, our first static tracking portfolio that priced the $340 call on the luxury goods company stock holds $H_O = 1.1482$ index options (along with $H_{Mkt} = -0.0772$ shares of the market index itself and $H_{RF} = 0.00558$ risk-free bonds). But if there's trading in the market index fund, then we can further decompose the index option into 0.613 shares of the market index and -0.0524 risk-free bonds (see Figure 2.36). Therefore, the 1.1482 units of the index option break down into 0.7038 units of the market index fund and -0.6016 risk-free bonds:

$$H_0 = 1.1482$$

$$= 1.1482 \times \begin{cases} H_{Mkt} = 0.613 \\ H_{RF} = -0.0524 \end{cases}$$

$$= \begin{cases} H_{Mkt} = 0.7038 \\ H_{RF} = -0.06016 \end{cases}$$

Figure 2.40 Decomposition of $340 Call on Luxury Goods Company Stock into a Different Set of Building Blocks

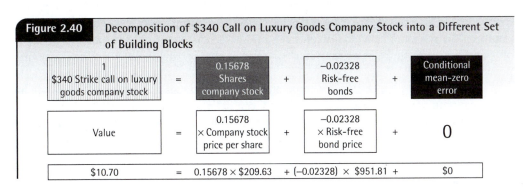

So indirectly, this first tracking portfolio consists of

$$H_{Mkt} = -0.0772 + 0.7038 = 0.627 \text{ units of the market index fund}$$
$$H_{RF} = 0.00558 - 0.06016 = -0.0546 \text{ risk-free bonds}$$

Approach 2: On the other hand, the second tracking portfolio that tracks the stock option dynamically using the underlying stock and the riskfree bond (shown in Figure 2.39) initially holds $H_{stock} = 0.15678$ shares of the stock (along with $H_{RF} = -0.02328$ risk-free bonds). But remember that we can track the stock itself with a static portfolio that is 4 units long the market index and -0.2 riskfree bonds. Thus we can decompose this alternative (and more familiar) tracking portfolio's position in the underlying stock even further:

$$H_{stock} = 0.15678$$
$$= 0.15678 \times \begin{cases} H_{Mkt} = 4 \\ H_{RF} = -0.2 \end{cases}$$
$$= \begin{cases} H_{Mkt} = 0.627 \\ H_{RF} = -0.031356 \end{cases}$$

So indirectly, this more familiar tracking portfolio consists of

$$H_{Mkt} = 0.627 \text{ units of the market index fund}$$
$$H_{RF} = -0.02328 - 0.031356 = -0.0546 \text{ risk-free bonds}$$

In reality, the two different dynamic tracking portfolios that price the call on the luxury goods company stock are identical: Both hold 0.627 units of the market index fund and -0.0546 risk-free bonds. The next two figures show this using our building blocks. Figure 2.41 breaks down the first tracking portfolio (the one consisting of the market index, the index option, and the riskfree bond); Figure 2.42 breaks down the second tracking portfolio (the one consisting of the underlying stock and the riskfree bond). At their molecular levels, these two tracking portfolios are identical.

What should you learn from this? If you have dynamic trading in claims on the common sources of uncertainty in the economy (and if those claims are well behaved), then your market is complete and every security (primary or derivative) is nothing more than a combination of claims on the sources of uncertainty plus conditional mean-zero error. All securities are really old wine in new bottles, and we can value any existing security by finding very simple tracking portfolios.

This has profound importance for corporate finance, because it tells us that *if* we are willing to make certain additional assumptions, *then* we can determine the capital market value of the cash flows from a new corporate investment *even if that investment is illiquid.* This is the heart and soul of the NPV rule, and it applies to whatever corporate investment you might think of (whether it be a real asset or an option on a real asset).

Figure 2.41 Decomposition of the Stock Option into Simple Building Blocks, Starting with the Tracking Portfolio Which Contains the Market Index, the Index Option, and the Risk-Free Bond

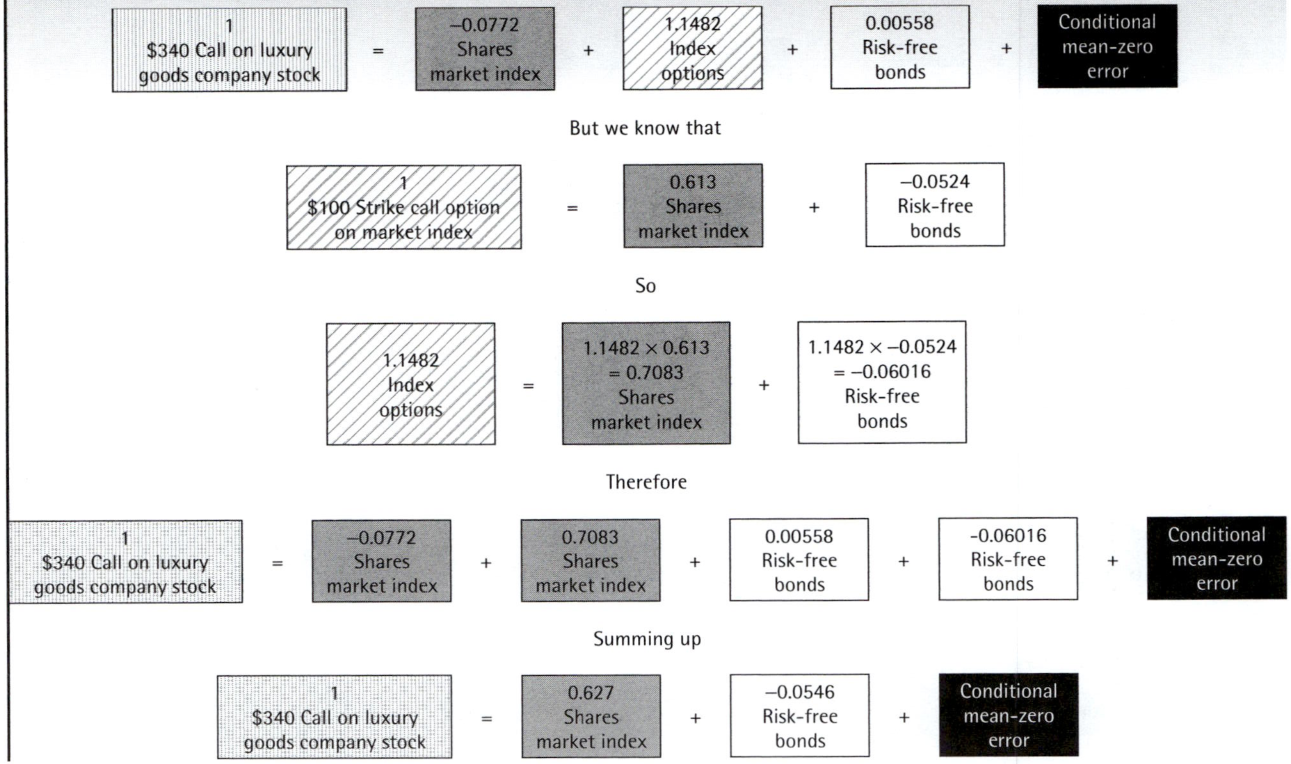

| 1 $340 Call on luxury goods company stock | = | −0.0772 Shares market index | + | 1.1482 Index options | + | 0.00558 Risk-free bonds | + | Conditional mean-zero error |

But we know that

| 1 $100 Strike call option on market index | = | 0.613 Shares market index | + | −0.0524 Risk-free bonds |

So

| 1.1482 Index options | = | 1.1482 × 0.613 = 0.7083 Shares market index | + | 1.1482 × −0.0524 = −0.06016 Risk-free bonds |

Therefore

| 1 $340 Call on luxury goods company stock | = | −0.0772 Shares market index | + | 0.7083 Shares market index | + | 0.00558 Risk-free bonds | + | −0.06016 Risk-free bonds | + | Conditional mean-zero error |

Summing up

| 1 $340 Call on luxury goods company stock | = | 0.627 Shares market index | + | −0.0546 Risk-free bonds | + | Conditional mean-zero error |

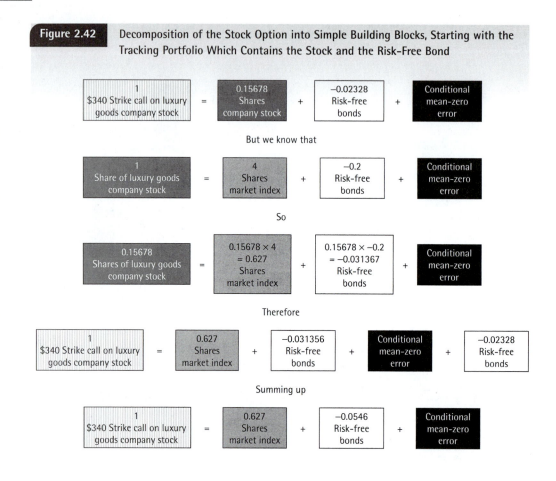

Figure 2.42 Decomposition of the Stock Option into Simple Building Blocks, Starting with the Tracking Portfolio Which Contains the Stock and the Risk-Free Bond

2.5 Summary

In securities markets, valuation of an existing security by arbitrage (including DCF and option pricing models) requires that the financial market be free of arbitrage opportunities. The fundamental theorem of asset pricing tells us that absence of arbitrage in the financial market is a sufficient (and necessary) condition for linear pricing to hold. Therefore, if we can recreate a security's cash flows with a tracking portfolio consisting of other traded claims, then the value of the security must equal the value of the tracking portfolio.

If the conditional mean cash flow on a security is zero (i.e., if its expected cash flow given every possible state of nature is zero), the security is worth zero today. A risky cash flow that has zero mean given all future states is worthless. We call this kind of risk *idiosyncratic risk.*

In arbitrage valuations, tracking portfolios need not be *perfect hedges* for the security being valued. That is, they don't have to match the security's cash flow exactly. Rather, the tracking portfolios must only match the *conditional mean cash flows* of the security (that is, the expected cash flow on the security in every possible state of nature). In other words, the only requirement for a tracking portfolio is that it has conditional mean-zero error. The conditional mean-zero error has no value because it can be diversified away.

If the conditional mean cash flows on a security are the same across all possible states of nature, the security will be priced to yield the risk-free rate of return. A security whose conditional mean cash flows are constant across all future macroeconomic states has no systematic risk; because of costless diversification, the holder receives no return for bearing any idiosyncratic risks associated with it.

If the conditional mean cash flows on a security are not the same across all states, then the security is exposed to systematic risk in some way. This is the risk we care about.

Discounted cash flow valuation (DCF) is a shortcut approach to an arbitrage valuation. It works only when the appropriate tracking portfolio is static. When you use the static CAPM to estimate a discount rate for a DCF valuation of an asset, you are actually determining the expected rate of return on a simple tracking portfolio that mimics the conditional mean cash flows on the asset in each future state of nature. (β) tells you how much of the tracking portfolio should be invested in the market index, and the rest $(1-\beta)$ should be invested in the risk-free asset. The static CAPM only works when these two assets are sufficient for tracking.

When the security you are tying to value has a nonlinear payoff, there are two alternative routes to valuing it by linear pricing. The first is to expand the set of molecular building blocks by creating options on the market index, and to use these nonlinear claims in static tracking portfolios. The second is to allow continuous trading in the economy's underlying sources of common risk and to create dynamic tracking portfolios. Both strategies act to complete the financial market. If there is only one source of common risk (and if information is revealed smoothly), then only *two frequently traded securities* are needed to complete the market: The market portfolio and a risk-free bond.

Finally, if a financial market is complete to the introduction of a new derivative on a security, then the tracking portfolio that values the new derivative need not contain the underlying risky security itself.

2.6 Bibliography

Black, Fisher, and Myron Scholes, 1973. "The Pricing of Options and Corporate Liabilities," *Journal of Political Economy* 81, 637–659.

Duffie, Darrel, and Chi-Fu Huang, 1985. "Implementing Arrow-Debreu Equilibria by Continuous Trading of Few Long-Lived Securities," *Econometrica* 53, 1337–1356.

Dybvig, Philip H., and Stephen A. Ross, 2003. "Arbitrage, State Prices and Portfolio Theory," in *Handbook of the Economics of Finance,* George Constantinides, Milton Harris and René Stulz (ed). Elsevier North-Holland.

Hirshleifer, David, and Tyler Shumway, 2003. "Good Day Sunshine: Stock Returns and the Weather," *Journal of Finance,* 1009–1032.

Ross, Stephen A., 1976. "Options and Efficiency," *Quarterly Journal of Economics* 90, 75–89.

Summers, Lawrence H., 1985. "On Economics and Finance," *Journal of Finance* 40 3, 633–635.

You can find the classic presentation of valuation under certainty and uncertainty in Hirshleifer, J., 1970. *Investment, Interest, and Capital,* Englewood Cliffs NJ: Prentice-Hall.

Appendix 2.1 | Solving for the Tracking Portfolio Holdings

Example 2.2. The Risk-Free Zero-Coupon Bond

We need the portfolio holdings H_{Mkt}, H_O, and H_{RF} such that the three equations in (2.9) equal the three possible values of the risk-free bond in Figure 2.15.

End-of-year value of tracking portfolio:

$$= \begin{cases} H_{Mkt} \times \$144.00 + H_O \times \$44 + H_{RF} \times \$1000.00 = \$150 & (2.A1.1) \\ H_{Mkt} \times \$102.00 + H_O \times \$2 + H_{RF} \times \$1000.00 = \$150 & (2.A1.2) \\ H_{Mkt} \times \$72.25 + H_O \times \$0 + H_{RF} \times \$1000.00 = \$150 & (2.A1.3) \end{cases}$$

When solving simultaneous equations, the trick is to eliminate all but one variable, solve for it, substitute in this solution for the variable, and repeat this process until all variables are solved. To eliminate variables, you multiply or divide any line by any constant, and then add or subtract that line from another line to eliminate a variable.

Here, all we have to do to eliminate a variable is to subtract one line from another. Suppose we subtract the (2.A1.2) from (2.A1.1):

$$\begin{array}{l} H_{Mkt} \times \$144.00 + H_O \times \$44 + H_{RF} \times \$1000.00 = \$150.00 \\ -(H_{Mkt} \times \$102.00 + H_O \times \$2 + H_{RF} \times \$1000.00 = \$150.00) \\ \hline H_{Mkt} \times \$42.00 \;\;+ H_O \times \$42 \qquad\qquad\qquad\qquad = \$0 \end{array} \qquad (2.A1.4)$$

Similarly, subtract (2.A1.3) from (2.A1.2):

$$\begin{array}{l} H_{Mkt} \times \$102.00 + H_O \times \$2 + H_{RF} \times \$1000.00 \;= \$150.00 \\ -(H_{Mkt} \times \$72.25 + H_O \times \$0 + H_{RF} \times \$1000.00 = \$150.00) \\ \hline H_{Mkt} \times \$29.75 \;\;+ H_O \times \$2 \qquad\qquad\qquad\qquad = \$0 \end{array} \qquad (2.A1.5)$$

Now multiply (2.A1.5) times 21,

$$H_{Mkt} \times \$624.75 \;\;+ H_O \times \$42 = \$0 \qquad (2.A1.6)$$

and subtract (2.A1.4) from (2.A1.6),

$$\begin{array}{l} H_{Mkt} \times \$624.75 + H_O \times \$42 = \$0 \\ -(H_{Mkt} \times \$42 + H_O \times \$42 \qquad\;\; = \$0) \\ \hline H_{Mkt} \times \$582.75 \qquad\qquad\qquad = \$0 \end{array} \qquad (2.A1.7)$$

This is easy to solve: $H_{Mkt} = 0$. Now plug $H_{Mkt} = 0$ into either (2.A1.4), (2.A1.5), or (2.A1.6), and get $H_O = 0$. Finally, substitute $H_{Mkt} = 0$ and $H_O = 0$ into either (2.A1.1), (2.A1.2), or (2.A1.3), and solve for H_{RF}, and you'll get $H_{RF} = 0.15$. For example, substitute $H_{Mkt} = 0$ and $H_O = 0$ into the boom equation (2.A1.1):

$$\begin{array}{r} 0 \times \$144.00 + 0 \times \$44 + H_{RF} \times \$1000.00 = \$150.00 \\ H_{RF} \times \$1000.00 = \$150.00 \\ H_{RF} = 0.15 \end{array}$$

You can verify that the solution $H_{Mkt} = 0$, $H_O = 0$, $H_{RF} = 0.15$ holds for all three equations.

Example 2.3. The Rain-Day Bond

We need the portfolio holdings H_{Mkt}, H_O, and H_{RF} such that the three equations in (2.9) equal the three conditional mean values of the rain-day bond in Figure 2.19:

End-of-year value of tracking portfolio:

$$= \begin{cases} H_{Mkt} \times \$144.00 + H_O \times \$44 + H_{RF} \times \$1000.00 = \$512.65 & (2.A1.8) \\ H_{Mkt} \times \$102.00 + H_O \times \$2 + H_{RF} \times \$1000.00 = \$512.65 & (2.A1.9) \\ H_{Mkt} \times \$72.25 + H_O \times \$0 + H_{RF} \times \$1000.00 = \$512.65 & (2.A1.10) \end{cases}$$

Use the exact same procedure as in Example 2.2. Subtract (2.A1.9) from (2.A1.8) and (2.A1.10) from (2.A1.9), and you get two equations identical to (2.A1.4) and (2.A1.5). Multiply (2.A1.5) times 21 to get (2.A1.6), subtract (2.A1.4) from (2.A1.6), and solve for H_{Mkt} to find $H_{Mkt} = 0$. Then use $H_{Mkt} = 0$ in either of the two-variable equations and find $H_O = 0$. Finally, Plug $H_{Mkt} = 0$ and $H_O = 0$ into any of the three equations (2.A1.8), (2.A1.9), or (2.A1.10), and find that HRF = 0.51265.

Example 2.4. The Equity Claim

We need to form a tracking portfolio such that

End-of-year value of tracking portfolio:

$$= \begin{cases} H_{Mkt} \times \$144.00 + H_O \times \$44 + H_{RF} \times \$1000.00 = \$376 & (2.A1.11) \\ H_{Mkt} \times \$102.00 + H_O \times \$2 + H_{RF} \times \$1000.00 = \$208 & (2.A1.12) \\ H_{Mkt} \times \$72.25 + H_O \times \$0 + H_{RF} \times \$1000.00 = \$89 & (2.A1.13) \end{cases}$$

To do this, first subtract (2.A1.12) from (2.A1.11):

$$\begin{array}{l} H_{Mkt} \times \$144.00 + H_O \times \$44 + H_{RF} \times \$1000.00 = \$376 \\ -(H_{Mkt} \times \$102.00 + H_O \times \$2 + H_{RF} \times \$1000.00 = \$208) \\ \hline H_{Mkt} \times \$42.00 + H_O \times \$42 \qquad\qquad\qquad = \$168 \end{array} \qquad (2.A1.14)$$

Now subtract (2.A1.13) from (2.A1.12)

$$\begin{array}{l} H_{Mkt} \times \$102.00 + H_O \times \$2 + H_{RF} \times \$1000.00 = \$208 \\ -(H_{Mkt} \times \$72.25 + H_O \times \$0 + H_{RF} \times \$1000.00 = \$89) \\ \hline H_{Mkt} \times \$29.75 + H_O \times \$2 \qquad\qquad\qquad = \$119 \end{array} \qquad (2.A1.15)$$

Now multiply (2.A1.15) times 21

$$H_{Mkt} \times \$624.75 + H_O \times \$42 = \$2{,}499 \qquad (2.A1.16)$$

and subtract (2.A1.15) from (2.A1.16):

$$\begin{array}{l} H_{Mkt} \times \$624.75 + H_O \times \$42 = \$2{,}499 \\ -(H_{Mkt} \times \$42 + H_O \times \$42 \quad = \$168) \\ \hline H_{Mkt} \times \$582.75 \qquad\qquad\quad = \$2{,}331 \end{array} \qquad (2.A1.17)$$

Solve (2.A1.17) to find that $H_{Mkt} = 4$. Plug this back into any of (2.A1.14), (2.A1.15) or (2.A1.16) to solve for H_O; I used (2.A1.15) to find

$$4 \times \$29.75 + H_O \times \$2 = \$119 \qquad (2.A1.18)$$

Solve (2.A1.18) to find that $H_O = 0$; plug $H_{Mkt} = 4$ and $H_O = 0$ back into any of the original three equations (2.A1.11), (2.A1.12), or (2.A1.13) to find $H_{RF} = -0.2$.

So, our tracking portfolio, which correctly tracks the equity, is long 4 units of the market index fund and short 0.2 unit of the risk-free bond.

Example 2.5. The Call Option on the Equity

We need to form a tracking portfolio such that
End-of-year value of tracking portfolio:

$$= \begin{cases} H_{Mkt} \times \$144.00 + H_O \times \$44 + H_{RF} \times \$1000.00 = \$45 & \text{(2.A1.19)} \\ H_{Mkt} \times \$102.00 + H_O \times \$2 + H_{RF} \times \$1000.00 = \$0 & \text{(2.A1.20)} \\ H_{Mkt} \times \$72.25 + H_O \times \$0 + H_{RF} \times \$1000.00 = \$0 & \text{(2.A1.21)} \end{cases}$$

Subtract (2.A1.20) from (2.A1.19)

$$\begin{array}{l} H_{Mkt} \times \$144.00 + H_O \times \$44 + H_{RF} \times \$1000.00 = \$45 \\ -(H_{Mkt} \times \$102.00 + H_O \times \$2 + H_{RF} \times \$1000.00 = \$0) \\ \hline H_{Mkt} \times \$42.00 + H_O \times \$42 \qquad\qquad\qquad = \$45 \end{array} \qquad \text{(2.A1.22)}$$

Subtract (2.A1.21) from (2.A1.20):

$$\begin{array}{l} H_{Mkt} \times \$102.00 + H_O \times \$2 + H_{RF} \times \$1000.00 = \$0 \\ -(H_{Mkt} \times \$72.25 + H_O \times \$0 + H_{RF} \times \$1000.00 = \$0) \\ \hline H_{Mkt} \times \$29.75 + H_O \times \$2 \qquad\qquad\qquad = \$0 \end{array} \qquad \text{(2.A1.23)}$$

Now multiply (2.A1.23) times 21

$$H_{Mkt} \times \$624.75 + H_O \times \$42 = \$0 \qquad \text{(2.A1.24)}$$

and subtract (2.A1.22) from (2.A1.24)

$$\begin{array}{l} H_{Mkt} \times \$624.75 + H_O \times \$42 = \$0 \\ -(H_{Mkt} \times \$42 + H_O \times \$42 \quad = \$45) \\ \hline H_{Mkt} \times \$582.75 \qquad\qquad\quad = -\$45 \end{array} \qquad \text{(2.A1.25)}$$

which tells us that $H_{Mkt} = -0.0772$. Now plug $H_{Mkt} = -0.0772$ into (A1.21), to get

$$-0.0772 \times \$72.25 + H_O \times \$0 + H_{RF} \times \$1000 = \$0$$

and solve, giving $H_{RF} = 0.00558$. Finally, plug $H_{Mkt} = -0.0772$ and $H_{RF} = 0.00558$ back into either (2.A1.19) or (2.A1.20) and solve to find that $H_O = 1.1482$.

Appendix 2.2 The Single-Period CAPM in Our Economy

There are a variety of ways to make assumptions and get the CAPM, but all of them end up with one punch line.[21] Given the assumptions, the optimal portfolio for each individual in the economy consists of only two things: A position in the risk-free bond, and a position in a maximally diversified fund of risky assets. While each individual's mix of risk-free bond and diversified risky fund would differ based on their risk aversion, the composition of the diversified fund of risky assets is exactly the same for everyone. It is the *market portfolio*.[22]

Given the necessary assumptions, we get the famous single-period CAPM in return-beta form:

$$E\{r_i\} = r + \beta_i[E\{r_{Mkt}\} - r]$$

where

$$\beta_i = \frac{cov(r_i, r_{Mkt})}{var(r_{Mkt})} \qquad (2.A2.1)$$

To use the CAPM in valuation of a future (potentially risky) cash flow, we calculate the expected value of the future cash flow *across macroeconomic states* and then discount at one plus the expected return given by the preceding CAPM return equation:

$$\text{DCF using CAPM } P_0 = \frac{E\{CF\}}{1 + r + \beta_i[E\{r_{Mkt}\} - r]} \qquad (2.A2.2)$$

If we try to calculate the beta of a new asset using Equation (2.A2.2), we're going to run into a problem: Calculation of the beta requires knowledge of future returns on the asset in each possible state of nature (so that the covariance with the market can be calculated), but knowledge of returns requires that we know the current price of the asset. To get around this problem, we need to use the CAPM in a more sophisticated (but absolutely equivalent) form.

To start, take Equation (2.A2.1) and recognize that by definition the return on asset i is simply the ending value of the asset divided by the beginning value, minus 1. In our notation, the ending value of asset i is its end-of-period cash flow, and its beginning value is its current price:

$$r_i \equiv \frac{CF_i}{P_0} - 1 \qquad (2.A2.3) \qquad\qquad (2.A2.3)$$

Substituting (2.A2.3) into the definition of asset i's beta (2.A2.1) gives an alternative expression for beta:

$$\beta_i = \frac{cov\left(\frac{CF_i}{P_0} - 1, r_{Mkt}\right)}{var(r_{Mkt})} \qquad (2.A2.4)$$

---

[21] For the single-period CAPM, assumptions either involve restrictions on investor utility functions (i.e., quadratic) or restrictions on probability distributions of returns on securities (e.g., multivariate normal). When we extend the discussion to a multiperiod economy, we'll need further assumptions (either log utility or a constant opportunity set) in order to generate the single-beta model. Whatever the case, however, the CAPM requires that the individuals in the economy share homogeneous expectations.

[22] This, in turn, implies a very specific relationship between the expected return on an individual's optimum portfolio and the standard deviation of that portfolio:

$$E\{r_{optimum\ portfolio}\} = r_F + \left\{\frac{E\{r_{Mkt}\} - r}{\sigma_{Mkt}}\right\}\sigma_{optimum\ portfolio}$$

The covariance between two random variables has some interesting features. If c is some constant,

$$cov(x + c, y) = cov(x, y)$$

and

$$cov\left(\frac{x}{c}, y\right) = \frac{1}{c} cov(x, y).$$

Using these, (2.A2.4) becomes

$$\beta_i = \frac{1}{P_0} \frac{cov(CF_i, r_{Mkt})}{var(r_{Mkt})} \qquad (2.A2.5)$$

If we then plug (2.A2.5) into the pricing equation (2.A2.2), we get

$$P_0 = \frac{E\{CF_i\}}{1 + r + \frac{1}{P_0} \frac{cov(CF_i, r_{Mkt})}{var(r_{Mkt})} [E\{r_{Mkt}\} - r]} \qquad (2.A2.6)$$

Simplifying (2.A2.6),

$$1 = \frac{E\{CF_i\}}{P_0(1 + r) + \frac{cov(CF_i, r_{Mkt})}{var(r_{Mkt})} [E\{r_{Mkt}\} - r]} \qquad (2.A2.7)$$

Finally, solve for P_0 on the left-hand side of (2.A2.7):

$$P_0 = \frac{1}{1 + r}\left[E\{CF_i\} - \frac{cov(CF_i, r_{Mkt})[E\{r_{Mkt}\} - r]}{var(r_{Mkt})}\right] \qquad (2.A2.8)$$

Equation (2.A2.8) is the CAPM in *price* form, and it is what we will use. This will give the exact same result as risk-adjusted discounting:

$$\frac{E\{CF_i\}}{1 + E\{r_i\}} = \frac{1}{1 + r}\left[E\{CF_i\} - \frac{cov(CF_i, r_{Mkt})[E\{r_{Mkt}\} - r]}{var(r_{Mkt})}\right] \qquad (2.A2.9)$$

Notice what's going on here: In the traditional form of risk-adjusted discounting (the left-hand side of (2.A2.9)), you discount the expected cash flow by a risk-adjusted discount rate (determined from the CAPM). In other words, the risk-adjustment takes place in the denominator. On the right-hand side of (2.A2.9), however, something different happens: You reduce the expected cash flow on the asset by some quantity, then discount this adjusted amount at the risk-free rate. In other words, the risk adjustment takes place in the *numerator,* with the CAPM telling you how many dollars (or euros, or whatever) to reduce the expected cash flow by in order to adjust for risk properly. This is why we call equation (2.A2.8) the *certainty equivalent* approach to valuation. This method is quite general, and it appears in all of the most popular MBA-level corporate finance texts (although we rarely ever present it to students).

In our hypothetical world, the risk-free rate is 5.06%, the market risk premium is 7.3% and the variance of returns on the market is 0.0669, so by (2.A2.8) the current value of any security will be

$$P_0 = \frac{1}{1.0506}\left\{E\{CF\} - \frac{cov(CF_i, r_{Mkt})[0.073]}{0.0669}\right\} \qquad (2.A2.10)$$

so to price new securities, we'll only need to calculate the covariance between the security's cash flows and the returns on the market. Equation (2.A2.10) will then give us the right value (as long as the static CAPM holds, which won't always be the case).

Example 2.1. The Coin-Flip Security

First, calculate the covariance between the cash flow on the coin-flip security and the return on the market:

$$cov(CF_{coin-flip}, r_{market}) = E\{(CF_{coin-flip} \times r_{market})\} - E\{CF_{coin-flip}\} \times E\{r_{market}\}$$
$$= E\{(CF_{coin-flip} \times r_{market})\} - \$0 \times 12.36\%$$
$$= E\{(CF_{coin-flip} \times r_{market})\}.$$

Evaluating this expression:

$$cov(CF_{coin-flip}, r_{market}) = E\{(CF_{coin-flip} \times r_{market})\}$$
$$= pr_{boom} \times pr_{heads} \times (CF_{heads} \times r_{boom}) + pr_{boom} \times pr_{tails} \times (CF_{tails} \times r_{boom})$$
$$+ pr_{stagnant} \times pr_{heads} \times (CF_{heads} \times r_{stagnant}) + pr_{stagnant} \times pr_{tails} \times (CF_{tails} \times r_{stagnant})$$
$$+ pr_{recession} \times pr_{heads} \times (CF_{heads} \times r_{recession}) + pr_{recession} \times pr_{tails} \times (CF_{tails} \times r_{recession})$$
$$= [pr_{heads} \times CF_{heads} + pr_{tails} \times CF_{tails}] \times [pr_{boom}$$
$$\times r_{boom} + pr_{stagnant} \times r_{stagnant} + pr_{recession} \times r_{recession}]$$
$$= [0.5 \times \$250 + 0.5 \times (-\$250)] \times [0.36 \times 44\% + 0.48$$
$$\times 2\% + 0.16 \times (-27.75\%)]$$
$$= \$0 \times 12.36\%$$
$$= 0.$$

So since the covariance between the cash flow on the coin-flip security and the return on the market is zero, we find the value of the coin-flip from the certainty-equivalent CAPM by substituting $E\{CF_{coin-flip}\} = \$0$ and $cov(CF_{coin-flip}, r_{Mkt}) = 0$ into (2.A2.10):

$$P_0 = \frac{1}{1.0506}\left[\$0 - \frac{0 \times [0.073]}{0.0669}\right]$$
$$= \frac{1}{1.0506}[\$0]$$
$$= \$0$$

The CAPM price of the coin-flip security is zero.

Example 2.2. The Risk-Free Zero-Coupon Bond

The covariance between the bond's cash flows and the return on the market is

$$cov(CF_{govt bond}, r_{market}) = E\{CF_{govt bond} \times r_{market}\} - E\{CF_{govt bond}\} \times E\{r_{market}\}$$

which requires that we calculate

$$E\{CF_{govt bond} \times r_{Market}\}$$
$$= pr_{Mkt boom} \times (CF_{boom} \times r_{Mkt boom}) + pr_{Mkt stagnant} \times (CF_{stagnant} \times r_{Mkt stagnant})$$
$$+ pr_{Mkt recession} \times (CF_{recession} \times r_{Mkt recession})$$
$$= 0.36 \times (150 \times 0.44) + 0.48 \times (150 \times 0.02) + 0.16 \times (150 \times (-0.2775))$$

$$= 0.36 \times (66) + 0.48 \times (3) - 0.16 \times (41.625)$$
$$= 23.76 + 1.44 - 6.66$$
$$= 18.54$$

which gives us

$$cov(CF_{govt\,bond},\, r_{market}) = E\{CF_{govt\,bond} \times r_{market}\} - E\{CF_{govt\,bond}\} \times E\{r_{market}\}$$
$$= 18.54 - 150 \times 0.1236$$
$$= 0$$

So by the certainty-equivalent form of the CAPM in (2.A2.10), the value of the bond is

$$P_0 = \frac{1}{1.0506}\left[\$150.00 - \frac{0 \times [0.073]}{0.0669}\right]$$
$$= \frac{1}{1.0506}[\$150.00]$$
$$= \$142.78$$

Now that we know the current value of the bond, we can calculate its beta using Equation (2.A2.5):

$$\beta_{govt\,bond} = \frac{1}{P_0} \times \frac{cov\,(CF_{govt\,bond},\, r_{Mkt})}{var\,(r_{Mkt})}$$
$$= \frac{1}{142.78} \times \frac{0}{0.0669}$$
$$= 0$$

·Note: You'd get the exact same result if you were to use the current price of $142.78 to calculate the return on the bond in each possible future state, then calculate beta the traditional way by calculating the covariance between the returns on the new bond and the returns on the market.

Example 2.3. The Rain-Day Bond

Again, we have to calculate the covariance between the cash flow on the rain-day bond (RDB) and the return on the market:

$$cov(CF_{RDB},\, r_{Mkt}) = E\{(CF_{RDB} \times r_{Mkt})\} - E\{CF_{RDB}\} \times E\{r_{Mkt}\}$$
$$= E\{(CF_{RDB} \times r_{Mkt})\} - 512.65 \times .1236$$

To evaluate the first term:

$$E\{(CF_{RDB},\, r_{Mkt})\} = pr_{boom} \times [pr_{\leq 120\,rain\,days} \times (525.30 \times 0.44) + pr_{>120\,rain\,days} \times (500 \times 0.44)]$$
$$+ pr_{stagnant} \times [pr_{\leq 120\,rain\,days} \times (525.30 \times 0.02) + pr_{>120\,rain\,days} \times (500 \times 0.02)]$$
$$+ pr_{recession} \times [pr_{\leq 120\,rain\,days} \times (525.30 \times -0.2775)$$
$$+ pr_{>120\,rain\,days} \times (500 \times -0.2775)]$$
$$= 0.36 \times [0.5 \times (231.13) + 0.5 \times (220)]$$
$$+ 0.48 \times [0.5 \times (10.51) + 0.5 \times (10)]$$
$$+ 0.16 \times [0.5 \times (-145.77) + 0.5 \times (-138.75)]$$
$$= 81.20 + 4.92 - 22.76$$
$$= 63.36$$

So

$$cov(CF_{RDB}, r_{Mkt}) = E\{(CF_{RDB} \times_{Mkt})\} - E\{CF_{RDB}\} \times E\{r_{Mkt}\}$$
$$= 63.36 - 512.65 \times .1236$$
$$= 63.36 - 63.36$$
$$= 0$$

We can now use the certainty-equivalent form of the CAPM from (2.A2.10). Since the expected cash flow on the rain-day bond is \$512.65 and the covariance between the cash flow on the rain-day bond and the return on the market is zero, the value of the rain-day bond is

$$P_0 = \frac{1}{1.0506}\left\{E\{CF_{RDB}\} - \frac{cov(CF_{RDB}, r_{Mkt})[0.073]}{0.0669}\right\}$$
$$= \frac{1}{1.0506}\left\{\$512.65 - \frac{0 \times [0.073]}{0.0669}\right\}$$
$$= \frac{\$512.65}{1.0506}$$
$$= \$487.95$$

So using (2.A2.5), the beta of the rain-day bond is zero:

$$\beta_{RDB} = \frac{1}{P_{RDB}} \times \frac{cov(CF_{RDB}, r_{Mkt})}{var(r_{Mkt})}$$
$$= \frac{1}{\$487.95} \times \frac{0}{0.0669}$$
$$= 0$$

Example 2.4. The Luxury Goods Company Stock

To price via the CAPM, we will need the covariance between the cash flow on the stock and the return on the market:

$$cov(CF_{equity}, r_{Mkt}) = E\{(CF_{equity} \times r_{Mkt})\} - E\{CF_{equity}\} \times E\{r_{Mkt}\}$$
$$= E\{(CF_{equity} \times r_{Mkt})\} - 249.44 \times 0.1236$$

We have to solve for the first term:

$$E\{(CF_{equity} \times r_{Mkt})\} = 0.36 \times 376 \times 0.44 + 0.48 \times 208 \times 0.02 + 0.16 \times 89 \times -.2775$$
$$= 59.56 + 1.99 - 3.95$$
$$= 57.60$$

so the covariance is

$$cov(CF_{equity}, r_{Mkt}) = E\{(CF_{equity} \times r_{Mkt})\} - E\{CF_{equity}\} \times E\{r_{Mkt}\}$$
$$= 57.60 - 249.44 \times 0.1236$$
$$= 26.77$$

Using our certainty-equivalent formula from (2.A2.10) with $E\{CF_{equity}\} = \$249.44$ and $cov(CF_{equity}, r_{Mkt}) = 26.77$ gives us

$$
\begin{aligned}
P_{equity} &= \frac{1}{1.0506}\left\{E\{CF_{equity}\} - \frac{cov\left(CF_{equity}, r_{Mkt}\right)[0.073]}{0.0669}\right\} \\
&= \frac{1}{1.0506}\left\{\$249.44 - \frac{26.77 \times [0.073]}{0.0669}\right\} \\
&= \frac{\$220.23}{1.0506} \\
&= \$209.63
\end{aligned}
$$

Given this price, we can determine the beta of the new equity from (2.A2.5)

$$
\begin{aligned}
\beta_{equity} &= \frac{1}{P_{equity}} \times \frac{cov\left(CF_{equity}, r_{Mkt}\right)}{var\left(r_{Mkt}\right)} \\
&= \frac{1}{\$209.63} \times \frac{26.77}{0.0669} \\
&= 1.908
\end{aligned}
$$

Example 2.5. The Call on the Luxury Goods Company Stock

To show that the static CAPM does *not* price the call option correctly, start by calculating the covariance between the call's cash flows and the return on the market:

$$
\begin{aligned}
cov(CF_{stock\,option}, r_{Mkt}) &= E\{(CF_{stock\,option} \times r_{Mkt}\} - E\{CF_{stock\,option}\} \times E\{r_{Mkt}\} \\
&= E\{(CF_{stock\,option} \times r_{Mkt}\} - 16.20 \times 0.1236
\end{aligned}
$$

To solve the first term,

$$
\begin{aligned}
E\{(CF_{stock\,option} \times r_{Mkt})\} &= 0.36 \times 45 \times 0.44 + 0.48 \times 0 \times 0.02 + 0.16 \times 0 \times -.2775 \\
&= 7.13 + 0 + 0 \\
&= 7.13
\end{aligned}
$$

so the covariance is

$$
\begin{aligned}
cov\left(CF_{stock\,option}, r_{Mkt}\right) &= E\{(CF_{stock\,option} \times r_{Mkt})\} - E\{CF_{stock\,option}\} \times E\{r_{Mkt}\} \\
&= 7.13 - 16.20 \times 0.1236 \\
&= 5.13
\end{aligned}
$$

Using our certainty-equivalent formula from (2.A2.10) with $E\{CF_{stock\,option}\} = \$16.20$ and $cov(CF_{stock\,option}, r_{Mkt}) = 5.13$ gives us

$$
\begin{aligned}
P_{stock\,option} &= \frac{1}{1.0506}\left\{E\{CF_{stock\,option}\} - \frac{cov\left(CF_{stock\,option}, r_{Mkt}\right)[0.073]}{0.0669}\right\} \\
&= \frac{1}{1.0506}\left\{\$16.20 - \frac{5.13 \times [0.073]}{0.0669}\right\} \\
&= \frac{\$10.60}{1.0506} \\
&= \$10.09
\end{aligned}
$$

Given this price, we can determine the static CAPM beta of the new equity from (2.A2.5)

$$\beta_{stock\,option} = \frac{1}{P_{stock\,option}} \times \frac{cov(CF_{stock\,option},\, r_{Mkt})}{var(r_{Mkt})}$$

$$= \frac{1}{\$10.09} \times \frac{5.13}{0.0669}$$

$$= 7.59$$

I reiterate that the static CAPM value calculated above is incorrect and admits an arbitrage opportunity; the static CAPM beta is therefore meaningless.

1. Suppose a project is expected to have annual revenues of $45,000.00 for the next 10 years, beginning next year. The discount rate for the project is based on a CAPM beta of 0.75. Assuming a risk-free return of 3% and an expected market portfolio return of 8%, what is the discount rate for the project? Further, assuming a cost of $300,000.00, what is the NPV (i.e., the discounted revenues less the cost) of the project?

2. Suppose there are two states of the world in the future: State A and State B. Each state has a 50% probability of occurring. Security X produces a cash flow of $3.00 in State A and $2.00 in State B. Security Y produces a cash flow of $4.00 in State A and $2.00 in State B. Assuming that both securities cost the same, create an arbitrage portfolio by going long in one security and short in the other security. Further, describe under what circumstances the portfolio produces revenue without any cost.

Suppose a third security, Security Z, pays $1.00 if State A occurs and zero otherwise. The cost of Security Z is $0.45. How can Security Z be introduced into the previous arbitrage portfolio to produce revenue today instead of in the future?

3. Suppose a security generates a cash flow of $75.00 one year from today and has a current price of $68.18. A new security generates a cash flow of $112.50 one year from today. Price the new security using a tracking portfolio approach and using a DCF approach.

4. Assume there are three possible future states for the economy (Boom, Stagnant, and Recession) with associated probabilities of 20%, 45%, and 35%. For each future state of the economy, a security pays either $40.00 or $20.00 with equal probability (i.e., a 50% chance of either payoff occurring).

   a. What is the expected future cash flow for any given future state of the economy?

   b. What is the expected future cash flow for the security?

   c. Further assuming the future outcomes are one year into the future, what is the current price of the security assuming a 5% annual discount rate?

   d. What is the conditional expected cash flow for each future state of nature? (*Note:* It will be the same for each state.)

   e. Assume that given any future state of nature, the $40.00 payoff is Event 1, and the $20.00 payoff is Event 2. What is the "conditional mean-zero idiosyncratic component" for the security based on the future payoffs in Event 1 and Event 2? (*Note:* It will be the same for each state.)

   f. What is the CAPM beta for this security?

5. Assume that the probability of a $40.00 payoff in Problem 4 is now 40% (with the associated probability of the $20.00 payoff being $60.00). Redo parts a through f of Problem 4 based on this new information.

6. Assume that there are two possible states of the future (Good and Bad) with associated probabilities of 40% and 60%. Given the Good state, the security pays off: $10.00 with

35% probability, $12.00 with 25%, and $8.00 with 40% probability. Given the Bad state, the security pays off: $2.00 with 50% probability and $0.00 with 50% probability.

    a. What are the expected payoffs given the Good state and the Bad state?

    b. What are the conditional expected payoffs for the security for each state of nature?

    c. What are the conditional mean-zero component payoffs for each future state of nature?

    d. Does this security have a CAPM beta of zero?

7. Assume there are two possible states of the future (Good and Bad) with associated probabilities of 55% and 45%. Given the Good state, the security pays off $10.00 with 40% probability and $8.00 with 60% probability. Given the Bad state, the security pays off $12.00 with 50% probability and $5.60 with 50% probability.

    a. What are the expected payoffs given the Good state and the Bad state?

    b. What is the expected future payoff for the security?

    c. What are the conditional mean-zero component payoffs for each future state of nature?

    d. Does this security have a CAPM beta of zero?

8. The table below represents three securities with their associated payoffs for three different future states of the economy (Boom, Stagnant, and Recession) that will occur one year from today.

Economy	Probability	Security 1 Payoffs	Security 2 Payoffs	Security 3 Payoffs
Boom	35%	$100.00	$500.00	$50.00
Stagnant	45%	$100.00	$300.00	$0.00
Recession	20%	$100.00	$200.00	$0.00

    a. Given an annual discount rate of 5% for Security 1, 14% for Security 2, and 45% for Security 3, what are the current prices of the three securities?

    b. A new security has a payoff of $85.00 in the Boom economy, a $60.00 payoff in the Stagnant economy, and a $50.00 payoff in the Recession economy. Find the tracking portfolio holdings: H_1, H_2, and H_3 that correspond to Securities 1, 2, and 3, respectively.

    (Suggestion) Notice that you will be solving three equations simultaneously:

$$H_1 \times \$100.00 + H_2 \times \$500.00 + H_3 \times \$50.00 = \$85.00$$
$$H_1 \times \$100.00 + H_2 \times \$300.00 + H_3 \times \$0.00 = \$60.00$$
$$H_1 \times \$100.00 + H_2 \times \$200.00 + H_3 \times \$0.00 = \$50.00$$

    In matrix notation, the three equations become:

$$\begin{bmatrix} \$100.00 & \$500.00 & \$50.00 \\ \$100.00 & \$300.00 & \$0.00 \\ \$100.00 & \$200.00 & \$0.00 \end{bmatrix} \times \begin{bmatrix} H_1 \\ H_2 \\ H_3 \end{bmatrix} = \begin{bmatrix} \$85.00 \\ \$60.00 \\ \$50.00 \end{bmatrix}$$

By inverting the first matrix and premultiplying the inverted matrix by the third matrix, a solution for the second matrix can be found. What is the price of the new security based on the price of the tracking portfolio?

c. Assuming Security 1 is the risk-free security and Security 2 is the market portfolio, what is the CAPM beta of the new security?

9. The table below represents three securities with their associated payoffs for three different future states of the economy (Boom, Stagnant, and Recession) that will occur one year from today. The table also contains the security's current prices.

Economy	Probability	Security 1 Payoffs	Security 2 Payoffs	Security 3 Payoffs
Boom	25%	$100.00	$500.00	$40.00
Stagnant	45%	$100.00	$350.00	$0.00
Recession	30%	$100.00	$150.00	$0.00
Current Price		$94.34	$282.33	$6.54

a. A particular security will pay either $200.00 or $100.00 in the Boom state with equal probability and zero otherwise. What holdings in Securities 1 through 3 (i.e., H_1, H_2, and H_3) will track this security?

b. A particular security will pay either $100.00 or $60.00 in the Stagnant state with equal probability and zero otherwise. What holdings in Securities 1 through 3 (i.e., H_1, H_2, and H_3) will track this security?

c. A particular security will pay either $50.00 or $0.00 in the Recession state with equal probability and zero otherwise. What holdings in Securities 1 through 3 (i.e., H_1, H_2, and H_3) will track this security?

d. What are the prices of the three securities in parts a through c?

10. Use the information from the table in Problem 9. A new security has the following payoffs: in the Boom state ($40.00 with 30% probability and $10.00 with 70% probability), in the Stagnant state ($20.00 with 60% probability and $10.00 with 40% probability), and in the Recession state ($25.00 with 35% probability and $15.00 with 65% probability). Determine the tracking portfolio holdings (i.e., H_1, H_2, and H_3) for the security.

11. In example 5, change the Boom economy litigation risk payouts from $304.00 to $280.00 and from $400.00 to $408.00.

a. Is the price of the Consumer Products Company Stock [QUERY2]affected by the change in the litigation risk? Why?

b. Reprice the call option from example 5. Because the variance of the litigation risk has changed, the option value changes.

12. A stock currently sells for $50.00. Every six months, the stock price can increase by 12% or decrease by 10%. Consequently, after six months, the stock price is either $56.00 [$50.00 × (1 + 12%)] or $45.00 [$50.00 × (1 − 10%)]. After one year, if the stock price was $56.00 after six months, the year-end price is either $62.72 [$56.00 × (1 + 12%)] or $50.40

[$56.00 \times (1 - 10\%)$]. Further, if the six-month price was $45.00, the year-end price is either $50.40 [$45.00 \times (1 + 12\%)$] or $40.50 [$45.00 \times (1 - 10\%)$].

A risk-free bond has a current price of $96.12. The bond will be worth $98.04 in six months and $100.00 one year from today. Given this information, price a one-year call option with a strike price of $50.00. Use the following steps:

a. Solve the two sets of simultaneous equations to find the holdings of the tracking portfolio when the six-month stock price is $56.00, and use the holdings of the tracking portfolio to solve for the option price at six months.

$$H_{STOCK} \times \$62.72 + H_{RF} \times \$100.00 = \$12.72 \ [max(\$62.27 - \$50.00, 0)]$$
$$H_{STOCK} \times \$50.40 + H_{RF} \times \$100.00 = \$0.40 \ [max(\$50.40 - \$50.00, 0)]$$

b. Solve the two sets of simultaneous equations to find the holdings of the tracking portfolio when the six-month stock price is $45.00, and use the holdings of the tracking portfolio to solve for the option price at six months.

$$H_{STOCK} \times \$50.40 + H_{RF} \times \$100.00 = \$0.40 \ [max(\$50.40 - \$50.00, 0)]$$
$$H_{STOCK} \times \$40.50 + H_{RF} \times \$100.00 = \$0.00 \ [max(\$40.50 - \$50.00, 0)]$$

c. Use the two option prices at six months found in parts a and b to solve for the current option price. (*Hint:* Create another set of simultaneous equations to solve for tracking portfolio holdings.)

13. In Britain, 19,475,430,000 bonds were sold, in which 1 out of every 30 bondholders received an interest payment. The interest payment (if received) was based on a lottery system in which various payments were awarded. The number of recipients and the cash value of the interest payment are displayed in the table below.

Interest Payment in Pounds	Number of Recipients
1,000,000.00	1
100,000.00	2
50,000.00	3
25,000.00	6
10,000.00	16
5,000.00	33
1,000.00	730
500.00	2190
100.00	11,129
50.00	635,071

Each bond costs one pound, and the interest is paid at the end of the month, which is when the bond matures. Calculate the expected monthly rate of interest for all of the bonds, and convert this calculation to an annual rate (by multiplying by 12). How should this rate compare to the risk-free rate in Britain?

3

VALUATION OF REAL ASSETS: WHAT CORPORATE FINANCE IS ALL ABOUT

A misunderstanding you run into is the idea that it is somehow inappropriate to use option pricing techniques in a corporate setting when you're dealing with non-traded assets. You hear this again and again from very sophisticated people. And it reflects a misunderstanding of what corporate finance is all about.

—Stewart Myers[1]

Stew Myers's quote (which comes from his keynote address at a conference that celebrated the 25th anniversary of his article[2] in which he first coined the term "real options") provides the motivation for this chapter. Many people—academics as well as practitioners—don't really understand the foundations of corporate finance, and this lack of good conceptual foundation translates directly into a large number of misconceptions.

In this chapter, I'll provide a heuristic explanation of the theory of *corporate* investment decisions. Although this may help you understand a lot of other things, my main objective is for you to learn exactly why option pricing techniques are every bit as legitimate in corporate investment analysis as the discounted cash flow (DCF) analyses you've been doing all along. By the end of the chapter, you should possess a deeper appreciation for Stewart's quote.

Chapter Plan

My teaching vehicle for this chapter will be a hypothetical firm that faces opportunities for growth investments. We'll first construct this firm, and we'll place it in our financial market economy from Chapter 2 (i.e., we'll assume that the company's existing securities trade in our financial market). Chapter 2 is an absolute prerequisite for this material, so if you have not worked through it carefully you need to go back and do so.

To make things easy, we'll assume that our firm is unlevered. Our first order of business will be to determine the financial market value of the firm's existing equity (or, equivalently, its assets). This is really just a reapplication of the material presented in Chapter 2; because the firm's equity claims are traded in our financial market, we can value them by arbitrage. I use this exercise to highlight several important concepts regarding the valuation of firms.

---

[1] Keynote Address at the University of Maryland Symposium on Real Options, April 18, 2002, as quoted in Arnold and Shockley (2003).

[2] Myers (1977).

Next, I'll turn to corporate finance and to the financial manager's investment decision. I'll introduce *two* new investment possibilities within the firm. The first opportunity will be a straightforward, now-or-never/no-flexibility project, and I'll use this example to illustrate how the manager *values* the new corporate project using prices from the financial market and then *evaluates* the project using the net present value (NPV) rule (see Chapter 1). I'll show that in this particular case, the DCF approach to valuation and the *static* NPV rule lead to the right decision.

The second example will be a growth opportunity that is not now-or-never/no-flexibility; instead, this one (if accepted) will create significant future flexibility for the firm. With this illustration, I can finally demonstrate what I claimed in Chapter 1: that the theory of valuation is the same for the growth option as for the static opportunity, but that the DCF *shortcut* to valuation won't work when the investment creates future flexibility. The existence of optionality in a corporate project does not change the fundamental principles of valuation—it only changes the practical approach.

In these two examples, we'll take for granted that the firm's investors unanimously want the firm's managers to follow the NPV rule (using the *true* NPV, of course). More specifically, we'll *assume* that the firm's investor's want managers to evaluate a potential project by comparing it to the investor's similar risk opportunity in the financial markets. Most people take this for granted, but it is not axiomatic at all. Investors will unanimously desire that managers use the NPV rule only under a certain set of conditions, which I'll explain in the final part of the chapter. The gist is that our idea of valuation by an arbitrage argument (DCF, option pricing, or whatever) requires that the corporate investment does not change financial market prices. The implication will be that application of option pricing techniques to the valuation of corporate projects will be entirely appropriate in any situation where maximization of *true* NPV is the appropriate goal of management. And this will bring us right back to Stewart Myers's quote.

3.1 Our Model of the World

We'll continue to work with our simple model economy that we used in Chapter 2. If you recall, we have a market index fund that is currently worth $100, an at-the-money call option on the market index fund with current value $11.42, and a risk-free bond presently priced at $951.81. At the end of the year, the value of the two risky securities depends on the state of nature, whereas the payoff on the risk-free bond is certain. The expected return on the market index is 12.36%, and the risk-free rate is 2.5% per six months or approximately 5.06% per year. Figure 3.1 summarizes the securities in our simple economy.

These three securities are the molecular building blocks in our economy. Our market is complete by construction and free of arbitrage by assumption, so the value of any other existing security must be equal to the value of a tracking portfolio that contains only these three building blocks (plus conditional mean-zero error). Moreover, if we can rebalance tracking portfolios after six months, then the index option is itself redundant and we can decompose any other existing security into only *two* building blocks—the market index and the risk-free bond—simply because frequent trading in the market index completes the market.

The point of this chapter is to demonstrate how and why corporate managers can use the financial markets to help make corporate investment decisions. I'll illustrate all of the important points via one hypothetical firm: a boutique consulting firm.

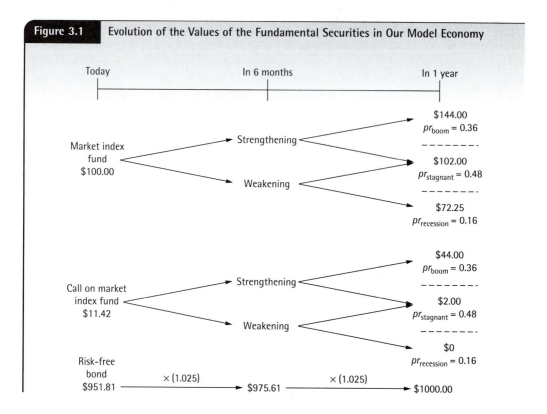

Figure 3.1   Evolution of the Values of the Fundamental Securities in Our Model Economy

Our Consulting Firm

Our consulting firm has $5 million in cash on hand, which it keeps in treasury bonds; the value of these bonds will be $5 million $\times (1.025)^2 = \$5,253,125$ for sure at the end of the year.[3] The other assets of the firm—its reputation and human capital—are in place to generate consulting cash flow.

Boutique consulting firms face both systematic and firm-specific cash flow risks. Revenues are quite sensitive to the overall state of the macroeconomy, and there's always the chance that a major client may defect to a competing firm. So we'll assume that the end-of-year value of all future consulting business cash flow depends both on the macroeconomic state of nature *and* whether or not its largest client defects (as detailed in Figure 3.2).

Make sure you understand what we've got here. The numbers in Figure 3.2 are the end-of-year present values of all future free cash flows from the consulting business given the different macroeconomic outcomes and client actions. In other words, they are the end-of-year values of the *consulting assets*. The end-of-year total value of the consulting firm will be the realized value of the consulting assets (from the table in Figure 3.2) plus $5,253,125 (the value of the cash on hand).

To value the consulting firm, we first need to calculate the end-of-year conditional mean values of the consulting assets, as shown in Figure 3.3.

Figure 3.4 shows that the outcomes of the firm-specific risk (whether or not the major client defects) cause a shock to the conditional mean that has an expected value of zero in each macroeconomic state, and hence is idiosyncratic risk.

---

[3] The risk-free bonds earn 2.5% every six months, or approximately 5.06% over the year.

Figure 3.2

End-of-Year Value of All Future Consulting Business Cash Flows

		Firm-Specific Risk Outcomes	
		Client Defects ($pr = 0.1$)	Client Stays ($pr = 0.9$)
Macroeconomic Outcomes	Boom ($pr = 0.36$)	$47.5 million	$62.5 million
	Stagnant ($pr = 0.48$)	$31 million	$41 million
	Recession ($pr = 0.16$)	$19.5 million	$25.75 million

Because the shocks to the conditional mean consulting asset values are idiosyncratic, they have no value, and we can ignore them in our valuation (if you don't remember why, go back and review Chapter 2). All we need to do is add in the end-of-year value of the firm's cash on hand, and we're ready to go. This has been done this for you in Figure 3.5.

We'll assume that our consulting firm has no debt, so the values in Figure 3.5 are the end-of-year conditional mean market capitalizations of the firm's equity given each possible macroeconomic state.[4]

We can now determine the financial market value of our consulting firm. The mechanics are simply a review of what we did in Chapter 2, but I want to make a couple of important observations along the way.

Figure 3.3   End-of-Year Value of Consulting Assets

		Firm-Specific Risk Outcomes		
		Client Defects ($pr = 0.1$)	Client Stays ($pr = 0.9$)	Conditional Mean
Macroeconomic Outcomes	Boom ($pr = 0.36$)	$47.5 million	$62.5 million	$0.1 \times \$47.5 + 0.9 \times \$62.5$ = $61 million
	Stagnant ($pr = 0.48$)	$31 million	$41 million	$0.1 \times \$31 + 0.9 \times \$41$ = $40 million
	Recession ($pr = 0.16$)	$19.5 million	$25.75 million	$0.1 \times \$19.5 + 0.9 \times \$25.75$ = $25.125 million

---

[4] If the firm is private, these are the possible values at which the firm could either sell its stock into the market in an IPO or to someone else in a competitive transaction at the end of the year. Either way, these are the possible values of the firm's assets in place at the end of the year.

Figure 3.4   End-of-Year Value of Consulting Assets (in millions)

| | | | Firm-Specific Risk Outcomes | | |
| | | | Idiosyncratic Shock to Conditional Mean (actual−conditional mean) | | |
		Conditional mean component	Client Defects ($pr = 0.1$)	Client Stays ($pr = 0.9$)	Conditional Mean of Idiosyncratic Component
Macroeconomic Outcomes	Boom ($pr = 0.36$)	$61	$47.5 − $61 = −$13.5	$62.5 − $61 = $1.5	$0.1 \times -$13.5 + 0.9 \times$ $1.5 = $0
	Stagnant ($pr = 0.48$)	$40	$31 − $40 = −$9	$41 − $40 = $1	$0.1 \times -$9 + 0.9 \times$ $1 = $0
	Recession $0.625 ($pr = 0.16$)	$25.125	$19.5 − $25.125 = −$5.625	$25.75 − $25.125 = $0.625	$0.1 \times -$5.625 + 0.9 \times$ = $0

This part has no value!

Valuing the Consulting Firm, Approach 1 (All-in-One)

Our firm is unlevered, so the value of its equity equals the value of its assets. Let's calculate the total market value of the equity. From what we learned in the last chapter, the conditional mean-zero shocks that will arise due to the client's actions are worthless in the financial markets because we can costlessly shed them by diversifying. So, to find the financial market price of the firm's equity, we need to find a tracking portfolio with holdings H_{Mkt} of the market index, H_O of the index option, and H_{RF} of the risk-free bond such that

End-of-year value of tracking portfolio:

$$= \begin{cases} H_{Mkt} \times \$144.00 + H_O \times \$44 + H_{RF} \times \$1000.00 = \$66,253,125 & \text{(Boom)} \\ H_{Mkt} \times \$102.00 + H_O \times \$2 + H_{RF} \times \$1000.00 = \$45,253,125 & \text{(Stagnant)} \\ H_{Mkt} \times \$72.25 + H_O \times \$0 + H_{RF} \times \$1000.00 = \$30,378,125 & \text{(Recession)} \end{cases}$$

Figure 3.5   End-of-Year Total Value of All Firm Assets

| | | End-of-Year Conditional Mean Values | | |
		Cash	Consulting Assets	Total
Macroeconomic Outcomes	Boom ($pr = 0.36$)	$5,253,125	$61,000,000	$66,253,125
	Stagnant ($pr = 0.48$)	$5,253,125	$40,000,000	$45,253,125
	Recession ($pr = 0.16$)	$5,253,125	$25,125,000	$30,378,125

It is relatively easy to work out that the appropriate tracking portfolio contains $H_{Mkt} = 500,000$ shares of the market index, $H_O = 0$ index options, and $H_{RF} = -5,746.87$ risk-free bonds (which I show in Appendix 3.2). Note that a short position in the risk-free bond is like borrowing, so the consulting firm's equity is really like a levered position in the market index. The total value of the tracking portfolio is

$$Current\ value\ of\ tracking\ portfolio = H_{Mkt} \times \$100 + H_O \times \$11.42 + H_{RF} \times \$951.81$$
$$= 500,000 \times \$100 + 0 \times \$11.42 - 5,746.87 \times \$951.81$$
$$= \$44,530,042$$

If there are no arbitrage opportunities in the financial markets, the financial market value of the consulting firm's stock is about $44.530 million.

Let's make sure we all understand what this number means and how to interpret it. When we say that the financial market value of the consulting firm's stock is $44.530 million, what we mean is that it would cost an investor $44.530 million to create a financial market portfolio with cash flows that behave like the conditional mean cash flows of the consulting firm. To create this portfolio, the investor only needs to put together our molecular building blocks that create conditional mean cash flows just like those of the consulting firm (with mean-zero error in each state). What do those building blocks look like here? Figure 3.6 gives our building-block representation of the tracking portfolio, just as we presented in Chapter 2.

And just as in Chapter 2, several points are not coincidental:

1. The tracking portfolio has

$$(500,000 \times \$100)/\$44,530,042 = 112.28\%$$

of its total value invested in the market index and

$$(-5,746.87 \times \$951.81)/\$44,530,042 = -12.28\%$$

invested in the risk-free bond (and nothing invested in the index option), so the expected return on the tracking portfolio is

$$E\{r^{tracking\ portfolio}\} = 1.1228 \times 12.36\% + (-0.1228) \times 5.06\%$$
$$= 13.256\%$$

2. The tracking portfolio with $H_{Mkt} = 500,000$, and $H_{RF} = -5,746.87$ represents the investors' or owners' equivalent opportunity in other financial market investments, and the expected return on this tracking portfolio is the investors' or owners' *opportunity cost of funds*.

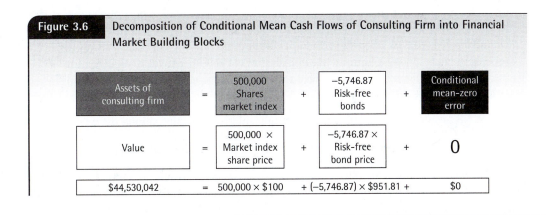

Figure 3.6 Decomposition of Conditional Mean Cash Flows of Consulting Firm into Financial Market Building Blocks

3. The expected value of the consulting company at the end of the year is

$$E\{V_{\text{consulting firm}}\} = 0.36 \times \$66,253,125 + 0.48 \times \$45,253,125 + 0.16 \times 30,378,125$$
$$= \$50,433,125$$

Had we discounted the expected end-of-year value of the consulting firm by the opportunity cost of funds in a DCF calculation, we would have arrived at the same answer:

$$\text{DCF value} = \frac{E\{V\}}{1 + r^{\bullet}}$$
$$= \frac{\$50,433,125}{1.13256} = \$44,530,042$$

In other words, the DCF value of the company is equal to the value of the tracking portfolio. To put it another way, the correct discount rate to use in a DCF valuation of the company is the expected return on the financial market tracking portfolio that mimics the firm's conditional mean cash flow.

4. Since the expected value of the company at the end of the year is $50,433,125 and the current arbitrage-free value of the company is $44,530,042, the expected return on the company's assets is

$$E\{r^{\text{consulting firm}}\} = \frac{\$50,433,125}{\$44,530,042} - 1 = 13.256\%$$

That is, the value of the firm implies that the expected return to its owners is identical to the expected return on the financial market tracking portfolio that mimics the firm's conditional mean cash flow.

5. If the capital asset pricing model (CAPM) holds, then the beta of the company's equity is 1.1228 (which I derive in Appendix 3.2). So, in a DCF valuation using the CAPM to estimate the risk-adjusted discount rate,

$$\text{DCF value using CAPM} = \frac{E\{V\}}{1 + r + \beta[E\{r_{\text{Mkt}}\} - r]}$$
$$= \frac{\$50,433,125}{1 + 0.0506 + 1.1228[0.1236 - 0.0506]}$$
$$= \frac{\$50,433,125}{1.13256} = \$44,530,042$$

Again, the CAPM return equation is nothing more than the equation for the expected return on a portfolio that has β% of its value invested in the market portfolio and $1 - \beta$% invested in the risk-free bond. When you calculate (or estimate) the company's hurdle rate via the CAPM, you are taking a shortcut to finding the tracking portfolio that exactly mimics the company's conditional mean cash flows. The CAPM will work here (if it holds in the economy) because the conditional mean cash flows on the equity are linear in the market index (as Figure 3.7 shows).

Figure 3.8 gives our visual depiction of the tight interrelationships among these points.

Valuing the Consulting Firm, Approach 2 (Divide-and-Conquer)

We could have valued the stock by valuing the firm's cash and consulting assets separately. The cash is obviously worth $5 million today; since the firm invests its cash in government bonds,

Figure 3.7

Linearity of Conditional Mean Cash Flows in Market Index

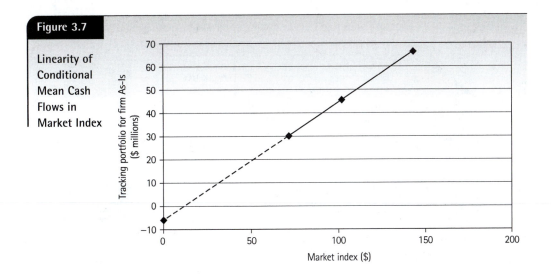

and each bond is worth \$951.81, the firm holds \$5 million/\$951.81 = 5,253.13 risk-free bonds. To value the consulting assets separately from the cash, we must form a tracking portfolio that tracks the conditional mean consulting asset values from Figure 3.3. So our tracking portfolio holdings must solve the simultaneous equations

Figure 3.8   Valuation of the Consulting Firm's Equity

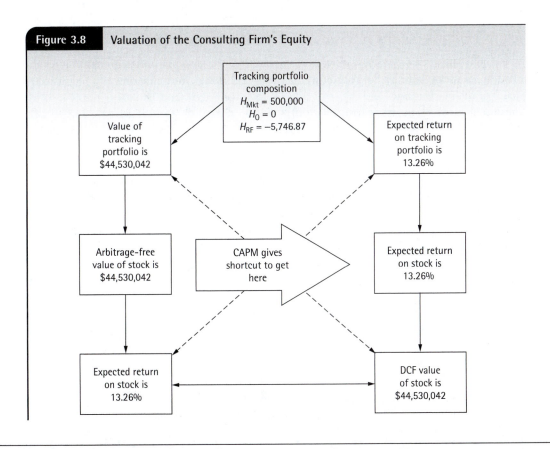

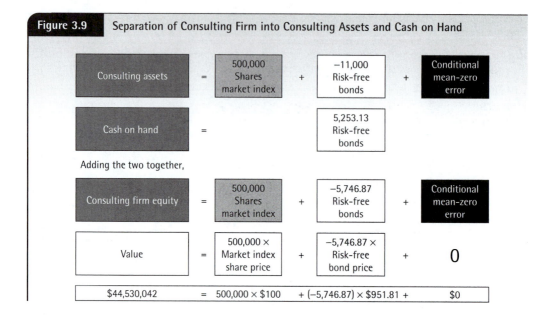

Figure 3.9   Separation of Consulting Firm into Consulting Assets and Cash on Hand

End-of-year value of tracking portfolio:

$$= \begin{cases} H_{Mkt} \times \$144.00 + H_0 \times \$44 + H_{RF} \times \$1000.00 = \$61,000,000 & \text{(Boom)} \\ H_{Mkt} \times \$102.00 + H_0 \times \$2 + H_{RF} \times \$1000.00 = \$40,000,000 & \text{(Stagnant)} \\ H_{Mkt} \times \$72.25 + H_0 \times \$0 + H_{RF} \times \$1000.00 = \$25,125,000 & \text{(Recession)} \end{cases}$$

This one is also pretty easy. As I show in Appendix 3.2, the tracking portfolio that mimics the conditional mean value of the consulting business cash flows alone contains $H_{Mkt} = 500,000$ shares of the market index and $H_{RF} = -11,000$ risk-free bonds (and no index options), so the consulting assets alone are worth $500,000 \times \$100 - 11,000 \times \$951.81 = \$39,530,042$. Adding this to the value of the company's cash gives a total enterprise value of $\$39,530,042 + \$5,000,000 = \$44,530,042$, exactly what we got before.

Let's explore this divide-and-conquer approach to the company valuation in several different ways. First, Figure 3.9 shows that the building blocks that make up the two pieces (cash-on-hand and consulting assets) combine to equal the building blocks that create the entire firm.

In other words, the value of the firm is nothing more than the sum of its parts. Or, in a more complex way, the value of a firm is just the sum of the values of the tracking portfolios that replicate each of the firm's parts. Even though we can't literally divide the firm into cash on hand and consulting assets, we can approach the valuation this way (else there would be an arbitrage opportunity). If the firm had other different business lines, we could value each individually and sum them all up.

The tracking portfolio that mimics the conditional mean cash flows on the consulting assets alone has $500,000 \times \$100/\$39,530,042 = 126.49\%$ of its total invested in the market index fund and $-11,000 \times \$951.81/\$39,530,042 = -26.49\%$ of its total invested in the risk-free bond. Therefore, the expected return on this tracking portfolio is

$$E\{r^{\text{tracking portfolio}}\} = 1.2649 \times 12.36\% + (-0.2649) \times 5.06\%$$
$$= 14.293\%$$

This is the investors' opportunity cost of funds for the consulting assets alone, and it tells us that the owners of the firm demand a higher rate of return on the consulting assets than they do on cash on hand (which should be obvious). You can check for yourself that the expected value of the consulting assets themselves is $45,180,000, so the DCF value of the consulting assets calculated using the 14.293% opportunity cost of funds is

$$\text{DCF value} = \frac{E\{V\}}{1 + r}$$

$$= \frac{\$45,180,000}{1.14293} = \$39,530,042$$

which is, of course, the value of the tracking portfolio. We can reconcile the opportunity cost of funds of the entire firm (13.256%) with the opportunity cost of funds for the consulting assets alone (14.293%) by observing that cash on hand, which has an opportunity cost of 5.06% (the risk-free rate) accounts for $5,000,000/$44,530,042 = 11.23% of the company's value while consulting assets account for the other $39,530,042/$44,530,042 = 88.77%, so the weighted-average of the opportunity cost of funds for the different pieces of the business is 13.256%:

$$0.1123 \times 5.06\% + 0.8877 \times 14.293\% = 13.256\%$$

The beta of the consulting assets is 1.2649. I show this in Appendix 3.2, but you can deduce this from the fact that (1) the tracking portfolio for the consulting assets contains only the market index and the risk-free bond, and (2) the tracking portfolio's weight in the market index is 126.49%. If we use this to value the consulting assets alone in a DCF valuation, we get $39.520 million.

$$\text{DCF value using CAPM} = \frac{E\{V_{\text{consulting assets}}\}}{1 + r + \beta[E\{r_{\text{Mkt}}\} - r]}$$

$$= \frac{\$45,180,000}{1 + 0.0506 + 1.2649[0.1236 - 0.0506]}$$

$$= \frac{\$45,180,000}{1.1429} = \$39,530,042$$

which is exactly what we got before. We can reconcile the beta of the entire firm (1.1228) with the beta of the consulting assets (1.2649) by remembering that the beta of the risk-free bond is zero, so the weighted average of the betas of the different pieces of the business is

$$0.1123 \times 0 + 0.8877 \times 1.2649 = 1.1228$$

The beta of a portfolio is just the weighted average of the betas of the assets in the portfolio.

What's the point of all of this? It is perfectly legitimate to divide a business into parts, do a valuation of each part by forming a financial market tracking portfolio that matches the conditional mean cash flow on each part, and then sum them all up. This leads to a very important result: If we add (or subtract) anything from the firm, we can just value the new piece (or the incremental change) by forming a financial market tracking portfolio that matches the *incremental* conditional mean cash flows that arise due to the new piece. The value of the firm after the change will be equal to the value of the firm before the change plus the value of this new piece. I'll illustrate this very important point with an example of a growth opportunity.

Before I get to that, however, I'd like to make three other equally important observations. First, in our divide-and-conquer valuation of the consulting assets, *we valued an illiquid asset.* The main asset that generates the firm's future cash flow is its human capital, and this human capital does not trade in a market. But this did not affect our approach at all: We valued the illiquid and nontraded consulting assets (the human capital) via an arbitrage argument in which we formed a financial market tracking portfolio that matched the conditional mean *cash flows* thrown off by the human capital. Although the *consultants* are illiquid, the cash flows they generate are liquid. (And I apologize for the tautology: Cash, by definition, is liquid.)

Moreover, when we valued the consulting assets (the human capital) in the financial market, we did *not* form a tracking portfolio that contained consultants, or even the stock of other consulting companies. Our tracking portfolio does not need to contain the asset being valued. All we need are a set of financial market securities that together span the cash flows thrown off by the consultants. (*Span* is just a fancy word meaning that we have appropriate building blocks to reconstruct the conditional mean cash flows with conditional mean-zero error).

It all boils down to this: cash is cash, and cash is king. The value of $1 of expected cash flow to an investor in a particular future macroeconomic state is the same whether the asset that throws off the cash is privately owned or publicly traded, and is the same whether the asset that generates the cash flow is illiquid or liquid. And the value of $1 of expected cash flow *in a particular future macroeconomic state* from consulting firm assets (human capital and reputation) is absolutely equal to the value of $1 of expected cash flow *in that same future macroeconomic state* from manufacturing assets, or from transportation industry assets, or from traded derivatives, or whatever. The source of the cash flows is irrelevant; all we care about are the cash flow *quantity, timing, and distribution across macroeconomic states of nature.*

And I remind you of one thing: This tracking portfolio approach is *exactly* what you've been doing every time you've done a DCF valuation.

> Major Result 9: Even though most corporate assets are illiquid and untraded, the claims on the cash flows thrown off by those assets (i.e., the firm's stocks and bonds) are liquid and tradable. We value the stocks and bonds of the firm by arbitrage using a tracking portfolio of financial market securities that correctly matches the conditional mean cash flows to those securities. The tracking portfolios don't need to hold the specific assets that generate the corporate cash flows.

3.2   Evaluating a Static Growth Opportunity at the Consulting Firm

We now get to corporate finance. Suppose that the managers of the firm face an opportunity to grow. How should they evaluate the opportunity? What decision rule should they use?

Anybody who's ever been through a finance course at any level would correctly say that the firm should calculate the NPV of the opportunity and invest if the NPV is greater than or equal to zero. But very few people understand what this actually means and why it works. Furthermore, most people are unaware of the conditions that must be met for shareholders to want managers to act in this way. My goal is to explain this as carefully as possible. The point of

| Figure 3.10 | End-of-Year Incremental Value of Immediate Growth Investment |

		Firm-Specific Risk Outcomes	
		Client Defects ($pr = 0.1$)	Client Stays ($pr = 0.9$)
Macroeconomic Outcomes	Boom ($pr = 0.36$)	$7,125,000	$9,375,000
	Stagnant ($pr = 0.48$)	$4,650,000	$6,150,000
	Recession ($pr = 0.16$)	$2,925,000	$3,862,500

this is *not* to show you how to calculate an NPV. Rather, my objective is to give you the *intuition and foundations.*

Suppose that our consulting firm is considering expanding by hiring more consultants, opening new offices, and so forth. The expansion would cost $5 million and would increase the end-of-year consulting asset values by 15% in every possible state of nature and given each firm-specific event. Should the firm do it?

Let's first do the evaluation of the growth investment using a static DCF approach to valuation. When we're through, I'll go back and show you what is *really* going on.

The end-of-year incremental values of the growth opportunity given each macroeconomic state of nature and each firm-specific event are shown in Figure 3.10. (I got these by simply multiplying the consulting asset values from Figure 3.2 by 15%). The expected incremental effect of the growth opportunity in one year will be

$$E\{\text{incremental value}\} = 0.36 \times [0.1 \times \$7,125,000 + 0.9 \times \$9,375,000]$$
$$+ 0.48 \times [0.1 \times \$4,650,000 + 0.9 \times \$6,150,000]$$
$$+ 0.16 \times [0.1 \times \$2,925,000 + 0.9 \times \$3,862,500]$$
$$= 0.36 \times \$9,150,000 + 0.48 \times \$6,000,000$$
$$+ 0.16 \times \$3,768,750$$
$$= \$6,777,000$$

To calculate the static NPV of the growth opportunity, we must discount this expected future incremental value by an appropriate risk-adjusted discount rate (to get the present value of the inflows), then subtract the $5,000,000 cash investment requirement. The appropriate risk-adjusted discount rate is a little tricky here. Even though the growth investment is scale enhancing, the beta of the project is *not* equal to the firm's overall beta of 1.1228 and so the investment's hurdle rate is *not* equal to the firm's overall hurdle rate of 13.256%. Why? Because the investment only enhances the scale of the consulting assets and *not* the firm's cash on hand. If you recall from the divide-and-conquer valuation of the entire firm, the consulting assets are riskier than the overall firm, simply because a part of the firm is cash (which is risk-free). In this case, the beta of the growth investment is equal to the beta of the consulting assets (1.2649), so the required rate of return on the new investment will be 14.293%. You don't have to trust me on this—I'll prove it to you a little later. In the meantime, let's finish the DCF valuation and the static NPV evaluation.

$$Static\,NPV = \frac{E\{\text{incremental value}\}}{1 + r_{incremental}} - I_{incremental}$$

$$= \frac{\$6,777,000}{1.14293} - \$5,000,000$$

$$= \$5,929,506 - \$5,000,000$$

$$= \$929,506$$

The result: The growth investment displays a static NPV of $929,506. If the static DCF has given us a good approximation of the project's true financial market value, then the opportunity creates value for the owners and should be taken.

I'm sure that this is the way you were taught to do project evaluation. It's the way I was taught and the approach I've seen in virtually every text I've looked at. What you probably don't know, however, is that when you follow this very standard procedure, you are actually doing something a bit more complex. The textbook DCF approach to the static NPV calculation actually is a shortcut to this more complex procedure:

1. Estimate the conditional mean incremental cash flows thrown off by the new investment in each macroeconomic state of nature.
2. Ask yourself how much money you would get if you were to sell these incremental cash flows as a new security in the financial market.
   a. Form a tracking portfolio of traded financial market securities that correctly matches the conditional mean cash flows on the new corporate investment.
   b. Assume that the new investment, if taken, would have no effect on the prices of the existing financial market securities (other than the firm's own equity).
   c. Add up the value of the tracking portfolio.
   d. Assume that the financial market allows no arbitrage opportunities, and conclude that the new investment must have the same value as the tracking portfolio. This is the financial market value of the project, which in a DCF valuation you would call the present value of the inflows.
3. Subtract the actual cost of the real investment from the financial market value of the incremental cash flows to arrive at the true NPV.
4. Invest if the true NPV is greater than or equal to zero; reject otherwise.

The critical insight, which many people miss, is that the financial market value of a project is equal to the value of a financial market tracking portfolio that mimics the project's incremental conditional mean free cash flows. If an investment has positive NPV, what it means is that the manager can buy the project's incremental conditional mean cash flows in the real asset market, resell them in the financial asset market, and make a profit.

If this sounds to you like an arbitrage, then you are catching on! NPV is really an arbitrage profit taken by managers on behalf of investors. Although we assume that the *financial market* admits no arbitrage opportunities, we freely allow there to be arbitrage opportunities in the market for real assets. Managers should follow the old saw: Buy low and sell high. If a manager can buy some cash flows in the real asset market for less than they are worth in the financial market, then the manager should do so. Value-creating managers are managers who find these opportunities.

Figure 3.11	End-of-Year Value of Consulting Firm with Growth Investment		
	Firm-Specific Risk Outcomes		
	Client Defects (pr = 0.1)	Client Stays (pr = 0.9)	Conditional Mean
Boom (pr = 0.36)	$47.5 mm × 1.15 = $54,625,000	$62.5 mm × 1.15 = $71,875,000	0.1 × $54.625 mm + 0.9 × $71.875 mm = $70,150,000
Stagnant (pr = 0.48)	$31 mm × 1.15 = $35,650,000	$41 mm × 1.15 = $47,150,000	0.1 × $35.650 mm + 0.9 × $47.150 mm = $46,000,000
Recession (pr = 0.16)	$19.5 mm × 1.15 = $22,425,000	$25.75 mm × 1.15 = $29,612,500	0.1 × $22.425 mm + 0.9 × $29.6125 mm = $28,893,750

(Macroeconomic Outcomes)

When I'm explaining this to students and managers, there are always one or two who object based on the grounds that firms don't sell new securities every time they make a growth investment. I'll show you that this doesn't matter. The intuition is simple: The incremental cash flows on the new investment change the total cash flows of the firm, and the incremental increase in the financial market value of the firm is exactly the same as the financial market value of those incremental cash flows (or else there would be an arbitrage opportunity).

To show you this, I need to do the tracking-portfolio valuation of the growth investment two different ways. First, I'm going to revalue the entire company assuming the firm makes the growth investment to show how the investment changes the owners' wealth. Then, I'll value the incremental effect of the growth investment separately to show that you get the same thing.

The first step in revaluing the entire company *with* the growth investment is to calculate the conditional mean cash flows on the entire company assuming the immediate growth investment has just been made. Remember that the growth investment increases the consulting business value by 15% no matter what happens, so we can calculate the conditional mean cash flows on the "grown" business, as I've done in Figure 3.11.

You can check for yourself that outcomes of the firm-specific risk (the client's action) cause conditional mean-zero shocks to these conditional mean cash flows, and hence are idiosyncratic and worthless. Since the firm must use all of its cash on hand to execute the growth investment, these are the conditional mean cash flows on all of the firm's assets, as shown in Figure 3.12.

To revalue the entire firm *with* the new opportunity, we need to find the tracking portfolio holdings H_{Mkt} shares of the market index, H_O index options, and H_{RF} risk-free bonds so that

End-of-year value of tracking portfolio:

$$= \begin{cases} H_{Mkt} \times \$144.00 + H_O \times \$44 + H_{RF} \times \$1000.00 = \$70,150,000 & \text{(boom)} \\ H_{Mkt} \times \$102.00 + H_O \times \$2 + H_{RF} \times \$1000.00 = \$46,000,000 & \text{(stagnant)} \\ H_{Mkt} \times \$72.25 + H_O \times \$0 + H_{RF} \times \$1000.00 = \$28,893,750 & \text{(recession)} \end{cases}$$

I show in Appendix 3.2 that the appropriate tracking portfolio contains H_{Mkt} = 575,000 shares of the market index, H_O = 0 index options, and H_{RF} = −12,650 risk-free bonds. The value of this particular tracking portfolio will be

Current value of tracking portfolio = $H_{Mkt} \times \$100 + H_O \times \$11.42 + H_{RF} \times \$951.81$

= 575,000 × $100 + 0 × $11.42 − 12,650 × $951.81

= $45,459,548

Figure 3.12	End-of-Year Value of All Consulting Firm Assets Given Growth Investment

			End-of-Year Conditional Mean Values	
		Cash	Consulting Business Cash Flows	Total
Macroeconomic Outcomes	Boom (*pr* = 0.36)	$0	$70,150,000	$70,150,000
	Stagnant (*pr* = 0.48)	$0	$46,000,000	$46,000,000
	Recession (*pr* = 0.16)	$0	$28,893,750	$28,893,750

So given our price taking, complete market, and no arbitrage assumptions, we must conclude that the total market value of the consulting firm's equity *with investment in the new project* is $45,459,548. This means, then, that the act of making the growth investment increases the total value of the firm by

$$\text{Change in firm value due to investment} = \text{Market value of firm with investment}$$
$$- \text{Market value of firm without investment}$$
$$= \$45,459,548 - \$44,530,042$$
$$= \$929,506$$

which is *exactly* equal to the static NPV we calculated before. The true NPV of an investment is the amount of wealth the investment *creates* for the owners of the firm. Here, the firm uses $5 million in cash (which is the investors' cash), but the value of the firm actually goes up. The firm value goes up because management is spending $5 million on something that is actually worth more than $5 million in the financial markets.

The tracking portfolio for the entire firm *with* the investment is somewhat different than the original tracking portfolio for the firm *without* the investment, and it is instructive to examine how the tracking portfolio changes. I've done this for you using our building block metaphor in Figure 3.13.

You can see in Figure 3.13 that when the firm gets the new growth investment, the tracking portfolio that mimics the firm's conditional mean cash flows increases its holdings in the market index by 75,000 shares and decreases its holdings in the risk-free bond by about 6,903.13 units. The value of this *change* in the tracking portfolio is

$$\text{Market value of incremental change in tracking portfolio} = 75{,}000 \times \$100 - 6{,}903.13 \times \$951.81$$
$$= \$929{,}506$$

which (except for rounding error) is the NPV of the investment! This result tells us that we should be able to apply our divide and conquer approach to evaluation of the new investment as well—simply split out the incremental change due to the new investment from the firm as is. That is what I'll demonstrate next.

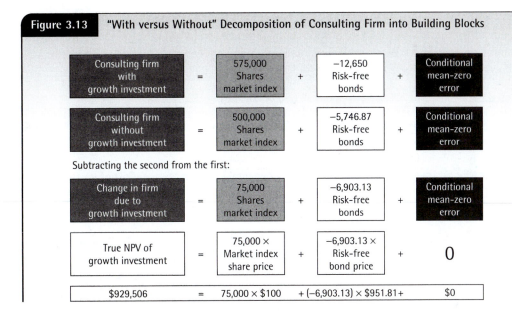

Figure 3.13   "With versus Without" Decomposition of Consulting Firm into Building Blocks

To evaluate the *incremental* effect of the growth investment, we must calculate its incremental effect on the firm's consulting assets. Here, we simply subtract the conditional mean future consulting assets *without* the growth opportunity from the conditional mean consulting assets *with* the growth opportunity. I've done this for you in Figure 3.14. (It is easy to check that the incremental change in each state is just 0.15 times the consulting asset values without the growth investment, as it should be since the growth investment increases the consulting business assets by 15%). To value the incremental change in the consulting assets, we need to form a financial market tracking portfolio containing H_{Mkt} shares of the market index, H_O index options, and H_{RF} risk-free bonds so that

End-of-year value of tracking portfolio:

$$= \begin{cases} H_{Mkt} \times \$144.00 + H_O \times \$44 + H_{RF} \times \$1000.00 = \$9,150,000 \quad \text{(Boom)} \\ H_{Mkt} \times \$102.00 + H_O \times \$2 + H_{RF} \times \$1000.00 = \$6,000,000 \quad \text{(Stagnant)} \\ H_{Mkt} \times \$72.25 + H_O \times \$0 + H_{RF} \times \$1000.00 = \$3,768,750 \quad \text{(Recession)} \end{cases}$$

Figure 3.14

Incremental Conditional-Mean Cash Flows Arising from Growth Investment			End-of-Year Conditional Mean Values of Consulting Assets		
			With Growth Investment	Without Growth Investment	Incremental Change
	Macroeconomic Outcomes	Boom (pr = 0.36)	$70,150,000	$61,000,000	$9,150,000
		Stagnant (pr = 0.48)	$46,000,000	$40,000,000	$6,000,000
		Recession (pr = 0.16)	$28,893,750	$25,125,000	$3,768,750

The correct tracking portfolio holdings which make all three equations work are H_{Mkt} = 75,000 shares of the index fund, H_O = 0 options on the index fund, and H_{RF} = −1,650 risk-free bonds—you can check for yourself that these holdings work (and I show this in Appendix 3.2). The value of this particular tracking portfolio is

$$75,000 \times \$100 - 1,650 \times \$951.81 = \$5,929,506$$

and we can conclude that the financial market value of the growth investment is $5,929,506. The true NPV of the investment opportunity is thus $929,506.

True NPV = True financial market value of incremental free cash fows − Cost of Investment
= $5,929,506 − $5,000,000
= $929,506

I've worked through all of this to demonstrate what I argued in Chapter 1: The present value of the inflows, or financial market price of the incremental cash flow, is the price that our investors would pay in order to buy those incremental cash flows on their own in the financial markets. The capital investment requirement is the price that the firm, which is investing on the behalf of the investor, must pay for those same cash flows in the real asset market. When the true NPV is positive, then managers can purchase a set of *incremental* cash flows (on the behalf of investors) in the real asset market for a lower price than the investors can purchase the "same" cash flows in the financial market. When true NPV is negative, it means that investors can buy the cash flows more cheaply in the financial markets than managers can in the real asset market.

True NPV = Financial market price of incremental cash inflows
− Real asset market price of those same incremental cash flows
= $5,929,506 − $5,000,000
= $929,506

There's no magic here. If the new investment is worth more than it costs, the difference flows into the pockets of the shareholders through an increase in the stock price. And the opposite is true as well: If the new investment is worth less than it costs, the difference flows out of the pockets of the shareholders through a decrease in the stock price.

> Major Result 10: The value of a new, illiquid corporate investment is simply the financial market price of the incremental conditional mean cash flows thrown off by the new investment.

> Major Result 11: The true NPV of a corporate investment is the difference between the financial market price of the investment's incremental conditional mean cash flows and the price the manager must pay for the cash flows in the real asset market. It is an arbitrage profit, and it accrues to the shareholders.

I'll reiterate one further point from Chapter 1. Many people incorrectly think that an NPV calculation requires a DCF calculation. As stated in Major Result 11 above, the true NPV of a new opportunity is the wealth that the new opportunity creates. To calculate the true NPV of a project, you have to do some sort of arbitrage valuation. But *any* arbitrage valuation approach, if correctly applied, will give you the true NPV; the key is to pick the right approach for each situation.

In the financial markets, there are many situations where you can estimate a discount rate and do a static DCF calculation in lieu of forming the tracking portfolio explicitly, and there are many others where you can't (like when dealing with options). The same holds true in corporate finance: There are many situations where we can estimate a hurdle rate and do a static DCF calculation as a shortcut to explicitly forming the tracking portfolio, and there are many other situations where we must form the tracking portfolio.

The static DCF approach to NPV worked in this example (the immediate growth opportunity at the consulting firm) because the growth opportunity is *static*—it is a one-shot investment with no future decisions or flexibilities. In other words, the static DCF approach worked because the growth investment is now-or-never/no-flexibility in nature. The static NPV tells us whether it is better to hardwire the investment's commitments immediately or discard the idea forever. Static NPV will *not* allow us to correctly evaluate whether we should wait or whether we should invest to learn and respond. When we introduce flexibilities (in the form of future growth *options*), we'll have to use the tracking portfolio approach in order to calculate the *true* NPV.

To conclude this section on the static growth opportunity, I've got a little housekeeping to do. I promised that I would prove that we used the right discount rate in our static DCF valuation of the new investment opportunity, and I will do that. I also need to reconcile the with-versus-without investment change in the overall firm's tracking portfolio with the incremental tracking portfolio. If these issues don't interest you, just skip ahead to the next section.

I'll first verify that 14.293% is the correct discount rate on the growth opportunity. The tracking portfolio for the incremental cash flows arising due to the growth investment, which represents the investor's similar alternative in the financial markets, has 75,000 × $100/$5.929 million = 126.49% of its value invested in the market index fund (with expected return = 12.36%) and −26.49% invested in the risk-free bond (with expected return = 5.06%), and 1.2649 × 12.36% −0.2649 × 5.06% = 14.293%. Since 14.293% is the expected return on the tracking portfolio that mimics the cash flows on the new project, it is also the correct discount rate to apply to the cash flows directly.

Moreover, the beta of the immediate growth is identical to the beta of the consulting asset in place because their tracking portfolios have identical weights. Knowing that the investment was perfectly scale-enhancing gave us a way to estimate the rate of return on the tracking portfolio without actually forming it so that we could take the DCF shortcut. I show that the beta of the growth investment is 1.2649 in the Appendix 3.2, but you should be able to infer this from the weights in the tracking portfolio.

3.3 A Delayed Growth Opportunity

Now let's change things up a bit. Instead of having now-or-never/no-flexibility growth opportunity, let's suppose that the consulting firm can spend a little money today, postpone the growth decision until the end of the year, then learn and respond by basing the end-of-the-year decision on what is learned in the interim. Perhaps the firm is busting at the seams, and delay in the expansion will require that the firm rent very expensive temporary office space at a cost of $600,000 for the year. But if the firm spends the $600,000 and delays the expansion decision, then management can learn the outcome of the macroeconomic risk and the client's decision *before* spending the $5 million on expansion. Delay is quite costly, but it allows the firm to avoid a bad outcome (investing in growth only to have revenues shrink). Intuitively, delay creates flexibility and flexibility is valuable. But which is more valuable: investing in immediate growth or investing in flexibility to postpone the decision? We know that immediate expansion is value creating. But is it the most valuable alternative? To answer these questions, we have to calculate the true NPV of the investment in flexibility.

Suppose that the firm does indeed decide to spend the $600,000 and put off the expansion decision. If the boom economy occurs, the consulting firm will find it valuable to grow regardless of whether or not the client defects, because the value of the growth opportunity will be greater than the cost ($5 million) either way (as you can see in Figure 3.10). And if the recession occurs, the consulting firm will not grow because the value of the growth opportunity will be less than its cost no matter what the client does. But if the economy turns out to be stagnant, then the firm's optimal policy depends on the resolution of the firm-specific risk: If the client defects in the stagnant economy, the growth opportunity will be worth only $4.65 million (or $0.35 million less than its cost), but if the client does not defect in the stagnant economy, then the growth opportunity will be worth $6.15 million (or $1.15 million more than its cost). Figure 3.15 shows the net payoffs from doing the right thing given every possible outcome: the value of the growth opportunity minus the cost of growth (if positive), and zero otherwise. Make sure you understand how I got each value.

How do we calculate the true NPV of the investment in flexibility? The same way we did when we valued the immediate growth investment—by arbitrage. The first step is to calculate the conditional mean incremental values of the future best decision based on what happens over the year, as shown in Figure 3.16.

Just to make sure you understand, Figure 3.17 shows that the shocks to the conditional mean caused by the outcome of the client's decision have zero mean in each macroeconomic state, and thus are idiosyncratic and have no value.

Figure 3.15	End-of-Year Net Incremental Value of Waiting	
	Firm-Specific Risk Outcomes	
	Client Defects (pr = 0.1)	Client Stays (pr = 0.9)
Boom (pr = 0.36)	*max* [$7,125,000 − $5,000,000; $0] = $2,125,000 (invest)	*max* [$9,375,000 − $5,000,000; $0] = $4,375,000 (invest)
Stagnant (pr = 0.48)	*max* [$4,650,000 − $5,000,000; $0] = $0 (don't invest)	*max* [$6,150,000 − $5,000,000; $0] = $1,150,000 (invest)
Recession (pr = 0.16)	*max* [$2,925,000 − $5,000,000; $0] = $0 (don't invest)	*max* [$3,862,500 − $5,000,000; $0] = $0 (don't invest)

Macroeconomic Outcomes

Figure 3.16	End-of-Year Net Incremental Value of Waiting

		Firm-Specific Risk Outcomes		
		Client Defects ($pr = 0.1$)	Client Stays ($pr = 0.9$)	Conditional Mean
Macroeconomic Outcomes	Boom ($pr = 0.36$)	$2,125,000	$4,375,000	$0.1 \times \$2.125$ mm $+ 0.9 \times \$4.375$ mm $= \$4,150,000$
	Stagnant ($pr = 0.48$)	$0	$1,150,000	$0.1 \times \$0 + 0.9 \times \$1.150$ mm $= \$1,035,000$
	Recession ($pr = 0.16$)	$0	$0	$0.1 \times \$0 + 0.9 \times \$0$ $= \$0$

Figure 3.17 gives the incremental conditional mean values of the learn-and-respond strategy given each state of nature. The true NPV of the investment in flexibility is simply the financial market price of these cash flows less the cost of waiting ($600,000). The financial market price of these conditional mean cash flows is the value of the financial market portfolio that replicates them.

Before we go on, let's notice something here. In Figure 3.18, I've plotted the conditional-mean payoff on the learn-and-respond investment against the value of the market index. I've also plotted the conditional mean value of the now-or-never/no-flexibility immediate opportunity against the value of the market index for comparison purposes.

What you should see in Figure 3.18 is that the conditional-mean payoff on the learn-and-respond investment (that is, the costly waiting alternative) is not linear in the market index. In fact, it has the familiar "hockey stick" profile of a call option. This is exactly what it is—a call

Figure 3.17	End-of-Year Net Incremental Value of Waiting (in millions)

		Conditional mean component	Firm-Specific Risk Outcomes		Conditional Mean of Idiosyncratic Component
			Idiosyncratic Shock to Conditional Mean (Actual − Conditional Mean)		
			Client Defects ($pr = 0.1$)	Client Stays ($pr = 0.9$)	
Macroeconomic Outcomes	Boom ($pr = 0.36$)	$4.150	$2.125 − \$4.150$ $= −\$2.025$	$4.375 − \$4.150$ $= \$0.225$	$0.1 \times −\$2.025 + 0.9 \times \$0.225$ $= \$0$
	Stagnant ($pr = 0.48$)	$1.035	$0 − \$1.035$ $= −\$1.035$	$1.150 − \$1.035$ $= \$0.115$	$0.1 \times −\$1.035 + 0.9 \times \$0.115$ $= \$0$
	Recession ($pr = 0.16$)	$0	$0 − \$0$ $= \$0$	$0 − \$0$ $= \$0$	$0.1 \times \$0 + 0.9 \times \$0$ $= \$0$

This part has no value!

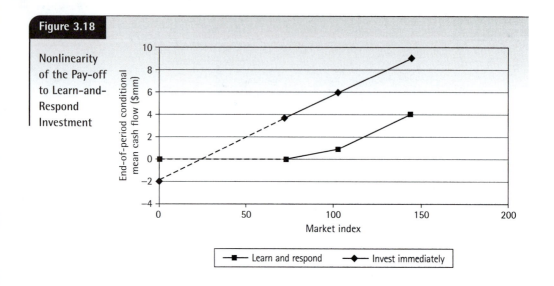

Figure 3.18

Nonlinearity of the Pay-off to Learn-and-Respond Investment

option. If the firm spends $600,000 and delays the decision, it effectively purchases this call option. An option's underlying asset is always what you get if you exercise the option; in this case, exercising the option entails actually making the growth investment in the future, and what the firm gets back is an incrementally larger firm. So in this case the underlying asset is the now-or-never/no-flexibility growth opportunity itself.

Figure 3.18 reminds us that the payoff on the real option (the costly growth option) is nonlinear, and so we can't value it with a static tracking portfolio that contains only two securities. Thus, a CAPM-based DCF won't work, as I'll prove to you shortly. We have two alternatives. The first, which we'll use right away, is to build a tracking portfolio that includes the market index option. The second, which I'll show in Appendix 3.1 for interested readers, is to allow frequent trading in the market index.

Let's do the valuation. Suppose we offer the financial markets a security with conditional mean cash flows of $4.150 million in the boom state, $1.035 million in the stagnant economy and $0 in the recession—either through a new security or by addition to the cash flows of the consulting firm's existing equity. What would the financial market pay for these new cash flows? To answer the question, we need to form a financial market tracking portfolio containing H_{Mkt} shares of the market index, H_O index options, and H_{RF} risk-free bonds so that

End-of-year value of tracking portfolio

$$
= \begin{cases}
H_{Mkt} \times \$144.00 + H_O \times \$44 + H_{RF} \times \$1000.00 = \$4,150,000 & \text{(boom)} \\
H_{Mkt} \times \$102.00 + H_O \times \$2 + H_{RF} \times \$1000.00 = \$1,035,000 & \text{(stagnant)} \\
H_{Mkt} \times \$72.25 + H_O \times \$0 + H_{RF} \times \$1000.00 = \$0 & \text{(recession)}
\end{cases}
$$

As I show in Appendix 3.2, the correct tracking portfolio has holdings of $H_{Mkt} = 31,951.95$, $H_O = 42,214.71$, and $H_{RF} = -2,308.53$ (again, I encourage you to verify that these holdings work). The value of this tracking portfolio is

$$31,951.95 \times \$100 + 42,214.71 \times \$11.42 + (-2,308.59) \times \$951.81 = \$1,480,071$$

Therefore, we can conclude that the financial market value of the investment in flexibility (that is, the true financial market value of the real option) is about $1.48 million. Since the cost of making the delay decision is $600,000, the *true* NPV of the investment in flexibility is

$$True\ NPV = \$1,480,071 - \$600,000$$
$$= \$880,071$$

Aha! The value that would be created by the investment in flexibility is *less than* the value that would be created by immediate investment! If the firm chooses to delay the decision, its value should increase by only $880,071 today; but if it chooses immediate investment, its value should increase by $929,506 today.

Now let's see how we could have gone wrong with a very naïve approach to valuing the real option. Many managers would look at the delay decision and apply the same discount rate as the immediate growth opportunity (which was 14.293%) in a DCF valuation. If you try to discount the expected cash flows on the delay strategy at 14.293%, you would get a very different answer:

$$\frac{0.36 \times \$4,150,000 + 0.48 \times \$1,035,000 + 0.16 \times \$0}{1.14293} - \$600,000$$
$$= \$1,741,839 - \$600,000$$
$$= \$1,141,839$$

which is way, way off of the true NPV of $880,071. Figure 3.19 collects our results for comparison purposes.

Notice what Figure 3.19 tells us. If the managers of the consulting firm rely on DCF to value the investment in flexibility (i.e., the delay strategy), they end up making the wrong decision. While it is true that flexibility has some value, and in this instance the investment in flexibility does create value, it does not create as much value as immediate investment. There's no way we could have uncovered this without doing the proper valuation of the investment in flexibility.

Why did static DCF lead to such a huge error? The problem was our discount rate. We had no justification whatsoever for discounting the expected cash flows from the investment in flexibility at 14.293%. As it turns out (and as you'll learn in later chapters), the delayed growth opportunity is much riskier than the immediate growth opportunity.

The important point here is that even though the delay strategy is an option, we approached its valuation in the same way that we approached valuation of the immediate growth decision—by arbitrage in the capital markets. There is not one whit of difference between valuation of an immediate investment in an illiquid corporate asset and valuation of an option on an illiquid corporate asset. One is harder than the other, but both rest on the same foundation: cash flow arbitrage.

Figure 3.19		
Static and True NPVs	*Static* NPV of investment in flexibility	$1,141,839
of Investment	*True* (or Static) NPV of immediate investment	$929,506
Alternatives	*True* NPV of investment in flexibility	$880,071

Now, we *could have* done this with a different tracking portfolio. We *could have* formed a tracking portfolio that contains the now-or-never/no-flexibility opportunity and the risk-free bond, and we would have arrived at *exactly* the same answer. I show this in Appendix 3.1 (which is advanced). If you have not seen the binomial model before, then I suggest you wait and only look at Appendix 3.1 after working through Chapter 4. Even though the now-or-never/no-flexibility immediate growth investment is not a traded asset, we can use it as a traded asset in our tracking portfolio simply because it is really a repackaging of the economy's building blocks (the market index, the index option, and the risk-free bond) which *are* traded. If there exists a traded financial market portfolio that tracks the conditional mean cash flow on a corporate investment, and trading is frequent, then there exists a traded financial market portfolio that tracks the conditional mean cash flows of *options* on that corporate investment even though the investment itself is not liquid. This is the *market adjusted disclaimer* (MAD) assumption of Copeland and Antikarov (2001), and it is completely legitimate.

As Stew Myers said in his quote at the beginning of this chapter, many people are completely misinformed about this. To understand why what I've done is perfectly legitimate and consistent with first principles, you need to understand the first principles themselves.

3.4   When Do Investors Want Managers to Maximize NPV?

The preceding examples illustrate the prescription we in finance give to all managers: Make decisions that maximize NPV. When managers ask us why, we say simply that maximization of NPV is what our owner-investors want us to do, because maximization of NPV maximizes their wealth.

We (your author included) tend to say this with an air of dogma, as if the NPV rule were handed down to us by some higher authority. This plays well in the classroom, but it hurts us in the long run. Investors unanimously desire the NPV rule only when certain conditions hold (i.e., only under certain assumptions). By skirting the assumptions required for the NPV rule to be proper, we've shortchanged our students of a very, very important insight: If our investors want us to use the NPV rule, then they want us to use option pricing techniques when our opportunities have option-like features.

The general paradigm behind the NPV rule is simple: Managers should use currently observed financial market prices to make decisions concerning new investment opportunities. This procedure allows managers to compare new corporate projects against the investors equivalent financial market opportunity. Remember that true NPV is an arbitrage profit: It is the difference between the financial market price of a new asset's cash flows and the manager's cost of buying those cash flows in the real asset market. The question we must ask is this: Under what conditions do investors want managers to value new illiquid corporate opportunities by comparison to a tracking portfolio containing liquid financial assets?

This question was a topic of great interest to academics in the 1970s, and the research on the question is known as the *unanimity* literature. It turns out that investors unanimously want managers to value illiquid corporate assets by arbitrage with a liquid financial market tracking portfolio as long as two conditions hold: (1) Managers act as *price takers* in the financial markets, and (2) the financial markets admit *no arbitrage opportunities*.[5]

---

[5] For thoroughly rigorous treatment, see Baron (1979a, 1979b), Fama (1972, 1978), Grossman and Stiglitz (1977), Jensen and Long (1972), and Leland (1974).

Figure 3.20	Assumptions Required for Investors to Unanimously Desire That Managers Follow the NPV Rule (i.e., value new investments via arbitrage with financial markets)

Assumption 1: Price Taking: The act of making the new investment does not change the prices of the financial market building blocks. This requires that
- The financial market is sufficiently complete; in other words, it is complete to the introduction of the cash flows from the new investment.
- The new investment does not change aggregate consumption in a material way.

Assumption 2: No Arbitrage: The financial market allows no arbitrage opportunities.

This result is very intuitive. The no-arbitrage assumption is necessary so that we can apply our linear pricing technique.[6] The price taking assumption assures that the manager's actions don't change the financial market equilibrium, so the manager can use the current prices of the financial market building blocks to predict the financial market value of the new project.

Finance theory tells us that there are two circumstances where managers could not act as price takers. The first would occur if the new corporate investment would create a stream of future incremental cash flows that could not be tracked with conditional mean-zero error by any portfolio strategy using existing financial market securities. In this case, the financial market is said to be *incomplete to the introduction of the new project's cash flows;* introduction of the new project's cash flows would change the financial market's equilibrium prices because it would change each investor's equilibrium demand for each financial market security.

A lot of people get hung up on the complete markets issue. There's a common misunderstanding that a complete financial market requires one distinct security for every possible future state of nature at every possible future point in time. Such a setup would be overkill, because of something I discussed in Chapter 2: You can always complete a market with options on the market portfolio, and you can create options on the market portfolio with a small number of securities as long as dynamic trading is possible. It is my personal opinion that, for all intents and purposes, investors can use derivatives to insure against every future state of nature that they care about.

The second circumstance that would violate price taking is not so benign, however. An important result we learn from general equilibrium theory is that the prices of all financial market securities will change if aggregate consumption changes, because an individual's risk aversion depends on the level of his or her endowments. We usually finesse this issue by assuming that a new corporate project is small relative to the economy so it really doesn't affect any investor's portfolio decision in a material way. But it is easy to imagine situations where corporate investments can change equilibrium prices by changing aggregate endowments, and such situations require completely different evaluation approaches.

To understand the importance of this section, you must realize that you've been implicitly making the assumptions listed in Figure 3.20 every time you've ever done an NPV calculation (whether or not you used DCF). That is, if you assume that maximization of NPV is the appropriate goal of managers, then you are implicitly assuming that the financial market is complete to the introduction of the new project, the new project is small, and the financial market admits no arbitrage opportunities.

---

[6] Moreover, financial market arbitrage opportunities would always dominate corporate investment opportunities.

Every time you ever use a DCF model to value a new corporate investment opportunity, you implicitly assume that there exists a liquid portfolio in the financial market that tracks the conditional mean cash flows thrown off by that opportunity. The liquidity of the corporate asset itself is irrelevant—if the assumptions of the NPV rule hold, then the claims on the asset's *cash flows* are liquid even though the asset itself may not be. In valuation, there is absolutely no reason to draw a distinction between a real asset and the cash flows it generates. This is why we can value the consulting firm's stock: Even though the consulting firms assets (its brand and its talent) are not liquid, the claims on the cash flows thrown off by those assets are liquid.

When you see it this way, then, you recognize that the only difference between corporate assets that can be valued without explicitly forming the capital market tracking portfolio (i.e., static investment opportunities, like the organic growth of the consulting firm), and corporate assets that require explicit formation of the capital market tracking portfolio (i.e., dynamic investment opportunities, like the option on delayed growth) is the composition of the tracking portfolios. If you recall, DCF is just a shortcut to arbitrage valuation, and it works when you can use an asset pricing model like the CAPM to tell you the return on the tracking portfolio. But this only works when the conditional mean cash flows on the asset in question are linear functions of the sources of common risk (e.g., in a CAPM world, they must be linear functions of the market portfolio).

We saw this in our examples in this chapter. The tracking portfolio for the firm's assets in place contained only the market index fund and the risk-free bond, so we know that the conditional mean cash flows of the assets in place are linear in the market index (our single source of common risk). Since the immediate investment opportunity is simply scale enhancing growth (it expands the consulting assets by 15% regardless of what happens in the future), we can value its cash flows by DCF using the hurdle rate on the firm's consulting assets in place because we know that the immediate growth opportunity's cash flows are also linear in the market index and are the same linear function as the consulting assets in place. The DCF approach to getting the value of the immediate growth opportunity is just a shortcut.

When we looked at the option on delayed growth, however, things changed. We saw quite clearly that the conditional mean cash flows from the option on delayed growth are not linear in the market index, and as a result, our tracking portfolio included the index option. There was no way to know the rate of return on this tracking portfolio without actually forming it, so we formed it. In principle, valuation of the growth option and valuation of the static growth opportunity are identical; the difference between the two valuations is merely a matter of technique.

The critical issue in valuing the option on delayed growth was not the illiquidity of the consulting firm's assets, but rather the existence of a capital market tracking portfolio that matched the growth option's conditional mean cash flow. The index option was necessary for the tracking portfolio, and without it we could not assume price taking. But the existence of the index option merely requires that there be frequent trading in the market index itself. Trading completes the financial markets, and complete financial markets allow for tracking of any cash flows (regardless of the liquidity of the source of those cash flows). (To see that there's another, much easier way to form tracking portfolios for corporate growth options, check out Appendix 3.1).

What this all means, then, is that even though we can't trade a corporate investment opportunity, we *can* trade claims on the *cash flows* thrown off by the corporate investment opportunity. If the financial market is complete to the introduction of claims on the *cash flows* from the new asset (which is required for unanimity and thus for the NPV rule to be desired by shareholders), then from a valuation perspective the new asset is nothing more than a combination of traded capital market securities plus conditional mean-zero noise. And if trading is allowed, then *we can price options on these same tracking portfolios of traded capital market securities.* Therefore, if illiquid corporate assets are equivalent to traded tracking portfolios of financial market securities, then options on those illiquid corporate assets are equivalent to options on the corresponding traded portfolios of financial securities.

To put it more bluntly, if you are willing to accept that maximization of NPV is the appropriate goal of management, then you have already made enough assumptions to justify application of option pricing techniques to the valuation of corporate projects whenever necessary. Moreover, if you reject real options based on some perceived impossibility in creating a suitable tracking portfolio, then you are implicitly rejecting the NPV rule as well.

> Major Result 12: If a firm's owners want management to maximize true NPV, then they want management to value any and all new investment opportunities by arbitrage with a tracking portfolio of financial market securities.

> Major Result 13: If the financial market is complete, then you can form liquid financial market tracking portfolios that correctly value options on illiquid corporate assets. (Remember that frequent trading completes the market.)

3.5 Two Misconceptions and Why They Are Wrong

When I wrote this chapter, one of my major goals was to dispel some very common misconceptions about corporate finance in general and option valuation in particular. I conclude this chapter by revisiting the two biggest misconceptions and summarizing why they are indeed wrong.

Misconception 1: Real options analysis is going to replace NPV in the corporate finance toolkit

- *Why this is wrong.* The true NPV of a corporate investment opportunity is the value it creates for the firm's owners. It is the difference between the financial market price of the opportunity's cash flows and the manager's cost of undertaking the opportunity. In some situations, an option pricing model is needed to ascertain the financial market price of the cash flows (real options analysis); in other situations, the discounted cash flow shortcut works perfectly well. In either case, the NPV rule holds.
- *The short response.* In some situations, real options analysis is the only way to estimate the true financial market value (and hence the true NPV) of a corporate opportunity. DCF and the static NPV rule will only sometimes get things right.
- *The difference between DCF and option pricing.* In DCF, the tracking portfolio is static; in real options valuation, the tracking portfolio changes over time. Both are applications of linear pricing (i.e., valuation by an arbitrage argument).
- *What to keep in mind.* When we use DCF to estimate NPV, we get the *static* NPV. The static NPV is fine in situations where the corporate opportunity is itself static (e.g., now-or-never/no-flexibility). When the corporate opportunity involves significant flexibility to make future decisions; however, the static NPV is a poor approximation to true value creation, and the true NPV calculation requires a dynamic approach (like option pricing).

Misconception 2: You can't price options on corporate assets, because corporate assets are illiquid and hence cannot be held in a hedge portfolio

- *Why this is wrong, part 1* (Liquidity of the asset versus liquidity of claims on its cash flows): In finance, the value of any asset (financial or real, primary or derivative) depends only on the cash flows it throws off and not on the physical nature of the asset itself. Arbitrage valuations of illiquid real assets require only that the *conditional mean cash flows* thrown off by the asset are reproducible via a financial market tracking portfolio. If they are not, then maximization of NPV is not necessarily the appropriate goal of management.

- *Why this is wrong, part 2* (Perfect hedging versus tracking). When you can hold the "underlying asset" in the tracking portfolio, you can get perfect hedging—that is, you track the resolutions of both the systematic risk and the idiosyncratic risk. But a conditional mean-zero error (the idiosyncratic risk) is valueless, and so perfect hedging is not necessary for any arbitrage valuation. If the financial market allows trading in the underlying sources of macroeconomic risk, then you can form a tracking portfolio that tracks the resolution of the systematic risk only and hence achieves tracking with mean-zero conditional error—which gives the same value as perfect hedging (since the conditional mean-zero risks are worthless).

- *What to keep in mind.* In pricing options on assets (financial or real), it is not necessary that the tracking portfolio actually contain the financial or real asset itself. There are potentially many ways to form a tracking portfolio; the only requirement is that it have mean-zero error given every macroeconomic state of nature. The most convenient way to form tracking portfolios for valuation of corporate growth options is to use the underlying illiquid project itself. This is the *Market Adjusted Disclaimer* (or MAD) assumption of Copeland and Antikarov (2001), and in Appendix 3.1 (which is advanced), I show that this is not an assumption at all—it is a theoretically appropriate procedure.

Unfortunately, these two misconceptions have been repeated so many times that they have become fact, much like the fictional knights and sorcerers in Don Quixote's books of chivalry became real in his mind. What's even more unfortunate is that more than a few influential (and otherwise sophisticated) people continue to spread the misinformation.

As I've said several times, my academic colleagues and I should accept much of the blame for the misunderstandings. Many of the erroneous notions concerning option pricing in general and real options in particular stem from the poor way we teach asset pricing and corporate finance at the undergraduate and MBA levels. It is essential that we update our pedagogies to better suit the more modern theory of asset pricing.

But I also have to pin a large part of the blame on the professional consulting community for overselling the real options paradigm. The term *option value* has superceded the term *strategic value* as the justification for otherwise unjustifiable corporate projects, and I've met many intelligent and honest managers who want no part of this (and as a result latch onto any possible grounds for rejection).

I'd like to close the chapter with another quote from Stewart Myers's keynote address at the University of Maryland Symposium on Real Options. This really sums it all up.

So you do have to make some assumptions about capital asset pricing and about the completeness of markets in order to value real options appropriately. Now some people who grow up in doing capital markets work get upset when they come inside the firm and things are not traded. . . . But that isn't the fault of the real options model. That's corporate finance, buddy!

—Stewart Myers[7]

3.6   Summary

There are two conditions that must be met for investors to unanimously desire that managers follow the NPV rule when evaluating new corporate investment opportunities. They are

Assumption 1: Price Taking—The act of making the new investment does not change the financial market prices. This requires that
  a. The financial market is sufficiently complete; in other words, it is complete to the introduction of the cash flows from the new investment.
  b. The new investment does not change aggregate consumption in a material way.

Assumption 2: No Arbitrage—The financial market allows no arbitrage opportunities.

Even though most corporate assets are illiquid and untraded, the claims on the cash flows thrown off by those assets (i.e., the firm's stocks and bonds) are liquid and tradable. We value the stocks and bonds of the firm by arbitrage using a tracking portfolio of financial market securities which correctly matches the conditional mean cash flows thrown off by the firm's illiquid assets. The tracking portfolios don't need to hold the specific assets that generate the cash flows, nor must they exhibit perfect tracking.

The value of a new, illiquid corporate investment is simply the financial market price of the conditional mean cash flows thrown off by the new investment. The true NPV of a corporate investment is the difference between the financial market price of the investment's incremental conditional mean cash flows and the price the manager must pay for the cash flows in the real asset market. The true NPV measures the wealth created or destroyed by a corporate investment, and it accrues directly to the shareholders.

If a firm's owners want management to maximize true NPV, then they want management to value any and all new investment opportunities by arbitrage with a tracking portfolio of financial market securities. That such a tracking portfolio exists is an assumption of the NPV rule.

3.7   Bibliography and Suggested Reading

Arnold, Thomas and Richard L. Shockley, Jr., 2003. "Real Options, Corporate Finance, and the Foundations of Value Maximization," *Journal of Applied Corporate Finance* 15(2), Winter 2003, 82–88.

Baron, David P., 1979a. "Investment Policy, Optimality, and the Mean-Variance Model," *Journal of Finance* 34(1), 207–232.

Baron, David P., 1979b. "On the Relationship Between Complete and Incomplete Financial Market Models," *International Economic Review* 20(1), 105–117.

---

[7] Keynote address at the University of Maryland Symposium on Real Options, April 18, 2002, as quoted in Arnold and Shockley (2003).

Copeland, Tom, and Vladimir Antikarov, 2001. *Real Options: A Practitioner's Guide,* Texere LLC. New York.

Fama, Eugene F., 1972. "Perfect Competition and Optimal Production Decisions Under Uncertainty," *Bell Journal of Economics* 3, 509–530.

Fama, Eugene F., 1978. "The Effects of a Firm's Investment and Financing Decisions on the Welfare of Its Security Holders," *American Economic Review* 68, 272–284.

Grossman, Sanford J., and Joseph E. Stiglitz, 1977. "On Value Maximization and Alternative Objectives of the Firm," *Journal of Finance* 32, 389–402.

Jensen, Michael C., and John B. Long, 1972. "Corporate Investments Under Uncertainty and Pareto Optimality in the Capital Markets," *Bell Journal of Economics* 3, 151–174.

Leland, Hayne E., 1974. "Production Theory and the Stock Market," *Bell Journal of Economics* 5, 125–144.

Myers, Stewart C., 1977. "Determinants of Corporate Borrowing," *Journal of Financial Economics* 5, 147–175.

Appendix 3.1   The Underlying Asset and the MAD Assumption (Advanced)

A point I've been trying to communicate all along through Chapters 2 and 3 is that the appropriate tracking portfolio for an investment opportunity (whether it be a static opportunity or an option) consists of rather basic financial market securities: the market index, the risk-free bond, and conditional mean-zero error (which has zero value).

However, as we go forward into practical applications, it will be necessary for us to form tracking portfolios that are not so basic (but still equally valid). If you worked through the advanced sections of Chapter 2, you saw that we *could* value the stock option by forming a tracking portfolio that consists of the underlying stock and the risk-free bond. The reason this works is because the stock is itself nothing more than a portfolio of the market index, the risk-free bond, and conditional mean-zero noise, and so when you break down the option tracking portfolio's stock holdings into the more fundamental building blocks of the economy, you get the same tracking portfolio that you would form if you just used the market index and the risk-free bond anyway.

In other words, the underlying asset for any option is really nothing more than a (sometimes complex) combination of the market index and the risk-free bond, and we can either work with these fundamental building blocks, *or* we can work with portfolios of them (like the stock) to create tracking portfolios.

To show how we'll use this in a real options setting, I need to assume that our financial market participants can trade after six months, and that our economy evolves in the same way that we assumed in Chapter 2 (Figure 3.21).

Now, we *know* that the tracking portfolio that mimics the conditional mean incremental cash flows on the immediate growth investment contains $H_{Mkt} = 75,000$ shares of the index fund, $H_O = 0$ options on the index fund, and $H_{RF} = -1,650$ risk-free bonds. So its value must evolve as shown in Figure 3.22.

In other words, the value of the immediate growth opportunity itself must evolve like in Figure 3.22, or else there will be an arbitrage opportunity. Be careful here—this is the *value* of the immediate growth opportunity and *not* its NPV.

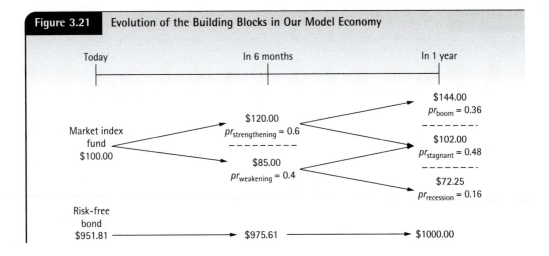

Figure 3.21   Evolution of the Building Blocks in Our Model Economy

The big question is this: Can we form a *dynamically changing* tracking portfolio that tracks the conditional mean payoffs on the growth option but contains only the risk-free bond and the now-or-never/no-flexibility immediate opportunity pictured in Figure 3.22? Yes.

Once again, you'll have to trust me on exactly how to do this until you've worked through the review of derivatives pricing (unless you already know how to work with the binomial model). I present the solutions in Figure 3.23.

So we can track (or replicate) the growth option with a portfolio that is initially long 0.77119 units of the now-or-never/no-flexibility immediate opportunity and short about 3,249 risk-free bonds. Why does this work? Because, as I hope you recall, we can further decompose the immediate opportunity down into 75,000 shares of the market index and −1,650 risk free bonds:

$$H_{\text{Immed. Growth Opp.}} = 0.77119$$

$$= 0.77119 \times \begin{cases} H_{\text{Mkt}} = 75,000 \\ H_{\text{RF}} = -1,650 \end{cases}$$

$$= \begin{cases} H_{\text{Mkt}} = 57,839.72 \\ H_{\text{RF}} = -1,272.47 \end{cases}$$

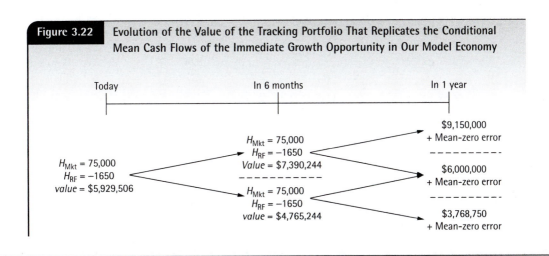

Figure 3.22   Evolution of the Value of the Tracking Portfolio That Replicates the Conditional Mean Cash Flows of the Immediate Growth Opportunity in Our Model Economy

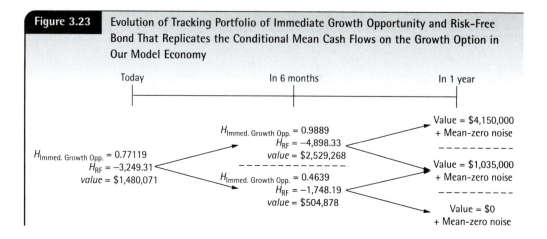

Figure 3.23 Evolution of Tracking Portfolio of Immediate Growth Opportunity and Risk-Free Bond That Replicates the Conditional Mean Cash Flows on the Growth Option in Our Model Economy

So, when we track the growth *option* with the underlying immediate growth opportunity and the risk-free bond, we are essentially replicating it with the economy's building blocks because our tracking portfolio indirectly holds

$$H_{Mkt} = 57,839.72$$
$$H_{RF} = -3,249.31 - 1,272.47 = -4,521.78$$

On the other hand, when we valued the growth option with the market index, the index option and the risk-free bond we found that the tracking portfolio contained $H_{Mkt} = 31,951.95$, $H_O = 42,214.71$, and $H_{RF} = -2,308.53$. And, as I mentioned in Chapter 2, when we can trade after six months then we can initially track the index option with the market index and the risk-free bond in the proportions:

$$1 \text{ index option tracked by} \begin{cases} H_{Mkt} = 0.613 \\ H_{RF} = -0.0524 \end{cases}$$

so the holdings of the index option in *this* tracking portfolio break down into

$$H_O = 42,214.71$$
$$= 42,214.71 \times \begin{cases} H_{Mkt} = 0.613 \\ H_{RF} = -0.0524 \end{cases}$$
$$= \begin{cases} H_{Mkt} = 25,887.77 \\ H_{RF} = -2,213.22 \end{cases}$$

and we can decompose this alternative tracking portfolio into

$$H_{Mkt} = 31,951.95 + 25,887.77 = 57,839.72$$
$$H_{RF} = -2,308.56 - 2,213.22 = -4,521.78$$

which is *exactly* the decomposed tracking portfolio that contained the immediate growth opportunity (as the underlying) and the risk-free bond.

The learning point of this illustration is extremely important: If we are valuing an option on a real asset, we can use that real asset itself (treated statically) as our underlying asset in a standard option tracking portfolio. In other words, when we are valuing an option on a corporate project, it is entirely appropriate to use the static DCF value of that project as the value of the underlying asset in the option analysis. The reason this works is because managers are price takers only in a sufficiently complete market, and in a sufficiently complete market the static project is nothing more than a portfolio containing the market index and the risk-free bond. This is the logic behind the *MAD assumption* given in Copeland and Antikarov (2001), and we will use this throughout all of our applications.

Please remember that price taking (and hence the complete markets assumption) is also necessary for DCF approach to the NPV rule, and that the financial market will be sufficiently complete as long as there is frequent trading in the sources of macroeconomic uncertainty (which in a CAPM world is just the market index) and the risk-free bond.

Appendix 3.2   Solving for the Tracking Portfolio Holdings

Valuing The Entire Firm

We need to find a tracking portfolio with holdings H_{Mkt} of the market index, H_O of the index option, and H_{RF} of the risk-free bond so that

End-of-year value of tracking portfolio

$$
= \begin{cases}
H_{Mkt} \times \$144.00 + H_O \times \$44 + H_{RF} \times \$1000.00 = \$66,253,125 & \text{(boom)} \\
H_{Mkt} \times \$102.00 + H_O \times \$2 + H_{RF} \times \$1000.00 = \$45,253,125 & \text{(stagnant)} \\
H_{Mkt} \times \$72.25 + H_O \times \$0 + H_{RF} \times \$1000.00 = \$30,378,125 & \text{(recession)}
\end{cases}
$$

We could solve these simultaneous equations by elimination like we did in Chapter 2, but there's another way: matrix algebra.

In matrix form, the system of equations looks like this:

$$
\begin{bmatrix}
\$144 & \$44 & \$1000 \\
\$102 & \$2 & \$1000 \\
\$72.25 & \$0 & \$1000
\end{bmatrix}
\times
\begin{bmatrix}
H_{Mkt} \\
H_O \\
H_{RF}
\end{bmatrix}
=
\begin{bmatrix}
\$66,253,125 \\
\$45,253,125 \\
\$30,378,125
\end{bmatrix}
$$

so the solution vector of tracking portfolio holdings H_{Mkt} of the market index, H_O of the index option, and H_{RF} of the risk-free bond is

$$
\begin{bmatrix}
H_{Mkt} \\
H_O \\
H_{RF}
\end{bmatrix}
=
\begin{bmatrix}
\$144 & \$44 & \$1000 \\
\$102 & \$2 & \$1000 \\
\$72.25 & \$0 & \$1000
\end{bmatrix}^{-1}
\times
\begin{bmatrix}
\$66,253,125 \\
\$45,253,125 \\
\$30,378,125
\end{bmatrix}
$$

$$
=
\begin{bmatrix}
-0.00172 & 0.03775 & -0.03604 \\
0.02553 & -0.06156 & 0.03604 \\
0.00012 & -0.00273 & 0.00360
\end{bmatrix}
\times
\begin{bmatrix}
66,253,125 \\
45,253,125 \\
30,378,125
\end{bmatrix}
=
\begin{bmatrix}
500,000 \\
0 \\
-5,746.87
\end{bmatrix}
$$

To give the general approach, suppose that there are M total states of nature at the end of the period and N assets. Index the states of nature by $m = 1, \ldots, M$ and the securities $n = 1, \ldots, N$, and let $V_{m,n}$ be the end-of-period value of security n in state m. Then the matrix $\mathbf{A}$ is the $M \times N$ matrix of end-of-period values of the market's fundamental securities.

$$\mathbf{A} = \begin{bmatrix} V_{1,1} & V_{1,2} & \cdots & V_{1,N} \\ V_{2,1} & V_{2,2} & \cdots & V_{2,N} \\ \vdots & \vdots & \ddots & \vdots \\ V_{M,1} & V_{M,2} & \cdots & V_{M,N} \end{bmatrix}$$

In our example, $M = 3$, $N = 3$ and

$$\mathbf{A} = \begin{bmatrix} V_{Boom,Mkt} & V_{Boom,O} & V_{Boom,RF} \\ V_{Stagnant,Mkt} & V_{Stagnant,O} & V_{Stagnant,RF} \\ V_{Recession,Mkt} & V_{Recession,O} & V_{Recession,RF} \end{bmatrix} = \begin{bmatrix} \$144 & \$44 & \$1000 \\ \$102 & \$2 & \$1000 \\ \$72.25 & \$0 & \$1000 \end{bmatrix}$$

Each column is one security, and each row is a state of nature.

Now let $\mathbf{H}$ be the $N \times 1$ vector of tracking portfolio holdings (i.e., the solution vector). In our example, there are $N = 3$ financial market securities to use in the tracking portfolio (the market index, the index option, and the risk-free bond), and so

$$\mathbf{H} = \begin{bmatrix} H_{Mkt} \\ H_{O} \\ H_{RF} \end{bmatrix}$$

Finally, let $\mathbf{W}$ be the $M \times 1$ vector of end-of-period conditional mean values of the asset under scrutiny (the firm as a whole, the immediate growth investment, the delayed growth investment, etc.). An entry in row m is the expected cash flow on the asset under scrutiny in state m. In our model, there are $M = 3$ states of nature, so

$$\mathbf{W} = \begin{bmatrix} V_{Boom,New\,Asset} \\ V_{Stagnant,New\,Asset} \\ V_{Recession,New\,Asset} \end{bmatrix} = \begin{bmatrix} \$66,253,125 \\ \$45,253,125 \\ \$30,378,125 \end{bmatrix}$$

In matrix form, we write the system of equations $\mathbf{AH} = \mathbf{W}$, so the solution vector $\mathbf{H}$ (if it exists) can be found through the operation $\mathbf{H} = \mathbf{A}^{-1}\mathbf{W}$. In all of our examples,

$$\mathbf{A}^{-1} = \begin{bmatrix} -0.00172 & 0.03775 & -0.03604 \\ 0.02553 & -0.06156 & 0.03604 \\ 0.00012 & -0.00273 & 0.00360 \end{bmatrix}$$

and so the only thing we need to do is to plug the appropriate $\mathbf{W}$ vector into the matrix equation

$$\begin{bmatrix} H_{Mkt} \\ H_{O} \\ H_{RF} \end{bmatrix} = \begin{bmatrix} \$144 & \$44 & \$1000 \\ \$102 & \$2 & \$1000 \\ \$72.25 & \$0 & \$1000 \end{bmatrix}^{-1} \times \mathbf{W}$$

$$= \begin{bmatrix} -0.00172 & 0.03775 & -0.03604 \\ 0.02553 & -0.06156 & 0.03604 \\ 0.00012 & -0.00273 & 0.00360 \end{bmatrix} \times \begin{bmatrix} V_{Boom,New\,Asset} \\ V_{Stagnant,New\,Asset} \\ V_{Recession,New\,Asset} \end{bmatrix} \quad (3.A1.1)$$

and do the matrix multiplication to get the solution vector of tracking portfolio weights.

To calculate the beta of the immediate investment opportunity, we must recall that in our economy the static CAPM pricing relationship is

$$P_0 = \frac{1}{1+r}\left[E\{CF_i\} - \frac{\text{cov}\,(CF_i, r_{Mkt})[E\{r_{Mkt}\} - r]}{\text{var}(r_{Mkt})}\right]$$

$$= \frac{1}{1.0506}\left\{E\{CF\} - \frac{\text{cov}\,(CF_i, r_{Mkt})[0.073]}{0.0669}\right\} \tag{3.A1.2}$$

and, from this price, we can calculate the static CAPM beta as

$$\beta_i = \frac{1}{P_0}\frac{\text{cov}\,(CF_i, r_{Mkt})}{\text{var}\,(r_{Mkt})} = \frac{1}{P_0}\frac{\text{cov}\,(CF_i, r_{Mkt})}{0.0669} \tag{3.A1.3}$$

To solve for the CAPM price of the firm as a whole, we recognize that the expected end-of-period value of the firm is $E\{CF_{Firm}\} = 50,433,125$. Since the expected return on the market is 12.36%, then the covariance between the end-of-period value of the firm and the return on the market portfolio is

$$\text{cov}\,(CF_{Firm}, r_{Market}) = E\{(CF_{Firm} \times r_{Market})\} - E\{CF_{Firm}\} \times E\{r_{Market}\}$$
$$= E\{(CF_{Firm} \times r_{Market})\} - 50,433,125 \times 0.1236$$
$$= E\{(CF_{Firm} \times r_{Market})\} - 6,233,534$$

To evaluate the first term,

$$E\{(CF_{Firm} \times r_{Mkt})\} = 0.36 \times 66,253,125 \times 0.44 + 0.48 \times 45,253,125 \times 0.02$$
$$+ \ 0.16 \times 30,378,125 \times -.2775$$
$$= 10,494,495 + 434,430 - 1,348,789$$
$$= 9,580,136$$

So, the covariance is

$$\text{cov}\,(CF_{Firm}, r_{Market}) = E\{(CF_{Firm} \times r_{Market})\} - E\{CF_{Firm}\} \times E\{r_{Market}\}$$
$$= 9,580,136 - 6,233,534$$
$$= 3,346,602$$

From (3.A1.2), the value of the entire firm is

$$P_0 = \frac{1}{1.0506}\left\{50,433,125 - \frac{3,346,602[0.073]}{0.0669}\right\}$$

$$= \frac{1}{1.0506}\{50,433,125 - 3,651,748\}$$

$$= \$44,530,042$$

From (3.A1.3), the static CAPM beta is

$$\beta_i = \frac{1}{44,530,042}\frac{3,346,602}{0.0669}$$

$$= 1.1228$$

Valuing the Firm's Consulting Assets

For the firm's consulting assets alone,

$$
W = \begin{bmatrix} V_{Boom,Consulting\,Assets} \\ V_{Stagnant,Consulting\,Assets} \\ V_{Recession,Consulting\,Assets} \end{bmatrix} = \begin{bmatrix} \$61,000,000 \\ \$40,000,000 \\ \$25,125,000 \end{bmatrix} \tag{3.A1.4}
$$

so plugging (3.A1.4) into (3.A1.1), our solution is

$$
\begin{bmatrix} H_{Mkt} \\ H_0 \\ H_{RF} \end{bmatrix} = \begin{bmatrix} \$144 & \$44 & \$1000 \\ \$102 & \$2 & \$1000 \\ \$72.25 & \$0 & \$1000 \end{bmatrix}^{-1} \times W
$$

$$
= \begin{bmatrix} -0.00172 & 0.03775 & -0.03604 \\ 0.02553 & -0.06156 & 0.03604 \\ 0.00012 & -0.00273 & 0.00360 \end{bmatrix} \times \begin{bmatrix} \$61,000,000 \\ \$40,000,000 \\ \$25,125,000 \end{bmatrix} = \begin{bmatrix} 500,000 \\ 0 \\ -11,000 \end{bmatrix}
$$

To solve for the CAPM price of the consulting assets, we recognize that the expected end-of-period value of the consulting assets is $E\{CF_{Consulting\,Assets}\} = \$45,180,000$. Since the expected return on the market is 12.36%, then the covariance between the end-of-period value of the consulting assets and the return on the market portfolio is

$$
\begin{aligned}
cov(CF_{Consulting\,Assets}, r_{Market}) &= E\{(CF_{Consulting\,Assets} \times r_{Market})\} - E\{CF_{Consulting\,Assets}\} \times E\{r_{Market}\} \\
&= E\{(CF_{Consulting\,Assets} \times r_{Market})\} - 45,180,000 \times 0.1236 \\
&= E\{(CF_{Consulting\,Assets} \times r_{Market})\} - 5,584,248
\end{aligned}
$$

To evaluate the first term,

$$
\begin{aligned}
E\{(CF_{Firm} \times r_{Mkt})\} &= 0.36 \times 61,000,000 \times 0.44 + 0.48 \times 40,000,000 \times 0.02 \\
&\quad + 0.16 \times 25,125,000 \times -.2775 \\
&= 9,662,400 + 384,000 - 1,115,550 \\
&= 8,930,850
\end{aligned}
$$

So the covariance is

$$
\begin{aligned}
cov(CF_{Firm}, r_{Market}) &= E\{(CF_{Firm} \times r_{Market})\} - E\{CF_{Firm}\} \times E\{r_{Market}\} \\
&= 8,930,850 - 5,584,248 \\
&= 3,346,602
\end{aligned}
$$

From Equation (3.A1.2), the value of the firm's consulting assets is

$$
\begin{aligned}
P_0 &= \frac{1}{1.0506}\left\{ 45,180,000 - \frac{3,346,602[0.073]}{0.0669} \right\} \\
&= \frac{1}{1.0506}\{ 45,180,000 - 3,651,748 \} \\
&= \$39,530,042
\end{aligned}
$$

From (3.A1.3), the static CAPM beta is

$$\beta_i = \frac{1}{39,530,042} \frac{3,346,602}{0.0669}$$

$$= 1.2649$$

Valuing the Entire Firm with the Immediate Growth Investment

For the entire firm with the immediate growth investment,

$$W = \begin{bmatrix} V_{Boom,Firm+} \\ V_{Stagnant,Firm+} \\ V_{Recession,Firm+} \end{bmatrix} = \begin{bmatrix} \$70,150,000 \\ \$46,000,000 \\ \$28,893,750 \end{bmatrix} \qquad (3.A1.5)$$

so plugging (3.A1.5) into (3.A1.1), our solution is

$$\begin{bmatrix} H_{Mkt} \\ H_0 \\ H_{RF} \end{bmatrix} = \begin{bmatrix} \$144 & \$44 & \$1000 \\ \$102 & \$2 & \$1000 \\ \$72.25 & \$0 & \$1000 \end{bmatrix}^{-1} \times W$$

$$= \begin{bmatrix} -0.00172 & 0.03775 & -0.03604 \\ 0.02553 & -0.06156 & 0.03604 \\ 0.00012 & -0.00273 & 0.00360 \end{bmatrix} \times \begin{bmatrix} \$70,150,000 \\ \$46,000,000 \\ \$28,893,750 \end{bmatrix} = \begin{bmatrix} 575,000 \\ 0 \\ -12,650 \end{bmatrix}$$

Valuing the Incremental Change Due to the Immediate Growth Investment

For the incremental change due to the immediate growth investment,

$$W = \begin{bmatrix} V_{Boom,Incremental} \\ V_{Stagnant,Incremental} \\ V_{Recession,Incremental} \end{bmatrix} = \begin{bmatrix} \$9,150,000 \\ \$6,000,000 \\ \$3,768,750 \end{bmatrix} \qquad (3.A1.6)$$

so plugging (3.A1.6) into (3.A1.1), our solution is

$$\begin{bmatrix} H_{Mkt} \\ H_0 \\ H_{RF} \end{bmatrix} = \begin{bmatrix} \$144 & \$44 & \$1000 \\ \$102 & \$2 & \$1000 \\ \$72.25 & \$0 & \$1000 \end{bmatrix}^{-1} \times W$$

$$= \begin{bmatrix} -0.00172 & 0.03775 & -0.03604 \\ 0.02553 & -0.06156 & 0.03604 \\ 0.00012 & -0.00273 & 0.00360 \end{bmatrix} \times \begin{bmatrix} \$9,150,000 \\ \$6,000,000 \\ \$3,768,750 \end{bmatrix} = \begin{bmatrix} 75,000 \\ 0 \\ -1,650 \end{bmatrix}$$

To solve for the CAPM price of the incremental effects of the immediate investment, we recognize that the expected end-of-period value of the incremental effect is $E\{CF_{Incremental}\} = \$6,777,000$. Since the expected return on the market is 12.36%, then the covariance between the end-of-period value of the incremental effect of the investment and the return on the market portfolio is

$$cov\left(CF_{Incremental}, r_{Market}\right) = E\{(CF \times r_{Market})\} - E\{CF_{Incremental}\} \times E\{r_{Market}\}$$

$$= E\{(CF_{Incremental} \times r_{Market})\} - 6,777,000 \times 0.1236$$

$$= E\{(CF_{Incremental} \times r_{Market})\} - 837,637$$

To evaluate the first term,

$$E\{(CF_{Incremental} \times r_{Mkt})\} = 0.36 \times 9{,}150{,}000 \times 0.44 + 0.48 \times 6{,}000{,}000 \times 0.02$$
$$+ \ 0.16 \times 3{,}768{,}750 \times -.2775$$
$$= \ 1{,}449{,}360 + 57{,}600 - 167{,}332$$
$$= \ 1{,}339{,}628$$

So the covariance is

$$cov(CF_{Incremental}, r_{Market}) = E\{(CF_{Incremental} \times r_{Market})\} - E\{CF_{Incremental}\} \times E\{r_{Market}\}$$
$$= \ 1{,}339{,}628 - 837{,}637$$
$$= \ 501{,}991$$

From Equation (3.A1.2), the value of the incremental effect of the growth investment is

$$P_0 = \frac{1}{1.0506}\left\{6{,}777{,}000 - \frac{501{,}991 \times [0.073]}{0.0669}\right\}$$

$$= \frac{1}{1.0506}\{6{,}777{,}000 - 547{,}762\}$$

$$= \$5{,}929{,}506$$

From (3.A1.3), the static CAPM beta is

$$\beta_i = \frac{1}{5{,}929{,}506}\frac{501{,}991}{0.0669}$$

$$= 1.2649$$

Valuing the Delayed Growth Option

For the delayed growth option,

$$W = \begin{bmatrix} V_{Boom,Delay} \\ V_{Stagnant,Delay} \\ V_{Recession,Delay} \end{bmatrix} = \begin{bmatrix} \$4{,}150{,}000 \\ \$1{,}035{,}000 \\ \$0 \end{bmatrix} \tag{3.A1.7}$$

and so plugging (3.A1.7) into (3.A1.1), our solution is

$$\begin{bmatrix} H_{Mkt} \\ H_0 \\ H_{RF} \end{bmatrix} = \begin{bmatrix} \$144 & \$44 & \$1000 \\ \$102 & \$2 & \$1000 \\ \$72.25 & \$0 & \$1000 \end{bmatrix}^{-1} \times W$$

$$= \begin{bmatrix} -0.00172 & 0.03775 & -0.03604 \\ 0.02553 & -0.06156 & 0.03604 \\ 0.00012 & -0.00273 & 0.00360 \end{bmatrix} \times \begin{bmatrix} \$4{,}150{,}000 \\ \$1{,}035{,}000 \\ \$0 \end{bmatrix} = \begin{bmatrix} 31{,}951.95 \\ 42{,}214.71 \\ -2{,}308.53 \end{bmatrix}$$

PROBLEMS

All of the problems here pertain to an economy with three future states (Boom, Stagnant, and Recession) with three securities (a market index, a risk-free security, and a put option on the market index with a strike at $200.00). The put option expires one year from today, which is also the same time horizon for the table below.

Future Economy	Probability	Market Index Level	Risk-Free Security	Index Option Value
Boom	20%	$600.00	$100.00	$0.00
Stagnant	60%	$350.00	$100.00	$0.00
Recession	20%	$150.00	$100.00	$50.00
Current Security Price		$315.79	$94.24	$6.58

1.

a. Find the state contingent returns for the market index, the risk-free security, and the index option (e.g., the return for the Boom state for the market index is $600.00 ÷ $315.79 − 1 = 90\%$) and the expected return for each security.

b. Find the value of a firm that has the following state contingent values: $8,000,000.00 (Boom), $6,000,000.00 (Stagnant), and $4,400,000.00 (Recession).

c. Find the CAPM beta for the firm.

2. Firm XYZ state contingent cash flows:

Future Economy	Event 1 (Probability = 60%)	Event 2 (Probability = 40%)
Boom	$5,000,000.00	$6,250,000.00
Stagnant	$4,000,000.00	$4,500,000.00
Recession	$3,000,000.00	$3,400,000.00

a. What are the mean-zero cash flows for Events 1 and 2 for each state of the economy?

b. Find the holdings for the tracking portfolio for the firm.

c. Value the firm, and find the firm's CAPM beta.

3. Firm ABC state contingent cash flows:

Future Economy	Event 1 (Probability = 20%)	Event 2 (Probability = 50%)	Event 3 (Probability = 30%)
Boom	$6,000,000.00	$3,000,000.00	$2,000,000.00
Stagnant	$2,750,000.00	$3,500,000.00	$2,500,000.00
Recession	$1,500,000.00	$2,500,000.00	$3,000,000.00

    a. What are the mean-zero cash flows for Events 1, 2, and 3 for each state of the economy?

    b. Find the holdings for the tracking portfolio for the firm.

    c. Find the value of the firm.

4. Firm BBB state contingent cash flows from assets in place:

Future Economy	Cash Position	Event 1 (Probability = 50%)	Event 2 (Probability = 50%)
Boom	$500,000.00	$2,000,000.00	$2,500,000.00
Stagnant	$500,000.00	$1,500,000.00	$2,250,000.00
Recession	$500,000.00	$1,000,000.00	$1,500,000.00

    a. Find the conditional mean asset value for each state of the economy.

    Firm CCC state contingent cash flows from assets in place:

Future Economy	Cash Position	Event 1 (Probability = 75%)	Event 2 (Probability = 25%)
Boom	$100,000.00	$3,000,000.00	$1,600,000.00
Stagnant	$100,000.00	$2,000,000.00	$3,150,000.00
Recession	$100,000.00	$1,800,000.00	$1,200,000.00

    b. Find the conditional mean asset value for each state of the economy.

    c. Why are these two firms equivalent in value?

5. Project A's incremental state contingent cash flows:

Future Economy	Event 1 (Probability = 50%)	Event 2 (Probability = 50%)
Boom	$70,000.00	$120,000.00
Stagnant	$50,000.00	$60,000.00
Recession	$30,000.00	$80,000.00

a. Find the value of the project's incremental cash flows using a tracking portfolio.
b. Find the discount rate for the project.
c. What is the NPV of the project given a cost of $60,000.00?

6. Project B's incremental state contingent cash flows:

	Event 1	Event 2
Future Economy	(Probability = 40%)	(Probability = 60%)
Boom	$60,000.00	$85,000.00
Stagnant	$65,000.00	$72,000.00
Recession	$35,000.00	$40,000.00

a. Find the value of the project's incremental cash flow.
b. Find the discount rate for the project.
c. What is the NPV of the project, given a cost of $55,000.00?

7. Firm TUV state contingent cash flows from assets in place:

		Event 1	Event 2
Future Economy	Cash Position	(Probability = 60%)	(Probability = 40%)
Boom	$1,000,000.00	$5,000,000.00	$6,000,000.00
Stagnant	$1,000,000.00	$2,000,000.00	$3,000,000.00
Recession	$1,000,000.00	$1,000,000.00	$1,500,000.00

a. Find the conditional mean asset value for each state of the economy, and value the firm using a tracking portfolio.

Firm TUV state contingent cash flows from assets in place after accepting a project with a cost of $500,000.00 (paid in cash):

		Event 1	Event 2
Future Economy	Cash Position	(Probability = 60%)	(Probability = 40%)
Boom	$500,000.00	$6,000,000.00	$6,500,000.00
Stagnant	$500,000.00	$2,200,000.00	$3,100,000.00
Recession	$500,000.00	$1,600,000.00	$800,000.00

b. Find the conditional mean asset value for each state of the economy, and revalue the firm with the project using a tracking portfolio.
c. What is the NPV of the project?

8. A firm currently has a value of $4,000,000.00. On accepting a project, the state contingent cash flows become $5,500,000.00 in the Boom economy, $4,800,000.00 in the Stagnant economy, and $4,240,000.00 in the Recession economy.

   a. Find the firm's value and CAPM beta with the project using a tracking portfolio.

   b. What is the NPV of the project?

9. Project A's incremental state contingent cash flows:

Future Economy	Event 1 (Probability = 50%)	Event 2 (Probability = 50%)
Boom	$80,000.00	$50,000.00
Stagnant	$40,000.00	−$10,000.00
Recession	$10,000.00	−$20,000.00

   a. What is the project's conditional cash flow for each state of the economy?

   b. What are the mean-zero cash flows for Events 1 and 2?

   c. Assuming a cost of $20,000.00 for the project, what is the project's NPV?

10. Suppose you could buy a right to delay the payment of the cost of the project in Problem 9 until you actually recognize the cash flow from the project. You could then decide to not accept the project if the cash flow was not greater than the $20,000.00 cost (a call option with a strike price of $20,000.00).

    a. How much is such an option worth? (*Hint:* Rework the table in Problem 9 considering when you would exercise the option and then value the option cash flows using a tracking portfolio.)

    b. Suppose the option costs $10,000.00. Should you purchase the option at this price?

11. Suppose the tracking portfolio for a project contains a position in the index option. Are the project cash flows linear relative to the market portfolio (market index) and the risk-free security?

12. Suppose a project has the following cash flows conditional on the state of the economy: $55,000.00 for the Boom economy, $35,000.00 for the Stagnant economy, and $22,000.00 for the Recession economy. The appropriate tracking portfolio has the following holdings in the market index, the risk-free security, and the index option: $H_{Mkt} = 80$, $H_{RF} = 70$, $H_O = 60$. What value for the Recession economy would make the project linear relative to the market index and the risk-free security? (*Hint:* Determine the value of the market index holdings and the risk-free security holdings relative to the Recession economy.)

3

THE BINOMIAL MODEL

4 MODELING UNCERTAINTY AND VALUING FLEXIBILITY

A key takeaway from Chapters 2 and 3, which is something I hope you knew before but now have a deeper appreciation of, is that the current *value* of an asset—whether it is a financial asset like a stock or a bond, a corporate project, or a derivative on a financial asset or a corporate project—is a function of what can happen to that asset's cash flows in the future, what can happen to the overall economy in the future, and, most important, the relationship between the two.

The problem for someone trying to value a risky asset is that the future is very obscure, and it seems as though the only thing we can confidently say about the future is that we will be surprised by what happens. Be that as it may, we live in a world where we need to attach values to risky assets, and valuation requires that we say something about what the future may bring. In other words, we must construct a *model* of the future (as I did in Chapters 2 and 3; see Figures 3.1 and 3.22).

A model is an abstract construction we use to describe the world, and the point of modeling is to simplify the world in order to help us make sense of things. You deal with models in your everyday life. Road and subway maps bear little likeness to the physical geography of a place, but they are very helpful in getting from point A to point B. Atomic elements are not really like little solar systems, but thinking of them that way helps students learn the principles of chemistry. Your credit score is an abstract number that is based only on a handful of observations about your personal history, but it is very useful to a lender who wants to predict your future behavior.

What these anecdotal examples show us is that modeling is all about *approximation*. Models rely on *assumptions* to simplify things, and every time you make an approximating assumption your model becomes less like the real world but more user friendly. A good model is a framework that helps users achieve their goals with the least amount of complexity.

Our goal in finance is valuation of risky future cash flows, and in this text we've already encountered one important abstraction that helps us manage the complexity of the real world: Our assumption that the financial market admits no arbitrage opportunities. The no-arbitrage assumption is not meant to describe the world exactly but rather to simplify it, and the benefit of the no arbitrage approximation is that it gives us the straightforward *linear pricing rule* model (via the fundamental theorem of asset pricing), which says that an asset's value must be equal to the value of a similar substitute portfolio of financial market building blocks. So, given this simplification, our valuation problem becomes easier: If we can find a way to decompose a risky asset into financial market building blocks, we can estimate its value with some confidence.

Now, finding an appropriate set of building blocks and learning how to put them together into an appropriate tracking portfolio is yet another difficulty. To get anywhere, we have to make further assumptions that describe what the future may hold. This is where the concepts of probabilities and probability distributions become handy, and when we make an assumption about the probability distribution of future events, we are making another simplifying abstraction that moves us further away from reality but closer to a usable model.

The tradition in finance is to assume that a normal distribution adequately describes potential future *changes* in the value of a risky asset (i.e., the asset's *returns*). We call this setting a *lognormal* world, for reasons that I'll explain later in the chapter. The assumption of lognormality simplifies the world by making the math easier, as the normal probability distribution is actually quite painless to work with. The modeling benefit of this simplification is that in a lognormal world with frequent trading and no arbitrage opportunities, building-block securities are easy to identify, and tracking portfolios become straightforward to form.

If you've seen any option pricing before, you've seen this in action—in a lognormal world with frequent trading, an option can be decomposed into a portfolio of only *two* building-block securities. The intuition here is that if you are willing to assume normally distributed returns, then over any very small time interval only *two* things can happen to a a risky asset's value: It can go up a little, or it can go down a little. As a result, only two things can happen to the value of a derivative on that risky asset because (by definition) a derivative's payoff is explicitly tied to the value of the underlying. Since two points define a line, then you can conclude that the derivative's value is linear in the value of the risky asset, and you only need two building blocks to recreate the line—the underlying risky asset and a risk-free bond.

This intuition motivates what we call the *binomial model*, which will be our workhorse for the rest of this book. In the binomial model, only two things can happen to the value of a risky asset over a brief amount of time: It can go up a little, or it can go down a little. The binomial model is really just a mechanical way of implementing our assumption of normally distributed returns, because when you link enough binomial models together in time, you get a nice lognormal world. An attractive feature of the binomial model is that it is at once simple to deal with and yet flexible enough to apply to a wide variety of different (and sometimes difficult) circumstances.

In my eyes, however, there's a more profound beauty to the binomial model: It allows me to explain to you something that I stated in Chapters 2 and 3, which you might have found either objectionable or confusing.

If you've ever studied option pricing before, then you've learned that the tracking portfolio that values an option requires only two building blocks: The *underlying risky asset* on which the option is written and a risk-free bond. You can think of these two building blocks as the molecules that, when put together correctly, reconstruct any option on the risky asset. But in Chapters 2 and 3, you saw that I priced options by forming tracking portfolios that contained the *financial market's building blocks:* The market index fund plus the risk-free bond. That is, my *molecules* in Chapters 2 and 3 were the market index and the risk-free bond, and I claimed that I could reconstruct any asset (including financial and real options) with frequent trading in them.

The binomial model can be used to demonstrate the connection between these two approaches. This all goes back to the fundamental theorem of asset pricing, which actually says something much more subtle (and much more important) than what I stated in Chapter 2. If the financial market admits no arbitrage opportunities, then according to the fundamental theorem there exists a primitive set of financial market *atomic building blocks* that, when put together correctly, make up the molecular building blocks (and, by force, every other financial market security). These atoms can be combined in one way to reconstruct a risk-free bond, in another way to re-create my market index fund, and in yet another way to replicate the underlying risky asset for any derivative. As a result, all derivatives can be decomposed into these few atomic building blocks; however you choose to form your tracking portfolio, you are using these atoms in one way or another. When you add to this our assumption of normally distributed returns, the world simplifies to the point that over any small interval of time you need only *two* of these atomic building blocks to track any derivative (or any primitive asset, for that matter). If you've seen option pricing before, then you've seen the shadows of these atomic building blocks—which you probably called risk-neutral probabilities.

Chapter Plan

This chapter provides a much lengthier presentation of the binomial model than you will find in a typical derivatives text. I have a very good reason for being so verbose. Practitioners in the field of financial derivatives find textbook option pricing models to be quite useful and, as a result, accept them without much worry about exactly *why* they work. To a typical corporate manager, however, derivative pricing models are mysterious black boxes. I believe that these corporate managers will be more willing to work with option pricing models when they develop more trust in them, and that trust will only come about through some intuition about what's really going on.

Rather than diving right into binomial option pricing, I'll start by showing you how and why the binomial model is a good way to put structure on the uncertain future. This is easy, and many people have told me that it helps their understanding.

Next, I will arbitrarily construct a single-step binomial tree, and we will spend a good deal of time learning the basics of valuation by arbitrage in it. We'll develop a general approach to building tracking portfolios, and at this point you can go back and work through the advanced sections of Chapters 2 and 3 (if you want to). My approach here will look very similar to Chapters 2 and 3, in that we'll value a corporate real option with two different tracking portfolios: a traditional tracking portfolio that contains the option's proximate underlying asset (the project itself) along with a risk-free bond, and a nontraditional tracking portfolio that contains the financial market's molecular building blocks (the market index fund and the risk-free bond).

Just as in Chapters 2 and 3, we'll get the same answer either way. An important objective of this chapter is to show you *why* they are the same. This leads into the section on risk-neutral pricing, which in my mind is the most important material in the book. In this section, you'll develop an even deeper understanding of what the term *risk* really means and how all valuation models actually work; the lessons here will allow me to stitch everything together. My hope is that this material will help you appreciate that option pricing models are quite appropriate in corporate finance.

Up to that point in the chapter, we'll still be working in a single-step binomial world. Before going any further, I'll walk you through three simplified corporate real options problems to show you how we'll be applying our option pricing models to corporate investments in flexibility. I find it beneficial to my students if I break away from theory a bit and demonstrate how we'll use it in practice before things get more complex. It seems to help them organize things in their minds.

After our three simplified real-world examples, we'll learn how to link individual binomial trials together into a multistep binomial tree and how to price multiperiod derivatives; all of the earlier principles will remain intact.

4.1 How a Binomial Model Approximates a Normal Distribution

Garish neon lights identify the business in Figure 4.1 When you enter, you encounter continuously clanging bells, stifling clouds of cigarette smoke, and hordes of addicted customers who are looking to change their financial status.

This is *not* a scene from Las Vegas. Rather, it is a very common sight in Tokyo, Nagoya, and all other major Japanese cities: A pachinko parlor. Although pachinko looks like a simple arcade game, it is actually a

Figure 4.1

© Getty Images, Inc.

very popular form of illegal (but tolerated) gambling among the Japanese.

Figure 4.2

© Getty Images, Inc.

The game is really very simple: A player like the woman in Figure 4.2 buys a box of little steel balls (11 mm in diameter, similar to large buckshot), and empties them into a machine. She then launches the balls into the very top of the machine in succession by turning a knob (see her right hand), and the balls cascade down through the playing area bouncing left and right off of nails that are spaced throughout. If a ball happens to fall into a special bin, the player wins more balls—which can be either replayed or redeemed for prizes like cigarettes and stuffed animals. The illegal aspect of pachinko occurs when the player reexchanges these prizes for cash in shady, but generally safe, back-alley transactions.

Even though the modern pachinko machine has spinning wheels, bumpers, and payoff bins from the top of the machine to the bottom, it operates on a very simple principle that illustrates the binomial model in an intuitive way. Consider a very primitive pachinko machine in which the playing area has nothing but nails, and the ball collection bins are only at the very bottom of the machine. In Figure 4.3, the black dots represent the nails in the pachinko game, and the boxes at the bottom are the collection bins for the balls.

When a player launches a ball into the machine, the ball drops from the top and immediately strikes the first nail (at the top of the pyramid of nails in Figure 4.3). When the ball strikes this nail, there are only two things that can happen: The ball can deflect off to the left, or the ball can deflect off to the right. See Figure 4.4 for a pictorial representation.

Now suppose, for the sake of the argument, that the ball deflects rightward off of the first nail. What then happens? As Figure 4.5 demonstrates, the ball encounters another nail, and again only two outcomes can occur: The ball deflects left, or the ball deflects right.

Now suppose that after striking the nail in the second row, the ball *again* deflects right. The ball encounters another nail (this one being the farthest right on the third row) and the ball can again only deflect right or left. After striking the nail on the third row, suppose the ball deflects right *again* (for the third straight time) and immediately encounters the right-most

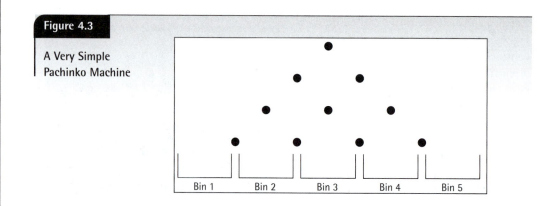

Figure 4.3

A Very Simple Pachinko Machine

Bin 1   Bin 2   Bin 3   Bin 4   Bin 5

Figure 4.4

When the Ball Encounters the First Nail, Only Two Events Can Occur

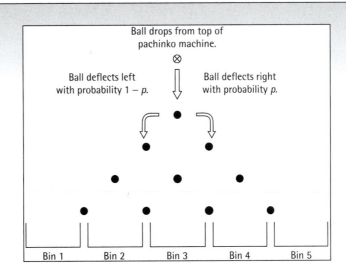

Ball drops from top of pachinko machine.

Ball deflects left with probability $1 - p$.

Ball deflects right with probability p.

Bin 1   Bin 2   Bin 3   Bin 4   Bin 5

nail on the fourth row. After striking the nail on the fourth row, the ball *again* deflects right (for the fourth straight time) and falls into Bin 5. Figure 4.6 depicts the ball's progress through the machine.

In our simple pachinko machine, the balls are symmetric, and there's an equal probability of deflection in each direction. So what is the probability that a ball ricochets right four times in a row and ends up in Bin 5? The answer is easy: $(0.5) \times (0.5) \times (0.5) \times (0.5) = 0.0625$. Further, notice that there is only one possible way for the ball to land in Bin 5: It must make four rightward deflections in a row and zero leftward deflections. So the probability of landing in Bin 5 is only .0625. In other words, if our player were to shoot 16 balls into the machine, she should expect only one of them to end up in Bin 5 (on average).

Figure 4.5

The Ball Continues through the Machine after Deflecting "Right" Off the First Nail

Ball drops from top of pachinko machine.

Ball deflects right off top nail.

Ball deflects left with probability $1 - p$.

Ball deflects right with probability p.

Bin 1   Bin 2   Bin 3   Bin 4   Bin 5

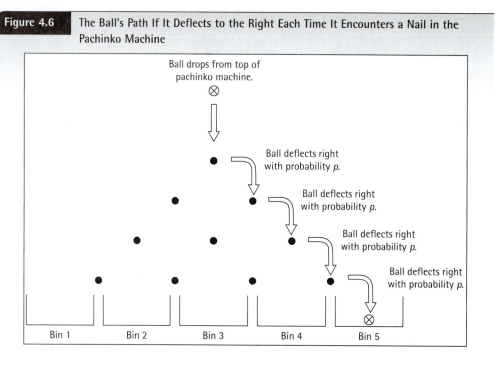

Figure 4.6 The Ball's Path If It Deflects to the Right Each Time It Encounters a Nail in the Pachinko Machine

Ball drops from top of pachinko machine.

Ball deflects right with probability p.

Ball deflects right with probability p.

Ball deflects right with probability p.

Ball deflects right with probability p.

Bin 1   Bin 2   Bin 3   Bin 4   Bin 5

The same logic works for Bin 1. To get there, a ball must deflect left four times in a row, which only occurs with probability .0625. There is only one possible path a ball can take to get to Bin 1: It must make four left deflections and zero right. So the likelihood of a ball landing in Bin 1 is only 625 out of 10,000, or 1 in 16. No wonder the big prizes are paid for balls collecting in very extreme places in the machine!

Now a harder question: What is the probability that a ball lands in Bin 4? Well, a ball could land in Bin 4 by falling into the machine and moving right, then right again, then right again, and then left after striking the last nail in row 4. What is the probability of this happening? Since left and right moves are equally likely, the probability of the ball moving right-right-right-left is $(0.5) \times (0.5) \times (0.5) \times (0.5) = 0.0625$. But this is not the answer to the question! Why? Right-right-right-left is *not* the only possible path that the ball can take to Bin 4. As Figure 4.7 shows, there are three other trips that the ball can take through the pachinko machine and still end up in Bin 4.

That's right—the ball can go R-R-R-L (which it does with probability 0.0625), or it can go R-R-L-R (with probability 0.0625), or R-L-R-R (with probability 0.0625), or L-R-R-R (with probability 0.0625). So the probability that a ball finishes the game in Bin 4 is $0.0625 + 0.0625 + 0.0625 + 0.0625 = 4 \times (0.0625) = 0.25$.

The same can be said for Bin 2. A ball can end up in Bin 2 by going L-L-L-R, L-L-R-L, L-R-L-L, or R-L-L-L. That is, three lefts and one right (no matter what order). So, the probability of ending up in Bin 2 is also 0.25, and our player should expect one out of every four balls played to end up there (on average).

Where are we so far? Well, Bins 2 and 4 are four times as likely as Bins 1 and 5. There's only one bin left: Bin 3. What is the probability that a ball ends up there? The shortcut to answer this problem is to realize that, by definition, the probabilities of all of the possible outcomes must sum to 1. Since the probability of Bins 1, 2, 4, and 5 are 0.0625, 0.25, 0.25, and 0.0625,

Figure 4.7 | The Four Possible Paths through the Pachinko Machine to Bin 4

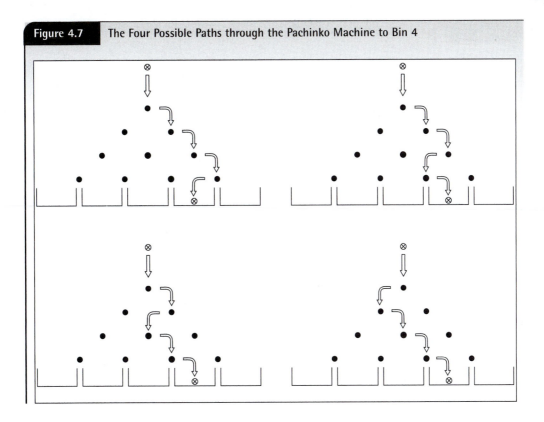

respectively, the probability of Bin 3 must be $1 - (0.0625 + 0.25 + 0.25 + 0.0625) = 1 - 0.625 = 0.375$. But let's prove it to ourselves.

There are *six* possible paths that a ball can take through the game and arrive at Bin 3:

R-R-L-L
R-L-L-R
R-L-R-L
L-R-L-R
L-R-R-L
L-L-R-R

which is shown in Figure 4.8.

Notice the pattern. Each possible path through the machine is equally likely, as long as the probabilities of left and right are the same. What differs is the number of paths throught the system. There are six routes that the ball can take to get to Bin 3, and the probability of each path is $(0.5) \times (0.5) \times (0.5) \times (0.5) = 0.0625$, so the probability that a ball ends up in Bin 3 is $6 \times 0.0625 = 0.375$.

To summarize what we know so far:

- Bin 1: probability = 0.0625, or 1 in 16.
- Bin 2: probability = 0.25, or 4 in 16.
- Bin 3: probability = 0.375, or 6 in 16.
- Bin 4: probabiltiy = 0.25, or 4 in 16.
- Bin 5: probability = 0.0625, or 1 in 16.

Figure 4.8   The Six Possible Paths through the Pachinko Machine to Bin 3

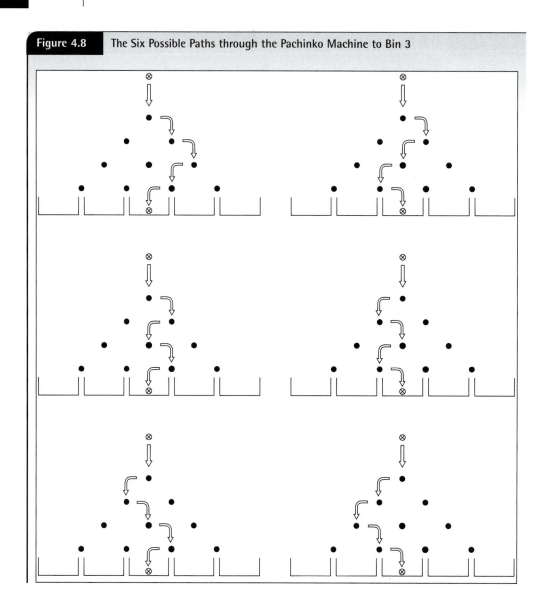

We can summarize these graphically, as I show in Figure 4.9. If our player shoots 16 balls into the machine, she should predict the outcome of the game shown in Figure 4.9.

You should notice that the probability distribution is symmetric around the middle bin, and that it is peaked in the middle as well. Because a bigger machine has more rows of nails, the probability distribution in the bottom becomes clearer as the machine gets larger.

The general result goes like this. If you have a pachinko machine with N rows of pins, then there will be $N + 1$ bins at the bottom. To end up in Bin $j + 1$ $\{j = 0, \ldots, N\}$, the ball must deflect to the right j times and to the left the other $(N - j)$ times. So if pr_R is the probability that a ball deflects off of any nail to the right (and thus $1 - pr_R$ is the probability that a ball deflects off of any nail to the left), then the probability that a played ball ends up in Bin $j + 1$

Figure 4.9

Predicted Destination
of 16 Balls Played
Through Our Simple
Pachinko Machine

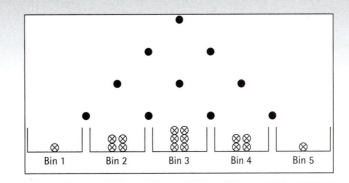

$\{j = 0, \ldots, N\}$ is given by

$$\binom{N}{j}(pr_R)^j(1 - pr_R)^{N-j} = \left(\frac{N!}{j!(N - j)!}\right)(pr_R)^j(1 - pr_R)^{N-j}$$

The first term calculates the number of possible paths that lead to bin $j + 1$, and the product of the second and third terms is the probability of any one path that leads to that bin. You can calculate this quickly using Microsoft Excel's function:

$$= \text{binomdist}\ (j, N, pr_R, false)$$

I used this to calculate the probability distribution for a pachinko machine with 10 rows of nails (and thus 11 possible collection bins at the bottom); I present the results in Figure 4.10.

The fascinating thing that you should be spotting in Figure 4.10 is that the distribution of balls in the bottom bins of the pachinko game looks like a bell curve, or a normal distribution. This is not a coincidence, but actually a mathematical result. The distribution of balls in the bottom bins is actually called a *binomial* distribution with N trials, where N represents the number of rows of nails in the game (i.e., the number of nails a ball can hit, or moves a ball can make). The important result, which is quite old in the field of probability, is that as the number trials N (or rows of nails) grows large, the distribution of balls in the bins approaches the normal distribution—which is the *limiting distribution* of the binomial. What you may not

Figure 4.10 Distribution of Balls in a 10-Row Pachinko Machine

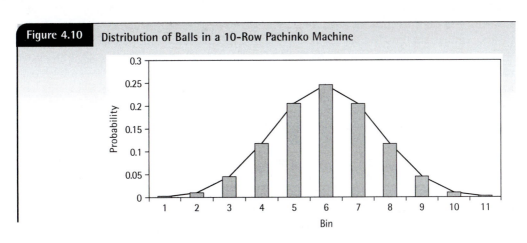

expect is that the pachinko game with only a few rows of nails gives an excellent approximation of the normal curve.[1]

How We'll Interpret the Pachinko Machine

The primitive pachinko machine I've described here generates a good approximation of a normal distribution with relatively few rows of nails. It is important that you understand exactly *what* this normal distribution describes. When we say that "the distribution of balls in the bottom of the pachinko machine is normal," we really mean that "a normal distribution describes the possible random *change* in the left-right position of a ball."

The words *change in position* are key here. In Figure 4.10, the ball begins play above Bin 6 in the very middle of the machine; Figure 4.10 tells us that the ball finishes the game in in the same left-right position (Bin 6) with about .25 probability. Further, Figure 4.10 says that there's roughly a 20% chance that the ball ends up one bin to the right of where it started, and roughly a 12% chance that the ball makes two net moves to the left during the game. Intuitively, it is very unlikely that a ball will end up very far to the left or to the right of center; the most likely place for the ball to end up is right in the middle (i.e., right where it starts—no net *change* in position).

The mean of the normal distribution does not have to be right where the ball starts (i.e., zero change in position). If we make the probability of a right deflection at each pin higher than the probability of a left deflection, then the mean will shift to the right (that is, the expected change in position will be nonzero). However, the *distribution of changes will remain normal* as long as (1) the probabilities are constant throughout the tree, and (2) the absolute size of the deflection to the left or right is the same throughout the tree.[2] In this case, we'll think of the normal distribution as describing the distribution of changes in location around the expected bin. Just keep the word *change* in mind.

How We'll Use the Pachinko Machine—Our Binomial Model

Our ultimate goal is to generate a range of possible future values of a risky asset and an associated probability for each possible outcome *that is consistent with the way we think about the world.* If we think that a normal distribution describes something random in the world, then the pachinko machine gives us an excellent way to approximate it and analyze it.

Financial economists think that the normal distribution adequately describes random *returns* on risky assets in most situations. Returns are changes, and the intuition in the binomial model translates directly into a way to approximate the normally distributed *changes* in an asset's value that might occur. Just turn the pachinko machine counterclockwise onto its side. *Right* moves in the pachinko machine are *positive returns* on an asset (or increases in its value), *left* moves in the machine are *negative returns* on the asset (or decreases in its value). The peak of the distribution is at the mean (or expected) *return* on the asset.

The beauty of the pachinko machine is that it is easy to construct—it is just a binomial process (like a coin flip), repeated over and over again. To understand the whole machine, all we need to master is the single binomial trial that occurs anywhere in the machine (and how they all link together).

---

[1] The primitive pachinko machine shown in this chapter is sometimes called a *quincunx*, and its use in teaching probability and statistics traces back to a British researcher named Sir Francis Galton (1822–1911). Galton, a cousin of Charles Darwin, built his quincunx (like my pachinko machine, but with more rows of nails) to experiment with randomness and to use as a visual tool in his lectures. The quincunx is still a great teaching aid, and you'll see it in many classes to this day.

[2] The binomial process can generate many other distributions if we relax either of these two restrictions.

Figure 4.11

The First
Event in the
Pachinko
Machine

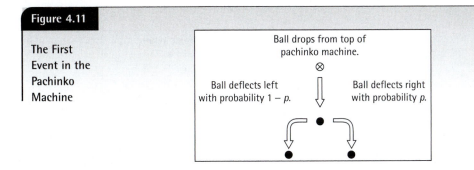

Just think about the very first nail at the top of the pachinko machine (Figure 4.11). Before the game ever starts, we *know* that the ball will strike the first nail. The randomness begins at that point. So the game really begins at the first nail, as I show in Figure 4.12.

This is the binomial trial that repeats itself over and over throughout the pachinko machine. We will reinterpret the nails in the machine as *asset values* and reinterpret moves to the right as *increases in value* and moves to the left as *decreases in value*. Compare Figure 4.12 with Figure 4.13.

The physical distance between rows of nails will represent time passing. For example, we might start by letting the time step be one year. A one-year binomial model is like a pachinko machine with only one row of nails and two collection bins, like I show in Figure 4.14.

Clearly this would be an extreme simplification, because there are only two possible outcomes at the end of the year. The way to make it slightly more realistic is simply to add a row of nails at the six-month mark. There will now be two rows of nails and three possible collection points (or terminal values), as I show in Figure 4.15.

Figure 4.15 is a pictorial representation of how our economy evolved in the advanced sections of Chapters 2 and 3. The three terminal states of the macroeconomy in Chapters 2 and 3 correspond to the three terminal nodes (or collection bins) in the figure. The earlier points in time are the rows of nails: The first nail is today, and the second row of nails is the six-month point in time. We'll learn that we can form a tracking portfolio at the first nail and then rebalance the tracking portfolio at the second row of nails (i.e., after the first time period has passed) so that it gives us the correct values at the end of the tree (in the collection bins), no matter which one we end up in.

Of course, we don't expect things to change as much over a six-month period as over a full year, so we'll have to adjust the magnitude of the up and down jumps when we cut the time step between rows of nails. That's not a problem. But still, there are only three outcomes. So add another row of nails, and let each time step be four months (as I show in Figure 4.16).

Figure 4.12

The Game
Begins at the
First Nail

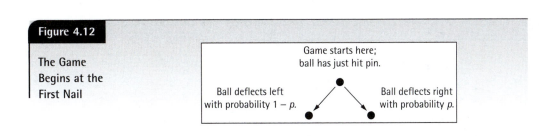

Figure 4.13

Right Is Up;
Left Is Down

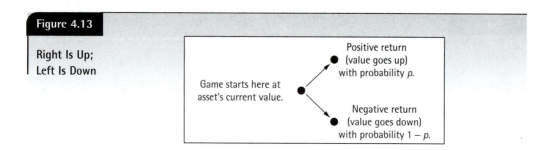

Now cut the year into four time periods (each three months long) to get five possible outcomes, as in Figure 4.17.

This is about as far as I can go drawing things out by hand. The essential issues are (1) that as I add time steps (or rows of nails), I increase the number of possible outcomes at the end of the game (or what we call the *binomial tree*), and (2) the probability distribution of *changes in the value of the asset* from M_0 to whatever comes about by the end of the tree (i.e., the distribution of *returns*) converges to a normal distribution.

The trick behind this model is to learn what goes on in one step of the binomial process. There's a lot of intuition here, so we'll go slowly. We'll spend a good deal of time understanding the single-step binomial model, and I'll even give you some simple real options examples using the single-step model before showing you how to create multistep trees.

4.2 Valuation by Arbitrage and Linear Pricing in the Single-Step Binomial Model

In this section, we'll learn how to price options (both real and financial) in a single-step binomial model. My presentation will not follow the standard approach, however. A typical derivatives text would proceed as follows: First, the author would present an arbitrary risky asset whose current value is known; next, the author would construct an arbitrary binomial model of that risky asset's future; finally, the author would demonstrate how to price derivatives on the risky asset in the binomial world.

Figure 4.14   A One-Period Binomial Model Is Like a Pachinko Machine with One Row of Nails and Two Collection Bins.

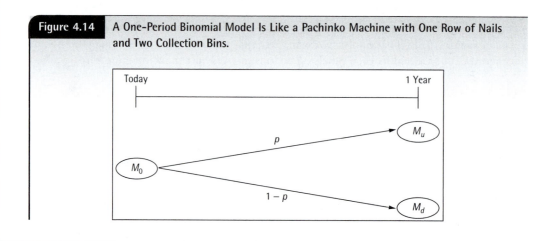

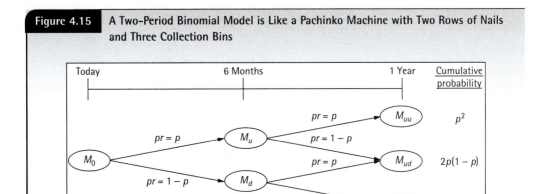

Figure 4.15 A Two-Period Binomial Model is Like a Pachinko Machine with Two Rows of Nails and Three Collection Bins

What derivatives texts pay no attention to, however, is that the current known price of the risky asset is determined by the equilibrium in the financial markets.[3] While this detail is not very important in the world of financial derivatives, it is important to a corporate manager who is trying to develop some intuition about how and why option pricing models work and why they are appropriate in a corporate setting. Therefore, I need to tie things back to what we learned in Chapters 2 and 3. So we'll start, once again, in our financial market, work our way into a risky corporate project, and then value an option on that project.

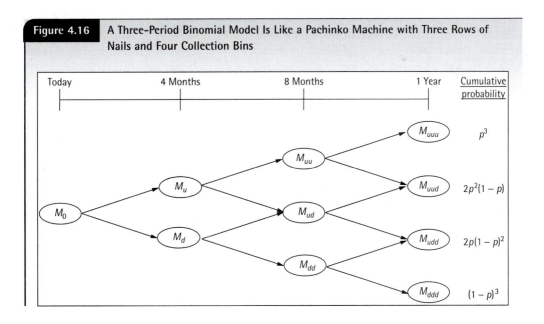

Figure 4.16 A Three-Period Binomial Model Is Like a Pachinko Machine with Three Rows of Nails and Four Collection Bins

[3] The fundamental theorem tells us that the following are equivalent: Absence of arbitrage, existence of a consistent positive linear pricing rule, and existence of an optimum consumption/investment choice for at least one agent who prefers more to less. The fundamental theorem is itself preference-free in the sense that it does not depend on any specific assumptions about preferences (beyond the axiom that agents prefer more to less), but it tells us that equilibrium is not far below the surface.

> **Figure 4.17** A Four–Period Binomial Model Is Like a Pachinko Machine with Four Rows of Nails and Five Collection Bins

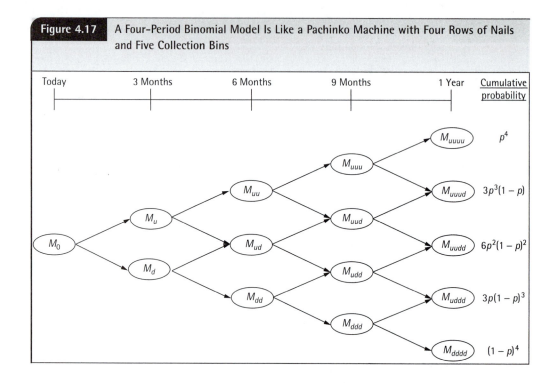

We're going to assume that we live in a world like our economy from Chapters 2 and 3, with one major change: We will assume that over a single period of time, only *two* things can happen to the macroeconomy. If we assume that there are only two potential economic states that can occur over a small amount of time (the economy goes up or down over that time period), we can implement our binomial model as I described in the previous section and get a very nice approximation of normally distributed future returns. The convenience of a binomial world is that over any individual step, tracking portfolios require only two building-block securities.

To keep the notation simple, I'm going to scale values such that the current price of one share of the market index fund is $1, and over the next time period, it can either go up to $2 or down to $0.50 with equal likelihood. Remember that this is the market portfolio, and it is a completely diversified investment in everything. When the index price goes up, overall wealth must be increasing, and the economy must be strengthening; similarly, when the index level goes down, overall wealth must be decreasing so the overall economy must be weakening. We therefore have two possible macroeconomic states of nature at the end of the period: A strengthening economy and a weakening economy. There are no potential idiosyncratic shocks to the market index in either of these states simply because the market portfolio is fully diversified.

The risk-free rate of return is 10% over the period, so we really don't need to nominate a bond price at all—if you invest $1 at the risk-free rate, at the end of the period your investment will be worth $1.10. The length of the time period is not relevant for the moment, but if you want, you can think of it as a year, a month, seven quarters, or whatever. We can represent the economy with a drawing, as in Figure 4.18.

In Figure 4.18, I've used the notation MKT_0 for the value of the market index today, MKT_{Up} for the value of the market index if the economy strengthens (i.e., in the up state), and MKT_{Dn}

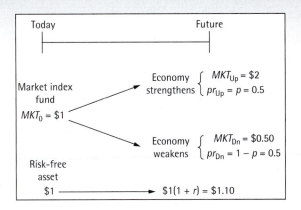

Figure 4.18 The Financial Market's Two Molecular Building Block Securities in Our Binomial Economy

for the value of the market index if the economy weakens (i.e., in the down state). This shorthand will be useful later when we derive some general results.

Notice that the expected return on the market is $0.5(\$2 - \$1)/\$1 + 0.5(\$0.5 - \$1)/\$1 =$ 25%. Since the risk-free rate of return is 10% over the period, the market risk premium is 15% over the period. In familiar terms, the equilibrium in this economy provides a 15% risk premium for every unit of market risk taken. The risk premium is positive because consumers are risk averse.

Pick any asset that exists in this arbitrage-free financial market. No matter what it is, if you can give me its conditional mean values in the strengthening and weakening states of the economy at the end of our time period, I can form a simple tracking portfolio today, containing only the market index fund and the risk-free bond, that gives the exact same state-contingent values at the end of the period and so must have the same value today (or else there's a violation of our no arbitrage assumption). I remind you that the tracking portfolio does not need to exhibit perfect tracking to give the correct arbitrage-free value of the asset. If the asset is a stock, then there might be firm-specific outcomes that affect the stock's price *within* each macroeconomic state of nature (like the litigation risk in our luxury goods company stock). But as long as we make sure that the state-contingent end-of-period values are *conditional means,* then the tracking errors caused by firm-specific outcomes will have an expected value of zero in each state and hence will be diversifiable and worthless. If you don't remember this lesson from Chapter 2, or if you skipped that chapter altogether, I urge you to go back and work through it before moving on.

If we add the assumptions necessary for corporate managers to act as price takers in the financial markets, then we can value new corporate projects the same way (see Chapter 3). Suppose a firm in this economy encounters a new now-or-never/no-flexibility investment opportunity, which we'll call the NONNF. If the managers invest in the NONNF, the project's end-of-period value will be determined by the joint resolution of the macroeconomic state of nature and a private (or firm-specific) risk. Like most corporate projects, the NONNF will generally do better if the economy strengthens than if the economy weakens. And conditional upon any state of nature, the NONNF will be worth more given a positive outcome of the firm-specific risk (which occurs with subjective probability 0.8) and less given a negative outcome of the firm-specific risk (which occurs with subjective probability 0.2). I've given the end-of-period values of the NONNF in Figure 4.19.

Figure 4.19   End-of-Period Values of the NONNF Opportunity

		Value Arising Due to Firm-Specific Risk Outcome		
		Positive $Pr_{POS} = 0.8$	Negative $Pr_{NEG} = 0.2$	Conditional Mean
Macro-economic outcomes	Economy strengthens	$5.30	$3.30	$0.8 \times \$5.30 + 0.2 \times \$3.30 = \$4.90$
	Economy weakens	$0.45	$0.20	$0.8 \times \$0.45 + 0.2 \times \$0.20 = \$0.40$

In order to exploit the NONNF opportunity, the firm's managers must invest $1.50 of investor capital today. Should they?

To evaluate the NONNF opportunity using the net present value (NPV) rule, we must assume that the corporate manager acts as a price taker in the arbitrage-free financial market. The first step in project evaluation is to determine the true financial market value the NONNF by arbitrage with an appropriate financial market tracking portfolio. As you can see from the calculation in Figure 4.19, the conditional mean values of the NONNF are $4.90 in the strengthening economy (or $NONNF_{Up} = \$4.90$) and $0.40 in the weakening economy (or $NONNF_{Dn} = \$0.40$). Figure 4.20 demonstrates that idiosyncratic (or firm-specific) *shocks* to the conditional means arising due to the outcomes of the private risk have zero mean in every state.

To value the NONNF, all we need to do is to find the tracking portfolio holdings H_{Mkt} units of the market index fund and $\$H_{RF}$ invested in the risk-free bond such that the end-of-period value of the tracking portfolio is $4.90 in the up state and $0.40 in the down state:

End-of-period value of tracking portfolio

$$= \begin{cases} H_{Mkt} \times \$2.00 + \$H_{RF} \times 1.10 = \$4.90 & \text{(strengthening economy)} \\ H_{Mkt} \times \$0.50 + \$H_{RF} \times 1.10 = \$0.40 & \text{(weakening economy)} \end{cases}$$

Figure 4.20   The Conditional Mean and Idiosyncratic Components of the NONNF's End-of-Period Value

			Value Arising Due to Private Risk Outcome		
		Conditional Mean Component	Idiosyncratic Shock to Conditional Mean (Actual − Conditional Mean)		Conditional Mean of Idiosyncratic Component
			Positive $Pr_{POS} = 0.8$	Negative $Pr_{NEG} = 0.2$	
Macroeconomic outcomes	Economy strengthens	$4.90	$5.30 − \$4.90 = \$0.40$	$3.30 − \$4.90 = -\$1.60$	$0.8 \times \$0.40 + 0.2 \times (-\$1.60) = \$0$
	Economy weakens	$0.40	$0.45 − \$0.40 = \$0.05$	$0.20 − \$0.40 = -\$0.20$	$0.8 \times \$0.05 + 0.2 \times (-\$0.20) = \$0$

This part has no value!

This is really easy to solve. If you subtract the second equation from the first, you get $H_{Mkt} \times \$1.50 = \$4.50$, so it must be that $H_{Mkt} = 3$. If you then plug $H_{Mkt} = 3$ back into the first equation, you have $\$H_{RF} \times 1.10 = -\$1.10$, so it must be that $\$H_{RF} = -\$1$. In other words, you can track the NONNF by borrowing $1 at the risk-free rate and buying 3 units of the market index. The market value of this tracking portfolio is

$$\text{Value of financial market tracking portfolio} = H_{Mkt} \times MKT_0 + \$H_{RF}$$
$$= 3 \times \$1 + (-\$1)$$
$$= \$2$$

so if we invoke our price-taking and no-arbitrage assumptions, the true financial market value of the NONNF must be $2.00.

Should the managers adopt the project? Since the true financial market value of the NONNF is $2.00, the true NPV of the NONNF must be $0.50 because $2.00 (the true financial market value of the NONNF) minus $1.50 (the corporate manager's cost of buying the NONNF in the real asset market) equals $0.50. Absent any other mutually exclusive projects, the managers should exploit this investment opportunity because it creates value for the firm's investors.

Recall a lesson from Chapters 2 and 3: Our tracking portfolio that correctly values the NONNF makes an error no matter what happens in the future. If the economy strengthens and the market goes up to $MKT_{Up} = \$2$, then the tracking portfolio will be worth $4.90 regardless of the outcome of the *NONNF*'s private risk. However, the NONNF itself is *never* worth $4.90 in the strengthening economic state: In that state, it will either be worth $5.30 (if the private risk outcome is positive) or $3.30 (if the private risk outcome is negative). Similarly, if the economy weakens and the market goes down to $MKT_{Dn} = \$0.50$, the tracking portfolio will be worth $0.40 regardless of the outcome of the NONNF's private risk. But in the weakening economic state, the NONNF itself will be worth either $0.45 or $0.20, given positive or negative outcome of the private risk, respectively. Fortunately for us, these tracking errors are completely unimportant to our valuation. The reason is that these errors are conditional mean zero (in other words, the expected error in every possible macroeconomic state of nature is zero), as shown in Figure 4.21.

| Figure 4.21 | The Tracking Portfolio Errors Have Zero Mean, Given Every Possible Future State of Nature |

			Tracking Portfolio Errors Arising Due to Private Risk Outcomes		
		Value of Tracking Portfolio	Tracking Error (Tracking Portfolio Value minus actual NONNF value)		Conditional Mean of Tracking Error
			Positive $Pr_{POS} = 0.8$	Negative $Pr_{NEG} = 0.2$	
Macroeconomic outcomes	Economy strengthens	$4.90	$4.90 − $5.30 = −$0.40	$4.90 − $3.30 = $1.60	$0.8 \times (-\$0.40) + 0.2 \times \$1.60$ = $0
	Economy weakens	$0.40	$0.40 − $0.45 = −$0.05	$0.40 − $0.20 = $0.20	$0.8 \times (-\$0.05) + 0.2 \times \$0.20$ = $0

This part has no value!

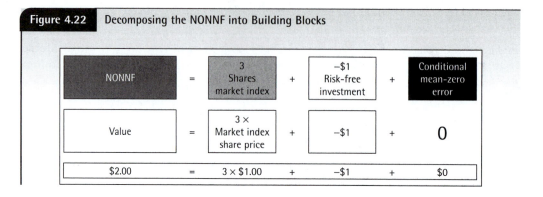

Figure 4.22   Decomposing the NONNF into Building Blocks

As discussed in Chapter 2, conditional mean-zero error is like a coin flip risk and has no value. I reiterate: We don't need to have perfect tracking to decompose an asset's cash flows into the financial market building blocks. As long as our tracking portfolio's expected error is zero in each macroeconomic state of nature, the value of the tracking portfolio must equal the value of the asset—else there's an arbitrage opportunity (buy the cheap one, sell the expensive one, and diversify away the conditional mean-zero tracking error). Figure 4.22 gives our building block interpretation. This will be *very* important as we go forward into real options valuation, for reasons you will see by the end of this section.

Since the current value of the NONNF opportunity is $NONNF_0 = \$2.00$, and since its conditional mean value is \$4.90 in the strengthening economic state (or $NONNF_{Up} = \$4.90$) and \$0.40 in the weakening economic state (or $NONNF_{Dn} = \$0.40$), we can construct a binomial model that describes the expected evolution of the NONNF as I've done in Figure 4.23.

An important observation in Figure 4.23 is that up and down movements of the NONNF correspond to the strengthening and weakening economies, respectively; this reflects the fact that the NONNF has a positive beta. You will see in the next few pages that if we want to value real options on the NONNF, we can work in the binomial world of our financial market (Figure 4.18), *or* we can work in the binomial world of Figure 4.23, and we'll get the same answer.

Figure 4.23   Binomial Model of How the Expected Value of the NONNF Project Evolves Over Time

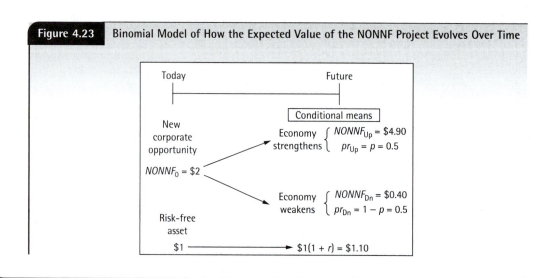

Before I do that, however, I'd like to show you that there is a shortcut way to construct Figure 4.23 using only the information in Figure 4.19 along with recognition that the risk-free rate of return is 10% and the market risk premium is 15%. Since the NONNF is a now-or-never/no-flexibility project, we can safely calculate its financial market value using discounted cash flow (DCF). To do so, we would first estimate its beta; I show in Appendix 4.3 that $\beta_{NONNF} = 1.5$. Since the risk-free rate of return is 10% and the market risk premium is 15%, the CAPM required rate of return on the NONNF would be

$$\bar{r}_{NONNF} = 0.10 + 1.5[0.15] = 32.5\%$$

Next, we would calculate the expected end-of-period value of the NONNF:

$$E\{V_{NONNF}\} = 0.5[0.8(\$5.30) + 0.2(\$3.30)] + 0.5[0.8(\$0.45) + 0.2(\$0.20)]$$
$$= \$2.65$$

and we would discount the expected value of the NONNF ($2.65) at the CAPM-determined required rate of return (32.5%) to get the current financial market value of the NONNF (which, in our notation, is $NONNF_0$):

$$NONNF_0 = \frac{E\{V_{NONNF}\}}{1 + \bar{r}_{NONNF}} = \frac{\$2.65}{1.325} = \$2.00$$

This is, of course, exactly what we got before.[4] We could then calculate the conditional mean values of the NONNF in each future state and quickly construct Figure 4.23 without having to model the financial market index itself. This is exactly how we'll work when valuing investments in flexibility when we get into the later chapters: We will first assume that our underlying project is now-or-never/no-flexibility with all decisions hardwired, we will then value this hypothetical project with DCF, and finally we will use it as our underlying asset.

Pricing a Real Option on the *NONNF*

Now let's do something fun. Let's suppose that the project is not really now-or-never, but rather that the firm can wait until the end of the period to make the decision. It is easy to see the potential benefit of this flexibility: By waiting, the firm can observe the outcome of the macroeconomic risk and the private risk (illustrated in Figure 4.19) *before* choosing to invest. But to make things interesting, let's assume that the cost of the project rises rather dramatically if the firm delays the investment. Specifically, let's assume that the project will require an investment of $3.50 if the firm waits until the end of the period to execute it (instead of the $1.50 required for immediate investment). Should the firm invest now or wait? Whichever creates more value for the firm's investors. What does your intuition tell you here? Is it worth waiting, even though the cost goes up so dramatically?

To determine the value of waiting, we have to ascertain exactly what the firm can learn by waiting and exactly what the firm will optimally do given what they learn. Here, by waiting, the firm gets to learn the end-of-period value of the project and then respond by investing $3.50, if and only if the learned value of the project exceeds $3.50. In other words, the act of waiting

---

[4] We can verify that 32.5% is indeed the required rate of return on the NONNF using what we learned about the tracking portfolio's contents. The tracking portfolio has $(3 \times \$1)/\$2 = 150\%$ of its total value invested in the market index, and $-\$1/\$2 = -50\%$ invested in the risk-free bond, so the expected return on the tracking portfolio is $1.50 \times 25\% + (-0.50) \times 10\% = 32.5\%$.

Figure 4.24   End-of-Period Values of the Call on the NONNF with Strike Price = $3.50

| | | Value Arising Due to Private Risk Outcome | | Conditional Mean |
		Positive $pr_{POS} = 0.8$	Negative $pr_{NEG} = 0.2$	
Macroeconomic outcomes	Economy strengthens	max [$5.30 − $3.50, $0] = $1.80	max [$3.30 − $3.50, $0] = $0	0.8 × $1.80 + 0.2 × $0 = $1.44
	Economy weakens	max [$0.45 − $3.50, $0] = $0	max [$0.20 − $3.50, $0] = $0	0.8 × $0 + 0.2 × $0 = $0

creates a call option on the NONNF with a strike price of $3.50. The end-of-period value of the call will be Max[*NONNF* − $3.50, $0], and that payoff depends on both the resolution of the macroeconomic uncertainty *and* the outcome of the NONNF's private risk. I've calculated the payoff on the call under all future contingencies in Figure 4.24. Notice that there's only one situation where waiting would result in subsequent investment in the project—if the economy strengthens and there's a positive outcome to the private risk.

Valuing the Real Option with a Traditional Tracking Portfolio

The traditional approach to valuing a call option is to form a tracking portfolio (or *hedge portfolio* or *arbitrage portfolio*) that contains the *underlying asset* and the risk-free bond, and this is what we'll do. What is the underlying asset? Well, it is always what you get if you ultimately exercise the option. In this example, the act of exercising the option is spending $3.50 at the end of the year to invest in the delayed project. What does management get back if they invest $3.50 at the end of the year? The NONNF, of course! So the underlying asset in this situation is the NONNF itself.

I know that there are some readers out there who are saying "Richard, you must be crazy—you can't do this, because you have to hedge four outcomes with only two securities." To those of you who may think this, I have two things to say: (1) As we learned in Chapters 2 and 3, we don't need perfect tracking—all we need is for our tracking portfolio to have an expected error of zero within each macroeconomic state of nature, and (2) there are only two macroeconomic states of nature. So, in reality, there are only *two* outcomes that we need to hedge: the conditional mean value of the option given the strengthening economy ($1.44) and the conditional mean value of the option given the weakening economy ($0). As long as the *conditional mean* value of our tracking portfolio matches up to the *conditional mean* value of the derivative in all macroeconomic states of nature, then the tracking error will be idiosyncratic, have no value, and will not impact our valuation one bit (as you'll soon see).

Figure 4.25 shows the evolution of the NONNF's conditional mean value as the economy changes, along with the evolution of the real option's conditional mean value as the economy changes. In other words, I've ignored the fact that there are two things that can happen within each macroeconomic state of nature to both the NONNF and the option on the NONNF, and instead I've focused only on the two possible macroeconomic states of nature and the conditional mean values of the NONNF and the real option in those two states. Notice that I'm using the notation RO_{Up} and RO_{Dn} to mean the conditional mean payoff on the real option in the up (strengthening economy) and down (weakening economy) states, respectively.

Figure 4.25 Evolution of Conditional Mean Value of Our NONNF and Associated Conditional Mean Values of Real Option on the NONNF

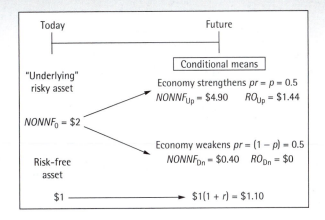

Now consider forming a tracking portfolio consisting of H_{NONNF} units of the underlying NONNF and $\$H_{RF}$ worth of risk-free bonds. At the end of the period, the *conditional mean* value of this tracking portfolio will be

$$H_{NONNF} \times NONNF_{Up} + \$H_{RF}(1 + r) = H_{NONNF} \times \$4.90 + \$H_{RF} \times (1.10)$$

if the economy strengthens, and

$$H_{NONNF} \times NONNF_{Dn} + \$H_{RF}(1 + r) = H_{NONNF} \times \$0.40 + \$H_{RF} \times (1.10)$$

if the economy weakens. To value the real option on the NONNF, all we need to do is find the holdings H_{NONNF} and $\$H_{RF}$ such that the end-of-period conditional mean value of the tracking portfolio equals the end-of-period conditional mean value of the real option in both states of nature:

End-of-period conditional mean value of portfolio

$$= \begin{cases} H_{NONNF} \times \$4.90 + \$H_{RF} \times (1.10) = \$1.44 & \text{(strengthening economy)} \\ H_{NONNF} \times \$0.40 + \$H_{RF} \times (1.10) = \$0 & \text{(weakening economy)} \end{cases} \quad (4.1)$$

Once we've located the appropriate holdings H_{NONNF} and $\$H_{RF}$, the value of the tracking portfolio today will be

$$H_{NONNF} \times NONNF_0 + \$H_{RF} = H_{NONNF} \times \$2.00 + \$H_{RF} \quad (4.2)$$

and, given our price-taking and no-arbitrage assumptions, this must be the value of the real option as well.

OK, let's roll. To find the appropriate H_{NONNF}, subtract the "weakening economy" equation in (4.1) from the "strengthening economy" equation. The result is

$$\begin{array}{ll} H_{NONNF} \times \$4.90 + \$H_{RF} \times (1.10) & = \$1.44 \\ -(H_{NONNF} \times \$0.40 + \$H_{RF} \times (1.10) & = \$0) \\ \hline H_{NONNF} \times \$4.50 & = \$1.44 \end{array}$$

and so the tracking portfolio must contain $H_{NONNF} = \$1.44/\$4.50 = 0.32$ units of the now-or-never/no-flexibility project. Now plugging this back into the "strengthening economy" equation in (4.1), we get

$$0.32 \times \$4.90 + \$H_{RF} \times (1.10) = \$1.44$$

or

$$\$H_{RF} = \frac{1}{1.10}[\$1.44 - 0.32(\$4.90)]$$
$$= \frac{-\$0.128}{1.10}$$
$$= -\$0.1164$$

which, due to the negative sign, is borrowing $0.1164 at the risk-free rate of return (with a promised repayment obligation of $0.128 at the end of the period). From Equation (4.2), the value of the tracking portfolio is therefore

$$0.32 \times \$2.00 + (-\$0.1164) = \$0.5236$$

What this tells us is that the firm should wait. The financial market value of *waiting* is $0.5236, and since there's no immediate cost to waiting then the true NPV of waiting is $0.5236. Remember that the true NPV of investing immediately is only $0.50. Waiting and investing immediately are mutually exclusive alternatives, so the NPV rule tells us that the best alternative is to wait even though waiting causes a dramatic rise in the cost of investment!

We need to make sure we got the tracking portfolio right, and to do so, we need to verify two things: (1) that the conditional mean end-of-period values of the tracking portfolio equal the conditional mean end-of-period values of the derivative, and (2) that the tracking error has zero mean in all macroeconomic states of nature. We'll do these two steps using tables. In Figure 4.26, I calculate the end-of-period value of the tracking portfolio given each possible macroeconomic state/private risk outcome combination, and then I calculate the mean value of the tracking portfolio conditional upon each macroeconomic state of nature. Notice that the conditional means are $1.44 in the up state and $0 in the down state, which is exactly what we wanted.

To show that the tracking errors have zero conditional mean, I've constructed Figure 4.27. In that table, each cell contains the difference between the actual end-of-period value of the tracking portfolio (from Figure 4.26) with the actual end-of-period value of the option on the NONNF (from Figure 4.24). Notice that even though the tracking portfolio makes an error in every macro state/private risk outcome contingency, the conditional mean error (i.e., the expected

Figure 4.26	Conditional Mean End-of-Period Values of Tracking Portfolio With $H_{NONNF} = 0.32$ Units of *NONNF* and $\$H_{RF} = -\$0.1164$ Invested in Risk-Free Bond at 10% Interest		
		Tracking Portfolio Value Arising Due to Private Risk Outcome	
		Positive $pr_{POS} = 0.8$	Negative $pr_{NEG} = 0.2$	Conditional Mean Value of Tracking Portfolio
Macroeconomic outcomes	Economy strengthens	$0.32 \times \$5.30$ $-\$0.128 = \$1.568$	$0.32 \times \$3.30$ $-\$0.128 = \$0.928$	$0.8 \times \$1.568$ $+ 0.2 \times \$0.928 = \$1.44$
	Economy weakens	$0.32 \times \$0.45$ $-\$0.128 = \$0.016$	$0.32 \times \$0.20$ $-\$0.128 = -\$0.064$	$0.8 \times \$0.016$ $+ 0.2 \times (-\$0.064) = \$0$

| Figure 4.27 | Conditional Mean End-of-Period Tracking Portfolio Errors (Actual tracking portfolio values from Figure 4.26, actual derivative values from Figure 4.24) |

		Tracking Error Arising Due to Private Risk Outcome (actual tracking portfolio value minus actual derivative value)		Conditional Mean Value of Tracking Error
		Positive $pr_{POS} = 0.8$	Negative $pr_{NEG} = 0.2$	
Macroeconomic outcomes	Economy strengthens	$1.568 − $1.80 = −$0.232	$0.928 − $0 = $0.928	0.8 × (−$0.232) + 0.2 × $0.928 = $0
	Economy weakens	$0.016 − $0 = $0.016	−$0.064 − $0 = −$0.064	0.8 × $0.016 + 0.2 × (−$0.064) = $0

error within each macroeconomic state) is zero. So, the tracking error is worthless, and it is irrelevant to our valuation of the derivative.

In this valuation, we've decomposed the real option on the NONNF into three simple building blocks: the NONNF itself, the risk-free investment, and conditional mean-zero error. Figure 4.28 shows our building-block metaphor.

Figure 4.28 illustrates application of the market adjusted disclaimer (or MAD assumption) discussed in Copeland and Antikarov (2001): The appropriate underlying asset for a real option on a project is the project itself, treated as a now-or-never/no-flexibility opportunity. The reason we can do this is that the underlying project (the NONNF) itself can be recreated by a tracking portfolio of financial market building blocks. If you worked through Chapters 2 and 3 carefully, this will be familiar to you, so you can either skim the next few paragraphs or skip forward to the generalization. The rest of you should just keep reading.

Reconciling with the More Basic Building Blocks

To illustrate why we can treat the now-or-never/no-flexibility project as our real option's underlying asset and put it in our tracking portfolio, I'll show you that we could have valued the real option (i.e., the $3.50 call option on the NONNF) using our more basic economic building blocks: the market index fund and the risk-free bond. Here, we need to find the tracking portfolio holdings H_{Mkt} units of the market index fund and $$H_{RF}$ investment in the risk-free asset such that

| Figure 4.28 | Decomposing the Real Option on the NONNF into Three Building Blocks: The NONNF Itself, the Risk-Free Investment, and Conditional Mean-Zero Error |

Real option on NONNF wtih strike = $3.50	=	0.32 Units NONNF	+	−$0.1164 Risk-free investment	+	Conditional mean-zero error
Value	=	0.32 × Market value of NONNF	+	−$0.1164	+	0
$0.5236	=	0.32 × $2.00	+	−$0.1164	+	$0

Figure 4.29   **Evolution of Market Index Value and Associated Conditional Mean Values of Real Option on the NONNF**

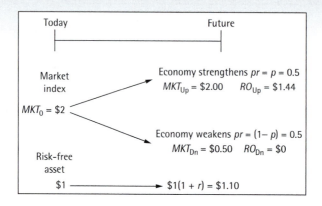

End-of-period value of tracking portfolio

$$= \begin{cases} H_{Mkt} \times MKT_{Up} + \$H_{RF} \times (1 + r) = RO_{Up} & \text{(strengthening economy)} \\ H_{Mkt} \times MKT_{Dn} + \$H_{RF} \times (1 + r) = RO_{Dn} & \text{(weakening economy)} \end{cases}$$

For our \$3.50 call option on the NONNF (the real option), $RO_{Up} = \$1.44$ and $RO_{Dn} = \$0$ (refer back to Figure 4.24 if you don't remember). And in our market, $MKT_0 = \$1$, $MKT_{Up} = \$2$, $MKT_{Dn} = \$0.50$ and $r = 10\%$. So we can look at our binomial world in the alternative way shown in Figure 4.29.

To value the real option in this context, we need to solve for H_{Mkt} and $\$H_{RF}$ such that

$$= \begin{cases} H_{Mkt} \times \$2.00 + \$H_{RF} \times (1.10) = \$1.44 & \text{(strengthening economy)} \\ H_{Mkt} \times \$0.50 + \$H_{RF} \times (1.10) = \$0 & \text{(weakening economy)} \end{cases} \qquad (4.3)$$

Once we've located the appropriate holdings H_{Mkt} and $\$H_{RF}$, the value of the tracking portfolio today will be

$$H_{Mkt} \times MKT_0 + \$H_{RF} = H_{Mkt} \times \$1.00 + \$H_{RF} \qquad (4.4)$$

and, given our price-taking and no-arbitrage assumptions, this must be the value of the real option as well.

Once again, solve simultaneous equations. To find the appropriate H_{Mkt}, subtract the weakening economy equation in (4.3) from the strengthening economy equation. The result is

$$\begin{array}{rl} H_{Mkt} \times \$2.00 + \$H_{RF} \times (1.10) = & \$1.44 \\ -(H_{Mkt} \times \$0.50 + \$H_{RF} \times (1.10) = & \$0) \\ \hline H_{Mkt} \times \$1.50 \qquad\qquad\qquad = & \$1.44 \end{array}$$

and so the tracking portfolio must contain $H_{Mkt} = \$1.44/\$1.50 = 0.96$ units of the market index fund. Now plug this back into the strengthening economy Equation in (4.3):

$$0.96 \times \$2.00 + \$H_{RF} \times (1.10) = \$1.44$$

or

$$\begin{aligned} \$H_{RF} &= \frac{1}{1.10}[\$1.44 - 0.96(\$2.00)] \\ &= \frac{-\$0.48}{1.10} \\ &= -\$0.4364 \end{aligned}$$

which, due to the negative sign, is borrowing $0.4364 at the risk-free rate of return (with a promised repayment obligation of $0.48 at the end of the period). From Equation (4.4), the value of the tracking portfolio is therefore

$$0.96 \times \$1.00 + (-\$0.4364) = \$0.5236$$

and so, given our price-taking and no-arbitrage assumptions, the value of the real option must also be $0.5236.

Notice that this is exactly the value of the real option that we calculated earlier when we used the NONNF as our underlying asset in our tracking portfolio. If it weren't, there would be an arbitrage opportunity. Figure 4.30 shows our visual building blocks interpretation.

To make sure you understand, I want to reconcile the building block decomposition of the real option on the NONNF in Figure 4.30 with the different building block decomposition of the same real option in Figure 4.28. This is simple. When we built a tracking portfolio the traditional way by combining the NONNF itself with the risk-free bond to track the real option on the NONNF, our tracking portfolio contained 0.32 units of the NONNF along with −$0.1164 invested in the risk-free bond (borrowing):

$$\text{Traditional tracking portfolio} = \begin{cases} H_{NONNF} = 0.32 \text{ units } NONNF \\ \$H_{RF} = -\$0.1164 \text{ invested in risk-free asset} \end{cases}$$

But recall the very first valuation we performed in this section: One unit of the NONNF decomposes into three units of the market index fund and −$1 invested in the risk-free bond (see Figure 4.22):

$$\text{One unit NONNF} = \begin{cases} H_{Mkt} = 3 \text{ shares market index fund} \\ \$H_{RF} = -\$1 \text{ invested in risk-free asset} \end{cases}$$

Figure 4.30	Decomposing the Real Option on the NONNF into Three Building Blocks: The Market Index Fund, the Risk-Free Investment, and Conditional Mean-Zero Error

Real option on NONNF wtih strike = $3.50	=	0.96 Units market index	+	−$0.4364 Risk-free investment	+	Conditional mean-zero error
Value	=	0.96 × Share price of market index	+	−$0.4364	+	0
$0.5236	=	0.96 × $1.00	+	−$0.4364	+	$0

So combining the two,

$$\text{Traditional tracking portfolio} = \begin{cases} 0.32 \times \text{One unit of NONNF} \\ -\$0.1164 \text{ invested in risk-free asset} \end{cases}$$

$$\begin{cases} 0.32 \times \begin{cases} 3 \text{ shares market index fund} \\ -\$1 \text{ invested in risk-free asset} \end{cases} \\ -\$0.1164 \text{ invested in risk-free asset} \end{cases}$$

$$= \begin{cases} 0.96 \text{ shares market index fund} \\ -\$0.32 \text{ invested in risk-free asset} \\ -\$0.1164 \text{ invested in risk-free asset} \end{cases}$$

$$= \begin{cases} 0.96 \text{ shares market index fund} = H_{Mkt} \\ -\$0.4364 \text{ invested in risk-free asset} = \$H_{RF} \end{cases}$$

$$= \text{Nontraditional tracking portfolio}$$

which shows that the two approaches are actually accomplishing the same thing: linear pricing by an arbitrage with a similar-risk financial market portfolio.

Whenever we work with a risky asset as our underlying in any option pricing model, we are *implicitly* working with a bundle of financial market building-block securities (plus conditional mean-zero error), even if we don't know it. The current arbitrage-free financial market value of *any* asset reflects the equilibrium values of the primitive building blocks (the market index and the risk-free bond). So if we can observe the arbitrage-free financial market value of a new corporate asset, then we can use that asset as the underlying in a derivatives valuation *even if the new asset itself is not traded*. The reason is simple: Even though the new asset is not traded, there exists an equivalent tracking portfolio of financial market building blocks which *is* traded—and (given our assumptions of price taking and arbitrage free markets) the new asset and its financial market tracking portfolio are substitutes.

In other words, we can dispense with our market index altogether when we form tracking portfolios to value options (financial or real). What I'll show you now is the general rule for forming an appropriate tracking portfolio using the underlying and the risk-free asset.

Generalization

In any binomial world, let UND_0 be the current arbitrage-free value of your *underlying* asset, UND_{Up} be the value of your underlying asset in the up state (i.e., the strengthening economy), and UND_{Dn} be the value of your underlying asset in the down state (i.e., the weakening economy). Furthermore, let $DERIV_{Up}$ be the value of a derivative on your underlying asset in the up state, and let $DERIV_{Dn}$ be the value of the same derivative on your underlying asset in the down state.[5] Finally, let r be the risk-free rate of return over the binomial time step. Figure 4.31 illustrates this.

---

[5] If there is idiosyncratic risk in either the derivative or the underlying, then these can be conditional means.

Figure 4.31

A Generalized Binomial World

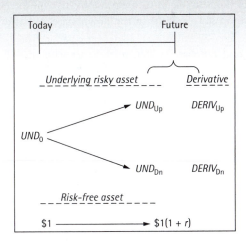

In this binomial world, the current arbitrage-free value of the derivative, $DERIV_0$, will be

$$DERIV_0 = \Delta \times UND_0 + \$\Psi \tag{4.5}$$

where Δ (the units of UND held in the tracking portfolio) and $\$\Psi$ (the tracking portfolio's investment in the risk-free asset) satisfy the following two simultaneous equations:

$$\Delta \times UND_{Up} + \$\Psi \times (1 + r) = DERIV_{Up} \tag{4.6}$$
$$\Delta \times UND_{Dn} + \$\Psi \times (1 + r) = DERIV_{Dn}$$

The general solutions for Δ and $\$\Psi$ are easy to generate. Subtract the second equation in (4.6) from the first to get

$$\Delta \times UND_{Up} + \$\Psi \times (1 + r) = DERIV_{Up}$$
$$-(\Delta \times UND_{Dn} + \$\Psi \times (1 + r) = DERIV_{Dn})$$
$$\Delta(UND_{Up} - UND_{Dn}) = (DERIV_{Up} - DERIV_{Dn})$$

so the solution for the units of the underlying in the tracking portfolio must be

$$\Delta = \frac{DERIV_{Up} - DERIV_{Dn}}{UND_{Up} - UND_{Dn}} \tag{4.7}$$

and now plug this back into the first equation in (4.6) and rearrange to get the solution for the tracking portfolio's investment in the risk-free asset:

$$\$\Psi = \frac{1}{1 + r}[DERIV_{Up} - \Delta \times UND_{Up}] \tag{4.8}$$

Valuing a derivative in this binomial world is a simple four-step process. First, determine the end-of-period state-contingent payoffs on the derivative. Second, use Equations (4.7) and (4.8) to solve for the tracking portfolio holdings Δ and $\$\Psi$. Third, plug these solutions into Equation (4.5) to get the value of the tracking portfolio. Finally, impose our no-arbitrage assumption (as well as the price-taking assumptions if in a corporate setting) and conclude that the value of the derivative must be equal to the value of the tracking portfolio.

Let's do some examples. In the first two examples, we'll price simple derivatives on the NONNF. In the third and fourth, we'll price derivatives on the market index.

Example 4.1

To see an illustration, let's suppose that you create a derivative on the NONNF with conditional mean payoff of $1 in the up state and $0 in the down state. What is the current value of this new derivative?

Here, $DERIV_{Up} = \$1$ and $DERIV_{Dn} = \$0$. In this case, the NONNF is our underlying asset so $UND_0 = \$2$, $UND_{Up} = \$4.90$, and $UND_{Dn} = \$0.40$ (see Figure 4.25). Finally, we know that $r = 10\%$. So Equation (4.7) tells us that the tracking portfolio that replicates this new derivative must be long 0.222 units of the underlying NONNF:

$$\Delta = \frac{DERIV_{Up} - DERIV_{Dn}}{UND_{Up} - UND_{Dn}} = \frac{\$1 - \$0}{\$4.90 - \$0.40} = \frac{\$1}{\$4.50} = 0.2222$$

Furthermore, Equation (4.8) indicates that the tracking portfolio must borrow $0.0808 at the risk-free rate of return:

$$\$\Psi = \frac{1}{1 + r}[DERIV_{Up} - \Delta \times UND_{Up}] = \frac{1}{1.10}[\$1 - (0.2222) \times \$4.90] = \frac{-\$0.0888}{1.10} = -\$0.0808$$

(The negative sign for the $\$\Psi$ solution means that you take a short position in the risk-free bond, or borrow $0.0808 at the risk-free rate of return; the promised end-of-period repayment of principal plus interest is $0.0808 \times 1.10 = \$0.0888$.) Using Equation (4.5), the current value of the derivative must be $0.3636:

$$DERIV_0 = \Delta \times UND_0 + \$\Psi = 0.2222 \times \$2 + (-\$0.0808) = \$0.3636$$

Example 4.2

For our next example, let's suppose that you create a derivative on the NONNF with conditional mean value of $0 in the up state (the strengthening economy) and $1 in the down state (the weakening economy). What is the current value of this new derivative?

Here, $DERIV_{Up} = \$0$ and $DERIV_{Dn} = \$1$. We've already determined that $UND_0 = \$2$, $UND_{Up} = \$4.90$, and $UND_{Dn} = \$0.40$. Finally, we know that $r = 10\%$. From Equation (4.7), the tracking portfolio that replicates this new derivative must be *short* 0.222 units of the UND:

$$\Delta = \frac{DERIV_{Up} - DERIV_{Dn}}{UND_{Up} - UND_{Dn}} = \frac{\$0 - \$1}{\$4.90 - \$0.40} = \frac{-\$1}{\$4.50} = -0.2222$$

(the negative sign for the Δ solution means that you take a short position in the UND). Furthermore, from Equation (4.8) we learn that the tracking portfolio must invest $0.9899 in the risk-free bond:

$$\$\Psi = \frac{1}{1 + r}[DERIV_{Up} - \Delta \times UND_{Up}] = \frac{1}{1.10}[\$0 - (-0.2222) \times \$4.90] = \$0.9899$$

(The positive sign for the $\$\Psi$ solution means that you take a long position in the risk-free bond, or lend at the risk-free rate of return.) From Equation (4.5) we must conclude that the current value of the derivative is $0.5455:

$$DERIV_0 = \Delta \times UND_0 + \$\Psi = -0.2222 \times \$2 + \$0.9899 = \$0.5455$$

Example 4.3

This example is a derivative written on the market index. It's very exotic, so I call it the *Richard.* The end-of-period value of the Richard is quite unique: It pays off the square of the market index value if the market index goes up, and the logarithm of the market index value if the market index goes down. In other words, if the market index (our underlying in this problem) goes up to \$2, the value of the Richard (our derivative in this case) will be $\$(2)^2 = \$4$; if the underlying (our market index) goes down to \$0.50, our derivative (the Richard) will be worth $\$\ln(0.50) = -\$0.6931$.[6] Since the market index is our underlying asset, we write that $UND_0 = \$1$, $UND_{Up} = \$2$, and $UND_{Dn} = \$0.50$. The Richard is the derivative, and so we can say its value when the underlying goes up is $DERIV_{Up} = \$4$, and its value when the underlying goes down is $DERIV_{Dn} = -\$0.6931$. Since we know that $r = 10\%$, we can use Equations (4.7) and (4.8) to work out that the appropriate tracking portfolio has $\Delta = 3.128$ units of the underlying asset (in other words, 3.128 shares of the market index)

$$\Delta = \frac{DERIV_{Up} - DERIV_{Dn}}{UND_{Up} - UND_{Dn}} = \frac{\$4 - (-\$0.6931)}{\$2 - \$0.50} = 3.128$$

and $-\$2.0509$ invested in the risk-free bond (that is, borrow \$2.0509 at 10% interest, and promise to repay $\$2.0509 \times 1.10 = \$2.256$).

$$\$\Psi = \frac{1}{1+r}[DERIV_{Up} - \Delta \times UND_{Up}] = \frac{1}{(1.10)}[\$4 - (3.128)\$2] = \frac{1}{(1.10)}(-\$2.256) = -\$2.0509$$

So given our no-arbitrage assumption, the value of the Richard must be equal to the value of the tracking portfolio, which Equation (4.5) tells us is \$1.077:

$$DERIV_0 = \Delta \times UND_0 + \$\Psi = 3.128 \times \$1 + (-\$2.0506) = \$1.077$$

I leave it to the reader to check that the tracking portfolio provides the right conditional mean payoffs in each macroeconomic state. I also urge the reader to confirm that we could have priced the Richard using the NONNF in our tracking portfolio (instead of the market index). Keep the derivative payoffs the same in the up and down states, but set $UND_0 = \$2$, $UND_{Up} = \$4.90$, and $UND_{Dn} = \$0.40$ and redo the tracking portfolio calculations. You'll get a different solution for Δ and $\$\Psi$, but you'll end up with the same value of the Richard (\$1.077). If you've gone this far, make sure you check to see that the tracking portfolio error has zero mean given each macro-economic state of nature.

Before we go to the last derivative example, I'd like to provide a geometric interpretation of why the tracking portfolio method works in our binomial world. To price the Richard, we constructed a tracking portfolio that contained 3.128 units of the market index fund and a promised debt obligation of \$2.256. So given *any* terminal value of the underlying, we can determine the corresponding value of the tracking portfolio. I've plotted the end-of-period value of the tracking portfolio given *any* ending market index value in Figure 4.32.

Notice that our tracking portfolio fits a line that passes through the two possible payoffs on the Richard in our simple economy. A well-known result of geometry is that any two points define a unique line. What we are doing with this simple method is reconstructing the *function*

---

[6] It is not uncommon to have a derivative with a future cash liability in some states of nature. Futures contracts, swaps, and short position in standard calls and puts are all examples of this.

Figure 4.32   End-of-Period Value of Tracking Portfolio as a Function of Market Index Value (Δ = 3.122, $\$\Psi$ = −$2.256)

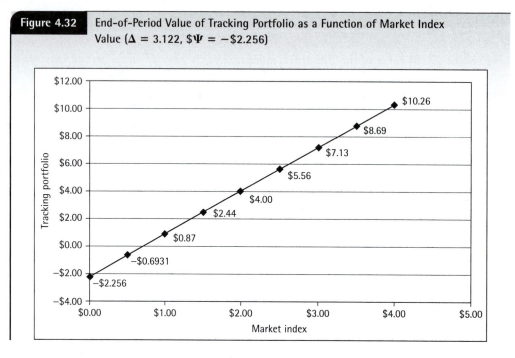

of the line that maps the value of the market index to the conditional mean payoffs on the Richard by using the information that is contained in the known parts. Note how we do this. We start with a plot of the conditional mean cash flows on the Richard against the corresponding end-of-period values of the market index, shown in Figure 4.33.

Figure 4.33   Plot of Conditional Mean Cash Flows on the "Richard" Derivative Against Possible Values of Market Index

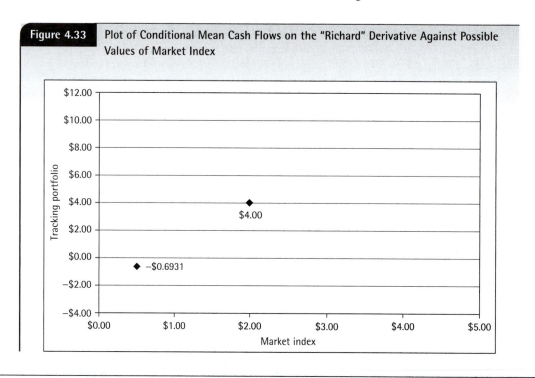

The slope of the line connecting the two points is the rise over the run, or

$$\frac{\$4 - (-\$0.6931)}{\$2 - \$0.5} = 3.128 = \Delta$$

And recall from Equation (4.7) that

$$\Delta = \frac{DERIV_{Up} - DERIV_{Dn}}{UND_{Up} - UND_{Dn}} = \frac{\$4 - (-\$0.6931)}{\$2 - \$0.5}$$

which is the very same thing! Further, once we know the slope we can solve for the intercept. Simply plug in a known point that the function passes through, like $(UND_{Up}, DERIV_{Up})$.

$$DERIV_{Up} = Intercept + 3.128 \times UND_{Up}$$

so

$$Intercept = DERIV_{Up} - 3.128 \times UND_{Up} = DERIV_{Up} - \Delta \times UND_{Up}$$

Recall from Equation (4.8) that

$$\$\Psi = \frac{1}{(1 + r)} [DERIV_{Up} - \Delta UND_{Up}].$$

This is just the *y*-intercept, time-adjusted by the risk-free discount factor $1/(1 + r)$. Our geometric result looks like this:

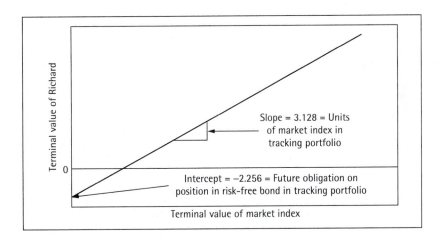

The geometric interpretation illustrates the essence of the binomial model: linearity. That is, any asset's conditional mean end-of-period value is linear in the market index. This translates nicely into a smooth real world, in a way you may have seen before.

If you've ever taken an introductory calculus class, you will recall that well-behaved functions are approximately linear at any point if you look at very small areas around that point. Once you accept the approximate linearity at a point, you can do things like calculate the slope of the function at that point by determining the slope of the line in the small region around that point:

$$\lim_{\Delta x \to 0} \frac{f(x + \Delta x) - f(x)}{(x + \Delta x) - x}$$

Figure 4.34	End-of-Period Values of Long and Short Forwards on Market Index Fund

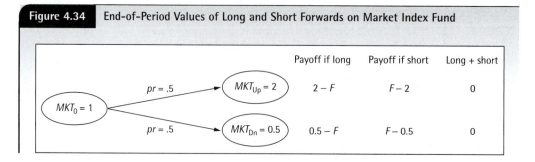

which is the standard definition of a mathematical derivative. This, in turn, allows you to perform tasks of integration (like determining the area under a curve) by constructing small rectangles and calculating their area. Approximating everything as linear over very small distances is a foundation of basic calculus.

This intuition applies to what we are doing *over time*. It is true that the world is complex, and that an asset's future value will not be drawn from a fixed number of discrete points but rather from a continuous distribution. But as long as we can shrink *time* down into small units, we can think of the world as being linear over that very small time period. And if the world is linear over that short time span, the binomial model is quite appropriate.

Example 4.4

Our final example will be another derivative written on the market index, but this one comes with a little twist. We're going to price a *forward* on the market index.[7] Recall that a forward purchase or sale is an agreement to purchase or sell an asset at a future date at a *prespecified* price. There is no exchange of money or asset at the current point in time, but the *forward price* is determined when the contract is struck. Let's denote the forward price by F. If you are long forward, you must pay F at the end of the period and receive a unit of the market index fund (regardless of its worth at that time). If you are short forward, you must deliver one unit of the market index fund at the end of the period and receive F in return. Figure 4.34 gives the end-of-period values of the long and short positions in a forward on the market index. In this case, the actual payoffs on the long and short positions are the conditional mean values, because there is no idiosyncratic outcome that can alter the payoffs in either state.

Since the payoffs on long and short positions are exact negatives of each other, a long and a short position at the same forward price exactly cancel each other out. Any gains to a party going long come at the expense of another party that is short, and vice versa.

The question is this: In our world, what is the forward price F that provides no free lunch? Whenever I pose this question to a class, I can be confident that at least one student in the class will quickly respond that F should equal $1.25, as that's the expected price of the underlying (the market index) at the time that forwards are settled up. You may think this, too. And if you do, you are wrong. If the forward price is $F = \$1.25$, then there's an arbitrage opportunity.

If the forward price is $1.25, then I'm going to go short forward (i.e., agree to deliver one share of the market index in the future and receive $1.25 at that time). Simultaneously, I'm

---

[7] In a world like our binomial economy where the risk-free rate of return is constant, the forward price will be identical to the futures price.

Figure 4.35	Arbitrage Profits If F = $1.25		
	CF today	CF if asset = $2	CF if asset = $0.5
Buy low–buy tracking portfolio			
Long 1 unit risky asset	−$1.000	$2.00	$0.50
Borrow $1.136	+$1.136	−$1.25	−$1.25
Sell high			
Short foward @ F = $1.25	$0.000	−$0.75	$0.75
Total cash flows	$0.136	$0.00	$0.00

going to borrow as much as I can against my future cash inflow. Since I'll have $1.25 guaranteed cash inflow in the future from my short forward position, I can borrow $1.25/1.10 = $1.136 today (and my repayment obligation will obviously be $1.25).

Finally, I'm going to use some of my borrowings to go ahead and buy one share of the market index fund, so I know I'll have a unit to deliver when my short position comes due. Figure 4.35 shows my overall position.

What Figure 4.35 indicates is that if the forward price is $1.25, then there is a money machine—I can make a $0.136 immediate profit with no future obligation by *synthetically replicating* (i.e., manufacturing) the forward position. Now you see why it is fair for me to borrow at the risk-free rate—if I'm truly arbitraging, I'm not taking any risk, but I am reaping a sure reward. Thus, the proper discount rate on the loan is the risk-free rate. But, of course, there are others who will do the same thing, and market prices will quickly adjust to the point where the arbitrage profits evaporate. So, at what forward price will there be no arbitrage opportunity?

We attack this just as before. In this case, the market index is our underlying asset so $UND_0 = \$1$, $UND_{Up} = \$2$, and $UND_{Dn} = \$0.50$. The derivative is the forward, and its payoff is $DERIV_{Up} = \$2 - F$ in the up state and $DERIV_{Dn} = \$0.50 - F$ (we'll solve for F at the end). The *delta* of the forward from Equation (4.7) is the number of units of the underlying held in the tracking portfolio, which is exactly 1:

$$\Delta = \frac{DERIV_{Up} - DERIV_{Dn}}{UND_{Up} - UND_{Dn}} = \frac{(\$2 - F) - (\$0.5 - F)}{\$2 - \$0.5} = 1$$

and the risk-free borrowing/lending in the tracking portfolio from Equation (4.8) is the present value of the forward price (whatever it may be):

$$\$\Psi = \frac{1}{(1 + r)} [DERIV_{Up} - \Delta UND_{Up}] = \frac{1}{(1.10)} [(\$2 - F) - 1 \times \$2] = \frac{-F}{(1.10)}$$

And here's the trick: Since no money changes hands right away, the current value of the forward must be zero so the tracking portfolio must be worth exactly zero. Using Equation (4.5), we can solve for the arbitrage-free forward price:

$$DERIV_0 = \Delta \times UND_0 + \$\Psi$$

$$\$0 = 1 \times \$1 + \left(\frac{-F}{1.10}\right)$$

$$F = \$1 \times (1.10) = \$1.10$$

I mentioned that many of my students will think that the correct forward price is $1.25 because the expected spot price is $1.25. What this example shows is that the forward price is *not* the expected value of the future spot price. In fact, the forward price does not explicitly involve the probabilities (or magnitudes) of an up or down movement. The forward price is simply $F = UND_0 (1 + r)$

The important point here is that the forward price is *forced* by the risk-free rate and the current value of the underlying. It is forced in this way because there is *always* a way to manufacture (i.e., track) the forward contract. The forward price is not the expected spot price in the future, nor is it the present value of the expected spot price.

$$F \neq \frac{p \times UND_{Up} + (1 - p) \times UND_{Dn}}{(1 + r)^t}$$
$$F = UND_0(1 + r)^t$$

(Of course, here we are assuming that there is costless storage of the underlying and that it yields no cash flow when holding it. We will relax these assumptions in Chapter 9 and see how they change the analysis.)

An Important Learning Point

There's one overarching learning point that you should take from all of the valuation examples we've done in this section. So far, we have valued several real options on the NONNF project, a forward on the market, and the strangest thing you've ever seen (the Richard) and we never once used a probability or a risk-adjusted discount rate. For all of these derivatives valuations, the only inputs we needed were the current price of the underlying asset, the underlying asset's conditional mean values in the up and down macroeconomic states, the derivative's conditional mean values in the up and down macroeconomic states, and the risk-free rate of return.

This is extremely general, and it is a point that I will hammer at several more times. In our binomial financial market, the value of *any asset* is *forced* by the current price of the market index fund, the risk-free rate of return, and the conditional mean payoffs on the asset. This is simply linear pricing in action. Where do the probabilities go? How does the risk adjustment take place?

As it turns out, the market does all of the hard work for us—if we can observe current market values, all that's left for us to do is to form appropriate tracking portfolios. What is really amazing (and time saving for us) is that the very tight structure of an arbitrage-free financial market gives us an incredibly simple way to form tracking portfolios in a binomial world—a way that is so simple that it often does not require even a calculator to compute. Moreover, this simplified approach will allow me to tie together the traditional and nontraditional tracking portfolio approaches to valuing the real option on the NONNF. To get to that simplification, we need to understand just how extraordinarily interconnected everything in an arbitrage-free market must be. That is the subject of the next section.

4.3   The Amazing Theory of Risk-Neutral Pricing

To value a derivative in our binomial world as pictured in Figure 4.31, all we need to do is use Equations (4.7) and (4.8) to solve for the tracking portfolio holdings and then plug these numbers into Equation (4.5) to get the value of the derivative. While it is true that the probabilities of future events and risk-adjusted rates of return do not appear anywhere in these three equations, you should not conclude that a derivative's value is invariant to the probability that it pays off or to its risk. Probabilities of future events and risk are important—we've simply found a way to do the valuation without needing to know them. I'll try to provide an intuitive explanation, and I'll follow that with a more formal presentation.

Where Have All the Probabilities Gone?

To get an idea of where the probabilities come into play, perform the following thought experiment. Suppose there are only two macrostates which capture the condition of the world at the end of next year: Global thermonuclear war (war) and peace on Earth (peace). At the time of this writing, the probability of war next year is quite slim. But what if war were to become a significant possibility?

If war were to become more likely, we would expect the prices of many goods to change. Items like tanning beds and snow blowers would become virtually worthless, while nonperishable foods, bottled water, and weapons would become quite valuable. As the probability of war changes, the price of water changes, and the price of any *derivative* written on water (such as a forward or an option) would change accordingly. The derivative's value is a direct function of the value of the underlying (water), and the equilibrium value of the underlying (water) is in turn a function of the market's aggregate assessment of the probabilities of future states (war and peace). So, when we value a derivative through the tracking portfolio method, we are implicitly capturing the probabilities of future states through our use of the current prices of the assets in our tracking portfolio. The competitive market for the tracking portfolio assets assesses the probabilities of future states and takes these into account in setting their equilibrium market prices. Thus, we don't need to even consider the probabilities of future states—that work has already been done for us through the market's valuation of the tracking assets.

In the context of our basic example from the previous section, the $1 equilibrium price of the market index depends critically on the probabilities of the future states. If the probabilities of future states change, the value of our market portfolio today will change. This will then change the value of any derivatives we might introduce.

But What About Risk?

We calculated the value of the forward, the Richard, and several other derivatives without ever using a risk-adjusted discount rate. How is this possible? The answer is exactly the same as for the issue of probabilities: The current equilibrium market values of the assets in the tracking portfolio already capture it. If the market's aggregate risk aversion changes, then the market value of the tracking assets will change, and the value of a derivative that is tracked by those assets must change as well.

I'd like to reiterate a point I made in Chapter 2. Whenever we do an arbitrage valuation (whether it is the valuation of a derivative or the DCF valuation of some new asset), we take the prices of existing securities as given. In other words, we ignore how the equilibrium comes about. But equilibrium is always right below the surface, and if anything changes the equilibrium, then the value of anything priced via an arbitrage argument will change as well. What goes into the determination of an equilibrium? Risk aversion, for one thing, along with beliefs about the future, endowments, utility of consumption, production opportunities, and investment opportunities.

Just *how* equilibrium prices account for risk aversion is a tremendously important issue and one that we need to understand to more fully comprehend the valuation of options (real and financial). In my mind, this next section is the most critical in the book.

Figure 4.36   The Evolution of the Market Index, and the Payoffs on the Red and Blue Derivatives

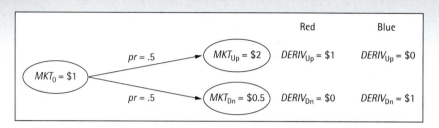

Two Very Important Derivatives

Maintaining the same economy we worked with in the previous section (illustrated in Figure 4.18), let's now consider two different derivatives. One we will call a Red, and the other we will call a Blue. The Red pays off $1 if the market index goes *up* in value and $0 otherwise; the Blue pays off $1 if the market goes *down* in value and $0 otherwise. I've drawn the evolution of the market index and the payoffs on the Red and the Blue derivatives in Figure 4.36; the risk-free rate of return is 10%.

There's a reason I call these particular derivatives the Red and the Blue. The Red pays off when the market is going up, when the economy is *Red hot*. The Blue, on the other hand, pays off when the market is going down—when we've *got the Blues*. Even though I can't use color in this text, I like using the titles *Red* and *Blue* as memory posts.

At first blush, the Red and the Blue look very similar. They both pay off $1 with 50% probability and $0 otherwise, so the expected value of each is $0.50. It turns out, however, that the Red and the Blue are very different.

Let's start by valuing the Red. Using Equations (4.7) and (4.8), the tracking portfolio for our Red will contain

$$\Delta(Red) = \frac{\$1 - \$0}{\$2 - \$0.5} = 0.6667 \text{ units of the market index}$$

and

$$\$\Psi(Red) = \frac{1}{(1.10)}[\$1 - .6667(\$2)] = -\frac{\$0.3334}{(1.10)} = -\$0.3031 \text{ invested in the risk-free asset.}$$

Therefore, (4.5) tells us that the current value of the Red must be $0.3636:

$$\text{Current value of Red} = 0.6667(\$1) + (-\$0.3031) = \$0.3636$$

Notice something here: This is the exact same answer we got for the derivative in Example 4.1. In that problem, the derivative had a conditional mean payoff of $1 if the NONNF went up and $0 if it went down. It is not coincidental that the values are the same. We will explore this at length in just a few moments.

Now let's turn to the Blue. Using Equations (4.7) and (4.8), we learn that our Blue tracking portfolio will contain

$$\Delta(Blue) = \frac{\$0 - \$1}{\$2 - \$0.5} = -0.6667 \text{ units of the market index}$$

and

$$\$\Psi(Blue) = \frac{1}{(1.10)} [\$0 - (-0.6667)(\$2)] = \frac{\$1.3334}{(1.10)} = \$1.2122 \text{ invested in the risk-free bond}$$

From Equation (4.5), the value of the Blue must be

$$\text{Current value of blue} = -0.6667(\$1) + \$1.2122 = \$0.5455$$

Before we go on, notice that the Blue derivative has a negative (i.e., short) position in the market index and a positive (long) position in the risk-free bond. In our geometric interpretation, the function has a positive intercept (a future *inflow*) and a negative slope. What this means is that we are *selling* (shorting) the underlying asset and using those proceeds, along with some more money, to *buy* the risk-free bond (i.e., to lend). The net cost of this portfolio is $0.5455, so that is what the derivative should be worth. The Blue is a *put option*, and puts always involve short positions in the underlying and long investment in the risk-free bond.

But back to the point. The first thing that you should have noticed is that the price of the Blue is *higher* than the price of the Red. How could this be? Each is equally likely (the probability of up equals the probability of down), and the payoff on each is $1, so the expected future cash flow on each is $0.50. Moreover, the standard deviation of cash flows is $0.50 for either one. How then could the Blue be worth more than the Red?

The answer to this question lies at the very heart of modern finance. Securities which pay off $1 in exactly one future state of nature and zero in all others (like the Red and the Blue) are called *state* securities, and in equilibrium their relative prices must obey the following relationship:[8]

$$\frac{\text{Current value of Blue}}{\text{Current value of Red}}$$
$$= \frac{pr(\text{Blue pays off}) \times \text{Marginal utility of consumption if Blue pays off}}{pr(\text{Red pays off}) \times \text{Marginal utility of consumption if Red pays off}} \quad (4.9)$$

Since we've constructed our world such that the Red and the Blue pay off with equal likelihood, then in our world of Figure 4.18, Equation (4.9) reduces to

$$\frac{\text{Current value of Blue}}{\text{Current value of Red}} = \frac{\text{Marginal utility of consumption if Blue pays off}}{\text{Marginal utility of consumption if Red pays off}} \quad (4.10)$$

which means that the difference in prices between the two must be explained by differences in marginal utility.

Perhaps the most basic assumption of economics is that individuals are risk averse; that is, uncertainty about future consumption decreases utility. Economists capture risk aversion by

---

[8] In the neoclassical consumer's consumption/investment choice problem, the following first-order condition must hold for every state ω:

$$\pi_\omega U'(c_\omega) = \lambda p_\omega$$

where π_ω, c_ω, and p_ω are the probability, consumption, and state price for state ω, and $\lambda = U_0'(c_0)$ is the marginal utility of wealth. So for any two distinct states $\omega \neq \omega'$,

$$\frac{\pi_\omega U'(c_\omega)}{\pi_{\omega'} U'(c_{\omega'})} = \frac{p_\omega}{p_{\omega'}}$$

The state prices can be shadow prices if the state securities are not traded directly.

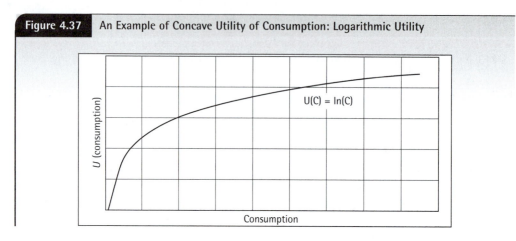

Figure 4.37 An Example of Concave Utility of Consumption: Logarithmic Utility

assuming that utility functions are *concave* in consumption (meaning that they are increasing, but increasing at a decreasing rate). As an example, consider the following concave utility function that we use quite frequently in economics:

$$U(C) = \ln(C)$$

(defined over $C > 0$). We call this logarithmic (or log) utility. Remember—this is just an example of concavity; see Figure 4.37.

If a consumer in our simple economy has a logarithmic utility function (as pictured in Figure 4.37), the consumer's *marginal utility of consumption* would be $U'(C) = 1/C$, shown in Figure 4.38.

Again, the specific function is just for illustration—the shape is what's important. What we can conclude from Equation (4.10) is that since the price of the Blue is greater than the price of the Red in our hypothetical economy, then marginal utility of consumption when the Blue pays off must be higher than the marginal utility of consumption when the Red pays off. By looking at Figure 4.38, we can see that marginal utility is decreasing in consumption—so it must be that the Blue pays off in low consumption states while the Red pays off in high consumption states. In other words, the up state is not just characterized by the market index going up, but more essentially by the entire economy strengthening. Similarly, the down state is not just the risky asset going down, but rather

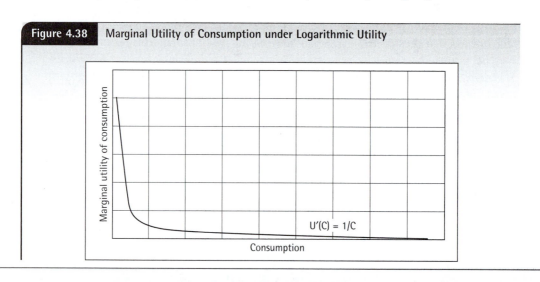

Figure 4.38 Marginal Utility of Consumption under Logarithmic Utility

the entire economy weakening. This is why I call them Red and Blue: The Red pays off when the economy is Red hot, while the Blue pays off when the economy's got the Blues. Remember?

The Red derivative pays off in high-consumption states, while the Blue derivative pays off in low-consumption states. As you can see from Figure 4.38, marginal utility is higher in low-consumption states. The marginal utility of the Blue is higher than the marginal utility of the Red, and so the price of the Blue must thus be higher than the price of the Red.

Amazing, isn't it! What is really intriguing, however, is the implication that this most basic analysis has on discount rates. Recall that the Red and the Blue pay off the same amount, $1, with equal probability, 50%. If both have the same expected cash flow but different prices, the discount rate used on the two derivatives must be the culprit. In fact, it must be that we are discounting the Blue at a *lower* rate of return than the Red:

$$\text{Current value of Red} = \frac{0.5(\$1) + 0.5(\$0)}{1 + r_{Red}} = \$0.3636 \quad \text{so} \quad r_{Red} = 37.5\%$$

$$\text{Current value of Blue} = \frac{0.5(\$0) + 0.5(\$1)}{1 + r_{Blue}} = \$0.5455 \quad \text{so} \quad r_{Blue} = -8.34\%.$$

That's right: The Red is riskier than the Blue. This is the most basic illustration of the notion of *risk* that I can think of: Risk is a function of the *distribution* of an asset's potential cash flows *across possible macroeconomic states*. More specifically, risk concerns how poorly an asset pays off in low-consumption states of nature. The more poorly an asset performs in low consumption states, the more risky it is. Because the Blue pays off well in the low consumption state, it is less risky than the Red.[9]

If you're keeping up, you probably noticed something interesting. The current price of the Blue, which is $0.5455, is actually higher than its expected payoff of $0.50. This, in turn, implies a negative discount rate for the Blue. Is it reasonable for people to pay more than the expected value of a risky asset and expect a negative rate of return?

Of course it is reasonable—this is why the insurance industry exists. If we purchase the Blue derivative, we are insuring against the economy going down—and since we have concave utility, we are willing to pay more for insurance against the economy going down than for insurance against the economy going up. My friend Scott Smart puts it intuitively: We're willing to pay more for insurance that pays off only when we are hungry (the Blue) than for insurance that pays off only when we are full (the Red).

Linear Pricing via Tracking Portfolios That Only Contain State Securities (the Red and the Blue)

When we break the world down like this, we see that every security is just a package of Reds and Blues. What this means, then, is that it is just as legitimate to form tracking portfolios using Reds and Blues as it is to use the market index and the risk-free bond (or any other underlying asset, for that matter) for our valuation problems. The Red and Blue state securities are the atomic particles that make up everything in the economy—including our original molecular building blocks (the market index and the risk-free bond).

---

[9] This is precisely why it is difficult to value options—real or financial—with decision trees. If the branches of a decision tree correspond with macroeconomic states of nature, then you must determine a unique risk-adjusted discount rate for each branch.

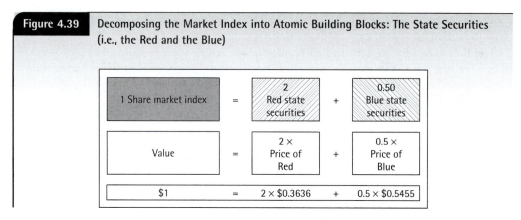

Figure 4.39   Decomposing the Market Index into Atomic Building Blocks: The State Securities (i.e., the Red and the Blue)

Let me show you. We can form an atomic tracking portfolio that tracks the market index by purchasing 2 Reds (giving us a $2 payoff in the up state but nothing in the down state) and $\frac{1}{2}$ of one Blue (giving us nothing in the up state but $0.50 payoff in the down state). Our total payoff, then, will exactly match the market index: $2 in the up state and $0.50 in the down state. Since a Red currently costs $0.3636, and a Blue currently costs $0.5455, the price of this tracking portfolio containing only Reds and Blues will be 2 × $0.3636 + 1/2 × $0.5455 = $1.00, which is exactly the current price of the market index fund share. In Figure 4.39, I show this using the building-blocks metaphor.

For a second illustration, build a tracking portfolio that contains exactly one Red and one Blue. This particular portfolio will pay off exactly $1 no matter what happens in the future, and its cost is 1($0.3636) + 1($0.5455) = $0.909. Since it is risk-free, it must be appropriate to discount the payoff on the portfolio at the risk-free rate, so it should be worth $1/(1.10) = $0.909. Exactly right. Our risk-free bond is really a portfolio of one Red and one Blue (see Figure 4.40).

For a third example, let's track our original NONNF with Reds and Blues. Recall that in Figure 4.23 the conditional mean end-of-period values of the NONNF are $4.90 in the strengthening economic state and $0.40 in the weakening economic state. To replicate this payoff structure with our atomic building blocks, simply buy 4.9 Reds and 0.4 Blues. The current value of this alternative tracking portfolio is 4.9($0.3636) + 0.4($0.5455) = $2, which is exactly the financial market value of the NONNF that we calculated before using an alternative tracking portfolio as well as via DCF (see Figure 4.41).

Figure 4.40   Decomposing the Risk-Free Bond into Atomic Building Blocks: The State Securities (i.e., the Red and the Blue)

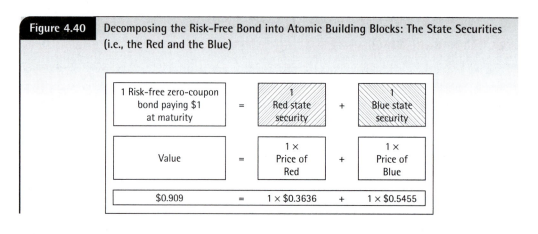

Figure 4.41   Decomposing the NONNF into Atomic Building Blocks: The State Securities (i.e., the Red and the Blue)

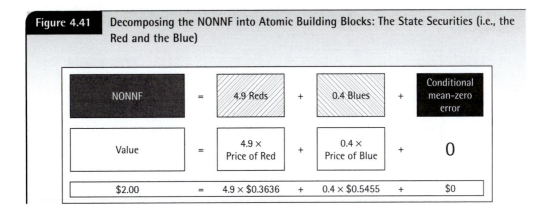

How about yet another example? Let's value the Richard with a tracking portfolio containing only Reds and the Blues. If you recall, the Richard pays off $DERIV_{Up} = \$4$ in the up state and $DERIV_{Dn} = -\$0.6931$ in the down state, so our tracking portfolio needs to be long 4 Reds and short 0.6931 Blues. The payoff on this portfolio will be $4(\$1) - .6931(\$0) = \$4$ in the up state and $4(\$0) - .6931(\$1) = -\$0.6931$ in the down state—the exact payoff pattern of the Richard. If this portfolio has the same payoff pattern as the Richard, then it must have the same price. Indeed it does: The cost of the portfolio is $4(\$0.3636) - .6931(\$0.5455) = \$1.077$. This neat result shows that the Richard is really just a portfolio of Reds and Blues (see Figure 4.42).

And here's one that you might find *really* amazing. If you recall, the conditional mean payoffs on our real option on the NONNF were $RO_{Up} = \$1.44$ in the strengthening economy state and $RO_{Dn} = \$0$ in the weakening economy state, and its current arbitrage-free price was $\$0.5236$. To replicate the conditional mean payoffs on this derivative with a tracking portfolio containing only Reds and Blues, we would need to go long 1.44 Reds and 0 Blues. The value of this tracking portfolio would be $1.44 \times (\$0.3636) + 0 \times (\$0.5455) = \$0.5236$, which is exactly what we got before. Figure 4.43 shows our decomposition of this particular real option into the atomic building blocks.

The really incredible point about our real option on the NONNF is that we valued it with three different tracking portfolios, yet we got the same answer each time. If you don't remember this, look back at Figure 4.28, Figure 4.30, and Figure 4.43.

Figure 4.42   Decomposing the Richard into Atomic Building Blocks: The State Securities (i.e., the Red and the Blue)

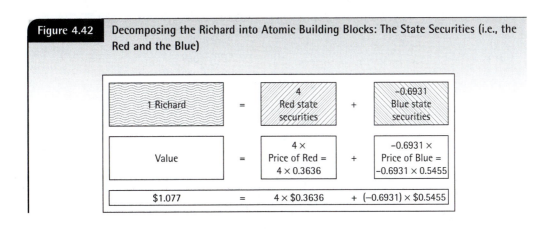

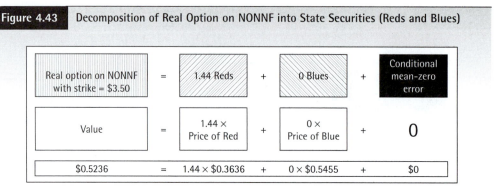

Figure 4.43   Decomposition of Real Option on NONNF into State Securities (Reds and Blues)

Real option on NONNF with strike = $3.50	=	1.44 Reds	+	0 Blues	+	Conditional mean–zero error
Value	=	1.44 × Price of Red	+	0 × Price of Blue	+	0
$0.5236	=	1.44 × $0.3636	+	0 × $0.5455	+	$0

In fact, we could redo every other example from this chapter, and we would find that tracking portfolios using Reds and Blues always have the exact same value as tracking portfolios containing the market index and the risk-free bond or tracking portfolios containing the NONNF and the risk-free bond. Why does this work? Because in reality, the market index and the risk-free bond and the NONNF are themselves just portfolios of the state securities (i.e., the Red and the Blue), so when we used those molecular building blocks we were implicitly using packages of the atomic building blocks.

For example, in our original valuation of the real option on the NONNF using the traditional tracking portfolio that contained the NONNF itself along with the risk-free bond, we found that

$$\text{Real option on NONNF} = \begin{cases} 0.32 \text{ units NONNF} \\ -\$0.1164 \text{ invested in risk-free asset @ 10\%} \end{cases}$$

(see Figure 4.28). Since we just learned that the NONNF is just a portfolio of Reds and Blues:

$$\text{NONNF} = \begin{cases} 4.9 \text{ Reds} \\ 0.4 \text{ Blues} \end{cases}$$

and since

$$\$1 \text{ invested in risk-free bond} = \begin{cases} 1.10 \text{ Reds} \\ 1.10 \text{ Blues} \end{cases}$$

(because every $1 invested in the risk-free bond pays $1.10 in the future), we can say that

$$\text{Real option on NONNF} = \begin{cases} 0.32 \times \begin{cases} 4.9 \text{ Reds} \\ 0.4 \text{ Blues} \end{cases} \\ -\$0.1164 \times \begin{cases} 1.10 \text{ Reds} \\ 1.10 \text{ Blues} \end{cases} \end{cases}$$

$$= \begin{cases} \begin{cases} 1.568 \text{ Reds} \\ 0.128 \text{ Blues} \end{cases} \\ \begin{cases} -0.128 \text{ Reds} \\ -0.128 \text{ Blues} \end{cases} \end{cases}$$

$$= \begin{cases} 1.44 \text{ Reds} \\ 0 \text{ Blues} \end{cases}$$

which is precisely the Red/Blue decomposition of the real option from Figure 4.43. Alternatively, we could have started with the nontraditional tracking portfolio which valued the real option on the NONNF using the market index and the risk-free bond:

$$\text{Real option on NONNF} = \begin{cases} 0.96 \text{ Units market index} \\ -\$0.4364 \text{ Invested in risk-free asset @ 10\%} \end{cases}$$

(see Figure 4.30). Since we just learned that the market index is really just a portfolio of Reds and Blues,

$$1 \text{ Unit market index fund} = \begin{cases} 2 \text{ Reds} \\ 0.5 \text{ Blues} \end{cases}$$

and since

$$\$1 \text{ Invested in risk-free bond} = \begin{cases} 1.10 \text{ Reds} \\ 1.10 \text{ Blues} \end{cases}$$

(because every \$1 invested in the risk-free bond pays \$1.10 in the future), we can say that

$$\text{Real option on NONNF} = \begin{cases} 0.96 \times \begin{cases} 2 \text{ Reds} \\ 0.5 \text{ Blues} \end{cases} \\ -\$0.4364 \times \begin{cases} 1.10 \text{ Reds} \\ 1.10 \text{ Blues} \end{cases} \end{cases}$$

$$= \begin{cases} \begin{cases} 1.92 \text{ Reds} \\ 0.48 \text{ Blues} \end{cases} \\ \begin{cases} -0.48 \text{ Reds} \\ -0.48 \text{ Blues} \end{cases} \end{cases}$$

$$= \begin{cases} 1.44 \text{ Reds} \\ 0 \text{ Blues} \end{cases}$$

which is, once again, exactly the same thing.

I cannot overstate the importance of this. Building tracking portfolios using only Reds and Blues is simple, because you always need 1 Red for every \$1 of payoff in the up state and 1 Blue for every \$1 of payoff in the down state no matter what you are trying to value. So, if we can find a way to come up with the equilibrium prices of the Red and the Blue, we can dispense with our underlying asset, as well as our molecular building blocks (the market index and risk-free bond), and just use the atomic building-block state securities in our tracking portfolios. Our valuation model will then look like Equation (4.11).

$$DERIV_0 = DERIV_{Up} \times \text{Current value of Red} + DERIV_{Dn} \times \text{Current value of Blue} \qquad (4.11)$$

As it turns out, there *is* a very easy way to calculate the equilibrium prices of the Reds and Blues—and many of you have been using this for quite some time (and using the Reds and Blues in your tracking portfolios) without even knowing that you were doing it.

A General Way to Value the Red and the Blue in Any Binomial Context

To see a very easy way to determine the equilibrium values of the Red and Blue state securities, let's do a little more algebra. In a binomial model, the general formulas for the tracking portfolio which tracks the Red are

$$\Delta(Red) = \frac{1 - 0}{UND_{Up} - UND_{Dn}} = \frac{1}{UND_{Up} - UND_{Dn}}$$

units of the underlying asset (whatever it may be), where I've used Equation (4.7) along with the general definition of the Red which implies that $DERIV_{Up} = 1$ and $DERIV_{Dn} = 0$, and

$$\$\Psi(Red) = \frac{1}{(1 + r)}\left[1 - \frac{1}{UND_{Up} - UND_{Dn}}(UND_{Up})\right]$$

investment in the risk-free bond, where I've used Equation (4.8) along with the solution for $\Delta(Red)$ we just calculated. Plugging our general solutions for $\Delta(Red)$ and $\$\psi(Red)$ into Equation (4.5), we get

$$\text{Current value of Red} = \Delta(Red) + \$\Psi(Red)$$

$$= \frac{1}{UND_{Up} - UND_{Dn}}UND_0 + \frac{1}{(1 + r)}\left[1 - \frac{UND_{Up}}{UND_{Up} - UND_{Dn}}\right]$$

which reduces to

$$\text{Current value of Red} = \frac{UND_0 \times (1 + r) - UND_{Dn}}{UND_{Up} \times (1 + r) - UND_{Dn}(1 + r)} \qquad (4.12)$$

But we can go even farther than this. Notice that $UND_{Up} = UND_0(1 + u)$, where u is the percentage return on the underlying in the up state. Similarly, $UND_{Dn} = UND_0(1 + d)$ where d is the percentage drop if the underlying goes down. If there is idiosyncratic risk in the underlying, u and d are *conditional mean* returns. If you make these substitutions into Equation (4.12), you will find that

$$\text{Current value of Red} = \frac{1}{1 + r}\left(\frac{r - d}{u - d}\right) \qquad (4.13)$$

Have you seen something like the right-hand side of Equation (4.13) before? If you've taken a derivatives class, you probably have. By the exact same method (which I don't include here, but you can work through it on your own), the value of the Blue state security is

$$\text{Current value of Blue} = \frac{1}{1 + r}\left(1 - \frac{r - d}{u - d}\right) \qquad (4.14)$$

This gives us an extremely easy-to-apply general procedure. In any binomial world, we can value any derivative via arbitrage by simply plugging Equations (4.13) and (4.14) into (4.11):

$$DERIV_0 = DERIV_{Up} \times \text{Current value of Red} + DERIV_{Dn} \times \text{Current value of Blue}$$

$$= DERIV_{Up} \times \frac{1}{1 + r}\left[\frac{r - d}{u - d}\right] + DERIV_{Dn} \times \frac{1}{1 + r}\left[1 - \frac{r - d}{u - d}\right] \qquad (4.15)$$

where r is the risk-free rate, u is the percentage return on the underlying if it goes up, and d is the percentage return on the underlying if it goes down. Moreover, this does not just work for derivatives—Equation (4.15) must hold for all assets in this binomial economy, else an arbitrage opportunity would exist.

Let's try a simple illustration. In our original economy, consider another asset with a conditional mean cash flow of $0.5 in the up state and $1.25 in the down state. One way to value this asset would be to build a molecular tracking portfolio as we did at the very beginning (it would be short 0.5 unit of the market index and long $1.3636 in the risk-free bond, so the value would be $-0.5(\$1) + \$1.3636 = \$0.8636$—check for yourself). But there is an easier way. Remember that in our economy, $r = 10\%$. Furthermore, if the market index goes up, it goes up by 100% ($\$2/\$1 - 1 = 100\%$), so $u = 100\%$; likewise, if the market index goes down, it goes down by -50% ($\$0.50/\$1 - 1 = -50\%$), so $d = -50\%$. Therefore, the current values of our atomic state securities are given by Equations (4.13) and (4.14):

$$\text{Value of Red} = \frac{1}{1+r}\left(\frac{r-d}{u-d}\right)$$

$$= \frac{1}{1.10}\left(\frac{0.10 - (-0.50)}{1.00 - (-0.50)}\right) = \frac{1}{1.10}\left(\frac{0.60}{1.50}\right) = \frac{0.40}{1.10} = \$0.3636$$

and

$$\text{Value of Blue} = \frac{1}{1+r}\left(1 - \frac{r-d}{u-d}\right)$$

$$= \frac{1}{1.10}\left(1 - \frac{0.10 - (-0.50)}{1.00 - (-0.50)}\right) = \frac{0.60}{1.10} = \$0.5455$$

So using Equation (4.11) or Equation (4.15), the value of this new derivative will be

$$DERIV_0 = DERIV_{Up} \times \text{Current value of Red} + DERIV_{Dn} \times \text{Current value of Blue}$$

$$= DERIV_{Up} \times \frac{1}{1+r}\left[\frac{r-d}{u-d}\right] + DERIV_{Dn} \times \frac{1}{1+r}\left[1 - \frac{r-d}{u-d}\right]$$

$$= 0.5 \times \$0.3636 + 1.25 \times \$0.5455 = \$0.8636$$

But we could have done this even another way. Sit down before you read this one—most people simply find this unbelievable. Instead of using the up and down returns on the *market index* to calculate u and d, we could have used the conditional mean returns on the *NONNF* to arrive at the correct values of the Red and Blue state securities. Remember that the arbitrage-free value of the NONNF is $NONNF_0 = \$2$, and that its conditional mean values in the strengthening economy (or up) and weakening economy (or down) states were $NONNF_{Up} = \$4.90$ and $NONNF_{Dn} = \$0.40$, respectively. Using the NONNF, $u = (\$4.90/\$2 - 1) = 145\%$ and $d = (\$0.40/\$2 - 1) = -80\%$, so Equations (4.13) and (4.14) give us

$$\text{Value of Red} = \frac{1}{1+r}\left(\frac{r-d}{u-d}\right) = \frac{1}{1.10}\left(\frac{0.10 - (-0.80)}{1.45 - (-0.80)}\right) = \frac{1}{1.10}\left(\frac{0.90}{2.25}\right) = \frac{0.40}{1.10} = \$0.3636$$

and

$$\text{Value of Blue} = \frac{1}{1+r}\left(1 - \frac{r-d}{u-d}\right) = \frac{1}{1.10}\left(1 - \frac{0.10 - (-0.80)}{1.45 - (-0.80)}\right) = \frac{0.60}{1.10} = \$0.5455$$

which are *the exact same prices for the Red and the Blue that we got when we used the market index to calculate them.*

The magic does not end there. We could have calculated the values of the Red and the Blue using the Richard. The Richard's current value is \$1.077, and its conditional mean payoff in the up state is \$4, so the up return on the Richard is $u = (\$4/\$1.077 - 1) = 271.4\%$; its conditional mean payoff in the down state is $-\$0.6931$, so its down return is $d = (-\$0.6931/\$1.077 - 1) = -164.35\%$. Again, using Equations (4.13) and (4.14),

$$\text{Value of Red} = \frac{1}{1 + r}\left(\frac{r - d}{u - d}\right) = \frac{1}{1.10}\left(\frac{0.10 - (-1.6435)}{2.714 - (-1.6435)}\right) = \frac{1}{1.10}\left(\frac{1.7435}{4.3575}\right) = \frac{0.40}{1.10} = \$0.3636$$

$$\text{Value of Blue} = \frac{1}{1 + r}\left(1 - \frac{r - d}{u - d}\right) = \frac{1}{1.10}\left(1 - \frac{0.10 - (-1.6435)}{2.714 - (-1.6435)}\right) = \frac{0.60}{1.10} = \$0.5455$$

Once again, exactly the same. You may be thinking that I'm cheating here; perhaps you suspect that I might have rigged the numbers to make this work out in this one extreme case, or that these results are just a matter of coincidence. I assure you that I'm innocent of all charges (at least all of these charges), and that the result here is completely general.

How can I be so bold to say this? Because what I've just demonstrated to you is a more general form of our old friend from Chapter 2: The fundamental theorem of asset pricing. We can now say it this way: If the financial market is free of arbitrage opportunities, then there exists at least one set of positive state prices (Reds and Blues in a binomial model) that consistently prices everything in the economy. Furthermore, if the financial market is complete then there is only *one* set of positive state prices that will work.[10]

This is really great news for us, because it tells us that we can dispense with tracking portfolios and attack the valuation of options (financial or real) using state prices. All we need is some way to find the prices of Reds and Blues, and if you look back at Equations (4.13) and (4.14), you'll see that we can calculate them as long as we know the risk-free rate of return, the current value of our underlying asset, and what happens to the underlying asset in the up and down states. Given the no-arbitrage and price-taking assumptions, the value of any new corporate project (whether it is a real asset like the NONNF or a real option like our option on the NONNF) must be consistent with these state prices.[11,12]

[10] This theorem works in the other direction as well: If there exists a set of positive state prices that consistently prices everything in the economy, then there exist no arbitrage opportunities. Moreover, there is a third condition that is both necessary and sufficient for the other two: There exists some agent who prefers more to less that has an optimum portfolio in the neoclassical portfolio choice problem mentioned in Note 8.

[11] Warning: Equations (4.13) and (4.14) give the prices of the state securities in the binomial world only if your underlying asset is costless to hold and provides no *convenience yield*. I'll explain those concepts and show you how to make an adjustment for them in Chapter 9. But for those of you who know something about convenience yield or *rate of return shortfall*, there's something I'd like to point out right now: The convenience yield on a risky asset and the convenience yield on a derivative on that risky asset may not be the same. This will arise in a real options context whenever we are considering options on a project that has fixed operating costs.

[12] Here's a proof. Suppose your market index fund is costless to hold and provides no dividends. Then its percentage return in the up state will be $u = MKT_{Up}/MKT_0 - 1$, and in the down state it will be $d = MKT_{Dn}/MKT_0 - 1$, so the price of the Red and the Blue will be

$$\text{Red} = \frac{1}{1 + r}\left[\frac{r - d}{u - d}\right] \qquad \text{Blue} = \frac{1}{1 + r}\left[1 - \frac{r - d}{u - d}\right]$$

Now consider any risky asset that is costless to store and provides no convenience yield from holding. Its current value is UND_0, its conditional mean value in the up state is UND_{Up}, and its conditional mean value in the down state is UND_{Dn}. If there are no arbitrage opportunities in the financial market, then it must be that this alternative risky asset is just a packaging of Reds and Blues:

$$UND_0 = UND_{Up} \times \frac{1}{1 + r}\left[\frac{r - d}{u - d}\right] + UND_{Dn} \times \frac{1}{1 + r}\left[1 - \frac{r - d}{u - d}\right]$$

There's just one little twist to how some people interpret the two state prices, and this alternative interpretation is so ubiquitous in finance that I'll adopt it for the rest of the text as well. If we inflate our state prices by one plus the risk-free rate of return, we get what a lot of people call *risk-neutral probabilities*, and we can use these risk-neutral probabilities in a very simple pricing model.

Risk-Neutral Probabilities

Let's do just a little bit more algebra. Recall from Equation (4.11) that we can decompose any derivative in our binomial world into a portfolio of Reds and Blues:

$$DERIV_0 = DERIV_{Up} \times \text{Current value of Red} + DERIV_{Dn} \times \text{Current value of Blue}$$

which gives us the shortcut pricing model in Equation (4.15):

$$DERIV_0 = DERIV_{Up} \times \frac{1}{1+r}\left[\frac{r-d}{u-d}\right] + DERIV_{Dn} \times \frac{1}{1+r}\left[1 - \frac{r-d}{u-d}\right]$$

What I'd like to do now is factor out the $(1 + r)$ in the denominator

$$DERIV_0 = \frac{DERIV_{Up} \times \left[\frac{r-d}{u-d}\right] + DERIV_{Dn} \times \left[1 - \frac{r-d}{u-d}\right]}{1+r}$$

and now make a simple substitution for the ratio that appears in both the price of the Red and the price of the Blue:

$$DERIV_0 = \frac{q \times DERIV_{Up} + (1-q) \times DERIV_{Dn}}{1+r}, \text{ where } q = \frac{r-d}{u-d} \qquad (4.16)$$

Equation (4.16) is called the *risk-neutral* pricing formula in the binomial model, and people use it every day to value derivatives. What most people don't know, however, is that the *risk-neutral probabilities* q and $1 - q$ are actually the prices of the Red and Blue state securities multiplied by $(1 + r)$.

So why do people call q and $1 - q$ risk-neutral probabilities? Because (1) they sum to one, just like subjective probabilities; (2) they are positive whenever the subjective probabilities of the corresponding states are positive; and (3) when you use them as if they actually are probabilities to calculate the expected return on any risky asset, you always end up with the risk-free rate of return. In other words, they make the risk premium on a risky asset appear to go away. Check this out.

If you recall, our market index return is $\$2/\$1 - 1 = 100\%$ if it goes up and $\$0.5/\$1 - 1 = -50\%$ if it goes down. Under the subjective (or physical)[13] probability measure $\{p, 1 - p\} = \{0.5, 0.5\}$, the expected return on our market index is 25% (and hence it carries

---

Next, define the percentage change on this alternative risky asset in the up state as the u' that solves $UND_{Up} = UND_0$ $(1 + u')$, and in the down state as $UND_{Dn} = UND_0 (1 + d')$. Using these substitutions and canceling out UND_0, we have

$$1 = \frac{1+u'}{1+r} \times \frac{r-d}{u-d} + \frac{1+d'}{1+r} \times \left[1 - \frac{r-d}{u-d}\right]$$

which, after only a little algebra, gives

$$\frac{r-d'}{u'-d'} = \frac{r-d}{u-d}$$

Thus, you get the same prices for the Red and the Blue whether you calculate them using the alternative risky asset or use the market index.

[13] It is tempting to use the term *true* probabilities here. However, the notion of probability is completely artificial, and there is no truth in a probability assessment. Everyone's probability assessment is subjective; we use the term *subjective probability* to indicate the market's aggregate assessment of the likelihood of each future state.

a risk premium):

$$E_p\{r_{Mkt}\} = 0.5 \times (+100\%) + 0.5 \times (-50\%) = 25\%$$

But using the risk-neutral probabilities $\{q, 1-q\} = \{0.4, 0.6\}$, the expected return on the market index is only 10%—which is identical to the risk-free rate:

$$E_q\{r_{Mkt}\} = 0.4 \times (+100\%) + 0.6 \times (-50\%) = 10\%$$

It doesn't stop there. If you recall, the current value of the Red is $0.3636, so its return is $1/$0.3636 - 1 = +175\%$ in the up state and $0/$0.3636 - 1 = -100\%$ in the down state. Under the subjective probability measure, the Red commands a large risk premium:

$$E_p\{r_{Red}\} = 0.5 \times (+175\%) + 0.5 \times (-100\%) = 37.5\%$$

But under the risk-neutral measure, the expected return on the Red is identical to the risk-free rate of return—just like the risky asset:

$$E_q\{r_{Red}\} = 0.4 \times (+175\%) + 0.6 \times (-100\%) = 10\%$$

It even holds for the Richard. Since the current value of the Richard is $1.077, its conditional mean return in the up state is $4/$1.077 - 1 = 271.4\%$, and its conditional mean return in the down state is $-$0.6931/$1.077 - 1 = -164.35\%$. So, under the subjective probability measure, the Richard commands a huge risk premium:

$$E_p\{r_{Richard}\} = 0.5 \times (+271.4\%) + 0.5 \times (-164.35\%) = 53.525\%$$

But, quite amazingly, the expected return on the Richard under the risk-neutral measure is equal to the risk-free rate of return of 10%, just like the market index and the Red:

$$E_q\{r_{Richard}\} = 0.4 \times (+271.4\%) + 0.6 \times (-164.35\%) = 10\%$$

This gives us the alternative interpretation I promised. In our binomial world, we can always value any derivative via a simple DCF valuation if we use the risk-neutral probabilities to calculate the expected future value of a derivative and then the risk-free rate of return to discount that expected future value. What's going on in Equation (4.16) is that the risk-neutral probabilities are actually adjusting for risk in the numerator, so the only thing we have to do in the denominator is adjust for time value of money (the risk-free rate of return).[14]

How the Risk–Neutral Probabilities Actually Adjust for Risk

Suppose you know the conditional mean cash flows on a risky asset in each of the two future states in our binomial world. There are two ways to go about determining the arbitrage-free value today.

If you know the subjective probabilities of the up and down states p and $1-p$, along with the required rate of return on the risky asset r_{Asset}, then you can do the arbitrage valuation by

[14] Because the risk-neutral probabilities make the expected return on everything appear to be the risk-free rate of return, economists call them *martingale probabilities*. Roughly speaking, a random variable is said to be a *martingale* if it is a fair game; that is, it is a martingale if its expected future value equals its current value. Now, under the risk-neutral probability measure the expected future value of a risky asset is *not* equal to its present value, but rather $(1 + r)$ times its present value. However, if we discount the asset's future conditional mean cash flows by the risk-free rate and *then* take the expected value using the risk-neutral probabilities, you get the asset's present value. So, the *discounted* price process of any risky asset is a martingale under the risk-neutral measure.

risk-adjusted discounting (as we learned in Chapter 2):

$$Asset_0 = \frac{p \times Asset_{Up} + [1 - p] \times Asset_{Dn}}{1 + r_{Asset}}$$

On the other hand, if you don't know the subjective probabilities or the risk-adjusted rate of return but you can extract the binomial economy's state prices, then you can use the risk-neutral pricing formula given in Equation (4.16) as your linear pricing approach:

$$Asset_0 = \frac{q \times Asset_{Up} + (1 - q) \times Asset_{Dn}}{1 + r}$$

The thing is, if there are no arbitrage opportunities then you will get the same answer either way, so

$$\frac{p \times Asset_{Up} + [1 - p] \times Asset_{Dn}}{1 + r_{Asset}} = \frac{q \times Asset_{Up} + (1 - q) \times Asset_{Dn}}{1 + r} \qquad (4.17)$$

By comparing the left-hand side of Equation (4.17) with the right-hand side, you see what I'm talking about. The left-hand side, which is the standard risk-adjusted discounting approach, accounts for both time value and risk in the denominator. The right-hand side, however, only adjusts for time value in the denominator because discounting takes place at the risk-free rate of return. So, to get the same answer, it must be that the risk-adjustment takes place in the numerator of the risk-neutral model. Now, the conditional mean cash flows on the asset are the same in either approach, so the only thing that could adjust for risk in the numerator of the right-hand side is the risk-neutral probability q.

To see this, we need one more way of looking at the Red and the Blue. Remember that the price of the Red is simply the market's price of $1 of cash flow to be received if the economy strengthens over the binomial step, an event that occurs with probability p. So we can write the price of the Red this way:

$$Red = \frac{p \times \$1}{1 + r_{Red}} = \frac{\$p}{1 + r_{Red}}$$

where r_{Red} is the implicit risk-adjusted discount rate on the Red. We can verify this in our economy, where (if you recall) the probability of the up step is 0.5, and the implicit discount rate on the Red is 37.5%.

$$Red = \frac{\$p}{1 + r_{Red}} = \frac{\$0.5}{1.375} = \$0.3636$$

We can do the same for the Blue, which has an implicit discount rate of -8.34%:

$$Blue = \frac{(1 - p) \times \$1}{1 + r_{Blue}} = \frac{\$0.5}{1 + (-0.0834)} = \frac{\$0.5}{0.9166} = \$0.5455$$

Finally, recall that q is just the price of the Red state security times 1 plus the risk-free rate of return, so we can write q a different way:

$$Red = \frac{1}{1 + r} \times \frac{r - d}{u - d} = \frac{1}{1 + r} \times q \quad \text{or} \quad q = (1 + r) \times Red,$$

so

$$q = (1 + r)\frac{p}{1 + r_{Red}}$$

By similar logic, we can express $1 - q$ as a function of the implicit discount rate on the Blue:

$$Blue = \frac{1}{1 + r} \times \left[1 - \frac{r - d}{u - d}\right] = \frac{1}{1 + r} \times (1 - q) \quad \text{or} \quad (1 - q) = (1 + r) \times Blue,$$

so

$$(1 - q) = (1 + r)\frac{(1 - p)}{1 + r_{Blue}}$$

Therefore, by plugging these new expressions for q and $(1 - q)$ into the risk-neutral pricing model (4.16), we see how the risk-adjustment actually takes place:

$$Asset_0 = \frac{q \times Asset_{Up} + (1 - q) \times Asset_{Dn}}{1 + r} = \frac{(1 + r)p\frac{Asset_{Up}}{1 + r_{Red}} + (1 + r)(1 - p)\frac{Asset_{Dn}}{1 + r_{Blue}}}{1 + r}$$

or

$$\frac{q \times Asset_{Up}}{1 + r} + \frac{(1 - q) \times Asset_{Dn}}{1 + r} = \frac{p \times Asset_{Up}}{1 + r_{Red}} + \frac{(1 - p) \times Asset_{Dn}}{1 + r_{Blue}} \tag{4.18}$$

Do you see what's happening in Equation (4.18)? In the risk-neutral model (the left-hand side), the risk-neutral probabilities effectively discount the up state (or strengthening economy) cash flows at one discount rate (the Red or up state or strengthening economy discount rate), and the down state (or weakening economy) cash flows at a different discount rate (the Blue or down state or weakening economy discount rate).

This is what actually goes on in *all* valuations in a world of uncertainty. If individuals are risk averse, then in equilibrium the risky cash flows that are associated with strong economic states are discounted at very high discount rates, while cash flows associated with weak economic states are discounted at low (or negative) discount rates (for the very reasons we talked about earlier).

What this tells us, then, is that "the" risk-adjusted discount rate to apply to a risky asset is really a nonlinear weighted average of the discount rates that the economy applies to the different states of nature:

$$\frac{1}{1 + r_{Asset}} = \frac{1}{p \times Asset_{Up} + (1 - p) \times Asset_{Dn}} \times \left[\frac{Asset_{Up}}{1 + r_{Red}} + \frac{Asset_{Dn}}{1 + r_{Blue}}\right] \tag{4.19}$$

An asset that pays off more in high consumption states gets more weight on the Red (high) discount rate; an asset that pays off more in low consumption states gets more weight on the Blue (low) discount rate.

Moreover, this notion of an asset paying off in high or low consumption states is precisely what *beta* measures: Assets with higher betas fare worse in low consumption states of nature; assets with low or negative betas fare better in low consumption states.

We can calculate the beta of a derivative easily using two basic and useful facts. First, the beta of a portfolio is simply the weighted average of the betas of the assets in the portfolio (where the weights are just the percentages of total portfolio value invested in each asset). Second, as we have shown, we can track a derivative with a portfolio of only two assets: the risky underlying asset and the risk-free bond. Since the tracking portfolio behaves exactly like the derivative, the beta of the tracking portfolio is the beta of the derivative. The beta of a derivative is then

$$\beta_{Derivative} = \%\ invested\ in\ underlying \times \beta_{Underlying} + \%\ invested\ in\ risk\text{-}free\ bond \times \beta_{risk\text{-}free\ bond}$$

$$\beta_{Deriv} = \frac{\Delta \times UND_0}{DERIV_0} \times \beta_{Und} + \frac{\$\Psi}{DERIV_0} \times \beta_{risk\text{-}free\ bond}$$

Since the beta of the risk-free bond is zero,

$$\beta_{Deriv} = \frac{\Delta \times UND_0}{DERIV_0} \times \beta_{Und} \tag{4.20}$$

If we find the value of the Red using the market index in our tracking portfolio, then $\Delta(Red) = 0.6667$, $UND_0 = \$1$, and the current value of the Red $= DERIV_0 = \$0.3636$, so using Equation 4.20,

$$\beta_{Red} = \frac{.6667 \times \$1}{\$0.3636} \beta_{Und} = 1.833 \beta_{Und} = 1.833$$

(since the beta of the market index is, by definition, 1). Doing the similar analysis for the Blue, $\Delta(Blue) = -0.6667$, $UND_0 = \$1$, and the current value of the Blue $= DERIV_0 = \$0.5455$, so

$$\beta_{Blue} = \frac{-.6667 \times \$1}{\$0.5455} \beta_{Und} = -1.222 \beta_{Und} = -1.222$$

In other words,

$$\beta_{Red} > \beta_{Und} > \beta_{Blue}$$

Remembering that the Red is a call on the market index and the Blue is a put on the market index, this illustrates the more general result that

$$\beta_{Call} > \beta_{Underlying} > \beta_{Put}$$

(for a positive-beta underlying asset). The Red is riskier than the market because the Red pays off only in high-consumption states, while the market index at least pays something ($0.5) in the low consumption state. The market is in turn more risky than the Blue, because the Blue pays off better than the market in the low consumption state. Calls are riskier than their underlying assets, and puts are less risky than the underlying.

For the Really Interested

If you are really interested in this stuff, here's an important relationship. Recall that we derived the beta of a derivative in Equation (4.20):

$$\beta_{Deriv} = \frac{\Delta \cdot UND_0}{DERIV_0} \times \beta_{Und}$$

We can insert some standard notation here, and rewrite this as

$$\beta_{Deriv} = \frac{\Delta \cdot UND_0}{DERIV_0} \times \beta_{Und} = \eta_{Deriv} \times \beta_{Und}$$

where we have defined the *elasticity* of the derivative (η_{Deriv}) as

$$\eta_{Deriv} = \frac{\Delta \cdot UND_0}{DERIV_0}$$

The elasticity η of a derivative is the percentage of the tracking portfolio's value that is invested in the underlying asset, and it has some very interesting features:

$$\beta_{Deriv} = \eta_{Deriv} \times \beta_{Und}$$

$$\sigma^2_{Deriv} = \eta^2_{Deriv} \times \sigma^2_{Und}$$

$$\sigma_{Deriv} = |\eta_{Deriv}| \times \sigma_{Und}$$

Furthermore, the elasticity of a call is *always* greater than 1.0, and the elasticity of a put is *virtually always* less than -1.0. So we can safely say the following:

- The beta of a call option is always greater (in absolute value) than the beta of the underlying asset.
- The beta of a put option is always the opposite sign of the beta of the underlying asset.
- The volatility of any option is always greater than the volatility of the underlying asset.

Before we go any further, I'll show you how we'll use all of this section's material in our capital budgeting problems. The next section will present three simple examples of real options, and we'll attack each one using our risk-neutral pricing approach. I'm doing this so that I can reinforce several important teaching points, and make a few more, before we get to the technical side of building binomial trees.

4.4 Three Simplified Real-World Examples

Now that we know how to work with each single step of the binomial model (and how each step works), our last task will be to learn how to link single-step binomial trials together to get a good approximation for the real world. Before we get to that, however, I find it useful to stop and reiterate our motivation by doing some very simple examples in a single-step binomial context. My students call this "putting numbers where the letters are."

I have two reasons for doing this. The most obvious reason is to review working with the binomial model. But my more subtle objective is to help you build intuition about how to frame valuation problems that contain significant optionality.

So don't get turned off by the limited-outcome nature of the examples, or by the fact that I don't tell you how to estimate the future state values. We'll handle those things in a later section. Let's just take this opportunity to stop, reflect on what we've learned so far, and think about how we are going to go forward.

Simplified Real World Case 1: Transcanal Cargo and the Asian Flu

Every year, cargo ships transport over 75 million tons of freight between Asia and the East coast of the United States via the Panama Canal. Exports from the United States to various Asian countries constitute 61% of this total.

You may not be aware that cartels dominate the global cargo shipping market. The cartels maximize total revenue by setting prices and allocating loads across members. Before 1997, the price of shipping 1 ton of freight between Asia and U.S. ports on the Gulf of Mexico was about $27.41.

But we all know that cartels are inherently fragile, and in 1997 some maverick firms from Taiwan and Korea broke ranks and negotiated prices directly with clients. The Asian financial crisis provided the impetus for the breakup, as decreased economic activity led to overcapacity in the transcanal shipping lanes. As a result, the price of shipping a ton of cargo on the same route fell to about $18.84 by March 1998. Of course, this forced down the market value of ships.

The good news for the import/export companies was obviously that their transportation prices dropped. The bad news, however, was that these companies were suddenly exposed to large uncertainties about future shipping prices. If the Asian crisis were to deepen any further, shipping prices could continue to fall. But if the Asian economy were to experience a quick turnaround, the cartels might reform and prices might jump back up.

Specifically, analysts concluded that given a continued weakening in the Asian economy, the expected price of shipping 1 ton of cargo between Asia and the U.S. ports on the Gulf of Mexico (in either direction) would be $12.95. On the other hand, given a rebound in the Asian economy, the expected price of shipping 1 ton of cargo on the transcanal route would revert back to $27.41. These are the conditional mean values of the price of shipping 1 ton of cargo in one year's time, and we can represent the possible evolution of shipping prices over the next year in a simple diagram:

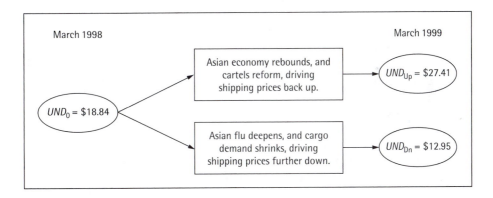

While the import/export (I/E) companies historically bought forward contracts on shipping, the situation I've outlined made some of them change their thinking. In March 1998, a few wanted the flexibility to take advantage of any further price declines, but at the same time they wanted to protect themselves against increases in shipping prices. So these companies approached the now-competitive ship owners and asked that the March 1999 price of shipping be capped at $18.84 per ton. In other words, if the Asian flu were to deepen and shipping prices were to fall below $18.84, the ship owners would charge the market price. But if the Asian economy were to rebound and shipping prices were to rise above $18.84, these particular I/E companies would only pay $18.84.

This is a one-sided deal. If shipping prices were to rise, the protected I/E companies would get to purchase something worth $27.41 (transport of 1 ton of cargo) for only $18.84. This gain

Figure 4.44   March 1999 Capped and Uncapped Cost of Transcanal Shipping

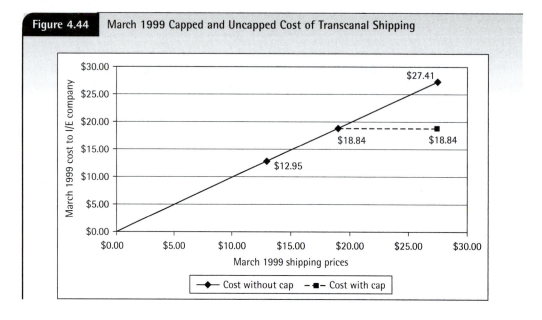

of $27.41 − $18.84 = $8.57 would come at the expense of the shipping companies, because they would be forced to accept only $18.84 for something worth $27.41. On the other hand, if shipping prices were to fall then the price cap would have no effect. So the shipping companies should demand an immediate fee for the price cap. But how much should they demand, and how much should the I/E companies be willing to pay?

Figure 4.44 shows the capped and uncapped cost to I/E companies against March 1999 shipping prices, with the dots connected. What you see in Figure 4.44 is that the price cap provides insurance against shipping prices rising above $18.84 per ton. The broken line presents the capped costs, and it is only visible for March 1999 shipping prices above $18.84 (because for prices below that, capped and uncapped costs are the same, and the broken line is hiding behind the solid line).

To attach a value to the cap itself, we need to know the incremental cash flows that accrue to the I/E company assuming it purchases one. The incremental cash flows arising from the cap are the vertical differences between the solid line (uncapped cost) and broken line (capped cost) in Figure 4.44. I've plotted these differences in Figure 4.45 and connected the dots.

When you look at it this way, you see that the price cap is actually a call option. The price cap gives the I/E companies the right, but not the obligation, to ship a ton of cargo between Asia and the U.S. Gulf Coast for $18.84. Since the price cap is actually a call, the true value of the cap should be equal to the option premium. We can value this option in our binomial model.

Let's be careful when defining the parameters of the call option. The underlying asset is always what you receive if you exercise the option. In this case, it is sufficient space on a ship for transportation of 1 ton of cargo between Asia and the U.S. Gulf Coast in March 1999. So $UND_0 = \$18.84$, $UND_{Up} = \$27.41$, and $UND_{Dn} = \$12.95$. If market prices of shipping go up, the cap will be in effect and the payoff to having the cap (i.e., the net gain that the protected I/E companies reap) will be $DERIV_{Up} = \$27.41 − \$18.84 = \$8.57$. If market prices fall, on the other hand, the cap will be worthless to the "protected" I/E companies and so $DERIV_{Dn} = \$0$.

Figure 4.45 | March 1999 Incremental Cash Flows Arising from Cap on Shipping Prices

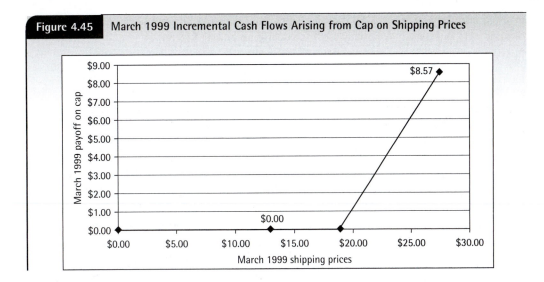

The maturity of the option is one year. The risk-free rate of return is simply the rate of return on a zero-coupon government bond with the same maturity as the option and in the same currency as the option's payoffs. Here, let's just assume it is 5% per year. The volatility of returns on the underlying is captured in our uncertainty about future prices—the more spread they are, the higher the volatility.

In terms of our simple binomial model, our problem looks like this:

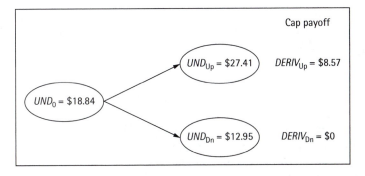

The most obvious way to attack this valuation problem is to form the tracking portfolio that creates the same conditional mean payoff as the cap. The tracking portfolio would contain

$$\Delta = \frac{DERIV_{Up} - DERIV_{Dn}}{UND_{Up} - UND_{Dn}} = \frac{\$8.57 - \$0}{\$27.41 - \$12.95} = 0.593$$

units of the underlying risky asset, and have

$$\$\Psi = \frac{1}{1 + r}[DERIV_{Up} - \Delta \times UND_{Up}]$$

$$= \frac{1}{(1.05)}[\$8.57 - (0.593)\$27.41] = -\$7.318$$

invested in the risk-free bond. So the value of this derivative (a European call on shipping 1 ton of cargo between Asia and the U.S. Gulf Coast in one year at $18.84) is

$$DERIV_0 = \Delta \times UND_0 + \$\Psi$$
$$= 0.593 \times \$18.84 + (-\$7.318) = \$3.85$$

In other words, the economic value of the price cap is $3.85 per ton. This is the most that the I/E company should be willing to pay, and it's the least that the shipping company should be willing to accept.

Can you really hold 0.593 unit of cargo shipping in a tracking portfolio? No. Does this really matter? Not at all. Remember the very important lesson from Chapter 3: When we value anything in corporate finance, we do so by comparison with a *financial market* tracking portfolio. So, in this example the delta of 0.593 means that our tracking portfolio that mimics the conditional mean payoffs on the price cap contains 0.593 units of a *financial market portfolio* that in turn mimics the conditional mean cost of shipping.

Notice that we could have priced this via the risk-neutral pricing formula in Equation (4.16). Since we're working in discrete time, $u = \$27.41/\$18.84 - 1 = 45.49\%$ and $d = \$12.95/\$18.84 - 1 = -31.26\%$, so

$$q = \frac{r - d}{u - d} = \frac{0.05 - (-0.3126)}{0.4549 - (-0.3126)} = 0.472$$

Thus,

$$DERIV_0 = \frac{q \times DERIV_{Up} + (1 - q) \times DERIV_{Dn}}{1 + r} = \frac{0.472 \times \$8.57 + 0.528 \times 0}{1.05} = \$3.85$$

The exact same answer. Why? Because of the fundamental theorem of asset pricing. The tracking portfolio valuation and the risk-neutral pricing valuation are really doing the same thing—valuation by arbitrage with a financial market tracking portfolio that displays the same conditional mean cash flows.

What is the beta of the price cap? Remember that the beta of a derivative is equal to the beta of the tracking portfolio used to price the derivative, and the beta of a portfolio is the weighted average beta of the items in the portfolio. So what are our weights? Well, our tracking portfolio is long 0.593 units of the risky underlying asset at a price of $18.84, so we are long an investment of $11.17 in the risky asset. The total invested in the portfolio is the cost of the portfolio (or the cost of the derivative) or $3.85, so the weight of the risky asset in our tracking portfolio is $11.17/$3.85 = 290%. The total invested in the risk-free bond is −$7.318 (we are short the risk-free bond, or borrowing) so the weight of the risk-free bond in our tracking portfolio is −$7.318/$3.85 = −190%. Notice that the weights sum to one as they should. So using Equation (4.20) the beta of our derivative is

$$\beta_{Deriv} = \%\ weight\ of\ risky\ asset \times \beta_{Und} = \frac{\Delta \cdot UND_0}{DERIV_0} \times \beta_{Und}$$

$$\beta_{Option\ On\ Shipping} = \frac{0.593 \times \$18.84}{\$3.85} \times \beta_{Shipping} = 290\% \times \beta_{Shipping} = 2.90 \cdot \beta_{Shipping}$$

The option on shipping has nearly three times as much beta risk as the shipping prices. Why? If you buy cargo shipping forward, you can lose *some* of your money in the down state; but if you invest in the option, you lose *all* of the money in the down state.

This highlights the problem with decision trees. A naïve analyst might forecast the subjective probabilities of the Asian economy strengthening or weakening, use these to calculate the expected payoff on the cap, and then discount at the required rate of return on a cargo ship. If you mastered the last section, you will immediately understand why this procedure would lead to the wrong valuation: The price cap (or option) only pays off if the economy improves, and outcomes contingent on the economy improving are discounted at a higher rate than outcomes contingent on the economy weakening. If you use the rate of return on the underlying to value the option in a standard DCF, you will make a huge mistake. In this case, you would use a discount rate that is much too low, and hence you would overvalue the price cap. (Remember the Reds and Blues? If you don't, go back to the last section.)

What happened in 1999? The postscript is quite interesting. The Asian economy continued to weaken, and shipping lines competed for less and less cargo. In the past, this sort of steep downturn in the shipping industry has led to the scrapping of older ships. But in 1999 the price of scrap metal plummeted as well, leaving supply of cargo ships high (and the value of ships, as well as the cost of shipping, low).

Nevertheless, there was an idiosyncratic outcome that supported prices a bit. The El Nino weather pattern that brought so much rain to the United States actually caused droughts in Central America. The droughts were so bad, in fact, that they affected the operation of the Panama Canal. The maximum draft of a ship allowed to pass through the Panama Canal dropped from $39\frac{1}{2}$ feet to 34 feet, which required that PANAMAX ship owners reduce cargo payloads through the canal by 20%. Since the number of canal passages cannot exceed 50 per day, the droughts effectively reduced the supply of shipping through the canal by one-fifth.

Simplified Real World Case 2: The Economic Value of Market Research[15]

In 1998, the U.S. market for whole bean and ground coffee was $2.8 billion, and coffee buyers made 80% of whole-bean and ground coffee purchases through the supermarket channel. Cunning Foods, a large marketer of brand-name grocery products, had an excellent position in this market with its extended Smart Home brand (over $680 million in annual sales). However, Cunning Foods did not have a super-premium brand on the grocery store shelves. Cunning had seen the explosive growth of private-label coffeehouses, and management projected that the super-premium coffee segment would grow because of changing consumer tastes toward a higher-quality coffee blend and because of "increased gourmet coffee awareness." Moreover, Cunning's main competitor (Proctor & Gamble) recently entered the super-premium coffee segment by purchasing Millstone Coffee and Brothers Coffee and offering these products on supermarket shelves at super-premium prices.

For these reasons, Cunning management explored the possibility of adding a super-premium gourmet coffee product to their own supermarket mix. After careful study, however, management concluded that the company couldn't simply extend the Smart Home brand into a much more expensive, super-premium whole-bean product because of the way it had positioned Smart Home. And building a new super-premium brand from scratch would be difficult. The only

---

15 *Note:* The information I used to write this example came from colleagues and former students at Indiana University who had been connected in various ways with the transaction. While I don't believe that I've been given any confidential information, I cannot verify the accuracy of the story. Hence, I've hidden the names of the parties. The numbers are my own estimates.

alternative, management concluded, was to purchase outright an existing gourmet coffee company with a regionally recognized brand, then use Cunning's power to put this new brand on supermarket shelves.

Cunning management charged their investment bankers with the task of discretely finding such a company to buy, and by late 1998 the investment bankers had found a potential acquisition candidate. At the same time, Cunning's analysts developed financial forecasts for the costs of actually putting the branded gourmet whole-bean coffee on the supermarket shelves (production facilities, distribution, etc.). Altogether, the capital required to buy the super-premium brand, ramp up production, and put it on supermarket shelves totaled $140 million.

Cunning management was not convinced about the desirability of the investment, however. Management was very unsure of the market's demand for gourmet coffee through the supermarket channel, and their own internal sales forecasts found the static present value of operating free cash flow to be only $110 million (yielding a static NPV of $110 − $140 = −$30 million). Nevertheless, they admitted that they were unsure of demand and that, in the best case, the present value of free cash flow could be as high as $152 million or, in the worst case, as low as $77 million. In other words, management's estimate of the *value* of a branded super-premium coffee product, distributed via the supermarket channel, was only $110 million; but it could be as high as $152 million or as low as $77 million. While the major part of this uncertainty was due to consumer taste, the value of the super-premium product was also dependent on the state of the macroeconomy. Luxury products do better in better economic times.

To address this uncertainty, management decided to do some market research *before* making a final decision. The problem with market research here was that Cunning needed a gourmet coffee product to test whether consumers would buy it through the supermarket channel. This is where Cunning management developed an ingenious idea: Use somebody else's brand. That "somebody else" was Orion Coffee.

Orion Coffee is a large and well-known super-gourmet coffee company. Orion originated as a chain of coffeehouses where customers would purchase brewed coffee, but Orion's management found that many coffeehouse customers would purchase whole-bean and ground coffee for home preparation. Orion's management believed there to be a large market for Orion's branded whole-bean coffee, but the company's coffeehouse focus limited the distribution potential for the product.

Cunning anticipated this and approached Orion with the proposition that Cunning, for a limited amount of time, would distribute Orion coffee through 80 carefully chosen supermarket stores. The purpose of the trial would be to see if consumers would purchase Orion coffee via the supermarket channel. If so, both Cunning and Orion could profit by combining Cunning's distribution power with Orion's brand name. The agreement would last for six months, and the parties would at that time reevaluate their temporary arrangement. Cunning agreed to fund and manage the entire market research project because of its expertise in the area.

In reality, Cunning had no intention of entering a long-term relationship with Orion. Cunning's only motivation in the deal was to learn whether consumers would purchase expensive coffee through the supermarket channel or not. If the results were favorable and the economy strengthened, Cunning would close the acquisition deal and put its own brand on the shelves at a cost of $140 million. If the results were unfavorable or the economy weakened, Cunning would simply walk away having spent only the cost of the market research.

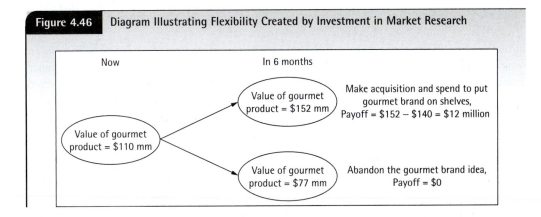

Figure 4.46 Diagram Illustrating Flexibility Created by Investment in Market Research

The problem is that market research is expensive. Cunning would have to sacrifice shelf space in order to stock the Orion whole coffee beans alongside its Smart Home products, and management would have to spend a good deal of money, time and effort inducing trial, gathering customer data, monitoring the program, doing follow-up purchase analysis, etc. This sort of research is so expensive, in fact, that free cash flows from sales of the tested product only cover a fraction of the market research costs.

Why would a company spend money on market research about a product with negative static NPV? Because the market research creates the flexibility to act in the future on better information. That is, the market study allows Cunning to learn more about the true demand for premium coffee through the grocery store distribution channel *before* spending $140 million to put its own gourmet coffee brand on the shelves. Diagramatically, the flexibility created by the market research investment looks like Figure 4.46.

In Figure 4.47, I've superimposed the information from the diagram in Figure 4.46 on a payoff graph. This will really help you see what market research buys in this particular example. What Figure 4.47 shows is that the market research creates a call option on the gourmet coffee brand. This gives us an important clue as to how Cunning management should evaluate the

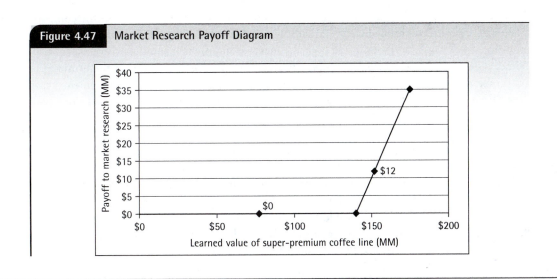

Figure 4.47 Market Research Payoff Diagram

investment in market research: The *most* that Cunning should be willing to spend on the research is the value of the option that the research creates!

Let's go straight to the valuation. The underlying is what you get if you exercise the option, which in this example is a new super-premium gourmet coffee product on the shelves in super-markets nationwide. The current value of the underlying is the current estimate of such a product's value: $110 million. If good things are learned during the market research, the underlying goes up to $152 and the payoff on the option created by the market research is $12; if bad things are learned during the market research, the underlying goes down to $77, and the payoff on the option created by the market research goes to $0.

Let's value the Cunning option using the risk-neutral probabilities approach. Using the numbers from Figure 4.46, we can quickly calculate that the size of the possible up step is 38% [($152 − $110)/$110], and the size of the possible down step is −30% [($77 − $110)/$110]. We will take the risk-free rate of return to be 2.5% per six months, so our risk-neutral probability q is

$$q = \frac{r - d}{u - d} = \frac{0.025 - (-0.30)}{0.38 - (-0.30)} = \frac{0.325}{0.68} = 0.48$$

and thus $(1 - q)$ is 0.52. Hence Equation (4.16) gives the value of the option that the market study creates:

$$\text{True value of market research} = \frac{q \times DERIV_{Up} + (1 - q) \times DERIV_{Dn}}{1 + r}$$

$$= \frac{0.48 \times \$12 \text{ mm} + 0.52 \times \$0}{1.025} = \$5.62 \text{ mm}$$

In other words, the market research creates value as long as it costs less than $5.62 million. If Cunning can do the research for less than $5.62 million, shareholders benefit. This is the value of learning, and learning investments constitute a large portion of corporate real option problems.

Why does this work? When the Cunning analyst performs the DCF analysis of the super-premium gourmet coffee product, she is really decomposing the conditional mean cash flows from the new product into a combination of financial market building blocks. If the company makes the investment immediately and simply watches what happens, it will learn after six months (after seeing the resolution of both the macroeconomic risk and the private risk of consumer taste) that the true value of the new product is either $152 million (in the up state) or $77 million (in the down state). So, from the financial market perspective, the incremental cash flows from an immediate investment in the super-premium coffee line are identical to a financial market portfolio containing 152 Red state securities and 77 Blue state securities, as shown in Figure 4.48.

In other words, there exists a traded portfolio of financial market securities (either the Reds and Blues themselves, or repackaging of the Reds and Blues into other securities like the market index fund and the risk-free bond) that replicates the conditional mean cash flows on the new product. The DCF value of a now-or-never/no-flexibility investment in the new product is equivalent to the value of this tracking portfolio. The relative illiquidity of the new product is completely unimportant—frequent trading in the financial market assures us that there exists a tracking portfolio of traded financial market securities that mimics its conditional mean cash flows.

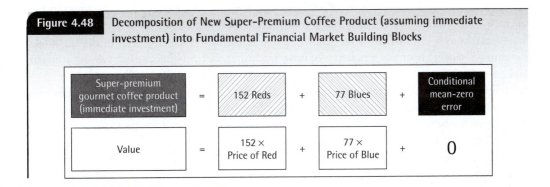

Figure 4.48 Decomposition of New Super-Premium Coffee Product (assuming immediate investment) into Fundamental Financial Market Building Blocks

When the analyst then turns to valuation of the market research, she will be valuing an option on the super-premium gourmet coffee product. Even though the underlying asset (a super-premium coffee product) is not traded in a liquid market, its tracking portfolio *is* traded (she used this tracking portfolio to do the now-or-never/no-flexibility DCF analysis; see Figure 4.48). So, since the *financial market* tracking portfolio trades, the analyst can freely think about the value of options on that tracking portfolio. And options on that tracking portfolio will be equivalent to options on the super-premium product that the tracking portfolio tracks.

An Important Learning Point

I'd like to review a very important point before we go to the third example. In the cargo example, the underlying source of uncertainty was the price of shipping 1 ton of cargo between Asia and the U.S. Gulf Coast. The market price was observable at the initiation of the option ($18.84), and the volatility of the underlying described how much the price could change over the life of the price cap. As the year progressed, everyone could watch the price of cargo shipping move, and by the end of the year, the uncertainty would be resolved.

In the market research example, however, things operated a little bit differently. Cunning started the market research activity with a *noisy estimate* of the value of a super-premium gourmet coffee line on the supermarket shelves, and as they engaged in the market research, their valuation would change due to macroeconomic outcomes (gourmet products are very sensitive to the state of the economy) and idiosyncratic outcomes (whether or not consumers will actually buy the product through the supermarket channel). In other words, the uncertainty was the *true* value of the super-premium product (which is related to the state of the macroeconomy as well as private risk). As time passed, the market research activity would reveal the true value, and the uncertainty would dissipate. The volatility is not so much how the value of the product can change over the life of the option, but rather how much Cunning's *estimate* could change (or, in other words, how *wrong* Cunning could be initially). Why would Cunning's estimate change? For two reasons. First, they would learn something about the macroeconomy. Second, they would learn something about true consumer demand for the product in the supermarket channel.

The similarity to a stock option is this: If you hold an option on a stock, you have the right to buy or sell that stock at a future date for a prespecified price. You do not know what the market price of the stock will be on the exercise date, but you learn about it over time. The current market value represents your current *understanding* about the expiration date price of the stock (discounted for risk and time value of money), and as time progresses your understanding about the expiration-date value of the stock becomes more certain (i.e., as you move closer and closer to the exercise date, the current price becomes a more precise estimate of the (discounted) exercise-date price). Uncertainty about the expiration date price is revealed to you in a smooth way until the very last instant, when you finally learn the expiration-date price of the stock with certainty. Volatility is simply a measure of how much things can change, or how wrong your initial estimate can be.

This is how most corporate real options work. There is a current understanding about the value of some asset, and that understanding may be wrong due to uncertainty. Any investment that allows the firm to decrease that uncertainty and learn more about the true value of the asset is a real option.

And for goodness sake, please remember that if you do a DCF valuation to estimate the value of the super-premium coffee line before the market research activity takes place, you are implicitly assuming that there exists a traded portfolio in the capital markets which tracks such an investment (because the DCF value of anything is just the value of the financial market portfolio that tracks it—remember?). If a traded portfolio that tracks a gourmet coffee line exists, which you are assuming, then options on that tracking portfolio exist as well. Thus, we can value options on the gourmet coffee line without additional assumptions.

Simplified Real World Case 3: Optimal Real Estate Development

The last example actually gives us a taste of what's to come. This one's a classic, and I've adapted it from a famous academic paper.[16]

Suppose we are considering buying a parcel of land that has been zoned for multifamily housing. We have determined that the best use of this land will be to build condominiums.

Our first decision involves the scale of our investment. The size of the lot dictates that we can only build three units per floor, and our issue is whether to build a two- or three-story building. A two-story building, which would have six units, would cost $80,000 per unit to build, while a three-story (nine-unit) complex would cost $90,000 per unit to build. As is usual in construction, cost per unit increases as the building gets taller, largely because of additional foundation and elevator costs. We will assume that fully rented condos just break even on a cash flow basis, so that they earn their entire required rate of return through expected capital gains (as opposed to any cash yield).[17]

Our second decision involves timing. In our market, the current value of a one-unit condominium is $100,000. What complicates matters is that the housing market is volatile, and it is possible that condo prices could increase over the next year. Of course, they could decrease as well. We have determined that the market value of a condominium will either increase to $150,000 next year or decrease to $90,000 next year with equal likelihood. The risk-free rate of return is 10%.

How much are we willing to pay for the land, and what is our optimum construction policy (in terms of scale and timing)?

In real-world problems like this, we will always start with a no-flexibility analysis. If we have to make our decision now (i.e., if this is a static now-or-never/no-flexibility opportunity), then

---

16 See Titman (1985).

17 If there were cash yield on owning fully developed condos, then there might be an incentive to exercise the option early. We will cover this in depth when we get to American options.

the static NPV of the condo development if we construct immediately would be

$$6 (\$100{,}000) - 6 (\$80{,}000) = \$120{,}000$$

if we build six units, or

$$9 (\$100{,}000) - 9 (\$90{,}000) = \$90{,}000$$

if we build nine units.

So, the optimal policy given no timing flexibility would be to build six units, and we would be willing to pay up to $120,000 for the property.

But flexibility changes matters and adds a lot of value to the process. The uncertainty here is the future value of condominiums in our market, and the flexibility is our ability to wait before we decide (that is, to delay) and also to alter the scale of our investment. Let's sketch it out.

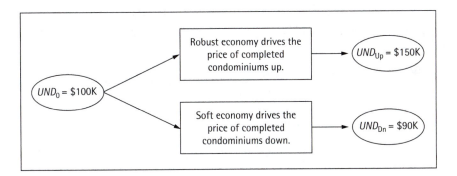

Suppose that we were to wait until next year to make our scale decision. What flexibility does waiting give us? The optimal development strategy, and its NPV, would then depend on the state of the housing market. If the condo market becomes robust, the NPV will be

$$6 (\$150{,}000 - \$80{,}000) = \$420{,}000$$

for a six-unit building, or

$$9 (\$150{,}000 - \$90{,}000) = \$540{,}000$$

for a nine-unit building.

Thus, if we wait and the market is robust we would build a nine-unit building. However, if the condo market becomes soft, the NPV of the development would be

$$6 (\$90{,}000 - \$80{,}000) = \$60{,}000$$

for a six-unit building, or

$$9 (\$90{,}000 - \$90{,}000) = \$0$$

for a nine-unit building.

So if we wait and the economy is soft, we would build a six-unit building. But the question is: Should we wait at all or should we go ahead with development immediately? In this example, we must choose between a real project (develop now) and a real option (wait to develop). Which is more valuable? To answer the question, we must value the option to wait.

Here, we have an option to build six or nine condo units in the future. The underlying is a fully developed condo project, so we know the price dynamics (the dynamics of a built condominium unit).

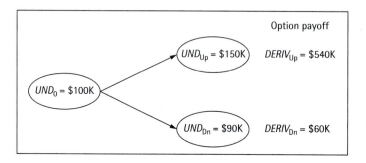

To price our development with the flexibility to wait, we need to use Equations (4.7) and (4.8) to build the financial market tracking portfolio that replicates the conditional mean cash flows from waiting:

$$\Delta = \frac{\$540,000 - \$60,000}{\$150,000 - \$90,000} = 8 \text{ units of the underlying asset}$$

and

$$\$\Psi = \frac{1}{(1.10)} \left[\$540,000 - 8\,(\$150,000) \right] = -\$600,000 \text{ of the risk-free bond (borrowing)}$$

The value of the tracking portfolio, which gives us the value of waiting to invest, is

$$DERIV_0 = 8\,(\$100,000) + (-\$600,000) = \$200,000$$

The value of developing right away is $120,000, but the value of waiting to develop is actually $200,000. The optimal investment strategy is to wait, build nine units if demand is strong, and build six if demand is weak. Therefore, the true financial market value of this piece of real estate is actually $200,000. Any price below $200,000 represents a value-creating investment for us. The *dynamic* NPV is positive for any real estate price below $200,000.

We could have valued the investment using the risk-neutral probability method from Equation (4.16) as well. Recognize that the underlying asset is a fully developed condo unit. The current price of a condo is $100,000, and if demand is robust, the price will go up to $150,000, so $u = 50\%$. If demand is soft, the price will fall to $90,000, so $d = -10\%$. The risk-free rate is 10%, so

$$q = \frac{r - d}{u - d} = \frac{.10 - (-.10)}{.50 - (-.10)} = \frac{1}{3}$$

Hence, we value the real option as

$$\text{Development option} = DERIV_0 = \frac{\dfrac{1}{3} \times \$540,000 + \dfrac{2}{3} \times \$60,000}{1.10} = \$200,000$$

Exactly the same thing.

This is a simple illustration of why investors choose to keep valuable real estate either undeveloped or underutilized (perhaps as a parking lot) even in markets where real estate sells at very high prices—the value of investing immediately may be positive, but the value of waiting is even higher. The real estate project competes with itself in time.

Just as everywhere else, we would have made a huge error had we tried to calculate the expected NPV of the development option using the required rate of return on condos. Given the current market price and future conditional mean values, the market's required rate of return on condo units must be 20%

$$\$100,000 = \frac{0.5 \times \$150,000 + 0.5 \times \$90,000}{1 + r_{Condo}} \qquad so \qquad r_{Condo} = 20\%$$

If we were to discount the expected payoffs from following the optimal investment strategy based on what happens to real estate prices using the 20% required rate of return on built condos, we would mistakenly believe that the condo development option is worth $250,000:

$$\frac{.5\,(\$540,000) + .5\,(\$60,000)}{1.20} = \$250,000$$

That is, we would have overvalued the land by more than one-quarter! We could not make this mistake too many times without going bust. The correct discount rate to use on the property with the option is 50%, but we could never know that without first valuing the option itself.

A Foretaste of What's to Come in this Book

Finally, let's make the problem a little more realistic. Suppose that we now have two periods. In the first year, the market prices of condos can go up to $150,000 or down to $90,000 just as happened before. In the second year, prices can change again:

- If the year-one price is $150,000 (robust), the market price of condos can go up to $225,000 (very robust) or down to $135,000 (mediocre)in the second year, with equal likelihood.
- If the year-one price is $90,000 (soft), the market price of condos can go up to $135,000 (mediocre) or down to $81,000 (very soft) in the second year, with equal likelihood.

What do we pay for the property now, and what is the optimal investment strategy? First, look at the decision tree in Figure 4.49.

Do you see how complex these decision diagrams can get with just a few points of flexibility? It is always a good idea to draw out a decision diagram, however, because it helps us identify the decisions we will have to make. Adding a second period makes the decision a bit more complex, because at Year 1 we can build or wait. If we build, we give up the flexibility to wait and see—and thus the static NPV of building at Year 1 must exceed the option value of waiting (not just zero). But this is exactly how we approached the current decision in the earlier one-period problem! So, to do the Year 1 problem, we just approach it as we've done before.

First, let's start at the end (just as we did before). Suppose we wait until Year 2 to do anything and we end up in the *very robust* state. Our NPV at that time would be

$$6\,(\$225,000 - \$80,000) = \$870,000$$

Figure 4.49	The Decision Tree for the Two–Period Condo Construction Option

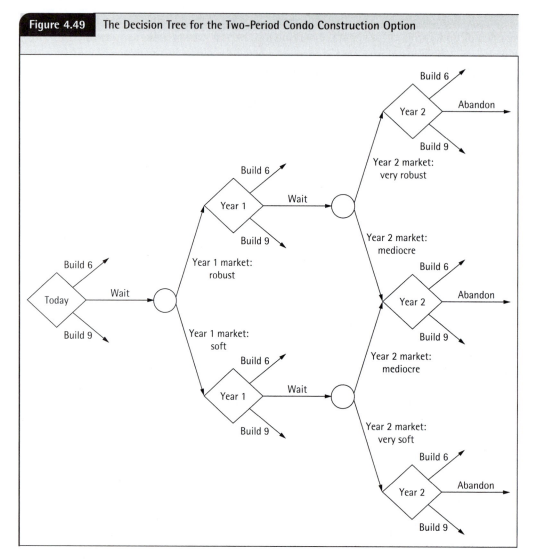

for a six-unit building, or

$$9\,(\$225{,}000 - \$90{,}000) = \$1{,}215{,}000$$

for a nine-unit building, or 0 if we abandon. So if we wait until Year 2 to build, and we end up in the *very robust* state, we will build a nine-unit building, and our NPV at that time will be $1,215,000.

Now suppose we wait until Year 2 to build, but we end up in the *mediocre* state. Our NPV at that time would be

$$6\,(\$135{,}000 - \$80{,}000) = \$330{,}000$$

for a six-unit building, or

$$9\,(\$135{,}000 - \$90{,}000) = \$405{,}000$$

for a nine-unit building, or 0 if we abandon. Again, if we wait until Year to 2 build, and we end up in the *mediocre* state, we will build a nine-unit building, and our NPV at that time will be $405,000.

Finally, suppose we wait until Year 2 to build, and we end up in the *very soft* state. Our NPV at that time would be

$$6 (\$81,000 - \$80,000) = \$6,000$$

for a six-unit building, or

$$9 (\$81,000 - \$90,000) = \$81,000$$

for a nine-unit building, or 0 if we abandon. So if we wait until Year 2 to decide, and we end up in the *very soft* state, we will only build a six-unit building, and our NPV at that time will be $6,000.

To summarize: If we wait until Year 2 to decide, we will

- Build a nine-unit building in the *very robust* state, and the NPV at that time will be $1,215,000.
- Build a nine-unit building in the *mediocre* state, and the NPV at that time will be $405,000.
- Build a six-unit building in the *very soft* state, and the NPV at that time will be $6,000.

However, if we only wait until Year 1 and then make our decision, we will

- Build a nine-unit building in the *robust* state, and the static NPV at that time will be $540,000.
- Build a six-unit building in the *soft* state, and the static NPV at that time will be $60,000.

Finally, if we invest today, we will build a six-unit building and today's static NPV will be $120,000.

But how do we decide whether to invest now, at Year 1, or at Year 2? The same way we approached the Year 1 problem. To proceed, let's sketch out how our underlying asset (built condominium) evolves over time (Figure 4.50).

Notice that I've already written in the flexibility payoffs (i.e., option payoffs) that we receive if we wait until Year 2 to decide. Suppose that we have not yet constructed as of Year 1, and we end up in the soft (UND_D = $90K) state. We then face a one-period problem just like before. We can go ahead and build a six-unit building for NPV = $60,000, or we can wait. We will build if the NPV of building exceeds the NPV of waiting, and we will wait if the option value of waiting exceeds $60,000 (the NPV of building immediately). So how do we calculate the option value of waiting? Exactly as we did in the one-period problem! Our new one-period binomial model will look like Figure 4.51.

You know how to do this problem! Let's do it the shortcut way. Here, the initial value of the underlying is $90,000, and if the underlying goes up, it increases by u% to $135,000. To solve for u,

$$\$90,000(1 + u\%) = \$135,000 \text{ so } u = 50\%$$

Similarly, if condos go down in value then we can find d:

$$\$90,000(1 + d\%) = \$81,000 \text{ so } d = -10\%.$$

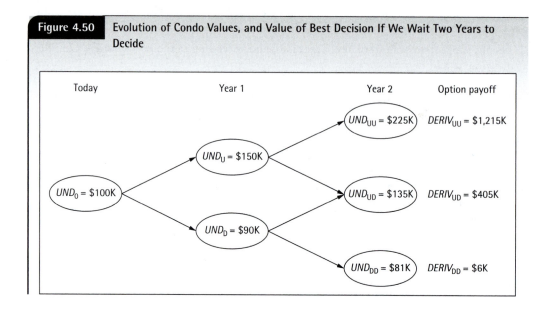

Figure 4.50   Evolution of Condo Values, and Value of Best Decision If We Wait Two Years to Decide

Today   Year 1   Year 2   Option payoff

$UND_0 = \$100K$

$UND_U = \$150K$

$UND_D = \$90K$

$UND_{UU} = \$225K$ $DERIV_{UU} = \$1,215K$

$UND_{UD} = \$135K$ $DERIV_{UD} = \$405K$

$UND_{DD} = \$81K$ $DERIV_{DD} = \$6K$

Finally, our risk-free rate of return is 10%. So we can calculate our risk-neutral probability q:

$$q = \frac{r - d}{u - d} = \frac{0.10 - (-0.10)}{0.50 - (-0.10)} = \frac{0.20}{0.60} = \frac{1}{3}$$

which implies that $1 - q = \frac{2}{3}$. Now we can solve for the value of the option to wait in the soft state at Year 1:

$$DERIV_D = \frac{\frac{1}{3} \times \$405,000 + \frac{2}{3} \times \$6,000}{1.10} = \$126,363$$

Aha! If we find ourselves in the soft state at year one, the NPV of investing immediately is $60,000, but the NPV of waiting is $126,363. So the best thing to do is wait!

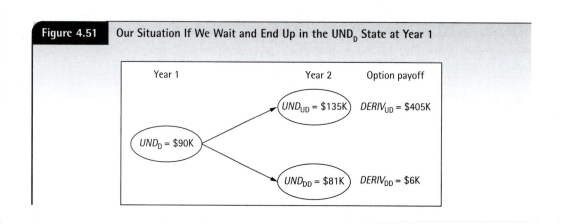

Figure 4.51   Our Situation If We Wait and End Up in the UND_D State at Year 1

Year 1   Year 2   Option payoff

$UND_D = \$90K$

$UND_{UD} = \$135K$ $DERIV_{UD} = \$405K$

$UND_{DD} = \$81K$ $DERIV_{DD} = \$6K$

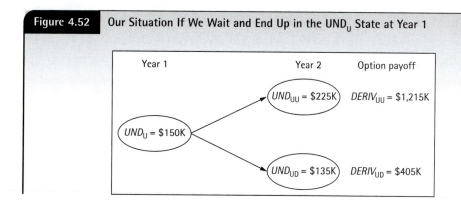

Figure 4.52   Our Situation If We Wait and End Up in the UND$_U$ State at Year 1

Now, suppose we are in the robust state ($UND_U = \$150K$) at time 1. We have a one-period problem that looks like Figure 4.52. And we proceed the same way. Recall that if we invest immediately in the robust state at Year 1, we will build a nine-unit building at an NPV of $540,000. We will wait if the NPV of waiting exceeds $540,000. What is the option value of waiting? I'll leave it to you to verify that $u = 50\%$ and $d = -10\%$ again, so $q = \frac{1}{3}$ and $(1 - q) = \frac{2}{3}$. The value of the option to wait is thus

$$DERIV_U = \frac{\dfrac{1}{3} \times \$1{,}215{,}000 + \dfrac{2}{3} \times \$405{,}000}{1.10} = \$613{,}636$$

Again, we wait—the NPV of waiting exceeds the NPV of investing immediately. Now, how do we analyze the initial decision as of today? Well, if we invest immediately, we will build a six-unit building at an NPV of $120,000. We will wait if the NPV of waiting exceeds the NPV of proceeding immediately. What is the value of the option to wait?

Again, I ask: What do we get if we wait? If we wait, and end up in the robust state, we will then receive an option that is worth $613,636. If we wait, and end up in the soft state, we will then receive an option that is worth $126,363. So our one-period problem now looks like Figure 4.53.

And now the problem is straightforward. As before, you can verify that $u = 50\%$, $d = -10\%$, so $q = \frac{1}{3}$ and $(1 - q) = \frac{2}{3}$. So, the value of the option today (and hence the value

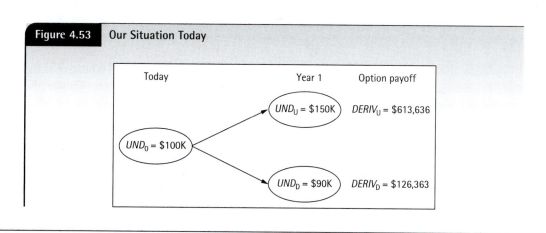

Figure 4.53   Our Situation Today

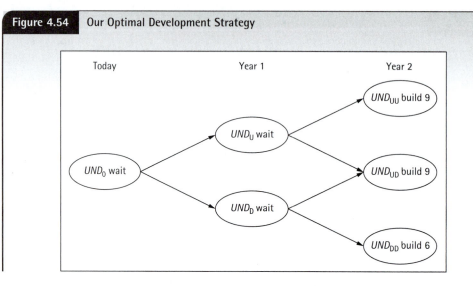

Figure 4.54   Our Optimal Development Strategy

Today   Year 1   Year 2

UND_{UU} build 9

UND_U wait

UND_0 wait

UND_{UD} build 9

UND_D wait

UND_{DD} build 6

of the land) is now

$$DERIV_0 = \frac{\frac{1}{3} \times \$613,636 + \frac{2}{3} \times \$126,363}{1.10} = \$262,533$$

The additional period added \$62K to the value of the option. This illustrates another important point: As the length of time before the option expires increases, the value of the option usually increases.

If we have two years to develop, we are willing to pay \$262,533 for the land, and our optimal development strategy will look like Figure 4.54.

4.5   Multistep Binomial Trees

Consider the following asset as it evolves through two periods of time, as shown in Figure 4.55. Here I've grown a two-period tree. You may assume that the subjective probability of any increase or decrease is always $\frac{1}{2}$. Notice that the tree has two branches out of each Time 1 state. This is called a *nonrecombinant* model—there is only one way to get to each end point, so if you know the end point, you know exactly what path it took to get there. Notice also that I've broken the one big tree down into three smaller trees, which I've outlined in dashed boxes numbered 1, 2, and 3.

Let's consider a European call on this risky asset, with strike price equal to 1 and expiration at the end of the second time step. I've written in the expiration-date payoffs on the option in Figure 4.56.

One of the great features of the binomial model is that we can consider each of individual binomial trials I've outlined earlier as their own single-step binomial game. To do this valuation, we simply start by cutting down the last trees and then clear-cutting the forest of trees backwards. For simplicity, we will assume that the risk-free rate is zero in this example.

Let's start with box number 2, which I've extracted for you in Figure 4.57. We will need to create a tracking portfolio that replicates the payoff of the derivative over the life of Binomial Game 2, no matter whether we end up in node UND_{UU} or UND_{UD}. At node

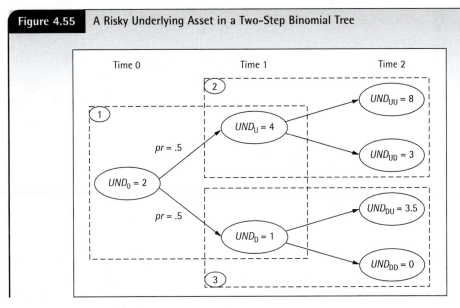

Figure 4.55 A Risky Underlying Asset in a Two-Step Binomial Tree

UND_U (which is the starting point in this analysis), Equations (4.7) and (4.8) tell us that our tracking portfolio will have

$$\Delta(\text{Game 2}) = \frac{7-2}{8-3} = 1 \text{ unit of the underlying risky asset}$$

and

$$\$\Psi(\text{Game 2}) = \frac{1}{(1+0)}\left[7-(1)8\right] = -\$1 \text{ invested in the risk-free bond}$$

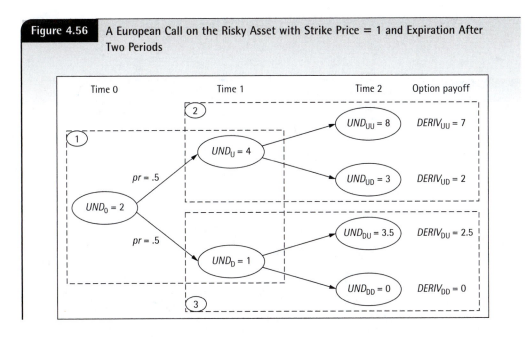

Figure 4.56 A European Call on the Risky Asset with Strike Price = 1 and Expiration After Two Periods

Figure 4.57   Binomial Game 2 Is a Single Step in Our Larger Binomial Tree

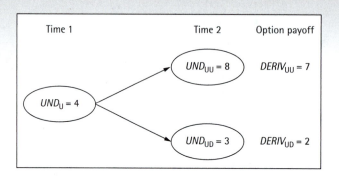

By Equation (4.5), our tracking portfolio at the beginning of Game 2 will be worth $1 \times$ $4.00 - $1 = 3, so we can say that if we get to the beginning of Game 2, our derivative will be worth $3 at that time. In other words, we can simplify Figure 4.56 as shown in Figure 4.58.

If, on the other hand, we find ourselves in Binomial Game 3 after one period (i.e., if the risky underlying asset drops in value over the first period), our situation will look like Figure 4.59.

If we find ourselves in Binomial Game 3 at Time 1, we will need a different tracking portfolio that pays off $0.50 in the UND_{UU} state and nothing in the UND_{DD} state. Again, we use Equations (4.7) and (4.8) to determine the tracking portfolio and then Equation (4.5) to solve the derivatives value at the beginning of this binomial game. In this case, our tracking portfolio will need

$$\Delta(\text{Game 3}) = \frac{2.5 - 0}{3.5 - 0} = .714 \text{ units of the underlying risky asset}$$

and

$$\$\Psi(\text{Game 3}) = \frac{1}{(1 + 0)}\left[2.5 - (.714)3.5\right] = \$0 \text{ invested in the risk-free bond}$$

Figure 4.58   Simplifying Our Multistep Binomial Tree by Pruning Away Branches from the End

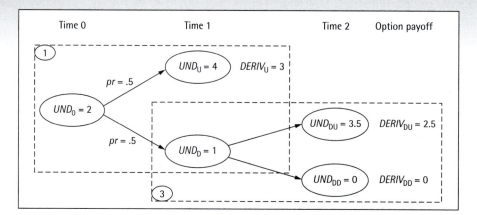

Figure 4.59 | **Binomial Game 3 Is Another Single Step in Our Larger Binomial Tree**

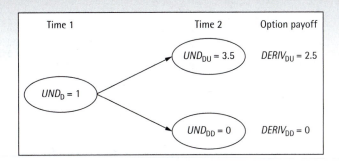

Time 1 | Time 2 | Option payoff

$UND_{DU} = 3.5$ $DERIV_{DU} = 2.5$

$UND_D = 1$

$UND_{DD} = 0$ $DERIV_{DD} = 0$

Our tracking portfolio at the beginning of Binomial Game 3 will thus be worth $0.714 \times$ $\$1.00 - \$0 = \$0.714$. In other words, if the risky asset goes down in the first period and we get to the beginning of Binomial Game 3, our derivative will be worth $\$0.714$ at that time.

You can prove to yourself that these portfolios indeed provide exactly the payoff structures needed to replicate the Time 2 payoff of the derivative. We can now prune back the branches into a one-tree problem (like our earlier example). In Binomial Game 1, if the asset goes up, we will have a derivative in Binomial Game 2 (worth $3); and if the asset goes down, we will have a derivative in Binomial Game 3 (worth $0.714). So our pruned tree looks like Figure 4.60.

Do you see what we've done? We've turned a complex problem into a very simple one, just by applying and reapplying what we learned about valuation in a single step of the binomial model. Now all that's left is to do the exercise one more time.

Initially (i.e., at the beginning of Binomial Game 1), we need a tracking portfolio that will be worth $3 if the risky underlying goes up over the first period, and $0.714 if it goes down. Using Equations (4.7), (4.8) and (4.5) one more time, the tracking portfolio that meets these criteria consists of

$$\Delta(\text{Game 1}) = \frac{3 - .714}{4 - 1} = \frac{2.286}{3} = 0.762 \text{ units of the underlying risky asset}$$

and

$$\$\Psi(\text{Game 1}) = \frac{1}{(1 + 0)}\left[3 - (.762)4\right] = -\$0.048 \text{ invested in the risk-free bond}$$

Figure 4.60

Clear–Cutting the Forest Backwards

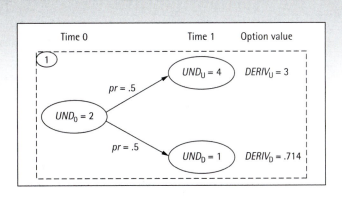

Time 0 | Time 1 | Option value

$UND_U = 4$ $DERIV_U = 3$

$pr = .5$

$UND_0 = 2$

$pr = .5$

$UND_D = 1$ $DERIV_D = .714$

Figure 4.61	Rebalancing the Tracking Portfolio as Necessary at Time 1 Is Costless.

	Game 1 Position	If Game 2 at Time 1			If Game 3 at Time 1		
		Needed	Change	Cash Flow	Needed	Change	Cash Flow
Units of Asset	0.762	1.000	+0.238	−$0.952	0.714	−0.048	+$0.048
Borrowing	−$0.048	−$1.000	−$0.952	+$0.952	$0.000	$0.048	−$0.048
				$0.0000			$0.0000

The value of the derivative at time 0 is thus the value of the initial tracking portfolio:

$$DERIV_0 = 0.762 \times \$2.00 - \$0.048 = \$1.476$$

Again, I'll leave it to you to show that the initial tracking portfolio gives us the payoff pattern we desire at Time 1. The point of this exercise, however, is more subtle.

Suppose we create the appropriate tracking portfolio at time 0. When we get to Time 1, we'll have to change our tracking portfolio to reflect the new tree in which we find ourselves. How does this affect our analysis? It doesn't, as Figure 4.61 demonstrates.

Rebalancing does not change our analysis! Once we have created the initial tracking portfolio, it is *always* costless to rebalance our position so that we ultimately have the payoff pattern required by the derivative—no matter how esoteric the derivative is!

I must tell you that I have skirted three issues here. First of all, we ignored any transactions costs that might arise from buying/selling the risky asset and the risk-free bond. This is not important for real options analysis, because in corporate finance we ignore the transactions costs of creating tracking portfolios (you've never worried about this in a DCF analysis, have you?)

Second, I assumed a zero risk-free rate of return. This was for convenience in the illustration, because if I assume a positive risk-free rate, there will sometimes be a very small rounding error in the cash flows from rebalancing.

Finally, we're working in a situation where there's perfect tracking. If the tracking portfolio exhibits imperfect tracking but has conditional mean-zero error, then there will be a cost to rebalancing the tracking portfolio *ex post*. However, the expected cost of rebalancing will be zero in every individual macroeconomic state of nature. Therefore, by the same reasons we uncovered in Chapter 2, the expected cost of rebalancing a tracking portfolio that tracks with conditional mean-zero error does not affect our valuation at all. The present value of a risky cash flow that has zero mean in all future states is exactly zero, just like the coin flip security.

What About Risk?

It is important to understand that the beta of our derivative actually changes over time. If you will recall, our initial tracking portfolio is long 0.762 unit of the asset (at $2 per unit) and borrows $0.048 at the risk-free rate. The net cash outflow from creating this tracking portfolio (and hence the cost of the derivative) is $1.476. Thus, our tracking portfolio has $1.524/$1.476 = 103.3% invested in the risky asset and −3.3% in the risk-free bond. The beta of this hedge portfolio is thus $1.033\beta_{UND}$:

$$\beta_{DERIV} = \frac{\Delta \cdot UND_0}{DERIV_0} \beta_{UND} = \frac{0.762 \times \$2}{\$1.476} \beta_{UND} = 1.033\beta_{UND}$$

Figure 4.62

The Beta of
Our Derivative
Is a Random
Variable

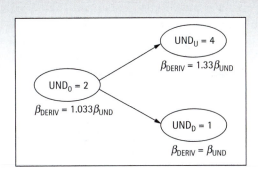

Would this give us the proper discount rate to use to value the derivative? NO! In Figure 4.62, I calculate the betas of the tracking portfolios at each node. The beta of the derivative changes, and it changes in very complex ways! The most important thing to be aware of is that the call's beta is never less than the beta of the underlying asset, and it changes randomly over time. The implication is straightforward: Since corporate growth opportunities are call options, they are riskier than their underlying assets. If we were to value the underlying asset using a positive beta, and we used this beta to calculate the value of the growth option on the asset, we would be over-estimating the value of the growth option.

We've understood derivatives from a probabilistic perspective for a century or more. The problem in developing a valuation model was figuring out a way to risk-adjust the future pay-offs. As you can see from the diagram in Figure 4.62, the beta of the derivative is itself a random variable. One of the real insights of the Black-Scholes contribution was to admit that we cannot know "the" risk-adjusted discount rate for a derivative, but instead that we must find another way to adjust for risk. We now understand that the Black-Scholes risk-free hedge is simply a portfolio of state securities (like the Reds and Blues from the earlier section), and that a necessary condition for the Black-Scholes to be applicable is for the financial market be free of arbitrage opportunities.

Figure 4.63   A Recombining Binomial Tree of Underlying Asset Values and a Different Derivative

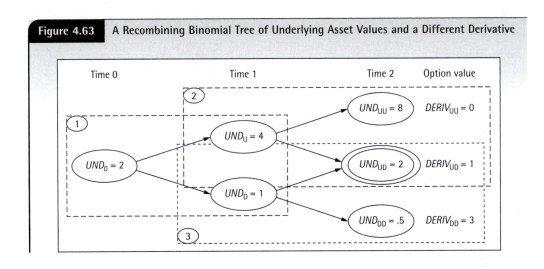

Another Example

Let's do another example, but this time let's use the risk-neutral pricing approach. Consider the two-period tree and corresponding derivative payoffs in Figure 4.63.

Notice that the tree in Figure 4.63 differs slightly from the tree in Figure 4.56, in that the new one *recombines*. That is, if the underlying goes up in value in the first period and then down in value in the second period, it will end up at the exact same price as if it evolved in the opposite manner (down then up). This is a very useful feature in a tree, because if the tree recombines, then the number of branches grows very slowly. In fact, if we let the tree grow even further to N total periods, there will be only $N + 1$ terminal states (in the nonrecombinant tree, there would be 2^N terminal states—a very large number even for $N = 10$). But even though recombination reduces the number of terminal states considerably, it does not reduce the accuracy of the model one bit—the recombinant binomial model approaches the limiting normal distribution just as quickly as one that does not recombine.

Further, notice that things are consistent throughout the tree in Figure 4.63. No matter where you are, $u = 100\%$ and $d = -50\%$, so our risk-neutral probability q will be

$$q = \frac{r - d}{u - d} = \frac{r - (-0.50)}{1.00 - (-0.50)} = \frac{r + 0.50}{1.50}$$

at every node in the tree! Thus, if we let our risk-free rate of return be 10% *per step*, the risk-neutral probability of the up and down moves will be $q = .40$ and $(1 - q) = .60$, respectively, everywhere in the tree. This will make the calculation easy as well.

If we clear-cut the forest from right-to-left, we reduce the two-step tree in Figure 4.63 to the one-step tree in Figure 4.64 because in Binomial Game 2

$$DERIV_U = \frac{q \times DERIV_{UU} + (1 - q) \times DERIV_{UD}}{1 + r} = \frac{.4(0) + .6(1)}{1.10} = \$0.5455$$

and in Binomial Game 3

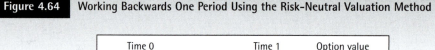

$$DERIV_D = \frac{q \times DERIV_{DU} + (1 - q) \times DERIV_{DD}}{1 + r} = \frac{.4(1) + .6(3)}{1.10} = \$2$$

Figure 4.64	Working Backwards One Period Using the Risk-Neutral Valuation Method

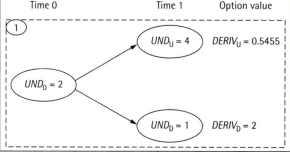

Notice that $DERIV_{UD}$ appears in both valuation equations—you can end up at UND_{UD} no matter what happens in the first time step.

Given these time-1 values, the value of the derivative at time zero is

$$DERIV_0 = \frac{q \times DERIV_U + (1 - q) \times DERIV_D}{1 + r} = \frac{.4(0.5455) + .6(2)}{1.10} = \$1.289$$

Notice what else we could have done:

$$DERIV_0 = \frac{q \times DERIV_U + (1 - q) \times DERIV_D}{1 + r}$$

$$= \frac{q \left[\frac{q \times DERIV_{UU} + (1 - q) \times DERIV_{UD}}{1 + r} \right] + (1 - q) \left[\frac{q \times DERIV_{UD} + (1 - q) \times DERIV_{DD}}{1 + r} \right]}{1 + r}$$

If we gather terms, we get

$$DERIV_0 = \frac{q^2}{(1 + r)^2} DERIV_{UU} + \frac{2q(1 - q)}{(1 + r)^2} DERIV_{UD} + \frac{(1 - q)^2}{(1 + r)^2} DERIV_{DD} \qquad (4.21)$$

which is a two-period version of our formula for valuation by state prices (i.e., forming a tracking portfolio with state securities). In Figure 4.63, there are *three* possible terminal states, so there are three state securities in Equation (4.21). The time-0 value of $1 of cash flow in the up-up state is $q^2/(1 + r)^2$; the time-0 value of $1 of cash flow in the up-down (or down-up) state is $2q(1 - q)/(1 + r)^2$; and the time-0 value of $1 of cash flow in the down-down state is $(1 - q)^2/(1 + r)^2$.

Of course, the state-pricing approach is absolutely equivalent to the risk-neutral probability approach because we just collect the denominator:

$$DERIV_0 = \frac{q^2 \times DERIV_{UU} + 2q(1 - q) \times DERIV_{UD} + (1 - q)^2 \times DERIV_{DD}}{(1 + r)^2} \qquad (4.22)$$

In our example

$$DERIV_0 = \frac{(.4)^2(0) + 2(.4)(.6)(1) + (.6)^2(3)}{(1.10)^2} = \$1.289$$

which gives us exactly the same answer. Does this mean anything? Yes. State pricing, risk-neutral pricing, and tracking portfolios are all identical in a multiperiod model, just as they are in a single period model. Let's find the patterns that allow us to take this great shortcut.

First, note that for every step (or period) in the recombinant tree, we add exactly one terminal state. In a one-step tree, there were two possible outcomes; in the two-step tree, there are three possible outcomes. The general result: If you have N steps in the recombinant tree, you will have $N + 1$ possible outcomes.

Second, we can calculate a risk-neutral probability for each outcome in an N-step tree! Let's do this by examining our two-step problem. In our two-step tree, what is the risk-neutral probability that the asset will end up in state UND_{UU}? Well, there is only one possible path to state

UND_{UU}—the asset must go up in value in the first step, with risk-neutral probability $(r - d)/(u - d)$, then must go up in the second period, again with risk-neutral probability $(r - d)/(u - d)$. Thus:

$$\text{Risk-neutral probability of } UND_{UU} = \left(\frac{r - d}{u - d}\right)\left(\frac{r - d}{u - d}\right) = q^2$$

Notice how q^2 enters the valuation Equations (4.21) and (4.22). Similarly, there is only one possible path to state UND_{DD}—the asset must go down in value twice (or up in value zero times). The risk-neutral probability of this happening is

$$\text{Risk-neutral probability of } UND_{DD} = \left(1 - \frac{r - d}{u - d}\right)\left(1 - \frac{r - d}{u - d}\right) = (1 - q)^2$$

Notice how $(1 - q)^2$ enters valuation Equations (4.21) and (4.22). Now, what is the risk-neutral probability of ending up at state UND_{UD} (the middle state)? Well, there are *two* possible ways of getting to node UND_{UD}: The asset could go up-down, which occurs with risk-neutral probability $q(1 - q)$; or the asset could go down-up, which occurs with risk-neutral probability $(1 - q)q$. Thus:

$$\text{Risk-neutral probability of } UND_{UD} = \left(\frac{r - d}{u - d}\right)\left(1 - \frac{r - d}{u - d}\right) + \left(1 - \frac{r - d}{u - d}\right)\left(\frac{r - d}{u - d}\right)$$
$$= 2q(1 - q)$$

Again, notice how $2q(1 - q)$ enters valuation Equations (4.21) and (4.22). Finally, note that $q^2 + 2q(1 - q) + (1 - q)^2 = 1$: The risk-neutral probabilities of all terminal states sum to 1. To summarize, in a two-step tree:

$$\text{Risk-neutral probability of } \begin{cases} \text{2 up and 0 down} = q^2 \\ \text{1 up and 1 down} = 2q(1 - q) \\ \text{0 up and 2 down} = (1 - q)^2 \end{cases}$$

If we extended the tree to *three* time-steps, there would be *four* possible terminal states. What are the risk-neutral probabilities of each of these states?

$$\text{Risk-neutral probability of } \begin{cases} \text{3 up and 0 down} = q^3 \\ \text{2 up and 1 down} = 3q^2(1 - q) \\ \text{1 up and 2 down} = 3q(1 - q)^2 \\ \text{0 up and 3 down} = (1 - q)^3 \end{cases}$$

Are you starting to see the pattern? The risk-neutral probability of up-up-up is $q \times q \times q = q^3$ and the risk-neutral probability of down-down-down is $(1 - q) \times (1 - q) \times (1 - q) = (1 - q)^3$, obviously. But why is the risk-neutral probability of two ups and one down equal to $3q^2(1 - q)$?

Think back to our pachinko machine. If you recall, in our pachinko machine there was only one possible path to the most extreme bins, but there were multiple paths to the middle bins. The same thing goes here. *One* possible way of getting two ups and one down is up-up-down, and this occurs with risk-neutral probability $q \times q \times (1 - q) = q^2(1 - q)$. But there are other ways of getting two ups and one down! A *second* possibility is for the asset to move up-down-up, and this occurs with risk-neutral probability $q \times (1 - q) \times q = q^2(1 - q)$. Finally, the *third* way for the asset to experience two ups and one down is down-up-up, which occurs with risk-neutral probability $(1 - q) \times q \times q = q^2(1 - q)$. There are three ways for the asset to make two up moves and one down move, and the risk-neutral probability of each is $q^2(1 - q)$, so the cumulative risk-neutral probability of two up moves and one down move is $3q^2(1 - q)$. Similarly, there are three ways of making one up move and two down moves, and the risk-neutral probability of each is $q(1 - q)^2$, so the cumulative risk-neutral probability of one up and two downs is $3q(1 - q)^2$.

The general rule is this: In an N-step recombinant tree in which q stays constant throughout the tree, the risk-neutral probability of a particular path in which the asset makes j up moves is

$$\text{Risk-neutral probability of a path with } j \text{ up steps out of } N \text{ total steps} = q^j(1 - q)^{N-j} \quad (4.23)$$

Moreover, the number of different paths the asset could take to make j up moves in an N-step tree is

$$\text{Number of paths through an } N\text{-step tree that have exactly } j \text{ up steps} = \binom{N}{j} = \frac{N!}{j!(N - j)!} \quad (4.24)$$

So, the risk-neutral probability of ending at a particular state is

$$\text{Risk-neutral probability of a state requiring } j \text{ up steps in an } N\text{-step tree} = \frac{N!}{j!(N - j)!}q^j(1 - q)^{N-j} \quad (4.25)$$

Microsoft Excel has the function $= \text{binomdist}(j, N, q, \text{false})$, which calculates Equation (4.25) for you, and a second function $= \text{combin}(N, j)$, which calculates $N!/[j! (N - j)!]$, Equation (4.24), for you.

Remember, the risk-neutral probability of a state is really the price of a state-security for that state times $(1 + r)^N$. So what the functions are really doing is valuing a portfolio of state securities, just like in the 2-step binomial model. The one difference is that here we no longer have simple Reds and Blues; rather, in an N-step tree, we have a rainbow of $N + 1$ state securities (because there are $N + 1$ things that can happen by the end of the tree). The Time 0 price of a state security that pays \$1 after j up steps in an N-step tree is thus

Current Price of \$1 to be received only if underlying goes up j times in an N-step tree

$$= \frac{1}{(1 + r)^N} \frac{N!}{j!(N - j)!} q^j(1 - q)^{N-j} \quad (4.26)$$

Let's make sure we understand this. To get the terminal state prices for our most recent two-step tree in Figure 4.63, start by counting the number of up steps required to get to each terminal state, as I've done for you in Figure 4.65.

Next, calculate the risk-neutral probability of actually observing a path that has j up steps. Using our notation that the risk-neutral probability of an up step in any single step of the tree is q, the risk-neutral probability of j up steps in an N-step tree is simply equal to $q^j(1 - q)^{N-j}$, as shown in Figure 4.66.

Next, use Equation (4.24) to calculate the number of possible paths that could be possibly taken to get to each terminal node. See Figure 4.67.

Figure 4.65   First, Count the Number of Up Steps Required to Get To Each Terminal State

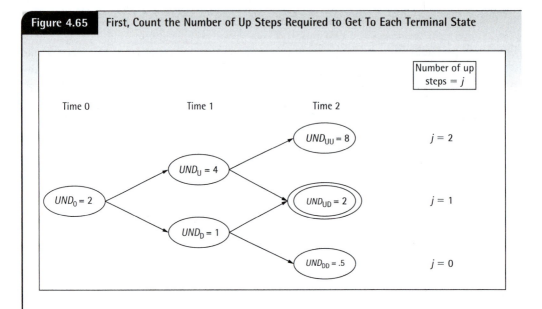

Finally, multiply the risk-neutral probability of j up steps times the number of possible paths with j up steps, and then divide this by $(1 + r)^N$ to get the state price (as you can see in Figure 4.68). It's that simple!

Let's check this result. Remember the derivative we priced in this tree (Figure 4.63)? If we multiply its Time 2 payoffs by the state prices, we get \$1.289—exactly the same price we calculated before. See my calculation in Figure 4.69.

You may be wondering why the state price for the middle state (\$0.3967) is higher than the state price for the low state (\$0.2975). Is this in conflict with my earlier story about risk-aversion (i.e., that risk-averse agents value consumption in bad states more than in better states)? Not at all. The reason that the state price in the middle state is so high here is that there are *two possible paths* to get to the same middle state. So in effect, there are really *two* middle

Figure 4.66   Next, Calculate the Risk-Neutral Probability of Any Path with j Up-Steps

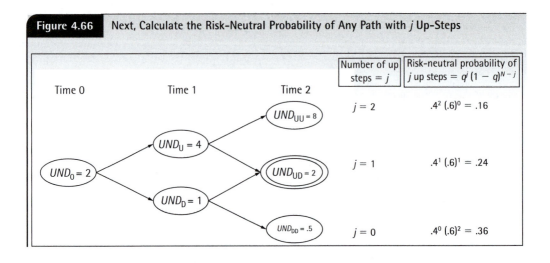

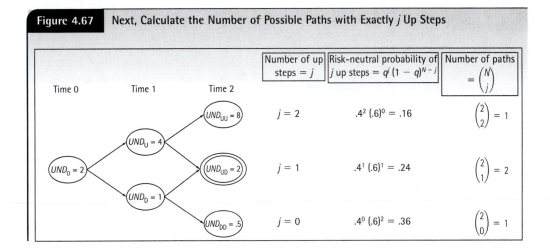

Figure 4.67 | Next, Calculate the Number of Possible Paths with Exactly *j* Up Steps

states, which look identical in our recombinant tree. If we let the tree evolve without recombining (as we did in the beginning of this lesson), there would be four states after two time steps—and the two middle states would have the same state price of $0.19835.

What Have We Learned So Far?

1. Extending the single-step binomial tree to a multistep binomial tree does not change the way we do our analysis. No matter where we find ourselves in the tree, we are always in a simple binomial game and we can price any derivative by arbitrage.
2. In a multistep tree, our risk-neutral probability *q* maintains the same meaning as in a single-step tree. It is really the way we adjust for risk: $q/(1 + r)$ is the price of a claim that pays $1 after an up move in the next step of the tree (and $0 otherwise), and $(1 - q)/(1 + r)$ is the price of a claim that pays $1 after a down move in the next step

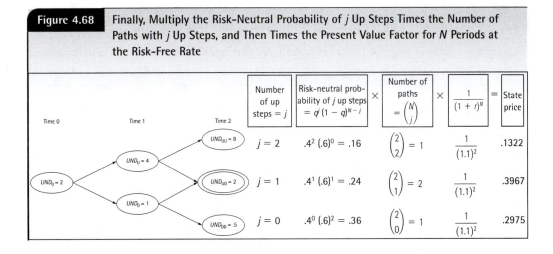

Figure 4.68 | Finally, Multiply the Risk-Neutral Probability of *j* Up Steps Times the Number of Paths with *j* Up Steps, and Then Times the Present Value Factor for *N* Periods at the Risk-Free Rate

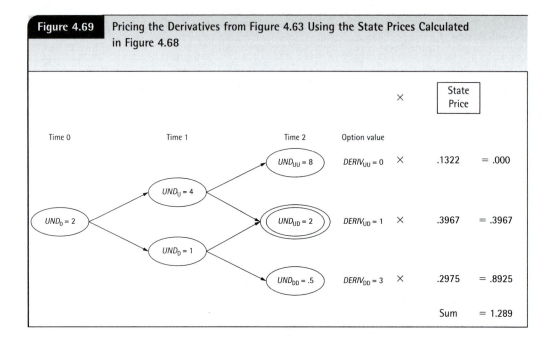

Figure 4.69   **Pricing the Derivatives from Figure 4.63 Using the State Prices Calculated in Figure 4.68**

of the tree. By calculating q, we get around the need to calculate a risk-adjusted discount rate when pricing a derivative.

3. If we build our trees in a clever way, our risk-neutral probability q will remain the same throughout the tree and hence we will need to calculate it only once.

4.6 How to Build Recombinant Binomial Trees

We're finally at the point where I can show you how to build multistep binomial trees that approximate a normal distribution for the *returns* on the underlying asset.

One Complication: Continuous Compounding and Discounting

There are a variety of ways to build binomial trees that approximate a normal distribution of asset returns very closely. Some are actually easier to work with than others. While I personally like the simplest models, I feel compelled to present to you the most common binomial model construction. The one complication that this brings up is that it uses continuous compounding. For those of you who are familiar with continuous compounding and discounting (and extracting simple rates of return from continuously-compounded values), just skip this section. For those of you that don't want to deal with continuous compounding at all, see Appendix 4.2 for a simpler tree building procedure.

Suppose you put \$1 in a bank CD that promises a 10% annual return, and you leave the money there for one year. How much do you have at the end of the year? This is easy: At the end of the year, you have

$$\$1(1 + r) = \$1(1.10) = \$1.10$$

I could have asked you a similar question: If you invest $1 in the CD today, and the bank promises to repay you $1.10 at the end of the year, what rate of return will you earn? To answer this, you solve for r:

$$\$1(1 + r) = \$1.10$$
$$(1 + r) = \frac{\$1.10}{\$1}$$
$$(1 + r) = 1.10, \text{ or } = 10\%$$

Now make the problem harder. Suppose you invest $1 in the one-year CD, and the bank promises you 10% (simple) interest compounded *semiannually*. What this means is that interest is credited every six months. You invest $1 today, and at the end of six months you earn 10%/2 = 5% interest on that $1. So at the end of six months, you have $1.05:

$$\$1(1 + r) = \$1(1.05) = \$1.05$$

The bank then reinvests that money for you, both the $1 principal and the $0.05 interest, at 5% for the next six months. At the end of the next six months, you have

$$\$1.05 \ (1 + r) = \$1.05 \ (1.05) = \$1.1025$$

To calculate it in one step:

$$\$1\left(1 + \frac{r}{2}\right)\left(1 + \frac{r}{2}\right) = \$1\left(1 + \frac{r}{2}\right)^2 = \$1(1.05)^2 = \$1.1025$$

Again, if the bank promises you $1.1025 at the end of the year with *semiannual compounding*, you would calculate the annual (simple) interest rate r as follows:

$$\$1\left(1 + \frac{r}{2}\right)\left(1 + \frac{r}{2}\right) = \$1\left(1 + \frac{r}{2}\right)^2 = \$1.1025$$
$$\left(1 + \frac{r}{2}\right)^2 = \frac{\$1.1025}{\$1}$$
$$\left(1 + \frac{r}{2}\right) = \sqrt{\frac{\$1.1025}{\$1}}$$
$$\left(1 + \frac{r}{2}\right) = 1.05, \text{ or}\left(1 + \frac{r}{2}\right) = 1.05, \text{ or } r = 10\%$$

Next, suppose the bank compounds the interest monthly. Given a simple annual rate of 10% per year, interest compounds at 10%/12 = .833% per month. Over the first month, your $1 investment grows to

$$\$1\left(1 + \frac{r}{12}\right) = \$1\left(1 + \frac{.10}{12}\right) = \$1(1.00833) = \$1.00833$$

You then reinvest the entire amount, and at the end of Month 2 you have

$$\$1.00833\left(1 + \frac{r}{12}\right) = \$1.00833(1.00833) = \$1(1.00833)(1.00833) = \$1(1.00833)^2 = \$1.016729$$

At the end of the year, your CD will be worth

$$\$1\left(1 + \frac{r}{12}\right)^{12} = \$1\left(1 + \frac{.10}{12}\right)^{12} = \$1(1.00833)^{12} = \$1.104713$$

If instead of promising an interest rate, the bank promises to repay you $1.104713 at the end of a year for a $1 investment today compounded monthly, you could figure the annual interest rate as

$$\$1\left(1 + \frac{r}{12}\right)^{12} = \$1.104713$$

$$\left(1 + \frac{r}{12}\right)^{12} = \frac{\$1.104713}{\$1}$$

$$\left(1 + \frac{r}{12}\right) = \sqrt[12]{\frac{\$1.104713}{\$1}}$$

$$\left(1 + \frac{r}{12}\right) = 1.00833, \frac{r}{12} = .00833, r = 10\%$$

You probably noticed that as you increase the number of compounding periods within the year, you increase the dollar payoff on the CD throughout the year because you earn interest on interest. This is the effect of compounding. The general rule is this: If you invest P_0 at a simple annual interest rate r for one year, and compounding takes place N times during the year, then the amount of money you have at the end of the year P_1 is given by

$$P_0\left(1 + \frac{r}{N}\right)^N = P_1$$

Similarly, if I tell you that an investment of P_0 turns into a payoff of P_1 over one year's time with compounding N times per year, you could solve for the simple annual rate of interest r as follows:

$$\left(1 + \frac{r}{N}\right) = \sqrt[N]{\frac{P_1}{P_0}}$$

You can make N larger and larger: compounding every week ($N = 52$), every day ($N = 365$), every hour ($N = 8,760$), every minute (N = 525,600), every second ($N = 31,536,000$). You could cut to nanoseconds if you like.

So what would happen if the bank were to promise interest compounded *continuously* over the year? Continuous compounding would mean that every instant of time, you earn interest on your invested money, and your principal and interest are then reinvested for the next instant of time. How much would you have at the end of the year?

This is actually easier than it sounds. Just think of what happens as N gets very large. Mathematicians have already worked it out for us:

$$\lim_{N\to\infty}\left(1 + \frac{r}{N}\right)^N = e^r$$

where e is the inverse of the logarithm function (antilogarithm) with natural base. If you invest $1, continuously compounded throughout the year at the simple annual interest rate of r%, by the end of the year you will have $1e^r$.

More generally, the future value of a cash flow CF, compounded *continuously* at the (simple) rate of return r per year for t years is

$$FV = CFe^{rt}$$

where t can be any number or fractions of years (e.g., $t = 2.25$ is two years and three months, $t = 0.5$ is one-half year). The present value of the same cash flow, discounted at a continuously compounded rate of r per year for t years, is

$$PV = CFe^{-rt}$$

Now turn the problem around. If you invest P_0 at the beginning of the year, interest compounds continuously, and by the end of the year you have P_1, what rate of return have you earned? Well, just use simple algebra:

$$P_0 e^r = P_1$$

$$e^r = \frac{P_1}{P_0}$$

$$r = \ln\left(\frac{P_1}{P_0}\right)$$

You extract the simple return from the continuously compounded result by taking the logarithm of the price relative (i.e., the price at the end of the year divided by the price at the beginning of the year). We call this the *log return*. As the asset value falls toward zero, the log return approaches $-\infty$ (rather than -100%, as in a simple return calculation). Our assumption of normally distributed returns actually applies only to *log returns*, because log returns are defined over $(-\infty, +\infty)$ as a normal random variable should be.

If your time period is of length t years, the calculation above gives you the periodic return but the annualized return requires a time adjustment:

$$r = \frac{1}{t}\ln\left(\frac{P_1}{P_0}\right)$$

For an example, suppose you invested $2 on January 1, 2000, in a CD, and at the end of November 2000 you had $2.30. What continuously compounded rate of return r have you earned on an annualized basis? Well, $P_0 = \$2$, $P_1 = \$2.30$, and $t = 11/12$. So since

$$P_0 e^{rt} = P_1$$

$$\$2.00 e^{r\frac{11}{12}} = \$2.30$$

$$e^{r\frac{11}{12}} = \frac{\$2.30}{\$2.00}$$

$$\ln\left(e^{r\frac{11}{12}}\right) = \ln\left(\frac{\$2.30}{\$2.00}\right)$$

$$r\frac{11}{12} = \ln(1.15), \quad \text{so} \quad r = 15.24\%$$

The Mathematics of Binomial Trees

Suppose the current (or starting) value of a risky asset is UND_0, which is known, and the random value of the asset at the end of the year is $\widetilde{UND}_1$ (the tilde designates that the asset's terminal value is a *random variable*). Recall that if you observe the value UND^*_1 at the end of the year, the log return earned over the year is

$$r^* = \ln\left(\frac{UND^*_1}{UND_0}\right)$$

Since the asset's terminal value is random, the log return over the period is random as well. We will assume that the distribution of possible log returns is normal. A normal distribution is completely characterized by its mean and variance, so you need to specify these up front. We will assume that the asset you want to model has log returns that are distributed normal with annual mean (or expected log return) m and annual standard deviation of log return σ.

$$\tilde{r} \equiv \ln\left(\frac{\widetilde{UND}_1}{UND_0}\right) \sim N(m, \sigma)$$

Since we are working in continuous compounding, we can look at any fraction of the year Δt. That is, we can look at the distribution of log returns and prices at $\Delta t = .5$ (meaning halfway through the year), $\Delta t = 11/12$ (meaning after 11 months), and so on. Over Δt years (or fraction of a year), the expected log return is $m \cdot \Delta t$. The variance in log returns over Δt years is $\sigma^2 \cdot \Delta t$, so the standard deviation of log returns over Δt years is $\sqrt{\sigma^2(\Delta t)} = \sigma\sqrt{\Delta t}$.

Even though the expected *log return* over Δt years is $m \cdot \Delta t$, the expected *value* of the asset after Δt years is *not* $UND_0 \times e^{m \cdot \Delta t}$. Why? Because if log returns are normally distributed, then the probability distribution of *values* is *lognormal*, and a lognormal distribution is not symmetric about its mean. Think of it this way: The price of a stock can go sky high during a year, but it cannot fall below zero. So the distribution of future values of the stock has a long right-hand tail (skewness), and this skewness affects the mean! A lognormal distribution is shown in Figure 4.70.

Do you see the right-hand skewness in Figure 4.70? Notice that the mean (expected value) is not at the peak—it is off to the right. The peak is the *median* value. The right-skewness of the

Figure 4.70

A Lognormal Probability Distribution

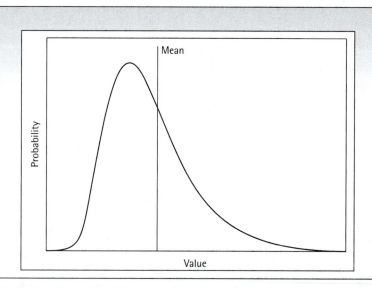

lognormal distribution makes the mean greater than the median; further, there is more probability mass below the mean than above! The *median* value is $UND_0 \times e^{m \cdot \Delta t}$, but the median is
really irrelevant to us.

Given the expected log return of $m \cdot \Delta t$ and the standard deviation in log return of $\sigma \sqrt{\Delta t}$,
the expected (or mean) *value* of the risky asset at the end of Δt years (or fractions of a year) is

$$E\{UND_{\Delta t}\} = UND_0 e^{(m+\frac{1}{2}\sigma^2) \cdot \Delta t} \qquad (4.27)$$

and the standard deviation of values after Δt years is

$$stdev\{UND_{\Delta t}\} = \left[UND_0 e^{(m+\frac{1}{2}\sigma^2) \cdot \Delta t}\right]\left(e^{\sigma^2 \cdot \Delta t} - 1\right)^{1/2} \qquad (4.28)$$

The $\frac{1}{2}\sigma^2$ term enters Equation (4.27) because of the skewness of the lognormal distribution. Since
asset values cannot fall below 0, if you want to add volatility (i.e., extreme outcomes) then you
have to add them to the right-hand tail of the distribution, which pulls the mean out to the right.

The expected log return is also called the *geometric mean return,* and it is not the risk-adjusted
rate of return on the asset. The risk-adjusted rate of return on an asset (or the required rate of
return for discounting) is the arithmetic mean return. The arithmetic mean return μ is defined
as the rate of return that relates the current asset price to the expected future price. Since the
expected value of the asset at the end of the year is

$$E\{UND_{\Delta t}\} = UND_0 e^{\left(m+\frac{1}{2}\sigma^2\right) \cdot \Delta t}$$

then the expected (or mean) arithmetic return μ satisfies

$$UND_0 e^{\mu \cdot \Delta t} = UND_0 e^{\left(m+\frac{1}{2}\sigma^2\right) \cdot \Delta t}$$

So obviously, the relationship between the annual arithmetic mean return μ and the geometric
(or log) mean return m is $\mu = m + .5\,\sigma^2$, or $m = \mu - .5\,\sigma^2$.[18],[19]

Now consider the binomial model where an asset starts with value UND_0 and moves up with
subjective probability p and down with subjective probability $1 - p$ over a period with length
Δt years (or fraction of a year):

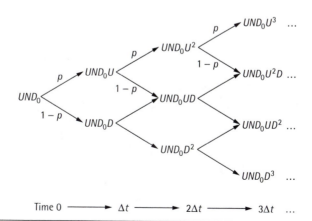

[18] The difference between the arithmetic and geometric mean returns comes about because of the order of operations. To
calculate the geometric mean return, first calculate the log return in each possible future state and then take the probability-
weighted average. To calculate the arithmetic mean return, first take the probability-weighted average of all possible future
values, divide by the current value of the asset, then take the logarithm of this price relative.

[19] Many textbook writers get sloppy and call the expected log return the "expected return". Be careful. Throughout this text, I
will use the notation m for the expected log return (or geometric mean return) and μ for the actual expected return (or
arithmetic mean return).

Notice what's going on. If the asset goes up, its prior value is multiplied by some number U, and if it goes down, its prior value is multiplied by some number D. We need to find values for U, D, and p such that for any Δt (any point in the tree), the distribution of random values is lognormally distributed with mean and standard deviation given in Equations (4.27) and (4.28). Here's where the relationship between normal and lognormal comes in handy. If the distribution of *values* is distributed lognormal with mean and standard deviation given in Equations (4.27) and (4.28), then the distribution of *log returns* over the period Δt will be normal with mean $m \cdot \Delta t$ and standard deviation $\sigma \sqrt{\Delta t}$. Remembering that we are working in continuous compounding, the expected log return of the asset at the end of the first time tick is

$$E\{log\,return\} = E\left\{\ln\left(\frac{\widetilde{UND_{\Delta t}}}{UND_0}\right)\right\}$$

$$= p\ln\left(\frac{UND_0 U}{UND_0}\right) + (1-p)\ln\left(\frac{UND_0 D}{UND_0}\right)$$

$$= p\ln U + (1-p)\ln D$$

and the variance of log returns is

$$var\{log\,return\} = var\left\{\ln\left(\frac{\widetilde{UND_{\Delta t}}}{UND_0}\right)\right\}$$

$$= p\left[\ln\left(\frac{UND_0 U}{UND_0}\right)\right]^2 + (1-p)\left[\ln\left(\frac{UND_0 D}{UND_0}\right)\right]^2 - \left[p\ln\left(\frac{UND_0 U}{UND_0}\right) - (1-p)\ln\left(\frac{UND_0 D}{UND_0}\right)\right]^2$$

$$= p\,(\ln U)^2 + (1-p)(\ln D)^2 - [p\ln U + (1-p)\ln D]^2$$

$$= p\,(1-p)(\ln U - \ln D)^2$$

where I have used the definition of the variance of a random variable $Var\{\tilde{x}\} = E\{x^2\} - (E\{x\})^2$. So, I need to find values for U, D, and p so that the binomial model gives us the right distribution of log returns; that is, such that over a period of length Δt

$$p\ln U + (1-p)\ln D = m \cdot \Delta t = (\mu - .5\sigma^2) \cdot \Delta t \tag{4.29}$$

and

$$p\,(1-p)(\ln U - \ln D)^2 = \sigma^2 \cdot \Delta t \tag{4.30}$$

This is an interesting situation—there are two equations to satisfy simultaneously, but *three* unknowns (U, D, and p). What this means is that there are an infinite number of solutions (combinations of U, D, and p) that will jointly work in Equations (4.29) and (4.30).

In this situation, we are free to be just a little bit arbitrary. Let's add the restriction $D = \frac{1}{U}$ so that the up and down multipliers are symmetric. In this case, our problem reduces to finding the U and p that simultaneously solve

$$(2p - 1)\ln U = m \cdot \Delta t = (\mu - .5\sigma^2) \cdot \Delta t \tag{4.31}$$

and

$$4p\,(1-p)(\ln U)^2 = \sigma^2 \cdot \Delta t \tag{4.32}$$

Do you remember how to solve simultaneous equations? Take one equation and perform some operation to it (multiply or divide it by something, raise it to a power, etc.), so that, when you add it to the other equation, one of the unknowns drops out. Here we'll square Equation (4.31) to get

$$(2p - 1)^2(\ln U)^2 = (m \cdot \Delta t)^2 = (\mu - .5\sigma^2)^2 \cdot (\Delta t)^2$$

so our simultaneous equations now look like this:

$$(4p^2 - 4p + 1)(\ln U)^2 = (m \cdot \Delta t)^2 = (\mu - .5\sigma^2)^2 \cdot (\Delta t)^2 \tag{4.33}$$

$$(4p - 4p^2)(\ln U)^2 = \sigma^2 \cdot \Delta t \tag{4.34}$$

Add Equations (4.33) and (4.34) together, and p disappears!

$$(\ln U)^2 = (\mu - .5\sigma^2)^2 \cdot (\Delta t)^2 + \sigma^2 \cdot \Delta t = (m \cdot \Delta t)^2 + \sigma^2 \cdot \Delta t \tag{4.35}$$

Substitute Equation (4.35) back into (4.31), and solve for p:

$$p = \frac{1}{2} + \frac{\frac{1}{2}}{\sqrt{\frac{\sigma^2 \cdot \Delta t}{(m \cdot \Delta t)^2} + 1}} = \frac{1}{2} + \frac{\frac{1}{2}}{\sqrt{\frac{\sigma^2}{m^2 \cdot \Delta t} + 1}} \tag{4.36}$$

and exponentiate (4.35) to solve for U:

$$U = e^{\sqrt{\sigma^2 \cdot \Delta t + (m \cdot \Delta t)^2}} \tag{4.37}$$

remembering in both cases that $m = \mu - .5\sigma^2$. Now the fun part: Think about what happens to Equations (4.36) and (4.37) when the time step Δt gets very small. As Δt approaches 0, $(\Delta t)^2$ approaches zero much faster. So, in the limit,

$$\lim_{\Delta t \to 0}(p) = \frac{1}{2} + \frac{1}{2}\frac{m}{\sigma}\sqrt{\Delta t} = \frac{1}{2} + \frac{(\mu - .5\sigma^2)}{2\sigma}\sqrt{\Delta t} \tag{4.38}$$

and

$$\lim_{\Delta t \to 0}(U) = e^{\sigma\sqrt{\Delta t}} \tag{4.39}$$

So we are there! To build a binomial tree of lognormally distributed asset *values*, where the *log returns* of the underlying asset are normally distributed with standard deviation σ and mean $m = \mu - .5\sigma^2$ per year (where μ is the arithmetic mean return or required rate of return you would use in a DCF to value an asset), use the following parameters:

- Pick a length of time Δt for each binomial time step:
- Set p, the subjective probability of an up step, to be

$$p = \frac{1}{2} + \frac{(\mu - .5\sigma^2)}{2\sigma}\sqrt{\Delta t}$$

- Set U, the multiplier for an up step, to be

$$U = e^{\sigma\sqrt{\Delta t}}$$

- And set D, the multiplier for a down step, to be

$$D = \frac{1}{U} = e^{-\sigma\sqrt{\Delta t}}$$

Remember—you don't really need to know p to price derivatives. I include it here because you *might* want to say something about the subjective probability that the option is exercised, or you might want to draw a picture of the real-world distribution of asset values to gain a heuristic understanding of σ. You do, however, need to know the risk-neutral probability q. To find q, remember that the current price of the underlying must equal the discounted expectation of its future value with the expectation taken using the risk-neutral probability measure and discounting at the risk-free rate:

$$UND_0 = \frac{q \times UND_{Up} + (1 - q) \times UND_{Dn}}{e^{r \cdot \Delta t}} \qquad (4.40)$$

Since $UND_{Up} = UND_0 \times U$ and $UND_{Dn} = UND_0 \times D$, Equation (4.40) reduces to

$$e^{r \cdot \Delta t} = q \times e^{\sigma \sqrt{\Delta t}} + (1 - q) \times e^{-\sigma \sqrt{\Delta t}} \qquad (4.41)$$

(where I've plugged in the solutions for U and D that we already found). From Equation (4.41), it is easy to solve for q:

$$q = \frac{e^{r \cdot \Delta t} - D}{U - D} \qquad (4.42)$$

Summary: How to Build and Use Binomial Trees

To build a binomial tree of underlying values and then value a European-style derivative written on that underlying, all you have to do is this:

1. Determine the initial value of the underlying asset UND_0.
2. Determine the annual volatility (standard deviation) of the *log returns* of the underlying asset σ.
3. Determine the time to expiration of the derivative T.
4. Determine how long you want each binomial step to be in terms of a fraction of a year. This is Δt. There will be $N = T/\Delta t$ steps in the tree; or, if you want N time steps over the entire T year period, $\Delta t = T/N$.
5. Determine the annual risk-free rate of return r.
6. Using σ and Δt, calculate the size of the up and down steps in your tree:

$$U = e^{\sigma \sqrt{\Delta t}}$$

$$D = \frac{1}{U} = e^{-\sigma \sqrt{\Delta t}}$$

7. Using your starting underlying value, build the first binomial step of the tree. If the asset goes up in value, its value goes to $UND_0 U$, and if it goes down in value, its value goes down to $UND_0 D$. From each of these values, only two things can happen: The asset can go up (multiply by U) or down (multiply by D). Keep building out the tree in this way for N periods of length Δt.
8. At the end of the tree, write down the payoffs on the derivative given each of the terminal underlying values.
9. Calculate the risk-neutral probability of up and down steps q and $1 - q$, respectively:

$$q = \frac{e^{r \cdot \Delta t} - D}{U - D}$$

10. Start at the very end of the tree, and look at each little binomial model. Calculate the expected present value of the derivative at the beginning of each little binomial tree, using the risk-neutral probability of up and down steps to get the expected value and discounting at the risk-free rate of return.

$$DERIV_0 = \frac{q \times DERIV_{Up} + (1 - q) \times DERIV_{Dn}}{e^{r \cdot \Delta t}}$$

11. Clear cut the forest of little binomial trees backward until you are left with the current value of the derivative.

I'll give you an example of tree building and show you what goes on in binomial trees in the final section of this chapter.

An Admitted Modeling Simplification (Advanced)

I don't like to hide things from my students or readers, so I want to be frank about a particular way in which the standard binomial model presented above abstracts from the real world and the way I described the world earlier in this chapter as well as in Chapters 2 and 3.

It is well known that the binomial approximation of the value of a European call option converges to the Black-Scholes (1973) model in the limit (i.e., as Δt gets small and the number of binomial steps gets large). The Black-Scholes model and the binomial approximation work very well to price options under certain *ideal conditions,* one of which is that the underlying asset's value can only change by a small amount over any short interval of time.[20] What this means, then, is that the Black-Scholes model and the binomial approximation are built on a tacit assumption that new information about the underlying asset's value arrives in a rather smooth, consistent way so that its value does not make large, sudden changes.

The real world does not usually work this way, as new information often arrives in surprise spurts. This is particularly true of firm-specific (or idiosyncratic) events, like the outcome of our luxury goods company's patent infringement lawsuit (in Chapter 2), or the consulting firm client's defection decision (in Chapter 3), or even the firm-specific component of the NONNF's risk (in this chapter). The outcomes of each of these events/risks would cause the asset's value to jump suddenly, and the potential for these sudden jumps would make the Black-Scholes model (as well as the binomial approximation) less precise and more of an approximation.

In a world with sudden jumps like this, *jump risk* affects the value of an option even if the jump is diversifiable and the outcome of the jump risk is unrelated to the state of the macroeconomy. The reason comes right from something I mentioned in Chapter 2: a mean-zero change in the idiosyncratic component of an asset's risk won't change the value of that asset, but it may change the value of an option written on that asset because it can change the conditional mean payoffs on the option (even though it does not change the conditional mean values of the asset itself).[21]

So in the way I've been describing the world, an appropriate interpretation would be that most assets (real or financial) face two sources of volatility: The volatility that comes from smooth arrival of new information (perhaps information about the macroeconomy), and the volatility that comes from discontinuous news about firm-specific outcomes (i.e., jump risk).

[20] More formally, the dynamics of the underlying asset's value (i.e., its price) must have a continuous sample path with probability 1.

[21] Merton (1976) explored what would happen if an investor were to use the Black-Scholes model in a world of jump risk. If the investor correctly estimates the true volatility of the stock (which would include the volatility of the jump parameter), then the Black-Scholes model will generally undervalue deep in-the-money and deep out-of-the-money options and overvalue at-the-money options.

What is important for us when using our binomial approximation to the real world is that our estimated volatility parameter σ reflect *both* sources of volatility. The appropriate volatility measure is not simply the standard deviation of an asset's conditional mean returns across macro-economic states, but rather the standard deviation of returns across all outcomes (both across states and within states). You'll see this in the next chapter. When necessary, like in the case of a drug in clinical trials, we'll explicitly model the jump risk component (i.e., the risk of technical success or failure in each stage) separately from the smooth risk component (information about the market demand for the drug).

4.7   A Binomial Tree Example

This section demonstrates elementary building of standard binomial trees. Along the way, I'll show you what is actually going on in the tree.

Suppose you own a piece of property in Florida, and similar parcels near yours have sold recently for $100,000. A developer has approached you and asked you for a one-year option to purchase the property. To value the option on the land, you need to model how the land's value might change over the next year. How do you do this? With our binomial model, of course!

Our binomial model is built on the assumption that the future random value of the land is best described by a lognormal distribution, and so that's an assumption we'll have to start with.

Figure 4.71 show's what we are trying to do: We want to build a binomial tree to model the randomness in future land prices given our assumption that future prices are lognormal (or that log returns are normal). The starting value of the asset is $100,000. Let's assume that the expected arithmetic return on land (i.e., the required rate of return on a land investment) is 10%; we won't need this immediately, but we'll use it later. Let's also assume that the standard

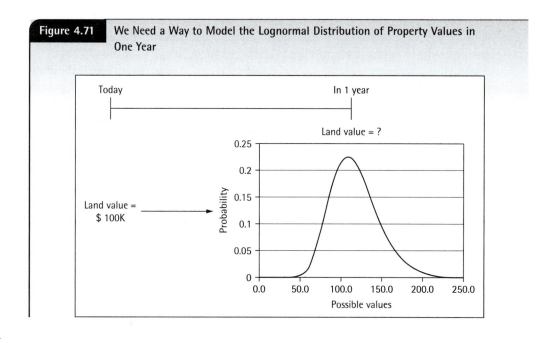

Figure 4.71   **We Need a Way to Model the Lognormal Distribution of Property Values in One Year**

deviation of log returns on land is 25% per year. Finally, let's build a 12-step tree. Since there is one year until the expiration of the option, each time step will be one month, so $\Delta t = 1/12 = 0.0833$.

Each up step in the tree will be

$$U = e^{\sigma\sqrt{\Delta t}} = e^{0.25\sqrt{0.0833}} = 1.075$$

and the down step is the reciprocal of the up step, or

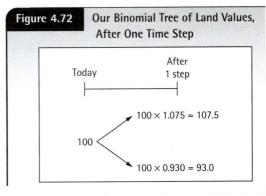

Figure 4.72   Our Binomial Tree of Land Values, After One Time Step

$$D = \frac{1}{U} = \frac{1}{1.075} = 0.930$$

So start building! After one time step, your tree looks like Figure 4.72.

Now just tack on a new binomial game with the same up and down steps at each of the ending nodes, and recall that the tree will recombine, as I've done in Figure 4.73.

Keep going. Figure 4.74 shows what happens when you add a third period.

Just repeat this procedure over and over until you've completed 12 time steps. Your final binomial tree will look like Figure 4.75.

Let's stop and notice a couple of things here before we go further. First, you see in Figure 4.75 that there are 13 possible states of nature after 12 time steps. This is exactly as it should be. Second, you'll notice that in the very high Time 12 states there are some fairly large values of the real estate. Don't worry about these—as I'll show you later, the probability of these values is extremely small. Finally, if you look across the "spine" of the tree, you see the value 100 repeated—it is at the very middle of every other time step. This happens because of the symmetric way we've built our U and D steps—if you go up then down, you end up right back where you started. As you'll see in Figure 4.76, this becomes a pattern in the tree:

Don't be fooled by this feature—the mean value at the end of the tree is *not* 100. To show you the mean value, I'll have to calculate the subjective probabilities of each up and down step, and then generate the subjective probability distribution at the end of the tree.

Figure 4.73   Our Binomial Tree of Land Values, After Two Time Steps

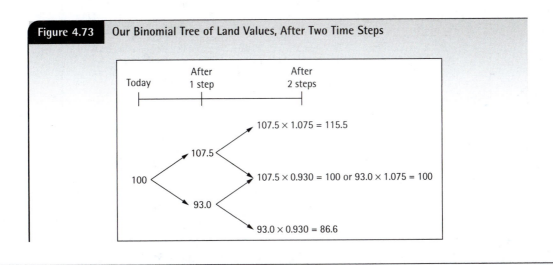

Figure 4.74   Our Binomial Tree of Land Values After Three Time Steps

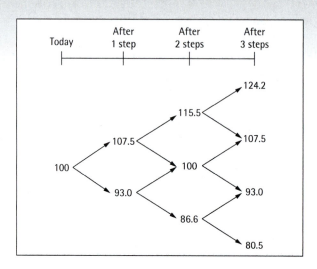

Given that the required rate of return on the real estate investment is 10% and the standard deviation of log returns is 25%, we can calculate the subjective probability of each up step using equation (4.38):

$$p = \frac{1}{2}\left(1 + \frac{\mu - .5\sigma^2}{\sigma}\sqrt{\Delta t}\right) = \frac{1}{2}\left(1 + \frac{0.10 - 0.5(0.25)}{0.25}\sqrt{0.0833}\right) = 0.54$$

Figure 4.75   Our Final Binomial Tree of Land Values, After 12 Steps (each of one month duration)

	_1_	_2_	_3_	_4_	_5_	_6_	_7_	_8_	_9_	_10_	_11_	_12_
												237.7
											221.2	
										205.8		205.8
sigma 0.25									191.5		191.5	
Δt 0.0833								178.1		178.1		178.1
u 1.0748							165.7		165.7		165.7	
d 0.9304						154.2		154.2		154.2		154.2
					143.5		143.5		143.5		143.5	
				133.5		133.5		133.5		133.5		133.5
			124.2		124.2		124.2		124.2		124.2	
		115.5		115.5		115.5		115.5		115.5		115.5
	107.5		107.5		107.5		107.5		107.5		107.5	
100.0		100.0		100.0		100.0		100.0		100.0		100.0
	93.0		93.0		93.0		93.0		93.0		93.0	
		86.6		86.6		86.6		86.6		86.6		86.6
			80.5		80.5		80.5		80.5		80.5	
				74.9		74.9		74.9		74.9		74.9
					69.7		69.7		69.7		69.7	
						64.9		64.9		64.9		64.9
							60.3		60.3		60.3	
								56.1		56.1		56.1
									52.2		52.2	
										48.6		48.6
											45.2	
												42.1

Figure 4.76 Our Method of Tree Building Leads to Constant Values Across "Spines"

		1	2	3	4	5	6	7	8	9	10	11	12
													237.7
												221.2	
											205.8		205.8
sigma 0.25										191.5		191.5	
Δt 0.0833									178.1		178.1		178.1
u 1.0748								165.7		165.7		165.7	
d 0.9304							154.2		154.2		154.2		154.2
						143.5		143.5		143.5		143.5	
					133.5		133.5		133.5		133.5		133.5
				124.2		124.2		124.2		124.2		124.2	
			115.5		115.5		115.5		115.5		115.5		115.5
		107.5		107.5		107.5		107.5		107.5		107.5	
	100.0		100.0		100.0		100.0		100.0		100.0		100.0
		93.0		93.0		93.0		93.0		93.0		93.0	
			86.6		86.6		86.6		86.6		86.6		86.6
				80.5		80.5		80.5		80.5		80.5	
					74.9		74.9		74.9		74.9		74.9
						69.7		69.7		69.7		69.7	
							64.9		64.9		64.9		64.9
								60.3		60.3		60.3	
									56.1		56.1		56.1
										52.2		52.2	
											48.6		48.6
												45.2	
													42.1

so the subjective probability of each down step is $1 - p = 1 - 0.54 = 0.46$. To calculate the subjective probability of reaching any of the thirteen terminal states, we simply count the number of up steps required to get to each state (call this number j) and calculate the binomial probability using the Microsoft Excel formula =binomdist(j, 12, 0.54, FALSE). I've done this for you in Figure 4.77.

You can see right away that the subjective probability of achieving 12 up steps in a row is quite small: 6 in 10,000. Also, notice that the vast majority of the probability mass is concentrated in the middle five states. Figure 4.78 presents an x-y plot with the end-of-tree values on the x-axis and subjective probabilities on the y-axis. I've done this to show you that our binomial tree approximates lognormal distribution very closely.

What is the mean of this lognormal distribution? To calculate this, we sum up the probability-weighted terminal values in the tree; see Figure 4.79.

The mean is $110,479.30. Notice that ln($110,479.30/$100,000) = 0.10; the log return calculated from the expected value is equal to the required rate of return on the land. 10% is the arithmetic mean return on the land, so in expectation the land should increase in value by 10%. Figure 4.79 shows us that it indeed does.

What would happen if we were to calculate the log return implied by each possible value at the end of the tree, then probability-weight these and add them up? I've done this for you in Figure 4.80.

The expected log return is 6.88%. Where does 6.88% come from? Well, 6.88% is the *geometric* mean return (or m in our notation), and its relationship to the required rate of return on the land of 10% (μ in our notation) comes from the mathematical formula

$$\mu - .5\sigma^2 = m$$

Figure 4.77   Calculating the Subjective Probability of Each Time 12 State in Our Binomial Tree

Parameters:

exp ret	10%
sigma	0.25
Δt	0.0833
u	1.0748
d	0.9304
p	0.54
1-p	0.46

1	2	3	4	5	6	7	8	9	10	11	12	Time 12 state	Up steps	Subjective probability of state
												237.7	12	0.0006
											221.2			
										205.8		205.8	11	0.0062
									191.5		191.5			
								178.1		178.1		178.1	10	0.0293
							165.7		165.7		165.7			
						154.2		154.2		154.2		154.2	9	0.0833
					143.5		143.5		143.5		143.5			
				133.5		133.5		133.5		133.5		133.5	8	0.1599
			124.2		124.2		124.2		124.2		124.2			
		115.5		115.5		115.5		115.5		115.5		115.5	7	0.2183
	107.5		107.5		107.5		107.5		107.5		107.5			
100.0		100.0		100.0		100.0		100.0		100.0		100.0	6	0.2172
	93.0		93.0		93.0		93.0		93.0		93.0			
		86.6		86.6		86.6		86.6		86.6		86.6	5	0.1588
			80.5		80.5		80.5		80.5		80.5			
				74.9		74.9		74.9		74.9		74.9	4	0.0846
					69.7		69.7		69.7		69.7			
						64.9		64.9		64.9		64.9	3	0.0321
							60.3		60.3		60.3			
								56.1		56.1		56.1	2	0.0082
									52.2		52.2			
										48.6		48.6	1	0.0013
											45.2			
												42.1	0	0.0001

In our example, we could have predicted this because $\mu = 10\%$ and $\sigma = 25\%$:

$$\mu - 0.5\sigma^2 = 0.10 - 0.5(0.25)^2 = 0.0688 = m$$

We can actually prove to ourselves that the standard deviation of *log returns* in our binomial tree is indeed 25%. The variance of log returns is given by

$$var\left[\ln\left(\frac{\widetilde{UND}}{UND_0}\right)\right] = E\left\{\ln\left(\frac{\widetilde{UND}}{UND_0}\right)^2\right\} - \left(E\left\{\ln\left(\frac{\widetilde{UND}}{UND_0}\right)\right\}\right)^2$$

Figure 4.78   The Probability Distribution of End-of-Tree Land Values Is Lognormal

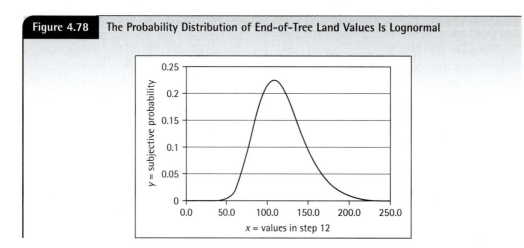

y = subjective probability

x = values in step 12

Figure 4.79 — Calculating the End-of-Tree Expected Value of the Underlying Asset

Parameters:

exp ret	10%
sigma	0.25
Δt	0.0833
u	1.0748
d	0.9304
p	0.54
1-p	0.46

1	2	3	4	5	6	7	8	9	10	11	12	12	Up steps	Subjective probability of state	Subjective probability weighted value
												237.7	12	0.0006	0.1452
											221.2				
										205.8		205.8	11	0.0062	1.2861
									191.5		191.5				
								178.1		178.1		178.1	10	0.0293	5.2221
							165.7		165.7		165.7				
						154.2		154.2		154.2		154.2	9	0.0833	12.8511
					143.5		143.5		143.5		143.5				
				133.5		133.5		133.5		133.5		133.5	8	0.1599	21.3471
			124.2		124.2		124.2		124.2		124.2				
		115.5		115.5		115.5		115.5		115.5		115.5	7	0.2183	25.2160
	107.5		107.5		107.5		107.5		107.5		107.5				
100.0		100.0		100.0		100.0		100.0		100.0		100.0	6	0.2172	21.7189
	93.0		93.0		93.0		93.0		93.0		93.0				
		86.6		86.6		86.6		86.6		86.6		86.6	5	0.1588	13.7438
			80.5		80.5		80.5		80.5		80.5				
				74.9		74.9		74.9		74.9		74.9	4	0.0846	6.3417
					69.7		69.7		69.7		69.7				
						64.9		64.9		64.9		64.9	3	0.0321	2.0808
							60.3		60.3		60.3				
								56.1		56.1		56.1	2	0.0082	0.4609
									52.2		52.2				
										48.6		48.6	1	0.0013	0.0619
											45.2				
												42.1	0	0.0001	0.0038

Sum = expected value → 110.4793

Figure 4.80 — Calculating the End-of-Tree Expected Log Return on the Underlying Asset

Parameters:

exp ret	10%
sigma	0.25
Δt	0.0833
u	1.0748
d	0.9304
p	0.54
1-p	0.46

1	2	3	4	5	6	7	8	9	10	11	12	12	Subjective probability of state	Log return	Probability weighted log return	Probability weighted log ret^2
												237.7	0.0006	0.8660	0.0005	0.000458
											221.2					
										205.8		205.8	0.0062	0.7217	0.0045	0.0032549
									191.5		191.5					
								178.1		178.1		178.1	0.0293	0.5774	0.0169	0.009772
							165.7		165.7		165.7					
						154.2		154.2		154.2		154.2	0.0833	0.4330	0.0361	0.0156274
					143.5		143.5		143.5		143.5					
				133.5		133.5		133.5		133.5		133.5	0.1599	0.2887	0.0462	0.0133287
			124.2		124.2		124.2		124.2		124.2					
		115.5		115.5		115.5		115.5		115.5		115.5	0.2183	0.1443	0.0315	0.0045473
	107.5		107.5		107.5		107.5		107.5		107.5					
100.0		100.0		100.0		100.0		100.0		100.0		100.0	0.2172	0.0000	0.0000	2.677E-33
	93.0		93.0		93.0		93.0		93.0		93.0					
		86.6		86.6		86.6		86.6		86.6		86.6	0.1588	-0.1443	-0.0229	0.0033079
			80.5		80.5		80.5		80.5		80.5					
				74.9		74.9		74.9		74.9		74.9	0.0846	-0.2887	-0.0244	0.0070533
					69.7		69.7		69.7		69.7					
						64.9		64.9		64.9		64.9	0.0321	-0.4330	-0.0139	0.0060158
							60.3		60.3		60.3					
								56.1		56.1		56.1	0.0082	-0.5774	-0.0047	0.0027365
									52.2		52.2					
										48.6		48.6	0.0013	-0.7217	-0.0009	0.0006631
											45.2					
												42.1	0.0001	-0.8660	-0.0001	6.786E-05

Sums = expected values → 0.0688 0.0668

that is, the variance is the average *squared* log return minus the squared *average* log return. We've already calculated the average log return to be 0.0688, so what we need is the first part of the calculation—the average squared log return. Notice that I've done this for you in Figure 4.80: The probability-weighted sum of the squared log returns is 0.0668. So the variance in log returns is

$$var\left[\ln\left(\frac{\widetilde{UND}}{UND_0}\right)\right] = E\left\{\ln\left(\frac{\widetilde{UND}}{UND_0}\right)^2\right\} - \left(E\left\{\ln\left(\frac{\widetilde{UND}}{UND_0}\right)\right\}\right)^2 = 0.0668 - (0.0688)^2 = 0.062$$

and hence the standard deviation of log returns is $\sqrt{0.062} = 25\%$. Exactly as it should be. If we do another *x-y* chart, this time with log returns on the *x*-axis but maintaining subjective probabilities on the *y*-axis, we get a picture as shown in Figure 4.81. This is a normal distribution with mean 0.10 and standard deviation 0.25. Exactly what we set out to construct!

Now let's shift gears and see what happens if we redo these calculations using the risk-neutral probability measure. Since our up step is $U = 1.075$, our down step is $D = 0.930$, the risk-free rate is 5%, and the length of time in each binomial step is $\Delta t = 0.0833$ years, the risk-neutral probability of the up and down steps are

$$q = \frac{e^{r \cdot \Delta t} - D}{U - D} = \frac{e^{0.05 \times 0.0833} - 0.930}{1.075 - 0.930} = 0.51$$

and

$$1 - q = 1 - 0.51 = 0.49$$

respectively. So if we know the number of up steps j required to get to any terminal state in our binomial tree, we can again use Equation (4.25) to calculate the risk-neutral probability of that state using Excel's =binomdist(j, 12, 0.51, FALSE) function. I've done this for you in Figure 4.82.

This may not mean much to you at first blush. But something important happens when we switch to the risk-neutral measure. Go back to our *x-y* plot of terminal values versus subjective probabilities, and superimpose a plot of the same values but with the associated risk-neutral probabilities on the *y*-axis. Figure 4.83 shows what happens.

Figure 4.81   The Probability Distribution of End-of-Tree Log Returns on the Underlying Is Normal

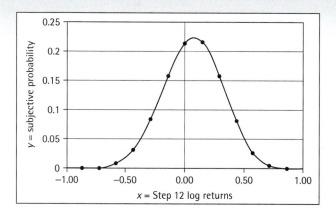

Figure 4.82   Calculating the Risk-Neutral Probabilities of the Time 12 States

	1	2	3	4	5	6	7	8	9	10	11	12	Up steps	R-N probability of state
												237.7	12	0.0003
risk-free	5%										221.2			
sigma	0.25									205.8		205.8	11	0.0036
Δt	0.0833								191.5		191.5			
u	1.0748							178.1		178.1		178.1	10	0.0191
d	0.9304						165.7		165.7		165.7			
q	0.511					154.2		154.2		154.2		154.2	9	0.0610
1-q	0.489				143.5		143.5		143.5		143.5			
				133.5		133.5		133.5		133.5		133.5	8	0.1315
			124.2		124.2		124.2		124.2		124.2			
		115.5		115.5		115.5		115.5		115.5		115.5	7	0.2014
	107.5		107.5		107.5		107.5		107.5		107.5			
100.0		100.0		100.0		100.0		100.0		100.0		100.0	6	0.2249
	93.0		93.0		93.0		93.0		93.0		93.0			
		86.6		86.6		86.6		86.6		86.6		86.6	5	0.1846
			80.5		80.5		80.5		80.5		80.5			
				74.9		74.9		74.9		74.9		74.9	4	0.1105
					69.7		69.7		69.7		69.7			
						64.9		64.9		64.9		64.9	3	0.0470
							60.3		60.3		60.3			
								56.1		56.1		56.1	2	0.0135
									52.2		52.2			
										48.6		48.6	1	0.0024
											45.2			
												42.1	0	0.0002

Do you see what happens? The risk-neutral probability measure is a leftward shift of the subjective probability measure. The magnitude of the shift reduces the expected value at the end of the tree in an important way, which we can learn from studying Figure 4.84.

Under the risk-neutral measure, the expected value is $105,127. Why is this significant? Because

$$\$100{,}000 \times e^{0.05} = \$105{,}127$$

That is, the expected change in the asset's value over the tree *using the risk-neutral probabilities* equals the risk-free rate.

You should suspect, then, that the shift to the risk-neutral measure transforms the probability distribution of log returns. It does. Figure 4.85 calculates the expected log return and expected squared log return under the risk-neutral (or martingale) probability measure.

Figure 4.83

Subjective and Risk–Neutral Probability

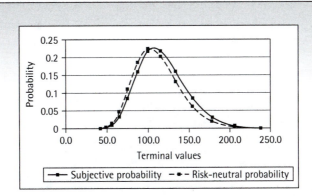

Probability (vertical axis: 0, 0.05, 0.1, 0.15, 0.2, 0.25) vs. Terminal values (horizontal axis: 0.0, 50.0, 100.0, 150.0, 200.0, 250.0)

Legend: —■— Subjective probability   –■– Risk-neutral probability

Figure 4.84 — Calculating the End-of-Tree Expected Value of the Underlying Using the Risk-Neutral Probability Measure

Parameters:

risk-free	5%
sigma	0.25
Δt	0.0833
u	1.0748
d	0.9304
q	0.511
1-q	0.489

Lattice (starting value 100.0) and end-of-tree expected value:

root	1	2	3	4	5	6	7	8	9	10	11	12	Up steps	R-N Probability of state	R-N Probability weighted value
												237.7	12	0.0003	0.0751
											221.2				
										205.8		205.8	11	0.0036	0.7472
									191.5		191.5				
								178.1		178.1		178.1	10	0.0191	3.4058
							165.7		165.7		165.7				
						154.2		154.2		154.2		154.2	9	0.0610	9.4088
					143.5		143.5		143.5		143.5				
				133.5		133.5		133.5		133.5		133.5	8	0.1315	17.5449
			124.2		124.2		124.2		124.2		124.2				
		115.5		115.5		115.5		115.5		115.5		115.5	7	0.2014	23.2649
	107.5		107.5		107.5		107.5		107.5		107.5				
100.0		100.0		100.0		100.0		100.0		100.0		100.0	6	0.2249	22.4947
	93.0		93.0		93.0		93.0		93.0		93.0				
		86.6		86.6		86.6		86.6		86.6		86.6	5	0.1846	15.9796
			80.5		80.5		80.5		80.5		80.5				
				74.9		74.9		74.9		74.9		74.9	4	0.1105	8.2771
					69.7		69.7		69.7		69.7				
						64.9		64.9		64.9		64.9	3	0.0470	3.0488
							60.3		60.3		60.3				
								56.1		56.1		56.1	2	0.0135	0.7580
									52.2		52.2				
										48.6		48.6	1	0.0024	0.1142
											45.2				
												42.1	0	0.0002	0.0079

Sum = expected value ────► 105.1271

Figure 4.85 — Calculating the Expected Log Return on the Underlying Asset Using the Risk-Neutral Probabilities

Parameters:

risk-free	5%
sigma	0.25
Δt	0.0833
u	1.0748
d	0.9304
q	0.511
1-q	0.489

Lattice (starting value 100.0) and expected log return:

root	1	2	3	4	5	6	7	8	9	10	11	12	R-N Probability of state	Log return	R-N Probability weighted log return	R-N Probability weighted log ret^2
												237.7	0.0003	0.8660	0.0003	0.000237
											221.2					
										205.8		205.8	0.0036	0.7217	0.0026	0.0018911
									191.5		191.5					
								178.1		178.1		178.1	0.0191	0.5774	0.0110	0.0063733
							165.7		165.7		165.7					
						154.2		154.2		154.2		154.2	0.0610	0.4330	0.0264	0.0114415
					143.5		143.5		143.5		143.5					
				133.5		133.5		133.5		133.5		133.5	0.1315	0.2887	0.0379	0.0109547
			124.2		124.2		124.2		124.2		124.2					
		115.5		115.5		115.5		115.5		115.5		115.5	0.2014	0.1443	0.0291	0.0041954
	107.5		107.5		107.5		107.5		107.5		107.5					
100.0		100.0		100.0		100.0		100.0		100.0		100.0	0.2249	0.0000	0.0000	2.773E-33
	93.0		93.0		93.0		93.0		93.0		93.0					
		86.6		86.6		86.6		86.6		86.6		86.6	0.1846	-0.1443	-0.0266	0.003846
			80.5		80.5		80.5		80.5		80.5					
				74.9		74.9		74.9		74.9		74.9	0.1105	-0.2887	-0.0319	0.0092059
					69.7		69.7		69.7		69.7					
						64.9		64.9		64.9		64.9	0.0470	-0.4330	-0.0204	0.0088142
							60.3		60.3		60.3					
								56.1		56.1		56.1	0.0135	-0.5774	-0.0078	0.0045009
									52.2		52.2					
										48.6		48.6	0.0024	-0.7217	-0.0017	0.0012243
											45.2					
												42.1	0.0002	-0.8660	-0.0002	0.0001407

Sums = expected values ────► 0.0188   0.0628

Figure 4.86   Subjective and Risk-Neutral Distributions of Log Returns

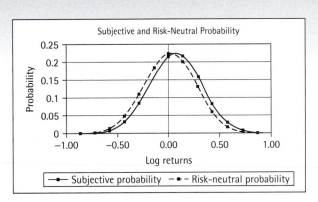

The expected log return under the risk-neutral measure is 1.88%. Where could 1.88% possibly come from? Well, the relationship between the geometric and arithmetic means extends to the case when the required rate of return is the risk-free rate. We can verify this using $\sigma = 25$:

$$0.05 - 0.5(0.25)^2 = 0.0188$$

This is why the term $r - 0.5\sigma^2$ appears in the Black-Scholes model—it is the expected log return under the risk-neutral measure. Why is it appropriate to use the subjective volatility of log returns in this calculation? Because the shift from the subjective measure to the risk-neutral measure *does not alter the volatility of log returns*:

$$var_Q\left[\ln\left(\frac{\widetilde{UND}}{UND_0}\right)\right] = E_Q\left\{\ln\left(\frac{\widetilde{UND}}{UND_0}\right)^2\right\} - \left(E_Q\left\{\ln\left(\frac{\widetilde{UND}}{UND_0}\right)\right\}\right)^2 = 0.0628 - (0.0188)^2 = 0.062$$

and so the standard deviation of log returns under the risk-neutral measure is $\sqrt{0.062} = 25\%$, just as it is under the subjective probability measure. We see that the change of measure only

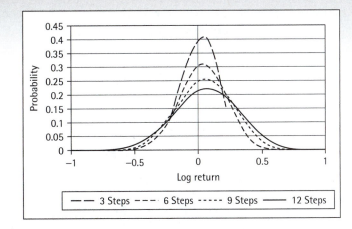

alters the mean of the distribution of log returns (and not its variance) with a simple chart (in Figure 4.86), which plots the two distributions of log returns.

Finally, I'd like to show you how quickly the binomial model approaches a normal distribution of log returns. In Figure 4.87, I've plotted the terminal distribution of log returns on the underlying in binomial trees with 3, 6, 9, and 12 steps.

What you see is that a 3-step tree does not give a very good approximation to a normal distribution, but a 9-step tree does. You can see the pattern: As you add steps to the tree, probability mass leaves the middle of the distribution and moves to the extreme tails. But as I mentioned before, the probabilities of large positive or negative returns are extremely small, so there's not much to be gained by building large trees. (And in Chapter 5, I'll show you a really neat trick that can get you very close approximations with few steps).

4.8   Bibliography

Black, Fisher, and Myron Scholes, 1973. "The Pricing of Options and Corporate Liabilities," *Journal of Political Economy* 81, 637–659.

Merton, Robert, 1976. "Option Pricing when Underlying Stock Returns are Discontinuous," *Journal of Financial Economics* 3, 125–144.

Titman, Sheridan, 1985. "Urban Land Prices Under Uncertainty," *American Economic Review* 75(3), 505–513.

Appendix   4.1   An Alternative Approach to Binomial Trees

There's a family of parameters U, D, and p that build trees correctly, and you will often encounter people who use a slightly different methodology. Remember, there are only two equations to solve:

$$p \ln U + (1 - p) \ln D = m \cdot \Delta t$$
$$p(1 - p)(\ln U - \ln D)^2 = \sigma^2 \cdot \Delta t$$

In the method I presented in the text, we arbitrarily set $D = \frac{1}{U}$ to find a solution, but we could have worked differently. Suppose instead that we force $p = .5$, and then solved for U and D. What would we get? Our equations change to

$$.5 \ln U + .5 \ln D = m \cdot \Delta t$$
$$.25 (\ln U - \ln D)^2 = \sigma^2 \cdot \Delta t$$

Once again, square the first equation to get

$$(\ln U)^2 + 2 \ln U \ln D + (\ln D)^2 = 4(m \cdot \Delta t)^2$$

add this to the second equation and solve for $\ln U$ to get

$$\ln U = \sqrt{2(m \cdot \Delta t)^2 + 2\sigma^2 \cdot \Delta t - (\ln D)^2}$$

substitute this back into the first equation, square both sides and collect terms to get

$$0 = 2(\ln D)^2 - 4m \cdot \Delta t \cdot \ln D - 2[(m \cdot \Delta t)^2 - \sigma^2 \cdot \Delta t]$$

Now use the quadratic formula to solve for $\ln D$:

$$\ln D = m \cdot \Delta t \pm \sigma \sqrt{\Delta t} = (\mu - .5\sigma^2) \cdot \Delta t \pm \sigma \sqrt{\Delta t}$$

You get the same thing if you solve for $\ln U$:

$$\ln U = m \cdot \Delta t \pm \sigma \sqrt{\Delta t} = (\mu - .5\sigma^2) \cdot \Delta t \pm \sigma \sqrt{\Delta t}$$

It is natural to think that an up step is bigger than a down step, so set $\ln U = m \cdot \Delta t + \sigma \sqrt{\Delta t}$, and you will find that $\ln D = m \cdot \Delta t - \sigma \sqrt{\Delta t}$. Now exponentiate both sides to get rid of the logarithm function, and you get the step sizes:

$$U = e^{m \cdot \Delta t + \sigma \sqrt{\Delta t}} = e^{(\mu - .5\sigma^2) \cdot \Delta t + \sigma \sqrt{\Delta t}}$$
$$D = e^{m \cdot \Delta t - \sigma \sqrt{\Delta t}} = e^{(\mu - .5\sigma^2) \cdot \Delta t - \sigma \sqrt{\Delta t}}$$

and build your tree remembering that we arbitrarily set the subjective probabilities of up and down equal to $\frac{1}{2}$.

Some people prefer this method of building trees because it clearly shows that the asset's return is drifting up in the tree (the mean return μ) and is shocked by the volatility σ. Others prefer it because of a technical reason. But this sort of tree building adds complications.

The most important complication is that you have to know the expected log return on the underlying asset. In order to get around this, you can invoke the risk-neutrality argument to come up with a risk-neutral tree along with the appropriate risk-neutral probability. It turns out that you can get the right answer by building the tree with up and down steps

$$U = e^{\left(r - \frac{1}{2}\sigma^2\right)\Delta t + \sigma \sqrt{\Delta t}}$$
$$D = e^{\left(r - \frac{1}{2}\sigma^2\right)\Delta t - \sigma \sqrt{\Delta t}}$$

where r is the arithmetic risk free return (do you see why?); and then applying the risk-free discount rate along with the risk-neutral probability

$$q = \frac{e^{0.5\sigma^2 \cdot \Delta t} - e^{-\sigma \sqrt{\Delta t}}}{e^{\sigma \sqrt{\Delta t}} - e^{-\sigma \sqrt{\Delta t}}}$$

The value of a derivative at the beginning of a binomial step is the same as before:

$$DERIV_0 = \frac{q \times DERIV_{Up} + (1 - q) \times DERIV_{Dn}}{e^{r \times \Delta t}}.$$

Appendix 4.2 | Another Alternative Approach (This One with Simple Discounting)

There's actually a very simple way to build binomial trees that gives virtually identical results as the two methods I described earlier. If you don't like working with e, this one's for you. I thank Phil Dybvig for showing me this.

If U and D are multiplicative up and down steps in a binomial tree, then the expected value of an asset with starting value UND_0 will be

$$E_P\{\widetilde{UND}\} = pUND_0U + (1 - p)UND_0D$$

under the subjective probability measure $\{p, 1 - p\}$, and

$$E_Q\{\widetilde{UND}\} = qUND_0U + (1 - q)UND_0D$$

under the risk-neutral probability measure $\{q, 1 - q\}$. Therefore, the expected gross return on the asset will be

$$\frac{E_P\{\widetilde{UND}\}}{UND_0} = pU + (1 - p)D = p(U - D) + D$$

under the subjective measure, and

$$\frac{E_Q\{\widetilde{UND}\}}{UND_0} = qU + (1 - q)D = q(U - D) + D$$

under the risk-neutral measure. Over the single binomial step, the variance in gross returns will be

$$var_P\left(\frac{\widetilde{UND}}{UND_0}\right) = p[U - (p[U - D] + D)]^2 + (1 - p)[D - (p[U - D] + D)]^2$$

$$= p(1 - p)^2(U - D)^2 + p^2(1 - p)(D - U)^2$$

under the subjective probability measure, and

$$var_Q\left(\frac{\widetilde{UND}}{UND_0}\right) = q(1 - q)^2(U - D)^2 + q^2(1 - q)(D - U)^2$$

under the risk-neutral measure.

Suppose the risky asset has an expected arithmetic return of μ% per year and standard deviation of returns of σ% per year, and also that the simple risk-free rate of return is r% per year. We need a subjective probability p, a risk-neutral probability q, a multiplicative up step U and a multiplicative down step D such that the expected return over any time step of length Δt years is $1 + \mu \cdot \Delta t$ under the subjective probability measure and $1 + r \cdot \Delta t$ under the risk-neutral probability measure, and the variance in returns is $\sigma^2 \cdot \Delta t$ under both measures.

In other words, under the risk-neutral measure $\{q, 1 - q\}$,

$$\frac{E_Q\{\widetilde{UND}\}}{UND_0} = q(U - D) + D = 1 + r \cdot \Delta t$$

and

$$var_Q\left(\frac{\widetilde{UND}}{UND_0}\right) = q(1 - q)^2(U - D)^2 + q^2(1 - q)(D - U)^2 = \sigma^2 \cdot \Delta t$$

We have three unknowns in these two equations, so let's arbitrarily set the risk-neutral probability $q = 0.5$. If you then solve these two equations for U and D, you'll find that

$$U = 1 + r \cdot \Delta t + \sigma\sqrt{\Delta t}$$
$$D = 1 + r \cdot \Delta t - \sigma\sqrt{\Delta t}$$

The risk-neutral pricing formula is

$$DERIV_0 = \frac{0.5 \times DERIV_{Up} + 0.5 \times DERIV_{Dn}}{1 + r \cdot \Delta t}$$

(because we've set $q = 0.5$, and thus $1 - q = 0.5$ as well). We can solve for the subjective probability p

$$p = \frac{1}{2}\left(1 + \frac{\mu - r}{\sigma}\sqrt{\Delta t}\right)$$

$$1 - p = \frac{1}{2}\left(1 - \frac{\mu - r}{\sigma}\sqrt{\Delta t}\right)$$

And you can check that under the subjective measure you get the same variance of returns (in the limit):

$$var_P\left(\frac{\widetilde{UND}}{UND_0}\right) = \sigma^2 \cdot \Delta t - (\mu - \sigma)^2 \cdot (\Delta t)^2$$

so

$$\lim_{\Delta t \to 0} Var_P\left(\frac{\widetilde{UND}}{UND_0}\right) = \sigma^2 \cdot \Delta t$$

   This binomial model works just as well as the ones presented earlier. There are two reasons I don't it use in the main text. First of all, the model I present in the text is the most popular form of the binomial model. Second, by setting the risk-neutral probability q to 0.5, we artificially make the state prices of the up and down states equal. This doesn't violate the equilibrium conditions, because if you recall the probability-weighted ratio of marginal utility of consumption must be equal to the ratio of state prices:

$$\frac{price\ of\ Red}{price\ of\ Blue} \equiv \frac{q}{1 - q} = \frac{p \times U'(Red)}{(1 - p) \times U'(Blue)}$$

or

$$\frac{q/p}{(1 - q)/(1 - p)} = \frac{U'(Red)}{U'(Blue)}$$

and even though we arbitrarily set $q = 1 - q$, we can see that $p > 1 - p$, so the marginal utility in the down (or Blue) state must be higher than the marginal utility in the up (or Red) state.
   Really advanced students will be interested to see that we can also define

$$\rho_U = \frac{q}{1 + r} \cdot \frac{1}{p} = \frac{Price\ of\ Red}{p}$$

and

$$\rho_D = \frac{1 - q}{1 + r} \cdot \frac{1}{1 - p} = \frac{Price\ of\ Blue}{1 - p}$$

The quantities $\{\rho_U, \rho_D,\}$ are collectively known by several names: the *state price density*, the *stochastic discount* factor, and the *pricing kernel*. They measure *priced relative scarcity*, and they can be used in yet another absolutely equivalent representation of linear pricing:

$$DERIV_0 = \rho_U \times p \times DERIV_{Up} + \rho_D \times (1 - p) \times DERIV_{Dn}$$

Appendix 4.3

To calculate the beta of the NONNF, we need to refer back to Appendix 2.2 where I derived the CAPM in price form. Equation (2.A2.8) gave us the CAPM price of a risky asset

$$P_0 = \frac{1}{1+r}\left[E\{CF\} - \frac{cov(CF,r_{Mkt})[r_{Mkt} - r]}{var(r_{Mkt})}\right]$$

while Equation (2.A2.5) gave us the beta of that asset:

$$\beta = \frac{1}{P_0}\frac{cov(CF,r_{Mkt})}{var(r_{Mkt})}$$

We'll first confirm that the CAPM price of the NONNF is indeed $2. In our problem, the expected return on the market is $r_{Mkt} = 25\%$, and the risk-free rate is $r = 10\%$. The probabilities of the up and down states are each 0.50; the market's return is 100% in the up state and 50% in the down state; and the value of the NONNF is $4.90 in the up state and $0.40 in the down state.

Given these inputs, the expected value of the NONNF is $E\{CF\} = \$2.65$. It is easy to calculate that $E\{CF \times r_{Mkt}\} = 2.35$ and $E\{r^2_{Mkt}\} = 0.625$, so

$$cov(CF,r_{Mkt}) = E\{CF \times r_{Mkt}\} - E\{CF\} \times E\{r_{Mkt}\}$$
$$= 2.35 - 2.65 \times .25 = 1.6875$$

$$var(r_{Mkt}) = E\{r^2_{Mkt}\} - E\{r_{Mkt}\}^2$$
$$= 0.625 - (0.25)^2 = 0.5625$$

Plugging everything into the price equation,

$$P_0 = \frac{1}{1.10}\left[\$2.65 - \frac{1.6875[0.15]}{0.5625}\right] = \$2.00$$

which confirms the price. Now filling in the beta equation,

$$\beta = \frac{1}{2}\frac{1.6875}{0.5625} = 1.5$$

1.

Row 0					1			
Row 1				1		1		
Row 2			1		2		1	
Row 3		1		3		3		1

The pyramid of numbers above is called Pascal's triangle. Starting with Row 2, each value within a row is the sum of the numbers from the previous row that are immediately to the left and to the right of the value in question. The outer numbers on each row are always equal to 1.

Notice that the Row 3 values correspond with the number of different ways in which a pachinko ball can arrive at bins: A_{uuu}, A_{uud}, A_{udd}, and A_{ddd}. In fact, Pascal's triangle is a method for determining the number of different paths a pachinko ball can take to arrive at a particular final destination.

Extend Pascal's triangle two more rows, and determine the number of different paths a pachinko ball can take to arrive at bins: A_{uuuuu}, A_{uuuud}, A_{uuudd}, A_{uuddd}, A_{udddd}, and A_{ddddd}.

2. Another method of determining the number of different paths a pachinko ball can take to arrive at a particular destination is to use a binomial coefficient, which is read as N choose M, where $M \le N$:

$$\binom{N}{M} = \frac{N!}{[M! \times (N - M)!]}$$

The exclamation point indicates a factorial (e.g., $5! = 5 \times 4 \times 3 \times 2 \times 1 = 120$; Note that $0! = 1$, and $1! = 1$). N corresponds to the number of interim time steps it takes to reach the final destination (i.e., rows of pins or the row number in Pascal's triangle). M indicates either the number of up or down movements the ball takes in arriving to its final destination.

For example, A_{udd} corresponds to a pachinko machine with three time steps ($N = 3$) and a path that requires one up movement ($M = 1$). The binomial coefficient $\binom{3}{1} = 3$, which corresponds to the three potential paths the pachinko ball could have taken: *udd*, *dud*, and *ddu*.

Using a binomial coefficient, what are the number of paths a pachinko ball can take to arrive at bin A_{uuuddd}?

3. Assuming that up and down movements have equal probability, which bin is more likely to accumulate pachinko balls, $A_{uuudddd}$ or $A_{uuddddd}$?

4. Which is greater, $\binom{3}{2}$ or $\binom{3}{1}$?

5. List the number of possible paths a pachinko ball can take to arrive at bin A_{uuudd}.

6. For bin A_{udd}, would the final value for the binomial coefficient be different if M is set to the number of down movements as opposed to the number of up movements?

7. Prove that $\binom{N}{M} = \binom{N}{N-M}$.

8. Suppose p equals 60%. What bin carries greater cumulative probability, A_{uddd} or A_{uuud}?

9. What are the associated binomial coefficients for the four values in the third row of Pascal's triangle (see Problem 1)?

10. Suppose there are four time steps within a binomial tree, and there exists a market index and a risk-free security, how many additional securities are necessary to complete the market for the different states of the economy that exist at the end of the tree? Further, under what conditions can these additional securities be generated from a portfolio of the market index and the risk-free security?

11. Suppose you have a security that has a current price of $10.00 and will either be $15.00 or $8.00 in exactly one year. Assuming the probability of each future price is 50%, what is the appropriate discount rate for the security? Further, what is the security's risk premium, assuming a 10% annual risk-free rate?

12. Suppose you have a security that has a current price of $10.00 and will either be $15.00 or $8.00 in exactly one year. What probabilities will reflect a 10% discount rate for the security? Assuming a risk-free rate of 10%, what is the one-year forward price? Is the forward price equal to the expected price of the security?

13. Suppose you have a security with a current price of $5.00 and will either be $7.00 or $4.00 in exactly one year. Assuming a risk-free rate of 5% and a risk-free bond price of $1.00, how many units ($\Delta$ and Ψ) of the security and the risk-free bond should be purchased to replicate a one-year forward contract? What is the current value of the forward contract?

14. Redo Problem 13, but assume that the current price of the risk-free bond is $10.00. Are the portfolio investments on a dollar basis the same as in Problem 13? Do the probabilities of the two outcomes matter in determining the investments in the portfolio?

15. Suppose you have a security that has a current price of $12.00 and will either be $15.00 or $10.80 one year into the future. After one year, a derivative security has a profit of $2.40 when the security price increases and a loss of $1.80 when the security price decreases. Assuming a 5% annual risk-free rate, what is the value of this derivative security? Is this derivative security similar to a forward contract, a call option, or a put option?

16. Suppose the derivative security in Problem 15 generates a profit of $2.40 when the price of the security increases and pays zero otherwise. What is the value of this derivative security? Is this derivative security similar to a forward contract, a call option, or a put option?

17. Suppose you have a security that has a current price of $25.00 and will either be $27.25 or $24.25 one year into the future. What is the value of a one-year put option with a

strike price of $26.00, assuming that it can only be exercised at maturity and the risk-free rate of interest is 4% annually?

18. Suppose a security has a current price of $20.00, and Investor A believes the future price of the security will either be $22.20 after one year or $18.00 after one year. Investor B believes the future price will be $23.00 after one year or $17.00 after one year. Given a 6% annual risk-free rate, the forward price of the security is $21.20. Does the forward contract cost one investor more money than the other investor? Defend your answer by comparing the cost of the tracking portfolio for each investor.

19. Suppose a security has a current price of $15.00, and Investor A expects the security price to increase by 10% in one year with 60% probability or decrease by 5% in one year with 40% probability. Investor B agrees with Investor A's values of the future prices but feels that the likelihood of either future price occurring is 50%. Assuming a 3% annual risk-free rate, what is the price of a one-year call option that has a strike price of $15.00 (assuming the call can only be exercised at maturity) for each of these investors? Do the differing probabilities assigned by these investors affect the price of the call option?

20. Suppose Investor B from Problem 19 desires to sell a one-year put option with a strike price of $15.00 for $0.56 (assume the option can only be exercised at maturity). Will there be anyone in the market willing to buy the put option from Investor B? (*Hint:* To answer the question, value the put using a tracking portfolio).

21. Suppose a security has a current price of $50.00 and will either be worth $55.00 or $45.00 one year into the future. Assuming a 5% annual risk-free rate and that the associated risk-free bond has a face value of $1.00, calculate the appropriate tracking portfolio weights (Δ and Ψ) for a one-year call option with a strike price of $40.00 (assume the option can only be exercised at maturity). Next, demonstrate that the tracking portfolio produces the correct future payoffs using an arbitrage table. Finally, price the option.

22. Redo Problem 21 using a one-year put option with a strike price of $60.00 that can only be exercised at maturity instead of a call option.

23. A security has a current price of $45.00 and is expected to increase in price to $50.00 or decrease in price to $42.75 in one year. Investor A believes that both future prices are equally likely. However, Investor B believes the $50.00 price will occur with 60% probability (correspondingly, the $42.75 price has a probability of 40%). Both investors agree on the current price and have access to a risk-free bond that pays 3% annual interest. What is the value of a derivative security that pays $1.00 when the $50.00 price occurs and $0.00 otherwise? Is the derivative security priced differently for each investor? Why or why not?

24. Price the same derivative security from Problem 23, except let the current price of the security for Investor B be $45.50 instead of $45.00 to reflect Investor B's more bullish views of the future. Is the derivative security priced differently for each investor? Why or why not?

25. A security has a current value of $30.00 and is expected to increase in price to $33.30 or decrease in price to $27.00 in one year. Assuming an annual risk-free rate of 5%, what is the price of a derivative security that pays $1.00 if the $33.30 security price should occur and zero otherwise? Further, what is the price of a derivative security that pays $1.00 if the $27.00 security price should occur and zero otherwise?

26. How will the values of the derivative securities in Problem 25 change if the $33.30 future security price increases to $35.00?

27. Suppose a security has two potential future prices: $52.00 and $45.00. Derivative Security A costs $0.36 and pays $1.00 when the $52.00 security price occurs and zero otherwise. Derivative Security B costs $0.58 when the $45.00 security price occurs and zero otherwise. Given these conditions, and assuming all maturities are for one year, what is the price of a call option with a strike price of $40.00 that can only be exercised at maturity? Further, what is the annual risk-free rate for a risk-free bond that pays $1.00 one year from today?

28. Suppose the low-consumption state has $C = 10$ units, and the high-consumption state has $C = 20$ units. Both states can occur with equal probability, and the associated utility function is $U(C) = \ln(C)$. Two derivative securities exist, High and Low, that each pay one dollar: High only pays the dollar when the high-consumption state occurs, and Low only pays the dollar when the low-consumption state occurs. Given that High has a price of $0.317, what is the price of Low?

29. Suppose the probability of the high-consumption state in Problem 28 became 55% (consequently, the probability of the low-consumption state becomes 45%). What is the new price for derivative security Low?

30. A security has a current price of $16.00 and is expected to increase in price to $20.00 or decrease in price to $14.00 after one year. Assuming an annual risk-free rate of 4%, what is the price of a one-year put option with a strike price of $18.00 that can only be exercised at maturity? Further, given a beta of 1.2 for the security, what is the beta for the put option?

31. Use the information from Problem 30, and perform the same requested calculations, except let the option be a call option instead of a put option.

32. Calculate the elasticity for the options in Problems 30 and 31.

33. A security's Treynor measure is defined as its risk premium divided by its beta. Given the elasticity relationship between a derivative security and its underlying asset, prove that the Treynor measure for a derivative security and its underlying asset are the same. (*Hint:* A security's risk premium is equal to the market risk premium multiplied by the security's beta.)

34. When reading different source material concerning risk-neutral pricing, it is not uncommon for $(1 - q)$ to be defined as $(u - r) \div (u - d)$. Demonstrate that this definition is the same as the definition in this text (i.e., $(1 - q) = [1 - (r - d) \div (u - d)]$).

    Note: Assume the current price of any risk-free bond used for calculations in Problems 35 through 51 is $1.00.

35. Using the risk-neutral valuation method, recalculate the value of the I/E company option discussed in Sect. 4.4 with a 4% annual risk-free rate rather than a 5% annual risk-free rate.

36. Assuming a 4% annual risk-free rate rather than a 5% annual risk-free for the I/E company option discussed in Sect. 4.4, answer the following questions. Does Δ change? Does the option beta increase or decrease? (*Hint:* Calculate the option's elasticity.)

37. What will be the value of the I/E company option discussed in Sect. 4.4 if the cap is set at $20.00 rather than $18.84? Use the tracking portfolio method to find the solution.

38. What is the value of the I/E company option discussed in the Sect. 4.4 if the future increased value of the underlying is $29.12 instead of $27.41? Use the tracking portfolio method to find the solution.

39. What will be the value of the I/E company option discussed in Sect. 4.4 if the future decreased value of the underlying is $9.86 instead of $12.95? Use the risk-neutral valuation method to find the solution.

40. Perform the equivalent tracking portfolio calculation to value the option for Cunning Foods, which is discussed in Sect. 4.4. *Note:* There may be some rounding error; however, the answer should be approximately $5.6 mm.

41. The option for Cunning Foods discussed in Sect. 4.4 is riskier than the underlying project. Calculate how much riskier the option is by calculating a multiplier for the underlying project beta. (*Hint:* This is the same as asking for the elasticity of the option.)

42. Suppose the final payoffs for the Cunning Foods option discussed in Sect. 4.4 are $147.00 mm and $112.00 mm. What is the value of the option given that the range of future values has decreased? Is the option more or less risky than it was before?

43. What will be the value of the real estate development option discussed in Sect. 4.4 if the increased value of the underlying is $110,000.00 rather than $150,000.00? Use the risk-neutral valuation method to find the solution. Should you still wait to develop?

44. What is the value of the real estate development option discussed in Sect. 4.4 if the annual risk-free rate is 5% rather than 10%? Use the risk-neutral valuation method to find the solution. Should you still wait to develop?

45. What is the elasticity of the real estate development option discussed in Sect. 4.4?

46. What is the elasticity of the real estate development option discussed in Sect. 4.4 if the annual risk-free rate is 5% rather than 10%?

47. The tree in Figure 4.58 has Δ of 1 and a Ψ of -1. Demonstrate with an arbitrage table that the tracking portfolio produces the desired future cash flows.

48. The tree in Figure 4.60 has Δ of 0.714 and a Ψ of 0. Demonstrate with an arbitrage table that the tracking portfolio produces the desired future cash flows.

49. The tree in Figure 4.61 has Δ of 0.762 and a Ψ of (-0.048). Demonstrate with an arbitrage table that the tracking portfolio produces the desired future cash flows.

50. Suppose you have a 4-step binomial tree. List the possible future outcomes at the end of the tree using u for upward movements and d for downward movements (e.g., up-up-up-up is *uuuu*). Further, assuming that $q = 55\%$, calculate the probability associated with each outcome.

51. Suppose you have a 5-step binomial tree with $q = 48\%$ and a risk-free rate of 1% for each step of the tree. What is the state price (i.e., a derivative security that pays $1.00 at a particular final node in the tree) for the path that follows up-up-up-down-down in no particular combination (e.g., up-down-up-up-down is also a valid path)?

52. Suppose you have a 4-step binomial tree. List the possible future outcomes at the end of the tree using u for upward movements and d for downward movements (e.g., up-up-up-up is $uuuu$). Further, let $x = \$1.00 \times [q \div (1 + r)]$, and let $y = \$1.00 \times [(1 - q) \div (1 + r)]$. Using x and y, calculate the associated state price for each final future outcome of the binomial tree.

53. Given the definitions for x and y in Problem 50, does $y = (1 - x)$?

54. Using continuous compounding, which of the following investments provides the most annual return (assuming we invest $100.00 today): One that

   a. Pays $109.42 in 18 months.
   b. Pays $123.37 in three years.
   c. Pays $191.55 in 10 years.
   d. Pays $104.08 in six months

55. Suppose the annual log return of a security is distributed normal with a mean of 9% and an annual variance of 6.25%. What is the expected price of the security one year from today, assuming the current price is $20.00?

56. Suppose the annual log return of a security is distributed normal with a mean of 10% and an annual standard deviation of 36%. What is the expected price of the security six months from today, assuming the current price is $30.00?

57. Calculate the value of the option in Sect. 4.7 using the 12-step tree and risk-neutral pricing.

58. Calculate the value of the option in Sect. 4.7 using a 12-step tree, risk-neutral pricing, and the alternative tree method from Appendix 3.1. *Note:* The answer will be different from the answer to Problem 57.

59. Calculate the value of the option in Sect. 4.7 using a 12-step tree, risk-neutral pricing, and the alternative tree method from Appendix 3.2. *Note:* You will need to adjust the annual risk-free rate to 5.1271% ($exp\,(5\%) - 1$), and the answer will be different from the answers to Problems 57 and 58.

60. Redo the tree in Problem 57 as a 4-step tree, and solve for the option price. You will notice that the price changes significantly, is the 4-step tree value for the option more correct than the 12-step tree value for the option? Why?

61. Adjust the 4-step binomial tree in Problem 60 to produce the "physical" probability distribution of the final prices. The values within the tree do not change; however, the probability of each final price will change. Calculate the expected log return and the variance of the log return. *Note:* The answers will differ from the calculations for the 12-step tree.

62. Recalculate the option value in Problem 57 using a 4-step binomial tree, risk-neutral pricing, and the alternative tree method from Appendix 4.1. *Note:* The answer will be different from the answer to Problem 60.

63. Adjust the 4-step tree in Problem 62 to allow the physical probability of an upward jump in price to be 0.50 (i.e., $p = 0.50$). Unlike Problem 61, the tree prices will change as well as the probabilities of the final prices. Calculate the expected log return and the variance of the log return.

64. Recalculate the option value in Problem 57 using a 4-step binomial tree, risk-neutral pricing, and the alternative tree method from Appendix 4.2. *Note:* You will need to adjust the annual risk-free rate to 5.1271% ($exp(5\%) - 1$), and the answer will be different from the answers to Problems 60 and 62.

65. Increase the volatility for the 12-step option tree in Problem 57 from 25% to 30%. Recalculate u, d, and q for the tree. Next, recalculate u, d, and q using the alternative tree method from Appendix 4.1.

66. Given u and d for the binomial trees in Problem 65, produce the 13 final node prices for both trees.

Our first in-depth corporate option valuation is a real-life case of investment in research and development at Boeing. I've gathered the details of the story from standard library research. The majority of the numbers, however, are my own estimates. *The Airline Monitor*, a trade journal, was a particularly useful resource to me in my development of reasonable approximations.

5.1 Background: Strategic Thinking and Strategic Investment

In the mid-1990s, Boeing executives undertook a strategic planning exercise to create a vision of what their company should be in the 21st century and determine what investments to pursue in order to make this vision a reality. The goal was to understand exactly what sorts of airplane products airlines and air freight companies would demand, and to figure out what Boeing could do to create a competitive advantage.

Two key observations forced the executives to spend a considerable amount of time thinking about the future of intercontinental commercial aviation. First, just about everyone agreed that demand for air transportation would continue to rise. Economic growth, particularly (but not exclusively) in Asia, would fuel a sustained increase in long-distance travel by both business-people and tourists as well as more use of air freight.[1]

The second observation, however, created substantial uncertainty about how people and freight would actually move between cities. An airport can only accommodate a fixed number of operations (takeoffs and landings) in a day due to regulations involving safety as well as local restrictions on operating hours. And in the mid-1990s, most of the world's gateway airports were *already* either at or very close to capacity.

It was clear to the Boeing executives that intercontinental capacity would have to increase somehow. What was unclear, however, was exactly how the improvement in capacity would come about. This, in turn, led to uncertainty about what kinds of planes the airlines and freight companies would demand.

After intense study, which included consultation with the airlines, expert economists, demographers, and scientists, the executives concluded that intercontinental commercial aviation (and demand for new airplanes) would take one of two very different paths over the next 30 years.

The first possible scenario would involve capacity increases through the proliferation of new gateway cities. This had already happened in trans-Atlantic aviation, as new routes such as

---

[1] Boeing estimated that aggregate air traffic would grow at 4.8% per year through 2020; whereas Airbus (Boeing's main competitor in the commercial aircraft product space) forecast a 4.9% annual growth rate over the same period. See Esty and Ghemawat (2002).

Cincinnati–Brussels arose to get around the choking that occurred in gateways like New York and London. If this scenario were to come true, airlines would demand new planes with improved fuel efficiency, extended range, and low cost-per-seat-mile. The airlines would not, however, be interested in significantly larger planes. This scenario would occur only if governments were willing to ease restrictions on entry points *and* spend money on runway and terminal improvements in smaller, less-congested airports.

In the competing scenario, however, governments would be unwilling and/or unable to expand smaller airports or to open new entry points. Under the second scenario, the only way to satisfy demand would be to somehow increase capacity at the gateways. Since runway additions are either politically or geographically impossible in most gateway cities, the only possible solution would be to actually accommodate more people and freight in each takeoff and landing operation. In other words, capacity would expand only by the airlines flying bigger planes. In this case, international carriers would demand *very large aircraft* (VLAs)—that is, planes that could accommodate more than 500 passengers—with good efficiency and range.

At the time, Boeing's largest passenger aircraft was its 400-seat 747. So, in January 1996, Boeing managers decided that they should initiate preliminary design of a new 800-seat super-jumbo jet, with the idea of presenting the new product to airlines in five years (i.e., in January 2001). Airlines could not commit to buying such a new plane without a detailed understanding of payload capabilities, maximum range, operating costs per seat mile, and (most important) price per plane; and Boeing could not provide these data to the airlines without a thorough preliminary design.

Preliminary R&D would involve the very detailed design of all of the components of the new plane, and even the building of a scale model for extensive wind tunnel testing. It would be a very expensive process, because it would require doing everything to construct a completely new type of plane, up to the point when the company must bend metal. The term "bend metal" is industry jargon for the point in time where there's no turning back—where the company makes huge capital expenditures and actually starts building the first plane. For the super-jumbo jet, the preliminary design costs would be substantial, as many new technologies (such as composite-material airframe design for strength with low weight) would have to be invented. I estimate that Boeing's original assessment was that preliminary R&D of the super-jumbo jet would cost $500 million.[2]

Privately, Boeing management felt that the first scenario (deregulation) was more likely, and that the necessary new planes would be either modifications to the 747 or straightforward designs of new planes using existing technologies. In fact, Boeing felt that the static net present value (NPV) of a super-jumbo jet product was negative, even ignoring the preliminary design costs.

5.2   Why the Super-Jumbo-Jet Concept Displayed Negative Static NPV

After extensive analysis, Boeing management estimated that the cost of rolling the first super-jumbo jet out of the hangar would be $20 billion *in addition to the cost of preliminary design.* That's right, $20 billion. This is the cost of bending metal (above and beyond the preliminary

---

[2] While I do not know either the projected or actual cost of Boeing's preliminary R&D effort, I do know that Airbus spent $700 million on the preliminary R&D of its A380. This number comes from an October 4, 2000, briefing to financial analysts by Airbus executives, as reported by Esty and Ghemawat (2002).

R&D costs). If Boeing were to actually bend metal, it would have to make back the capital commitment, plus an appropriate return, by selling a very large volume of planes at a sales price above the marginal cost of production.[3]

Why so much? Well, part of this cost would be the expense of creating an entirely new facility in which to build the monster plane. When Boeing developed the 747 in the late 1960s, the company was forced to build an entirely new production facility that ended up being the world's largest industrial building at the time—and which accounted for 20% of the 747's capital investment. In addition, Boeing would have to build intelligent machines to automate many parts of the construction. The remainder is simply the high cost of translating design into reality by building a prototype.[4]

Boeing estimates the demand for its products through a proprietary in-house model that the company calls the *Current Market Outlook* (CMO). The CMO starts with a detailed economic analysis and forecast for 12 distinct regions around the world. The outputs from this exercise become inputs for a forecast of traffic flows in 51 inter- and intraregional markets around the world. Boeing used the traffic-flow forecasts from the CMO, along with competitive analysis, to estimate the incremental free cash flows that would be reasonably expected to arise from a super-jumbo-jet product.

The incremental cash flow generated by a super-jumbo-jet product would be a function of both demand for the jet and Boeing's pricing power. Demand and pricing power would themselves be determined by two more primitive variables: The overall health of the global economy in the early 21st century (particularly in Asia) and the presence or absence of a competing product from Airbus. To determine the cash returns from selling a super-jumbo-jet product, management broke the world down into a manageable (but rather large) set of possible contingencies. I've simplified things to only two possible levels of economic activity (strong and weak), but rest assured that Boeing took a more thorough approach.

Let's assume for this illustration that Boeing executives believed the global economy would be strong in January 2001 with probability $\frac{2}{3}$, and would be weak at that time with probability $\frac{1}{3}$. Given that Boeing did not know Airbus's intention, ability to raise financing, or technological capabilities, Boeing management estimated that Airbus would also complete preliminary R&D of a super-jumbo jet with probability $\frac{1}{2}$. Given these probabilities, Boeing estimated the cumulative present value of the incremental free cash flows on the super-jumbo (over and above the cost of preliminary design and bending metal) in each contingency. Figure 5.1 provides the estimates for the four contingencies upon which I will focus.

Let me be careful to tell you how Boeing might have done the analysis I summarize with Figure 5.1. Management would have given each scenario to a team of financial analysts and told each team to develop a free cash flow model for their scenario only.

---

[3] You'll find an excellent illustration of just how poor the super-jumbo jet's economics were (and still are) in Esty and Ghemawat (2002). For a back-of-the-envelope approximation, assume that Airbus will make a $32 million incremental free cash flow on each unit of its own super-jumbo product (the A380) sold. If the company's real cost of capital is 11%, Airbus will have to sell 70 planes per year for 40 years to recover the capital investment. In comparison, Boeing has sold 1,400 747's since the plane's first flight in 1970—for an average of only 40 per year. (Airbus's current list price for the A380 is $284 million, but buyers typically pay only 75% of list; $32 million is thus a 15% profit margin on typical postdiscount prices.)

[4] In an article reporting the A380's maiden flight in April 2005, *International Herald Tribune* reported that Airbus's launch-date (December 2000) estimate for the plane's capital cost was €14 billion, but that total expenditures on the new plane had exceeded that amount by €1 billion (making the total cost €15 billion, or roughly $19 billion at the day's foreign exchange rate). See Phillips (2005).

Take the *strong economy/no Airbus entry* scenario as an example. The analysis team would put themselves into a world in 2001 in which the global economy is strong and where there's no competition from Airbus. The team would then forecast the number of planes that could be sold over the life span of the product (say, 25–40 years), the selling price per plane, the cost of production, any other net rev-

Figure 5.1

Expected 2001 Present Value of Boeing's Incremental Free Cash Flow from Selling Super-Jumbo-Jet Aircraft in Each of Four Scenarios, Using Information Available in 1996

		Global economy	
		Strong (*pr* = 2/3)	Weak (*pr* = 1/3)
Entry of Airbus	No (*pr* = 1/2)	$30 billion	$18 billion
	Yes (*pr* = 1/2)	$12 billion	$9 billion

enues that might be generated from selling replacement parts and maintenance services, and the like, and then discount these back at an appropriate risk-adjusted cost of capital. Obviously, in a strong global economy with no competitor, both units sold and price would be high. This gave a January 2001 free cash flow value of $30 billion for this scenario. *Important:* These values assume that the $20 billion capital investment has already been made. In other words, they are the PV of the free cash inflows as of January 2001, with work on the first plane underway.

Given these four scenario values, we can see that the expected January 2001 financial market value of the super-jumbo-jet business (i.e., the expected 2001 discounted cash flow (DCF) value of the incremental cash inflows from selling planes) *based only on the information available as of January 1996* was $18.5 billion:

E{2001 Financial market value of super-jumbo-jet business | info available in 1996}

$$= \frac{2}{3} \times \frac{1}{2} \times \$30 \text{ billion} + \frac{2}{3} \times \frac{1}{2} \times \$12 \text{ billion} + \frac{1}{3} \times \frac{1}{2} \times \$18 \text{ billion} + \frac{1}{3} \times \frac{1}{2} \times \$9 \text{ billion}$$

$$= \$18.5 \text{ billion}$$

Let's make sure we get this straight. This analysis was being done in 1996, and the managers were forecasting what they would encounter in 2001, when they would have to make the final go/no-go decision (i.e., the decision to spend $20 billion and bend metal). What this tells us, then, is that in 1996 Boeing's managers believed that the 2001 opportunity to invest $20 billion in a super-jumbo-jet product would ultimately show a negative static NPV.

E{2001 Static NPV of $20 billion investment in super-jumbo plane | info available in 1996}

$$= \$18.5 \text{ billion} - \$20 \text{ billion}$$
$$= -\$1.5 \text{ billion}$$

In other words, in 1996 Boeing's managers believed that the super-jumbo-jet business would ultimately be a destroyer of value. Nevertheless, Boeing went forward with the preliminary design anyway. Why did management decide to do the preliminary design even though they thought they'd never build the plane? Why would the company even consider doing the preliminary R&D? Preliminary R&D would not generate any cash inflows on its own, so wouldn't this just be throwing good money after bad?

5.3   The Static NPV of the Investment in Preliminary R&D

As discussed in Chapter 1, a static NPV evaluation of the 1996 investment in preliminary R&D requires that we treat the entire project as if it were now-or-never/no-flexibility. In other words, we must hard-wire all future decisions, then ask whether it is better to invest immediately and commit fully to those decisions or to do nothing and throw away the opportunity forever.

In this case, there's only one future decision to make: The 2001 decision to either enter the super-jumbo-jet business or ignore it from that point forward. Figure 5.2 shows how static NPV analysis forces us to think about the problem as a choice among three mutually exclusive bets: Invest in preliminary design with a commitment to building the super-jumbo jet, invest in preliminary design with a commitment to *not* building the super-jumbo jet, or do nothing at all.

The first way to hard-wire the 2001 decision is to commit to investing the $20 billion in 2001 no matter what. Given this commitment and a WACC of 13%, the 1996 static NPV of the preliminary R&D investment is the discounted value of the future commitment (i.e., the expected 2001 static NPV of the $20 billion investment in the super-jumbo jet based on what is known as of 1996) minus the cost of the preliminary R&D:

1996 Static NPV of investment in preliminary R&D given commitment to invest in 2001

$$= \frac{-\$1.5 \text{ billion}}{(1.13)^5} - \$\text{Cost of peliminary R\&D}$$

$$= -\$814 \text{ million} - \$500 \text{ million}$$

$$= -\$1.314 \text{ billion}$$

The second way to hard-wire the 2001 decision is to commit to doing nothing at that time (i.e., to commit to never building the super-jumbo jet at all). Given this commitment, the 1996 static

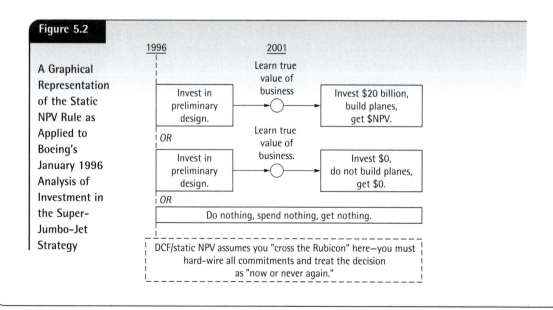

Figure 5.2

A Graphical Representation of the Static NPV Rule as Applied to Boeing's January 1996 Analysis of Investment in the Super-Jumbo-Jet Strategy

NPV of the preliminary R&D investment is the discounted value of the future commitment (which in this case is $0) minus the cost of the preliminary R&D:

1996 Static NPV of investment in preliminary R&D given commitment to not invest in 2001

$$= \frac{\$0}{(1.13)^5} - \$Cost\ of\ peliminary\ R\&D$$

$$= -\$500\ million$$

No matter what the cost of preliminary R&D may be, the second hard-wired alternative (committing to do nothing in 2001) is better than the first. Therefore, if the company were forced to make a bet, then we can conclude that *in expectation* (i.e., *on average*) a commitment to doing nothing in 2001 was better for the shareholder than a commitment to building planes in 2001.

Be that as it may, the second committed sequence of decisions (invest in preliminary R&D but never build super-jumbo-jet planes) displays negative static NPV no matter what the cost of preliminary R&D, so the static NPV rule tells us to reject this investment in favor of the third alternative: Do nothing at all, and never revisit the decision.

Yet in 1996, Boeing's Board of Directors approved the very large investment in preliminary R&D in spite of its negative static NPV. Why? Because the Board knew that the company had to be ready for both of the industry's possible future scenarios. Boeing could not offer a super-jumbo jet to airlines without having done preliminary design, and therefore a decision to *not* do the preliminary design would be equivalent to a commitment to *not* offer a super-jumbo-jet product regardless of whether or not it would be demanded. Boeing knew that its main competitor, Airbus, was also thinking about preliminary R&D of a super-jumbo-jet product, and it would be just as disastrous for Boeing to cede a good market for super-jumbo jets to Airbus as it would be for the company to try to sell the behemoths in a weak market for them.

In other words, the preliminary design was strategic, in that it would allow Boeing to play the super-jumbo-jet strategy *in case such a strategy were to become valuable in the future*. But how much is strategy worth? How much shareholder money should be spent in the name of strategy? That's exactly what we are going to estimate in the next section.

Why was the static NPV analysis inconsistent with management's intuition? Because DCF and static NPV are not appropriate in this situation. As I've just showed you, static NPV analysis forces the company to treat the decision as a now-or-never/no-flexibility bet. But the preliminary R&D investment was not a static bet; rather it was strategic because it created flexibility. For the reasons discussed in Chapter 1, DCF and static NPV cannot value and evaluate the flexibility gained by this investment.

5.4 Creation of a Strategy = Creation of an Option

When the Boeing executives decided that the investment in preliminary design was strategic, what they intuitively captured was that it created an *option* to make a valuable future investment. Let me explain this as carefully as possible.

Figure 5.2, which provides a graphical representation of what goes on in a static NPV analysis, is not an accurate picture of how Boeing will actually behave. By investing in preliminary R&D, Boeing is *not* making a commitment to spend $20 billion and build planes, nor is it making a commitment to not build planes. Rather, by spending money on preliminary design in 1996, Boeing purchases *the right but not the obligation* to spend $20 billion in January 2001. If Boeing learns by January 2001 that a super-jumbo-jet product is worth more than $20 billion,

Figure 5.3   **A More Accurate Picture of How Boeing Will Behave in 2001 If It Invests in Preliminary R&D in 1996**

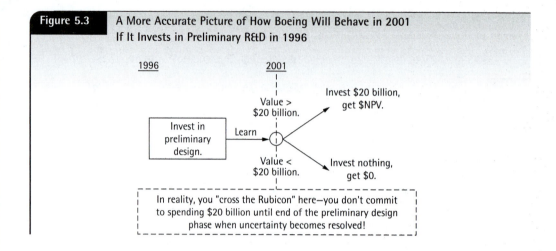

it will exercise its right by spending the $20 billion at that time and keeping the difference (the learned true NPV as of 2001). If Boeing learns by January 2001 that a super-jumbo-jet product is worth less than $20 billion, the company will walk away and focus on other, more promising strategies.

When we look at it this way, we see that the investment in preliminary design actually buys Boeing *two* things. First, it buys Boeing five more years before a decision must be made. But second, and more important, it gives Boeing better information on which management can base the $20 billion capital investment decision. Without the preliminary design, Boeing can never learn whether or not the airlines demand the product (and at what price); that is, they are out of the game by default. But *with* the preliminary design, the company gets to see the demand and pricing of a super-jumbo-jet product *before* making a big capital investment decision. Figure 5.3 illustrates this very important point.

The preliminary design expenditure purchases *the right but not the obligation* to invest $20 billion in a super-jumbo-jet product in January 2001, based on whatever is known by that time. The strategy will be to make the best decision based on what the company actually learns. Recognizing that the January 2001 observed value of the new product (the true financial market value of its future incremental free cash inflows from that point forward) can be anything, we can draw the January 2001 payoff on the strategy created by the preliminary R&D investment as shown in Figure 5.4.

The payoff pattern in Figure 5.4 is, of course, the payoff diagram for a call option. More specifically, it is a five-year call, with a strike price of $20 billion, written on a super-jumbo-jet product. If Boeing invests in preliminary design, it purchases this call. Once we recognize this correspondence between the strategy being purchased and a call option, we can determine the economic value of the preliminary design itself.

Even though the preliminary design generates no cash inflow on its own, it

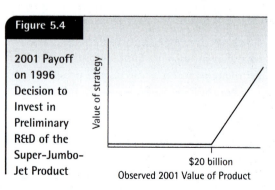

Figure 5.4

2001 Payoff on 1996 Decision to Invest in Preliminary R&D of the Super-Jumbo-Jet Product

has value because it creates an option (or a strategy). *The value of this option is the most Boeing should spend on preliminary design.* If the option created is worth more than the cost of the preliminary design, then the true NPV of the investment in preliminary R&D is positive, and the preliminary design phase creates value for the shareholders. In other words, the super-jumbo-jet strategy is valuable in January 1996 *if and only if* Boeing can complete the preliminary R&D for a cost that is less than the value of the option it creates.

5.5 Valuing the Option

How do we value the option that the preliminary design creates? Let's think intuitively for a minute. The basic underlying uncertainty is the 2001 value of a super-jumbo-jet product (as shown in Figure 5.4), and the flexibility that management buys is the ability to observe this value (via demand and price) and then decide whether or not to actually spend $20 billion and launch the product. Remember that the *value* of the product is the present value of the incremental free cash flows from selling it (i.e., the financial market value of the product's incremental cash inflows). So, in a decision diagram form, the strategy created by preliminary R&D looks like Figure 5.5.

Of course, decision trees are not risk-adjusted, and we need to approach this with an option model (our binomial model). What do we need to know to do this analysis? The current value of the underlying asset, the volatility of changes in the value of the underlying, the exercise price of the option, the risk-free rate of return, and the time to the maturity of the option.

The last three variables are easy to find. The time to maturity of the option is five years (Boeing will exercise or not in five years—in January 2001 after they have observed demand). The yield on a five-year risk-free bond was 7% at the time. Finally, the exercise price of the option is $20 billion. If demand is sufficiently high, the company will invest the $20 billion in a full-scale launch and take whatever value is there. If demand is not sufficiently high, Boeing will just walk away.

Now to the more difficult issues. How do we determine the current value of the underlying? Well, to answer this, we need to know exactly what the underlying is. The underlying asset is always what you will own if you exercise the option. Here, exercising the option involves spending $20 billion to fully develop and launch a super-jumbo-jet product, so if we exercise the option, what we will have is a fully developed super-jumbo-jet product in 2001.

Therefore, in this particular case, what is meant by the term *value of the underlying asset* is *value of a fully developed super-jumbo-jet product in 2001.* And if you will recall, we've already estimated that as of January 1996 (the day this analysis was done, thus the day we are valuing

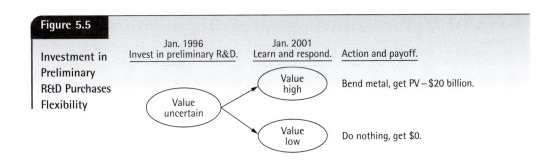

Figure 5.5

Investment in Preliminary R&D Purchases Flexibility

Jan. 1996
Invest in preliminary R&D.

Jan. 2001
Learn and respond.

Action and payoff.

Value uncertain

Value high → Bend metal, get PV – $20 billion.

Value low → Do nothing, get $0.

the option), the *expected* January 2001 value of a fully developed super-jumbo-jet product is $18.5 billion. This is not exactly what we need, however. The starting value in our binomial tree must be the *current* value of the underlying asset, which in this case is the January 1996 value of the incremental free cash flows from selling super-jumbo jets starting in January 2001.

To get the *current* (January 1996) value of the fully developed super-jumbo-jet product, we must take the contemporaneous estimate of the jet product's expected January 2001 exercise-date value ($18.5 billion) and discount it back at the project's required rate of return (13%) to appropriately adjust for time value. Why? Because of the way we build our binomial trees. Recall from Chapter 4 that one thing that happens in a binomial tree is that the expected value of the underlying asset increases through the tree at the asset's required rate of return. So, because we want the expected value of the super-jumbo-jet product to be $18.5 billion in January 2001, we must start our binomial tree with a January 1996 value of $10.04 billion.

$$1996 \text{ Value of underlying} = \frac{\text{Expected 2001 value of underlying}}{(1.13)^5}$$

$$= \frac{\$18.5 \text{ billion}}{(1.13)^5}$$

$$= \$10.04 \text{ billion}$$

I round this down to $10 billion for the rest of the analysis to keep the presentation simple.

This thought process confuses a lot of people, so let me reiterate the logic. To get the *current* (January 1996) value of the underlying, we start by supposing that Boeing has already committed to spend the $20 billion plus the preliminary R&D costs to fully design and complete the project. In this no-flexibility case, Boeing commits to investing in a super-jumbo-jet product in January 2001 regardless of what the world looks like at that time. The plane's January 2001 *value* (after completion of the R&D and investment of the $20 billion) will be the present value of the incremental free cash flows from that point forward; in other words, the product's January 2001 value will be what someone else would be willing to pay for the business if Boeing had already spent the $20 billion. As of January 1996, we expect that number to be $18.5 billion when January 2001 actually arrives. So the current (or starting) value of the underlying asset is the current (January 1996) estimate of the expected 2001 value of the plane, discounted for time value and calculated using only the information currently at hand (January 1996). In other words, it is the *no-flexibility* present value of the inflows, appropriately discounted for time value.

Thus, in January 1996 there exists a financial market tracking portfolio that tracks the value of a commitment to invest in a super-jumbo jet in January 2001 regardless of what is learned. The January 1996 value of that tracking portfolio is $10 billion, so the current (or starting) value of the underlying is $10 billion.

This is the general approach that we will often use to begin a real-option analysis—we almost always start with a *static* or *no-flexibility* valuation of the future cash inflows (not including the investment/strike/exercise price).[5] The 1996 expected present value of the inflows from selling

---

[5] Novices tend to make two mistakes here: They use the static NPV as the starting value of the underlying, and they condition the starting value of the underlying assuming success (i.e., they recognize that the project will only generate cash flows if the option is exercised, and so calculate the value of the underlying using its expected value given exercise on the exercise date). Both are egregious. If you use the static NPV as the starting value of your underlying asset, you will end up double-counting the strike price; moreover, if your initial NPV estimate is negative, it will always be negative in your binomial tree. If you calculate the starting value of the underlying conditional upon success, you are using information that is not available—you don't know whether the product will be successful or not.

planes is $10 billion based on what is known at that time; as time marches forward, this *estimate* of the 2001 present value of the inflows from selling planes will change based on what Boeing learns. In expectation, it will rise at the required rate of return of 13% per year. But it can deviate from that based on the volatility of changes (which describes Boeing's uncertainty in the estimate).

Well then, what is the annual volatility of changes (or returns) in the underlying's value? That is easy for us to estimate as well, using management's estimates about demand. First, we need to switch from asset *values* to asset *returns*. In the *strong economy/no Airbus entry* state, the return on the underlying (i.e., the *change* in Boeing's understanding about its value from the purchase of the option in January 1996 to the exercise date in January 2001) would be ($30 bn/$10 bn − 1) = 200% over five years. Similarly, in the *strong economy/yes Airbus entry* state, the five-year return would be ($12 bn/$10 bn − 1) = 20%. In the *weak economy/no Airbus entry* state, the five-year return would be ($18 bn/$10 bn − 1) = 80%. Finally, in the *weak economy/yes Airbus entry* state, the five-year return would be ($9 bn/$10 bn − 1) = −10%. So the expected return on the underlying asset over five years is

$$\mu_{5\text{-year return}} = \frac{2}{3} \times \frac{1}{2} \times (200\%) + \frac{2}{3} \times \frac{1}{2} \times (20\%)$$

$$+ \frac{1}{3} \times \frac{1}{2} \times (80\%) + \frac{1}{3} \times \frac{1}{2} \times (-10\%) = 85\%$$

Why do we need the expected return over five years? So that we can calculate the *variance* in returns over five years:

$$\sigma^2_{5\text{-year return}} = \frac{2}{3} \times \frac{1}{2} \times (2.00 - 0.85)^2 + \frac{2}{3} \times \frac{1}{2} \times (0.20 - 0.85)^2$$

$$+ \frac{1}{3} \times \frac{1}{2}(0.80 - 0.85)^2 + \frac{1}{3} \times \frac{1}{2} \times (-0.10 - 0.85)^2 = 0.7325$$

Since the five-year variance in returns (or more properly in the change in Boeing's understanding of the value of the super-jumbo jet) is 0.7325, the one-year variance is 0.7325/5 = 0.1465. Therefore, the *annual* standard deviation in returns is $(0.1465)^{1/2}$ = 38.27% per year. We'll round this to an annual volatility estimate of σ = 38% per year.

Two Advanced Points

You might notice that the compound annual growth rate (CAGR) is $(1.85)^{1/5} -1$ = 13%, which is the cost of capital we used to generate the starting value of the underlying. In other words, the underlying is expected to increase in value at its required rate of return—there is no convenience yield or dividend yield. (When there is a convenience or dividend yield, the asset's expected value will increase at its required rate of return less the convenience or dividend yield. We will cover this issue, along with storage costs, when we come to American options).

Also, if you calculate the five-year expected *log* return you will get

$$m_{\text{return}} = \frac{2}{3} \times \frac{1}{2} \times \ln\left(\frac{\$30}{\$10}\right) + \frac{2}{3} \times \frac{1}{2} \times \ln\left(\frac{\$12}{\$10}\right)$$

$$+ \frac{1}{3} \times \frac{1}{2} \times \ln\left(\frac{\$18}{\$10}\right) + \frac{1}{3} \times \frac{1}{2} \times \ln\left(\frac{\$9}{\$10}\right) = 0.50$$

Figure 5.6	Binomial Tree of Values of Super-Jumbo-Jet Product (in billions)

Jan-96	Jan-97	Jan-98	Jan-99	Jan-00	Jan-01
$10.00					

We can account for the difference between the five-year arithmetic mean return μ_{return} = 85% and the five-year log (geometric) return m = 50% by the relationship between the two that we established earlier: $m = \mu - .5\sigma^2$

$$m = \mu - .5\sigma^2 \quad \text{so} \quad .50 = .85 - .5\sigma^2 \quad \text{or} \quad \sigma^2_{5\text{-year}} \approx .7$$

$$\sigma^2_{1\text{-year}} \approx .7/5 = .14 \quad \text{so} \quad \sigma_{1\text{-year}} \approx 38\%$$

(where I've done a little rounding).

Back to the Story

The hard part is now over. We can grow a tree of underlying values using what we learned in Chapter 4. For ease of presentation, I'll present the analysis to you in a 5-step binomial tree. Since there are five years to maturity of the option, and since we'll be using five time steps in the tree, each time step will be of length Δt = 1 year.[6] In practice, you will get a more precise answer by building a tree with more steps; however, I'll show at the end of this chapter that it is not necessary at all to build extremely large trees.

Recall that in our binomial model, the size of an up step is

$$U = e^{\sigma\sqrt{\Delta t}}$$

where σ is the annual standard deviation in returns on the underlying, and Δt is the length of each step (in fractions of a year). Since we are assuming σ = 38%, and building our tree such that Δt = 1, our up and down steps are

$$U = e^{.38\sqrt{1}} = 1.462$$

and

$$D = 1/U = 1/1.462 = 0.684$$

We can now set up our tree. The starting point in time is January 1996, when the value of the underlying is $10 billion. The five subsequent points in time will be January 1997, 1998, 1999, 2000, and 2001 (when the decision must be made). Figure 5.6 shows the initial setup of the binomial tree of underlying values.

Next, let the tree grow by one time step. Since U = 1.462, the value of the underlying in January 1997, if it moves up from the starting value in January 1996, will be $10.00 × 1.462 = $14.62 billion. On the other hand, if the underlying moves down during the first year, then its January 1997 value will be $10.00 × 0.684 = $6.84 billion. See Figure 5.7.

Notice that in Figure 5.7 I've collapsed the tree downwards: An up move is not physically up on the page, but rather across (to the right, or east, if you will); a down move remains a move downward on the page (to the southeast). This is a common convention, and it is useful for two

[6] $\Delta t = T/N$ = 5 years/5 steps = 1 year per step.

Figure 5.7	Binomial Tree of Values of Super–Jumbo-Jet Product (in billions)

Jan-96	Jan-97
$10.00	$14.62 = $10.00 × 1.462
	$6.84 = $10.00 × 0.684

reasons. First, it saves space on the page and makes presentation slightly easier. Second (but equally valuable), it makes the tree very easy to construct in a spreadsheet program such as Microsoft Excel. Every move to the right is an up move, which is (in this case) 1.462 times the value immediately to the left. Since the tree recombines (up then down is the same as down then up) and the up moves stay the same size, you can complete most of the tree by simply copying this up-move formula across to the right. You'll catch on as I complete the tree. Figure 5.8 shows the calculation for the next time step (January 1998).

Do you see what is going on? Notice the middle state at January 1998. To get there, you have to have one up move and one down move (in any order), so you can get there by either going down from $14.62 in January 1997 or going up from $6.84 in January 1997. Comparing Figure 5.7 with Figure 5.8, we can see that every move to the right (or east) is simply a multiplication by 1.462; every move to the southeast is a multiplication by 0.462. Excel allows you to copy and paste these formulas, and that makes completing the tree very easy. Figures 5.9, 5.10, and 5.11 extend the process to the third, fourth, and final time points in our tree, respectively.

Figure 5.11 is our completed binomial tree of underlying values. Remember that this is a *model* in which we are *assuming* that the unknown January 2001 value of the super-jumbo-jet product will be drawn from a lognormal distribution with certain parameters, and that we are *approximating* this distribution via our binomial technique. I've translated the discrete view of the world from Figure 5.1 into an approximate lognormal distribution of possible values in Figure 5.11. It is not at all essential that the values in our binomial tree in Figure 5.11 match up exactly with the discrete estimates in Figure 5.1. Management's estimates in Figure 5.1 were noisy approximations; moreover, they actually performed that analysis over a larger possible number of outcomes.

While I'm on this subject of the interpretation of the tree, let me warn you about one thing: Do not become overly concerned with the very large value in the highest terminal state (in this

Figure 5.8	Binomial Tree of Values of Super–Jumbo-Jet Product (in billions)

Jan-96	Jan-97	Jan-98
$10.00	$14.62	$21.38 = $14.62 × 1.462
	$6.84	$10.00 = $6.84 × 1.462 or = $14.62 × 0.684
		$4.68 = $6.84 × 0.684

Figure 5.9	Binomial Tree of Values of Super–Jumbo-Jet Product (in billions)

Jan-96	Jan-97	Jan-98	Jan-99
$10.00	$14.62	$21.38	$31.27 = $21.38 × 1.462
	$6.84	$10.00	$14.62 = $10.00 × 1.462
		$4.68	$6.84 = $4.68 × 1.462
			$3.20 = $4.68 × 0.684

Figure 5.10	Binomial Tree of Values of Super-Jumbo-Jet Product (in billions)				
	Jan-96	Jan-97	Jan-98	Jan-99	Jan-00
	$10.00	$14.62	$21.38	$31.27	$45.72 = $31.27 × 1.462
		$6.84	$10.00	$14.62	$21.38 = $14.62 × 1.462
			$4.68	$6.84	$10.00 = $6.84 × 1.462
				$3.20	$4.68 = $3.20 × 1.462
					$2.19 = $3.20 × 0.684

Figure 5.11	Binomial Tree of Values of Super-Jumbo-Jet Product (in billions)					
	Jan-96	Jan-97	Jan-98	Jan-99	Jan-00	Jan-01
	$10.00	$14.62	$21.38	$31.27	$45.72	$66.86
		$6.84	$10.00	$14.62	$21.38	$31.27
			$4.68	$6.84	$10.00	$14.62
				$3.20	$4.68	$6.84
					$2.19	$3.20
						$1.50

case, $66.86 billion in January 2001). The assumption of lognormal terminal values implies that there is a very small probability of an extremely large value, and the binomial model simply reflects this. If you build a tree with more steps, you'll actually get even higher extreme values—but they will occur with very low likelihood. The extreme values are always there when you assume lognormality (e.g., every time you use the Black-Scholes model), but you only see them when you use the binomial model.

Finally, keep in mind the way we built the tree. A horizontal move to the right is an up move, and a diagonal move down and right is a down move; remember that you can't move in a north-easterly direction.

Now, to value the real option on the super-jumbo jet that Boeing creates by investing in pre-liminary R&D, we start at the terminal node and work backward. At 2001 management must make a *now-or-never* decision. They will launch if they find themselves in a terminal state where the PV of the operating cash flows is greater than the cost of bending metal ($20 billion), and they will walk away otherwise. The payoff in the terminal time step in the tree is *max*[underlying value −$20, 0]. So we start our calculation by building an *option value tree* and plugging this value into all of the states at the last date. Figure 5.12 demonstrates.

Next we clearcut the forest, rolling backwards in time, using our binomial risk-neutral pricing model from Chapter 4. At any point in time *t*, the value of the real option is

$$DERIV_t = \frac{q \times DERIV_{Up\,at\,t+\Delta t} + (1 - q) \times DERIV_{Dn\,at\,t+\Delta t}}{e^{r \times \Delta t}}$$

In other words, in any state at any time point before January 2001, the value of the option on the super-jumbo jet is simply the expected present value of what can happen over the next bino-mial step—with the expectation taken using the risk-neutral probabilities and the discounting done at the risk-free rate of return.

Figure 5.12

Binomial Tree of Values of Super-Jumbo-Jet Product (in billions)

	Jan-96	Jan-97	Jan-98	Jan-99	Jan-00	Jan-01
	$10.00	$14.62	$21.38	$31.27	$45.72	$66.86
		$6.84	$10.00	$14.62	$21.38	$31.27
			$4.68	$6.84	$10.00	$14.62
				$3.20	$4.68	$6.84
					$2.19	$3.20
						$1.50

Value of Option on Super-Jumbo-Jet Product (in billions)

Jan-96	Jan-97	Jan-98	Jan-99	Jan-00	Jan-01
	= max [$66.86 − $20, $0] = $46.86				$46.86
	= max [$31.27 − $20, $0] = $11.27				$11.27
	= max [$14.62 − $20, $0] = $0				$0.00
					$0.00
					$0.00
					$0.00

Recall that in our binomial construction, the risk-neutral probability of an up move is

$$q = \frac{e^{r \times \Delta t} - D}{U - D} = \frac{1.0725 - .684}{1.462 - .684} = .499$$

Since $q = .499$, $(1 - q) = .501$. Furthermore, the risk-free discount rate over any step is

$$e^{r \times \Delta t} = e^{0.07 \times 1} = 1.0725$$

Finally, these quantities do not change throughout the tree.

For an illustration of the very first calculation, suppose we are in the very highest possible state at January 2000. In Figure 5.12, the value of the underlying at this point is $45.72 billion. If the underlying goes up, the option on the super-jumbo jet will be worth $46.86 billion; but if the underlying goes down, the option on the super-jumbo jet will be worth only $11.27 billion. So the value of the *option* in the highest state at January 2000 is

$$\frac{(0.499)(\$46.86) + (0.501)(\$11.27)}{1.0725} = \$27.07$$

and so we plug this into our option value tree, which I've done for you in Figure 5.13.

Figure 5.13

Value of Option on Super-Jumbo-Jet Product (in billions)

	Jan-96	Jan-97	Jan-98	Jan-99	Jan-00	Jan-01
					$27.07	$46.86
	= [0.499 × $46.86 + 0.501 × $11.27]/1.0725					$11.27
						$0.00
						$0.00
						$0.00
						$0.00

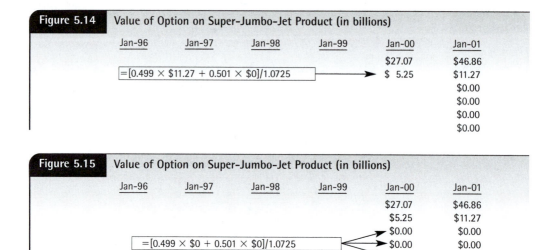

Figure 5.14 Value of Option on Super-Jumbo-Jet Product (in billions)

Jan-96	Jan-97	Jan-98	Jan-99	Jan-00	Jan-01
					$46.86
				$27.07	$11.27
=[0.499 × $11.27 + 0.501 × $0]/1.0725				$ 5.25	$0.00
					$0.00
					$0.00
					$0.00

Figure 5.15 Value of Option on Super-Jumbo-Jet Product (in billions)

Jan-96	Jan-97	Jan-98	Jan-99	Jan-00	Jan-01
				$27.07	$46.86
				$5.25	$11.27
				$0.00	$0.00
=[0.499 × $0 + 0.501 × $0]/1.0725				$0.00	$0.00
				$0.00	$0.00
					$0.00

We proceed by doing the same exercise for the next state down at January 2000 (see Figure 5.14).

$$\frac{(0.499)(\$11.27) \ + \ (0.501)(\$0)}{1.0725} = \$5.25$$

Notice that the remaining states at January 2000 must have zero value because all states that follow them in time have zero value. So, we can complete the January 2000 column of the option value tree, as I've done for you in Figure 5.15.

We then roll back to January 1999. I've done the work for you in Figure 5.16; make sure you follow each calculation.

Continue clear-cutting the forest back to January 1998 using q and $(1 - q)$ to calculate the expected end-of-period values and $e^{r \times \Delta t}$ as the discount factor. Figure 5.17 shows the values you

Figure 5.16 Value of Option on Super-Jumbo-Jet Product (in billions)

Jan-96	Jan-97	Jan-98	Jan-99	Jan-00	Jan-01
=[0.499 × $27.07 + 0.501 × $5.25]/1.0725			$15.05	$27.07	$46.86
=[0.499 × $5.25 + 0.501 × $0]/1.0725			$2.44	$5.25	$11.27
=[0.499 × $0 + 0.501 × $0]/1.0725			$0.00	$0.00	$0.00
			$0.00	$0.00	$0.00
				$0.00	$0.00
					$0.00

Figure 5.17 Value of Option on Super-Jumbo-Jet Product (in billions)

Jan-96	Jan-97	Jan-98	Jan-99	Jan-00	Jan-01
=[0.499 × $15.05 + 0.501 × $2.44]/1.0725		$8.15	$15.05	$27.07	$46.86
=[0.499 × $2.44 + 0.501 × $0]/1.0725		$1.14	$2.44	$5.25	$11.27
=[0.499 × $0 + 0.501 × $0]/1.0725		$0.00	$0.00	$0.00	$0.00
			$0.00	$0.00	$0.00
				$0.00	$0.00
					$0.00

Figure 5.18	Value of Option on Super-Jumbo-Jet Product (in billions)					
	Jan-96	Jan-97	Jan-98	Jan-99	Jan-00	Jan-01
	$2.26	$4.32	$8.15	$15.05	$27.07	$46.86
		$0.53	$1.14	$2.44	$5.25	$11.27
			$0.00	$0.00	$0.00	$0.00
				$0.00	$0.00	$0.00
					$0.00	$0.00
						$0.00

$$= [0.499 \times \$4.32 + 0.501 \times \$0.53]/1.0725$$

should get, along with calculations. Again, make sure you follow the logic—this is the last time in the book that I will proceed so deliberately.

Apply the same procedure to complete the two possible option values in January 1997, and then finally to find the current (January 1996) value of the option on the super-jumbo jet, as I've done for you in Figure 5.18. This is what Boeing "buys" if the company spends money on the preliminary R&D.

That is, we estimate the true financial market value of the preliminary R&D to be $2.26 billion. Therefore, our estimate of the *true* NPV of the investment in preliminary R&D is

> *True* NPV of investment in preliminary R&D
>
> = True financial market value of preliminary R&D — Cost of investment
>
> = $2.26 billion — Cost of preliminary R&D
>
> = $2.26 billion — $500 million
>
> = $1.76 billion

In other words, preliminary design is a value-creating investment for Boeing shareholders as long as Boeing can successfully complete it at a cost of anything less than $2.26 billion. Preliminary design is not worth doing if it requires more than $2.26 billion. Why is preliminary design valuable in and of itself? Because the purchase of preliminary design is actually the purchase of an option—an option to later purchase a fully designed and launched super-jumbo-jet product for a strike of $20 billion with better information.

Remember that we characterized the preliminary R&D investment as an investment in a *strategy*. What this analysis tells us is that the strategy created by the preliminary design is worth $2.26 billion, so the most Boeing's shareholders want management to spend to buy the strategy is $2.26 billion.

The Same Valuation, Using State Securities

Before we go further, let's recalculate the value of this option using our state-price approach. In a recombinant binomial tree with continuous compounding of interest, the value of a state security that pays $1 after j up moves and 0 otherwise is

$$\text{(number of paths with } j \text{ up moves)} \times e^{-rt} q^j (1 - q)^{N-j}, \quad \text{or}$$

$$\frac{N!}{j!(N - j)!} \left[\frac{1}{e^{rt}} q^j (1 - q)^{N-j} \right]$$

For the underlying to reach the extreme upper value of $66.86 billion, it must go up five times in a row in five total steps, so $N = 5$ and $j = 5$. Therefore, the value of a state security that pays $1 if the underlying reaches $66.86 billion is

$$\frac{5!}{5!(0!)}\left[\frac{1}{e^{.07\times5}}(.499)^5(.501)^0\right] = \$0.0218$$

Just over 2 cents. We will need 46.86 billion of these state securities to replicate the real option's payoff in this state. Similarly, the value of a state security that pays $1 if the underlying reaches $31.27 billion (and 0 otherwise) is

$$\frac{5!}{4!(1!)}\left[\frac{1}{e^{.07\times5}}(.499)^4(.501)^1\right] = \$0.1094$$

about 11 cents, and we will need 11.27 billion of these to replicate the real option's payoff in this state. We will not need any further state securities to replicate the payoff on the product option, so we need no further calculation. The value of this tracking portfolio of state securities is

$$46.86 \text{ billion} \times \$0.0218 + 11.27 \text{ billion} \times \$0.1094 = \$2.26 \text{ billion}$$

Exactly the same answer, which should not be a surprise.

Valuation Using the Black–Scholes Model

The option created by the preliminary R&D expenditure is a simple European call, and we could have valued it through the Black–Scholes model. The Black–Scholes value of a European call on an asset that generates no cash income and bears no storage cost is

$$C = S \times N(d_1) - Ke^{-rT} \times N(d_2) \tag{5.1}$$

where S is the current value of the underlying asset, K is the strike price, r is the risk-free rate of return per year, and T is the time in years until the option expires.

The terms $N(d_1)$ and $N(d_2)$ are the cumulative probabilities that a unit normal random variable (i.e., a normally distributed random variable with mean $= 0$ and standard deviation $= 1$) takes a realized value less than or equal to d_1 and d_2, respectively, where

$$d_1 = \frac{\ln\left(\frac{S}{K}\right) + (r + 0.5\sigma^2)T}{\sigma\sqrt{T}} \tag{5.2}$$

and

$$d_2 = d_1 - \sigma\sqrt{T} \tag{5.3}$$

and σ is the annual standard deviation of log returns on the underlying asset.

In our case, $S = \$10$ billion, $K = \$20$ billion, $r = 7\%$, $T = 5$ (years), and $\sigma = 38\%$. Plugging these into Equations (5.2) and (5.3) to solve for d_1 and d_2, and then using Equation (5.1), we can find that the Black–Scholes valuation of the option on the super-jumbo-jet product is

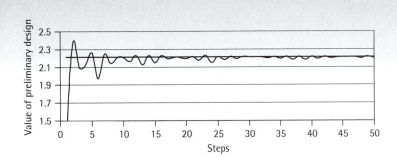

Figure 5.19

Convergence
of Binomial to
Black-Scholes

$2.214 billion, which is very close to our binomial valuation. In this case, we were only about 2% off—although there's no guarantee that we'll always get this much precision in such a small tree.

The Black-Scholes value is the limit of the binomial model's approximate solution as the number of steps in the binomial model approaches infinity. If we need to, we can improve on our binomial estimate by increasing the number of steps in a year (and thus decreasing the size of each time step). Adding steps makes the terminal distribution of asset values become more and more lognormal, and the precision of the binomial model (relative to the Black-Scholes) increases accordingly. But how many steps should we take in practice? Less than you might think!

Figure 5.19 shows the plot of the binomial model valuation, using trees ranging from only 1 step (5 years long) to 50 steps (each $\frac{1}{10}$ of a year long). The squiggly line represents the binomial model's valuation, and the straight line is the Black-Scholes theoretical value. Look at what happens.

The first thing you should notice from Figure 5.19 is that the binomial model converges to the Black-Scholes pretty quickly, so large trees are not really necessary. The second feature that you probably notice is that the binomial model's valuation oscillates around the Black-Scholes value of the option. The reason for the oscillation is as follows. When we increase the number of steps in a binomial model from N to $N + 1$, we add exactly one additional terminal state (we move from $N + 1$ possible outcomes to $N + 2$). The newly added terminal is either an *in-the-money* state (which will increase the value of the option) or an *out-of-the-money* state (which will decrease the value of the option). Thus, after adding an in-the-money state, we tend to overshoot the theoretical value of the option, and after adding an out-of-the-money state, we tend to undershoot the theoretical value.

We can actually use this oscillation to our advantage. Consider doing *two* binomial valuations of the option, one with N steps and one with $N + 1$ steps, and taking the average of the two. Does this improve precision without necessitating a many-step tree? Yes. Check out Figure 5.20, where for every N I've plotted the average of the N-step tree value and the $N - 1$ step tree value.

Wow! With only a few steps we can get very close to the theoretical value. As a matter of fact, if we average the 4-step tree value ($2.12 billion) with the 5-step tree value ($2.26 billion), we get $2.19—within 0.9% of the Black-Scholes value. By going out as far as 9 and 10 steps and averaging the value, we get $2.21 billion—within 0.2% of the theoretical price.

This observation is of added importance if you are building your binomial model in Microsoft Excel. In Excel, recalculation occurs every time you hit the enter key (if you have set

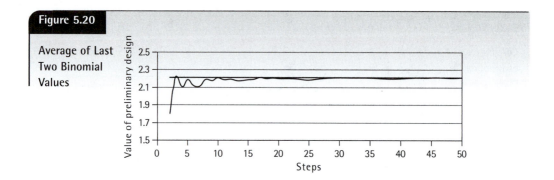

Figure 5.20

Average of Last Two Binomial Values

Value of preliminary design (y-axis): 1.5, 1.7, 1.9, 2.1, 2.3, 2.5

Steps (x-axis): 0, 5, 10, 15, 20, 25, 30, 35, 40, 45, 50

your program to automatic recalculation). But the wise programmers at Microsoft have determined that they can save processing time by only recalculating those cells that change due to a change in the worksheet. Now, what constitutes a change is arbitrary, and Microsoft has decided that if the value of a cell does not change in the *first x significant digits,* then no cells that are linked to that cell will be recalculated. I don't know what x is, but my experience tells me that it is not tiny. In fact, I've found that I *cannot* build a binomial tree with more than 50 steps in Microsoft Excel without having some cells fail to recalculate when I make changes. The moral: If it is important to get within fractions of a cent, write your own code in a compiler that allows for double-precision mathematics.

Why Didn't We Use the Black-Scholes to Begin With?

The Black-Scholes model gives a very precise answer to a very specific issue: the valuation of a European call or put. It works great for simple corporate growth options (like the one in this chapter), but it is not applicable in a multitude of other interesting and important situations. In fact, there will be only one more example in this book where the Black-Scholes will work—and that will be in Chapter 6, where our objective will be to learn something about estimation of the volatility parameter.

On the other hand, the binomial model is flexible enough to handle a wide variety of situations—*if* you know how to use it correctly. We're going to spend a lot of time in the remaining chapters learning how to fit nonstandard situations into the binomial approach, but what you'll see as you work through the rest of the book is that *problem framing* is always the first (and usually the most difficult) issue. My pedagogical goal in the Boeing example was to focus on framing: how we should go about reducing the problem into a manageable question that we can answer with our basic tool (the binomial approach).

5.6   Postscript

Boeing undertook the initial preliminary design stage, with a real options analysis like the one I've presented in this chapter to support the decision. By 1998, the worst possible situation developed: The global economy weakened considerably (in particular the Asian economies), and Airbus simultaneously offered the A-3-XX, which could be configured to carry between 481 and 656 passengers.

Boeing ultimately decided that there would be limited demand for a super-jumbo jet for at least 20 years. What Boeing learned about the airline market is instructive. Most of their potential customers determined that the future of the global airline industry would be one of further deregulation and increased competition. Even though slots at the world's major airports are fixed and are not expected to be expanded over the next 20 years, strategic analysts at the world's major airlines have concluded that as regulations ease and competition increases, the best strategy will be to add flights (either by making the airports more efficient, increasing flight offerings at slow times of the day, or by going to new airports altogether). Boeing concluded that the only industry structure in which airlines would utilize a super-jumbo jet would be a tightly regulated one, which was unlikely to occur.

As you might predict, Boeing mothballed the super-jumbo-jet project and focused its attention on a new class of planes (its 7E7 Dreamliner line) that bring the flight distance and speed capabilities of the 747 (about 8,500 nautical miles at mach 0.85) to smaller planes with substantially greater fuel efficiency. The 7E7s will accommodate between 217 and 257 passengers on these long flights, will improve cargo capacity by 40–60%, and at the same time use 20% less fuel for similar operations than any other large plane. Boeing is designing this new plane specifically for the long-distance point-to-point market, which it believes will account for most new demand over the next couple of decades.

The Airbus A-3-XX (now called the A380) is designed to be a double-decked plane, with 10-across seating for coach class on the main deck (in that oh-so-desirable 3-4-3 configuration), nine-across seating on the upper deck for super-coach seating (3-3-3), and six-across seating (2-2-2) in business class (upstairs) and first class (downstairs).

Customer response to the A380 was mixed. Three long-distance carriers (Singapore Airlines, Quantas Airways, and Emirates Airlines) made early commitments to purchase a total of 63 planes. It is widely rumored, however, that Airbus gave these three carriers very steep discounts to secure their orders. In fact, at least two published reports indicate that Airbus was willing to sell these first 63 planes at only $135–$140 million each (which is roughly equal to the lowest discounted price on the cheapest 747).[7] Since then, Airbus has received only 49 more firm orders for passenger versions of the plane and 25 firm orders for cargo versions (as of July 2005).[8]

Furthermore, it turns out that there are significant technical problems with the super-jumbo jet. At it stood in 2005 only around 15 airports in the United States could even accommodate a takeoff and landing of an A380; moreover, only *six* of those had expressed a desire to actually accept the plane (four for passenger flights and two for freight). The problem appears to be cost, as welcoming airports would have to spend a significant amount of money on runway/taxiway upgrades as well as terminal improvements and yet would only see two or three A380 landings per day.[9] Experts estimate that the 15 U.S. airports would have to spend at least $7.5 billion just to widen their runways so that the A380's engines would always be over tarmac (and this doesn't consider the potential for having to completely rebuild the runways to handle the plane's weight, or the cost of new jetway and waiting facilities that would accommodate 550–600 embarking and disembarking passengers).[10]

---

7 See Matlack, C., S Holmes, and C. Dawson, "Given 'Em Away," *Business Week*, March 5, 2001, p. 52; and The Lehman Brothers Equity Research Report, October 2, 2000, p. 3.

8 *Airliner World*, June 2005, p. 47.

9 "Airports Mull New Superjumbo Hassles," cnn.com, Thursday, February 15, 2005, posted 14:39 GMT.

10 Willis Limited, *Global Aviation Bulletin*, Issue 37, June 1, 2001, p. 5.

Moreover, the plane could engender significant spillover costs. At San Francisco International, the parallel runways are so close together that one of them will have to be temporarily shut down every time an A380 wants to take off or land.[11] And any airport that accepts the plane must provide increased labor and facilities to deal with the larger spikes in passenger arrivals and departures: everything from customs and immigration to baggage handling, check-in counters, and security will be affected.

Finally, there are issues of emergency exit safety. The A380 is equipped with 16 exit doors, and because the A380 is a double-decker plane, its upper emergency exits require huge slides that descend steeply from a very high door (and which, in some instances, traverse right in front of the jet engines). Many aviation observers and experts don't believe that the plane, with only 16 exit doors, can be evacuated in 90 seconds with one-half of the exits inoperable (as required by the FAA for commercial flight in the United States).[12]

Airbus has resorted to politics and pander to get around these issues. The company unsuccessfully lobbied the FAA to allow it to prove the plane's emergency evacuation performance via computer simulation (as opposed to actual trials), claiming oddly that minor gains in the safety of human subjects employed in the trials outweighed the safety of potential passengers whose survival might actually depend on the slides.[13] And Airbus purposefully chose American suppliers of components for the plane so that it could recite the well-worn script of job creation—in a recent speech, Airbus CEO Noël Forgeard stated boldly that the A380 would create 60,000 new jobs in the United States.[14] I will go on the record as being skeptical of this number.

Be that as it may, the A380 will move people and freight as soon as Airbus can deliver the first one.[15] And if you fly between London and Asia, or between the United States west coast and Australia, or into and out of the Middle East, you may well get to experience this remarkable feat of engineering. Only time will tell whether or not the plane's financial returns justify the huge investment.

5.7 Two Important Final Points

Even though Boeing created an option that expired unexercised, the company's decision to invest in the preliminary design of the super-jumbo jet was the correct one, and the sophisticated option-based analysis used by Boeing will ultimately lead to better use of capital and value creation. Many (if not most) corporate growth options will go unexercised. But if firms like Boeing continually purchase growth options for amounts less than true values, shareholders will

---

[11] "Airports Mull New Superjumbo Hassles," cnn.com, Thursday, February 15, 2005, posted 14:39 GMT.

[12] The number of emergency exits is a critical issue for Airbus, because each additional door adds significant drag to the plane. To compensate for the added drag, the plane's engines must generate more thrust and thus burn more fuel. This puts the designer into a perplexing problem: Either add more fuel, which increases the empty weight of the plane (and thus decreases the number of passengers that can be flown), accept a shorter maximum flight distance, or find other ways to take weight out of the plane.

[13] Webster (2001).

[14] Noël Forgeard, in a speech to employees of Goodrich Aerospace in Cleveland, as quoted by *Flug Review Online*, May 6, 2001.

[15] It is unclear exactly when this will be. Only hours after the plane's maiden flight on April 27, 2005, Airbus announced that its first scheduled delivery–to Singapore Airlines for the London-Singapore-Sydney route–would be delayed for at least six months. At least part of the delay is attributable to excess weight. See "Airbus Needs 'Several Years' to Hit A380 Delivery Schedule," *Seattle Post-Intelligencer*, June 15, 2005; and "Airbus Details A380's Production Delays," *Flight International*, June 21, 2005.

ultimately be made better off. The key for everyone is to avoid overpayment for these options. This can easily happen when *strategy* is the overriding argument.

We should also be careful about the outputs of the analysis. Our result that the preliminary design is worth $2.26 billion is only as good as the assumptions we made to get to it. What I've found, and many of my friends have found as well, is that the real benefit of the real option analysis is not the number that comes out of the calculations, but rather the discipline that it imposes on management's thinking. Instead of relying on claims that a project has so-called strategic value, real option analysis allows the manager to ask, "What does the world have to look like in order for this strategy to have value?" That's a giant step forward, and we'll explore it in our next case study.

5.8 Bibliography

"Airbus Bets the Company," *The Economist,* March 18, 2000, p. 17.

"Airbus Details A380's Production Delays," *Flight International,* June 21, 2005.

"Airbus Needs 'Several Years' to Hit A380 Delivery Schedule," *Seattle Post-Intelligencer,* June 15, 2005.

"Airbus Successfully Completes World's Biggest Jet's First Flight," *The Wall Street Journal,* April 28, 2005, p. A5.

The Airline Monitor, Report for January/February 2000.

The Airline Monitor, Report for January/February 2001.

"Airports Mull New Superjumbo Hassles," cnn.com, February 15, 2005.

"Boeing Loses Singapore Airlines Jet Order to European Rival Airbus Industrie," *The Seattle Times,* December 19, 2000, p. D1.

"Boeing to Shelve Superjumbo," *Reuters News,* March 28, 2001.

Cole, J., "Airbus Prepares to 'Bet the Company' as it Builds a Huge New Jet," *The Wall Street Journal,* November 3, 1999, p. A1.

Cole, J., F. Rose, and C. Goldsmith, "Boeing's 747 Decision Shifts Rivalry with Airbus," *The Wall Street Journal,* January 22, 1997, p. A3.

Credit Suisse First Boston Equity Research Report, "Global Commercial Aerospace Monthly," May 2000.

"European Aeronautic Defence and Space Company (EADS)," *Credit Suisse First Boston Equity Research Report,* March 2001.

"Airbus A3XX: The Business Case for the Double Decker," *Dresdner Kleinwort Benson Aerospace and Defense Equity Research Report,* May 8, 2000.

"Emirates Announces $15bn Aircraft Order," *Financial Times,* November 5, 2001.

Esty, B.C., and Kane, M., "Airbus A3XX: Developing the World's Largest Commercial Jet," *Harvard Business School Publishing* case No. 201-028, 2001.

Esty, B. C., and P. Ghemawat, "Airbus vs. Boeing in Super Jumbos: A Case of Failed Preemption," unpublished manuscript, Harvard Business School, 2002.

Matlack, C., S. Holmes, and C. Dawson, "Giving 'Em Away?," *Business Week,* March 5, 2001, p. 52.

"Boeing Company," *Morgan Stanley Dean Witter Equity Research Report,* March 20, 2001.

Phillips, Don, "Huge but Quiet Airbus Makes First Test Flight," *International Herald Tribune,* April 28, 2005, p. 11.

Rothman, A., "Airbus Chief Justifies Customer Discounts," *The Seattle Times,* March 24, 2001, p. E1.

"Superjumbo," *Airliner World,* July 2005, 42–59.

Webster, B., "Airbus in Fear of Full Emergency Test," *The Times,* June 18, 2001.

Willis Limited, *Global Aviation Bulletin,* Issue 37, 1 June, 2001, p. 5.

PROBLEMS

1. Calculate the remaining four state prices (i.e., the state price is the value of security that pays $1.00 in a particular final state in a binomial tree) for the binomial tree discussed in the chapter.

2. Revalue Boeing's option given a strike price of $30 billion and a strike price of $12 billion.

3. Generate a new tree for Boeing's option with a volatility of 45% annually rather than 38% annually. Revalue the option, and determine if R&D should commence at a cost of $2.7 billion.

4. Use the state price method of option valuation to calculate the option value in Problem 3.

5. Suppose a project is dependent on whether there is a good economy and whether a competitor enters the market. If there is no competitor, the project will produce $50 million in a good economy and $15 million in a poor economy. If there is a competitor, the project will produce $30 million in a good economy and $10 million in a poor economy. The probability of a good economy is 60%, versus 40% for a poor economy; and the probability for a competitor to enter the market is 30%, versus 70% for no competitor.

   a. Find the expected value of the cash flow from the project.

   b. Assume the project cannot begin for three years and has a risk-adjusted discount rate of 18%. Calculate the present value of the project's expected cash flow.

   c. Using the calculation from part b, calculate the expected three-year holding-period return, the variance of the three-year holding-period return, and the standard deviation of the three-year holding-period return.

   d. Adjust the variance and the standard deviation in part c to annual terms.

6. Assume that the project in Problem 5 is valuable if it can generate a cash flow above $25 million. A decision on whether to develop the project at a cost of $6.5 million needs to be made today if the project is to be implemented in three years. Given a 5% annual risk-free rate and the calculations from Problem 5, generate a binomial tree (each stage of the tree being one year) to value the development option and make a decision.

7. Assume that management believes the option in Problem 6 only has a cost of $3 million instead of $6.5 million. Further, the annual volatility is believed to be 30%, which is much lower than the volatility used in Problem 6. Recalculate the value of developing the project and determine if it is feasible under this new scenario.

8. A project is expected to produce cash flows of $60 million, $40 million, or $12 million assuming the economy is good (20% probability), average (50% probability), or poor (30% probability), respectively. If a competitor enters the market (30% probability), the respective cash flows reduce to $40 million, $25 million, and $10 million. Given a risk-adjusted discount rate of 16% and an eight-year horizon for beginning the project, what is the present value of the expected payoff for the project?

9. Compute the annual holding-period variance and standard deviation for the project in Problem 8.

10. What are the state prices for the final nodes of an 8-step binomial tree that models the project cash flows (each stage being one year), assuming an annual risk-free rate of 4% and using the calculations from Problem 9?

11. Use the state prices in Problem 10 to determine the value of developing the project from Problem 8 today, assuming the cost of the project is $35 million.

6

PLATFORM INVESTMENTS:
A LESSON ON VOLATILITY ESTIMATION

The Boeing case (Chapter 5) provides a simple and elegant illustration of how we can use standard option-pricing techniques to value corporate investment opportunities that create future flexibility. Boeing's investment in preliminary R&D purchases a future cash flow pattern that looks just like a European call option, and so we can value that investment as if it were a European call—exactly the way the financial markets would.

There's more to Chapter 5 than meets the eye, however. Even though valuation of options on financial assets is identical in theory to valuation of options on real assets, a lesson we learn from the Boeing case is that we have to think a little differently when we are dealing with a real option. We use the same *models* to value financial and real options; the difference lies in how we go about implementing those models.

The first place we had to think carefully was when we estimated the initial value of the underlying. Remember, to exercise this option Boeing would have to spend $20 billion (the strike price) in January 2001; if Boeing were to do so, it would receive back in exchange a super-jumbo-jet product. So, the underlying asset is itself a super-jumbo-jet product, and the *value* of that product at any point in time is whatever the financial markets would be willing to pay for the future free cash flows that product is expected to generate.

Intuitively, we could say that there exists a traded financial market portfolio that would generate the same future cash flows (in terms of quantity, timing, and risk) as a super-jumbo-jet product. We formed that tracking portfolio on January 1, 1996, based only on what we knew at that time and found that its value was $10 billion. Thus, the value of a super-jumbo-jet product on that day was $10 billion, and so the starting value of our underlying asset was $10 billion as well.

It helps a lot to think about the underlying asset and its tracking portfolio as being interchangeable, because this makes the volatility of a real asset more intuitive. And estimation of the volatility parameter was the second place in the Boeing case where we had to think very carefully.

The key insight is that as time marches on, and as new information arrives about the expected free cash flows from selling super-jumbo jets, the present value of the product's free cash flows will change. Since the present value of the product's free cash flows is really the value of the financial market tracking portfolio that mimics those cash flows, it follows that as new information arrives, the value of the product's tracking portfolio changes.

When we speak of the *volatility of returns* on an asset, what we mean is the standard deviation of the probability distribution that describes the potential changes in the asset's value. And since the super-jumbo-jet product (the asset, in this case real) and its tracking portfolio are interchangeable, we can think about the volatility of returns on the underlying as the standard deviation of potential changes in the value of its *tracking portfolio.*

This is *exactly* how we approximated the volatility parameter in the Boeing example. Management's estimates of what the future might bring, along with the probabilities of those outcomes, allowed us to construct a probability distribution of the potential January 2001 *values* of the super jumbo jet's tracking portfolio. This, in turn, gave us a probability distribution of the potential *changes* in the tracking portfolio's value between January 1996 and January 2001—that is, a probability distribution of the *returns* on the tracking portfolio over that period. The annualized standard deviation of this probability distribution of returns is the volatility of returns on the tracking portfolio; since the super-jumbo-jet product and its tracking portfolio are interchangeable, we thus have the volatility of returns on our underlying asset (which we estimated to be 38%).

The subtle point in the Boeing case is that we were able to extract our estimate for the volatility of returns on the underlying from management's *intuition* about the future. This is a powerful concept, one that we will explore in this chapter.

Estimating the Volatility Parameter

When first confronting a real options valuation problem, many corporate managers become frustrated with their inability to calculate the underlying asset's return volatility. Some of this frustration undoubtedly comes from their procedure, as many managers believe that the *only* way to estimate the volatility of an asset's returns is to observe a historical time series of the asset's value, translate that time series of values into a time series of returns, then calculate the standard deviation of those observed returns.[1]

Relying solely on historically observed returns is not the only way to estimate the volatility parameter in an option valuation. In fact, it is not how sophisticated traders of financial derivatives work. Although financial options traders may know the historical volatility of returns on an underlying stock, they would never blindly use this statistic in their own valuations. Instead, they only use the historical volatility as a starting point, and they consciously adjust it to reflect

---

[1] Such a procedure actually involves another step: A silent prayer that the future will look like the past.

their own subjective assessment of what the future might bring. In other words, they use their own intuition about the world to estimate the volatility of a stock's returns, and they base their option trading strategies around this intuitively generated parameter.

In my mind, the practical problem with volatility in the real options context is not that it can't be estimated precisely but rather that we haven't developed any heuristic ways of thinking about it to help us arrive at a good approximation. My point in this chapter is to show you a way that I think has promise.

The basis of my idea is my belief that managers possess a lot of information about the future potential for a project, and they usually have some intuition (often based on experience) that tells them how likely it is that a project will succeed spectacularly, be mediocre, or fail. If this intuition is available, we should use it. But we won't use it to arrive at a precise volatility parameter and then proceed with valuation of the option. Rather, we will value the real option with an arbitrary volatility parameter, and then we will do two things.

First of all, we will search for a *range* of volatilities that make our binomial model of the future approximately consistent with the manager's intuition about the real-world future. Second, we will determine the *break-even* volatility parameter, see what it implies about the future of the world, see where it falls relative to our range, and ask the manager "Is this reasonable?" or "Is the world really this uncertain?"

To demonstrate this, I'll show you one more example of a simple corporate growth option. My point here is to get to the volatility estimation issue, so I won't dwell on the specifics. I will tell you, however, that this case is based on a true story that I've had to alter only slightly to make my teaching point (as well as to respect the company's concerns for confidentiality).

6.1 The Problem for This Chapter: A Platform Investment

Companies of all sorts launch new products that display unquestionably negative static net present value (NPV). Why would they do so? The answer is usually that the new offering is strategic: The launch of the negative-NPV first-generation product produces the opportunity to later launch subsequent-generation products that might create value. These kinds of trial balloon activities are often called *platform investments,* and they usually involve some new kind of product technology for which demand is very difficult to ascertain.

In these situations, it is easy for managers to argue that their new platform investments are strategic and should be exploited at once: The static NPV calculation only measures the cash flow value of the first generation product and completely misses the value of the concomitant follow-on opportunities. But the hard question is then, How much should the company be willing to lose on the first-generation product in order to implement the strategy? How much is strategy worth to the firm's shareholders? By explicitly recognizing that the follow-on opportunities are options, we can supplement the manager's intuition with a scientific way of addressing this problem.

Here's the example we will use. In June 2000, an American server and router company determined that a particular part of its proprietary operating system software could be scaled down and applied to a new type of consumer electronics product. The design phase of the first generation of this new product would take about 15 months and would cost, in present value terms, about $40.4 million. The first-generation product's launch would occur on September 30, 2001. Based on inputs from marketing, as well as the firm's policy of a 25% hurdle rate (which I believe

Figure 6.1   Static NPV Analysis of First-Generation Product

	6/30/2000	Q3'00	Q4'00	Q1'01	Q2'01	Q3'01	Q4'01	Q1'02	Q2'02	Q3'02	Q4'02	Q1'03	Q2'03
						After Tax Incremental Cash Flows in $000							
First-generation													
Development costs June 30, 2000, PV at 25%	40,359	3,642	2,708	14,500	17,645	10,721							
Operating cash flows June 30, 2000, PV at 25%	31,677						(4,570)	5,550	28,990	20,880			
NPV of first-generation	(8,682)												

is far too high, but I'll use anyway), the company's financial analysts estimated the June 2000 present value of the expected operating free cash flows (after taxes) over the short life of the product to be only about $31.7 million. Hence, the first-generation product had a static NPV of nearly −$8.7 million. Figure 6.1 provides a summary of the static NPV analysis of the first-generation product.

What you see in Figure 6.1 is that the firm forecast the first-generation product's cash flows to end after only one year of sales.[2] This short life cycle is typical of high-technology products: Given a launch on September 30, 2001, the company's marketing department determined that the product would be virtually obsolete by September 30, 2002. If the product turned out to be a dud, the company would liquidate the inventory from the first production run and move on to other opportunities. If the product turned out to be a success, low-cost competitors would quickly respond with a similar offering at a discounted price; to maintain a competitive advantage in this situation, our company would have to launch a second-generation product with more technology.

The Potential Second-Generation Product

The second-generation product, if pursued, would take nine months to develop. Since the second-generation product would need to be on the shelves by September 30, 2002 (the forecast obsolescence date of the first generation product), its development would have to begin by December 31, 2001.

The cost of developing the second-generation product (mostly engineering headcount) was fairly easy for the company to predict—about $65.5 million when discounted back to the second-generation decision date of December 31, 2001, or about $46.9 million when discounted back to June 30, 2000. Forecasting the operating cash flows on the second-generation product was a bit harder, but management came up with an estimated June 2000 present value of about $45 million. So the second-generation product had a negative NPV, just as the first-generation product did. Figure 6.2 gives the static NPV analysis of the second-generation product. Notice in Figure 6.2 that the static NPV of the second-generation product is negative no matter what point in time is used for the analysis. The *current* (June 30, 2000) value of the

---

[2] In this analysis, changes to net working capital are included in operating cash flows. The negative operating cash flow in Q4'01 reflects a necessary inventory and receivables buildup; as the company sells down the inventory and collects its receivables in the last two quarters of the first-generation product's sales, cash flows bulge. Sales are positive in the first quarter; they are just being masked by the net working capital effect.

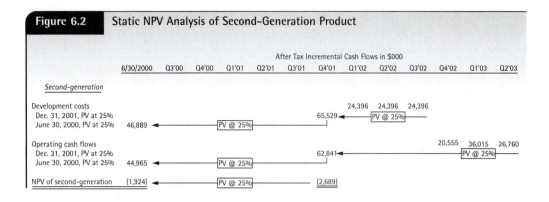

Figure 6.2 Static NPV Analysis of Second-Generation Product

After Tax Incremental Cash Flows in $000

	6/30/2000	Q3'00	Q4'00	Q1'01	Q2'01	Q3'01	Q4'01	Q1'02	Q2'02	Q3'02	Q4'02	Q1'03	Q2'03
Second-generation													
Development costs								24,396	24,396	24,396			
Dec. 31, 2001, PV at 25%						65,529	PV @ 25%						
June 30, 2000, PV at 25%	46,889	PV @ 25%											
Operating cash flows											20,555	36,015	26,760
Dec. 31, 2001, PV at 25%						62,841	PV @ 25%						
June 30, 2000, PV at 25%	44,965	PV @ 25%											
NPV of second-generation	(1,924)	PV @ 25%			(2,689)								

second-generation product is about $45 million, and the current cost of development is about $46.9 million, so the current static NPV is about -1.9 million. All figures grow in time value by the 25% discount rate, so the expected decision date NPV (i.e., the static NPV calculated at December 31, 2001) is about $-\$1.9$ million $\times (1.25)^{1.5} = -\$2.7$ million.

From a completely static perspective, the entire strategy was a dog. Why, then, did management invest in the first-generation product anyway? The company knew intuitively that the first-generation product would produce more than cash flow—it would generate information about demand for the company's proprietary technology and new brand. Strong acceptance of the first-generation product would signal strong demand for later products; tepid acceptance of the product would signal that the company should abandon the new market strategy. So, the company did not have to immediately commit to the second-generation development expenditures. Rather, management could wait to observe the early results from sales of the first-generation technology before making this decision.

Being well-trained in finance, the CFO of the company wanted more than casual claims of strategic value—he wanted hard numbers. The first task of the finance and marketing groups was to sketch out the problem, and I've reproduced their decision diagram in Figure 6.3.

We've seen this picture before, only in a different context. Notice how this looks just like the gourmet coffee example, where the investment in market research allowed management to learn about the market for the product before committing capital to developing it. Notice how it also looks like the Boeing R&D example, where Boeing's investment in preliminary R&D on a super-jumbo jet created no cash flow but rather information about market demand for the plane—information that would be used to make a more informed go/no-go decision.

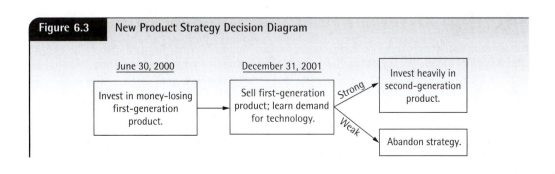

Figure 6.3 New Product Strategy Decision Diagram

Once again, we have a standard corporate growth option, which is a call option. When we look at things in a dynamic context, we realize that the company would only invest in the second-generation product if the first-generation product were a hit. The act of exercising this option is simply spending the development costs of the second-generation product, and so the underlying (what you get back in return) is the second-generation product (or, more precisely, the operating cash flows from the second-generation product). Launch of the first-generation product creates cash flows on its own as well as an option on the second generation product, so the *true* NPV of the strategy consists of the *static* NPV of the first generation product *plus* the value of the option on the second-generation product.

Of course, the real-world strategy would not end there. Launch of the second-generation product would create an option on a third-generation, and development of the third-generation product would create an option on a fourth generation, and so on. We will learn how to deal with these chains of decisions in Chapter 7. The point of this chapter is to teach you something about the volatility of the underlying asset. So, for the time being, we'll just assume that the second-generation product is the final step in this particular strategy (or that the cash flow value of the second-generation includes all future option values).

When the marketing and finance groups presented Figure 6.1 and Figure 6.2 to senior management, they provided some additional information: an estimation of the *best case,* the *worst case,* and some *more likely* cases for the product along with a subjective assessment of just how likely these outcomes might be. The worst case scenario involved demand substantially below expectation, in which case the free cash flows from the second-generation product would be less than one-half of the forecast (i.e., less than about $31.4 million); based on past experience, management knew to expect this about 25% of the time. On the other hand, the best case would be for a blockbuster second-generation product with free cash flows in excess of three times the original forecast (i.e., greater than about $188.2 million), and management believed that about 1 out of every 20 new products could achieve blockbuster status. A good case would be for the second-generation product to have free cash flows in excess of two times the original forecast (i.e., greater than about $125.5 million); management subjectively assigned a 1-in-8 probability to this scenario. Finally, management believed that there was only a 1-in-3 chance of actually launching the second-generation product at all on December 31, 2001. The critical insight is that immediate launch of the first-generation product allows management to learn which of these scenarios occurs *before* investing in development of the second-generation product. Figure 6.4 summarizes management's intuition about the potential for this very risky venture.

The data presented in Figure 6.4, which come from management's intuition and past experience, are extremely valuable and we can use them to help with our option analysis. Keep them in mind—we'll come back to them later when we analyze our volatility parameter.

Figure 6.4	Various Scenarios for Second Generation Product: Present Value of Free Cash Flows as of Decision Date (12/31/01) and Associated Subjective Probabilities Assigned by Management		
		December 31, 2001 Value of 2G Operating Cash Flows	Subjective Probability
Best case scenario	$> 3 \times$ Expected Value	$> \$188.2$ million	1-in-20 (5%)
Good scenario	$> 2 \times$ Expected Value	$> \$125.5$ million	1-in-8 (12.5%)
Actual launch		$> \$65.5$ million	1-in-3 (33%)
Worst case scenario	$< \frac{1}{2} \times$ Expected Value	$< \$31.4$ million	1-in-4 (25%)

Valuation of the Platform Option Created by the First-Generation Product

Let's pin down the parameters of the option problem. If management initiates development of the first-generation product on June 30, 2000, then they create the option to start development of the second-generation production on December 31, 2001. So the maturity of the option is 18 months, or 1.5 years. We'll take the risk-free rate over the 18-month period to be 5% per year.

We have to be very careful with the strike price. In any option problem, whether financial or real, the strike price is the amount of money that is paid (or committed) *on the date of exercise.* For example, if you purchase a one-year European call option on Starbucks stock with a strike of, say, $100, then you pay precisely $100 if you choose to exercise in one year's time. The strike is not given in present value terms; rather it is the nominal amount that you will write on the check when you exercise.

Look back at Figure 6.2, at the investment cost of the second-generation product. By developing the first-generation product starting on June 30, 2000, management creates the *right but not the obligation* to spend the capital investment necessary for the second generation product <u>on December 31, 2001.</u> When management reaches its date with destiny on December 31, 2001, $65.529 million is the present value of the cost of continuing. So, $65.529 million is the appropriate strike price for the option on the second-generation product—it is the amount that management must "write on the check" on the exercise date to exercise the option.

Please make sure you understand that the strike price for the option on the second-generation product is <u>not</u> the June 30, 2000, present value of the second-generation development costs ($46.889 million); $46.889 million is the discounted value of the strike, and if you use this you will substantially overstate the value of the real growth option.

But what about the current value of the underlying asset? Again, we have to be very careful. Remember that the underlying asset is what you get back if you exercise the option. In this case, management exercises the option when they commit to spending $65.529 million on December 31, 2001. So what does management get back if, on December 31, 2001, they decide to spend the $65.529 million? The answer is obvious—they get back the second-generation product. The underlying asset is the second-generation product, and the *value* of the underlying asset is the present value of the free cash flows management will expect to be thrown off by the second-generation product.

But here's where we have to be extremely careful. The appropriate input for our option problem is the *current* value of the underlying asset, and what we mean by *current* value is the expected free cash flows from the underlying asset <u>discounted all the way back to the day that management *creates* the option</u>—in this case, June 30, 2000. Looking back at Figure 6.2, we see that this is $44.965 million. The starting value of the underlying is <u>not</u> the exercise-date present value of the expected cash flows ($62.841 million).

Why? To understand this, we need to remember what went on in our binomial trees. Recall from Chapter 4 that the expected value of the underlying asset increases through the binomial tree at the asset's required rate of return. In other words, if we start our binomial analysis in this example on June 30, 2000, with an underlying value of UND_0, the *expected* value of the second-generation product on the exercise date of December 31, 2001, will be $UND_0(1.25)^{1.5}$, because the required rate of return on the second-generation product is 25% (the discount rate we used to value it), and the time between June 30, 2000, and December 31, 2001, is 18 months, or 1.5 years. Figure 6.2 shows us that we need the expected value of the second-generation product's free cash flows to be $62.841 million on December 31, 2001, so the current or starting value of our underlying asset must satisfy

$$UND_0(1.25)^{1.5} = \$62.841 \text{ mm}$$

$$UND_0 = \frac{\$62.841 \text{ mm}}{(1.25)^{1.5}} = \$44.965 \text{ mm}$$

For an intuitive way to think about this, consider once again a $100 Starbucks call. When you value that one-year European call on Starbucks stock with a $100 strike price, the number you use for the current value of the underlying is the *current* price of Starbucks stock—*not* the expected value of the stock on the day of exercise. The current price of a stock is the present value of its future expected price (plus the present value of any dividends received in the meantime, of course).

Just keep this in mind: The strike price is the present value of the capital commitments discounted back to the exercise date, while the current value of the underlying is the present value of the expected free cash flows thrown off by the underlying asset discounted all the way back to the day that the option is being valued. Figure 6.5 shows this point visually.

Be careful—novices make two errors here. The first error some make is to take the NPV of the second-generation product as the starting value of the underlying. This is incorrect, because the strike price captures the capital investments required for the second-generation product, and the strike is not paid unless management actually exercises the option. Using the NPV of the underlying as the current value of the underlying forces the assumption that management commits the capital investment regardless of what is learned (and potentially double-counts the

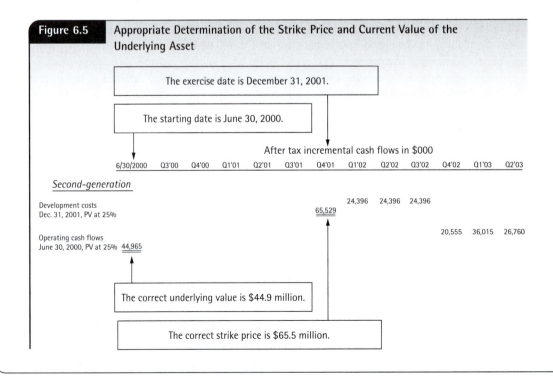

Figure 6.5   Appropriate Determination of the Strike Price and Current Value of the Underlying Asset

strike price). Remember, only use the present value of the operating cash flows (i.e., what you get back *if* you spend the strike).[3]

The second (and more frequent) error some make is in the time value of the underlying and the strike. As I've mentioned above, the proper starting or current value of the underlying is the June 2000 discounted value of the free cash flows, or $44.9 million, while the proper strike price is the December 2001 discounted value of the development costs, or $65.5 million (and *not* the June 2000 value of $46.9 million). The binomial model (and the Black-Scholes model) take time value into account. So, to keep it straight: Use the current PV of the expected free cash inflows as the starting value, and the exercise-date PV of the investment costs as the strike.

With that warning, let's move on. If we start our binomial analysis with a June 30, 2000, value of the underlying (the second-generation product) of $44.965 million, then the *mean,* or expected value, of the underlying on the exercise date will be $62.841 million. This is only an estimate based on what we know as of June 30, 2000, and we describe the uncertainty in that estimate through our volatility parameter (which is the point of this chapter).[4]

Remember that in the real options context, the value of the underlying is our current *understanding* of its future cash flows, and the volatility of the underlying represents how much our understanding can *change,* or how much there is to learn. Low volatility implies great confidence in our current estimate, whereas high volatility admits that our current estimate could be quite wrong. Like I mentioned at the beginning of this chapter, a lot of practitioners get bogged down in an effort to pin down a precise volatility estimate. What I'd like to do is start with an arbitrary volatility (here 100%), do the analysis, and then go back and try to calibrate our volatility estimate using management's intuition (which was captured to some extent in Figure 6.4).

Let's briefly review the parameters of our analysis:

- The starting value of the underlying is $UND_0 = \$44.9$ million.
- The volatility of returns (or log changes) in the underlying is $\sigma = 100\%$.
- The time to expiration of the option is 18 months (or $T = 1.5$ years).
- The strike price on the option is $K = \$65.5$ million.
- The risk-free rate is 5%.

Just to keep things simple, I'll build a 6-step binomial tree ($N = 6$); you'll get a more precise valuation with more steps. Since $T = 1.5$ and $N = 6$, each time step will be $\Delta t = T/N = 1.5$ years/6 steps $= 0.25$ year per step, or $\Delta t = \frac{1}{4}$ year. These parameters lead to the following calculations:

- The size of an up step u is $U = e^{\sigma\sqrt{\Delta T}} = e^{1.00\sqrt{1/4}} = 1.649$.
- The size of a down step is $D = 1/U = 0.607$.
- The discount rate between steps is $e^{r\times\Delta t} = e^{(0.05)(1/4)} = 1.013$.
- The risk-neutral probability of an up move is $q = (e^{r\times\Delta t} - D)/(U - D) = 0.39$.
- The risk-neutral probability of a down more is $1 - q = 0.61$.

---

[3] Moreover, if your NPV is negative (as in this case), and you start your binomial tree with a negative number, every number in the tree will be negative and the option will be worthless as it will never be exercised.

[4] We assume that the exercise-date *value* of the underlying is described by a lognormal probability distribution function. Remember that the volatility parameter is not the standard deviation of that distribution, but rather the annualized standard deviation of log changes (returns) from the starting value to each possible terminal value with the same associated probability.

Figure 6.6   Binomial Tree of Underlying (2G product) Values ($millions)

6/30/2000	1	2	3	4	5	12/31/2001
44.9	74.0	122.1	201.2	331.8	547.0	901.8
	27.2	44.9	74.0	122.1	201.2	331.8
		16.5	27.2	44.9	74.0	122.1
			10.0	16.5	27.2	44.9
				6.1	10.0	16.5
					3.7	6.1
						2.2

Figure 6.7

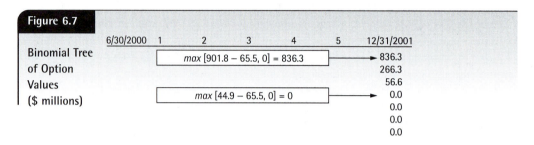

Binomial Tree of Option Values ($ millions)

6/30/2000	1	2	3	4	5	12/31/2001
		max [901.8 − 65.5, 0] = 836.3			→	836.3
						266.3
						56.6
		max [44.9 − 65.5, 0] = 0			→	0.0
						0.0
						0.0
						0.0

The first step is to build the binomial tree for 6 steps with a starting value of $44.9 million, an up-step size of 1.649, and a down-step size of 0.607. Figure 6.6 presents the binomial tree of second-generation product values.

Next, we start at the end and work backward. At the end of the 6th quarter (on December 31, 2001), the company will launch the second generation product if and only if the observed value of the free cash flows at that time is greater than $65.5 million. So we create a tree of option values, and we fill in the values for the exercise date as *max* [value of underlying − $65.5, $0]. See Figure 6.7.

The next step is to clear-cut the forest back using the risk-neutral probabilities of the up and down moves ($q = 0.39$ and $1 − q = 0.61$, respectively) and the risk-free discount factor 1.013. Figure 6.8 documents the work for quarter 5.

Now repeat the process for quarter 4, as I show in Figure 6.9.

Once we've clear-cut the forest all the way back to the beginning, we get the value of the *option to initiate the second-generation product*. I show the final result in Figure 6.10.

The interpretation is this: Given our assumptions (and in particular, our 100% per year volatility assumption), the option to launch the second-generation product is worth $17.6 million! So given our assumptions so far, the *true* NPV of the first-generation product is its own static

Figure 6.8

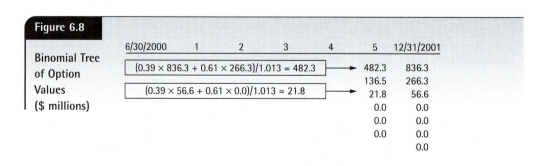

Binomial Tree of Option Values ($ millions)

6/30/2000	1	2	3	4	5	12/31/2001
	(0.39 × 836.3 + 0.61 × 266.3)/1.013 = 482.3			→	482.3	836.3
					136.5	266.3
	(0.39 × 56.6 + 0.61 × 0.0)/1.013 = 21.8			→	21.8	56.6
					0.0	0.0
					0.0	0.0
					0.0	0.0
						0.0

Figure 6.9		Binomial Tree of Option Values ($millions)					
6/30/2000	1	2	3	4	5	12/31/2001	
(0.39 × 482.3 + 0.61 × 136.5)/1.013 = 267.9			→ 267.9	482.3	836.3		
				65.7	136.5	266.3	
(0.39 × 21.8 + 0.61 × 0.0)/1.013 = 8.4			→ 8.4	21.8	56.6		
				0.0	0.0	0.0	
				0.0	0.0	0.0	
					0.0	0.0	
						0.0	

Figure 6.10		Binomial Tree of Option Values ($millions)					
6/30/2000	1	2	3	4	5	12/31/2001	
17.6	36.3	73.2	142.7	267.9	482.3	836.3	
	6.0	13.6	30.3	65.7	136.5	266.3	
		1.2	3.2	8.4	21.8	56.6	
			0.0	0.0	0.0	0.0	
				0.0	0.0	0.0	
					0.0	0.0	
						0.0	

NPV on a stand-alone basis *plus* the value of the option it creates on the second generation product: −$8.6 million +$17.6 million = $9 million. This is really the value of the strategy, and it tells us that we would be willing to lose even more on the first-generation project in order to have the option on the second generation.

This example, which is rooted in a real-world situation, shows why many high-technology and e-commerce businesses have such high stock market valuations in spite of negative expected earnings or even negative expected cash flows. Even if the current expected NPV of future possible projects is negative, the options on those projects can be quite valuable. It also explains why these stocks are so volatile—as you move through the option value tree in Figure 6.10, you see huge movements up and down in value based on small changes in information about the value of the second-generation product (Figure 6.6).

But that's not the point of this chapter. I promised you I'd try to develop a heuristic way of approaching the volatility estimate. The intuition behind my idea here is that the volatility estimate (along with the required return on the underlying asset) makes very specific statements about the likelihood of various future events. If managers have their own subjective assessments about the likelihood of those events (like those we collected in Figure 6.4), then we should be able to match up the volatility estimate with management's beliefs.

6.2   A Way to Calibrate the Volatility Parameter

It all starts with our *assumption* that log returns are described by a normal distribution. If you recall from the review of derivatives pricing, our method of building binomial trees rests on the assumption that log returns are distributed normal with mean log return m per year and standard deviation of log returns σ per year. This, in turn, implies that the expiration-date *values* of the underlying asset are described by a lognormal distribution with very specific probabilities of various values occuring.

Since log returns come from a normal distribution with mean m and standard deviation σ, then the probability of actually observing a log return less than r^* over a period of T years is

$$\Pr\left[\ln\left(\frac{UND_T}{UND_0}\right) < r^*\right] = N\left(\frac{r^* - mT}{\sigma\sqrt{T}}\right)$$

where $N(\bullet)$ is the cumulative probability distribution function of a normal random variable with mean 0 and standard deviation 1. This is easy to evaluate with Excel's built-in function $= normsdist ((r^* - mT)/\sigma\sqrt{T})$. The first thing we need to recall is that m, the mean annual log return, is the geometric mean return on the underlying asset. We arrive at m through its relationship with the arithmetic mean annual return on the asset (i.e., the asset's required rate of return): $m = \mu - .5\sigma^2$. So, we can rewrite the probability of observing a log return less than r^* to be

$$\Pr\left[\ln\left(\frac{UND_T}{UND_0}\right) < r^*\right] = N\left(\frac{r^* - (\mu - .5\sigma^2)T}{\sigma\sqrt{T}}\right)$$

For example, we can calculate the cumulative probability that the learned value of the second-generation product falls short of the exercise price (i.e., the probability that we don't continue into the second-generation product). The probability of learning a value less than the strike price K is equal to the probability of seeing a log return less than $\ln(K/UND_0)$:

$$\Pr\left[\ln\left(\frac{UND_T}{UND_0}\right) < \ln\left(\frac{K}{UND_0}\right)\right] = N\left(\frac{\ln(K/UND_0) - (\mu - .5\sigma^2)T}{\sigma\sqrt{T}}\right)$$

This is easy to evaluate under our assumptions. Since the strike is $K = \$65.5$, the current value of the underlying is $UND_0 = \$44.9$, the required rate of return on the underlying is $\mu = 0.25$, the standard deviation of log returns on the underlying is $\sigma = 1.00$, and the time to maturity of the option is $T = 1.5$, then the probability that this option dies out of the money is

$$\Pr\left[\ln\left(\frac{UND_T}{UND_0}\right) < \ln\left(\frac{65.5}{44.9}\right)\right] = N\left(\frac{\ln(65.5/44.9) - (0.25 - 0.5(1.00)^2) \cdot 1.5}{1.00\sqrt{1.5}}\right)$$

$$= N\left(\frac{0.378 - (-0.375)}{1.225}\right)$$

$$= N(0.615)$$

$$= 0.73$$

(where I evaluated the unit normal CDF in Excel using $= normsdist(0.615)$). What this tells us is that under the assumption of 100% volatility, there is a roughly 3-in-4 chance that the company won't develop the second-generation product, or equivalently only about a 1-in-4 chance that it will.

Many managers think more in terms of how likely it is that we exceed certain extreme values. So we can rearrange the probability statement above to tell us the probability of *exceeding* some value, like the strike price. Since $1 - N(x) = N(-x)$,

$$\Pr\left[\ln\left(\frac{UND_T}{UND_0}\right) > \ln\left(\frac{K}{UND_0}\right)\right] = N\left(-\frac{\ln(K/UND_0) - (\mu - .5\sigma^2)T}{\sigma\sqrt{T}}\right)$$

$$= N\left(\frac{-\ln(K/UND_0) + (\mu - .5\sigma^2)T}{\sigma\sqrt{T}}\right)$$

$$= N\left(\frac{\ln(UND_0/K) + (\mu - .5\sigma^2)T}{\sigma\sqrt{T}}\right)$$

(This may be familiar to you. If you replace the required rate of return on the asset μ with the risk-free rate r, you get the $N(d_2)$ expression from the Black-Scholes model. In the Black-Scholes model, $N(d_2)$ is the cumulative probability that the underlying exceeds the strike price under the risk-neutral probability measure.)

But we don't have to restrict ourselves to the probability that the underlying exceeds (or falls short of) the strike—we can do this exercise for *any* potential value of the underlying Z. The probability that we learn a value of the underlying greater than Z is given by

$$\Pr\left[\ln\left(\frac{UND_T}{UND_0}\right) > \ln\left(\frac{Z}{UND_0}\right)\right] = N\left(\frac{\ln(UND_0/Z) + (\mu - .5\sigma^2)T}{\sigma\sqrt{T}}\right)$$

We can pick some potential outcome (perhaps our best case scenario) and vary σ until we match the probability of exceeding that outcome with management's subjective assessment. For example, the cumulative probability that the second-generation product turns out to be worth at least $188.2 million at December 31, 2001, is

- 0.1% (or about 1-in-1,000) for $\sigma = 30\%$
- 2.1% (or about 1-in-50) for $\sigma = 50\%$
- 4.8% (or about 1-in-21) for $\sigma = 70\%$
- 6.5% (or about 1-in-15) for $\sigma = 90\%$

As far as this scenario goes, it looks like a volatility of roughly 70% gives a likelihood that matches up with management's intuition about the best case scenario in Figure 6.4.

It doesn't stop there. With this in hand, management can then go back to the cash flow forecasts and examine what would be necessary (pricing, market size, market share, etc.) for the second generation to be worth $188.2 million. It's a lot easier for managers to understand the likelihood of some operating parameter (such as a million unit sales, or a total market size of two million units, etc.) than the meaning of the volatility of log returns.

Of course, we should repeat this process of all the potential scenarios that management laid out. I've done this, and I've put the results in Figure 6.11.

The first thing we see in Figure 6.11 is that no one volatility assumption is going to sync exactly with management's priors about every single scenario—we can't expect management intuition to exactly match a lognormal distribution. But that's not important. What *is* important in Figure 6.11 is the fact that all of management's subjective beliefs are matched by a volatility parameter in the 60–80% range, with the evidence seeming to favor something in the middle. At 70% volatility,

Figure 6.11	Cumulative Probabilities of Various Outcomes Implied by Different Volatility Assumptions					
				Cumulative Probability Implied by Volatility		
Scenario	Outcome	Management Subjective Probability	50%	60%	70%	80%
Best Case	>$188.2mm	5%	2.1%	3.5%	4.8%	5.8%
Good Case	>$125.5mm	12.5%	8.5%	10.5%	11.7%	12.5%
Launch	>$65.5 mm	33%	37.8%	35.5%	33.3%	31.1%
Worst Case	<$31.4 mm	25%	18.6%	26.4%	33.5%	39.8%

the real option is worth about $10.6 million. This gives us more confidence that the platform investment is a good one, even though the static NPV of the first stage is −$8.7 million.

The General Idea

In the following chart, I've put various learned values of the second-generation product on the *x*-axis and the cumulative probabilities of exceeding those values on the *y*-axis for five different volatility levels.

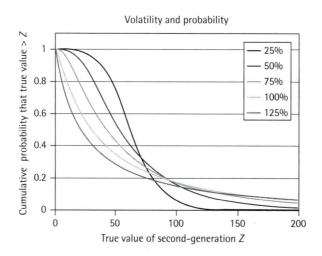

What you can see from this chart is that as volatility increases, the likelihood of exceeding high values increases (although the effects are not as strong as you might suspect). But notice what else goes on—as volatility increases, the probability of exceeding very low values *decreases*; what this means then is that volatility increases, the likelihood of falling below low values increases. For example, the probability that the December 2001 value of the second-generation product turns out to be *less than* $31.4 million is

- 0.2% (or roughly 1-in-500) for $\sigma = 30\%$
- 6% (or roughly 1-in-17) for $\sigma = 50\%$
- 18.4% (or roughly 1-in-5) for $\sigma = 70\%$
- 31.5% (or roughly 1-in-3) for $\sigma = 90\%$

Strategies with high probabilities of failure, but high payoffs if successful, are high-volatility projects.

6.3 Break-Even Volatility

Another very useful thing we can do with this sort of analysis is figure out the *break-even* volatility (i.e., the volatility estimate required to make the value of the option on the second-generation product equal to the negative static NPV of the first-generation product), and explore what sort of world that volatility describes. In our problem here, the first-generation product loses about

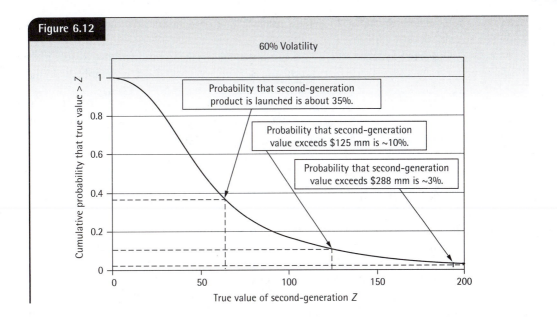

Figure 6.12

60% Volatility

Cumulative probability that true value > Z (y-axis)

True value of second-generation Z (x-axis)

Probability that second-generation product is launched is about 35%.

Probability that second-generation value exceeds $125 mm is ~10%.

Probability that second-generation value exceeds $288 mm is ~3%.

$8.7 million on an expected cash flow basis (its own static NPV) but also creates the valuable option. At what volatility is the option worth $8.7 million, so that the true NPV of the whole strategy is zero?

The answer to this question is that a volatility of about 60% makes the entire strategy have zero true NPV (check for yourself).[5] But what does 60% volatility mean? Again, we should develop our cumulative probabilities. I've done this and accumulated the results in Figure 6.12.

For this particular strategy to be valuable, there has to be some uncertainty in the world—and a picture like Figure 6.12 helps management see what that is. How likely is it that the world would evolve in a way that the second-generation product would be worth more than, say, $188 million? If management believes it is a better than 1-in-33 bet, then 60% volatility is too low, and the option is worth more than it costs. We don't need a precise estimate of the volatility of the second generation product. All we need is some assurance that there's enough uncertainty.

Combining this break-even volatility analysis with the results in Figure 6.11 provides some comfort that this strategy is valuable. Management's intuition seems to favor a volatility estimate in the 60–80% range, and the minimum volatility required for the investment to be zero true NPV is about 60%.

6.4 A Word of Caution

Finally, I'd like to share a word of caution with you. I see many consultants who suggest that a firm (such as this one) should use the volatility of its stock returns as the volatility input for its real options. I don't think that this is a very good idea at all. The volatility of returns on a stock will be significantly lower than the volatility of returns on a company's individual projects simply

[5] Using the Black-Scholes model, I find that an option value of $8.7 million reveals an implied volatility of 61.1%.

due to the effects of diversification. Individual projects have tremendous uncertainty, and there's no reason to avoid high volatilities.

Moreover, it seems to me that many managers are misinformed about just how volatile their stocks actually are. While it is true that the volatility of the S&P 500 index is roughly 20%, the simple average of the vols of the 500 stocks in the index is around 50% (again, diversification shows its power). And if you look for firms with only a few products (like some of the biotech firms), you will find volatilities in excess of 150% per year. And there are commodities like electric power where the volatility is 50–60% per month (or more than 200% per year).

6.5   An Added Difficulty

Of course, this technology company's problem is more complex. The company may not have to begin development of the second-generation product on September 30, 2001; instead, it may be that the company has the additional flexibility to wait and only commit the second-generation development costs *if and when* it becomes propitious to do so. This timing feature, which is the characteristic of an *American* option, makes the flexibility even more valuable.

We'll learn how to handle the optimal timing decision in Part 5 of the book, but I'll give you a little preview of the topic now. When faced with the ability to delay exercise of an option, an option holder will always do so unless waiting is sufficiently costly. If waiting to exercise is costly, then at each point in the binomial analysis we must decide whether the benefits of waiting exceed the cost, and we delay the decision as long as they do.

In the case of our high-tech company, waiting might be costly if there is a threat of a competitor entering the market first and thereby eroding the value of our company's second-generation product. In industries where the competitive rivalry is intense *and* the opportunities are not exclusive to one player, we tend to see early exercise of real options as preemptive/defensive mechanisms. On the other hand, when competitive rivalry is low and a firm has some exclusivity over a new product, we will expect the cost of waiting to be low, and thus our firm will probably wait and learn.

6.6   Summary

In valuation of financial options, the hardest parameter to estimate is the volatility of returns on the underlying asset. This conceptual problem compounds when we move into the realm of real options, because the mechanical volatility estimation techniques we've developed for financial options are usually inapplicable in the real options context.

Many managers become frustrated at their inability to mechanically generate a point estimate of the volatility of returns on a real asset, and this frustration often leads them to avoid the real options approach altogether. In fact, one of the consistent criticisms of the approach is that there's no way to know precisely the volatility of a real asset. But we've heard this objection before in another context, and we've since learned that it is without merit.

Around 50 years ago, when the academic finance community began to urge managers to use risk-adjusted discounting for project valuation (as opposed to the existing standards such as accounting rates of return and payback periods), reluctant practitioners objected vehemently on two grounds. One common protestation was that "similar substitutes" for corporate projects did not exist in financial markets. We now know that this is not an issue (although, as I've discussed at length, people still use it to reject real options analysis). The second problem that managers raised was that every project should theoretically have its own unique risk-adjusted discount rate, and that it is virtually impossible to precisely estimate the correct discount rate to use on every new project.

Although it is true that every project should theoretically have its own unique discount rate, determining the precise opportunity cost of a project is not really necessary. Rather, we've come up with a wide variety of heuristic ways to approximate a project's discount rate. We take a lot of shortcuts when we do a DCF analysis, but what we've learned over the last half-century is that the benefits we achieve through the use of the model far exceed the cost of the approximations (as long as we use the model in the right situations).

So, in my mind, the practical problem with volatility is not that it can't be estimated precisely, but rather that we haven't developed any heuristic ways of thinking about it to get a good approximation. My teaching objective in this chapter was to show you how to use management's intuition about the future to calibrate the volatility estimate so that our model of the uncertainty about the underlying asset would be consistent with management's intuition about how the world works.

PROBLEMS

1. A colleague looks at the option valued in the chapter for the server and router company and states that the option can be valued by discounting the expected future payoff for the option over all of the final nodes of the tree using the risk-free rate. Demonstrate that your colleague is correct by performing the calculation.

2. When evaluating the likelihood of the option described in the chapter to finish out-of-the-money, an assumption of 100% (annual) volatility was used. Does the option have a better chance of finishing in the money if the volatility is increased to 200% annually? Provide an appropriate calculation to validate your answer.

3. Evaluate the probability that the option discussed in the chapter will be profitable assuming a volatility of 150% annually. Further, what is the probability that the project valued by the option is worth more than $300 million?

4. Evaluate the probability that the second-generation project discussed in the chapter is worth less than $30 million assuming an annual volatility of 150%.

5. A project has two stages that each cost $200,000.00 currently (i.e., $200,000.00 is the present value of the cost of the project). However, the first stage will only produce $125,000.00 (in present value terms) in operating cash flows, and the second stage will only produce $185,000.00 (in present value terms) in operating cash flows. After Stage 1, the firm has the option to abandon Stage 2. Assuming a discount rate of 20% annually, and a project duration of three years for Stage 1, when viewing Stage 2 as option, what is the current value of the underlying security for the option, and what is the strike price for the option?

6. Assuming an annual volatility of 60% and an annual risk-free rate of 6%, use a 3-step binomial tree to the value the option described in Problem 5.

7. Redo Problem 6 using a 6-step binomial tree.

8. What is the probability that the option valued in Problem 6 will finish out-of-the-money?

9. A colleague has contacted you in regard to a real option analysis he is performing. The colleague states that the project has two phases, which both have negative NPVs (–$153,000.00 and –$210,000.00, respectively). The colleague is using the second NPV value as the current value of the underlying security for the option valuation (i.e., the second phase can be abandoned after the first phase) but cannot figure out what to use as a strike price. What should you tell your colleague to correct his analysis?

10. Your colleague in Problem 9 does not understand your answer and has e-mailed you the components of his analysis:

Phase 1 (2 years):

PV(operating cash flows @ 21%) = $1,225,625.00

PV(costs @ 21%) = $1,378,625.00

NPV(Phase 1) = −$153,000.00

Phase 2 (9 years):

PV(operating cash flows @ 21%) = $4,698,045.00

PV(costs @ 21%) = $4,908,045.00

NPV(Phase 2): −$210,000.00

a. What should be the price of the underlying security?

b. What should be the strike price for the option?

c. Assuming an annual volatility of 56%, what is the probability that the option will finish in-the-money? Further, what is the probability that Phase 2 will be worth more than $10,000,000.00?

When you read the platform investments case in Chapter 6, it probably occurred to you that the technology company's flexibility created by the money-losing first-generation product might not end with the decision to either launch the second-generation product or walk away. Instead, launch of the second-generation product might "purchase" an option to later launch a third-generation product, and the decision to launch the third-generation product might create an option on a fourth-generation technology, and so on. The point of this chapter is to show you how to handle valuation of corporate investments that create a chain of future decisions.

Many corporate investments are not undertaken to create one-off options in the future, but rather to create strategies that entail multiple *tollgates.* Once again, the key issue is *learning and responding;* a staged strategy allows a firm to resolve uncertainty in phases. In the typical structure, the firm establishes tollgates at key points in time where it can digest what it has learned so far—and where it can then use that information to make a new investment decision. In general, you can think of an investment at each tollgate as a purchase of information that can be gleaned during the *next* phase. Since that information will be used to make a more informed investment decision at the subsequent tollgate, each investment in the sequence purchases an option (a sequence of them, actually) on all later phases.

Examples of this are everywhere, and I list but a few here.

- When large firms invest in enterprise resource planning (ERP) software, they often try out the system in one or two small subsidiaries just to see if it works within their computing systems and if their employees can handle the change. If so, the companies then try it in a larger setting (perhaps a regional head-quarters) to see if the system delivers the promised efficiencies. A final decision to adopt the software nationally or globally takes place only after seeing success at all earlier stages.
- When Gatorade introduced its Propel Fitness Water, it did so only in stages. The first stage, in 1998, was very basic market research, which entailed focus-group testing of nine flavors with five variations. Then, in 1999, the company engaged in more expensive test marketing by actually selling the product through 47 outlets (namely, 7-Eleven convenience) stores in Colorado Springs, Colorado. Next, the company rolled out the product in the southern United

States in 2001. The decision to launch the product on a national basis only came about in April of 2002.[1]

- Pharmaceutical research and development proceeds through very well-defined stages in which the drug company learns both about its technical ability to deliver the concept drug as well as the potential market for the drug. (This problem has a special wrinkle, and we will cover it in Chapter 8).

The common feature that you see in all of these examples, as well as in many others you might personally know of, is that each involves a sequence of increasingly large, irreversible capital investments. Staging the strategy allows the firm to resolve uncertainty a bit at a time—the firm spends a small amount of capital when uncertainty is large, then increases the commitment (or walks away) as the uncertainty begins to resolve, and only makes the very large investments when the odds are truly favorable.

Our goal in this chapter is to learn how to value one of these investments at an early stage. How much is it worth to a company to test an ERP in a small subsidiary? What is the value that Gatorade gets from doing expensive test marketing in Colorado Springs? Does investment in early-stage clinical trials of a new drug create or destory value? These are the sorts of problems you should be able to attack after working through this chapter and the next.

7.1   Some Background—The Supermarket Industry

During the 1990s, food prices in U.S. supermarkets grew at more than twice the rate of the producer price index. This was attributable mainly to consolidation in the grocery business, and the result was a steady increase in the overall profitability of the industry. By the late 1990s, only three major supermarket chains remained: Kroger (and its various subsidiaries, such as Ralph's and Fred Meyer), Albertson's, and Safeway (which now includes Von's and Randall's). These chains sold groceries thorough a variety of store formats, with most new investment going into construction of 50,000 ft^2 grocery-pharmacy units. Figure 7.1 presents operating characteristics of the three chains as of the late 1990s.

By 1998, the traditional grocers were feeling the heat from a very different competitor: Wal-Mart. *Wal-Mart Supercenters,* which were 180,000 ft^2 stores combining grocery with discount retailing, were attracting grocery shoppers who were willing to forego convenience for significant savings: It was estimated that grocery prices at Wal-Mart Supercenters were between 8% and 27% less than at the three major chains (even after discounts such as customer loyalty programs and specials). Wal-Mart could offer such low prices not only because of its extraordinary buying power but also

Figure 7.1	Operating Characteristics of U.S. Grocery Chains, Late 1990s		
	Sales/ft²/week	Gross Margin (% of Sales)	SG&A Expense (% of Sales)
Kroger	N/A	25.5%	18.6%
Safeway	$7.71	29.2%	20.7%
Albertson's	$6.88	28.4%	21.0%

[1] I thank Ece Aksuyek, Chris Imwalle, and Ting Zheng (all KSOB MBA 2003) for their research on this example.

because of its low-cost distribution system, inventory tracking, and ability to control operating costs. For Wal-Mart's U.S. operations (which include its regular discount stores as well as its Supercenters), sales per square foot per week (sales/ft²/week) were about $7.82, gross margin was about 21% of sales, and selling, general & administrative expense (SG&A) expenses were only 16.3% of sales.[2]

Our Investment—Wal-Mart's New Platform[3]

On June 1, 1998, Wal-Mart announced a completely new format called *Wal-Mart Neighborhood Markets*. These new stores would be 40,000 ft² facilities, with 60% of the floor space devoted to grocery, produce, and delicatessen, and the remainder to pharmacy, health and beauty, and pet supplies. While the Supercenters attracted highly price-sensitive shoppers who were willing to drive fairly far from home to get big savings, the Neighborhood Markets would be located closer to the consumer (like traditional grocery stores) and would target the many customers who were willing to pay more for convenience. The idea behind the concept was to attack the traditional grocery chains head-on: by using its strategic advantages (buying power, distribution strength, and cost control), Wal-Mart could undercut the prices of the existing grocery chains and yet profit as much or even more. The stores would be strategically placed so as to maximize market share gain and leverage from the distribution structure of the Supercenters.

There's no public information about Wal-Mart's assessment of the potential size of the chain. Since Kroger, Albertson's, and Safeway had about 2,500, 2,300, and 1,700 storefronts, respectively, I've estimated that 2,000 Neighborhood Markets could be built over a 10-year period, though it is quite possible that the chain could end up being larger (if Wal-Mart's actions serve to drive out one of the three competitors, as many predict). Figure 7.2 presents my static discounted cash flow (DCF) analysis of Wal-Mart's investment in the Neighborhood Markets concept, based on the following assumptions:

- The analysis is performed on June 30, 1998.
- 200 stores would be built per year for 10 years.
- Each store would be 40,000 ft².
- June 30, 1998, construction costs were $200/ft² (Wal-Mart's average construction cost) and would rise at the inflation rate of 2% per year.
- Capital expenditures on storefronts would be depreciated on a straight-line basis over seven years.
- Sales revenue would be $8/ft²/week, or $416/ft²/year, and would rise at the inflation rate of 2% per year.
- Gross profit would be 24% of sales.
- SG&A expense would be 17% of sales.
- Taxes would be levied at Wal-Mart's incremental rate of 37.2%.
- Net working capital requirements are 15.6% of sales (Wal-Mart's average).
- The nominal weighted average cast of capital (WACC) for the analysis is 12.1%, which combines Wal-Mart's real WACC of 9.9% with the inflation rate of 2%.[4]

---

[2] By 2002, the 1200 Wal-Mart Supercenters sold more groceries than any of the traditional chains.

[3] I adapted this case study from a term paper submitted by my students Nick Churi, Kerri Koellner, and Scott Smaistrla (all MBA Class of 2000 at the Kelley School of Business at Indiana University) in the spring semester of 2000. Most of the data come from the Food Marketing Institute (www.fmi.org) and the public SEC filings of Wal-Mart, Albertsons, Kroger, and Safeway. All figures are my own estimates.

[4] $(1.099) \times (1.02) = 1.121$

Figure 7.2 DCF Valuation of Wal-Mart Neighborhood Markets (fiscal years ending in June)

	1999	2000	2001	2002	2003	2004	2005	2006	2007	2008	2009	2010	2011	2012	2013	2014
Number of new stores	200	200	200	200	200	200	200	200	200	200	2000	2000	2000	2000	2000	2000
Total stores	200	400	600	800	1000	1200	1400	1600	1800	2000	2000	2000	2000	2000	2000	2000
Sales/sqft	416.00	424.32	432.81	441.46	450.29	459.30	468.48	477.85	487.41	497.16	507.10	517.24	527.59	538.14	548.90	559.88
Sales (mm)	$3,328	$6,789	$10,387	$14,127	$18,012	$22,046	$26,235	$30,583	$35,094	$39,773	$40,568	$41,379	$42,207	$43,051	$43,912	$44,790
Operating CFs (in mm)																
Gross profit	$799	$1,629	$2,493	$3,390	$4,323	$5,291	$6,296	$7,340	$8,422	$9,545	$9,736	$9,931	$10,130	$10,332	$10,539	$10,750
SG&A	566	1,154	1,766	2,402	3,062	3,748	4,460	5,199	5,966	6,761	6,897	7,035	7,175	7,319	7,465	7,614
Depreciation	229	462	700	942	1,189	1,442	1,699	1,733	1,768	1,803	1,561	1,313	1,061	804	541	273
Pretax profit	4	14	28	47	71	101	137	408	689	981	1,279	1,583	1,894	2,210	2,533	2,862
Tax @ 37.2%	2	5	10	17	27	38	51	152	256	365	476	589	704	822	942	1,065
Operating income after tax	3	8	17	29	45	64	86	256	432	616	803	994	1,189	1,388	1,591	1,797
Add back depreciation	229	462	700	942	1,189	1,442	1,699	1,733	1,768	1,803	1,561	1,313	1,061	804	541	273
FCF from operations	231	470	717	971	1,234	1,506	1,785	1,989	2,200	2,419	2,364	2,308	2,250	2,191	2,132	2,071
Continuation value																20,915
PV	206	374	509	615	697	759	803	798	787	772	673	586	510	443	384	3,697
6/98 PV of operating CF	$12,614															
Investing CFs (in mm)																
Change in NWC	$519	$540	$561	$583	$606	$629	$653	$678	$704	$730	$124	$127	$129	$132	$134	$137
PPE investment	1,600	1,632	1,665	1,698	1,732	1,767	1,802	1,838	1,875	1,912	0	0	0	0	0	0
Total investments	(2,119)	(2,172)	(2,226)	(2,281)	(2,338)	(2,396)	(2,455)	(2,516)	(2,578)	(2,642)	(124)	(127)	(129)	(132)	(134)	(137)
Continuation value																(1,384)
PV	(1,890)	(1,728)	(1,580)	(1,445)	(1,321)	(1,207)	(1,104)	(1,009)	(922)	(843)	(35)	(32)	(29)	(27)	(24)	(245)
6/98 PV of investments	($13,443)															
6/98 NPV (in mm)	($829)															

309

Given very reasonable estimates for the performance of the Neighborhood Markets, including gross margins significantly higher than at the Supercenters and SG&A significantly lower than the competition, the static net present value (NPV) of the potential investment was negative. Wal-Mart would need higher gross margins and perhaps lower costs to make this a value-creating enterprise, but there was substantial uncertainty about its ability to do this. To keep costs low, the Neighborhood Markets would have to offer far fewer choices than the 35,000 SKUs typically inventoried in a supermarket.[5] Moreover, Wal-Mart's business model was notorious for its indifference toward personalized customer service (the meat counters in the Neighborhood Markets would not be staffed). Finally, the competing chains were retrenching with aims of creating loyalty among their customers (either through cleanliness, service, or loyalty programs). On the other hand, history has proven time and again that the hearts of American consumers are very close to their wallets. In addition, Wal-Mart's ability to operate with exactly zero unionized employees could turn out to be a huge advantage, as increases in union-demanded pension and health-care expenditures were already hurting profits at the big three grocers.

Before going forward, let's remind ourselves of how we should interpret the −$829 million static NPV of the investment in the Wal-Mart Neighborhood Markets. The static NPV analysis allows us to compare two alternative courses of action: Either an immediate commitment to an investment with all future decisions hard-wired in, or an immediate commitment to never investing in the project at all. All-or-nothing, now-or-never. What Figure 7.2 tells us is that if forced to choose between (1) immediately committing $13.443 billion for development of the new chain and (2) throwing away the concept once and for all, Wal-Mart's investors would be better off in expectation (i.e., on average) if they choose the latter. And if the decision is all-or-nothing/now-or-never, then the static NPV result provides the right decision.

The key for us and for management, however, is the "in expectation/on average" part. The project is risky, and based on what was known in June 1998, the opportunity was not worth the risk. But as we discussed just two paragraphs ago, there was substantial uncertainty about the inputs for the DCF valuation and the static NPV analysis. It *could* turn out that the format has higher sales/per square foot, higher margins, lower SG&A expenses, and perhaps even capacity for more stores—in which case the Neighborhood Markets would create a lot of value. On the other hand, things could turn out to be even worse than anticipated, meaning Wal-Mart could destroy even more value. Was there a way to resolve some of this uncertainty before making an all-or-nothing/now-or-never decision?

Wal-Mart's Staging Strategy

Wal-Mart management recognized the uncertainty, and rather than abandoning the concept altogether, they took a staged approach to its development. In June 1998, Wal-Mart decided to open only five Neighborhood Markets, at a cost of about $60 million total, in Arkansas. These stores would be used as a laboratory, and after two years of study, management would have better information about whether the retailing concept would. Then, in June 2000, management would decide whether or not to build 40 more test stores in Oklahoma, Texas, and west Tennessee at a total cost of $400 million *based on what was learned from the first five test stores.*

---

[5] The *Wall Street Journal* provided this anecdotal example: "In barbeque-crazy Memphis, a Kroger store offered 13 types of locally made barbecue sauces, while the Wal-Mart supercenter had three." ("Wal-Mart Tops Grocery List with its Supercenter Format," by Patricia Callahan and Ann Zimmerman, *Wall Street Journal*, May 27, 2003).

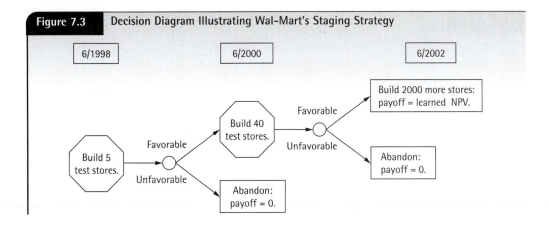

Figure 7.3 | **Decision Diagram Illustrating Wal-Mart's Staging Strategy**

The 40 additional test stores would allow management to learn more about the value of the strategy. The decision to launch a 2,000-store chain would not be made until June 2002, when results from the second-stage of testing were completely digested.

If a 2,000-store chain displays negative static NPV, then 5- and 45-store chains will also. Why, then, would Wal-Mart management decide to invest in a five-store chain of Neighborhood Markets? Once again, we see the same story. The first five stores are test stores, and investment in the test stores buys two things. First, it buys the cash flow from the test stores. Second, it buys information about a 2,000-store chain. The testing program allows Wal-Mart to delay its investment decision concerning the 2,000-store chain until a point in time when the company has better information about the economics of such an investment.

So the cost of the test stores must be measured against the flexibility benefit they create. The test-store program creates an option on a 2,000-store chain, and the initial investment in five test stores has positive *true* NPV if the option it creates is worth more than what is spent. But the problem here is very different from the problems in the previous two chapters, because investment in the five test stores creates the ability to make *two* future decisions: The decision to build 40 more test stores in 1998 and, if 40 stores are built in 1998, the decision to build 2,000 stores in 2002. Let's sketch out the flexibilities that the staged investment program creates. Figure 7.3 presents a decision diagram for the entire strategy.

This is really interesting, because there are actually *two* options here. To see this, we need to work backwards. First, look at year 2000 and the decision whether to build 40 additional test stores (i.e., the second phase of testing). I've carved out this part of the problem for you in Figure 7.4.

Figure 7.4

The Last Two Years of the Decision Diagram

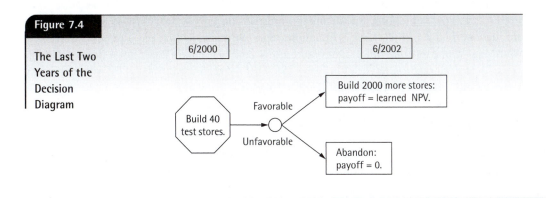

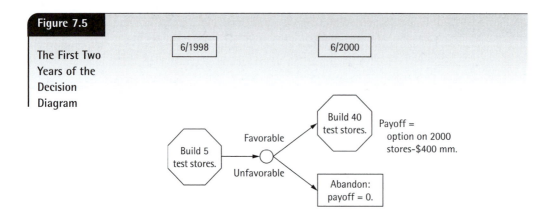

Figure 7.5

The First Two Years of the Decision Diagram

If Wal-Mart builds the second phase of 40 additional test stores in June 2000 (at a cost of $400 million), they will *create the option* to build 2,000 more stores in 2002 *if conditions are right*. In 2002, they will exercise this option if the value of doing so exceeds the cost of building at that time. The exercise price is the 2002 nominal cost of construction, and the underlying asset is a 2,000-store chain. So, the decision to invest $400 mm in 2000 in 40 additional test stores should be measured against the value of the option it creates—not just the value of the cash flow from the test stores.

Now work backward to 1998. I've re-drawn the decision diagram for you in Figure 7.5. If Wal-Mart builds the five test stores in 1998, it will create the option to spend $400 million on 40 more test stores in 2000 *if conditions are right*. Of course, the decision to build 40 more test stores in 2000 creates an option on 2,000 stores in 2002, so the underlying asset for this earlier option is actually itself an option! The investment in the first five test stores creates a strategy that is really an *option on an option*. The cost of initiating this strategy in 1998 is $60 million. Does the value exceed the cost? Is it the right thing to do? Does the testing create value for Wal-Mart shareholders? To answer these questions, we need to know how to value options written on other options. This is straightforward in the binomial model.

7.2   Option Valuation

The critical insight that you must have when dealing with options-on-options like this is that *there is only one true underlying asset*. The essential underlying asset is what you will receive if you exercise the <u>very last option</u> (or, in other words, if you choose to continue at every tollgate throughout the life of the strategy). In our example, we'll assume that the June 2002 decision at Wal-Mart will be to either build 2,000 more stores (and hence have 2,045 total stores, including those 45 built during testing) or walk away. So the act of exercising in June 2002 will be the commitment of capital for 200 stores per year for 10 years starting at that time. The *current* value of this underlying asset is the June 1998 discounted value of the free cash inflows that would be generated <u>from a June 2002 launch of the chain</u> (using only the information that is known in 1998). This is a little bit tricky because we're working in an environment with inflation.

In June 1998, Wal-Mart management would use the same information from the DCF in Figure 7.2 to project what would happen if they delayed the project four years until June 2002.

Figure 7.6 Forecast 2002 DCF Valuation of Wal-Mart Neighborhood Markets (fiscal years ending in June)

	2003	2004	2005	2006	2007	2008	2009	2010	2011	2012	2013	2014	2015	2016	2017	2018
Number of new stores	200	200	200	200	200	200	200	200	200	200	0	0	0	0	0	0
Total stores	200	400	600	800	1000	1200	1400	1600	1800	2000	2000	2000	2000	2000	2000	2000
Sales/sqft	$450.29	$459.30	$468.48	$477.85	$487.41	$497.16	$507.10	$517.24	$527.59	$538.14	$548.90	$559.88	$571.08	$582.50	$594.15	$606.03
Sales (mm)	$3,602	$7,349	$11,244	$15,291	$19,496	$23,864	$28,398	$33,104	$37,986	$43,051	$43,912	$44,790	$45,686	$46,600	$47,532	$48,483
Operating CFs (in mm)																
Gross profit	$865	$1,764	$2,698	$3,670	$4,679	$5,727	$6,815	$7,945	$9,117	$10,332	$10,539	$10,750	$10,965	$11,184	$11,408	$11,636
SG&A	612	1,249	1,911	2,600	3,314	4,057	4,828	5,628	6,458	7,319	7,465	7,614	7,767	7,922	8,080	8,242
Depreciation	247	500	757	1,020	1,288	1,561	1,839	1,876	1,914	1,952	1,689	1,422	1,148	870	586	296
Pretax profit	5	15	30	51	77	110	148	441	745	1,062	1,384	1,714	2,050	2,392	2,742	3,098
Tax @ 37.2%	2	5	11	19	29	41	55	164	277	395	515	638	762	890	1,020	1,152
Operating income after tax	3	9	19	32	48	69	93	277	468	667	869	1,076	1,287	1,502	1,722	1,946
Add back depreciation	247	500	757	1,020	1,288	1,561	1,839	1,876	1,914	1,952	1,689	1,422	1,148	870	586	296
CF from operations	250	509	776	1,052	1,336	1,630	1,933	2,153	2,382	2,619	2,559	2,498	2,436	2,372	2,307	2,241
Continuation value																22,639
PV	223	405	551	666	755	821	869	864	852	836	729	634	552	479	416	4,002
6/02 PV of operating CF	**$13,654**															
Investing CFs (in mm)																
Change in NWC	$562	$584	$608	$631	$656	$681	$707	$734	$762	$790	$134	$137	$140	$143	$145	$148
PPE investment	1,732	1,767	1,802	1,838	1,875	1,912	1,950	1,989	2,029	2,070	0	0	0	0	0	0
Total investments	(2,294)	(2,351)	(2,409)	(2,469)	(2,531)	(2,593)	(2,658)	(2,724)	(2,791)	(2,860)	(134)	(137)	(140)	(143)	(145)	(148)
Continuation value																(1,498)
PV	(2,046)	(1,871)	(1,711)	(1,564)	(1,430)	(1,307)	(1,195)	(1,092)	(999)	(913)	(38)	(35)	(32)	(29)	(26)	(265)
6/02 PV of investments	**($14,551)**															
6/02 NPV (in mm)	**($897)**															

313

Figure 7.6 presents the DCF analysis rolled forward in time by four years. Inflation will change the cash inflows through its effect on sales per square foot: The 1999 estimate was $416, and $416(1.02)^4 = $450.29, so the 2003 sales per square foot will be $450.29, and that cost will increase at the 2% inflation rate thereafter. (Notice that on the original DCF, the 2003 sales/ft² was this same number.) Inflation will also change construction costs, as the 1999 cost of $200/ft² will rise to $200(1.02)^4 = $216.49 in 2003 and continue to rise at 2% thereafter.

The June 2002 exercise price on the option to build 2,000 stores at that time is **$14,551 million**—the capital that would be committed in *nominal dollars on the date of exercise* (i.e., in June 2002) to build 2,000 more Neighborhood Markets. Notice that inflation has increased the capital commitment by exactly 2% per year: $13,443(1.02)^4 = $14,551. Remember that the exercise price is always in nominal dollars spent at the time of exercise.

Now the question that confuses many students. What is the current value of the underlying asset? Let's walk through this very carefully. The underlying asset is always what you get if you exercise the option, right? In this case, it is the free cash flows from a 2,000-store Neighborhood Markets chain *begun in June 2002*. The June 2002 present value of these expected free cash flows is $13,654 million. Is this the starting value of the underlying? Of course not—this is the expected value of the underlying in June 2002, and we're doing the analysis in June 1998. We need the current (or June 1998) discounted value of this expectation. Since the nominal WACC on this project is 12.1%, then the starting value (i.e., June 1998 value) of the underlying asset is $8,647,

$$\frac{\$13,654.21}{(1.121)^4} = \$8,646.57$$

This is where many students get confused. Some will look at our original June 1998 DCF (see Figure 7.2) and see that the present value of the free cash flows from a 2,000-store chain at that time is $12,614, and then mistakenly assume that this must be the June 1998 starting value of the underlying. This is incorrect, and the reason it is wrong is because it ignores time value of money. $12,614 is the June 1998 value of a 2,000-store chain *begun immediately* (i.e., begun in June 1998). But the underlying asset here is not the value of a chain begun in June 1998, but rather the *June 1998 value of a 2,000-store chain begun in June 2002*. This is why we calculate the June 2002 free cash flow value and then discount this back at the nominal WACC to June 1998.

Some students partially understand this, but argue that we should take the June 1998 DCF value of an immediately started chain ($12,614) then discount this quantity at the nominal WACC of 12.1% for four years to account for the delayed start. This is incorrect because it misses the effects of inflation. The correct starting value of the underlying is $8,647, and its relationship to the June 1998 value of a chain begun immediately is through the *real* WACC of 9.9%, that is:

$$\$8,647(1.099)^4 = \$12,614$$

It is true that the time value of money here is 12.1% in nominal terms. But the June 1998 value of the underlying does <u>not</u> drop by 12.1% for every year of delay, because inflation *increases* the nominal value of the cash flows by 2% per year. Notice that the inflation rate of 2% gives us the relationship between the June 1998 value of a chain begun immediately ($12,614; see Figure 7.2) and the June 2002 value of a chain begun immediately ($13,654; see Figure 7.6):

$$\$12,614(1.02)^4 = \$13,654$$

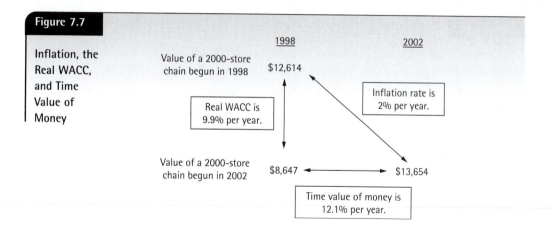

Figure 7.7

Inflation, the Real WACC, and Time Value of Money

Value of a 2000-store chain begun in 1998 — 1998 — $12,614

Real WACC is 9.9% per year.

Inflation rate is 2% per year. — 2002

Value of a 2000-store chain begun in 2002 — $8,647 — $13,654

Time value of money is 12.1% per year.

The inflation rate also explains the difference between the June 1998 static NPV (−$829; see Figure 7.2) and the June 2002 static NPV (−$897; see Figure 7.6):

$$-\$829(1.02)^4 = -\$897$$

The relationship is easy to summarize. The June 1998 value of any future cash flows *falls* at the real discount rate of 9.9% per year for every year the project is delayed. The start-date nominal present value of any future cash flows *rises* at the 2% inflation rate per year for every year the project is delayed. The difference between the two increases at the nominal WACC of 12.1% per year, as shown in Figure 7.7.

Thus, the starting value of the ultimate underlying asset is $8,647 million, and the June 2002 strike price (the strike price on the very last option) is $14,551 million. The way we do the valuation of an option-on-an-option is simply to start with the very last option on the ultimate underlying asset, working as if it were the *only* option available. Build the binomial model of the underlying, begin in the last year, ask "would I exercise or not," and write the payoffs into the last period of the binomial tree of option values. Then, using your risk-neutral probabilities and risk-free discount rate, work backwards in the binomial tree of option values, taking the expected value (using the risk-neutral probabilities) and discounting (at the risk-free rate).

The process works exactly like a standard European option *until you get back to the point where the next-to-last option expires*. In our case, this will be June 2000. In June 2000, Wal-Mart must decide whether to spend $400 million on the second-stage testing (40 stores) or abandon. To continue *forward* in time, it must spend $400 million. What it gets back is the option on the June 2002 rollout (which it will know the value of) plus the static NPV of the 40 test stores themselves. We'll ignore the cash implications of the test stores, so the decision will be simple. In each state in June 2000, we simply compare the cost of continuing ($400 million) with what is returned if we do continue (the option). If the option value is greater than $400 million, spend the $400 million, buy it, and keep the difference; if the option value is less than $400 million, just walk away. Thus, the June 2000 entries in the binomial tree of option values will be

max(June 2000 value of June 2002 option on 2,000 stores−$400 million, $0)

From there, you continue working backward with the *same* risk-neutral probabilities and the same discount rate as before.

Figure 7.8	Binomial Tree of Values of a 2,000–Store Chain Begun in June 2002 (in $mm)							
Jun-98	Dec-98	Jun-99	Dec-99	Jun-00	Dec-00	Jun-01	Dec-01	Jun-02
8,647	12,315	17,537	24,975	35,568	50,653	72,136	102,730	146,300
	6,072	8,647	12,315	17,537	24,975	35,568	50,653	72,136
		4,264	6,072	8,647	12,315	17,537	24,975	35,568
			2,994	4,264	6,072	8,647	12,315	17,537
				2,102	2,994	4,264	6,072	8,647
					1,476	2,102	2,994	4,264
						1,037	1,476	2,102
							728	1,037
								511

That may sound confusing, but it is actually quite easy. Let me walk you through it. We're standing at June 1998, our underlying asset (a 2,000-store chain begun in 2002) is currently worth $8,647 million, our final exercise date is four years away (June 2002) and our final exercise price is $14,551 million. Let's build a binomial tree with eight total steps (or two steps per year just to keep things presentable), so each time step will be $\Delta t = \frac{1}{2}$. We'll use a risk-free rate of $r = 5\%$. Rather than trying to pin down a volatility estimate, let's just start with $\sigma = 50\%$ per year and analyze it later. In our tree, each up step will be

$$U = e^{\sigma \sqrt{\Delta t}} = e^{0.50\sqrt{1/2}} = 1.424$$

and each down step will be

$$D = \frac{1}{U} = 0.702$$

so our binomial tree of values of a 2,000-store chain will look like the one in Figure 7.8.

We will use this tree of values of a 2,000-store chain to develop a tree of strategy values, which will include all of the options to continue or abandon. It will look like the chart in Figure 7.9.

Notice what I've done here—I've put dark gray highlights at the points in time at which I must make a decision whether to continue, and above the tree in those columns, I've written the costs of continuing (the exercise prices). As I mentioned before, we work from the end

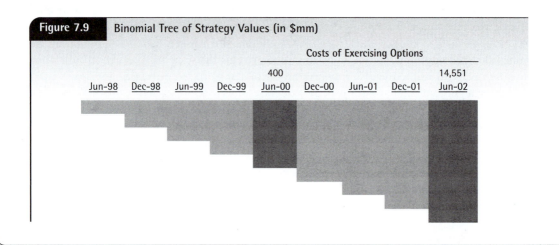

| Figure 7.9 | Binomial Tree of Strategy Values (in $mm) |

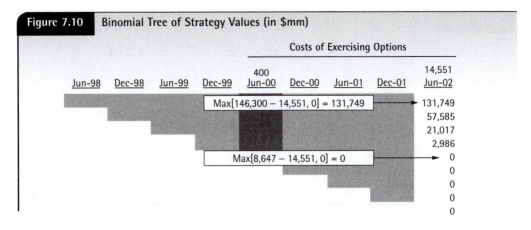

Figure 7.10 | Binomial Tree of Strategy Values (in $mm)

backwards. Simply treat the last option (the June 2002 option to launch the entire 2,000-store chain) as a European call. Figure 7.10 shows the first step.

Next, we work backwards calculating the expected value of each binomial outcome using the risk-neutral probabilities and discounting this at the risk-free rate of return. The risk-free discount rate over any step of our tree will be

$$e^{r \times \Delta t} = e^{0.05(1/2)} = 1.0253$$

and the risk-neutral probability of an up step in our model is

$$q = \frac{e^{r \times \Delta t} - D}{U - D} = \frac{1.0253 - 0.702}{1.424 - 0.702} = 0.448$$

so the risk-neutral probability of a down step is $(1-q) = (1-0.448) = 0.552$. Therefore the December 2001 values of the June 2002 option on 2,000 stores will be as shown in Figure 7.11.

We keep working backwards this way until we've finished back through December 2000. I've done this for you in Figure 7.12.

Remember what we've got here: Each of these entries represents a state-contingent value of the June 2002 option on the 2,000-store chain. Remember as well that the option on a 2,000-store chain is itself the underlying asset for the option to build 40 test stores, which must be exercised in June of 2000 at a price of $400 million. So *if* we spend $400 million in June 2000, this

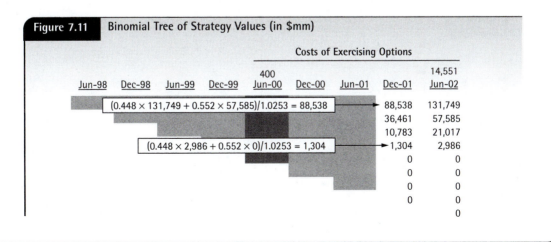

Figure 7.11 | Binomial Tree of Strategy Values (in $mm)

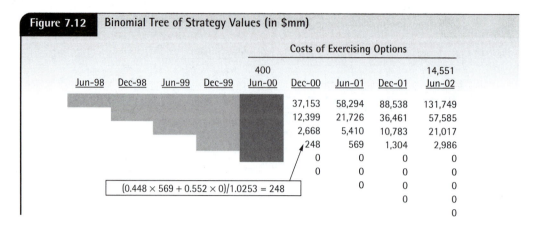

Figure 7.12 Binomial Tree of Strategy Values (in $mm)

Costs of Exercising Options

				400				14,551
Jun-98	Dec-98	Jun-99	Dec-99	Jun-00	Dec-00	Jun-01	Dec-01	Jun-02
					37,153	58,294	88,538	131,749
					12,399	21,726	36,461	57,585
					2,668	5,410	10,783	21,017
					248	569	1,304	2,986
					0	0	0	0
					0	0	0	0
						0	0	0
							0	0
								0

$(0.448 \times 569 + 0.552 \times 0)/1.0253 = 248$

is what we get back. Therefore, we have to work backward again with our risk-neutral probabilities and our risk-free discount rate to get the June 2000 value of the option on 2,000 stores. But this time, we compare this value to the cost of purchasing it ($400 million). If the June 2000 value of the option on 2,000 stores is worth more than $400 million, buy it and write in the option value minus $400 million. If the option on 2,000 stores is not worth at least $400 million, don't buy it—abandon the Neighborhood Markets strategy—and write in a value of 0. So, the June 2000 entries in the binomial tree of strategy values will be

$$max \text{ (June 2000 value of June 2002 option on 2,000 stores} - \$400 \text{ mm, 0)}$$

If there were any anticipated positive or negative cash flow from the 40 test stores themselves, it would be added in here (but we'll ignore that because of the very small size of the test stores relative to the overall project). If you do this step, you'll get what I show in Figure 7.13.

Notice what happens here—you continue in the high states, and you abandon in the low ones (which I've highlighted in dark gray). There are two important points to see. If you notice from my documentation, there's one abandonment state (the highest dark gray state) where the option is still valuable, but its value is below the cost of continuing. There would be more of these in a tree with smaller time slices. This is a case of cutting your losses early, and this is where staging really adds value over and above a single-shot European option. Second, recall that each of the

Figure 7.13 Binomial Tree of Strategy Values (in $mm)

Costs of Exercising Options

				400				14,551
Jun-98	Dec-98	Jun-99	Dec-99	Jun-00	Dec-00	Jun-01	Dec-01	Jun-02
				22,499	37,153	58,294	88,538	131,749
				6,450	12,399	21,726	36,461	57,585
				899	2,668	5,410	10,783	21,017
				0	248	569	1,304	2,986
				0	0	0	0	0
					0	0	0	0
						0	0	0
							0	0
								0

Continue value =
$[(0.448 \times 37,153 + 0.552 \times 12,399)/1.0253] - 400 = 22,499$
Abandon value = 0
  So continue! Value = 22,499

Continue value =
$[(0.448 \times 248 + 0.552 \times 0)/1.0253] - 400 = -289$
Abandon value = 0
  So abandon! value = 0

states in the strategy value tree corresponds with an updated estimate of the ultimate value of a 2,000-store chain (the original tree of underlying asset values, given in Figure 7.8). If you look at the lowest continuation state in Figure 7.13 (where the value of continuing is $899 million), and search for the corresponding value in the original tree of the underlying asset (Figure 7.8), you'll see that in this state you are continuing with the project even though you only think the 2,000-store chain is worth $8,647 in present value terms, or $8,647(1.121)^2 = $10,886$ in expected future value at the time of exercise, when the strike will be $14,551. In other words, the June 2002 option on the 2,000-store chain is *out-of-the-money*, but you continue anyway. Why? Because there's still uncertainty—there's still the chance that you'll learn something good, and the value of learning exceeds the cost. The higher the volatility estimate in your model, the more you'll see this in a staged investment problem.

We're not done here. We still have to find the current (June 1998) value of the strategy. Let's make sure we understand one point. To work backwards one period from the June 2000 values above to the December 1999 values of the strategy, simply take the expected values using the same risk-neutral probabilities as before and discount at the risk-free rate. People who aren't familiar with the asset-pricing foundation of the binomial model sometimes think that the risk-neutral probabilities need to be recalculated here. They do not, because *there is only one ultimate underlying asset,* remember? The risk-neutral probabilities are really the prices of $1 of consumption in the up and down states (grossed up by one plus the risk-free discount rate). They are determined by the way the underlying asset covaries with the overall economy. Adding layers of options on options does not change the risk-return relationship in the overall economy one bit (if it did, you couldn't do any sort of arbitrage valuation). The up and down states are not altered, so their prices are not altered, and hence the risk-neutral probabilities are the same. I show the next set of calculations in Figure 7.14.

Repeating this process all the way back to June 1998, we find that the dynamic value of the Neighborhood Markets strategy created by the initial investment in five test stores is more than $2.272 billion (given the assumptions we've put in), as I show in Figure 7.15. Since the cost of the five test stores is only $60 million, we can say that the *true NPV* of the Neighborhood Markets strategy is $2.212 billion!

A Simple Analysis of the Volatility Variable

Our analysis rested on an assumption of 50% volatility per year. What does that mean? Well, it implies a certain view of the future.

Figure 7.14   Binomial Tree of Strategy Values (in $mm)

				Costs of Exercising Options					
				400					14,551
Jun-98	Dec-98	Jun-99	Dec-99	Jun-00	Dec-00	Jun-01	Dec-01	Jun-02
			13,297	22,499	37,153	58,294	88,538	131,749
$(0.448 \times 22,499 + 0.552 \times 6,450)/1.0253 = 13,297$			3,300	6,450	12,399	21,726	36,461	57,585
			392	899	2,668	5,410	10,783	21,017
$(0.448 \times 899 + 0.552 \times 0)/1.0253 = 392$			0	0	248	569	1,304	2,986
				0	0	0	0	0
					0	0	0	0
					0	0	0	0
						0	0	0
								0

Figure 7.15	Binomial Tree of Strategy Values (in $mm)							
					Costs of Exercising Options			
				400				14,551
Jun-98	Dec-98	Jun-99	Dec-99	Jun-00	Dec-00	Jun-01	Dec-01	Jun-02
2,272	4,200	7,582	13,297	22,499	37,153	58,294	88,538	131,749
	813	1,652	3,300	6,450	12,399	21,726	36,461	57,585
		171	392	899	2,668	5,410	10,783	21,017
			0	0	248	569	1,304	2,986
				0	0	0	0	0
					0	0	0	0
						0	0	0
							0	0
								0

Suppose management felt that a great (but achievable) outcome would be to learn that they could actually generate a 27% gross margin on sales with only 16.3% SG&A expense. If you plug these back into the 2002 DCF model (see Figure 7.6), you'll find that together they imply a 2002 learned value of the 2,000-store chain equal to $19.3 billion (before the capital investment). Furthermore, suppose management believed that there was an outside chance that they could achieve these extremes *and* actually find out that the market would support a 3,000-store chain. This would imply 2002 value of $28.9 billion (again before the capital investment). How likely are these values, and what volatilities support them?

The volatility estimate makes specific implications. Figure 7.16 shows various volatilities across the *x*-axis and the associated probability that the value of the underlying exceeds $28.9 billion and $19.3 billion in June 2002 using the technique described in Chapter 6.

A volatility of 50% implies about a 2-in-9 chance of the good case and a 1-in-9 chance of the outstanding case. Dropping the volatility to 40% lowers the likelihood of the first case to about 1-in-9 and the second case to about 1-in-25, and lowers the strategy value to about $1.4 billion. Raising the volatility to 60%, on the other hand, increases the likelihood of the first case to about 1-in-3 and the second to about 1-in-5, and also raises the value of the strategy to about

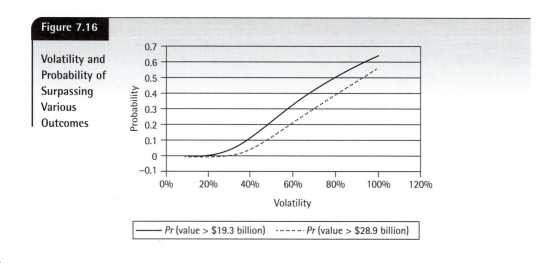

Figure 7.16

Volatility and Probability of Surpassing Various Outcomes

—— Pr (value > $19.3 billion)   ······· Pr (value > $28.9 billion)

$2.9 billion. A similar exercise can be done for worst case scenarios and for the likelihoods that the project fails. This sort of exercise can really help management match up the analysis to the way they view the real world.[6]

Of course, this case was a no-brainer. Wal-Mart management did not need an option model to tell them whether or not to invest in the test stores, simply because they knew that they had a very valuable business platform, and that it most surely was transportable into other businesses. But there are many instances where investments in early stages of new strategies are significant, and it is unclear whether there is real strategic value in the investments at all. An analysis like this will never be the final arbiter of such an investment decision—there are just too many approximations to make. The benefit of a model like this, however, is that it forces management to be more scientific about what the world must look like (i.e., what assumptions must be made) for a strategy to actually be valuable. Also, it can help management set up the strategic process such that decisions points and learning coincide.

---

[6] What amazes me is that even if we accept the volatility estimate to be 100%, the Neighborhood Markets strategy is just a drop in the bucket to Wal-Mart shareholders: The $5.2 billion value implied by a 100% volatility would represent just over $1 per share of Wal-Mart's stock price (which was about $40 per share in 1998 and $56 per share in July 2003). The company's stock price assumes an extraordinary growth rate.

1. Suppose Wal-Mart intended to delay the opening of the 2,000-store expansion project for an additional two years. What would be the current value of the underlying asset for the compound option discussed in the chapter?

2. The present value of the operating cash flows a project can generate is $1,278 million. Assuming a nominal WACC of 12% annually and an annual inflation rate of 3%, what would the present value of the project's operating cash flows become, assuming the project is delayed three years?

3. Suppose a project has three phases with separate NPVs for each phase: NPV(Phase 1) = −$10,345.00, NPV(Phase 2) = −$70,872.00, and NPV(Phase 3) = −$12,345,098.00. Either of the later phases can only occur if the previous phases have already occurred. Phase 1 will last three years, and Phase 2 will last two years.

   Assume that the NPVs are calculated relative to when the given phase is expected to begin (i.e., the NPV for Phase 3 is calculated five years into the future). The expense portions of the NPV calculations are $20,000.00, $100,000.00, and $52,000,000.00 for the respective phases. Further, the nominal WACC for the projects is 15.2% annually, and the annual expected rate of inflation is 1%.

   Determine the two strike prices at Year 3 and Year 5 for the compound option analysis relevant to this project. Further, determine the current value of the underlying security for this compound option.

4. Redo Problem 3, assuming the NPV values are in current dollars.

5. Company ABC has just made your firm the following offer with a cost of $100 million Two years from today, a second investment of $600 million can be made, or the deal can be terminated. Assuming the deal is not terminated, a third payment of $1,200 million will allow for the outright purchase of Company ABC two years from the second payment.

   Your analysts constructed the following binomial tree to model the operating cash flows of Company ABC, assuming a risk-free rate of 4% annually and an upward probability measure (p) of 35.56% (all values are in millions).

Year 0	Year 1	Year 2	Year 3	Year 4
567.00	1200.34	2541.12	5379.55	11388.50
	267.83	567.00	1200.34	2541.12
		126.51	267.83	567.00
			59.76	126.51
				28.23

Viewing the deal as a series of call options, determine the value of the deal, and make a decision on accepting the deal.

6. The tree in Problem 5 was constructed based on an annual volatility of 75%. Reproduce the tree given a 70% annual volatility, and determine if the deal is acceptable.

7. Given the analysis from Problem 6 and the original analysis performed in Problem 5, the sensitivity of the deal value to volatility becomes very apparent. A second round of negotiations increases the initial payment to $200 million and lowers the second payment from $600 million to $300 million. Assuming an annual volatility of 70% (i.e., the same assumption from Problem 6), is the deal acceptable?

8. Your company desires to calculate the value of an existing joint venture with Company XYZ. The joint venture requires a payment of $300 million next year (Year 1), $900 million the following year (Year 2), and a final payment of $2,500 million that purchases Company XYZ the next year (Year 3). At any point when a payment is due, the venture can be terminated. The binomial tree below models the value of the operating cash flows of Company XYZ, assuming a 4% annual risk-free rate and an up probability (p) of 37.92% (all values are in millions).

Year 0	Year 0.5	Year 1.0	Year 1.5	Year 2.0	Year 2.5	Year 3
832.00	1464.86	2579.12	4540.94	7995.02	14076.47	24783.79
	472.55	832.00	1464.86	2579.12	4540.94	7995.02
		268.40	472.55	832.00	1464.86	2579.12
			152.44	268.40	472.55	832.00
				86.58	152.44	268.40
					49.18	86.58
						27.93

What is the value of the joint venture?

9. Firm QRS wishes to buy your rights to the joint venture from Problem 8 for $55 million. Assuming that you believe the analysis in Problem 8 is correct, should you sell the rights to Firm QRS? Given Firm QRS's price for the joint venture, does Firm QRS believe the volatility used in your calculation of the value is too high or too low?

10. Assume that Firm QRS believes the volatility of the joint venture discussed in Problem 8 to be 85% annually. What is the value of the joint venture to QRS? Did QRS pay too much for the rights in Problem 9?

EARLY-STAGE PHARMACEUTICAL R&D: THE INTERACTION OF MARKET AND TECHNICAL RISK

The lesson from the Wal-Mart Neighborhood Markets case is that we can view staged investments, which proceed from tollgate to tollgate, as options-on-options. Once we recognize this structure, we can value investment strategies of this sort at any intermediate stage (subject to our ability to pin down the specifics of the problem, of course).

Everyone's favorite example of such a problem is the valuation of pharmaceutical or biotechnological research and development projects. Throughout development of a compound, managers and scientists have numerous opportunities to evaluate whether to press onward through the next stage of development (and spend a substantial amount of cash) or to discontinue the project altogether.

If you try to evaluate an early-stage investment in pharma or biotech R&D using discounted cash flow (DCF), you will almost certainly conclude that the project displays negative static NPV and therefore that the investment should not be made. Yet pharmaceutical and biotechnology companies spend billions of dollars per year on research and development, and there is empirical evidence that the market values of these companies are positively related to their R&D commitments. Furthermore, transfers of rights to certain compounds in early stages of development (through licensing agreements or outright sales) occur frequently at prices well above DCF values.

You should know by now why DCF will not work well in this sort of setting. The DCF valuation technique and the static NPV rule assume that managers must make a single *now or never* decision at the point of the valuation—either commit to the entire project immediately or walk away forever. This traditional static analysis, which compresses all future decisions to one stream of hard-wired commitments before the process has begun, misses the high level of flexibility in management decisions throughout the pharmaceutical R&D process. An options approach to the valuation captures the flexibility of management to only invest the large sums of capital (which typically occur in late stages of development) when things look promising, and to avoid investment when the outlook is poor.

As I said, just about everyone uses the pharma/biotech R&D process as an intuitive example of a corporate investment that purchases optionality. Unfortunately, this is a tricky problem to actually attack. The dynamics of the R&D process create a significant stumbling block: framing the problem. If you are going to apply an option model to any situation, you have to put *more* structure on the problem than you would in the DCF setting.[1] That is, you have to carefully specify what the problem actually looks like—what the flexibilities are, where they occur in time, how much must be spent at each tollgate, what is the ultimate underlying asset and what is its current value, what are the relevant uncertainties, and the like.

If we can overcome the problem-framing difficulty, however, we can learn some valuable lessons from the analysis of a specific problem. Pharma/biotech R&D projects present a particular issue which is common in many other types of corporate investments. The complexity in these sorts of problems stems from the fact that the risk of such projects comes from *two* distinct sources, and we need an approach that can keep track of both of them.

8.1   Market Risk and Technical Risk

First of all, drugs are exposed to market risk (just as are sales revenues at Wal-Mart Neighborhood Markets—though perhaps to a different degree). Valuation of a marketed drug amounts to projecting the number of "scribbles on a doctor's prescription pad" as well as the free cash flow value of each of those scribbles over the drug's expected life cycle. This is notoriously difficult to do when the drug is in early stages of development and FDA approval is many years away because it requires estimates of (1) the number of people who actually suffer from the disease targeted by the potential drug, (2) the number of those people who will be diagnosed with the disease, (3) the number of those diagnosed who will be prescribed the drug, (4) the number of those receiving the drug who stay on the prescription (and for how long), and (5) *the value-added price which the drug can command.*[2] As a compound progresses from early research to FDA approval and manufacturing, the drug company learns more and more about the actual market value of selling the new drug; at each tollgate, a *part* of the decision to continue or discontinue is based on what has been learned about the market potential for the new drug.[3]

---

[1] I make this point because a lot of practitioners have been led to believe just the opposite—that the options approach to valuation is applicable to amorphous, difficult-to-define problems. For evidence of this, just open up any of the "soft" practitioner-oriented books on the subject. This, in my opinion, is one of the biggest reason why so many managers are so strongly opposed to using the real options paradigm: They've come to decide, through bad experience, that the emperor has no clothes. And in these amorphous situations, they are right. A valuation approach can help to put discipline on a thought process and to add organization and structure to a problem, but it cannot add fundamental information that does not exist.

[2] This last point about value-added pricing is extremely important, because it explains why marketed prescription drugs have nonzero betas. Pricing ultimately depends on the value added by the drug to the patient, which depends in part on the macroeconomic state of nature. If people are willing to pay more for the therapy when the economy is strong, or if governments will pay more when tax revenues are high, then the future cash flows are exposed to systematic risk. There is empirical evidence to support this: The equity betas of pharmaceutical and biotechnology firms are positive. Moreover, rich countries spend more of their wealth on prescription drugs than do poor countries.

[3] Here's an example of a firm discontinuing clinical trials of a drug that was technically successful but showed disappointing market potential: "Dr. Reddy's Laboratories (NYSE: RDY) announced today that Novo Nordisk has decided to terminate further clinical development of its partial PPAR (peroxisome proliferator activated receptor) gamma agonist balaglitazone (DRF 2593), an oral treatment for patients with type-2 diabetes. Novo Nordisk has decided to terminate further clinical development of balaglitazone, as the preclinical results did not suggest a sufficient competitive advantage for balaglitazone compared to similar, marketed products within this therapeutic category." *Source*: BioSpace.com, October 27, 2004.

The second source of risk, which is the new wrinkle we introduce in this chapter, is technical risk (which some people call *private* risk). The technical risk in a drug is simply the uncertainty about whether or not the compound will do what the scientists intend for it to do. As I will describe next, each tollgate of the R&D process aligns with a natural point in time when the company learns something about the efficacy of the drug. Therefore, at each tollgate, a second part of the decision to continue or discontinue is based on what has been learned about the technical potential for the new drug. Does it treat the targeted disease? Does it have adverse side effects? The answers to these questions are resolutions of technical risk. So at each tollgate, a *second part* of the decision to continue or discontinue is based on what has been learned about the *technical potential* for the new drug.

If the R&D process for a new drug contains no technical risk, then the analysis proceeds just like the Wal-Mart Neighborhood Markets problem. In fact, I'll first do the valuation under the assumption of no technical risk just to review the procedure. We'll calculate the beta of the strategy at each tollgate in which the project continues, and we will learn that the beta of the project generally drops as the project proceeds along the success path.

To introduce the effect of technical risk on our project valuation, we'll have to apply what we learned about idiosyncratic risk in Chapter 2. Specifically, we'll have to estimate the likelihood of technical success or failure at each tollgate, then adjust the value of the underlying asset in each state at a tollgate by the corresponding probability of success at that tollgate so that the resolution of technical risk is conditional mean zero (or idiosyncratic).

When we go back and recalculate our project betas after introducing technical risk, we will see something extremely important (but widely unknown): In a multistage option problem, *technical risk* in later stages affects the *market risk* of the project in earlier stages. That is, *the beta of the drug development project at early stages depends on the likelihood of technical success in the later stages.*[4] What we'll see is that the beta risk in the early stages of an R&D program is <u>very</u> sensitive to the likelihood of technical success at later stages. This helps to explain the enormous volatility of the stocks of small pharma and biotech companies whose only assets are early-stage compounds. It also tells us that we *cannot* value early-stage R&D in a simple decision tree in which we assume 100% technical success and then probability-weight this quantity by the actual probability of technical success.

The problem we'll analyze is a real-life example of an actual R&D investment at a genomics-based drug discovery and development company. To maintain strict confidentiality, we'll call the company Biotech.com, disguise the details about the compound under consideration, and sanitize the data in order to protect a company that has been generous enough to provide information that makes this discussion very realistic.

Our Problem: Valuation of an R&D Opportunity at Biotech.com[5]

Biotech.com has a very important business unit called *Discovery*. The mission of the Discovery unit is to undertake intelligent scientific research to identify compounds that may be used in prescription drugs for a wide variety of illnesses. Much of this research focuses on the areas of

---

[4] The reason, for those who want it right away, is that the likelihood of technical success in a late stage affects the value of making a decision to continue or discontinue at an earlier, intermediate stage. As the likelihood of technical success in the late stage drops, the value of continuing at an intermediate tollgate falls in every possible state of nature at that tollgate, and there exist some macroeconomic states at the intermediate tollgate where you would optimally continue the project given a high probability of later technical success but optimally discontinue given a lower probability of later technical success. So the probability of technical success in a late stage influences the *moneyness* of the options on the intermediate stages. As we learned in Chapter 4, out-of-the-money calls have higher betas than in-the-money calls. Thus, as you decrease the likelihood of technical success in a late stage of an R&D program, you increase the beta of the project at its early stages.

[5] To write this example, I've drawn heavily from an outstanding term paper submitted by Thomas Coburn and Brian Cole (both Kelley School of Business MBA, Class of 2004).

expertise of the company's scientists, and Biotech.com funds research into general concepts that management feels are promising for the discovery of new compounds.

In late 2003, the Discovery unit presented Biotech.com management with an attractive new compound that could possibly be used as a prescription drug therapy for a particular illness. At this point, the compound is ready to pass from the Discovery unit to the *Development* unit, and management must decide whether to commit substantial resources (both financial and human) in order to see if the compound can be developed into an actual prescription drug. From this point forward the R&D program becomes somewhat standard, and the pharma and biotech industries have historical data that make the duration and cost of further development along a success path somewhat predictable. This is really the first point in a potential drug's life where we can use an option model to arrive at a value, because it is the first point where the problem becomes concrete. Our analysis takes place on December 31, 2003, and we put ourselves in the place of Biotech.com management. Should we initiate the development of this compound into a new drug, or should we pass?

Turning this compound into a new drug would require the successful completion of five general stages of R&D, which would take eight years and cost $211 million (*not including* launch costs). I briefly describe each stage next.

1. *Preclinical Trials.* In preclinical trials, Biotech.com scientists will test the safety and effectiveness of the compound through the use of laboratory and animal trials. The preclinical trials will take one year and $6 million to complete. Historically, the industry-wide rate of technical failures in preclinical trials is about 25%.

2. *Phase I/IND:* If the compound passes successfully through preclinical trials *and* the drug's marketability still looks good, Biotech.com will spend an additional $15 million to complete Phase I clinical trials (small-scale trials on human subjects to test for safety) and to prepare the Investigational New Drug (IND) application for the FDA. This stage takes about 1.5 years. Historically, about one-half of all new compounds that begin Phase I clinical trials fail due to technical reasons. The FDA's approval of the IND includes very strict guidelines for the conduct of any further clinical trials as well as how the data from those trials must be collected.

3. *Phase II Clinical Trials:* If the FDA approves the IND application *and* the market potential of the drug still looks profitable after the Phase I trials are over, Biotech.com will spend $25 million on Phase II clinical trials. The Phase II trials explore the effectiveness of different dosage schedules and are usually performed with patients affected by the targeted disease. This will take two years. On average, the technical success rate in Phase II is about $\frac{2}{3}$ (that is, $\frac{1}{3}$ of all new drugs that enter Phase II clinical trials are discontinued either during or immediately after the trials due to technical failures).

4. *Phase III Clinical Trials:* If the drug passes successfully through the Phase II clinical trials *and* its marketability still appears good, Biotech.com will spend $150 million on Phase III clinical trials. The Phase III trials are large-scale, double-blind, placebo-controlled studies that evaluate both the safety and efficacy of the drug. The trials use a pool of both healthy volunteers and people suffering from the targeted disease. The data from the trials are collected for presentation to the FDA. Historically, Phase III trials fail due to technical reasons about 50% of the time.

5. *NDA Filing:* If the drug passes through the Phase III clinical trials with success *and* the drug still appears profitable, Biotech.com will commit an additional $15 million to prepare documentation of the drug and its success in the clinical trials for submission of the New

Figure 8.1 Timeline for Biotech.com's Drug-Approval Process

	Today	Preclinical		IND and Phase I			Phase II				Phase III					NDA	
	31-Dec-03	Jun-04	Dec-04	Jun-05	Dec-05	Jun-06	Dec-06	Jun-07	Dec-07	Jun-08	Dec-08	Jun-09	Dec-09	Jun-10	Dec-10	Jun-11	Dec-11
Probability of success	Already here	75%		50%			67%				50%					95%	
Decision given success	Go to preclinical?	Go to IND/Phase I?		Go to Phase II?			Go to Phase III?				Go to NDA?					Go to launch?	
Cost (mm)	$6	$15		$25			$150				$15					$50	

Drug Application (NDA) to the FDA. This will take approximately one year. The FDA rejects about 5% of all NDA submissions.

If the FDA approves the NDA *and* the profit potential for the drug still appears sufficiently high, the company must make one further investment: a $50 million commitment to actually launch the drug as a marketed product. This $50 million includes creation of samples, advertising to physicians, a buildup of inventory, and a marketing campaign targeted at both prescribing physicians as well as the general public. In addition, there are often further regulatory matters (such as the final packaging) that must clear the FDA. Figure 8.1 shows the timeline, along with key decision dates (or tollgates) and amounts that must be spent at each point to continue the process.

Our job is to evaluate whether Biotech.com should spend the $6 million and initiate the process (by beginning preclinical trials). Is the financial market value of this opportunity greater than $6 million? We'll see. We'll also calculate the beta of the opportunity so that we can understand how its market risk may change as it progresses through the R&D program.

8.2 Static NPV

Let's begin with a static NPV analysis. I'll do this for two reasons. First, I'd like to show how the decision changes when we explicitly recognize the value of optionality. Second, we'll use the present value of the expected free cash inflows as the starting value of our underlying asset.

The conventional approach to a static NPV analysis of a drug R&D program involves two steps: Calculation of the expected present value of the free cash flows from selling the drug, and calculation of the present value of the expected investment cost. I'll do these two steps separately.

In a purely static analysis, we first calculate the DCF value of the free cash flows from selling the drug *assuming* that the entire R&D program is successful through final launch of the product. We then weight this number by the cumulative probability of technical success through launch and finally discount at the proper WACC for a new drug.

If Biotech.com launches the drug at the end of 2011, the new product will follow a normal life cycle: Expected sales revenues are $20 million in the first six months (January–June 2012), $60 million for the next six months (July–December 2012), $125 million for the next six months (January–June 2013), and $200 million for the following six months (July–December 2013). The company expects sales growth to slow at that point, with expected sales of $250 million for each six-month period in 2014 and $275 million for each six-month period in 2015. At that point, management expects sales to begin to slow as competing products arrive. Specifically, the company expects sales to drop by 10% in each six-month period from January 2016 through June 2018, and then by 20% in each six-month period thereafter in perpetuity. Manufacturing

Figure 8.2		Time Period		Sales Revenue (mm)
Assumptions	January–June	2012		$20
about Cash Flows	July–December	2012		$60
on Marketed	January–June	2013		$125
Drug	July–December	2013		$200
	January–June	2014		$250
	July–December	2014		$250
	January–June	2015		$275
	July–December	2015		$275
	Percentage growth every six months through June 2018			−10%
	Perpetual growth every year after June 2018			−20%
	Direct expenses of making and selling drug as a percentage of revenues			20%
	Marginal tax rate			18%
	Hurdle rate for marketed drug			14%

and selling expenses will be 20% of sales revenues in all periods, the company's marginal tax rate is 18%, and the WACC for this type of drug is 14%. Figure 8.2 summarizes the assumptions made by Biotech.com.

Based on these assumptions, the expected launch-date (December 31, 2011) value of the new drug *assuming technical success through launch* is $1,101.10 million. This is the DCF value Biotech.com expects to see on December 31, 2011, *if* the drug makes it all the way through the R&D process. If we discount this back to the decision date (December 31, 2003) at the weighted average cost of capital for this drug, we find that the present value of the expected free cash flows from selling the drug *assuming technical success through launch* is $386.00 million. (This is an important number—keep it in mind). Figure 8.3 provides the DCF calculation.

Our next step will be to determine the present value of the expected cost of completing all stages of the R&D process and taking the drug to market. This is quite easy—we simply multiply the cost of each stage by the probability of reaching that stage, then discount the product back. Since I'm showing you the conventional approach here, I'll show what most people do: They discount these probability-weighted stage costs at the risk-free rate. The conventional argument (with which I do not agree) is that the continue/discontinue decisions at each stage are purely driven by resolution of technical risk and hence the investment costs at each stage bear no market risk.

To get the technical probability that Biotech.com makes an investment to initiate any particular stage of the R&D process, simply take the product of the probabilities of success of all prior stages. For example, the probability that Biotech.com spends $15 million on the Phase I/IND phase is simply the probability that the new drug passes successfully through the preclinical phase: 75%. So the expected investment in Phase I/IND is 0.75 × $15 million = $11.25 million. Similarly, the probability that Biotech.com invests $25 million in the Phase II trials equals the probability of technical success in preclinical trials (0.75) times the probability of technical success in Phase I/IND (0.50), or 0.375; therefore, the expected investment in Phase II trials is 0.375 × $25 million = $9.38 million. We calculate the expected cost of each of the remaining stages, then discount each back to December 31, 2003 at the risk-free rate of 5%. Figure 8.4 shows two things. First, the probability of technical success through all stages of R&D is only 0.1188. Second, the discounted value of the expected investments in R&D and launch is $60.47 million.

Figure 8.3   DCF Valuation of New Drug at Biotech.com Assuming Technical Success through Launch (in millions)

Annual hurdle rate   14.00%
6-month hurdle rate   6.77%

	Today 31-Dec-03	Launch 31-Dec-11	2012-1	2012-2	2013-1	2013-2	2014-1	2014-2	2015-1	2015-2	2016-1	2016-2	2017-1	2017-2	2018-1
Sales revenue			$20.00	$60.00	$125.00	$200.00	$250.00	$250.00	$275.00	$275.00	$247.50	$222.75	$200.48	$180.43	$162.38
Direct expenses			$4.00	$12.00	$25.00	$40.00	$50.00	$50.00	$55.00	$55.00	$49.50	$44.55	$40.10	$36.09	$32.48
Gross margin			$16.00	$48.00	$100.00	$160.00	$200.00	$200.00	$220.00	$220.00	$198.00	$178.20	$160.38	$144.34	$129.91
Taxes			$2.88	$8.64	$18.00	$28.80	$36.00	$36.00	$39.60	$39.60	$35.64	$32.08	$28.87	$25.98	$23.38
Free cash flow			$13.12	$39.36	$82.00	$131.20	$164.00	$164.00	$180.40	$180.40	$162.36	$146.12	$131.51	$118.36	$106.52
Terminal value															$250.65
Total FCF			$13.12	$39.36	$82.00	$131.20	$164.00	$164.00	$180.40	$180.40	$162.36	$146.12	$131.51	$118.36	$357.17
Exp. PV at launch		$1,101.10													
PV today	$386.00														

Figure 8.4	Present Value of the Expected Cost of Development					
	Assumptions About Clinical Trials			Probability of	Expected	Discounted Expected
Phase	Duration	Success Likelihood	Cost (mm)	Expenditure	Cost	Cost
Discovery	Already Completed					
Preclinical development	1 Year	75.00%	$6	100.00%	$6.00	$6.00
IND filing and Phase I	1.5 Years	50.00%	$15	75.00%	$11.25	$10.71
Phase II	2 Years	66.67%	$25	37.50%	$9.38	$8.30
Phase III	2.5 Years	50.00%	$150	25.00%	$37.50	$30.11
NDA filing	1 Year	95.00%	$15	12.50%	$1.88	$1.33
Launch	Immediate		$50	11.88%	$5.94	$4.02
			Present Value of Expected Costs of Development			$60.47

We can now finish the static NPV analysis. Since the present value of the expected free cash flows from selling the drug *assuming technical success throughout the R&D process* is $386 million, and since the probability of technical success throughout the program is 11.88%, the probability-weighted present value of the expected free cash inflows is 0.1188 × $386 million = $45.84 million. Therefore, the static NPV of the new drug at December 31, 2003 (and *after* the $6 million investment in preclinical development), is $45.84 million − $60.47 million = −$14.63 million. From the static NPV viewpoint, one would expect the development of this drug to be value destroying.[6]

It should not surprise you that we get a negative static NPV here. The reason is simple: The static NPV analysis forces the assumption that we commit to investment in each stage of development as long as we've achieved technical success in all prior stages, and then, if we make it through FDA approval, we launch the drug regardless of its profit potential. That is, we spend the development costs (in expectation in this setting), and then, if we're technically successful, we market the drug—good or bad. *On average,* the expected free cash flow from selling the drug will not return the shareholders' investments in development at an appropriate rate.

But we (the managers of Biotech.com) are *not* going to play the averages here. Admittedly, we most likely will be forced to discontinue at some point in time before launch due to purely technical reasons. But we will not be blind to the market potential of a successfully developed drug. If at any point during the development of the drug we learn that the ultimate market potential for the drug is poor, we will stop investing and walk away.[7]

If you don't see this, then perform the following thought experiment. Let's suppose we get through all stages of R&D successfully, and the FDA approves the drug. All that will be left to do at that point is to spend $50 million and launch the new product. If at that point the present value of the free cash flows from selling the drug turns out to be only $45 million, we will

---

[6] The static NPV is negative even if you discount the expected development costs at the WACC of 14%. In my opinion, there is market risk in the development cost—but not as much as in the cash flows from a new drug. As we'll see in the option analysis, a part of the decision to continue at each stage will depend on the (risky) market potential for the new drug—so there will be some relationship between the cost of development and the macroeconomic state of nature.

[7] Here's another example of a company doing just that: "Pfizer Inc. said today that it is ceasing the clinical development of sumanirole, a compound under investigation for the treatment of Parkinson's disease and restless leg syndrome. The decision is based on results of recent studies that failed to sufficiently distinguish sumanirole from currently available therapies. While the compound may still prove effective in these conditions, it did not meet Pfizer's criteria for continued development." *Source:* PRNewswire-First Call, July 21, 2004.

not spend the $50 million at all—we will walk away having spent a lot on development, but not yielding to the temptation to let sunk costs alter our go-forward decisions.

So the probability of spending the $50 million launch cost is actually *less than* 0.1188, and hence the expected present value of the launch cost is less than the $4.02 million calculated in Figure 8.4. The same goes for all the other development costs. Moreover, we will only spend any of the development costs as long as the true net present value (NPV) is positive, based on what we know *about the market value of the drug* at each tollgate. This is the option value of staging the R&D process, and it turns out to be significant.

8.3   Framing and Analyzing the Problem, Assuming No Technical Risk

We'll begin our analysis of the option value of the new drug at Biotech.com by assuming that there is no technical risk—that is, that there is a 100% expected success rate through each stage of the R&D process. I want to take this intermediate step for several reasons. First, I want to review the procedure for a staged investment (like the Wal-Mart example). Second, I want to highlight the fact that the continue/quit decision at any tollgate depends on more than just the outcome of the scientific investigation. Finally, the solution in the 100% technical success scenario gives us a baseline to which we can compare the results that incorporate technical risk.

Let's go through the process of framing the problem, just to make sure we've got it right. Assuming 100% technical success in all R&D stages, the very last decision that we (management) will have to make will be the December 31, 2011 decision to either (1) spend $50 million to launch the new drug or (2) walk away. If we invest the $50 million, we get back the free cash flow value of selling the new drug in the marketplace. If we walk away, we get zero. This decision will be easy—when we get there, we can use a static NPV analysis and invest in launch only if launch has positive NPV. We don't know today exactly which choice we will make on December 31, 2011; all we know (or at least assume) is that we will make the best decision on that date given whatever we learn by then.

Moving backwards in time, the next-earlier decision will be the December 31, 2010 decision to either (1) invest $15 million in the NDA application, or (2) walk away. Obviously, if we walk away at that point, our payoff will be zero. But what do we get back if we invest the $15 million in the NDA application? Figure 8.5 helps us answer this question.

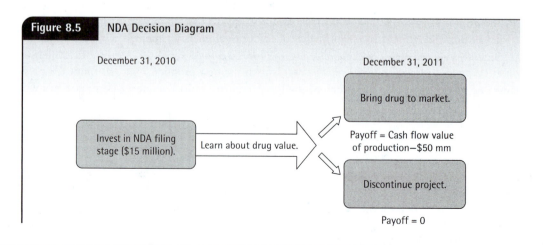

Figure 8.5   NDA Decision Diagram

December 31, 2010

December 31, 2011

Invest in NDA filing stage ($15 million).

Learn about drug value.

Bring drug to market.

Payoff = Cash flow value of production−$50 mm

Discontinue project.

Payoff = 0

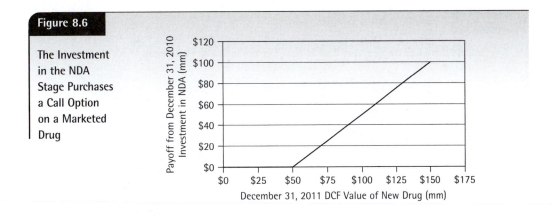

Figure 8.6

The Investment in the NDA Stage Purchases a Call Option on a Marketed Drug

Figure 8.5 shows us that if we spend $15 million on the NDA filing on December 31, 2010, we will get back the ability to make a nonnegative NPV decision one year later. If, by the end of the year, we learn that the DCF value of selling the new drug is greater than $50 million, we will spend the $50 million launch cost and take the positive NPV (whatever it may be). If, on the other hand, the DCF value of selling the new drug is less than $50 million, we will optimally choose to walk away, and the incremental value implication for Biotech.com will be zero. Figure 8.6 plots the payoff diagram for the $15 million investment in the NDA on December 31, 2010.

The plot in Figure 8.6 is, of course, the payoff diagram for a standard call option. By spending $15 million on the NDA filing on December 31, 2010, Biotech.com will purchase this call. What are its parameters? The time to maturity is one year. The strike price is $50 million. The underlying asset is what will be received back in exchange for the strike price, which is a marketed new drug—so the value of the underlying is the December 31, 2010 expected present value of the free cash flows from selling the new drug starting on 2011 *based on what is known about them at December 31, 2010.* The volatility is simply the uncertainty in the December 31, 2010 estimate of the December 31, 2011 value of these cash flows. The risk-free rate is, well, the risk-free rate. That's it. Investment in the NDA filing buys a one-year European call on a marketed new drug with a $50 million strike price. If this option is worth more than $15 million on December 31, 2010, Biotech.com will make the investment; if not, the company will walk away.

Now let's move back to the next-earlier decision in time: the June 30, 2008 decision to either (1) invest $150 million in Phase III clinical trials or (2) walk away from the project. Again, the net payoff from walking away is zero. But what will the company's shareholders get on June 30, 2008, if management spends the $150 million on the Phase III clinical trials? Figure 8.7 gives a clue.

Figure 8.7 makes the large investment in Phase III clinical trials look very much like the investment in the NDA application: It allows for learning, then a later decision. But, just as in the Wal-Mart Neighborhood Markets case, this earlier investment has a very unique implication. If, by the end of the Phase III clinical trials, Biotech.com learns that an investment in the NDA is worth more than $15 million, management will spend the $15 million, file the NDA, and take back the difference. What we just learned in the previous paragraph is that the investment in the NDA investment *purchases a call option on a marketed new drug.* So in other words, at the end of the Phase III clinical trials, management will spend $15 million on the NDA application *if a one-year call on a marketed new drug with a $50 million strike* is worth more than $15 million. Figure 8.8 shows the payoff diagram for the $150 million investment in Phase III trials on June 30, 2008.

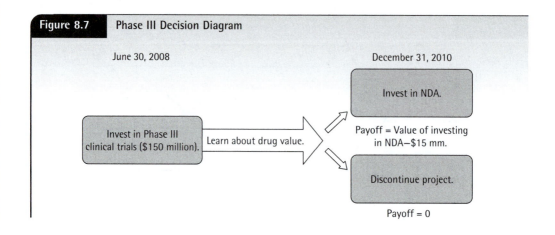

Figure 8.7   Phase III Decision Diagram

June 30, 2008   December 31, 2010

Invest in Phase III clinical trials ($150 million). — Learn about drug value. →

Invest in NDA.

Payoff = Value of investing in NDA–$15 mm.

Discontinue project.

Payoff = 0

Again, we see the payoff diagram for a call option: The $150 million investment in Phase III clinical trials buys a 2.5 year call option. The twist here is that the underlying asset is not cash flow, but rather is an option—if Biotech.com exercises the option pictured in Figure 8.8 by investing $15 million in the NDA filing on December 31, 2010, the shareholders receive in return a one-year option on a fully marketed drug with a strike price of $50 million. So, the $150 million investment in Phase III clinical trials purchases an *option-on-an-option* (see Figure 8.9). The underlying asset is itself an option, and the starting value of the underlying is the June 30, 2008 value of this option. Biotech.com management should spend the $150 million on Phase III if and only if this option-on-an-option-on-a-marketed drug is worth more than $150 million. We can handle the valuation of this compound option easily in our binomial analysis, just as in the Wal-Mart case.

If you understand up to this point, then you know what happens next (and if you don't, go back and review Chapter 7). The next-earlier tollgate, the June 30, 2006 decision to invest $25 million in Phase II clinical trials, purchases an option-on-an-option-on-an-option on a marketed drug and should be evaluated accordingly. The next earlier decision, the December 31, 2004 potential investment of $15 million in Phase I, adds another layer of optionality. So,the current decision (spend $6 million on preclinical trials) represents the purchase of an

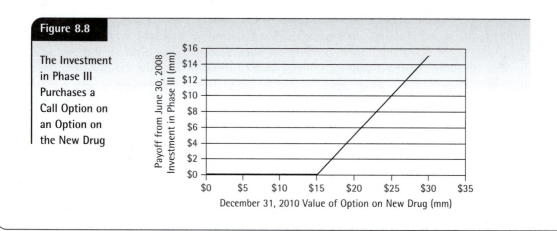

Figure 8.8

The Investment in Phase III Purchases a Call Option on an Option on the New Drug

Payoff from June 30, 2008 Investment in Phase III (mm)

December 31, 2010 Value of Option on New Drug (mm)

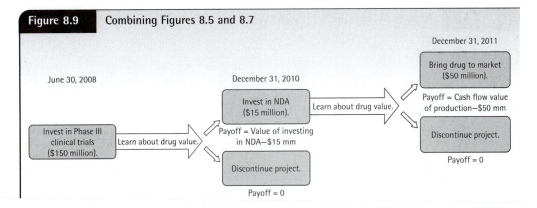

Figure 8.9   Combining Figures 8.5 and 8.7

option-on-an-option-on-an-option-on-an-option-on-an-option on a marketed new drug. It's easier to show this using a diagram like Figure 8.10.

Now that we understand the structure of the problem assuming no technical risk, we can turn to the valuation. Again, it works just like the Wal-Mart example (but with more intermediate options).

To get the parameters we need, we start by assuming that the very last decision (whether to launch on December 31, 2011, at a cost of $50 million at that time) is the *only* option. This is eight years away, and if we ultimately spend the $50 million strike price, we get back a marketed new drug. Given what we know right now (December 31, 2003), the launch-date expected value of a new drug is $1,101.10 million so the *current* value of our underlying asset is the present value of this, or $386 million (see Figure 8.3). This will be the starting value of the underlying asset in our binomial tree.

The other parameter we need for modeling our learning about the marketability of the new drug (remember, we're assuming no technical risk) is the volatility of changes in our estimate of its value. Keep in mind that the volatility parameter describes how "wrong" our launch-date expected value ($1,101.10 million) could turn out to be. In this example we'll estimate the volatility in a bit more scientific way, using the lesson from Chapter 6.

The senior managers at Biotech.com understand from experience that their estimate of the launch-date value of a successful new drug ($1,101.10 million) could turn out to be very wrong. Based on past experience (which includes development and launch of drugs aimed at similar

Figure 8.10   Decision Diagram for Entire Drug Development Timeline

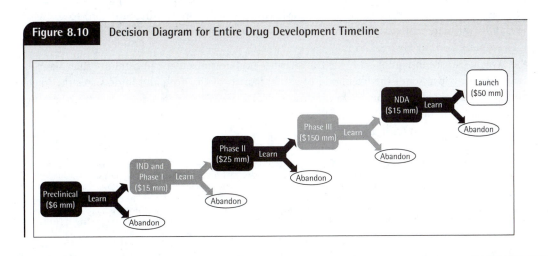

Figure 8.11	Probabilities Implied by Different Volatilities				
		Management's Prior	30%	50%	70%
New drug worth > $50 mm on launch date		0.95	0.999	0.936	0.728
New drug worth > $2,202.2 mm on launch date		0.125	0.124	0.126	0.096
New drug worth > $4,404.4 mm on launch date		0.05	0.024	0.051	0.049

diseases), the managers believe that the drug will be worth at least the launch cost of $50 million with 95% probability. (This squares up with the general observation that most, but not all, successfully developed drugs are launched and marketed). Historically, about one out of every eight new drugs has turned out to be worth over twice as much as anticipated, so senior management assigns a prior probability of 12.5% as the likelihood that the drug turns out to be worth more than $2,202.20 million on 12/31/2011. Finally, when pressed on the point, the senior managers believe that there is about a 1-in-20 chance that the drug could be worth four times as much as anticipated—and hence assign a prior probability of 5% to the event that the drug is worth more than $4,404.4 million on launch date. It is worthwhile to repeat what these probabilities represent. They are management's view of the future, conditioned on actually making it to launch. Hence, although we are currently considering the case with no technical risk, we will be able to use these same probabilities when considering the problem with technical risk.

We can use these prior probabilities to come up with a reasonable estimate of the volatility parameter. Recall from Chapter 6 that the probability the underlying asset exceeds value Z on the exercise date is

$$N\left(\frac{\ln(UND_0/Z) + (\mu - .5\sigma^2)T}{\sigma\sqrt{T}}\right)$$

where $N(x)$ is the cumulative probability that a unit-normal random variable (i.e., a normal random variable with mean zero and standard deviation 1) is less than or equal to x, UND_0 is the current value of the underlying asset ($386 million), μ is the required rate of return on the asset per year (14%), T is the number of years until the exercise date (eight), and σ is the volatility estimate (the volatility of log changes in the value of the underlying). I performed this calculation for different estimates of σ (using Microsoft Excel's =normsdist function) to see what volatility estimate matches up the most closely with management's probability assessments. My results are shown in Figure 8.11.

As you can see in Figure 8.11, a 30% volatility underestimates the uncertainty that management faces: It overstates the likelihood of actual launch of the drug and understates the likelihood of the very high outcome. On the other side, a 70% volatility forces too much uncertainty (particularly on the downside). The 50% volatility estimate seems to fit management's priors the best, and that is what we'll use here in this analysis.[8]

---

[8] The very careful reader may notice that I'm mixing discrete compounding (using 14% as my annually compounded discount rate to get the DCF value of the underlying asset) with continuous compounding (using 14% as the continuously compounded rate of return μ in the preceding probability calculations). While this is true, I wish to point out that it does not make much of a difference. If 14% is the annually compounded required rate of return on our underlying asset, then the equivalent continuously compounded required rate of return is $\ln(1.14) = 13.1\%$. As a proof, note that $386e^{0.131\times8} = \$1,101.10$. Using $\mu = 13.1\%$ and $\sigma = 50\%$, the probabilities that the underlying asset exceeds $50 mm, $2,202.20 mm, and $4,404.40 mm on January 1, 2012 are 0.93, 0.12, and 0.05, respectively.

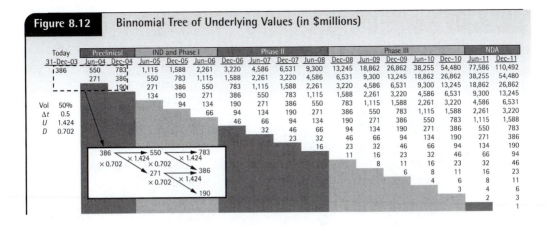

Figure 8.12   Binomial Tree of Underlying Values (in $millions)

Armed with our volatility estimate of $\sigma = 50\%$, we only need to decide how long each step will be in our binomial tree, and then we'll be on our way. We'll need to be a bit finer here than in the past, so I'm going to build a 16-step tree with each time step representing six months. Since our length of time will be $\Delta t = 0.5$ years, our up and down step sizes will be

$$U = e^{\sigma\sqrt{\Delta t}} = e^{0.50\sqrt{0.5}} = 1.424 \quad \text{and} \quad D = \frac{1}{U} = 0.702$$

Combining these tree parameters with our starting value of $386 million yields a binomial tree of underlying values that looks like Figure 8.12.

Before we value the compound option (the investment in the preclinical trials) assuming no technical risk, let me remind you of a couple of things. The binomial tree in Figure 8.12 models how we (the management at Biotech.com) will learn about the true value of a marketed drug. The expected value increases year by year from the starting value of $386 million to the launch-date expectation of $1,101.10 million, and the volatility of *returns* of 50% per year creates a probability distribution over launch-date values just as I described earlier. Don't worry about the existence of extremely large values at the end of the tree. The probability of reaching the $110 billion state is negligible. The large values are there simply because we've built a tree with a lot of steps, and the assumption of a continuous distribution (the normal distribution of log returns) always implies that there is a very small probability of *any* large value.

Now we can figure out what Biotech.com gets back if management spends $6 million on preclinical trials (assuming no technical risk). As always, we start at the final expiration date and work backward. On December 31, 2011, we will spend $50 million on launch if and only if we find out by that time that the cash flow value of selling the drug is greater than this. So we set up a binomial tree of option values, and in every state in the very last time period we write in the maximum of the value of the underlying minus $50 million or zero. This is shown in Figure 8.13, with a couple of example calculations.

We now work one step backwards, calculating the value of the option in June 2011 as the expected present value of the December 2011 payoffs (that we just determined), properly adjusting for risk through the risk-neutral probabilities and discounting at the risk-free rate of 5%. Given a risk-free rate of 5% and a time-step of $\frac{1}{2}$ year, the risk-free time value factor is

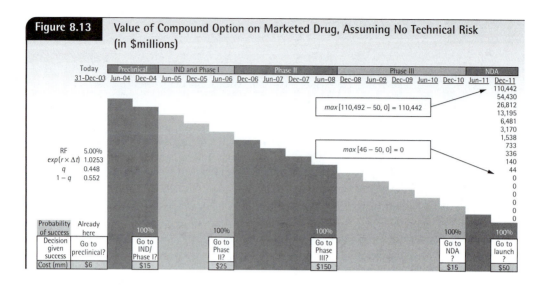

Figure 8.13 Value of Compound Option on Marketed Drug, Assuming No Technical Risk (in $millions)

$e^{r \times \Delta t} = e^{0.05/2} = 1.0253$, so the risk-neutral probabilities of the up and down steps are

$$q = \frac{e^{r \times \Delta t} - D}{U - D} = \frac{1.0253 - 0.702}{1.424 - 0.702} = 0.448 \quad \text{and} \quad 1 - q = 0.552$$

Using these, the June 2011 values of the compound option on the marketed new drug are shown in Figure 8.14.

We now move back to the end of December 2010, which is the tollgate at the end of Phase III clinical trials. At this point, we (management) will decide whether or not to spend $15 million on the NDA filing and keep the option on the marketed product alive. Since we're assuming no technical risk, the only relevant uncertainty is that which is described in our binomial tree of

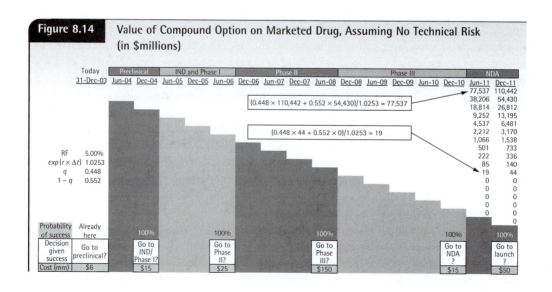

Figure 8.14 Value of Compound Option on Marketed Drug, Assuming No Technical Risk (in $millions)

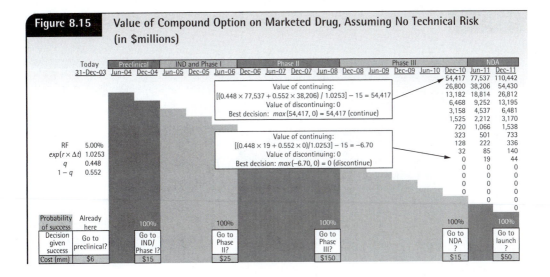

Figure 8.15 Value of Compound Option on Marketed Drug, Assuming No Technical Risk (in $millions)

underlying values, so we will exercise this option-on-an-option (i.e., spend the $15 million on the NDA filing and get back the simple option on the marketed product) if the compound option is worth more than $15 million at that time. So, in each state in December 2010, we must first calculate the value of the option (just as we did in the last step), and then write into our binomial tree either (1) the value of the option just calculated minus the $15 million cost of continuing or (2) zero, whichever is larger. Figure 8.15 shows the results with a couple of sample calculations.

In the next four time steps backward, we have no decision to make, so the value of the option in each state is the discounted expectation of its value in the two following states, again using the risk-neutral probabilities to adjust for risk and the risk-free discount rate to account for time value. Figure 8.16 shows the results back to the end of December 2008 with sample calculations.

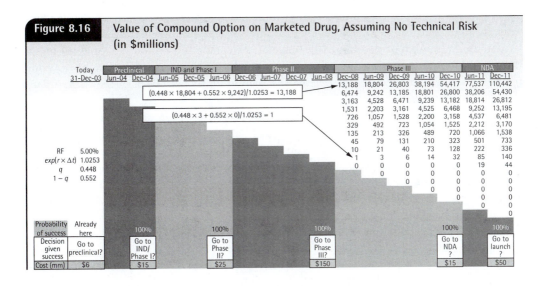

Figure 8.16 Value of Compound Option on Marketed Drug, Assuming No Technical Risk (in $millions)

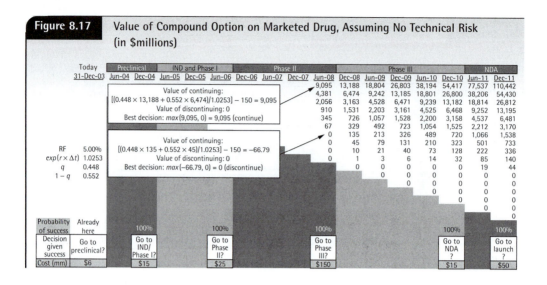

Figure 8.17 Value of Compound Option on Marketed Drug, Assuming No Technical Risk (in $millions)

At the end of June 2008 we have a big decision to make: Spend $150 million on Phase III clinical trials and keep the strategy alive, or discontinue and preserve our capital for a more compelling investment. This works just like the December 2010 decision. We first have to calculate the value of keeping the option alive, just as if there were no decision. We then write into our compound option value tree either (1) the value of keeping the compound option alive minus $150 million or (2) zero, whichever is larger. Figure 8.17 demonstrates this.

As you can see in Figure 8.17, there are several June 2008 states of nature in which we will optimally discontinue the trials simply because the market potential does not look good enough to support a $150 million investment in Phase III clinical trials, *even though we are assuming 100% technical success in all stages of R&D.*

The rest of the analysis is the same: Always work backwards in time, using the risk-neutral probabilities to calculate the compound option's expected value at the end of any binomial step to adjust for risk, then discounting at the risk-free rate of return to account for time value. In June 2006 and December 2004, there are continue/terminate decisions to make, so write in the maximum of this value (the value of the compound option if kept alive) minus the cost of continuing, or zero. In all other time steps, just write in the value of the compound option if kept alive. I've completed the analysis all the way back to the current decision date in Figure 8.18.

Figure 8.18 shows that the financial market value of investment in preclinical trials (i.e., the value we get back if we make the investment) is $217 million, <u>assuming no technical risk</u>. Since the cost of initiating the preclinical trials is $6 million, then the true NPV of initiating the R&D process for turning this compound into a new drug is $217 million − $6 million = $211 million <u>assuming no technical risk</u>. Of course, the risk that the compound fails somewhere in the R&D process lowers this value substantially. We'll turn to that problem shortly, but before we do, I'd like to show one more thing.

In Chapter 4, I showed how to calculate the beta of a derivative:

$$\beta_{\text{Derivative}} = \eta_{\text{Derivative}} \times \beta_{\text{Underlying}}$$

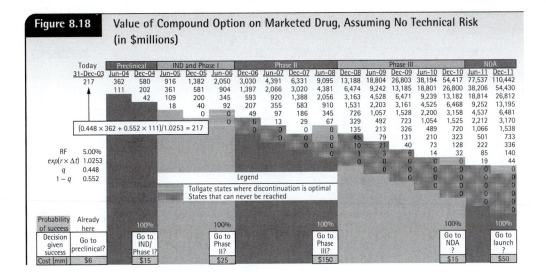

Figure 8.18 Value of Compound Option on Marketed Drug, Assuming No Technical Risk (in $millions)

	Today	Preclinical		IND and Phase I			Phase II				Phase III				NDA	
	31-Dec-03	Jun-04	Dec-04	Jun-05	Dec-05	Jun-06	Dec-06	Jun-07	Dec-07	Jun-08	Dec-08	Jun-09	Dec-09	Jun-10	Dec-10	Jun-11	Dec-11
	217	362	580	916	1,382	2,050	3,030	4,391	6,331	9,095	13,188	18,804	26,803	38,194	54,417	77,537	110,442
		111	202	361	581	904	1,397	2,066	3,020	4,381	6,474	9,242	13,185	18,801	26,800	38,206	54,430
			42	109	200	345	593	920	1,388	2,056	3,163	4,528	6,471	9,239	13,182	18,814	26,812
				18	40	92	207	355	583	910	1,531	2,203	3,161	4,525	6,468	9,252	13,195
					0	0	49	97	186	345	726	1,057	1,528	2,200	3,158	4,537	6,481
						0	6	13	29	67	329	492	723	1,054	1,525	2,212	3,170
							0	0	0	0	135	213	326	489	720	1,066	1,538
								0	0	0	45	79	131	210	323	501	733
									0	0	10	21	40	73	128	222	336
										0	1	3	6	14	32	85	140
											0	0	0	0	0	19	44
												0	0	0	0	0	0
													0	0	0	0	0
														0	0	0	0
															0	0	0
																0	0

$(0.448 \times 362 + 0.552 \times 111)/1.0253 = 217$

RF	5.00%
$\exp(r \times \Delta t)$	1.0253
q	0.448
$1-q$	0.552

Legend

Tollgate states where discontinuation is optimal
States that can never be reached

Probability of success	Already here	100%		100%		100%			100%	100%
Decision given success	Go to preclinical?	Go to IND/Phase I?		Go to Phase II?		Go to Phase III?			Go to NDA?	Go to launch?
Cost (mm)	$6	$15		$25		$150			$15	$50

where $\eta_{\text{Derivative}}$ is the elasticity of the derivative. Notice that the elasticity of the derivative is just a beta multiplier: It measures how the derivative magnifies the beta risk of the underlying asset. The elasticity of a derivative is easy to calculate at any point in time:

$$\eta = \Delta \times \frac{\text{Value of underlying}}{\text{Value of derivative}}$$

where Δ is the number of units of the underlying asset held in the tracking portfolio that mimics the derivative. As I hope you remember, the delta of a derivative can be calculated at any time state in a binomial model as follows:

$$\Delta = \frac{DERIV_{\text{up}} - DERIV_{\text{dn}}}{UND_{\text{up}} - UND_{\text{dn}}}$$

The numerator in this expression is the value of the derivative if the underlying goes up over the next binomial time step minus the value of the derivative if the underlying goes down over the same time step. The denominator is the value of the underlying itself if it goes up over the next time step minus its value if it goes down over the same time step. Using this, I've calculated the elasticity (i.e., the beta multiplier) of our compound option at every point in time. Figure 8.19 presents my results. Note that if we exercise the final option and launch the drug in 2011, we will own the asset itself, so our beta multiplier is 1.0. Note further that if we discontinue at any point in time, we will no longer have the investment so its beta is not material.

Let's make sure we understand the interpretation here—the elasticity of 1.60 as of today means that if we undertake the investment in preclinical trials, the beta risk of our project will be 1.6 times the beta risk of the drug itself (assuming 100% technical success). This is greater than 1.0 simply because we are dealing with call options (which always have elasticities greater than 1.0).

Notice what happens as you move through time. If things turn out just as expected, the underlying asset moves roughly through the middle of the tree. What you see scanning through the middle states at each decision point is that the elasticity of the investment drops over time. This is normal for successful development of a new drug. But notice also what else you see—if

Figure 8.19 Elasticity (Beta Multiplier) of the Compound Option, Assuming No Technical Rick

Today	Preclinical		IND and Phase I			Phase II				Phase III					NDA	
31-Dec-03	Jun-04	Dec-04	Jun-05	Dec-05	Jun-06	Dec-06	Jun-07	Dec-07	Jun-08	Dec-08	Jun-09	Dec-09	Jun-10	Dec-10	Jun-11	Dec-11
1.60	1.45	1.33	1.21	1.15	1.10	1.06	1.04	1.03	1.02	1.00	1.00	1.00	1.00	1.00	1.00	1.00
	2.00	1.73	1.46	1.33	1.23	1.14	1.09	1.07	1.05	1.01	1.01	1.00	1.00	1.00	1.00	1.00
		3.02	2.03	1.75	1.55	1.32	1.21	1.14	1.10	1.02	1.01	1.01	1.01	1.00	1.00	1.00
			3.17	3.17	2.38	1.72	1.55	1.34	1.23	1.04	1.03	1.02	1.01	1.01	1.01	1.00
				W	A	2.37	2.24	2.06	1.60	1.08	1.05	1.04	1.03	1.02	1.01	1.00
					A	AA	3.17	3.17	4.03	1.17	1.12	1.08	1.06	1.04	1.02	1.00
						AA	AA	W	A	1.38	1.27	1.18	1.12	1.09	1.05	1.00
							AA	AA	A	1.61	1.45	1.29	1.19	1.10	1.10	1.00
								AA	AA	AA	2.07	1.80	1.49	1.22	1.22	1.00
									AA	AA	AA	3.17	2.81	1.57	1.57	1.00
										AA	AA	AA	AA	3.17	3.17	1.00
											AA	AA	AA	A	A	A
												AA	AA	AA	AA	AA
													AA	AA	AA	AA
														AA	AA	AA
															AA	AA
																AA

W = Project is alive but worthless at this state.
A = Project is optimally discontinued at this tollgate state.
AA = Project has been discontinued before reaching this point.

the learned market value of the new drug moves down close to states in which we will discontinue the project, the elasticity of the compound option goes *up*. This is simply because the option is going out-of-the-money, and out-of-the-money calls have higher elasticities. Moreover, notice that the beta can drop very quickly if you learn very good things, but it can rise very quickly if you learn very bad things. For expected learning, the beta changes in a more smooth way.

But there's more. The elasticity not only gives us the relationship between the beta of a derivative and the beta of the underlying asset, it also gives us the relationship between the total volatility of the derivative and the total volatility of the underlying asset:

$$\sigma_{\text{Derivative}} = \eta_{\text{Derivative}} \times \sigma_{\text{Underlying}}$$

So, suppose our business at Biotech.com consists only of this one project, and we have no debt. The return volatility of our stock should be 1.6 times the return volatility of a new drug—or $1.6 \times 50\% = 80\%$. Even with no technical risk and no leverage, our stock will be very volatile (and as you'll see, technical risk actually makes this multiplier larger)!

8.4 How to Deal with Technical Risk in the R&D Process

In the earlier analysis (where we assumed no technical risk), the only source of uncertainty was the market value of the new drug, and so, at every tollgate, we based the continue/discontinue decision solely on the drug's market potential. But this is only part of the story. Technical risk in the R&D process means that when Biotech.com's managers actually get to a tollgate, the drug may have failed that step of the R&D process, and no decision will be available at all.

Technical risk is unrelated to the macroeconomic state of nature, and we handle it just as we handled asset- or firm-specific risks in Chapters 2 and 3. Do you remember how we handled the rain-day risk in our rain-day bonds, or the litigation risk in our risky stock, or the risk of client defection in our consulting firm with a growth opportunity? We valued each of those assets (financial in the first two cases, real in the third) by determining the conditional mean cash flows within each macroeconomic state of nature, and recognizing that the remaining risk within each state is conditional-mean zero (or idiosyncratic) and thus has no value. We do exactly the same

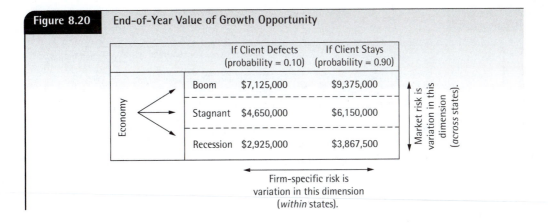

Figure 8.20 End-of-Year Value of Growth Opportunity

	If Client Defects (probability = 0.10)	If Client Stays (probability = 0.90)
Boom	$7,125,000	$9,375,000
Stagnant	$4,650,000	$6,150,000
Recession	$2,925,000	$3,867,500

Economy

Market risk is variation in this dimension (*across* states).

Firm-specific risk is variation in this dimension (*within* states).

thing here. (If you skipped those chapters, I strongly suggest that you go back and read them before going on.)

The example of the delayed growth opportunity at the consulting firm that faces the random risk of client defection (from Chapter 3, Section 3.2) provides the right model for dealing with both market and technical risk in the R&D process, and I'd like to review it briefly here. If you recall, the consulting firm has a potential growth opportunity which it can exercise at the end of the year at a cost of $5 million. The actual value of the growth opportunity depends on the strength of the macroeconomy *and* whether or not the major client defects to another firm. Figure 8.20 summarizes those numbers.

Figure 8.20 shows the two dimensions of risk (market risk and firm-specific risk) and how they interact. No matter what the client does, the value of the growth opportunity is positively correlated with the overall economy—but the growth opportunity is more valuable if the client stays (regardless of how the economy performs).

If the growth opportunity requires a $5 million investment, then the firm will optimally exercise it in the boom economy and optimally pass on it in the recession no matter what the client does. The stagnant economic outcome, however, provides a very interesting case because the firm's optimal exercise decision will depend on what the client does: If the client stays, the

Figure 8.21 End-of-Year Net Payoff from Optimal Exercise of Growth Opportunity [*max*(Value −$5 mm, $0)]

	If Client Defects (probability = 0.10)	If Client Stays (probability = 0.90)	Conditional Mean
Boom	$2,125,000	$4,375,000	$4,150,000
Stagnant	$0	$1,150,000	$1,035,000
Recession	$0	$0	$0

Economy

Market risk is variation in this dimension (*across* states).

Firm-specific risk is variation in this dimension (*within* states).

Figure 8.22	Decomposing the Consulting Firm's Growth Opportunity

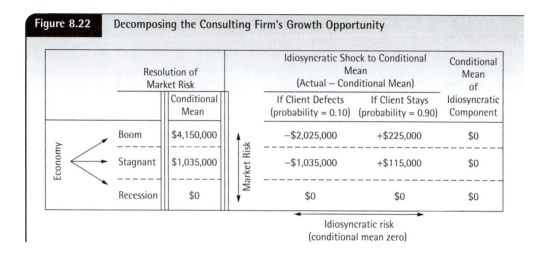

growth opportunity will have a positive NPV; but if the client defects, the opportunity will be value destroying. Figure 8.21 shows the net payoffs from the optimal exercise decision given each possible resolution of both the market risk and the firm-specific risk.

As I hope you recall, we value the growth opportunity under both market and firm-specific risk by calculating the conditional mean cash flow from optimal exercise of the growth opportunity in each macroeconomic state, and then finding the financial-market portfolio that gives the same expected cash flow in each macroeconomic state; by the no-arbitrage assumption, the value of the growth option will be equal to the value of this capital market portfolio. The reason that we don't have to consider the firm-specific risk dimension is because it is now idiosyncratic—its expected value is zero in all states of nature, as Figure 8.22 shows.

Since the effect of the client defection risk in Figure 8.22 has zero mean in all states of nature, it must have zero value today—so today's value of the growth opportunity is equal to the value of a capital market portfolio strategy that pays off an expected value of $4,150,000 in the boom economy, $1,035,000 in the stagnant economy, and $0 in the recession economy.

I'll reiterate. The key step in valuing the growth opportunity with both market and firm-specific risk was to transform the firm-specific risk (the risk of the client's action) into an idiosyncratic (or conditional-mean zero) risk. To do this, we had to calculate the optimal exercise strategy and payoffs given each possible scenario (each combination of economic state and client action), then calculate expected values *within* each economic state.

We do the exact same thing when dealing with market and technical risk in an R&D process. We capture market risk through our binomial tree of underlying values, then capture technical risk as an exogenous shock in each macro state. Now you see why it is necessary to build the binomial tree of underlying values under the assumption of no technical risk.

I'd like to demonstrate this procedure in general terms before we turn back to the new drug at Biotech.com. Let's suppose that we are one time step before a tollgate and the current value of the underlying asset in our binomial tree is UND. Over the next binomial time-step, we will learn *two* things: (1) whether the underlying asset goes up (to UND_{up}) or down (to UND_{dn}) and (2) whether the compound succeeds in the current stage of R&D or fails. If the compound is successful (which occurs with probability p_{tech}), then to continue the R&D process, we must spend K; if the compound fails at the current stage, we have no decision, and our payoff is zero. Figure 8.23 summarizes this.

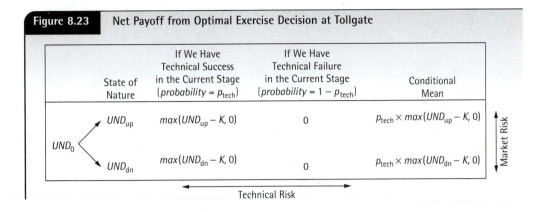

Figure 8.23 — Net Payoff from Optimal Exercise Decision at Tollgate

	State of Nature	If We Have Technical Success in the Current Stage (probability = p_{tech})	If We Have Technical Failure in the Current Stage (probability = $1 - p_{tech}$)	Conditional Mean
UND_0	UND_{up}	$max(UND_{up} - K, 0)$	0	$p_{tech} \times max(UND_{up} - K, 0)$
	UND_{dn}	$max(UND_{dn} - K, 0)$	0	$p_{tech} \times max(UND_{dn} - K, 0)$

Technical Risk

Market Risk

Using the conditional means from Figure 8.23, we can break away the idiosyncratic portion of the risk over the next stage, as Figure 8.24 demonstrates.

Make sure you understand how to construct this. Here is how I got the entries to Figure 8.24:

- The conditional means of the resolution of market risk in Figure 8.24 come right from the last column of Figure 8.23.
- The max and min terms in the resolution of technical risk simply reflect that there's only a shock due to the resolution of technical risk if $UND_i > K$ (where i = up or dn). Let's take this one step at a time.
  - If $UND_i > K$, technical success in the current stage causes a positive shock, added to the conditional mean, and calculated as follows:

$$p_{tech}(UND_i - K) + shock = (UND_i - K)$$

therefore,

$$shock = (UND_i - K) - p_{tech}(UND_i - K) = (1 - p_{tech})(UND_i - K)$$

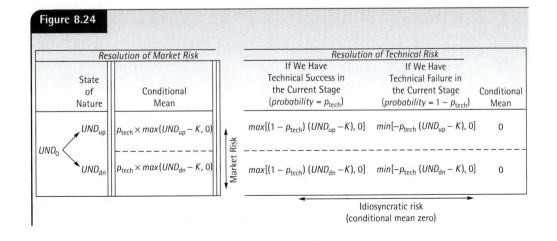

Figure 8.24

	Resolution of Market Risk			Resolution of Technical Risk		
State of Nature		Conditional Mean		If We Have Technical Success in the Current Stage (probability = p_{tech})	If We Have Technical Failure in the Current Stage (probability = $1 - p_{tech}$)	Conditional Mean
UND_{up}		$p_{tech} \times max(UND_{up} - K, 0)$		$max[(1 - p_{tech})(UND_{up} - K), 0]$	$min[-p_{tech}(UND_{up} - K), 0]$	0
UND_{dn}		$p_{tech} \times max(UND_{dn} - K, 0)$		$max[(1 - p_{tech})(UND_{dn} - K), 0]$	$min[-p_{tech}(UND_{dn} - K), 0]$	0

UND_0

Market Risk

Idiosyncratic risk (conditional mean zero)

- If $UND_i \leq K$, then you won't exercise the option to continue even if there is technical success. Here, the conditional mean is zero, and the shock is zero (and we certainly don't want technical success to enter as a negative shock!).

Hence, we can concisely express the two different cases ($UND_i > K$ and $UND_i \leq K$) for the value of the shock caused by technical success as

$$max[(1 - p_{tech})(UND_i - K), 0]$$

- Similarly, technical failure in the current stage causes a negative shock only when $UND_i > K$.
  - When $UND_i > K$, technical failure reduces the conditional mean to zero so

$$p_{tech}(UND_i - K) + shock = 0$$

and therefore

$$shock = 0 - p_{tech}(UND_i - K) = -p_{tech}(UND_i - K)$$

- When $UND_i \leq K$, the conditional mean is zero anyway, and the option will not be exercised regardless of the resolution of technical risk. Therefore, the shock is zero (again, we don't want technical failure to enter as a positive shock!).

Therefore, we concisely express the two different cases ($UND_i > K$ and $UND_i \leq K$) for the value of the shock caused by technical failure as

$$min[-p_{tech}(UND_i - K), 0]$$

- To show that the conditional mean of the idiosyncratic risk is zero in all states, just consider the two cases. First of all, if $UND_{up} > K$ then

$$max[(1 - p_{tech})(UND_{up} - K), 0] = (1 - p_{tech})(UND_{up} - K)$$

and

$$min[-p_{tech}(UND_{up} - K), 0] = -p_{tech}(UND_{up} - K),$$

so the conditional mean is

$$p_{tech}(1 - p_{tech})(UND_{up} - K) + (1 - p_{tech})(-p_{tech})(UND_{up} - K) = 0$$

If, on the other hand, $UND_{up} < K$, then $max[(1 - p_{tech})(UND_{up} - K), 0] = 0$ and

$$min[-p_{tech}(UND_{up} - K), 0] = 0$$

so the conditional mean is

$$p_{tech} \times 0 + (1 - p_{tech}) \times 0 = 0$$

The same two arguments hold for $UND_{dn} > K$ and $UND_{dn} \leq K$

Notice where this leaves us. All we care about are the conditional mean payoffs associated with the resolution of market risk. As we can see from Figure 8.23 or Figure 8.24, these are simply the option payoffs given technical success multiplied by the probability of technical success. For example, the conditional mean payoff if the underlying goes up is

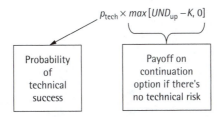

$$p_{tech} \times max[UND_{up} - K, 0]$$

Probability of technical success

Payoff on continuation option if there's no technical risk

Therefore, to incorporate technical risk into our R&D compound option, we start at the end as usual and work our way backwards toward the last tollgate. At this very last tollgate, we calculate the optimal exercise strategy and payoff from exercise of the option at the tollgate, assuming 100% technical success (just like in a standard problem), and then probability-weight this by the probability of technical success associated with that tollgate:

$$p_{tech}^N max[UND - K^N, 0]$$

Here, p_{tech}^N is the probability of technical success in the Nth stage, and K^N is the cost of continuing—exercising—at the tollgate which occurs at the end of that stage. Working backwards in the binomial tree, at any earlier nontollgate state, the value of the compound option is the standard binomial option pricing formula

$$\frac{q \times DERIV_{up} + (1 - q) \times DERIV_{dn}}{e^{r \times \Delta t}}.$$

When you get to an earlier tollgate stage (we'll call it the ith tollgate), the value of the compound option is

$$p_{tech}^i \times max[\text{value of continuing}, 0]$$

where p_{tech}^i is the probability of technical success over the ith stage. If the cost of continuing at the tollgate at the end of the ith stage is K^i, then the value of continuing at that tollgate will be

$$\frac{q \times DERIV_{up} + (1 - q) \times DERIV_{dn}}{e^{r \times \Delta t}} - K^i$$

Don't let the notation put you off. These are simple formulae to use, as you will see in the next section.

8.5 Valuation of Our R&D Investment with Technical Risk

Let's get right to it. We start with the same underlying asset, and the same binomial tree, as in the case with no technical risk. The only change is how we work with the tree. Figure 8.25 provides our original tree of the market value of the marketed new drug (our underlying) along with the probabilities of technical success in each stage and the amounts that must be spent to continue at each tollgate.

Once again, start at the very end—but this time use what we just learned. Suppose we've reached the end of December 2011, just before we learn the outcome of the NDA filing. If the

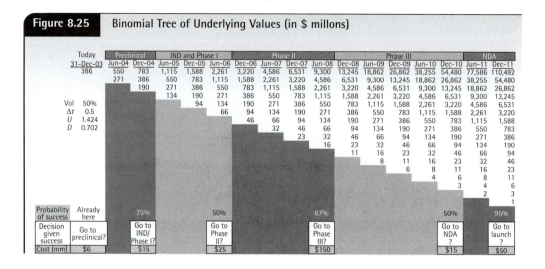

Figure 8.25 Binomial Tree of Underlying Values (in $ millons)

FDA approves the NDA (which we expect with probability 0.95), we will invest $50 million and launch the new drug in all states of nature in which its market value is greater than $50 million. So, in each December 2011 state, calculate the maximum of the market value of the new drug minus the $50 million launch cost or zero, then multiply this by the probability of technical success in the NDA stage (0.95). I've done this for all December 2011 states in Figure 8.26, and I've provided some sample calculations.

We now work backwards one time step to the end of June 2011. Since there's no decision to be made here, this calculation works in our usual way: In every state, simply take the expected present value of the two outcomes that can occur over the next period, using the risk-neutral probabilities to adjust for risk and the risk-free discount rate to adjust for time value of money. Since we have not changed our underlying asset (a marketed new drug) at all, we don't change the risk-neutral probabilities. Remember that the risk-neutral probabilities are really just the state prices of the Red and Blue state securities (compounded out at the risk-free rate). Technical

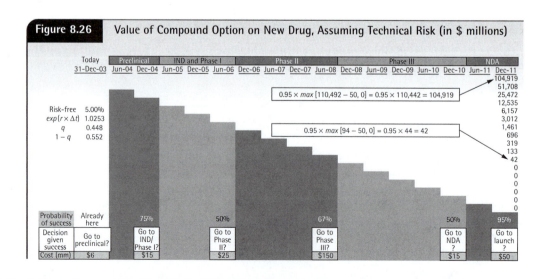

Figure 8.26 Value of Compound Option on New Drug, Assuming Technical Risk (in $ millions)

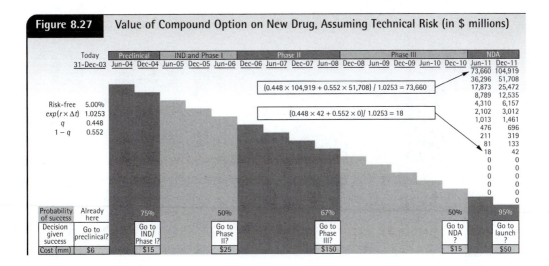

Figure 8.27 Value of Compound Option on New Drug, Assuming Technical Risk (in $ millions)

risk does not change these—it only changes the number of each that we need in order to correctly track our option. Figure 8.27 provides some sample calculations for June 2011.

The end of December 2010 marks the end of the Phase III clinical trials (if the drug gets that far) and therefore the resolution of the technical risk in that stage. If you recall, about 50% of all drugs that make it to Phase III clinical trials actually succeed in those trials. So with 0.50 probability, the Phase III trials end successfully, and we have the opportunity to continue. To continue, we must spend $15 million to prepare the NDA filing. In each state in December 2010, we must perform a 2-step procedure: (1) calculate the payoff from the optimal continue/discontinue strategy *given* technical success in the Phase III clinical trials, and then (2) multiply this number by the probability of technical success in Phase III. The payoff from the optimal continue/discontinue strategy given technical success is simply the maximum of the option value minus the cost of continuing ($15 million) or zero, and the option value in any state at December 2010 is simply the expected present value of the two things that could happen

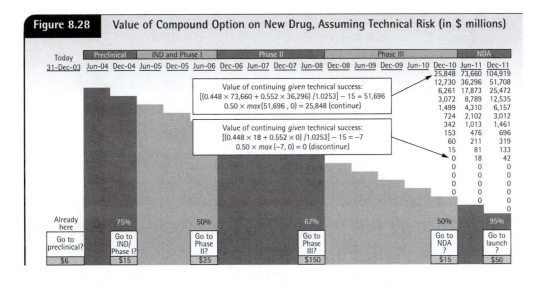

Figure 8.28 Value of Compound Option on New Drug, Assuming Technical Risk (in $ millions)

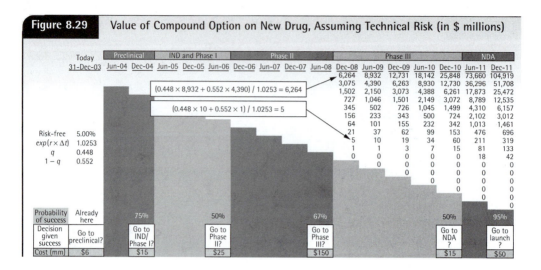

Figure 8.29 Value of Compound Option on New Drug, Assuming Technical Risk (in $ millions)

from there in June 2011. Figure 8.28 shows several example calculations. Make sure you understand what I've done here, as this is the key to the whole issue of technical risk.

We now work backwards through the Phase III time periods, using the risk-neutral probabilities and the risk-free discount rate. Figure 8.29 illustrates.

At the end of June 2008, we once again encounter a point in time where we must calculate the optimal continue/discontinue strategy and then adjust for the likelihood of technical success (this time, the 0.67 probability of success in Phase II clinical trials). Figure 8.30 shows this.

You've probably got it now. Just continue this process all the way back, making sure to weight your payoffs from continuing appropriately at the end of the Phase I and preclinical stages. Figure 8.31 shows the completed analysis, where I have *not* subtracted the $6 million cost of the preclinical trials from today's option value.

Figure 8.31 tells us that the investment in the preclinical trials actually purchases a compound option that is worth $8.96 million. Since the preclinical trials cost $6 million, the right thing to do is initiate them; the *true* NPV of the investment is $2.96 million.

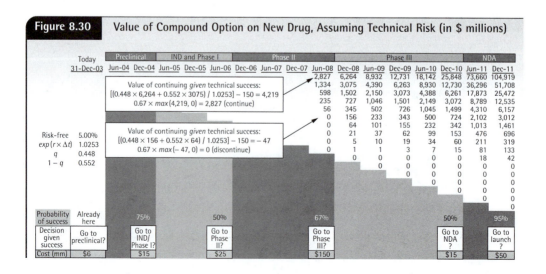

Figure 8.30 Value of Compound Option on New Drug, Assuming Technical Risk (in $ millions)

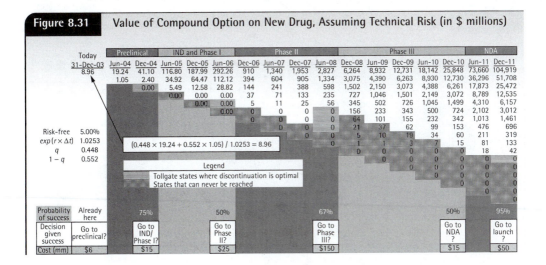

Figure 8.31 — Value of Compound Option on New Drug, Assuming Technical Risk (in $ millions)

	Today 31-Dec-03	Preclinical Jun-04	Dec-04	IND and Phase I Jun-05	Dec-05	Jun-06	Phase II Dec-06	Jun-07	Dec-07	Jun-08	Phase III Dec-08	Jun-09	Dec-09	Jun-10	Dec-10	NDA Jun-11	Dec-11
	8.96	19.24	41.10	116.80	187.99	292.26	910	1,340	1,953	2,827	6,264	8,932	12,731	18,142	25,848	73,660	104,919
		1.05	2.40	34.92	64.47	112.12	394	604	905	1,334	3,075	4,390	6,263	8,930	12,730	36,296	51,708
			0.00	5.49	12.58	28.82	144	241	388	598	1,502	2,150	3,073	4,388	6,261	17,873	25,472
				0.00	0.00	0.00	37	71	133	235	727	1,046	1,501	2,149	3,072	8,789	12,535
					0.00	0.00	5	11	25	56	345	502	726	1,045	1,499	4,310	6,157
						0.00	0	0	0	0	156	233	343	500	724	2,102	3,012
							0	0	0	0	64	101	155	232	342	1,013	1,461
								0	0	0	21	37	62	99	153	476	696
									0	0	5	10	19	34	60	211	319
										0	1	3	7	15	81	133
											0	0	0	18	42
												0	0	0	0
													0	0	0
														0	0
															0

Risk-free 5.00%
exp(r × Δt) 1.0253
q 0.448
1 − q 0.552

(0.448 × 19.24 + 0.552 × 1.05) / 1.0253 = 8.96

Legend
Tollgate states where discontinuation is optimal
States that can never be reached

Probability of success	Already here	75%	50%	67%	50%	95%
Decision given success	Go to preclinical?	Go to IND/Phase I?	Go to Phase II?	Go to Phase III?	Go to NDA?	Go to launch?
Cost (mm)	$6	$15	$25	$150	$15	$50

Comparisons to the Case with No Technical Risk

There are some critical lessons to be learned from comparing the results that recognize technical risk in the R&D process with the results that assumed no technical risk. Firstly (and most obviously), the introduction of technical risk reduced the value of the compound option from $217 million (Figure 8.18) to $8.96 million (Figure 8.31). This is a no-brainer.

What may not be so obvious, however, is the magnitude of the reduction. If you recall, the cumulative probability of technical success through all stages of the R&D process was 11.88% (see Figure 8.4). An incorrect way to approach this problem would have been to take the answer we got assuming no technical risk ($217 million; see Figure 8.18) and then multiply this by the cumulative probability of success (11.88%), to get 0.1188 × $217 million = $25.78 million. As you can see, this method would have wildly overstated the value of the option.

Why? Because the mere existence of technical risk causes us to discontinue the project earlier than we would without technical risk. You can see this by comparing Figure 8.31 (the compound option tree with technical risk) against Figure 8.18 (the compound option tree with no technical risk). I've reconstructed the exhibits in Figure 8.32 so that you can easily see what I'm talking about.

In Figure 8.32, the cells crossed out with horizontal lines are the states of nature at each tollgate where we optimally discontinue the R&D process of this drug and move on to something more valuable. The important cells, though, are the ones I've outlined in bold in the *no-technical-risk* tree. These are the states of nature where we would optimally <u>continue</u> if there were no technical risk, but where <u>the mere presence of technical risk in later stages causes us to optimally discontinue.</u> The end result is that technical risk in late stages makes the project less valuable in early stages, and hence causes us to discontinue it more often than if technical success were a sure thing. The lower the likelihood of technical success in the late stages of R&D, the more likely we are to terminate the R&D process at earlier tollgates. In other words, ***the likelihood of technical success or failure in later stages of the R&D process directly affects the moneyness of the compound option in earlier stages. As the probability of technical success in a later stage drops, the moneyness of the compound option in earlier stages drops as well.***

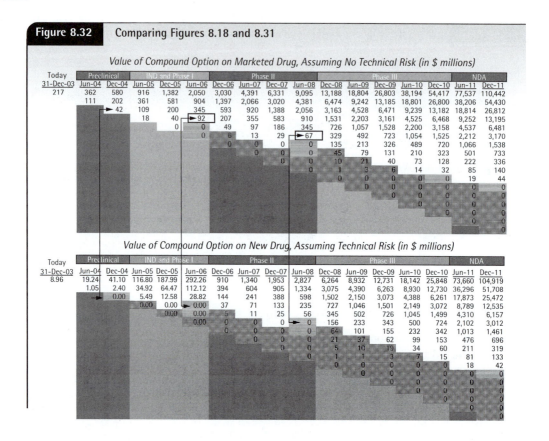

Figure 8.32   Comparing Figures 8.18 and 8.31

Value of Compound Option on Marketed Drug, Assuming No Technical Risk (in $ millions)

Value of Compound Option on New Drug, Assuming Technical Risk (in $ millions)

Now, if you were paying attention in Chapter 4, you will recall that the beta of an option is a function of its moneyness: As a call option goes deeper out of the money, its elasticity increases—which means its beta increases and its volatility increases. What this means, then, is that technical risk in later stages of the R&D process **_indirectly affects the beta of the R&D process in earlier stages._** We can see this by recalculating the elasticity (or beta multiplier) of the option at each time state under technical risk, which I've done for you in Figure 8.33.

Figure 8.33   Elasticity (Beta Multiplier) of the Compound Option, with Technical Risk

Today 31-Dec-03	Preclinical		IND and Phase I			Phase II				Phase III					NDA	
	Jun-04	Dec-04	Jun-05	Dec-05	Jun-06	Dec-06	Jun-07	Dec-07	Jun-08	Dec-08	Jun-09	Dec-09	Jun-10	Dec-10	Jun-11	Dec-11
2.81	2.79	2.76	1.46	1.33	2.45	1.12	1.08	1.06	1.56	1.00	1.00	1.00	1.00	2.00	1.00	1.00
	3.17	16.97	2.06	1.79	3.09	1.28	1.19	1.13	1.63	1.01	1.01	1.00	1.00	2.00	1.00	1.00
		A	3.17	3.17	5.13	1.64	1.46	1.30	1.80	1.02	1.01	1.01	1.01	2.01	1.00	1.00
			AA	W	A	2.27	2.11	1.86	2.25	1.04	1.03	1.02	1.01	2.02	1.01	1.00
				AA	A	AA	3.17	3.17	4.63	1.06	1.06	1.04	1.03	2.04	1.01	1.00
					AA	AA	AA	W	A	1.17	1.12	1.08	1.06	2.08	1.02	1.00
						AA	AA	AA	A	AA	1.27	1.18	1.13	2.18	1.05	1.00
							AA	AA	AA	AA	AA	1.45	1.30	2.39	1.10	1.00
								AA	AA	AA	AA	AA	1.82	3.00	1.22	1.00
									AA	AA	AA	AA	AA	5.77	1.57	1.00
										AA	AA	AA	AA	AA	3.17	1.00
											AA	AA	AA	AA	AA	A
												AA	AA	AA	AA	AA
													AA	AA	AA	AA
														AA	AA	AA
															AA	AA
																AA

W = Project is alive but worthless at this state.
A = Project is optimally discontinued at this tollgate state.
AA = Project has been discontinued before reaching this point.

Figure 8.34 Elasticity (Beta Multiplier) of the Compound Option, with Greater Technical Risk in NDA Stage

Today	Preclinical		IND and Phase I			Phase II				Phase III					NDA	
31-Dec-03	Jun-04	Dec-04	Jun-05	Dec-05	Jun-06	Dec-06	Jun-07	Dec-07	Jun-08	Dec-08	Jun-09	Dec-09	Jun-10	Dec-10	Jun-11	Dec-11
2.99	2.99	2.88	1.49	1.35	2.48	1.13	1.09	1.06	1.57	1.00	1.00	1.00	1.00	2.00	1.00	1.00
	3.17	36.93	2.10	1.85	3.16	1.30	1.20	1.13	1.64	1.01	1.01	1.00	1.00	2.00	1.00	1.00
		A	3.17	3.17	5.46	1.67	1.50	1.32	1.81	1.02	1.01	1.01	1.01	2.01	1.00	1.00
			AA	W	A	2.31	2.16	1.94	2.31	1.04	1.03	1.02	1.01	2.02	1.01	1.00
				AA	A	AA	3.17	3.17	5.16	1.08	1.06	1.04	1.03	2.04	1.01	1.00
					AA	AA	AA	W	A	1.18	1.12	1.08	1.06	2.08	1.02	1.00
						AA	AA	AA	A	A	1.28	1.19	1.13	2.18	1.05	1.00
							AA	AA	AA	AA	AA	1.46	1.30	2.40	1.10	1.00
								AA	AA	AA	AA	AA	1.85	3.02	1.22	1.00
									AA	AA	AA	AA	AA	5.93	1.57	1.00
										AA	AA	AA	AA	AA	3.17	1.00
											AA	AA	AA	AA	AA	A
												AA	AA	AA	AA	AA
													AA	AA	AA	AA

W = Project is alive but worthless at this state.
A = Project is optimally discontinued at this tollgate state.
AA = Project has been discontinued before reaching this point.

I remind you that the elasticity of the compound option today (December 31, 2003), assuming no technical risk, was 1.60. Why did incorporating technical risk make the beta of the R&D program go up? Because the technical risk in later stages affected our decision to continue or discontinue in some macroeconomic states at earlier tollgates (shown in Figure 8.32). Remember our extremely important lesson from Chapter 4: Cash flows that are received in strong economic states are discounted more heavily than those received in weaker economic states. Technical risk in later stages of the R&D process causes us to discontinue the program at earlier stages in intermediate economic states (see Figure 8.32)—which means that we only exercise the option in *stronger* economic states where discount rates are higher (and hence the beta is higher).

The effect of technical risk in later stages is to magnify not only the project beta in earlier stages but also the volatility of total returns on the project. If this single project were our firm's only asset, and if our firm were unlevered, then the volatility of our equity returns would be 2.81 × 50% = 140.5%. There are single-drug biotech firms traded in the OTC market, and their returns are *very* sensitive to both results in the clinical trials (when information comes out) *and* to the overall movements in the market.

To show the point in one further way, I've redone the entire analysis, assuming only a 90% likelihood of success in the NDA stage. You would expect that a lower likelihood of technical success in the last stage would translate through to a lower option value today, and indeed it does: When there's only a 90% chance of making it through the NDA filing successfully, today's value of entering the preclinical trials falls to $7.5 million, and so the NPV of investing in the preclinical trials falls to $1.5 million. But what most people would not expect is that the beta of the R&D program rises. Figure 8.34 shows that this one small change in the likelihood of technical risk in the last stage increases the elasticity of the project today from 2.81 to 2.99.

8.6 Summary

The key point you should take from this is that *market risk and technical risk interact.* It is simply not appropriate to treat them separately in a multistage option problem, because they work jointly to affect our optimal exercise or discontinue decisions (and hence to affect the beta of the compound option). For a rigorous theoretical treatment of this issue, I point the interested reader to Berk, Green, and Naik (2004). The intuition that comes out of their model is *exactly* as I've given it here: Technical risk interacts with market risk to affect the moneyness of a compound option in its early stages, and hence the technical risk affects the beta of the compound option.

Jonathan Berk likes to use another thought experiment to illustrate this point. Suppose you've got a plot of land which you *think* might have an oil deposit under it. You've decided to do some test drilling to learn for sure—a process that will take one year. So over the next year, you will learn two things: (1) you will learn how much oil can be extracted from your property, and (2) you will learn the market price of oil (which will change from now until then). Think about how these interact to affect your decision to actually develop the property. If you learn that there's not much oil to be extracted from your property, you will only develop the oilfield if oil prices are very high (because you have to cover a very large fixed cost of drilling—the strike price). But if you learn that the deposit has a *lot* of oil which can be extracted, you will definitely develop the oilfield if prices are high, and you might develop it if prices are medium. So the likelihood of a purely idiosyncratic outcome—high or low quantity of oil in your deposit—affects the measure of the set of macroeconomic states (oil prices) in which you actually exercise the option. In other words, the ex-ante likelihood of having a large quantity of oil in your deposit affects the moneyness of your option today, and hence affects the market risk of the test drilling activity.

8.7   Bibliography

Berk, Jonathan, Richard Green, and Vasant Naik (2004). "Valuation and Return Dynamics of New Ventures," *Review of Financial Studies* 17, 1–35.

Coburn, Thomas A., and Brian D. Cole (2003). "Valuing a 'Cure in the Rough': Analysis of Real Options in Biotech Development with Dynamic Efficacy Failure Possibilities." Unpublished manuscript, Indiana University.

PROBLEMS

Note: Problems with asterisks require a spreadsheet package.

1. In Figures 8.23 and 8.24, the conditional mean for the payoff metric is $p_{tech}^{*} \times max\,[UND_i - K, 0]$ (where $i =$ up or dn). By subtracting the conditional mean from each possible outcome, the idiosyncratic risk can be eliminated: (assuming technical success with probability p_{tech}), $max\,[UND_i - K, 0] - p_{tech} \times^{*} max[UND_i - K, 0]$ and (assuming technical failure with probability $(1 - p_{tech})$), $0 - p_{tech}^{*} \times max[UND_i - K, 0]$. However, this is not what is specifically illustrated in Figure 8.24. Demonstrate that the conditional mean of the idiosyncratic risk is still zero using these equations for the outcomes.

2.* Reproduce the option pricing tree in the chapter, assuming the probability for technical success at the NDA stage is 90% and not 95%.

3.* Reproduce the option pricing tree in the chapter, assuming the probability of technical failure at the end of Phase I is 40% instead of 50%, and that the cost of going to Phase II is $30 million instead of $25 million. *Hint:* Use the same tree from the chapter as it corresponds to Dec.-06 through Dec.-11.

4.* Reproduce the option pricing tree in the chapter, assuming the cost of going to Phase I is $10 million instead of $15 million. *Hint:* Use the same tree from the chapter as it corresponds to Jun.-05 through Dec.-11.

5. If the value of launching a new drug 10 years from today is $1,250 million, what is the current value of the project (i.e., the spot price from which a binomial tree of future project values emerges), assuming a WACC of 16.25% and a risk-free rate of 5%?

6.* Project Y has two phases of development. The initial phase lasts one year and will cost $5 million today. The second phase, if launched, will cost $10 million and last two years. Assuming the value of the project is $40 million if it is launched after the two phases of development, what is the current value of launching a successful project with a WACC of 10%? Given a volatility of 40% annually and a risk-free rate of 4% annually, and using six-month increments, find the NPV of initiating the development of Project Y using binomial trees.

7.* What happens to the NPV of developing the project in Problem 6, if after the first phase, there is a 60% chance of failure? (Produce the appropriate option pricing tree to justify your answer.)

8.* Continuing with Problems 6 and 7, what happens to the NPV of developing the project, if after the second phase there is a 20% chance of failure in addition to the 60% chance of failure after Phase I? (Produce the appropriate option pricing tree to justify your answer.)

In addition, approximately what strike price at the end of Phase II would make developing the project have an NPV of zero (e.g., the strike price could be a licensing fee or a tax)?

9.*   Project Z has three phases of development. The initial phase lasts one year and will cost $10 million today. The second phase, if launched, will cost $10 million and will also last one year. The third phase, if launched, will cost $20 million and will also last one year. Assuming the value of the project is $60 million if it is launched after the three phases of development, what is the current value of launching a successful project with a WACC of 16%? Given a volatility of 60% annually and a risk-free rate of 4% annually, and using six-month increments, find the NPV of initiating the development of Project Z using binomial trees.

10.*   Suppose there is a 10% chance of failure after each phase in Problem 9. What is the NPV of developing Project Z? (Produce the appropriate option pricing tree to justify your answer.)

What is the NPV if the chance of failure is 30%, but only after the final phase of the project?

What is the NPV, if the chance of failure is 30%, but only after Phase I of the project?

PART 5

AMERICAN-STYLE REAL OPTIONS

9 INTRODUCTION TO AMERICAN OPTIONS

In all of our examples up to now, we've focused on problems where the "dates with destiny" are fixed in time. For example, Boeing's January 1996 investment in preliminary R&D created the January 2001 flexibility to decide whether or not to fully develop the super-jumbo jet. And Wal-Mart's tollgates for expanding to 40 and then 100 Neighborhood Markets occurred at precise points in time. We never considered Boeing's flexibility to commit to (or walk away from) the project early, nor did we consider Wal-Mart's flexibility to expedite or delay the tollgate decisions.

There were two reasons that we avoided *timing* decisions up to this point. First, many projects really don't have much flexibility in their investment-decision schedules. Second, the possibility of early exercise requires an additional complexity, and I wanted us to master the basic European-style option before we moved on to what are called American-style options.

As I've mentioned, most corporate growth options are calls. An important feature of call options is that even if you have the ability to exercise them early, you will always wait to exercise them *unless there is a sufficiently high cost of waiting*. While it is pretty easy to demonstrate (and understand) the cost of waiting in the world of stock options, it is a good deal harder to explain in the world of commodity options, and it can be downright bewildering in the world of real options. So I'm going to take a very measured approach. Stay with me here—this is important material.

9.1   Our Basic Binomial Model—A Review

Let's go back to our binomial model. If you recall, we used the following notation:

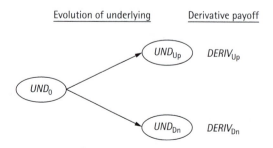

We also had borrowing and lending at the risk-free rate r. Since we're now familiar with continuous compounding, we'll use it exclusively so the present value of \$1 received t years from now is e^{-rt}.

Our first derivatives problem was a forward contract. The state-contingent payoffs for the forward are

	Long Forward	Short Forward
$DERIV_{Up}$	$UND_{Up} - F_t$	$F_t - UND_{Up}$
$DERIV_{Dn}$	$UND_{Dn} - F_t$	$F_t - UND_{Dn}$

where F_t is the currently prevailing price for delivery t years forward. I'm sure you recall that we were able to determine the forward price F_t via an arbitrage argument. Specifically, the forward price F_t should be set such that there's no arbitrage profit available from going short the forward and long the tracking portfolio.

	CF Today	CF If UND_{Up}	CF If UND_{Dn}
Buy low–buy tracking portfolio			
Long 1 unit risky asset	$-UND_0$	UND_{Up}	UND_{Dn}
Borrow PV of F_t	$+F_t \times e^{-rt}$	$-\$F_t$	$-\$F_t$
Sell high–short forward			
Short forward @ F_t	\$0.00	$F_t - UND_{Up}$	$F_t - UND_{Dn}$
Total cash flows	$\underline{F_t \times e^{-rt} - UND_0}$	$\underline{\$0.00}$	$\underline{\$0.00}$

To preclude arbitrage, the *CF Today* column must sum to zero, so the arbitrage-free forward price must be

$$F_t = UND_0 \times e^{rt}$$

(Of course, you'd get the exact same answer if you set things up where you short the tracking portfolio and go long forwards).

This result relies critically on the assumption that there are no costs to holding the underlying asset, and that there are no cash yields or benefits received from holding it. We will relax these assumptions and see what happens. There's a critical difference between risky assets held for investment purposes and assets held for productive purposes, so we'll deal with each in turn.

9.2   Storage Costs on Assets Held for Investment Purposes

Some risky assets that are held for investment involve costly storage. A great example is gold. If you invest in gold, you never actually see your bullion. Rather, your gold broker will safeguard your gold for you in a secure warehouse and issue you a warehouse receipt. Of course, safeguarding large quantities of gold is not cheap, so the gold broker charges you a fee for the service.

Does costly storage of gold enter the value of derivatives written on gold? Yes. The easiest way to demonstrate this is to look at what happens to gold forwards when gold is costly to store. Let's think about gold as our risky asset in our binomial model. Assume that the current price is \$354 per ounce, and that it can go up to \$360 or down to \$348 over the next one month. Furthermore, suppose that the risk-free rate of interest is 1.5% per year, and that the cost of storing one ounce of gold is $0.06 per month (i.e., 6¢ per month), which is paid in advance.

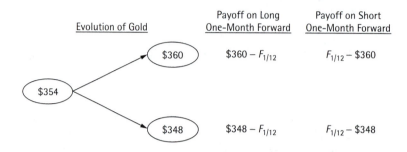

	Evolution of Gold	Payoff on Long One-Month Forward	Payoff on Short One-Month Forward
	$360	$360 − $F_{1/12}$	$F_{1/12}$ − $360
$354			
	$348	$348 − $F_{1/12}$	$F_{1/12}$ − $348

If you were to ignore the costly storage and calculate the one-month forward price of gold as $F_t = UND_0 \times e^{rt} = \$354 \times e^{0.015/12} = \$354.44$, you would be creating an arbitrage opportunity. In this case, an investor who is holding gold would actually prefer to get rid of the gold and just hold the forward contract, because by doing so the investor could save the cost of storage and yet still earn the exact same future state-contingent cash flows! So in this situation, an investor with gold will (1) go long one forward on gold at $354.44, (2) sell one unit of gold in the spot market at $354, (3) save the $0.06 storage cost (this is an incremental gain), and (4) lend the PV of the forward price $354.44 \times e^{-0.015/12} = \$354$. Here's the arbitrage table:

	CF Today	CF If Gold = $360	CF If Gold = $348
Sell High			
Sell 1 unit gold; buy back later	+$354	−$360	−$348
Save storage cost over period	+$0.06		
Lend PV of $F_{1/12}$	−$354	+$354.44	+$354.44
Buy low			
Long forward on gold	$0.00	$360 − $354.44	$348 − $354.44
Total cash flows	+$0.06	$0.00	$0.00

So $354.44 must not be the correct forward price for gold when there's costly storage. Remember that the mantra of arbitrage is *buy low, sell high,* and in our example this means buying the forward and selling the tracking portfolio. Therefore, the forward must be too cheap—that is, the forward price must be higher than $354.44. But how much higher?

Well, if you are thinking you'll recognize that the present value of the forward price $F_{1/12}$ must equal $354.06 so that the first column sums to zero (the last two columns will sum to zero regardless of $F_{1/12}$). Therefore, $\$354.06 = F_{1/12} \times e^{-0.015/12}$ so $F_{1/12} = \$354.06 \times e^{0.015/12} = \$354.50$. If you plug this in above, you'll see that there are no arbitrage opportunities. Notice what happened: The 6¢/unit storage cost pushed *up* the arbitrage-free forward price by roughly 6¢.

We can generalize this. When the cost of storage is quoted as $S per unit stored, paid in advance, then the forward price F_t makes the following arbitrage table hold:

	CF Today	CF in Future given $\widetilde{UND}$
Buy low-buy tracking portfolio		
Long 1 unit risky asset	$-UND_0$	$\widetilde{UND}$
Borrow PV of F_t	$+F_t \times e^{-rt}$	$-F_t$
Pay storage cost	$-S$	
Sell high		
Short forward at F_t	$0.00	$F_t - \widetilde{UND}$
Total cash flows	$F_t \times e^{-rt} - UND_0 - S$	0.00

Notice that the tracking portfolio exactly offsets the short forward position in the future no matter what value the risky asset takes—we don't have to be in a binomial world for this to work. The CF Today column must sum to zero for there to be no arbitrage opportunities. So now, with costly storage S per unit of the risky asset, the correct forward price becomes

$$F_t = (UND_0 + S)e^{rt}$$

If you pay the storage costs in arrears (at the end of time) rather than in advance, you get the same answer if you let S be the *present value* of the storage costs (taken at the risk-free rate, since you pay them no matter which state occurs).

If the storage cost is not stated in dollars per unit but rather as a continuously compounded *percentage* of the value of the underlying ($s\%$), then the relationship is

$$F_t = UND_0 \times e^{(r+s)t}$$

This is a very common way of quoting things, so let's calculate it from our data.

$$\$354.50 = \$354e^{(0.015+s)\times 1/12}$$

So

$$\ln\left(\frac{\$354.50}{\$354.00}\right) = \ln\left(e^{(0.015+s)/12}\right)$$
$$0.0014 = (0.015 + s)/12$$
$$s = .002$$

or the cost of storage of gold is roughly 0.2% per year.[1]

The point you should remember is that when storage is costly, the owners of the risky asset must pay the cost of storage, while owners of derivatives on the asset do not. This will drive forward and futures prices up. Call options will also become more expensive because storage costs will make the call's tracking portfolio more expensive (long the underlying plus borrowing—remember?).

9.3 Known Cash Income from Assets Held for Investment Purposes

When looking at assets held for investment purposes, the opposite of costly storage is known cash income or known cash yield. The cash income/yield must be perfectly predictable (just as the storage cost was known with certainty). The simplest example is a stock that is trading cum-dividend. If you own the stock and hold it until the ex-date, you get the dividend. But if you own a call on the stock that expires at or after the ex-date, you *don't* get the dividend. So we should expect the existence of a known dividend to affect the value of derivatives written on the stock.

Let's do a quick example. Suppose there's a stock that is trading cum-dividend but will go ex-dividend within the next month. The stock's current price is $120.00, but its future price may change—it can take any positive value $\widehat{UND}$. Suppose further that the present value of the known future dividend is $2.00, and that the current risk-free rate of return is 2%. What's the correct price for one-month forward delivery of the stock (i.e., the one-month forward price of the stock)?

---

[1] I'm writing this on July 31, 2003. I actually used the near-term (August) futures price as the spot and the September futures as the one month. Forwards and futures are not exactly the same in a world where the risk-free rate can change randomly. But they are very close over short horizons.

Again, let's start by supposing that the forward price follows the relationship $F_t = UND_0 \times e^{rt}$. In this case, we would have $F_{1/12} = \$120.00 \times e^{0.02/12} = \$120.20$. Again, this will create an easy arbitrage opportunity. Simply buy the tracking portfolio (buy one share of stock, receive the dividend, and borrow the present value of the forward price $\$120.20 \times e^{-0.02/12} = \$120.00$; at the same time, go short a forward on the stock at the forward price of $\$120.20$.

	CF Today	CF in Future If Stock = $\widetilde{UND}$
Buy low-buy tracking portfolio		
Long 1 unit stock	−$120.00	$\widetilde{UND}$
Receive dividend payment	+$2.00	
Borrow PV of F_t	+120.00	−$120.20
Sell high		
Short forward at F_t	$0	$120.20 − $\widetilde{UND}$
Total cash flows	+$2.00	$0.00

The arbitrage profit of $2.00 tells us that the forward price of $120.20 is not correct. But is it too low or too high? Well, remember that to eat the free lunch, we buy low and sell high. In this case, we bought the tracking portfolio and sold forward, so the forward must be too expensive—that is, the forward price is too high.

The known cash income (that is, the dividend) must push the forward price *down*. But how far? Well, once again the forward price $F_{1/12}$ must be set so that the CF Today column sums to zero; that is, the present value of the forward price must be $118.00. So $F_{1/12} \times e^{-0.02/12} = \$118.00$, and this means that $F_{1/12} = \$118.20$. Plug this into the table above, and you'll see that it is right. The $2.00 known cash yield on the underlying pushes the forward price down by about $2.00.

Again we can generalize. If the present value of the known cash income on the underlying is C per unit, then the arbitrage-free forward price F_t makes the following table hold.

	CF Today	CF in Future If Asset = $\widetilde{UND}$
Buy low-buy tracking portfolio		
Long 1 unit risky asset	$-UND_0$	$\widetilde{UND}$
Borrow PV of F_t	$+F_t \times e^{-rt}$	$-F_t$
Receive PV of known cash income	$+C$	
Sell high		
Short forward at F_t	$0.00	$F_t - \widetilde{UND}$
Total cash flows	$0.00	$0.00

For the *CF Today* column to sum up to zero, the forward price F_t must be

$$F_t = (UND_0 - C)e^{rt}$$

The known cash income can also be expressed as a continuously paid known cash *yield* (return) denominated in percent $c\%$, and when doing it this way the forward price will be

$$F_t = UND_0 \times e^{(r-c)t}$$

Let's back out the cash yield from our example:

$$\$118.20 = \$120.00 \times e^{(0.02-c)/12}$$

$$\ln\left[\frac{\$118.20}{\$120.00}\right] = (0.02 - c)/12$$

$$-0.18 = 0.02 - c$$

$$c = 20\%$$

The first important point here is that presence of known cash income (or yield) from holding the risky asset drives the forward price *down*. The same thing will happen to a European call—if a firm makes a surprise announcement of a special dividend payment to stockholders, European calls on the stock will drop in value.

The example of dividend-paying stocks give us a second important point. The current price of the stock is the present value of its expected future price *plus* the present value of any expected dividends. So the overall return on a stock can be divvied up into two pieces: the capital gain return and the dividend yield (or cash yield). The required rate of return on a stock is the sum of the two. What this means is that when the dividend yield is positive, the expected capital appreciation in the stock is *less than* its required rate of return.

For example, suppose you have a stock with required rate of return equal to 15% per year. If the stock's dividend yield is 3% per year, then the expected appreciation in the stock price is only 12% over the next year. The dividend yield (or cash yield) creates what is known as a *rate of return shortfall* in the stock.

The third important point, which I'll demonstrate at some length, is that presence of a dividend yield (or cash income, or rate of return shortfall) may make the holder of a call option on the stock want to exercise the call early. If the call option is an American call, it *may* behoove the option holder to exercise early and capture the cash income (along with the expected capital gain yield) rather than keep the option alive.

Let's build some intuition about this through an example. Suppose the current price of a company's stock is $25, and that the volatility of returns on the stock is 40% per year. In a binomial model with one time step per year, the up step will be

$$U = e^{\sigma\sqrt{\Delta t}} = e^{0.4\sqrt{1}} = 1.49$$

and the down step will be

$$D = \frac{1}{U} = \frac{1}{1.49} = 0.67$$

If the risk-free rate of return is 5% per year, then the risk-free time value factor over one binomial step will be

$$e^{r \times \Delta t} = e^{0.05 \times (1)} = 1.051$$

so the risk-neutral probability of an up step will be

$$q = \frac{e^{r \times \Delta t} - D}{U - D} = \frac{1.051 - 0.67}{1.49 - 0.67} = 0.465$$

and the risk-neutral probability of a down-step will be $1 - q = 0.535$. The one-step binomial model for the stock looks like this:

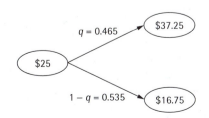

Now suppose we have a one-year *American* call option on the stock with a strike price of $20. An American option is one that may be exercised at any time—not just upon its expiration. To value an American call in the binomial model, we need two steps.

1. First, we need to value the option if it is exercised immediately. This is easy: If we exercise the call right away, we must pay $20 for a $25 stock and hence the value of the call *if exercised immediately* is $25 − $20 = $5.
2. Second, we need to value the option if we delay exercise and keep the option alive. This is easy as well, because you just treat the option as a European option over this step of the binomial tree.

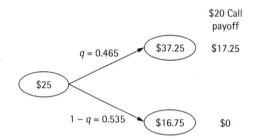

The value of the call *if kept alive* is

$$\frac{q \times DERIV_{up} + (1 - q) \times DERIV_{Dn}}{e^{r \times \Delta t}} = \frac{0.465 \times \$17.25 + 0.535 \times \$0}{1.051} = \$7.63$$

The value of the option at the beginning of this binomial trial is the maximum of the two: $DERIV_0 = max$ [value if kept alive, value if exercised] $= max$ [$7.63, $5.00] = $7.63, and the optimal thing to do is to keep the option alive.

Now let's make the problem a bit more interesting. Let's suppose that the company plans to pay a $1 dividend later today. The dividend (which is tax-free to the shareholder) will be financed by an asset sale, so the assets that remain will still have 40% volatility and our binomial parameters U, D, q, and $1 - q$ will stay the same. But the dividend will impact the stock price: When it is paid later today, the stock price will drop by $1 to $24. A stockholder is indifferent to this transaction. But is an option holder indifferent? Diagrammatically, the binomial model now looks like this:

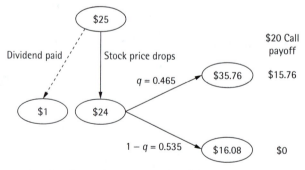

Notice that after the stock price drop, the magnitude of the up step has remained at $U = 1.49$, but because the stock price has dropped, the up value of the stock is only $24 × 1.49 = $35.76. Similarly, after the dividend and concomitant stock price drop, the down value is only $24 × 0.67 = $16.08.

This change in the stock price dynamics changes the value of the American option on the stock. Let's work again in two steps.

1. First, notice that if we exercise immediately the payoff is still $25 − $20 = $5, so the value of the option *if exercised immediately* remains at $5.
2. What's the value of the option if kept alive?

$$\text{Value if kept alive} = \frac{0.465 \times \$15.76 + 0.535 \times \$0}{1.051} = \$6.97$$

In this case, the best decision is to keep the option alive and so $DERIV_0 = \$6.97$. But notice what happened here. The anticipated payment of the dividend doesn't change the value of the option if exercised immediately, simply because if you exercise immediately, you'll own the stock and hence get the dividend. But the coming dividend payment *does* affect the value of the option *if the option is left alive,* because the option holder does *not* get the benefit from the dividend, but *does* experience the value erosion effect of the dividend on the stock price (and as we all know, European calls decrease in value as the underlying asset decreases in value). The best thing to do here is still to keep the option alive; but the $1 dividend decreases the value of the option.

Now let's really make it interesting. Suppose that instead of a $1 dividend, the company announces that it will pay a $5 special dividend later today. Our binomial model now looks like this:

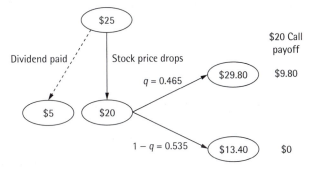

The value of exercising the option immediately remains at $5 ($25 − $20 = $5), but the value of the option if kept alive drops even further:

$$\text{Value if kept alive} = \frac{0.465 \times \$9.80 + 0.535 \times \$0}{1.051} = \$4.34$$

So now, with a large dividend payment about to be made, the best thing for us to do is to kill the option by exercising it immediately. What we are doing is giving up the option value in exchange for the cash dividend. The value of the option in this case is $DERIV_0 = max$[value if kept alive, value if exercised] = max[$4.34, $5.00] = $5.00 and the optimal strategy is to exercise the option immediately.

Figure 9.1 traces out the value of exercising immediately versus the value of keeping the option alive in our example for dividend levels from $0 to $10. The value of the option if exercised immediately is fixed at $5, but the value of the option if left alive decreases as the dividend increases. At a dividend of about $4, the option holder would be indifferent between the two strategies. For dividends less than $4, the option is worth more alive than dead; for dividends greater than $4, the option should be exercised, and its value is $5.

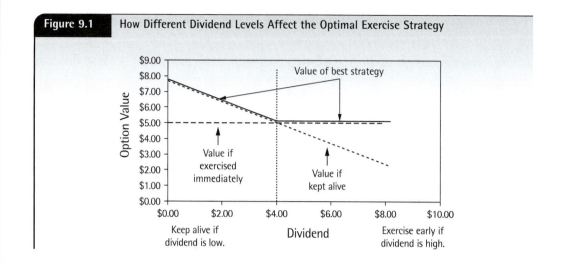

Figure 9.1 How Different Dividend Levels Affect the Optimal Exercise Strategy

The general result is this: Known income or cash yield on the underlying asset reduces the value of a call option on the asset. If the income or cash yield on the asset is sufficiently high, then the option holder may be better off by exercising the option early and capturing the cash income (if possible) than by waiting and keeping the option alive.

So whenever you have an American call option, you face a trade-off between the value of waiting (the option value) and the cost of waiting (the cash income that you give up by waiting). Obviously, if there's no cash income lost from waiting, you'll wait. This is why you never exercise early an American call on a nondividend paying stock. But if you lose cash income by waiting (and experience the concomitant value erosion or rate of return shortfall in the underlying), then you may find it optimal to kill your option and exercise early.

Early Exercise of Real Options: A Sneak Peak

In the real options context, remember that your underlying asset is always what you get back if you exercise your option. If your underlying asset is such that it would generate cash flow if you own it but you lose the cash flow if you don't own it, then your optimal strategy *may* be to invest early.

Later in the book, we'll look at an example of a firm that could build a factory and receive a tax credit. There was tremendous uncertainty in the value of the factory output, and the firm didn't want to lose more on the output than it made back in the tax credit. So, the company looked at the project as an option to build the factory in the future when more information about the value of the output became available. But there was a cost of waiting, as the tax credit would last only 10 calendar years—so each year of waiting to learn more about output prices cost the firm a year of tax credits (which is cash income). At any given point in time, the best strategy trades off the benefit of waiting (the value of the option to make a decision in the future with better information) against the cost of waiting (the lost tax shield). The value of having/ creating the option in the first place will be a function of the optimal exercise strategy.

Another example (which we won't cover, but which is very intuitive) would be a company with a new product. Waiting to launch in order to perform additional research may be valuable in making a more informed decision, but there may be a cost of waiting if there's a threat that a rival firm will enter the market first and steal market share. If the firm goes ahead and launches, it gets the cash flow from the product but bears the uncertainty of its value. If the firm waits to invest, it mitigates the uncertainty but loses cash flow. The optimal timing decision reflects a tradeoff of these two issues.

9.4 Storage Costs and Known Cash Income on Assets Held for Production

Assets held for use in production (like oil or aluminum) are costly to store, and we should expect costly storage to affect derivatives written on them just as it does on assets held for investment purposes. But an interesting phenomenon occurs quite frequently that can lead to something that *looks* like cash income on the productive asset—and triggers early exercise of American calls on it—even though the productive asset doesn't directly generate known cash income.

To demonstrate this, let's think about crude oil. After extraction, crude oil transits to large storage tanks and then into refineries where it is distilled into various refined products (like jet fuel and gasoline). Because refining is a high fixed cost, spread-type business, refineries tend to run at maximum capacity virtually all of the time. So the storage tanks exist for operational reasons: Crude arrives irregularly in boatloads, and the tanks hold the oil so that it can be delivered in a smooth, continuous stream into the refinery. Obviously, constructing and maintaining storage tanks is costly.

Sometimes, vertically integrated crude oil producers have so much oil that they exhaust their own storage capacity and have to lease storage space in the tanks of other companies. The cost of this temporary storage can be about $0.25 per barrel per month. We should, absent any other issues (to be discussed later), expect the forward price of oil to follow the relationship we established earlier:

$$F_t = (UND_0 + S) \times e^{rt}$$

For example, if the spot price of oil is $30.65, the storage cost is $0.25 per month, and the risk-free rate of interest is 1.5% per year, then we might expect the one-month forward price of oil to be

$$F_t = (UND_0 + S)e^{rt} = (\$30.65 + \$0.25)e^{0.015/12} = \$30.94$$

Let's make sure we understand the actual arbitrage activity that would drive the forward price up this high. Suppose that the one-month forward did not reflect the $0.25 cost of storage and was $F_t = UND_0 e^{rt} = \$30.65e^{.015/12} = \$30.69$. Just as with gold, the holder of oil could sell oil on the spot market, invest the proceeds at the risk-free rate, go long one forward on oil, and pocket the storage cost savings.[2]

	CF Today	CF in Future: Oil Price = $\tilde{O}$
Sell High		
Sell 1 unit oil; buy back later	+$30.65	−$\tilde{O}$
Save storage cost over period	+$0.25	
Lend PV of $F_{1/12}$	−$30.65	+$30.69
Buy low		
Long forward on oil	$0.00	$\tilde{O}$ − $30.69
Total cash flows	+$0.25	$0.00

[2] A holder of oil that is paying to use someone else's storage would simply save the storage cost. A holder of oil that is using their own storage could sell oil out of the tanks and then rent that storage space to someone else.

The key to this arbitrage is that the owners of oil (typically the vertically integrated producer/ refiners) must be willing to sell oil out of their storage tanks and replace it with "paper oil" (i.e., a forward contract on oil). The thing is, this would sometimes be unwise.

The problem with this arbitrage will arise in times of shortages (or anticipated shortages). Suppose that instead of the tanks being very full, there's a general shortage of crude oil and a refiner's storage tanks are getting low. In this case, selling the oil out of the tank might lead to a situation where the refining company can't run its refinery. As I mentioned before, refiners want to run their refineries at full capacity as much as possible because of the very high fixed-cost nature of the facilities—once the fixed costs are covered, the refining spread is free cash flow (before taxes, etc.). So, let's suppose that refineries find their tanks very low, down to the point where they only have just enough crude to operate the refinery until the next shipment arrives. If they sell even one barrel of oil into the spot market to capture an arbitrage profit there, they lose the free cash flow they would have generated from running that oil through the refinery. If the free cash flow generated by running one barrel of crude through the refinery is, say, $0.59, then the holders of oil will *not* find an arbitrage opportunity when the forward price is $30.69.

	CF Today	CF in Future: Oil Price = $\tilde{O}$
Sell High		
Sell 1 bbl oil; Buy back later	+$30.65	−$\tilde{O}$
Save storage cost over period	+$0.25	
Lend PV of F_t	−$30.65	+$30.69
Lose FCF of refining that bbl	−$0.59	
Buy low		
Long forward on oil	$0.00	$\tilde{O}$ − $30.69
Total cash flows	−$0.34	$0.00

In this case, the forward price of oil will *not* be driven up to reflect the cost of storage, because the people who have the ability to do the arbitrage (the refiners with oil in their tanks) bear a very high cost of doing so ($0.59 lost FCF per bbl sold into the arbitrage activity). This lost production value is called the *convenience income* on an asset like oil, and it leads to situations where forward prices are below the spot price (a phenomenon known as *backwardation*).

When there is a convenience income of $$C$ per barrel in addition to storage costs, what is the arbitrage-proof forward price? Well, let's go back to our arbitrage table.

	CF Today	CF in Future: Asset Value = $\widetilde{UND}$
Sell high-sell tracking portfolio		
Sell 1 unit risky asset; buy back later	UND_0	−$\widetilde{UND}$
Lend PV of F_t	−$F_t \times e^{-rt}$	+F_t
Save storage cost	+S	
Lose convenience income	−C	
Buy low		
Long forward at F_t	$0.00	$\widetilde{UND}$ − F_t
Total cash flows	$UND_0 − F_t \times e^{-rt} + S − C$	$0.00

To preclude arbitrage, the CF Today column must sum up to zero, so it must be that

$$F_t = (UND_0 + S − C)e^{rt}$$

The convenience income in commodities is frequently referred to as a continuously compounded *percentage return c%*; in this formulation, it is called the *convenience yield*. When costly storage and convenience yield are quoted in percent, the arbitrage-free forward price is

$$F_t = UND_0 \times e^{(r+s−c)t}$$

To further complicate matters, the standard practice is to work with a *net* convenience yield, which is the net of $c - s$ (the convenience yield minus the costly storage rate). If *ncy%* is the net convenience yield, then the forward price is

$$F_t = UND_0 \times e^{(r-ncy)t}$$

You can always use this; just keep in mind that a negative *ncy* represents costly storage that exceeds the convenience yield, while a positive *ncy* represents convenience yield that exceeds the costly storage.

We frequently use this to back out the net convenience yield from the forward curve. For example, if the spot price of oil is \$30.65, the one-month forward is \$30.35 and the risk-free rate is 1.5%, then the net convenience yield in oil is

$$F_t = UND_0 e^{(r-ncy)t}$$
$$\$30.35 = \$30.65 e^{(.015-ncy)/12}$$
$$\ln\left[\frac{\$30.35}{\$30.65}\right] = (0.015 - ncy)/12$$
$$-0.118 = 0.015 - ncy$$
$$ncy = 13.3\%$$

That the number is positive tells us that the convenience yield in oil swamps its cost of storage. This is quite often the case in oil (as well as many other commodities), for the exact reasons I've discussed—when supplies get short, producers that use the asset want to hold their inventories, and they are willing to forego the free lunch in the forward/futures markets in order to protect their operating cash flows.

Convenience yield on a productive asset looks (and works) just like known cash yield on a financial asset. It drives down the value of calls and gives the holder of American call options a reason to consider exercising early (because it represents a cost of waiting).

This sort of convenience yield appears in the canonical examples of real options (i.e., investments in the extractive industries, such as oil well and mine development). Undeveloped oil wells are actually American call options on developed oil wells (with strike price equal to development costs), and if there were no convenience yield in the underlying oil field, no one would ever exercise the option to develop wells.[3] Convenience yield in oil is a necessary condition for oil well development.

9.5 Yet Another Way to Think About Cash Yield or Convenience Yield

Teaching students about convenience yield is one of the trickiest problems I've faced as a professor. I'll lay out another intuition to help those that are still struggling.

When you are looking at any asset, whether it is a financial asset, a commodity, or a real asset, there's an intuitive way to understand whether or not it displays a convenience yield (or cash yield). Just ask the following question: If I lend this asset to someone else, and the loan is completely default-risk-free (either because of the creditworthiness of the borrower or because they've fully collateralized the loan), what rate of return *in excess of the risk-free rate* do I charge on the loan?

---

[3] I'll point out here that convenience yield in oil and convenience yield on an undeveloped oil field are really two different things. Fixed costs involved in operating an oil field magnify the convenience yield on oil. We'll see this later.

Let's work through a couple of examples. Suppose you own a stock that pays a known dividend yield of 2%. If you lend the stock to someone else, *they* get the dividend, not you; when they give you back the stock, it is worth less (all other things equal) simply because the company has disgorged cash. So even if the loan is risk-free, you suffer an opportunity loss of 2% by lending because you've lost the dividend yield. To bribe you into lending the stock, the borrower must pay you the risk-free rate *plus* the dividend yield of 2%. Therefore, the convenience yield on the stock is 2%.

Now suppose you own a factory that turns aluminum into end-user products, so you keep an inventory of aluminum. If you lend the aluminum to someone during a time of tight supply, and then you can't operate your production facility because you don't have the inputs, you suffer an opportunity loss. So you would charge the borrower the risk-free rate plus a premium that would compensate you for the opportunity loss. The factory's free cash flow lost from not having the aluminum input is the convenience yield.

Finally, think about the problem that automobile rental companies face. When you rent an automobile, you are really just taking out a short-term unsecured loan. Instead of borrowing cash, you borrow a car—and the rental agency requires that you repay the loan "in kind" (by bringing back the car) and pay interest in cash (through the rental fee). Even if the loan is free of credit risk, the rental company must charge you something much higher than the risk-free rate of interest. Why? Because the car loses value while in your possession. At a bare minimum, the rental fee must recompensate the lender (the rental company) for the erosion in the value of the car while you have it *plus* the interest cost of the loan. In a competitive rental market, the excess you pay for a rental over and above the cost of funds is compensation for the value erosion in the asset—that is, it is the convenience yield on a car. The car is worth less when you bring it back than when you take it out, and you must compensate the rental agency for this benefit that *you* capture while renting.

9.6 How to Handle Net Convenience Yield in the Binomial Model

There are actually two ways to deal with a net convenience yield (which can be negative, in the case of costly storage only) in our binomial model. The first way is to adjust the binomial tree for the convenience yield and then apply the same risk-neutral probabilities that we've developed before (just as in our earlier example of the dividend-paying stock). The alternative way is to build binomial trees ignoring the net convenience yield, and then apply risk-neutral probabilities that are adjusted to capture the convenience yield. In either case, the objective is to make the expected value of the underlying *using the risk-neutral probabilities* equal to the forward price.

Let's do a couple of quick examples using oil. Our spot oil price is $30.65, and the *net* convenience yield on oil is 13.3% per year. To build binomial trees, we'll need the volatility of oil, which I'll assume is 25%; given $\sigma = 25\%$, the up and down step sizes over a one-month step of a binomial tree will be $U = e^{0.25\sqrt{1/12}} = 1.075$ and $D = 1/U = 0.930$.

The first method is to adjust the binomial tree for the convenience yield and use our standard calculation for the risk-neutral probabilities. To do this, we need to treat the convenience yield as a constant percentage of the price of oil, and reduce the price of oil by the percentage monthly net convenience yield at all future nodes. (If we tried to reduce values in the tree by a dollar amount, our tree would no longer recombine.) Here's our tree after one step:

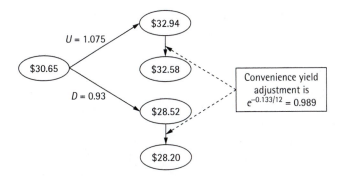

With this setup, our risk-neutral probabilities are

$$q = \frac{e^{r \times \Delta t} - D}{U - D} = \frac{e^{0.015/12} - 0.930}{1.075 - 0.930} = 0.49$$

and

$$1 - q = 0.51$$

Notice that if we use the risk-neutral probabilities to calculate the expected value of oil, we get the forward price:

$$0.49 \times \$32.58 + 0.51 \times \$28.20 = \$30.35$$

which is just as it should be—the risk-neutral probabilities make the expected value of anything equal to its forward price.[4]

Using this setup, what is the price of a $30 American call on oil? First, we calculate the value of leaving the option alive. Our option payoffs are

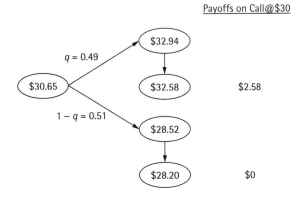

Payoffs on Call@$30

The value of this call *if kept alive* is

$$\frac{0.49 \times \$2.58 + 0.51 \times \$0}{1.00125} = \$1.26$$

---

[4] To get to the current market price of $30.65, you have to discount the forward price *plus* the convenience yield adjustment at the risk-free rate. Remember that the convenience yield is just like a dividend—it accrues to whoever possesses the asset.

The value of the option *if exercised immediately* is the current value of oil minus the strike price, or

$$\$30.65 - \$30 = \$0.65$$

The value of the option takes the maximum of the two, which is clearly the strategy of leaving the option alive (i.e., $DERIV_0 = \$1.26$). In this case, it is better to give up the convenience yield and hold the option. If we're working backward in a larger binomial tree, $1.26 becomes the value of the derivative at this node (where the spot price of oil is $30.65).

The second method of handling the convenience yield is by ignoring it in our binomial tree, but capturing it in our risk-neutral probability. Our binomial tree will look like this:

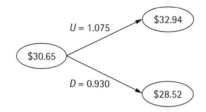

Our risk-neutral probabilities now look like this:

$$q = \frac{e^{(r-ncy)\times\Delta t} - D}{U - D} = \frac{e^{(0.015-0.133)/12} - 0.930}{1.075 - 0.930} = 0.414$$

and

$$1 - q = 0.586$$

To check that this is right, calculate the expected value of the underlying using the risk-neutral probabilities:

$$0.414 \times \$32.94 + 0.586 \times \$28.52 = \$30.35$$

We get the forward price—exactly what we want.

This time, let's value a $29 American call on oil. Once again, the first step is to calculate the value of the option if left alive. Our payoffs look look like this:

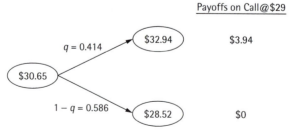

The value of the call *if kept alive* is

$$\frac{0.414 \times \$3.94 + 0.586 \times \$0}{1.00125} = \$1.63$$

but the value of the call *if exercised immediately* is $30.65 - $29.00 = $1.65. In this case, the value of the flexibility is lower than the cost of waiting, and hence the optimal thing to do is exercise the option immediately. The value of the option at the beginning of the tree is the early-exercise value (i.e., $DERIV_0 = $1.65), and if we were working backward in a larger binomial tree, $1.65 would become the value of the option at this particular node.

Note that in a 1-step binomial model, the two preceding methods will not give exactly the same answers, but will be off by a very small amount. The reason is that they converge to the theoretical answer (the continuous-time limit) in slightly different ways. As you cut time into smaller and smaller slices and build multiple steps in your trees, the values provided by the two methods get closer and closer.

9.7   Convenience Yield in Corporate Growth Options with Early Exercise Flexibility

In the world of real options, the convenience yield or known-cash returns or rate-of-return shortfall issue presents itself in many different guises. *Sometimes* it looks like a cash income or cash return, and in these cases, we will capture its effects by manipulating the binomial tree (just as we did in the dividend-paying stock example). *Other times* it looks more like traditional convenience yield in a commodity, and we handle this by building our binomial trees just as we've done before, but adjusting our risk-neutral probabilities for it. Practitioners often encounter unnecessary difficulty because they try to force the commodity-type model into situations that call for a different approach. Knowing how to approach a new problem comes from having a good intuition about how our models work; this, in turn, comes from practice.

We'll first look at a straightforward problem that is the classic in real options analysis: an extractive industry where there's convenience yield in the commodity (Chapter 10). My example is admittedly simplified; the point is not to teach you about mining or oil well development, but rather to teach you about the basics of valuing a real option when there's a clearly defined convenience yield in the underlying. We'll then look at a very interesting example of an option to abandon a foreign subsidiary (Chapter 11).

We'll then turn to the trickier (but more interesting) examples of real options where there's a known cash return on the underlying that will be lost if the option is not exercised (Chapters 12–15). The remarkable thing about these examples (the fab shells at Intel, the multiple choices in a pollution compliance strategy, and the tax shield investment at Koch Industries) is that we'll have the potential for early exercise even though the asset we're modeling in our binomial tree does not exhibit an obvious convenience yield.

1. Assuming a risk-free rate of 4% per annum, what is the six-month forward price of a commodity that currently sells for $275.00? What is the six-month forward price of the commodity, assuming there are storage costs of $3.67 paid in arrears? What is the six-month forward price, assuming the storage costs are paid immediately?

2. Assuming a 3% annual risk-free rate, a commodity spot price of $326.50, and a one-year forward price of $339.72, what is the value of the storage costs: if paid immediately, in arrears, or as a yield?

3. A particular stock has a current price of $62.00 and will pay a $2.00 dividend in four months. What is the six-month forward price of the stock assuming an annual risk-free rate of 5% and an annual discount rate of 14% on the stock?

4. What is the annual dividend yield implied from the forward contract and spot price in Problem 3?

5. Suppose a stock has a current spot price of $23.95 with an annual volatility of 35%. Produce a single-stage binomial tree to value a one-year call option with a strike price of $22.50 (risk-free rate is 6% APR). If a dividend is to be paid today, at what value for the dividend would the investor be indifferent to exercising the option now versus at expiration? (*Note:* Use Excel's Goal Seek function.)

6. Redo Problem 5, assuming an annual volatility of 40%.

7. If the option in Problem 5 has a strike price of $20.00, will an immediate dividend of $3.95 make the investor indifferent to early exercise?

8. Commodity ZZZ has a current price of $89.25 per unit and a one-year forward price of $82.39. Assuming a risk-free rate of 4% APR, what is the annual net convenience yield on the commodity?

9. Based on the information in Problem 8 and an assumed annual volatility of 28%, use a one-stage binomial tree to price a one-year call option with a strike price of $90.00. Use the method described in this chapter in which the forecasted prices are adjusted by the net convenience yield.

10. Redo Problem 9, but use the method in which the net convenience yield is incorporated into the risk-neutral probability measures. *Note:* As mentioned in the text, your answer will vary from the answer in Problem 9. However, both techniques will converge to the same answer as more intermediate stages are added to the binomial tree.

10 VALUATION AND OPTIMAL DEVELOPMENT OF A COAL MINE

We'll start our investigation of American-style real options by looking at the canonical real options problem: valuation of an option to develop a plot of land into a commodity-producing mine or well. Since we can choose to develop at any time, the value of the undeveloped property (i.e., the option) will depend on the optimal development strategy. If there's a convenience yield in our underlying, we may develop early—and our European option valuation method won't be appropriate. In this example (as well as the case in Chapter 11), we'll capture the convenience yield in our underlying asset by adjusting our risk-neutral probabilities in the manner I described in Chapter 9.

The point of this chapter is to lay out the general procedure that one might use in this sort of situation. The primary source of uncertainty will be the market price of the commodity that the mine or well will produce. What we'll do is model that uncertainty in our standard binomial framework, then translate each of those potential commodity prices into the value of a brand-new mine or well. This state-contingent value of a brand new mine or well will form the basis of our decision to exercise the development option immediately or wait to develop in the future. The added step (modeling the primary source of uncertainty—the commodity price—then translating this into the value of our real "underlying" asset—the mine) is necessary; one of the key learning objectives of this chapter is for you to see why.

I'm a firm believer in full disclosure, and I'll admit right up front that I'll be taking a modeling shortcut in order to make my teaching point: I'll be modeling coal prices in our standard binomial process, which assumes that the asset being modeled is lognormal. Many commodities, including coal, are thought to have *mean reverting* prices. There are ways to handle mean reversion in *trinomial* trees, and I've shown these to my MBA students on several occasions. For now, my goal is not to teach you about mean-reverting processes but rather to show you how to handle the early exercise feature in American-style real options. If you can do it in the standard binomial setup, you can do it in any other lattice formulation.

10.1 Introduction and Background

The earliest adopters of the real options paradigm were the major players in the extractive industries (particularly the oil industry). There are two reasons for this. First, the major oil companies have a long tradition of approaching problems from a decision-theoretic basis; option models, because they correctly adjust for risk, were a natural extension. Second, the extractive industries are closely related to the commodities markets, and it is somewhat intuitive to think that the owner of a *developed* well or mine has an option on the underground commodity with strike price equal to the incremental cost of extraction. Unfortunately, the option to turn off and on an oil well is rarely valuable because the marginal costs of extraction are rather low, and the costs of shutting off a mine are often quite high.

The more important problem in the extractive industries is to attach a value to an *undeveloped* property. Extractive firms enter auctions to either buy or lease the rights to properties that can be developed into wells or mines, and the big question involves how much they should be willing to bid in these auctions. The *value* of the property (before development) to the extractive company depends on the company's *strategy* for developing it. The extractive company *could* develop the property immediately, and in this case the value of winning the auction would be the static net present value (NPV) of the immediate development decision less the winning bid price. The static NPV of the developed property would provide the upper bound on how much the firm should be willing to pay at the auction *if they are committed to "now or never" development.*

But it should be obvious by this point in the book that the static NPV might not provide the true value of owning the rights to the property, because it assumes that the commitment to development is made immediately. Just as in the condo development example in Chapter 4, the optimal strategy may be to *wait* to develop the property. If you win the auction for the rights to the property, you are not making a commitment to develop. Rather, you are purchasing the ability to develop *if and when conditions are appropriate.* So if you win the auction, you purchase an *option on a developed property.* The strike price is the cost of development, and the underlying asset is a brand-spanking-new mine or well (with a full life of extraction ahead of it).

I want to highlight part of the last sentence: *the underlying asset is a brand-spanking-new mine or well (with a full life of extraction ahead of it).* The underlying asset is *not* the commodity itself (like oil or gold), but rather a developed property ready to produce the commodity (like an oil well or a gold mine). This may seem like splitting hairs, but I promise you it is not. If you operate an oil well, your sales revenues are tied directly to the cost of oil. But if there are any fixed costs involved in operating your well, then your bottom-line free cash flow will not be a linear function of the market price of oil. Rather, your bottom line cash flow will behave much like the equity of a levered firm—it will be more volatile than your revenue stream, and the volatility will depend on the degree of leverage (fixed costs) and will be random.

Nevertheless, the market price of the oil or gold will be the key uncertainty you face when making the decision as to whether to develop the property or not, because the value of the mine or well will be a deterministic function of the spot and forward prices of the commodity. So what we have to do is model the market price of the commodity in a binomial tree, then translate the modeled spot prices into values of a just-opened mine or well as we work backward in our option analysis.

Of course, the option to develop the property is an American call, and you won't exercise it early unless there's a cost of waiting. The point of this chapter is to show you how to do this when the commodity in question displays a convenience yield. In this case, we will build our binomial trees just as we've always done before, then capture the effects of the convenience yield in our risk-neutral probabilities.

10.2 Our Problem: An Option on a Coal Mine

In December 2000, a major coal company faced a decision concerning its future production. An auction for a 20-year lease on some Wyoming property was nearing, and management wanted to know the maximum the firm should be willing to bid for the lease.

The lease offered the winner of the auction a very interesting (but somewhat complex) proposition. The winner of the lease would have 10 years to actually develop the mine. Once development takes place (if ever at all), the leaseholder may extract 25 million tons of coal per year for exactly 10 years. If development did not take place by December of 2010 (10 years down the road), then the lease would end at that time.

The economics of the property were straightforward, as much was already known about the coal deposits and the extraction rate. If developed, the average extraction cost would be $4.00 per ton. Development of the property would cost $125 million, as new roads for trucking the coal away from the mine as well as new mining equipment would be necessary. There would be no reclamation costs at the end of the life of the mine.

At the time of the auction, the spot price of this quality coal for Wyoming delivery was $4.58. Furthermore, the forward curve for coal looked like that shown in Figure 10.1.

Notice that I've plotted the actual forward curve (the solid line) and the *forward w/ zero net CY* curve (the dotted line). This *forward w/ zero net CY* curve is the arbitrage-free forward curve we would expect to see if there were no net convenience yield (that is, if $ncy = 0\%$). The thing to observe here is that the actual forward price of coal was *below* what one would expect with no net convenience yield. One might believe that coal should be costly to store (in which case the actual forward curve would be *above* the $ncy = 0$ curve). So what this tells us is that there was actually a *convenience yield* associated with holding coal. The holders of coal inventories—mostly electric utilities—experience a cash loss if they run short of coal, and this slightly dominates the cost of coal storage.[1]

We can infer the net convenience yield on coal from the forward curve if we know the risk-free rate of interest, because we know the relationship

$$UND_0 \cdot e^{(r-ncy)\cdot t} = F_t$$

If the risk-free rate at 12/2000 were 6% per year, then the convenience yield over the first year would have been the c that solved

$$\$4.58 \cdot e^{(.06-ncy)\cdot 1} = \$4.70, \quad \text{or}$$
$$ncy = 3.5\%$$

---

[1] So, even though the forward curve for coal exhibits what is known as *contango* (an upward slope, with forwards above the spot), there is a net convenience yield in coal. Positive net convenience yield does not necessarily imply an inverted market.

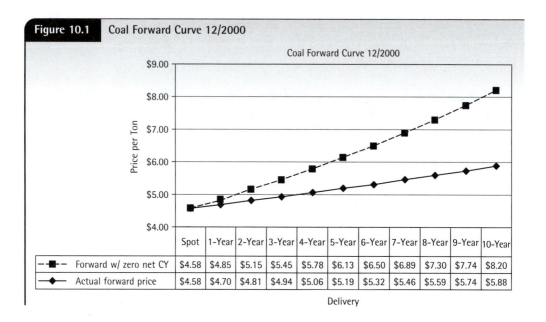

Figure 10.1 Coal Forward Curve 12/2000

Coal Forward Curve 12/2000

Price per Ton

	Spot	1-Year	2-Year	3-Year	4-Year	5-Year	6-Year	7-Year	8-Year	9-Year	10-Year
Forward w/ zero net CY	$4.58	$4.85	$5.15	$5.45	$5.78	$6.13	$6.50	$6.89	$7.30	$7.74	$8.20
Actual forward price	$4.58	$4.70	$4.81	$4.94	$5.06	$5.19	$5.32	$5.46	$5.59	$5.74	$5.88

Delivery

Notice that in the 12/2000 forward curve presented above, the convenience yield per year is constant. The convenience yield over the period (t_1, t_2) is

$$F_{t_1} \cdot e^{(r-ncy)[t_2 - t_1]} = F_{t_2}$$

so, for example

$$\$4.70 \cdot e^{(.06 - ncy) \cdot 1} = \$4.81, \quad \text{or}$$

$$ncy = 3.5\%$$

So, for our example, the net convenience yield on coal will be 3.5% per year. We will assume that this is a fixed parameter; that is, no matter what happens to the market price of coal, the net convenience yield will be 3.5%.

Static DCF and Static NPV

In this case, management might have started with a discounted cash value (DCF) analysis of the mine. Given a 10-year straight line depreciation schedule, a 40% marginal tax rate, and an assumption of no net working capital impact, the static DCF value of the mine (assuming immediate opening) would have been about $170 million, and its static NPV would have been about $45 million, as I show in Figure 10.2.

Take a careful look at how I've done the static DCF analysis in Figure 10.2. I have not built out the revenues based on *expected* future coal prices, but rather based on *forward* prices of coal. This is quite important, because you'll recall that forward prices contain no risk premium. So, the appropriate discount rate to apply to them (or to any free cash flows derived from them) is the risk-free rate of return. This is why I discounted all the expected cash flows at the risk-free rate. If you use expected future prices of coal, you would need a risk-adjusted discount rate that

Figure 10.2 DCF Analysis of Coal Mine

Mine Assumptions

Tons/year (mm)	25	
Extr. cost/ton	$4.00	
Development (mm)	$125	Date developed	Dec-00
Reclamation (mm)	$0	Spot coal price/ton	$4.58
		Convenience yield	3.5
Cost inflation	0%	Risk-free rate	6%
		Marginal tax rate	40%

	Dec-00	Dec-01	Dec-02	Dec-03	Dec-04	Dec-05	Dec-06	Dec-07	Dec-08	Dec-09	Dec-10
Forward price/ton		$4.70	$4.81	$4.94	$5.06	$5.19	$5.32	$5.46	$5.59	$5.74	$5.88
Extraction cost/ton		$4.00	$4.00	$4.00	$4.00	$4.00	$4.00	$4.00	$4.00	$4.00	$4.00
Marketing margin		$0.70	$0.81	$0.94	$1.06	$1.19	$1.32	$1.46	$1.59	$1.74	$1.88
MM tons production		25	25	25	25	25	25	25	25	25	25
Op. income (mm)		$17.40	$20.37	$23.42	$26.54	$29.75	$33.03	$36.40	$39.85	$43.39	$47.02
Less: depr. (mm)		($12.50)	($12.50)	($12.50)	($12.50)	($12.50)	($12.50)	($12.50)	($12.50)	($12.50)	($12.50)
Income B4 tax (mm)		$4.90	$7.87	$10.92	$14.04	$17.25	$20.53	$23.90	$27.35	$30.89	$34.52
Less: tax (mm)		($1.96)	($3.15)	($4.37)	($5.62)	($6.90)	($8.21)	($9.56)	($10.94)	($12.36)	($13.81)
NI (mm)		$2.94	$4.72	$6.55	$8.43	$10.35	$12.32	$14.34	$16.41	$18.53	$20.71
Add back: depr.		$12.50	$12.50	$12.50	$12.50	$12.50	$12.50	$12.50	$12.50	$12.50	$12.50
Free cash flow (mm)		$15.44	$17.22	$19.05	$20.93	$22.85	$24.82	$26.84	$28.91	$31.03	$33.21
PV at risk-free rate		$14.57	$15.33	$16.00	$16.57	$17.07	$17.50	$17.85	$18.14	$18.37	$18.55
Present value (mm)	$169.93										
Dev. cost (mm)	($125.00)										
Static NPV (mm)	$44.93										

reflects both the market risk in the revenues *and* the degree of operating leverage—but you should get exactly the same thing.[2]

Be that as it may, a static NPV analysis would tell us that, given the current economic conditions and our assumptions about the mine, the most that the company should bid in the auction for the lease is about $45 million. Any larger winning bid would result in value destruction from a static perspective.

Of course, this is a very naïve approach. The winner of the auction is not necessarily making a commitment to immediately invest $125 million and begin extraction. Rather, the winner of the auction gets some very valuable flexibility: The winner can open the mine immediately or wait until some optimum future time. The mine investment *competes with itself in time,* and this flexibility to wait actually adds substantial value to the lease.

Framing the Undeveloped Mine as an Option

Let's fit the mine into an option framework. If we own the lease, then we have the *option* to develop when we want. Development costs $125 million, so the act of developing is the exercise of the option, and hence $125 million is the strike price.

The underlying asset is always what you get if you exercise, and in this case, the underlying would be a fully developed, brand-new mine with 10 years of production ahead of it. If the coal company were to immediately exercise upon winning the auction, the value of the underlying would be the PV of the operating cash flows from the mine that were estimated earlier: About $170 million. In the earlier examples, I treated this as the starting value of the underlying, then built a binomial tree based on an assumption about the uncertainty (volatility). Here, we have an interesting case: At any point, the DCF value of the underlying (a just-developed mine) is a deterministic function of something else that is observable (the spot price of coal). Our uncertainty in this case is not with respect to the mine, but simply about how coal prices will evolve in the future.

So what we will do here is model the evolution of spot coal prices by building a binomial tree for spot coal. (The observed volatility of changes in coal prices is only about 15% per year, so our volatility will be 15%.) Then, for each node in the binomial tree of coal prices, we will calculate the value of a brand-new mine, given that particular spot price and a net convenience yield of 3.5%. The convenience yield on coal does *not* enter our binomial tree of coal prices; rather, it enters into the risk-neutral probabilities of up and down steps. When we take this approach, the risk-neutral probability of an up step will be[3]

$$q = \frac{e^{(r-ncy)\Delta t} - D}{U - D}$$

In this case, the complexity of the lease contract actually makes the option valuation simpler. The mine must be developed by December 2010 (i.e., within 10 years) or the lease terminates, so the flexibility ends in exactly 10 years. In other words, the time to expiration of the option is

---

[2] This does assume that the financial markets and the coal commodity market are perfectly integrated. In some commodity markets (particularly electricity), it appears that there's an imbalance between the demand for long forward positions and the supply of the opposite side (short positions). When this happens, the forward price no longer derives from an arbitrage argument, but rather arises in an equilibrium in which a premium is offered to parties willing to step in and make markets clear. In that case, you have to find a way to figure out what the risk premium on the commodity is.

[3] Notice here that I'm assuming that the convenience yield is fixed. This assumption can be relaxed: The convenience yield can change over time in a deterministic way, or even can be made a function of the (random) spot price of coal. If you allow c to be either time-dependent or state-dependent (or both), then your risk-neutral probability q also becomes time-dependent and/or state-dependent.

10 years. (Remember that the leaseholder can develop the mine any time before expiration and then mine for 10 years.)

To summarize our parameters:

- The underlying uncertainty is with respect to the spot price of coal:
  - The current spot price of coal is $4.58 per ton.
  - The net convenience yield on coal is 3.5%, and this is fixed.
  - The volatility of log changes in coal prices is 15% per year.
- The relationship between the spot/forward price of coal and the value of a just-developed mine (our true underlying asset) is given in the DCF analysis of Figure 10.2.
- The strike price is $125 million.
- The time to maturity of the option is 10 years.
- The risk-free rate of return is 6% per year.

Modeling Uncertainty

We will build a binomial tree of coal prices with one step per year for 10 years, so $\Delta t = 1$. Hence, our up and down steps will be

$$U = e^{\sigma\sqrt{\Delta t}} = e^{0.15\sqrt{1}} = 1.1618$$

$$D = \frac{1}{U} = \frac{1}{1.1618} = 0.8607$$

This gives us a binomial tree of coal prices that looks like Figure 10.3.

The risk-neutral probability of an up step in this tree will be

$$q = \frac{e^{(r-ncy)\Delta t} - D}{U - D} = \frac{e^{(0.06-0.035)} - 0.8607}{1.1618 - 0.8607} = 0.55$$

and so the risk-neutral probability of a down-step in the tree will be $(1 - q) = 0.45$; the risk-free time value factor over each step will be $e^{r \times \Delta t} = e^{0.06} = 1.062$.

Analysis

Now that we understand the problem, we can proceed with the valuation. As always, we start at the end and work backwards. Begin in December 2010, in the highest coal price state ($20.53).

| Figure 10.3 | Binomial Tree of Coal Prices |

Dec-00	Dec-01	Dec-02	Dec-03	Dec-04	Dec-05	Dec-06	Dec-07	Dec-08	Dec-09	Dec-10
$4.58	$5.32	$6.18	$7.18	$8.35	$9.70	$11.26	$13.09	$15.21	$17.67	$20.53
	$3.94	$4.58	$5.32	$6.18	$7.18	$8.35	$9.70	$11.26	$13.09	$15.21
		$3.39	$3.94	$4.58	$5.32	$6.18	$7.18	$8.35	$9.70	$11.26
			$2.92	$3.39	$3.94	$4.58	$5.32	$6.18	$7.18	$8.35
				$2.51	$2.92	$3.39	$3.94	$4.58	$5.32	$6.18
					$2.16	$2.51	$2.92	$3.39	$3.94	$4.58
						$1.86	$2.16	$2.51	$2.92	$3.39
							$1.60	$1.86	$2.16	$2.51
								$1.38	$1.60	$1.86
									$1.19	$1.38
										$1.02

Figure 10.4 Binomial Tree of Coal Prices

	Dec-00	Dec-01	Dec-02	Dec-03	Dec-04	Dec-05	Dec-06	Dec-07	Dec-08	Dec-09	Dec-10
	$4.58	$5.32	$6.18	$7.18	$8.35	$9.70	$11.26	$13.09	$15.21	$17.67	$20.53
		$3.94	$4.58	$5.32	$6.18	$7.18	$8.35	$9.70	$11.26	$13.09	$15.21
			$3.39	$3.94	$4.58	$5.32	$6.18	$7.18	$8.35	$9.70	$11.26
				$2.92	$3.39	$3.94	$4.58	$5.32	$6.18	$7.18	$8.35
					$2.51	$2.92	$3.39	$3.94	$4.58	$5.32	$6.18
						$2.16	$2.51	$2.92	$3.39	$3.94	$4.58
							$1.86	$2.16	$2.51	$2.92	$3.39
								$1.60	$1.86	$2.16	$2.51
									$1.38	$1.60	$1.86
										$1.19	$1.38
											$1.02

Mine Assumptions

Tons/year (mm)	25	Date developed	Dec-10
Extr. cost/ton	$4.00	Spot coal price/ton	$20.53
Development (mm)	$125	Convenience yield	3.5%
Reclamation (mm)	$0	Risk-free rate	6%
Cost inflation	0%	Marginal tax rate	40%

	Dec-10	Dec-11	Dec-12	Dec-13	Dec-14	Dec-15	Dec-16	Dec-17	Dec-18	Dec-19	Dec-20
Forward price/ton		$21.05	$21.58	$22.13	$22.69	$23.26	$23.85	$24.46	$25.08	$25.71	$26.36
Extraction cost/ton		$4.00	$4.00	$4.00	$4.00	$4.00	$4.00	$4.00	$4.00	$4.00	$4.00
Marketing margin		$17.05	$17.58	$18.13	$18.69	$19.26	$19.85	$20.46	$21.08	$21.71	$22.36
MM tons production		25	25	25	25	25	25	25	25	25	25
Op. income (mm)		$426.24	$439.56	$453.22	$467.23	$481.59	$496.31	$511.41	$526.88	$542.75	$559.03
Less: depr. (mm)		($12.50)	($12.50)	($12.50)	($12.50)	($12.50)	($12.50)	($12.50)	($12.50)	($12.50)	($12.50)
Income B4 tax (mm)		$413.74	$427.06	$440.72	$454.73	$469.09	$483.81	$498.91	$514.38	$530.25	$546.53
Less: tax (mm)		($165.50)	($170.83)	($176.29)	($181.89)	($187.64)	($193.52)	($199.56)	($205.75)	($212.10)	($218.61)
NI (mm)		$248.25	$256.24	$264.43	$272.84	$281.45	$290.29	$299.34	$308.63	$318.15	$327.92
Add back: depr.		$12.50	$12.50	$12.50	$12.50	$12.50	$12.50	$12.50	$12.50	$12.50	$12.50
Free cash flow (mm)		$260.75	$268.74	$276.93	$285.34	$293.95	$302.79	$311.84	$321.13	$330.65	$340.42
PV at risk-free rate		$245.99	$239.18	$232.52	$226.01	$219.66	$213.45	$207.39	$201.48	$195.71	$190.09
Present value (mm)	$2,171.48										

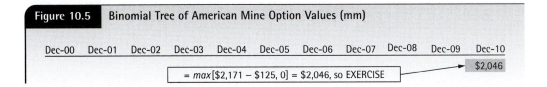

Figure 10.5   Binomial Tree of American Mine Option Values (mm)

| Dec-00 | Dec-01 | Dec-02 | Dec-03 | Dec-04 | Dec-05 | Dec-06 | Dec-07 | Dec-08 | Dec-09 | Dec-10 |

= *max*[$2,171 − $125, 0] = $2,046, so EXERCISE → $2,046

At this point, we ask ourselves the following question: If we get to December 2010 without having developed the mine yet, and at that time we see a spot price of coal equal to $20.53, would we spend $125 million and develop? Or would we just walk away from the project altogether?

The answer is "it depends." On what? Well, it depends on what we get back for our $125 million investment at that time. This is actually quite easy to calculate. Just create a static DCF model exactly like what we've done in Figure 10.2, but starting at December 2010 with a coal spot price of $20.53. I've done this in Figure 10.4, and you'll see that the December 2010 PV of the inflows of a new coal mine, given a spot price at that time equal to $20.53, a risk-free rate of 6%, and a constant 3.5% net convenience yield, is $2,171 million. Notice that we want the PV of the inflows, and *not* the NPV, because it is the value of what we get back (an open mine) *if* we exercise the option by spending $125 million to develop the mine.

Obviously, if we get to December 2010 without having developed already, and we see a spot price of $20.53 (and a corresponding new mine value of $2,171 million), we will develop. That is, we will exercise the option. The payoff to developing at that time and in that coal price state is $2,171 million − $125 million = $2,046 million. Enter this as the December 2010 top-state value in our binomial tree of option prices, and keep track of the fact that we do in fact exercise at that point in time. I keep track of exercise states by shading them; see Figure 10.5.

Now do the same thing for the rest of the December 2010 coal prices. Remember, just consider what would happen if you got to 2010 without having already developed. Plug each 2010 coal price into the DCF model, and compare the PV of the cash flows from a new mine against the cost of developing ($125 million). If the PV of the cash flows is greater than $125 million, spend the money and enter the difference in the option value tree (and shade the cell). If the PV of the cash flows is less than the $125 million, let the option die and put $0 in the option value tree. When you complete year 2010, you'll have the beginnings of a binomial tree of option values that looks like this:

Binomial Tree of American Mine Option Values (mm)

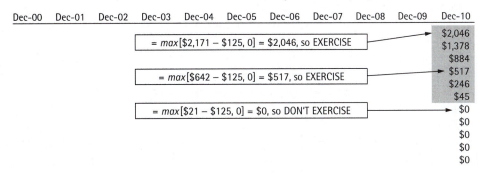

| Dec-00 | Dec-01 | Dec-02 | Dec-03 | Dec-04 | Dec-05 | Dec-06 | Dec-07 | Dec-08 | Dec-09 | Dec-10 |

= *max*[$2,171 − $125, 0] = $2,046, so EXERCISE → $2,046
$1,378
$884
= *max*[$642 − $125, 0] = $517, so EXERCISE → $517
$246
$45
= *max*[$21 − $125, 0] = $0, so DON'T EXERCISE → $0
$0
$0
$0
$0

Now we have to work backwards in the tree to December 2009. Remember that this is an American option, so in each state in 2009, we have to ask ourselves what we would do if we got there without already having developed: Would we rather (1) develop the property immediately (at a cost of $125 million) or (2) postpone the development decision and keep the option alive? The value we put in the option value tree is the maximum value of the two alternatives.

Let's take a look at the very top state in December 2009, when the spot price of coal is $17.67. If we leave the option alive, and coal prices go up (to $20.53), we will develop the mine in the next year and receive a payoff at that time of $2,046 million. If we leave the option alive, and prices go down (to $15.21), we will again develop but only receive back $1,378 million. So the value of *keeping the option alive and postponing development* given a spot price of $17.67 in December 2009 is

$$\frac{q \times DERIV_{Up} + (1 - q) \times DERIV_{Dn}}{e^{r \times \Delta t}} = \frac{0.55 \times \$2,046 + 0.45 \times \$1,378}{1.062} = \$1,644$$

To get the value of developing immediately, we put the spot price of $17.67 into our DCF model with a starting date of December 2009. If you do this, you'll find that the December 2009 free cash flow value of a just-opened mine is $1,812 million. I've done this for you in Figure 10.6.

So, if we haven't developed the mine by 2009, and we see a spot price of coal of $17.67 at that time, the payoff to us from developing immediately is the value of the mine in that time-state minus the cost of developing, or $1,812 million − $125 million = $1,687 million.

Now make the comparison. If we get to December 2009 without having opened the mine, and we see a spot price of $17.67 at that time, the payoff to us if we develop immediately is $1,687 million, and the payoff to us if we postpone the development decision is $1,644 million. So the best thing for us to do is invest, and the value in our tree will be $1,687 million. Make sure you highlight it to keep track of the exercise decision, as I've done in Figure 10.7

Do the same thing for all of the different possible spot prices at December 2009, and you'll end up with a tree of option values that looks like the one in Figure 10.8.

From this point on, it just gets tedious (although you can make the work much easier if you learn to use Excel's DataTable function, especially if you plan on changing the parameters later). In each successively earlier year, assume that you have gotten there without opening the mine, and ask yourself whether you would be better off by postponing the development decision further or by developing immediately. Write in the maximum value of the two, and shade the states in which your optimal decision is an early exercise. You'll eventually get a tree of option values that looks like the one in Figure 10.9.

This picture tells us a couple of very interesting things. First, the value of an *option* on a mine is about $142 million. What this means is that the *true* value of winning the auction is $142 million minus the winning bid price, so $142 is the maximum we should be willing to bid in the auction. Notice that this is over three times the maximum bid estimated from the static NPV perspective. Second, even though the static NPV was positive, the most valuable thing for the company to do if it wins the auction is *wait until later to develop*. How long should it wait? Well, the places in Figure 10.9 where the option value could cross over from the white areas into the shaded areas trace out what is called the *optimal exercise boundary*, and we can go back and identify the coal-price states that we would need to see to trigger early exercise. Figure 10.10 shows what it looks like.

What Figure 10.10 says is that we need to wait for a substantial rise in prices before we trigger early exercise. Notice we won't develop unless we see a price of at least $8.35 per ton early in the

Figure 10.6 Binomial Tree of Coal Prices

Dec-00	Dec-01	Dec-02	Dec-03	Dec-04	Dec-05	Dec-06	Dec-07	Dec-08	Dec-09	Dec-10
$4.58	$5.32	$6.18	$7.18	$8.35	$9.70	$11.26	$13.09	$15.21	$17.67	$20.53
	$3.94	$4.58	$5.32	$6.18	$7.18	$8.35	$9.70	$11.26	$13.09	$15.21
		$3.39	$3.94	$4.58	$5.32	$6.18	$7.18	$8.35	$9.70	$11.26
			$2.92	$3.39	$3.94	$4.58	$5.32	$6.18	$7.18	$8.35
				$2.51	$2.92	$3.39	$3.94	$4.58	$5.32	$6.18
					$2.16	$2.51	$2.92	$3.39	$3.94	$4.58
						$1.86	$2.16	$2.51	$2.92	$3.39
							$1.60	$1.86	$2.16	$2.51
								$1.38	$1.60	$1.86
									$1.19	$1.38
										$1.02

Mine Assumptions

Tons/year (mm)	25	Date developed	Dec-09
Extr. cost/ton	$4.00	Spot coal price/ton	$17.67
Development (mm)	$125	Convenience yield	3.5%
Reclamation (mm)	$0	Risk-free rate	6%
Cost inflation	0%	Marginal tax rate	40%

	Dec-09	Dec-10	Dec-11	Dec-12	Dec-13	Dec-14	Dec-15	Dec-16	Dec-17	Dec-18	Dec-19
Forward price/ton		$18.12	$18.58	$19.05	$19.53	$20.02	$20.53	$21.05	$21.58	$22.13	$22.69
Extraction cost/ton		$4.00	$4.00	$4.00	$4.00	$4.00	$4.00	$4.00	$4.00	$4.00	$4.00
Marketing margin		$14.12	$14.58	$15.05	$15.53	$16.02	$16.53	$17.05	$17.58	$18.13	$18.69
MM tons production		25	25	25	25	25	25	25	25	25	25
Op. income (mm)		$352.93	$364.40	$376.16	$388.21	$400.57	$413.24	$426.23	$439.55	$453.21	$467.22
Less: depr. (mm)		($12.50)	($12.50)	($12.50)	($12.50)	($12.50)	($12.50)	($12.50)	($12.50)	($12.50)	($12.50)
Income B4 tax (mm)		$340.43	$351.90	$363.66	$375.71	$388.07	$400.74	$413.73	$427.05	$440.71	$454.72
Less: tax (mm)		($136.17)	($140.76)	($145.46)	($150.28)	($155.23)	($160.30)	($165.49)	($170.82)	($176.29)	($181.89)
NI (mm)		$204.26	$211.14	$218.19	$225.43	$232.84	$240.44	$248.24	$256.23	$264.43	$272.83
Add back: depr.		$12.50	$12.50	$12.50	$12.50	$12.50	$12.50	$12.50	$12.50	$12.50	$12.50
Free cash flow (mm)		$216.76	$223.64	$230.69	$237.93	$245.34	$252.94	$260.74	$268.73	$276.93	$285.33
PV at risk-free rate		$204.49	$199.04	$193.69	$188.46	$183.33	$178.32	$173.41	$168.61	$163.91	$159.33
Present value (mm)	$1,812.58										

Figure 10.7   Binomial Tree of American Mine Option Values (mm)

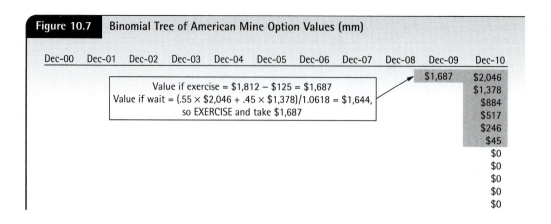

Value if exercise = $1,812 – $125 = $1,687
Value if wait = (.55 × $2,046 + .45 × $1,378)/1.0618 = $1,644,
so EXERCISE and take $1,687

Dec-00	Dec-01	Dec-02	Dec-03	Dec-04	Dec-05	Dec-06	Dec-07	Dec-08	Dec-09	Dec-10
									$1,687	$2,046
										$1,378
										$884
										$517
										$246
										$45
										$0
										$0
										$0
										$0
										$0

Figure 10.8   Binomial Tree of American Mine Option Values (mm)

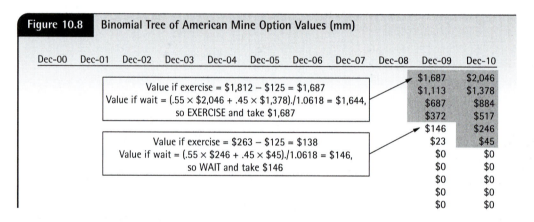

Value if exercise = $1,812 – $125 = $1,687
Value if wait = (.55 × $2,046 + .45 × $1,378)./1.0618 = $1,644,
so EXERCISE and take $1,687

Value if exercise = $263 – $125 = $138
Value if wait = (.55 × $246 + .45 × $45)./1.0618 = $146,
so WAIT and take $146

Dec-00	Dec-01	Dec-02	Dec-03	Dec-04	Dec-05	Dec-06	Dec-07	Dec-08	Dec-09	Dec-10
									$1,687	$2,046
									$1,113	$1,378
									$687	$884
									$372	$517
									$146	$246
									$23	$45
									$0	$0
									$0	$0
									$0	$0
									$0	$0
									$0	$0

Figure 10.9   Binomial Tree of American Mine Option Values (mm)

Dec-00	Dec-01	Dec-02	Dec-03	Dec-04	Dec-05	Dec-06	Dec-07	Dec-08	Dec-09	Dec-10
$142	$201	$279	$383	$517	$687	$884	$1,113	$1,378	$1,687	$2,046
	$91	$133	$192	$273	$379	$517	$687	$884	$1,113	$1,378
		$52	$80	$122	$182	$264	$375	$517	$687	$884
			$25	$41	$67	$107	$167	$254	$372	$517
				$9	$16	$28	$49	$85	$146	$246
					$2	$3	$6	$12	$23	$45
						$0	$0	$0	$0	$0
							$0	$0	$0	$0
								$0	$0	$0
									$0	$0
										$0

life of the lease, but later in the life of the lease we will exercise at lower and lower thresholds (until 2010, when we exercise in any positive static NPV state as it becomes now-or-never at that time). The optimal exercise boundary displays the trade-off between the benefit and cost of waiting. As the spot price of coal gets very high, the benefit of waiting becomes small because we know we'll develop in the future (and there's little risk of prices falling into the value-destroying area) and the cost of waiting is the convenience yield on having coal in hand (and not just in the ground).

Figure 10.10 Optimal Exercise Boundary

Dec-00	Dec-01	Dec-02	Dec-03	Dec-04	Dec-05	Dec-06	Dec-07	Dec-08	Dec-09	Dec-10
$4.58	$5.32	$6.18	$7.18	$8.35	$9.70	$11.26	$13.09	$15.21	$17.67	$20.53
	$3.94	$4.58	$5.32	$6.18	$7.18	$8.35	$9.70	$11.26	$13.09	$15.21
		$3.39	$3.94	$4.58	$5.32	$6.18	$7.18	$8.35	$9.70	$11.20
			$2.92	$3.39	$3.94	$4.58	$5.32	$6.18	$7.18	$8.35
				$2.51	$2.92	$3.39	$3.94	$4.58	$5.32	$6.18
Develop the Mine.					$2.16	$2.51	$2.92	$3.39	$3.94	$4.58
Mine Already Open.						$1.86	$2.16	$2.51	$2.92	$3.39
							$1.60	$1.86	$2.16	$2.51
								$1.38	$1.60	$1.86
									$1.19	$1.38
										$1.02

It is interesting to note that the value of a 10-year *European* option on a coal mine (with all of the same assumptions as above) is only $103 million. The ability to exercise early creates value because it allows the option holder to capture the convenience yield.

This should tell you that the option value is sensitive to the convenience yield. And it is. But some people get the intuition wrong here. The early exercise feature adds value over and above the value of an otherwise identical European option whenever early exercise is possible (which requires a positive net convenience yield). But an increase in the convenience yield increases the cost of waiting and hence makes you exercise *earlier*. The *earlier* you tend to exercise, the *less* the call is worth. So an increase in the convenience yield *decreases* the value of an American call. For example, if we were to raise the convenience yield to 6% (but keep all other assumptions constant), we'd lower the real option value to only $59 million (and exercise in the first few years at a price of $7.18 or above). In the extreme case of a very high convenience yield, you may find that the best decision is to exercise right away at the time of analysis; in this case, the option value collapses to the static DCF value.

10.3 A Brief, But Important, Final Observation

At this point you might be wondering why we went through the effort of translating coal prices into new mine values at each step working backwards. Couldn't we have just taken December 2000 present value of the free cash inflows ($170 million), used this as our starting value of our underlying, and used the volatility of coal to give us up and down steps so that we could build a binomial tree of new mine values?

The answer is no. There's a big difference between a large pile of coal on top of the ground and coal that is still in a mine. A mine has fixed operating and extraction costs.

Because of the operating leverage in a mine, the volatility of returns on the *mine* will not be the same as the volatility of returns on *coal*. Furthermore, the volatility of returns on a *new mine* will depend on the level of the coal price, as the degree of operating leverage in the mine decreases as its total value increases (just like the equity in a levered firm).[4]

---

[4] In this problem, the extraction costs provide the operating leverage. Had we treated them as a percent of the spot price of coal (as opposed to a fixed dollar amount), the effect would have actually reversed slightly because of the depreciation tax shield.

The upshot is simple: the value of a mine full of coal behaves differently from the value of a pile of coal above the ground. The value of well full of oil behaves differently from the value of a tank full of oil above the ground. Therefore, we should expect an option on a mine full of coal (or a well full of oil) to behave differently from an option on a pile of coal (or a tank full of oil). Operating leverage will not only change the value of the option—it will change the optimal timing decision as well. Keep this in mind when working on your own problems.

PROBLEMS

Discrete-Time Annuity Simplification of Free Cash Flow Analysis

If forward prices are inputs into a series of N discounted cash flows, the discounted cash flows can be evaluated in the following manner assuming discounting at the risk-free rate (let S be the spot price):

$$\frac{S \times (1 + r)}{(1 + r) \times (1 + ncy)} + \frac{S \times (1 + r)^2}{(1 + r)^2 \times (1 + ncy)^2} + \cdots + \frac{S \times (1 + r)^N}{(1 + r)^N \times (1 + ncy)^N}$$

$$= \frac{S}{(1 + ncy)} + \frac{S}{(1 + ncy)^2} + \cdots + \frac{S}{(1 + ncy)^N}$$

$$= \frac{S}{ncy}\left[1 - \frac{1}{(1 + ncy)^N}\right]$$

This is a present value annuity using the net convenience yield as the discount rate.

Assuming production capability of Q units and the free cash flow is a constant proportion k of revenue, then the present value of a series of free cash flows based on N forward prices is

$$= \frac{k \times Q \times S}{ncy}\left[1 - \frac{1}{(1 + ncy)^N}\right]$$

1. Assuming a risk-free rate of 6% APR, what is the annual net convenience yield if the current spot price of a commodity is $5.87 and the six-month forward price is $6.01? What is the annual net convenience yield if the six-month forward price is $5.78?

2. Using the annuity simplification above, solve for a multiplier (call it C) that when C is multiplied by the spot price, the value of the discounted free cash flows is generated. Based on what is stated in the chapter, are the discounted free cash flows simply a multiple of the spot price in reality? That is, does the annuity simplification have some onerous assumptions?

3. A mining company can develop land with a commitment of $500 million, which will allow it to extract 10,000,000 units of metal for a 20-year period. The government is considering selling the rights to develop land over a five-year period. As soon as development occurs, the mining company has the right to mine the land for 20 years. Assuming a risk-free rate of 5% APR, a net convenience yield of 8% APR, a spot price of $35.26, and that free cash flows are 15% of revenue, what is the value of the multiplier C discussed in Problem 2? What is the NPV of developing the land today? If the government starts the bidding for the rights to develop the land at $60 million, should the mining company pursue developing the land based on NPV?

4. Based on the information in Problem 3 and assuming the per unit price of the metal has a volatility of 35% per annum, value the development rights using a five-stage binomial tree. If a bid on $100 million will obtain the rights, should the mining firm make this bid?

5. Redo Problem 4 with a volatility of 20% per annum.

6. In Problems 4 and 5, what is the minimum spot price that will lead to early exercise? In which tree can early exercise occur the soonest?

7. What would the value of the land rights be in Problem 4 if development could only occur at the end of the fifth year (i.e., like a European option)?

8. Suppose in valuing the land rights in Problem 4, there was also the potential (a 10% chance) that the government could stop the entire program (assuming development has not occurred) at the end of the second year (i.e., preventing development in Year 3 and beyond). What would the value of the land rights be now? (*Hint:* See Chapter 8, and view the government shutdown as technical risk.)

   Clarification note: If development starts in Year 1 or Year 2, the mining company would be allowed to proceed with mining for the next 20 years.

   Would early exercise of the rights in Year 1 or Year 2 occur under these conditions?

9. Suppose the risk of a government shutdown of the program in Problem 8 was 50%, would early exercise of the rights in Year 1 or Year 2 occur? Calculate the appropriate option pricing binomial tree to justify your answer.

10. If the government was definitely going to shut-down the program in Problem 4 after two years, effectively making the land rights available for a two-year period instead of a five-year period, would the land rights carry any value (assume no minimum bid specified)? (Answer does not need any calculations.)

11

WHEN DO YOU ABANDON A MONEY-LOSING BUSINESS? AN AMERICAN OPTION WITH FOREIGN CURRENCY RISK

It's not uncommon for managers to face the uncomfortable decision of whether or not to close down a money-losing business line or subsidiary. Intuitively, managers know that there's value to keeping a poorly performing business alive just because "things might turn around." But how long do you wait before leaving a market? To what extent are your investors willing to lose cash in order to wait for the possibility of better times? Just how bad do things have to be before you should pull the plug?

In this chapter, we'll examine a situation where a once-profitable subsidiary of a major international company has become a money loser because of adverse foreign exchange (FX) rate movements. The firm must decide whether to shut down the subsidiary immediately and stop the cash bleeding or leave it alive a little longer in case the FX rate becomes more favorable. What we'll see is that the business looks bad from a static DCF perspective, but when we examine the optimal abandonment policy, we'll conclude that the subsidiary is worth more alive than dead![1]

There are several learning objectives in this chapter. First, I want you to learn what abandonment options look like and how to spot them. Second, I want you to use the abandonment option example to develop a deeper intuition about how American options work in general. Third, I want to show you how to model foreign exchange risk in a binomial tree.

11.1 Historical Background

In the early part of the 20th century, Argentina was relatively small (its population was only about 8 million) but quite wealthy. Its vast endowment of fertile farmlands, combined with substantial rail infrastructure and refrigerated shipping capabilities, made it Europe's main supplier of grain and meat. By the 1930s, its per capita gross domestic product (GDP) was equal to that of France.

But the 1930s brought a global slump in agricultural commodity prices. Many countries reverted to protectionist agricultural policies to support their own farmers, and Argentina's economy faltered as a direct result. A military coup in 1943 led to decades of political instability as well as bad fiscal and monetary policy. The economy decayed almost continuously as the country lurched from one military coup to another.

---

[1] To write this chapter, I've drawn heavily from a term paper submitted by Michael Todorow and Marx Xavier, both Kelley School of Business MBA class of 2003.

Even though democracy returned in 1983, the economy did not recover. Inflation became a major problem, and the inflation rate hit 200% *per month* in the late 1980s.

The country elected President Carlos Menem in 1989, and Menem immediately initiated a very bold economic plan that included privatization of state-owned industries, lowering of trade tariffs, and encouragement of foreign investment. Menem's most daring policy, though, was to peg the Argentine peso (ARS) at a one-to-one conversion rate with the U.S. dollar (US$). Combined with very strict limits on money printing, this policy worked at taming inflation; in fact, Argentina experienced slight *deflation* in 1999.

The problem with the one-for-one peg was that it overvalued the ARS and made Argentina's exports far too expensive to be competitive. Another global slump in agricultural commodity prices didn't help things. As the country's exports fell, the government's ability to repay US$-denominated debt deteriorated. In December 2001, the government was forced to abandon the one-for-one peg (an act considered unspeakable only one year earlier), and the ARS quickly weakened to about 28.5¢ (or 3.5 per 1US$).

11.2 Mead Johnson

Mead Johnson, one of the world's largest marketers of formulas for infants, babies and toddlers, expanded into Argentina in the mid-1990s. Initially, this division was profitable. Unfortunately, the devaluation of the ARS turned Mead Johnson's Argentine business upside down, because the company did not produce formula locally but rather purchased it with US$ from a factory in northern Mexico. The weakening of the ARS relative to the US$ effectively increased Mead Johnson's costs of formula by a factor of 3.5, and turned what was a money-making division into a cash sink.

As I mentioned in Chapter 1, you can think of this issue in two different ways. One way is to think about the Argentine division's cash flows translated back into US$. The fall in the ARS from a value of $1.00 to $0.285 did nothing to the US$ cost of producing formula, but it cut the division's US$ revenues by over 70%. Equivalently, you can think of things in terms of ARS as the local (Argentine) managers would have. The weakening of the ARS from 1 per US$ to 3.5 per US$ did nothing to the Argentine division's ARS-denominated revenues, but more than tripled its ARS-denominated cost of goods sold. I'll work through the example this way.

Whichever way you think about it, however, you should realize that Mead Johnson could not cure the problem by simply raising prices because their Argentine competitors produced formula locally. The currency risk created a *strategic* exposure for Mead Johnson, and the effect of the currency devaluation was a reduction in the value of Mead Johnson's Argentina strategy. Since the weakening of the ARS raised costs so drastically, the Argentine subsidiary quickly turned from one of positive free cash flow generation (in ARS) to one of negative free cash flow generation. In other words, corporate headquarters was subsidizing the Argentine division.

In Figure 11.2, I present a static valuation of Mead Johnson's Argentine subsidiary, in ARS, given my own estimates as of December 31, 2002; I list my assumptions in Figure 11.1. I've assumed that the previous six months' sales were ARS 7.1 million and that the previous six months' operating expenses were ARS 3.240 million. To keep things from getting too complex, I've assumed that these would grow only at the expected Argentine inflation rate of 6%. The previous six months' cost of goods sold were US$ 1.1 million, and I've assumed that these would grow only at the expected US$ inflation rate of 2%. I've made the standard corporate finance approximation that depreciation

Figure 11.1

Assumptions for Static DCF Valuation

Annual ARS risk-free rate	12.20%
Annual ARS expected inflation	6.00%
Annual US$ risk-free rate	2.20%
Annual US$ expected inflation	2.00%
Spot ARS/USD	3.380
Previous 6-month Sales (ARS 000)	7,100
Previous 6-month COGS ($ 000)	1,100
Previous 6-month Op Exp (ARS 000)	3,240
NWC as % of Sales	10%
Subsidiary cost of capital (ARS)	20%

expense equals incremental capital investment, and I've assumed that net working capital equals 10% of sales and that the subsidiary's tax rate was 35%.

In my valuation in Figure 11.2, I've used arbitrage-free *forward* foreign exchange rates to convert the subsidiary's dollar-based expected cost of goods sold to ARS. If you are thinking about an exchange rate in what is called *direct quotation* (i.e., in units of domestic currency per one unit of foreign currency), then the *foreign* risk-free rate of interest looks just like a convenience yield in the equation for the forward FX rate:

$$F_t = UND_0 e^{(r_{domestic} - r_{foreign})t}$$

where UND_0 is the spot FX rate in units of local currency per unit of foreign currency, t is the length of time (in years) between now and the date of forward delivery, and F_t is the t-year forward price (i.e., how much local currency will be given or received in exchange for 1 unit of foreign currency). On December 31, 2002, the spot ARS/US$ FX rate was 3.38, the annual ARS risk-free rate was 12.2%, and the annual US$ risk-free rate was 2.2%, so the six month forward price of US$ 1 was

$$F_{0.5} = 3.380 e^{(0.122 - 0.022) \times 0.5} = 3.553$$

I generated all of the remaining forwards in exactly the same way. (Please note that this construction assumes that the ARS and US$ yield curves are flat. If you want interest rate risk and sloped yield curves, you need a more advanced way of building binomial trees.)

Foreign exchange risk is *not* the only source of risk in the Argentine division's cash flows. The subsidiary's sales revenue itself is driven by macroeconomic conditions, so we must discount the unit's free cash flows at a risk-adjusted, ARS discount rate. For the analysis, I've assumed an ARS cost of capital of 20% per year (or 9.54% per six months). This may sound high to some, but a credit crunch caused ARS denominated funds to be quite expensive at the time.

Given all of these assumptions, the static value of Mead Johnson's Argentine division was about ARS −10.9 million on December 31, 2002.

On December 31, 2002, a static NPV analysis would tell Mead Johnson to close the Argentine division immediately. In a static NPV analysis of the decision to close, the incremental cash flows from closing the division would be the negative of the cash flows generated in Figure 11.2, so the static present value of the incremental cash inflows from a decision to close would be *positive* ARS 10.9 million. Given any cash outlay required to close the business, the static NPV of abandoning immediately is

Static NPV of abandoning = *ARS* 10.9 million − Cash outlay required to abandon

Figure 11.2 Static DCF Valuation of Mead Johnson's Argentina Subsidiary as of December 31, 2002

	Dec-02	Jun-03	Dec-03	Jun-04	Dec-04	Jun-05	Dec-05	Jun-06	Dec-06	Jun-07	Dec-07	Jun-08	Dec-08
Years of inflation and discounting		0.5	1.0	1.5	2.0	2.5	3.0	3.5	4.0	4.5	5.0	5.5	6.0
Sales (ARS 000)		7,310	7,526	7,748	7,978	8,213	8,456	8,706	8,964	9,229	9,501	9,782	10,071
COGS (USD 000)		1,111	1,122	1,133	1,144	1,156	1,167	1,179	1,191	1,203	1,214	1,227	1,239
ARS/USD forward	3.380	3.553	3.735	3.927	4.128	4.340	4.563	4.796	5.042	5.301	5.573	5.858	6.159
COGS (ARS 000)		3,948	4,191	4,450	4,725	5,016	5,326	5,655	6,004	6,374	6,768	7,186	7,629
Gross margin (ARS 000)		3,362	3,335	3,299	3,253	3,197	3,130	3,051	2,960	2,854	2,733	2,597	2,442
Total op expenses (ARS 000)		3,336	3,434	3,536	3,640	3,748	3,859	3,973	4,090	4,211	4,336	4,464	4,596
Profit before tax (ARS 000)		27	−100	−237	−388	−551	−729	−922	−1,131	−1,357	−1,602	−1,867	−2,154
Tax @35% (ARS 000)		9	−35	−83	−136	−193	−255	−323	−396	−475	−561	−654	−754
Profit after tax (ARS 000)		17	−65	−154	−252	−358	−474	−599	−735	−882	−1,042	−1,214	−1,400
+DEPR − CAPEX (ARS 000)		0	0	0	0	0	0	0	0	0	0	0	0
Less: Add. to NWC (ARS 000)		−21	−22	−22	−23	−24	−24	−25	−26	−26	−27	−28	−29
Free cash flow (ARS 000)		−4	−86	−177	−275	−382	−498	−624	−761	−909	−1,069	−1,242	−1,429
Terminal value (ARS 000)													−22,330
Static DCF value (ARS 000)	−10,869												

In other words, as long as the cash outlays required to shutter the operation are less than ARS 10.9 million, then the best thing to do from a purely static perspective is to walk away from the Argentine business immediately. The Argentine business is naturally short US$ and long ARS, and it has to buy US$ at the ARS/US$ FX rate every six months. In other words, it is naturally short the ARS/US$ FX rate. Given the current forward structure, the continued purchase of US$ with ARS makes the business unjustifiable from a static DCF basis.

But, by now you should know that the static DCF valuation and static NPV analysis might not tell the entire story. The static NPV analysis assumes that the abandonment decision is *now or never/no flexibility*, and it allows no possibility of waiting a while to see if things get better. The static DCF valuation in Figure 11.2 implicitly assumes that Mead Johnson leaves its Argentina division alive *forever*, and the static NPV analysis compares this value against the value of shutting the division immediately. If the only alternatives that Mead Johnson managers have are (1) shut the division immediately or (2) commit to leaving it open forever, then the static NPV analysis gives the right decision rule.

The static NPV analysis is clearly inappropriate in this case, because we know that Mead Johnson has a *third* alternative: Keep the division alive for a little while longer, and reevaluate the decision among all *three* alternatives at a later date (close, commit to keep open forever, or continue to wait). Because static DCF valuation forces us to hard-wire all future decision, we can't use static NPV to evaluate the third alternative.

Most managers would recognize this, and it is pretty intuitive that a decision to keep the division open for, say, six more months is only a commitment to bleed cash for six months until a better decision can be made. The cost of continuing is the expected cash loss over the time until the company expects to reevaluate the decision; the benefit of continuing is the value of the option to make an informed decision on that reevaluation date.

The problem for us, though, is figuring out exactly how long the business should be kept open (or, in other words, how bad things have to be in order to justify closing the business). It's always easy to think that one's luck is about to change, and it's particularly easy for a manager who is gambling with someone else's money to think that good times are just around the corner. What we want to do here is ascertain just how long the firm's owners want Mead Johnson to keep the Argentine division alive. Specifically, just how bad does the ARS/US$ FX rate have to be to trigger abandonment? How much cash drain should the shareholders tolerate?

11.3 Modeling Uncertainty

The source of uncertainty we care about here is the ARS/US$ FX rate. Obviously, there are more uncertainties in the business (local demand, etc.); dealing with multiple uncertainties requires a *rainbow option* model, which I won't cover in this book, but which you can read about in several other places.[2] Our strategy will be just like that used in Chapter 10. We'll build a binomial tree of ARS/US$ spot foreign exchange rates that maintains the appropriate forward structure. Given this lattice of FX rates, we'll be able to calculate the cost of leaving the business open for another six months at any point as well as the value of doing so (which will be the value of the option to make the decision in the next period).

---

[2] I refer the academic readers to the papers by Boyle, Evnine, and Gibbs (1989) and Chen, Chung, and Yang (2002) for lattice techniques.

When we start our binomial analysis, however, we immediately confront one big problem: We have to pick a future date when the flexibility will end and a *now-or-never* decision must be made. You can get around this with a more mathematical analysis that treats this situation as a perpetual option, but this book is intended for practitioners, and I want to stay with the binomial model. So I'm going to arbitrarily state that the flexibility ends in six years (i.e., December 31, 2008). This will no doubt damper the value of the flexibility somewhat, but I'd like to keep the presentation simple. My goal here is to help you learn the general method of approach; if you like, you can get a more precise analysis by extending the tree out farther into the future.

I'll build a six-year binomial tree of ARS/US$ FX rates, with two steps per year (or one per six months), assuming that the volatility of log changes in the ARS/US$ FX rate is 20% per year. Later, we'll see how different volatility assumptions change the optimal abandonment policy. Given $\sigma = 20\%$ and $\Delta t = 0.5$, the size of an up step will be

$$U = e^{\sigma\sqrt{\Delta t}} = e^{0.2\sqrt{0.5}} = 1.152$$

and the size of each down step will be $D = 1/U = 0.868$, so the binomial tree of ARS/US$ FX rates looks like what I show in Figure 11.3.

Once again, I point out that this assumes flat yield curves for both ARS and US$ risk-free investments, and also that a normal distribution describes log changes in the ARS/US$ FX rate (so that the rate itself comes from a lognormal distribution).

Since the foreign risk-free rate acts like a convenience yield on the foreign currency, we'll have to adjust our risk-neutral probabilities for it (just as we do when dealing with commodities). Our risk-neutral probability of each up step will be

$$q = \frac{e^{(r_{domestic} - r_{foreign}) \times \Delta t} - D}{U - D} = \frac{e^{(0.122 - 0.022) \times 0.5} - 0.868}{1.152 - 0.868} = 0.645$$

and the risk-neutral probability of a down step will be 0.355. Keep in mind here, however, that an up step in the ARS/US$ FX rate is actually a down step in the value of Mead Johnson's Argentine business.

| Figure 11.3 | Binomial Tree of Spot ARS/US$ FX Rates |

Dec-02	Jun-03	Dec-03	Jun-04	Dec-04	Jun-05	Dec-05	Jun-06	Dec-06	Jun-07	Dec-07	Jun-08	Dec-08
3.38	3.893	4.485	5.166	5.951	6.855	7.896	9.096	10.478	12.069	13.903	16.015	18.448
	2.934	3.380	3.893	4.485	5.166	5.951	6.855	7.896	9.096	10.478	12.069	13.903
		2.547	2.934	3.380	3.893	4.485	5.166	5.951	6.855	7.896	9.096	10.478
			2.211	2.547	2.934	3.380	3.893	4.485	5.166	5.951	6.855	7.896
				1.920	2.211	2.547	2.934	3.380	3.893	4.485	5.166	5.951
					1.667	1.920	2.211	2.547	2.934	3.380	3.893	4.485
						1.447	1.667	1.920	2.211	2.547	2.934	3.380
							1.256	1.447	1.667	1.920	2.211	2.547
								1.090	1.256	1.447	1.667	1.920
									0.947	1.090	1.256	1.447
										0.822	0.947	1.090
											0.713	0.822
												0.619

11.4 Option Analysis

What I want to do now is start at the very end of the binomial tree of spot FX rates (Dec-2008 in Figure 11.3), and translate each spot FX rate at that time into a value of the Argentine business if left open from that time onward. Here's my strategy: Given every possible spot FX rate at that time (December 31, 2008), create a DCF spreadsheet to calculate the static value of the Argentine subsidiary at that time and in that FX state.

For example, the highest (or worst) Dec-2008 FX rate state is where the price of US$1 is ARS 18.448. To generate the Dec-2008 DCF value of the subsidiary given a spot ARS/US$ FX rate of 18.448 at that time, we have to construct a new spreadsheet that uses our assumptions from Figure 11.1 but that correctly adjusts for expected inflation between now (December 31, 2002) and then (December 31, 2008). I've done this one for you in Figure 11.4, and in that figure, you'll see that the DCF value of an open business in this particular time-FX state (time = December 31, 2008; FX = 18.448) is ARS −250.678 million.

Make sure you notice how I've accounted for expected inflation in the static DCF analysis in Figure 11.4. An example might help you. In our original assumptions, we asserted that sales revenue for the six months ending December 31, 2002 was ARS 7,100 and that this was expected to grow at the Argentine expected inflation rate of 6% per year. So by the six-month period ending on December 31, 2008, sales would be expected to grow by the 6% inflation rate for six years, or to ARS $7,100 \times (1.06)^6 =$ ARS 10,071. Recall that the standard corporate finance approach is to assume that cash flows are received at the *end* of each period, so we must compound this ARS 10,071 out for six more months of inflation to get the expected sales for the *next* six months ending Jun-09: ARS $10,071 \times (1.06)^{0.5} =$ ARS 10,369. Operating expenses and cost of goods sold must be adjusted in the same way, with the exception that COGS uses the US$ inflation rate of 2%.

What do we do with this result of the static DCF analysis in Figure 11.4? Remember, we're arbitrarily forcing a now-or-never/no-flexibility decision onto the model at December 31, 2008 (supposing that we get there at all without already having closed the division). So we take the value of the business if left alive in that time-state (ARS −250.678 million), and compare it to the cash consequence of closing the business immediately. Whichever is larger (or less negative) is the best static decision at that time, and the payoff to the best strategy is simply the larger (or less negative) of these two values.

For the moment, we are going to assume that there is no direct cash consequence (costs involved in laying off employees, etc.) or direct cash benefit (asset sale proceeds) from closing the division. So if we get to December 31, 2008, without having already closed the division, and we see a spot price of dollars of ARS 18.448 at that time, an open business would have a value of ARS −250.678 million, while a closed business would have a value of ARS 0 (the cash consequence of abandoning), and so the optimal thing to do would be to close the business at that time, and the value of the business would be zero. Create a binomial tree to keep track of the dynamic value of the subsidiary, and enter 0 as the value of the subsidiary in the highest FX state at Dec-08. I've done this for you, with documentation of the procedure, at the bottom of Figure 11.4.

If you do this for all of the December 31, 2008, FX-rate states, you'll get a picture that looks like Figure 11.5. What Figure 11.5 shows is that if the ARS strengthens versus the dollar, the business is valuable, and we will want to keep it open (exactly in line with our intuition); whereas if the ARS weakens, the best thing to do will be to close the business if we have not already done so.

Figure 11.4 Expected December 31, 2008, Static DCF Value of Open Argentine Subsidiary Given a Spot ARS/US$ FX Rate of 18.448

	Dec-08	Jun-09	Dec-09	Jun-10	Dec-10	Jun-11	Dec-11	Jun-12	Dec-12	Jun-13	Dec-13	Jun-14	Dec-14
Years of inflation and discounting		0.5	1.0	1.5	2.0	2.5	3.0	3.5	4.0	4.5	5.0	5.5	6.0
Sales (ARS 000)		10,369	10,676	10,991	11,316	11,651	11,995	12,350	12,715	13,091	13,478	13,876	14,287
COGS (USD 000)		1,251	1,264	1,276	1,289	1,302	1,315	1,328	1,341	1,354	1,368	1,381	1,395
ARS/USD forward	(18.448)	19.393	20.388	21.433	22.532	23.687	24.902	26.178	27.521	28.932	30.415	31.974	33.614
COGS (ARS 000)		24,263	25,761	27,351	29,040	30,832	32,736	34,757	36,902	39,180	41,599	44,167	46,893
Gross margin (ARS 000)		−13,894	−15,085	−16,360	−17,723	−19,181	−20,740	−22,407	−24,187	−26,089	−28,121	−30,290	−32,607
Total op expenses (ARS 000)		4,732	4,872	5,016	5,164	5,317	5,474	5,636	5,802	5,974	6,150	6,332	6,520
Profit before tax (ARS 000)		−18,626	−19,957	−21,376	−22,887	−24,498	−26,214	−28,042	−29,989	−32,063	−34,271	−36,623	−39,126
Tax @35% (ARS 000)		−6,519	−6,985	−7,481	−8,011	−8,574	−9,175	−9,815	−10,496	−11,222	−11,995	−12,818	−13,694
Profit after tax (ARS 000)		−12,107	−12,972	−13,894	−14,877	−15,924	−17,039	−18,228	−19,493	−20,841	−22,276	−23,805	−25,432
+DEPR − CAPEX (ARS 000)		0	0	0	0	0	0	0	0	0	0	0	0
Less: Add. to NWC (ARS 000)		−30	−31	−32	−32	−33	−34	−35	−37	−38	−39	−40	−41
Free cash flow (ARS 000)		−12,137	−13,003	−13,926	−14,909	−15,957	−17,074	−18,263	−19,530	−20,879	−22,315	−23,845	−25,473
Terminal value (ARS 000)													−398,076
Static DCF value (ARS 000)	(−250,678)												

Binomial Tree of Dynamic Value of Subsidiary (ARS 000)

Dec-02	Jun-03	Dec-03	Jun-04	Dec-04	Jun-05	Dec-05	Jun-06	Dec-06	Jun-07	Dec-07	Jun-08	Dec-08
		(−250,678)										0

max [−250,678 (keep open), 0 (abandon]] = 0
abandon.

Figure 11.5	Binomial Tree of Dynamic Value of Subsidiary (ARS 000)

Dec-02 Jun-03 Dec-03 Jun-04 Dec-04 Jun-05 Dec-05 Jun-06 Dec-06 Jun-07 Dec-07 Jun-08 Dec-08

```
                                                                                    0
                                                                                    0
                                                                                    0
                                                                                    0
                                                                                    0
                                                                                    0
                                                                                    0
                                                                               12,935
                                                                               23,339
                                                                               31,180
                                                                               37,090
                                                                               41,543
                                                                               44,900
```

(When you do this yourself, I encourage you to use Microsoft Excel's *DataTable* feature. It will make your life a lot easier, particularly when you want to go back and change assumptions).

Working Backwards

To make the next step backwards in the tree, We have to be just a little bit careful and a little bit clever. Let's think about it for a second. At any earlier point, we have two alternatives: (1) shut the business down immediately or (2) keep the business open for one more period and reevaluate the abandonment decision at the end of that period. Our goal is to make the decision that maximizes the value of the business (open or shut), and so we need to ascertain the value of the subsidiary under each alternative.

The Value of the Business If Abandoned

If we abandon the business, the valuation is easy: We will get the cash consequence of closing the subsidiary (whatever it may be). For the time being, I'm going to assume that there's no direct cash cost required to shut the business (like severance payments, contract buyouts, fines, etc.), and there's no direct cash benefit from closing it either (like liquidation values of fixed assets and inventory). With this assumption, the value of a closed subsidiary is zero. (Later on, we'll relax this and see how it changes the optimal decision).

The Value of the Business If Kept Alive

The other alternative is to keep the business alive for one more period and then reevaluate the decision afterward. What is the value of the business if we keep it alive for one more period? Well, two things happen if we keep the business alive. First, we get the current period's cash flow (whatever it may be). Second, we get the present value of the expected business value at the end of the period, *given the optimal decision at that time*. Let's just break it down.

The Expected Cash Flows if the Business Is Kept Alive If you go back to the original spreadsheet in Figure 11.2, you'll see that the expected free cash flow in any six-month period (in ARS 000) is composed of a very simple set of inflation-adjusted costs and revenues. In any six-month period, expected sales revenues are ARS $7{,}100 \times (1.06)^T$, where T is the length of time (in years) between December 31, 2002, and the *end* of the period in question. For example, expected sales revenue in the period ending June 30, 2004 is ARS $7{,}100 \times (1.06)^{1.5} =$ ARS 7,748 (because there are 1.5 years of expected inflation, at the Argentine inflation rate, between December 31, 2002 and June 30, 2004). Similarly, expected operating expenses are ARS $3{,}240 \times (1.06)^T$ and expected contributions to net working capital are ARS $-10\% \times 7{,}100 \times [(1.06)^T - (1.06)^{T-0.5}]$ (where the number in brackets calculates the expected change in sales from the preceding period). Since cost of goods sold are in US\$, the expected cost of good sold in ARS is US\$$1{,}100 \times (1.02)^T \times F$, where F is the arbitrage-free forward price of US\$ (in ARS). Thus, given the effect of taxes, the expected cash flow over any six-month period (in ARS 000) is

$$[7{,}100 \times (1.06)^T - 1{,}100 \times (1.02)^T \times F - 3{,}240 \times (1.06)^T](1 - 0.35)$$
$$- 7{,}100 \times 10\% \times [(1.06)^T - (1.06)^{T-0.5}] \tag{11.1}$$

We have to keep in mind that we've built our DCF model using the standard approach that cash flows are received at the *end* of each period. Moreover, the source of uncertainty that we are modeling is the random spot ARS/US\$ FX rate, and the *actual* free cash flow over any six-month period will depend on the *actual* realization of the ARS/US\$ FX rate at the end of that period. So, at any point in time where the spot ARS/US\$ FX rate is UND_0, the *actual* free cash flow over the *next* six-month period will be

$$[7{,}100 \times (1.06)^T - 1{,}100 \times (1.02)^T \times UND_{Up} - 3{,}240 \times (1.06)^T](1 - 0.35)$$
$$- 7{,}100 \times 10\% \times [(1.06)^T - (1.06)^{T-0.5}] \tag{11.2}$$

if the spot FX rate goes up, and

$$[7{,}100 \times (1.06)^T - 1{,}100 \times (1.02)^T \times UND_{Dn} - 3{,}240 \times (1.06)^T](1 - 0.35)$$
$$- 7{,}100 \times 10\% \times [(1.06)^T - (1.06)^{T-0.5}] \tag{11.3}$$

if the spot FX rate goes down, where $UND_{Up} = UND_0 \times U = UND_0 \times e^{\sigma \sqrt{0.5}}$ and $UND_{Dn} = UND_0 \times D = UND_0 \times e^{-\sigma \sqrt{0.5}}$. What we care about, though, is the expected free cash flow from operating the business over the next six-month period, so we can take the expectation of Equations (11.2) and (11.3) using our risk-neutral probabilities q and $(1 - q)$. If we do this, we get

$$[7{,}100(1.06)^T - 1{,}100(1.02)^T \{q \times UND_{Up} + (1 - q) \times UND_{Dn}\} - 3{,}240(1.06)^T](1 - 0.35)$$
$$- 7{,}100 \times 10\% \times [(1.06)^T - (1.06)^{T-0.5}] \tag{11.4}$$

Equation (11.4) is very easy to evaluate, however, because we know that the expected value of an asset *under the risk-neutral measure* is equal to its arbitrage-free forward price

$$\{q \times UND_{Up} + (1 - q) \times UND_{Dn}\} = F_{\Delta t} \tag{11.5}$$

So, since our asset is the ARS/US\$ FX rate, the quantity in (11.5) will be

$$\{q \times UND_{Up} + (1 - q) \times UND_{Dn}\} = UND_0 \times e^{(r_{ARS} - r_{US\$}) \times 0.5} \tag{11.6}$$

and so, given a spot ARS/US$ FX rate of UND_0 at a point in time $(T - 0.5)$ years from December 31, 2002, the expected free cash flow from keeping the business open over the next year will be

$$[7,100(1.06)^T - 1,100(1.02)^T \times UND_0 \times e^{(r_{ARS}-r_{US\$})\times 0.5} - 3,240(1.06)^T](1 - 0.35)$$
$$- 7,100 \times 10\% \times [(1.06)^T - (1.06)^{T-0.5}] \tag{11.7}$$

and the *present value* of the expected cash flow from keeping the business open one more period is the quantity in Equation (11.7) discounted for 0.5 year at the company's cost of capital (20% in our case).

To show you an example that should confirm to you that my structure is correct, consider the date of this analysis: December 31, 2002. On December 31, 2002, the spot FX rate is 3.380. What we want to calculate is the expected cash flow to be received on June 30, 2003, from keeping the business open one more period, so $T = 0.5$. Since the arbitrage-free forward FX rate is

$$UND_0 \times e^{(r_{ARS}-r_{US\$})\times 0.5} = 3.380 \times e^{(0.122-0.022)\times 0.5} = 3.553 \tag{11.8}$$

we can set up a simple spreadsheet that calculates the expected cash flow for an open business over the next six months as described by Equation (11.7) and then discounts the result back for six months of time value. I've done this for you in Figure 11.6.

What I want you to notice in Figure 11.6 is that the expected cash flows over the first six months are *exactly* the same as in the original DCF analysis of Figure 11.2. I point this out simply to give you some comfort that my Equation (11.7) is correct; you should check for yourself that this always works. When we discount the expected FCF given to us by Equation (11.7) by the 20% cost of capital for six months, we get what we want—the present value of the

Figure 11.6		
	Beginning of period date	Dec-02
December 31,	Spot FX rate	3.38
2002 Expected	Years of inflation since 12/31/2002	0.0
Free Cash Flow	End of period date	Jun-03
from Keeping	Years of inflation since 12/31/2002	0.5
Business Open		
Six More	Expected sales (ARS 000)	7,310
Months, Given	Expected COGS ($ 000)	1,111
Spot ARS/US$	6-Month forward FX rate	3.553
FX Rate = 3.380		
	Expected COGS (ARS 000)	3,948
	Expected gross margin (ARS 000)	3,362
	Expected operating expenses (ARS 000)	3,336
	Expected profit before tax (ARS 000)	27
	Expected tax @35% (ARS 000)	9
	Expected profit after tax (ARS 000)	17
	+DEPR − CAPEX (ARS 000)	0
	Less: exp. add. to NWC (ARS 000)	−21
	Expected free cash flow (ARS 000)	−4
	Discounted for 6 months (ARS 000)	
	= Cost of contining	−3

expected cash flow that the business would throw off (or consume) if left open for six more months. When this is a negative number (as in Figure 11.6), you can interpret it as the *cost of continuing for one more period.*

The PV of the Expected Business Value at the End of the Period, Given the Best Decision at That Time This part is easy. If we keep the business open for one more period, we are maintaining the option to close it (or keep it alive for yet another period) at the end of the period. Hence, the PV of the expected business value at the end of the period given the best decision at that time is simply the value of the option:

$$\frac{q \times DERIV_{\text{Up}} + (1 - q) \times DERIV_{\text{Dn}}}{e^{r \times \Delta t}} \qquad (11.9)$$

where $DERIV_{\text{Up}}$ is the value of the best decision at the end of the period given an up move in the FX rate, and $DERIV_{\text{Dn}}$ is the value of the best decision at the end of the period given a down move in the FX rate; we get these from the Dynamic Subsidiary Value binomial tree that we began constructing in Figure 11.5.

Summary: How We Work Backwards

To work backwards in our binomial tree of dynamic subsidiary values (see Figure 11.5) we first calculate the value of keeping the business alive. This has two parts: the cash flow from keeping the business alive for six more months (which we get from the spreadsheet that we built using Equation [11.7], as I did in Figure 11.6) *plus* the value of keeping the abandonment option alive (which we calculate using our standard binomial pricing model, as in Equation [11.9]). Second, we calculate the cash consequence of abandoning the business immediately (which we are currently assuming to be zero). The optimal decision is the larger of these, and we enter the larger value in our dynamic subsidiary value binomial tree (which we began in Figure 11.5), making sure to keep track of the states in which we optimally abandon.

Let me do the first one for you. Suppose we are at the highest ARS/US$ FX rate state at June 30, 2008. In this June 30, 2008, state, the spot ARS/US$ rate is 16.015 (see Figure 11.3). Given a spot FX rate of 16.015 in June 30, 2008, the PV of the expected cash flow from keeping the business open over one more six-month period is ARS −9.153 million (as I show in Figure 11.7).

The value of keeping the abandonment option alive in this time-state is

$$\frac{q \times DERIV_{\text{Up}} + (1 - q) \times DERIV_{\text{Dn}}}{e^{r \times \Delta t}} = \frac{0.645 \times 0 + 0.355 \times 0}{1.063} = 0$$

(because the dynamic value of the business is zero in both the up and down states that follow a spot FX rate of 16.015 in June 2002, and because of the parameters we've assumed):

$$e^{r \times \Delta t} = e^{0.122 \times 0.5} = 1.063$$

$$q = \frac{e^{(r-c) \times \Delta t} - D}{U - D} = \frac{e^{(0.122 - 0.022) \times 0.5} - 0.868}{1.152 - 0.868} = 0.645$$

Therefore, the total value of keeping the business open for one more period is ARS −9.153 million + ARS 0 = ARS − 9.153 million.

Figure 11.7

June 30, 2008
Expected Free
Cash Flow from
Keeping Business
Open Six More
Months, Given
Spot ARS/US$
FX Rate = 16.015

Beginning of period date	Jun-08
Spot FX rate	16.015
Years of inflation since 12/31/2002	5.5
End of period date	Dec-08
Years of inflation since 12/31/2002	6.0
Expected sales (ARS 000)	10,071
Expected COGS ($ 000)	1,239
6-Month forward FX rate	16.836
Expected COGS (ARS 000)	20,856
Expected gross margin (ARS 000)	−10,784
Expected operating expenses (ARS 000)	4,596
Expected profit before tax (ARS 000)	−15,380
Expected tax @35% (ARS 000)	−5,383
Expected profit after tax (ARS 000)	−9,997
+DEPR − CAPEX (ARS 000)	0
Less: exp. add. to NWC (ARS 000)	−29
Expected free cash flow (ARS 000)	−10,026
Discounted for 6 months (ARS 000)	
= Cost of continuing	−9,153

On the other hand, the cash consequence of abandoning the business immediately is ARS 0, so the optimal thing to do in this time-FX rate state is to abandon the business. Its dynamic value in this state is zero, and we enter this (along with shading to note that we do abandon) into our tree of dynamic subsidiary values, as shown in Figure 11.8.

Let me do another one for you. Suppose that we end up in the June 2008 state that has a spot FX rate of 2.934. The PV of the expected free cash flow over the next six months will be ARS 0.955 million (a *positive* number, which I document in Figure 11.9).

The value of keeping the abandonment option alive in this time-state is ARS 4,316 million (be careful of rounding):

$$\frac{0.645 \times 0 + 0.355 \times 12,935}{1.063} = 4,316$$

Therefore, the dynamic value of the business if left open is ARS 0.955 million + ARS 4,316 million = ARS 5.271 million. The cash consequence of closing the business is ARS 0, so the business should be kept open, and its dynamic value is ARS 5.271 million. See Figure 11.10.

Now all you do is repeat this procedure iteratively backwards. In every period, you are assessing a trade-off: Do you take the business cash flow over the next six months plus the option to abandon at the end of that period, or do you abandon immediately and take zero? If you work the entire analysis backwards to December 31, 2002, you should get a binomial tree of dynamic subsidiary values that looks like the one in Figure 11.11.

We can learn several things from Figure 11.11. First, Figure 11.11 shows us that (given our assumptions) the subsidiary should *not* be closed on December 31, 2002, even though its static DCF value is ARS −10.869 million (see Figure 11.2). Second, when we explicitly account for the value of the option to close at a later date, the value of the business rises from ARS −10.869 million to ARS 1.485 million—in other words, the value of the option to

Figure 11.8 Optimal Decision in Jun-08 If the Spot FX Is 16.015 at That Time

Binomial Tree of Spot ARS/US$ FX Rates

Dec-02	Jun-03	Dec-03	Jun-04	Dec-04	Jun-05	Dec-05	Jun-06	Dec-06	Jun-07	Dec-07	Jun-08	Dec-08
3.38	3.893	4.485	5.166	5.951	6.855	7.896	9.096	10.478	12.069	13.903	16.015	18.448
	2.934	3.380	3.893	4.485	5.166	5.951	6.855	7.896	9.096	10.478	12.069	13.903
		2.547	2.934	3.380	3.893	4.485	5.166	5.951	6.855	7.896	9.096	10.478
			2.211	2.547	2.934	3.380	3.893	4.485	5.166	5.951	6.855	7.896
				1.920	2.211	2.547	2.934	3.380	3.893	4.485	5.166	5.951
					1.667	1.920	2.211	2.547	2.934	3.380	3.893	4.485
						1.447	1.667	1.920	2.211	2.547	2.934	3.380
							1.256	1.447	1.667	1.920	2.211	2.547
								1.090	1.447	1.667	1.920	1.447
									0.947	1.090	1.256	1.447
										0.822	1.090	1.090
											0.713	0.822
												0.619

Binomial Tree of Dynamic Value of Subsidiary (ARS 000)

Dec-02	Jun-03	Dec-03	Jun-04	Dec-04	Jun-05	Dec-05	Jun-06	Dec-06	Jun-07	Dec-07	Jun-08	Dec-08
											0	0
											0	0
											0	0
											0	0
											0	0
											214	0
											5,271	0
											17,155	12,935
											26,509	23,339
											33,559	31,180
											38,872	37,090
											42,876	41,543
												44,900

In *this* time-FX rate state, the PV of the expected cash flow from keeping the business open six more months is ARS −9.153 million (Figure 11.7), and the value of the abandonment option is $(0.645 \times 0 + 0.355 \times 0)/1.063$ = ARS 0. So, the total of the business if kept alive is ARS −9.153 million + ARS 0 = ARS − 9.153 million. The cash consequence of abandoning the business immediately is ARS 0. Therefore, the value of the best decision is

max [ARS − 9.153 million (keep open), ARS 0 (abandon)] = 0

and the optimal strategy is to close the business at once.

Figure 11.9

June 30, 2008, Expected Free Cash Flow from Keeping Business Open Six More Months, Given Spot ARS/US$ FX Rate = 2.934

Beginning of period date	Jun-08
Spot FX rate	2.934
Years of inflation since 12/31/2002	5.5
End of period date	Dec-08
Years of inflation since 12/31/2002	6.0
Expected sales (ARS 000)	10,071
Expected COGS ($ 000)	1,239
6-Month forward FX rate	3.085
Expected COGS (ARS 000)	3,821
Expected gross margin (ARS 000)	6,250
Expected operating expenses (ARS 000)	4,596
Expected profit before tax (ARS 000)	1,654
Expected tax @35% (ARS 000)	579
Expected profit after tax (ARS 000)	1,075
+DEPR − CAPEX (ARS 000)	0
Less: exp. add. to NWC (ARS 000)	−29
Expected free cash flow (ARS 000)	1,046
Discounted for 6 months (ARS 000)	
= Cost of continuing	955

Figure 11.10 Optimal Decision in Jun-08 if the Spot FX Is 2.934 at That Time

Binomial Tree of Spot ARS/US$ FX Rates

Dec-02	Jun-03	Dec-03	Jun-04	Dec-04	Jun-05	Dec-05	Jun-06	Dec-06	Jun-07	Dec-07	Jun-08	Dec-08
3.38	3.893	4.485	5.166	5.951	6.855	7.896	9.096	10.478	12.069	13.903	16.015	18.448
	2.934	3.380	3.893	4.485	5.166	5.951	6.855	7.896	9.096	10.478	12.069	13.903
		2.547	2.934	3.380	3.893	4.485	5.166	5.951	6.855	7.896	9.096	10.478
			2.211	2.547	2.934	3.380	3.893	4.485	5.166	5.951	6.855	7.896
				1.920	2.211	2.547	2.934	3.380	3.893	4.485	5.166	5.951
					1.667	1.920	2.211	2.547	2.934	3.380	3.893	4.485
						1.447	1.667	1.920	2.211	2.547	2.934	3.380
							1.256	1.447	1.667	1.920	2.211	2.547
								1.090	1.256	1.447	1.667	1.920
									0.947	1.090	1.256	1.447
										0.822	0.947	1.090
											0.713	0.822
												0.619

Binomial Tree of Dynamic Value of Subsidiary (ARS 000)

Dec-02	Jun-03	Dec-03	Jun-04	Dec-04	Jun-05	Dec-05	Jun-06	Dec-06	Jun-07	Dec-07	Jun-08	Dec-08

In *this* time-FX rate state, the PV of the expected cash flow from keeping the business open six more months is ARS 0.955 million (Figure 11.9), and the value of the abandonment option is $(0.645 \times 0 + 0.355 \times 12{,}935)/1.063 = $ ARS 4.316 million. So the total of the business if kept alive is ARS 0.955 million + ARS 4.316 million = ARS 5.271 million. The cash consequence of abandoning the business immediately is ARS 0. Therefore, the value of the best decision is

   max [ARS 5.271 million (keep open), ARS 0 (abandon)] = ARS 5.271 million

and the optimal strategy is to leave the business open.

Jun-08 / Dec-08 values:

Jun-08	Dec-08
0	0
0	0
0	0
0	0
0	0
214	0
5,271	0
17,155	12,935
26,509	23,339
33,559	31,180
38,872	37,090
42,876	41,543
	44,900

Figure 11.11 Binomial Tree of Dynamic Value of Subsidiary (ARS 000)

Dec-02	Jun-03	Dec-03	Jun-04	Dec-04	Jun-05	Dec-05	Jun-06	Dec-06	Jun-07	Dec-07	Jun-08	Dec-08
1,485	328	0	0	0	0	0	0	0	0	0	0	0
	3,865	1,933	560	0	0	0	0	0	0	0	0	0
		7,005	4,505	2,359	775	0	0	0	0	0	0	0
			10,762	7,837	5,088	2,709	929	0	0	0	0	0
				15,076	11,857	8,614	5,530	2,855	902	0	0	0
					19,879	16,579	13,020	9,313	5,666	2,432	214	0
						24,938	21,878	18,400	14,481	10,105	5,271	0
							29,770	27,202	24,262	20,922	17,155	12,935
								33,925	31,780	29,315	26,509	23,339
									37,446	35,641	33,559	31,180
										40,409	38,872	37,090
											42,876	41,543
												44,900

▨ Abandon in this state.

Figure 11.12

June 30, 2003, Expected Free Cash Flow from Keeping Business Open Six More Months, Given Spot ARS/US$ FX Rate = 3.893

Beginning of period date	Jun-03
Spot FX rate	3.893
Years of inflation since 12/31/2002	0.5
End of period date	Dec-03
Years of inflation since 12/31/2002	1.0
Expected sales (ARS 000)	7,526
Expected COGS ($ 000)	1,122
6-Month forward FX rate	4.093
Expected COGS (ARS 000)	4,592
Expected gross margin (ARS 000)	2,934
Expected operating expenses (ARS 000)	3,434
Expected profit before tax (ARS 000)	−501
Expected tax @35% (ARS 000)	−175
Expected profit after tax (ARS 000)	−326
+DEPR −CAPEX (ARS 000)	0
Less exp. add. to NWC (ARS 000)	−22
Expected free cash flow (ARS 000)	−347
Discounted for 6 months (ARS 000)	
= Cost of continuing	−317

abandon the business later is ARS 12,354 million! Finally, we can learn something very important by doing a little digging. Examine what happens if things get *worse* after the first six months—that is, the spot price of US$ goes *up,* and we end up in the highest FX rate state in June of 2003 (3.893; see Figure 11.3). Given a spot rate of 3.893 ARS/US$ in June-03, the PV of the expected cash flow from continuing for another six months is ARS −317,000 (as shown in Figure 11.12).

Yet, even though the cash burn from continuing in this state is huge, Figure 11.11 tells us that we optimally continue anyway. Why? Because the value of the option to abandon later is sufficiently high:

$$\frac{0.645 \times 0 + 0.355 \times 1,933}{1.063} = 645$$

In other words, keeping the business alive in this time-FX rate state costs ARS 317,000, but it purchases an option that is worth ARS 645,000. This is the trade-off that we will make every period. When the cost of keeping the business open one more period is greater than the value of the option we get by keeping it open, we will abandon.

How bad does the FX rate have to get to justify abandonment? We can find out by going back and using the results of Figure 11.11 to overlay the optimal exercise boundary (the places we cross over into the gray regions of Figure 11.11) onto our original binomial tree of FX rates. I've done this for you in Figure 11.13.

What you see in Figure 11.13 is that, given the assumptions we've made about the economics of the business and the dynamics of the ARS/US$ FX rate, Mead Johnson should keep the business open as long as one US$ costs less than about ARS 4.485 (or, in other words, as long as the ARS is worth at least $0.223).

Figure 11.13	Binomial Tree of Spot ARS/US$ FX Rates, With Optimal Exercise Boundary

Dec-02	Jun-03	Dec-03	Jun-04	Dec-04	Jun-05	Dec-05	Jun-06	Dec-06	Jun-07	Dec-07	Jun-08	Dec-08
3.38	3.893	4.485	5.166	5.951	6.855	7.896	9.096	10.478	12.069	13.903	16.015	18.448
	2.934	3.380	3.893	4.485	5.166	5.951	6.855	7.896	9.096	10.478	12.069	13.903
		2.547	2.934	3.380	3.893	4.485	5.166	5.951	6.855	7.896	9.096	10.478
			2.211	2.547	2.934	3.380	3.893	4.485	5.166	5.951	6.855	7.896
				1.920	2.211	2.547	2.934	3.380	3.893	4.485	5.166	5.951
					1.667	1.920	2.211	2.547	2.934	3.380	3.893	4.485
						1.447	1.667	1.920	2.211	2.547	2.934	3.380
							1.256	1.447	1.667	1.920	2.211	2.547
								1.090	1.256	1.447	1.667	1.920
									0.947	1.090	1.256	1.447
										0.822	0.947	1.090
											0.713	0.822
												0.619

▒ Abandon in this state.
═ Subsidiary already abandoned.

And do you know what happened? The Argentine peso actually strengthened remarkably over the first few months of 2003, going from 3.38 (or about 29.6¢) on January 1 to 2.975 (or about 33.6¢) by July 1, and it has remained around this level up to the day I'm writing this chapter. So not only was keeping the subsidiary open the right thing to do, it actually paid off for the company!

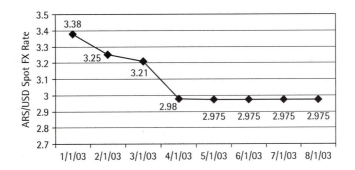

11.5 Comparative Statics

We can learn a lot by changing the parameters and looking at what happens to both the dynamic value of the subsidiary and the optimal exercise boundary.

Cash Consequence of Abandoning

Suppose there's a cash outflow required if the company closes the subsidiary. Specifically, let's see what happens if Mead Johnson were to lose ARS 4,000,000 due to an abandonment decision (in lost assets, or fines, or severance, or employee relocation costs, or whatever).

Figure 11.14 Valuation of the Subsidiary Assuming an ARS 4 Million Cost of Abandonment

Binomial Tree of Dynamic Value of Subsidiary (ARS 000)

Dec-02	Jun-03	Dec-03	Jun-04	Dec-04	Jun-05	Dec-05	Jun-06	Dec-06	Jun-07	Dec-07	Jun-08	Dec-08
−1,134	−2,896	−3,951	−4,000	−4,000	−4,000	−4,000	−4,000	−4,000	−4,000	−4,000	−4,000	−4,000
	1,880	−539	−2,493	−3,745	−4,000	−4,000	−4,000	−4,000	−4,000	−4,000	−4,000	−4,000
		5,554	2,652	24	−2,129	−3,566	−4,000	−4,000	−4,000	−4,000	−4,000	−4,000
			9,786	6,533	3,373	495	−1,872	−3,465	−4,000	−4,000	−4,000	−4,000
				14,522	11,068	7,504	3,992	765	−1,873	−3,566	−4,000	−4,000
					19,655	16,234	12,492	8,510	4,449	605	−2,505	−4,000
						24,895	21,806	18,282	14,286	9,784	4,742	−871
							29,770	27,202	24,262	20,922	17,155	12,935
								33,925	31,780	29,315	26,509	23,339
									37,446	35,641	33,559	31,180
										40,409	38,872	37,090
											42,876	41,543
												44,900

Abandon in this state.

Optimal Exercise Boundary Given ARS 4 Million Cost of Abandonment

Dec-02	Jun-03	Dec-03	Jun-04	Dec-04	Jun-05	Dec-05	Jun-06	Dec-06	Jun-07	Dec-07	Jun-08	Dec-08
3.38	3.893	4.485	5.166	5.951	6.855	7.896	9.096	10.478	12.069	13.903	16.015	18.448
	2.934	3.380	3.893	4.485	5.166	5.951	6.855	7.896	9.096	10.478	12.069	13.903
		2.547	2.934	3.380	3.893	4.485	5.166	5.951	6.855	7.896	9.096	10.478
			2.211	2.547	2.934	3.380	3.893	4.485	5.166	5.951	6.855	7.896
				1.920	2.211	2.547	2.934	3.380	3.893	4.485	5.166	5.951
					1.667	1.920	2.211	2.547	2.934	3.380	3.893	4.485
						1.447	1.667	1.920	2.211	2.547	2.934	3.380
							1.256	1.447	1.667	1.920	2.211	2.547
								1.090	1.256	1.447	1.667	1.920
									0.947	1.090	1.256	1.447
										0.822	0.947	1.090
											0.713	0.822
												0.619

Abandon in this state.
Subsidiary already abandoned.

If the cash cost of closing the subsidiary is ARS 4 million, then the dynamic value of the subsidiary will fall all the way to ARS −1.134 million; however, Mead Johnson would optimally keep the division open anyway, because the cost of abandoning would swamp the benefit of abandoning. Figure 11.14 gives the new dynamic subsidiary value tree and new optimal exercise boundary. When abandonment is costly in and of itself, the abandonment option is less valuable, and yet we wait *longer* to abandon.

On the other hand, if there's a direct cash inflow from abandonment (perhaps from selling assets), then the dynamic value of the subsidiary goes up, the value of the abandonment option goes up, and yet we abandon *earlier*.

Volatility

If we drop the volatility of the ARS/US$ FX rate to 10% (and return to our original assumption of no cash consequence of abandonment), the value of the abandonment option drops, the dynamic subsidiary value drops to ARS 97 million, and we abandon earlier and at lower FX rates, as Figure 11.15 summarizes.

Figure 11.15 Valuation of the Subsidiary Assuming a 10% Volatility

Binomial Tree of Dynamic Value of Subsidiary (ARS 000)

Dec-02	Jun-03	Dec-03	Jun-04	Dec-04	Jun-05	Dec-05	Jun-06	Dec-06	Jun-07	Dec-07	Jun-08	Dec-08
97	0	0	0	0	0	0	0	0	0	0	0	0
	689	290	48	0	0	0	0	0	0	0	0	0
		1,742	1,105	582	202	0	0	0	0	0	0	0
			3,139	2,314	1,574	943	450	124	0	0	0	0
				4,786	3,766	2,814	1,955	1,216	626	212	0	0
					6,853	5,576	4,328	3,143	2,061	1,132	419	0
						9,883	8,371	6,792	5,154	3,466	1,742	0
							14,167	12,781	11,319	9,784	8,182	6,519
								18,282	17,050	15,746	14,372	12,935
									22,026	20,922	19,747	18,504
										25,415	24,412	23,339
											28,462	27,537
												31,180

Abandon in this state.

Binomial Tree of Spot ARS/US$ FX Rates and Optimal Exercise Boundary, Given 10% Volatility

Dec-02	Jun-03	Dec-03	Jun-04	Dec-04	Jun-05	Dec-05	Jun-06	Dec-06	Jun-07	Dec-07	Jun-08	Dec-08
3.38	3.628	3.893	4.179	4.485	4.814	5.166	5.545	5.951	6.387	6.855	7.357	7.896
	3.149	3.380	3.628	3.893	4.179	4.485	4.814	5.166	5.545	5.951	6.387	6.855
		2.934	3.149	3.380	3.628	3.893	4.179	4.485	4.814	5.166	5.545	5.951
			2.734	2.934	3.149	3.380	3.628	3.893	4.179	4.485	4.814	5.166
				2.547	2.734	2.934	3.149	3.380	3.628	3.893	4.179	4.485
					2.373	2.547	2.734	2.934	3.149	3.380	3.628	3.893
						2.211	2.373	2.547	2.734	2.934	3.149	3.380
							2.060	2.211	2.373	2.547	2.734	2.934
								1.920	2.060	2.211	2.373	2.547
									1.789	1.920	2.060	2.211
										1.667	1.789	1.920
											1.553	1.667
												1.447

Abandon in this time-state.
Subsidiary already abandoned.

On the other hand, if we increase volatility to 60%, the value of the abandonment option goes up, the dynamic value of the subsidiary jumps to ARS 13.977 million, and we wait longer and for worse FX rates to abandon, as shown in Figure 11.16.

Figure 11.16   Valuation of the Subsidiary Assuming a 60% Volatility

Binomial Tree of Dynamic Value of Subsidiary (ARS 000)

Dec-02	Jun-03	Dec-03	Jun-04	Dec-04	Jun-05	Dec-05	Jun-06	Dec-06	Jun-07	Dec-07	Jun-08	Dec-08
13,977	6,198	125	0	0	0	0	0	0	0	0	0	0
	22,066	14,317	6,284	81	0	0	0	0	0	0	0	0
		29,381	22,475	14,380	6,126	0	0	0	0	0	0	0
			35,676	29,902	22,533	13,985	5,557	0	0	0	0	0
				40,936	36,393	30,108	22,024	12,707	4,028	0	0	0
					45,185	41,889	36,951	29,926	20,580	9,545	0	0
						48,440	46,286	42,838	37,514	29,474	17,526	0
							50,769	49,490	47,359	44,002	38,872	31,180
								52,350	51,603	50,288	48,168	44,900
									53,419	52,979	52,147	50,772
										54,131	53,850	53,286
											54,579	54,362
												54,822

▨ Abandon in this state.

Binomial Tree of Spot ARS/US$ FX Rates And Optimal Abandonment Boundary, Given Volatility = 60%

Dec-02	Jun-03	Dec-03	Jun-04	Dec-04	Jun-05	Dec-05	Jun-06	Dec-06	Jun-07	Dec-07	Jun-08	Dec-08
3.38	5.166	7.896	12.069	18.448	28.196	43.097	65.837	100.68	153.89	235.22	359.52	549.520
	2.211	3.380	5.166	7.896	12.069	18.448	28.196	43.097	65.873	100.68	153.89	235.219
		1.447	2.211	3.380	5.166	7.896	12.069	18.448	28.196	43.097	65.873	100.684
			0.947	1.447	2.211	3.380	5.166	7.896	12.069	18.448	28.196	43.097
				0.619	0.947	1.447	2.211	3.380	5.166	7.896	12.069	18.448
					0.405	0.619	0.947	1.447	2.211	3.380	5.166	7.896
						0.265	0.405	0.619	0.947	1.447	2.211	3.380
							0.173	0.265	0.405	0.619	0.947	1.447
								0.113	0.173	0.265	0.405	0.619
									0.074	0.113	0.173	0.265
										0.049	0.074	0.113
											0.032	0.049
												0.021

▨ Abandon in this time.
═ Subsidiary already abandoned.

11.6   References

Boyle, P., J. Evnine, and S. Gibbs, 1989. "Numerical Evaluation of Multivariate Contingent Claims," *Review of Financial Studies* 2(2), 241–450.

Chen, R., S. Chung, and T. Yang, 2002. "Option Pricing in a Multi-Asset, Complete Market Economy," *Journal of Financial and Quantitative Analysis* 37(4), 649–667.

PROBLEMS

Adapting techniques developed in Arnold and James (2000), the pro forma analysis performed in Figure 11.2 becomes a function of the initial sales level (7,100), the initial COGS level (US$1,100), the initial operating expense level (3,240), the initial exchange rate (3.380), and the working capital based on a percentage of sales (10%).

$$NPV = -10{,}869.23 = [7{,}100 - 3{,}240] \times 10.157781 - [1{,}100 \times 3.380]$$
$$\times 13.383451 - [7{,}100 \times 10\%] \times 0.448726$$

Note: The coefficients: 10.157781, 13.383451, and 0.448726 remain constant if model parameters from the pro forma analysis other than the five function inputs remain constant.

Arnold, T., and J. James, 2000. "Finding Firm Value without a Pro Forma Analysis," *Financial Analysts Journal* (March/April), 77–84.

1. Using the NPV calculation for Figure 11.2 based on the Arnold-James technique, solve for the exchange rate that will make the NPV equal to zero.

2. Reproduce the NPV calculation of Figure 11.4 using the Arnold-James technique described above. Next, determine what exchange rate will set the NPV equal to zero.

   Note: Let Dec-08 sales be 10,071.49, let Dec-08 COGS (USD) be 1,2378.78, and let the exchange rate be 18.4476 to provide greater accuracy in the calculation.

3. If Problem 2 also included ARS 4 million abandonment cost, what exchange rate will set the NPV equal to – ARS 4 million (−4,000 in the units used in the exercise)?

4. Extend the ARS/US$ binomial tree (Figure 11.3) two more periods. (*Hint:* Take advantage of the patterns that exist in the tree already.) Based on this extended tree, what are the 15 final node values (i.e., Dec-09) for the associated subsidiary value binomial tree? (Hint: Determine the exchange rate that sets the NPV to equal zero.)

   Note: Let Dec-09 sales be 10,675.77, let Dec-09 COGS (USD) be 1,263.55, and let Dec-09 operating expenses be 4,871.76.

5. In Figure 11.11, produce the associated calculations for finding the value of 214 in the Jun-08 column of the subsidiary value binomial tree. *Note:* There may be rounding error due to the exchange rate being truncated.

6. In Figure 11.14, produce the associated calculations for finding the value of −2,505 in the Jun-08 column of the subsidiary value binomial tree. *Note:* There may be rounding error due to the exchange rate being truncated.

7. In Figure 11.14, produce the associated calculations for finding the value of 4,742 in the Jun-08 column of the subsidiary value binomial tree. *Note:* There may be rounding error due to the exchange rate being truncated.

8. In Figure 11.15, produce the associated calculations for finding the value of 450 in the Jun-06 column of the subsidiary value binomial tree. *Note:* There may be rounding error due to the exchange rate being truncated. (*Hint:* Remember to adjust probabilities.)

9. In Figure 11.16, produce the associated calculations for finding the value of 29,902 in the Dec-04 column of the subsidiary value binomial tree. *Note:* There may be rounding error due to the exchange rate being truncated. (*Hint:* Remember to adjust probabilities.)

12

VALUE EROSION AS CONVENIENCE YIELD: THE INCREDIBLE SHRINKING OIL WELL

An extremely important takeaway from Chapters 9 and 10 is the result that American call options are never exercised early unless there's a convenience yield in the underlying asset. Convenience yield (or rate of return shortfall) creates a cost of waiting, and without it you're always better off keeping an American call alive.

Recognizing this, you might understand how surprised I was in November 2004 to read that several small oil and gas development firms in Texas were spending significant amounts of capital to redevelop oil wells that had been abandoned (or "shut in") by major oil companies many years earlier, in spite of the fact that oil futures prices did not display a net convenience yield.

For example, a 12-employee company out of Corpus Christy, Texas, called Dewbre Petroleum spent about $750,000 to reopen a well that had been shut in by Atlantic Richfield in the 1980s even though the oil futures reflected a net cost of carry at the time (i.e., a negative net convenience yield). Press reports attributed the activity to a bump in spot prices, but I knew better—high spot prices alone are *not* enough to trigger exercise of an American call, and an option to redevelop a shut-in well is fundamentally no different from an option to develop a new one. Existence of convenience yield is a necessary condition for early exercise of either, and I was quite interested to find out why these companies appeared to be acting suboptimally.[1]

I did some digging, and I learned something very important. As it turns out, companies like Dewbre were acting rationally after all. The shut-in wells presented a very unique complication that created the effect of a convenience yield: The leases on these properties were still active but about to expire. As each year passes, the remaining lease term gets smaller and smaller, and in the eyes of the leaseholder the underlying asset (a redeveloped oil well) effectively shrinks in size. This shrinkage in the value of the well (to the leaseholder) serves to create a rate of return shortfall that induces early exercise of the American call.

---

[1] Kennett, Jim, "Small Drillers Rush to Tap Oil While Crude Prices are High," *Seattle Times*, November 1, 2004.

Let me make one thing perfectly clear before going any further. While the specific problem I'm about to show you focuses on an extractive industry (oil well development), the principle I'm trying to get across is much more general. This is not just a story about oil well development. Rather, it is a story about *any* situation where you stand to lose something by waiting to exercise an American call.

12.1 Background

In the United States, laws that govern the ownership of underground minerals and hydrocarbons are very complex.[2] Nevertheless, the standard process for securing rights to hydrocarbons works as follows.

Production companies use sophisticated scientific techniques to ascertain where hydrocarbon reserves are most likely to be. They then employ people known in the business as *landmen* to locate the owners of the mineral rights under a particular parcel of property, verify the ownership of those rights, and then negotiate a mineral lease, which transfers ownership of the hydrocarbons from the legitimate owner to the leaseholder.[3] The mineral lease typically involves a bonus payment, which is a lump sum price per acre paid to the owner of the mineral rights, along with a royalty agreement. Mineral leases are never perpetual, but rather have fixed time horizons. Leases may be renegotiated at any time, but this typically involves a new bonus payment along with renegotiation of the royalty.

Once an oil well has been developed, the production company always has the option to abandon it if economic conditions so dictate (an analysis like the one in Chapter 11 would predict when optimal abandonment would take place). Production companies typically plug abandoned wells with concrete to prevent leakage; once plugged, the mineral leaseholder has an option to redevelop.

To redevelop a plugged well, one must only drill out the concrete. The cost of redevelopment is nontrivial but significantly less than the cost of drilling a new well. A lot of bad things can happen to a well that has been shut in for an extended amount of time, however, and the expected production quantities from redeveloped wells are usually small. For this reason, large exploration and development companies usually don't redevelop wells; this job is left to small companies like Dewbre, who sublet the mineral rights for the remainder of the original lease's life. Reopening a well is a rather quick process, typically taking only 10–12 days of time.

12.2 Our Problem

We'll consider a plugged well that has four years remaining on its mineral lease. We'll assume that the well can produce 100,000 barrels of crude per year, with a per-barrel extraction cost of $5 and revenue-related payments (royalties, severance taxes, and ad valorem taxes) equal to 25%

---

[2] Most states distinguish between surface ownership of a property and mineral ownership (rights to the minerals under the property). In Louisiana, for example, a party that sells the surface ownership of a parcel of land may, under certain conditions, retain ownership of the minerals under the property for 10 years plus one day.

[3] This alone does not give the leaseholder the right to enter the property or drill on it. That requires another lease of surface rights.

Figure 12.1	Static DCF Valuation of an Immediately Reopened Well				

	Year	0	1	2	3	4
Spot crude		$45.00				
Forward crude			$47.31	$49.73	$52.28	$54.96
Barrels produced			100,000	100,000	100,000	100,000
Revenue			$4,730,720	$4,973,269	$5,228,254	$5,496,312
Less: extr. cost			500,000	500,000	500,000	500,000
Less: sev./royalty			1,182,680	1,243,317	1,307,064	1,374,078
Operating income			3,048,040	3,229,952	3,421,191	3,622,234
Less: fixed costs			2,920,000	2,920,000	2,920,000	2,920,000
Profit before tax			128,040	309,952	501,191	702,234
Tax expense			44,814	108,483	175,417	245,782
Free cash flow			$83,226	$201,469	$325,774	$456,452
PV of inflows		$915,571				

of production revenue.[4] These are deductible from taxable income; the tax rate is 35%. The major fixed expense of operating a small well is the rental of a rig, which is $8,000 per day (or $2,920,000 per year).

To calculate revenues, we will need to know spot and forward prices for crude. We'll assume a spot price of crude of $45 per barrel, with a net convenience yield of exactly zero. Given a 5% risk-free rate of return, the one-, two-, three-, and four-year forward prices for crude will be

$$F_1 = \$45 \times e^{(0.05-0.00)\times 1} = \$47.31$$
$$F_2 = \$45 \times e^{(0.05-0.00)\times 2} = \$49.73$$
$$F_3 = \$45 \times e^{(0.05-0.00)\times 3} = \$52.28$$
$$F_4 = \$45 \times e^{(0.05-0.00)\times 4} = \$54.96$$

The well costs $750,000 to redevelop. For this illustration, I'm going to ignore depreciation as it would only add an unnecessary nuisance to the option problem; if you like, you may think of it as if the redevelopment costs are expensed rather than capitalized, and that the cost I quote is an after-tax number. I'll also assume that there are no net working capital commitments involved in operating the well.

Static NPV Analysis of Opportunity to Redevelop

Figure 12.1 presents my static discounted cash flow (DCF) valuation of the immediately redeveloped well. In my DCF valuation, the only source of risk is oil price risk. Since I've valued the well off of the oil forward curve, the appropriate discount rate to use in the analysis is the risk-free rate (which we've assumed to be 5%). In Figure 12.1, I've discounted the future cash flows assuming *continuous compounding of returns* so that I can make one teaching point (which you'll see very shortly).[5] Given continuous discounting, the current value of an immediately reopened well is $915,571.

---

[4] In the United States, it is typical for a well operator to pay $\frac{1}{7}$ of the well's revenues as a royalty to the party that owns the mineral rights. Furthermore, states (and even counties) add a variety of taxes at the wellhead. For example, the state of Wyoming charges a 6% severance (or excise) tax, an ad valorem tax of between 5.9% and 7% (depending on the school district in which the well sits), and a small conservation tax, all levied against revenues.

[5] With continuous compounding, the PV factor for a cash flow to be received T years in the future is e^{-rT}.

Before we go any further, I want to remind everyone of a standard convention in corporate finance: When we create a spreadsheet of free cash flows (like Figure 12.1), we impose the artificial short cut that a period's total cash flows are received at the *end* of that period. In reality, the cash flows from a well would be received throughout the year; we'd get a closer and closer approximation of the exact static DCF value if we slimmed our time periods down into months, or weeks, or even days. However, the benefit from doing so is small. Just keep in mind that, for example, $83,226 is the expected cash flow over the entire first year—not really to be received in one lump sum at the end of the year.

Given a static DCF value of $915,571, the static net present value (NPV) of redeveloping the well is $915,571 − $750,000 = $165,571. Remember that this only compares *now* versus *never again*. If our only alternatives are to either (1) develop the well immediately at a cost of $750,000 or (2) ignore the opportunity forever from this point forward, the static NPV analysis tells us that the best choice is the former. But we know that there's a third choice here: Do nothing today, and reevaluate the decision in the future (say, at the end of one year).

Based on what we learned in Chapters 9 and 10, you may be thinking that we should wait to develop since we've assumed that the net convenience yield on crude is zero. As you'll see later on, this may not be correct. It *may* be optimal for us to develop this well early for one very important reason: With this particular investment opportunity, there's another huge cost of waiting. Specifically, if we wait one year to develop, the opportunity changes from a well with four years of production to a well with only three. In other words, the well *shrinks* as we wait. Our optimal development decision must take this shrinkage into account.

12.3 Modeling the Uncertainty in the Value of the Shrinking Well

As in the coal mine example of Chapter 10, we start our analysis of the option on the shrinking well by modeling the single source of uncertainty (which in this case is the spot market price of oil) in a standard binomial tree. We then take each potential spot price of oil at each future date and translate this into the value of our underlying (a redeveloped well). We have to make sure we capture the shrinkage of our well over time, so our approach will be slightly different from the coal mine problem in Chapter 10.

Here, we'll maintain our assumption that the current spot price of oil is $45 per barrel and that there's no net convenience yield built into forward prices. We'll add the assumption that the volatility of oil (i.e., the standard deviation of log changes in its price) is 30%. To keep the illustration simple, I'll build my binomial analysis using only one time step per year so $\Delta t = 1$. With these assumptions, our tree parameters are $U = e^{\sigma\sqrt{\Delta t}} = e^{0.30\sqrt{1}} = 1.3499$ and $D = 1/U = 0.7408$; I provide our resulting tree of spot oil prices in Figure 12.2.

Figure 12.2					
	0	1	2	3	4
Binomial Tree	$45.00	$60.74	$82.00	$110.68	$149.41
of Oil Prices		$33.34	$45.00	$60.74	$82.00
			$24.70	$33.34	$45.00
				$18.30	$24.70
					$13.55

Since we're assuming for this illustration that there's no net convenience yield on oil and that the risk-free rate is 5%, our risk-neutral probability of an up step will be

$$q = \frac{e^{(r-ncy) \times \Delta t} - D}{U - D} = \frac{e^{(0.05-0) \times 1} - 0.7408}{1.3499 - 0.7408} = 0.51$$

and the risk-neutral probability of a down-step will be $1 - q = 0.49$.

Observe that this structure gives us forward prices that are consistent with those in our static DCF analysis above. For example, the expected Year-1 price of oil under the risk-neutral probability measure is $0.51 \times \$60.74 + 0.49 \times \$33.34 = \$47.31$, which is exactly the forward price we used to determine the Year-1 expected cash flows in our DCF valuation in Figure 12.1. If you calculate the expected oil prices from the binomial tree values in Years 2, 3, and 4, you will get the forward prices for those years that we used in our static DCF valuation. In other words, the binomial tree synchs up with our DCF valuation (a point that you'll see again in just a few paragraphs).

What we'll do next is use the binomial tree of spot oil prices (Figure 12.2) to determine the *current year's* cash flow in each time-spot price state. We simply use the same assumptions as in our DCF analysis of Figure 12.1 but focus our attention only on a single year's cash flow given a spot price of oil for that year. For example, if the spot price of oil in Year 4 is $149.41 (its highest state in that year), then the free cash flow received during that year from an open well would be $5,060,506, as shown in Figure 12.3.

For another example, suppose the spot price of oil in Year 3 turns out to be $18.30 (its lowest possible state in that year). This would translate to a Year-3 free cash flow from an open well of −$1,331,008; this value is negative simply because the mine's net operating income would not cover its fixed cost in a year when oil prices are so low (as I document in Figure 12.4).

Figure 12.3

	Year	4
Year-4 Free Cash Flow from Open Well If Spot Oil Price = $149.41	Spot crude	$149.41
	Barrels produced	100,000
	Revenue	$14,940,526
	Less: extr. cost	500,000
	Less: sev./royalty	3,735,132
	Operating income	10,705,395
	Less: fixed costs	2,920,000
	Profit before tax	7,785,395
	Tax expense	2,724,888
	Free cash flow	$5,060,506

We repeat this procedure for every time-price state, making sure to put each resulting value into the appropriate spot in a binomial tree of current year's cash flow from an open well. Figure 12.5 documents the result. Once again, I encourage you to use Microsoft Excel's *DataTable* feature to automate this process for you when you do it yourself.

Why do we have $0 for year 0? Remember—the standard convention is to number each time period at its very end. The Year-1 values are the cash flows that we would earn over Year 1 given the two different possible oil prices from our binomial tree; by convention, we approximate their values by assuming that they are received at the time marked 1 which is the end of Year 1. Time 0 is today—right now—and the well is not yet open.

We'll use Figure 12.5 to create a binomial tree of values of an open but shrinking well,

Figure 12.4

	Year	3
Year-3 Free Cash Flow from Open Well If Spot Oil Price = $18.30	Spot crude	$18.30
	Barrels produced	100,000
	Revenue	$1,829,563
	Less: extr. cost	500,000
	Less: sev./royalty	457,391
	Operating income	872,173
	Less: fixed costs	2,920,000
	Profit before tax	−2,047,827
	Tax expense	−716,740
	Free cash flow	−$1,331,088

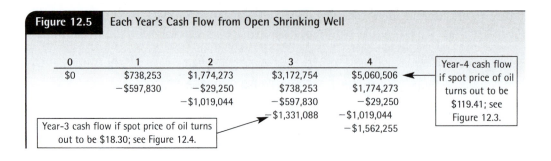

Figure 12.5   Each Year's Cash Flow from Open Shrinking Well

0	1	2	3	4
$0	$738,253	$1,774,273	$3,172,754	$5,060,506
	-$597,830	-$29,250	$738,253	$1,774,273
		-$1,019,044	-$597,830	-$29,250
			-$1,331,088	-$1,019,044
				-$1,562,255

Year-4 cash flow if spot price of oil turns out to be $119.41; see Figure 12.3.

Year-3 cash flow if spot price of oil turns out to be $18.30; see Figure 12.4.

which will be our underlying asset for the option problem. What makes this problem slightly different from the coal mine example in Chapter 10 is that the value of an open well depends on how many more years of operation are left. If you recall, we assumed in Chapter 10 that we could open the coal mine at any time over the next 10 years, and that, once opened, the mine would produce coal for 10 years. Therefore, valuation of a brand-new mine opened today and a new mine opened next year were very similar in approach. Here, however, we'll get four years of production if we open the well today but only three years of production if we open it next year. As time passes, the underlying asset changes in a unique way—it shrinks—and we must model this shrinkage.

Capturing the shrinkage in the well's value is not hard, as long as we are careful. All we have to remember is that the value of an open well in any given time-spot price state is simply the expected present value of the well's remaining free cash flows. Figure 12.5 gives us all the data we need.

We'll start at the end and work backwards. At the end of Year 4, an open well would be absolutely worthless to us since the lease ends and the well reverts to the owner at that time. So, construct a new binomial tree to record the value of an open well, and put in $0 for every spot oil price state at the end of Year 4. (Now you see why I've been so careful to point out the convention concerning the timing of the cash flows. What we're doing here is valuing the well on an ongoing basis right at the end of the year, *after* all of the year's cash flows have been received. At that point, the well's value is only determined by its expected cash flows in all future years.) Figure 12.6 shows the first step.

Now we work backwards. If the well is open at the end of Year 3, what do we get? The expected present value of all future cash flows, of course. What constitutes the expected present value of all future cash flows? Two things: (1) the expected cash flow to be received over the coming year plus (2) the expected value of the open well at the end of the coming year. Let's place ourselves in the highest spot price state at the end of Year 3, where the spot price of oil is $110.68, and think through this intuitively.

If we have an open well in the $110.68 spot price state at the end of Year 3, only two things can happen: Either the spot price of oil goes up over the next year to $149.41, or the spot price of oil goes down over the next year to $82.00. What do we get in each case?

- If the spot price of oil goes up over the next year to $149.41, we'll get the Year-4 cash flows of $5,060,506, and then at the end of Year 4 we'll have a well that is worth $0.
- If, on the other hand, the spot price of oil goes down over the next year to $82.00, we'll get the Year-4 cash flows of $1,774,273, and again at the end of Year 4, we'll have a well that is worth $0.

Figure 12.6	Step 1 of Valuing the Open Shrinking Well

Binomial Tree of Oil Prices

0	1	2	3	4
$45.00	$60.74	$82.00	$110.68	$149.41
	$33.34	$45.00	$60.74	$82.00
		$24.70	$33.34	$45.00
			$18.30	$24.70
				$13.55

Each Year's Cash Flow from Open Shrinking Well

0	1	2	3	4
$0	$738,253	$1,774,273	$3,172,754	$5,060,506
	−$597,830	−$29,250	$738,253	$1,774,273
		−$1,019,044	−$597,830	−$29,250
			−$1,331,088	−$1,019,044
				−$1,562,255

Value of an Open Shrinking Well

0	1	2	3	4
0	1	2	3	4
				$0
				$0
				$0
				$0
				$0

Therefore, the value of an open (but shrinking) well in the $110.68/barrel state at the end of Year 3 is simply the expected present value of these two sums. We take the expectation using our risk-neutral probabilities of up and down movements in the spot price of oil, and then we discount at the risk-free rate. In our problem, $q = 0.51$, $1 − q = 0.49$, and $e^{r \times \Delta t} = 1.051$, so the value of an open well in this time-spot price state is

$$\frac{0.51 \times (\$5,060,506 + \$0) + 0.49 \times (\$1,774,273 + \$0)}{1.051} = \$3,281,171$$

In Figure 12.7, I've entered this result as the value of an open shrinking well in the highest spot price state at the end of Year 3. I've documented the calculation, and I've shown an additional example. Make sure you follow.

Let's work through one more step back to make sure we're all at the same level of incompetence. Suppose that, at the end of Year 2, we have an open well and find ourselves in the highest spot-price state in our binomial tree ($82.00). What would be the value of the well? Again, only two things can happen: The spot price of oil can go up, or it can go down.

- If the spot price of oil goes up to $110.68, then we get two things by the end of Year 3:
  1. Year-3 cash flows equal to $3,172,754.
  2. The value of an open but shrinking well in the $110.68 spot price state at the end of Year 3 (i.e., the expected present value of all cash flows to be received after Year 3), which is $3,281,171 (as Figure 12.7 shows).
- If, on the other hand, the spot price of oil goes down to $60.74, we again get two things:
  1. Year-3 cash flows equal to $738,253.
  2. The value of an open but shrinking well in the $60.74 spot price state at the end of Year 3 (i.e., the expected present value of all cash flows to be received after Year 3), which is $846,670 (as Figure 12.7 shows).

Figure 12.7   Step 2 of Valuing the Open Shrinking Well

Binomial Tree of Oil Prices

0	1	2	3	4
$45.00	$60.74	$82.00	$110.68	$149.41
	$33.34	$45.00	$60.74	$82.00
		$24.70	$33.34	$45.00
			$18.30	$24.70
				$13.55

Each Year's Cash Flow from Open Shrinking Well

0	1	2	3	4
$0	$738,253	$1,774,273	$3,172,754	$5,060,506
	−$597,830	−$29,250	$738,253	$1,774,273
		−$1,019,044	−$597,830	−$29,250
			−$1,331,088	−$1,019,044
				−$1,562,255

Value of an Open Shrinking Well

0	1	2	3	4
0			$3,281,171	$0
	[0.51 × ($5,060,506 + $0) + 0.49 × ($1,774,273 + $0)]/1.051		$846,670	$0
			−$489,413	$0
	[0.51 × (−$1,019,044 + $0) + 0.49 × (−$1,562,255 + $0)]/1.051		−$1,222,671	$0
				$0

Therefore, the value of an open (but shrinking) well in the $82/barrel state at the end of Year 2 is simply the expected present value of these two sums (where the expectation is taken under the risk-neutral probability measure, and discounting occurs at the risk-free rate):

$$\frac{0.51 \times (\$3,172,754 + \$3,281,171) + 0.49 \times (\$738,253 + \$846,670)}{1.051} = \$3,868,510$$

In Figure 12.8, I've entered this value in the appropriate place in our tree of open but shrinking well values, and I've completed the analysis for the other two states at the end of Year 2. Again, make sure you follow the documentation.

Figure 12.8   Step 3 of Valuing the Open Shrinking Well

Each Year's Cash from Open Shrinking Well

0	1	2	3	4
$0	$738,253	$1,774,273	$3,172,754	$5,060,506
	−$597,830	−$29,250	$738,253	$1,774,273
		−$1,019,044	−$597,830	−$29,250
			−$1,331,088	−$1,019,044
				−$1,562,255

Value of an Open Shrinking Well

0	1	2	3	4
0		$3,868,510	$3,281,171	$0
[0.51 × ($3,172,754 + $3,281,171) + 0.49 × ($738,253 + $846,670)]/1.051		$261,463	$846,670	$0
		−$1,718,126	−$489,413	$0
[0.51 × ($738,253 + $846,670) + 0.49 × (−$597,830 + −$489,413)]/1.051			−$1,222,671	$0
				$0

Figure 12.9					
	0	1	2	3	4
Value of an	$915,571	$2,844,368	$3,868,510	$3,281,171	$0
Open Shrinking		−$1,163,881	$261,463	$846,670	$0
Well			−$1,718,126	−$489,413	$0
				−$1,222,671	$0
					$0

If you follow what I've done in Figure 12.7 and Figure 12.8, you can complete the value of an open shrinking well tree all the way back to today (Time 0). I show the finished product in Figure 12.9.

Figure 12.9 presents the evolution of our risky real asset that underlies our option on the shrinking well. Notice that in Figure 12.9, the value of a well that is opened right now (Time 0) is $915,571, which is *exactly* the same as the current value of a well in our static DCF analysis of Figure 12.1. This is the reason I used continuous discounting to take present values in Figure 12.1—I wanted to show you that our binomial model of valuation is perfectly consistent with static DCF (if done correctly).[6]

12.4 Valuing the American Option on the Shrinking Well

The rest of the problem is straightforward. Taking our underlying asset value tree (Figure 12.9), we simply start at the end and work backwards, at each date asking whether it is better to spend the $750,000 development cost (the strike price) immediately and get back a shrinking well or wait and make the best decision at the end of the next period. It should be obvious to you that if we wait until the end of Year 4, the option dies unexpired, and we have a net payoff of zero regardless of the state of nature. The first real calculation occurs at the end of Year 3.

The decision at the end of Year 3 is pretty easy. If we get to that point without having developed the well, doing so would cost us $750,000 and would get us a well with only one year of production left in return. Waiting longer, on the other hand, gets us the expected present value of the option to make the best decision at the end of Year 4. However, in this case waiting gets

---

[6] Some technically inclined readers might object that our underlying risky asset (the shrinking well) as modeled in Figure 12.9 does not appear to follow a martingale under the risk-neutral measure. You have to be careful here. When you have a convenience yield, then the asset's *total expected return* (which includes both capital gain *and* convenience yield) must equal the risk-free rate under the risk-neutral measure. Take what happens over the first year as an example. If you are fastidious with rounding, you'll find that the Time-0 expected value of the well at the end of Year 1 is $879,287 and the Time-0 expected cash flow to be received from the well over the first year is $83,226 (all taken under the risk-neutral measure, of course). Therefore, the total Time-0 risk-neutral expectation of the Time-1 value *plus* convenience yield is $962,513; hence, the expected log return over the first year under the risk-neutral measure is ln($962,513/$915,571) = 5%, which is the risk-free rate. Or, I can put it another way. Using simple compounding over the first year, the well itself is expected (under the risk-neutral measure) to suffer capital *loss* of ($879,287/$915,571 − 1) = −3.96% but generate a cash return (like a dividend yield) of ($83,226/$915,571−1) = 9.09%; −3.96% + 9.09% = 5.13%, and exp(0.05) = 1.0513. Either way, the discounted shrinking well does follow a martingale.

Figure 12.10	Step 1 of Valuing the Option on the Shrinking Well

Value of Open Shrinking Well

0	1	2	3	4
$915,571	$2,844,368	$3,868,510	$3,281,171	$0
	−$1,163,881	$261,463	$846,670	$0
		−$1,718,126	−$489,413	$0
			−$1,222,671	$0
				$0

Value of Option on Shrinking Well

0	1	2	3	4
			$2,531,171	$0
			$96,670	$0
			$0	$0
			$0	$0
				$0

Value if exercise =
$3,128,171 − $750,000 = $2,531,171
Value if wait = (0.51 × $0 + 0.49 × $0)/1.051 = $0
max [$2,531,171, $0] = $2,531,171 Exercise.

us nothing because we know that the option will be worth $0 at the end of Year 4 no matter what happens. So at the end of Year 3, we'll invest whenever the value of the shrinking well is greater than the cost of reopening it. I've done this for you in Figure 12.10, and added grey shading to note where we exercise early. You'll see that the optimum thing to do in Year 3 (if we get there and have not yet reopened the well) is to redevelop the well if the spot price of oil is in the highest two states, but not in the lowest two states.

What about the end of Year 2? We do the same thing. In the highest oil price state at the end of Year 2, an open well would be worth $3,868,510, and so the payoff to reopening immediately would be $3,868,510 − $750,000 = $3,118,510. If we wait, on the other hand, we have an option whose value will be $2,531,171 at the end of Year 3 if oil prices rise, or $96,670 at the end of Year 3 if oil prices fall. Given our risk-neutral probabilities and the risk-free rate, the value of this option will be

$$\frac{0.51 \times \$2,531,171 + 0.49 \times \$96,670}{1.051} = \$1,272,397$$

Therefore, if we reach the end of Year 2 without reopening the well and then find ourselves in the highest oil-price state at that time, the best thing to do is immediately reopen the well and own a real asset worth $3,118,510 (as opposed to waiting and owning a real option worth $1,272,397). I documented this calculation (along with one other Year-2 calculation) and added shading to indicate optimal early exercise points at the end of Year 2, in Figure 12.11.

The remainder of the option analysis works exactly the same way. I've completed the tree of option values for you and constructed the optimal exercise boundary based on spot oil prices in Figure 12.12.

Just as I promised you, the shrinkage in the size of the well as time passes acts just as a convenience yield and drives us to exercise the option on the well early. Given our parameters, the current value of the option on the shrinking well is $1,026,117; the best thing to do for the meantime is to leave the well closed unless oil prices rise to $60.74.

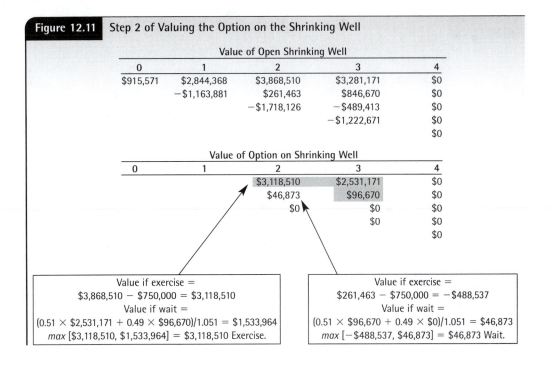

Figure 12.11   Step 2 of Valuing the Option on the Shrinking Well

Value of Open Shrinking Well

0	1	2	3	4
$915,571	$2,844,368	$3,868,510	$3,281,171	$0
	−$1,163,881	$261,463	$846,670	$0
		−$1,718,126	−$489,413	$0
			−$1,222,671	$0
				$0

Value of Option on Shrinking Well

0	1	2	3	4
		$3,118,510	$2,531,171	$0
		$46,873	$96,670	$0
		$0	$0	$0
			$0	$0
				$0

Value if exercise =
$3,868,510 − $750,000 = $3,118,510
Value if wait =
(0.51 × $2,531,171 + 0.49 × $96,670)/1.051 = $1,533,964
max [$3,118,510, $1,533,964] = $3,118,510 Exercise.

Value if exercise =
$261,463 − $750,000 = −$488,537
Value if wait =
(0.51 × $96,670 + 0.49 × $0)/1.051 = $46,873
max [−$488,537, $46,873] = $46,873 Wait.

I want to assure you that the early exercise possibility in this problem comes about solely because of the potential shrinkage in the underlying well. We've built no convenience yield whatsoever into oil prices, and yet we still get early exercise. In the appendix at the end of this chapter, I show that if the well does not shrink as time passes (but rather remains a four-year well no matter when it is reopened), then there will be no early exercise whatsoever unless we build a positive net convenience yield into the crude oil forward curve.

Figure 12.12   The Optimal Exercise Boundary

Value of Option on Shrinking Well

0	1	2	3	4
$1,026,117	$2,094,368	$3,118,510	$2,531,171	$0
	$22,728	$46,873	$96,670	$0
		$0	$0	$0
			$0	$0
				$0

Binomial Tree of Oil Prices

0	1	2	3	4
$45.00	$60.74	$82.00	$110.68	$149.41
	$33.34	$45.00	$60.74	$82.00
		$24.70	$33.34	$45.00
			$18.30	$24.70
				$13.55

Reopen well.
Well already reopened.

Figure 12.13   **Repeating the Analysis Assuming 130,000 bbl/yr Production**

Value of Option on Shrinking Well with 130,000 bbl/yr Production

0	1	2	3	4
$2,453,359	$4,494,610	$5,335,907	$4,057,153	$0
	$313,595	$646,747	$892,301	$0
		$0	$0	$0
			$0	$0
				$0

Binomial Tree of Oil Prices

0	1	2	3	4
$45.00	$60.74	$82.00	$110.68	$149.41
	$33.34	$45.00	$60.74	$82.00
		$24.70	$33.34	$45.00
			$18.30	$24.70
				$13.55

Reopen well.
Well already reopened.

12.5 Comparative Statics

I hear grumbling in the classroom. "Richard, you motivated this problem by telling us that small producers were reopening wells right away. Your option analysis in Figure 12.12 says to wait a little longer before reopening." Calm down. My *example* well should not be reopened immediately, but there are others that should (and there are others that should be kept closed even longer). We can see this by just changing the parameters a little.

First, if we increase the annual production of the well from 100,000 barrels to 130,000 barrels, the optimal thing to do is to reopen the well immediately (as I show in Figure 12.13).

Why? Simple. If we increase the annual production, the option goes deeper into the money, and the cost of waiting increases much faster than does the option value of waiting. We'll get the same effect if we return to our assumption of 100,000 barrels/year production, but raise the current spot price of oil to $55 (which I shown in Figure 12.14). As the spot price of oil rises, the cost of waiting rises and poorer-quality shut-in wells become more attractive.

Figure 12.14   **Repeating the Analysis Assuming Spot Oil = $55**

Value of Option on Shrinking Well with Spot Oil = $55

0	1	2	3	4
$2,115,571	$4,068,536	$4,895,075	$3,730,228	$0
	$235,877	$486,463	$754,726	$0
		$0	$0	$0
			$0	$0
				$0

Binomial Tree of Oil Prices

0	1	2	3	4
$55.00	$74.24	$100.22	$135.28	$182.61
	$40.75	$55.00	$74.24	$100.22
		$30.18	$40.75	$55.00
			$22.36	$30.18
				$16.57

Reopen well.
Well already reopened.

| Figure 12.15 | Repeating the Analysis Assuming Fixed Cost = $3,650,000 |

Value of Option on Shrinking Well with Fixed Cost = $3,650,000

0	1	2	3	4
$526,129	$1,085,068	$2,237,806	$2,079,813	$0
	$0	$0	$0	$0
		$0	$0	$0
			$0	$0
				$0

Binomial Tree of Oil Prices

0	1	2	3	4
$45.00	$60.74	$82.00	$110.68	$149.41
	$33.34	$45.00	$60,74	$82.00
		$24.70	$33.34	$45.00
			$18.30	$24.70
				$13.55

Reopen well.
Well already reopened.

On the other hand, things that make the economics of a shrinking well poorer will cause the owner of the lease to wait even longer to reopen. For example, if we return to our original parameters but increase fixed costs of renting a rig from $8,000/day to $10,000/day (which is what happens when prices rise and more wells become open), we'll have to see higher spot prices in order to justify reopening the well and the value of the option on the well drops, as I show in Figure 12.15.

12.6 The Grand Lesson

I've pitched this story in terms of an option on an oil well for purely pedagogical reasons. Specifically, I wanted to create a very easy transition from the canonical mining problem that we covered in Chapter 10 to the more general real-world problems we'll be covering in the last three chapters of the book. By treating this as a "shrinking well" (or, equivalently, a "shrinking mine"), I've changed only one thing from the canonical mining problem—I've added value erosion to our underlying asset.

The big lesson is this: *Anything* that erodes the value of a real asset over time may make you exercise an American call on that real asset early. Some potential sources of such erosion are economic depreciation of a real asset that generates cash flow from usage, investment-related tax shields that vanish after a certain year, or even the threat of a competitor entering your market and eroding your potential market share. Whenever there's a "use it or lose it" facet to a growth option, you may find it valuable to exercise early.

Appendix 12.1

If the well does not shrink, but rather has four years of production left regardless of when it is open, the problem proceeds exactly like the coal mine problem in Chapter 10. Begin by analyzing the decision at Year 4: If we reach Year 4 without having reopened the well, would we spend $750,000 and get back a nonshrinking, four-year well, or would we let the option die? Get the value of a nonshrinking, four-year well in each Year-4 oil price state simply by plugging each Year-4 spot oil price into the original DCF valuation model (see Figure 12.1).

Figure 12.16 Value of Option on Brand-New, Nonshrinking Well

0	1	2	3	4
$2,754,640	$4,819,563	$8,198,959	$13,393,475	$20,524,597
	$895,741	$1,809,905	$3,655,469	$7,379,664
		$38,927	$80,282	$165,571
			$0	$0
				$0

Then work backward. In each earlier time-price state, compare the value of investing immediately (which you get by plugging the current spot oil price into the DCF model of Figure 12.1 and subtracting $750,000) or the value of waiting (the standard option valuation method, using risk-neutral probabilities and the risk-free discount rate). The optimal decision is the maximum of the two; keep track of exercise points by shading in gray.

I present the solution, based on our original set of parameters, in Figure 12.16. Notice that in this case (where there's no convenience yield in oil *and* no shrinkage in the well), there are no states in which we optimally exercise the option on the well early.

I want to stress here that the *only* way that we can change the parameters of the nonshrinking well problem so as to induce early exercise is to introduce net convenience yield into the forward curve for oil. There are *no* parameter settings that will cause early exercise as long as the net convenience yield is zero. Figure 12.17 presents the result if the net convenience yield on oil is 3%.

Introduction of the net convenience yield causes the value of the option on the nonshrinking well to drop and concomitantly leads to a potential for early exercise, just as in Chapter 10.

Figure 12.17 Value of Option on Brand-New, Nonshrinking Well with *ncy* = 3%

0	1	2	3	4
$1,749,128	$3,397,484	$6,385,782	$11,425,340	$18,434,680
	$517,837	$1,186,736	$2,719,662	$6,232,693
		$0	$0	$0
			$0	$0
				$0

PROBLEMS

1. In Figure 12.2, what is the expected price of a barrel of oil at the end of Year 4? Is the expected price different from the futures price? (*Hint:* Rounding error of up to $0.05 is a common problem.)

2. In Figure 12.2, what is the expected price of a barrel of oil at the end of Year 4, assuming a convenience yield of 2% per annum? Is the expected price different from the futures price? Remember to adjust the futures price with the convenience yield. (*Hint:* Rounding error of up to $0.05 is a common problem.)

3. Redo Figure 12.3 for a spot price of $82.00 (the second highest spot price in the fourth year of the binomial tree). (*Hint:* Expect rounding error of about $300.00 due to imprecision with the spot price of $82.00.)

4. In Figure 12.9, provide the calculation to find the option value in Year 2 when the spot price of oil is $60.74. (*Hint:* Expect rounding error of about $3,000.00 due to imprecision in the probability inputs.)

5. Redo the binomial tree in Figure 12.2 with a volatility of 35% per annum. Does the expected price at the end of Year 1 still correspond to the associated futures price (provide numerical evidence)? (*Hint:* Use four decimal place precision throughout the tree to reduce rounding error in Problems 6 through 9.)

6. Using the binomial tree in Problem 5, develop an associated tree similar to Figure 12.5 (use the same assumptions in regard to production from the chapter). To expedite matters, use the following equation for the calculation of free cash flow based on the spot oil price derived from Figures 12.3 and 12.4:

   Free cash flow = {price × 75,000 − 3,420,000} × (1 − 35%)

7. Using the binomial tree in Problem 6, develop an associated tree similar to Figure 12.9. Does the value of the well still correspond to the DCF analysis from earlier in the chapter (assume some rounding error within $1,100.00)? (*Hint:* Use 1.0513 as the discount factor instead of 1.051.)

8. Using the binomial tree in Problem 7, value the real option for developing the shut-in well. (*Hint:* Use 1.0513 as the discount factor instead of 1.051.)

9. Redo Problem 8, assuming the cost of developing a shut-in well is $1,000,000.00 instead of $750,000.00. (*Hint:* Use 1.0513 as the discount factor instead of 1.051.)

CONVENIENCE YIELD AS SHRINKAGE IN THE UNDERLYING: VALUATION OF A TAX CREDIT INVESTMENT AT KOCH INDUSTRIES[1]

Koch Industries is the largest private corporation in the United States and one of the biggest businesses in the world.[2] The company's 2005 sales revenue, $80 billion, was slightly larger than that of Home Depot ($73 billion) and Honda Motor ($78 billion), over twice that of Microsoft ($38 billion) and Dow Chemical ($40 billion), nearly four times the sales of The Coca-Cola Company ($21 billion), and not far below Conoco-Phillips ($118 billion).[3]

Koch concentrates its business interests in oil, natural gas, specialty chemicals, and other energy products, as well as a wide variety of financial derivatives designed to promote a more stable and liquid market for these commodities. It also has substantial activities in ranching, securities, and venture investing. In 2005, Koch paid $13.8 billion in cash (and assumed $7 billion in debt) to acquire all of the assets of Georgia-Pacific, a paper and forest products company that had been one of the country's 100 largest public firms.

13.1 Background

Within its minerals subsidiary, Koch provides an array of services to the coal industry. In 1994, Koch had the opportunity to invest in a new but unproven technology for turning coal dust (or *fines*) into coal *briquettes* for use in energy production. The particular allure of this investment was that it would generate a side effect: A very large tax credit for converting hazardous waste into an alternative energy source. In fact, as you'll see in this chapter, the potential tax credit was expected to be far more valuable than the briquetting business. To put it quite bluntly, this investment was a tax play. The uncertainty was the marketability of the briquettes themselves, and the risk was that the company could possibly destroy more value in the briquette business than it would create via the tax shield.

---

[1] The original idea for this case came from a term paper submitted in the Spring of 1999 by my students Monica Chawla, Ben Lasoi, and Ed Seguine (all Kelley School of Business MBA 1999). I've estimated the parameters as best as I can from public data sources, but you should keep in mind that they are only approximations. The point here is to demonstrate a general methodology when there's known cash income on the underlying that would be lost due to waiting.

[2] The pronunciation of Koch is "coke." Charles and David Koch, along with their charitable foundations and the charitable foundation of their late father Fred Koch (who founded the company in 1940), own the majority of the company. J. Howard Marshall, late husband of celebrity Anna Nicole Smith, owned 15% of the company prior to his death. The two other Koch brothers, Frederick and William (winner of the 1992 America's Cup yacht race) sold their interests in the company to Charles and David for $1.1 billion in 1983.

[3] The Koch sales estimate comes from Hoovers.com; all other revenue numbers are from Forbes.

To understand the potential appeal of briquetting, it is necessary that you understand just a bit about the process of coal production itself. Don't worry—this is not another case about mining. Instead, it is about optimal exercise strategy when the underlying asset shrinks in value. In this example, our shrinking asset will be the tax credit!

Everything You Always Wanted to Know About Coal Production*

*But Were Afraid to Ask

Mined coal can contain a significant amount of inorganic sulfur and noncombustible ash. Since end users (electricity producers, steel mills, etc.) require a product that meets certain standards of quality and consistency, most mine operators around the world perform what is known as *beneficiation* (or *washing*) to prepare the coal for delivery.

Beneficiation involves crushing mined coal into smaller pieces and immersing it in water. Since pure coal and the undesired materials have different densities, the impurities separate from the coal and leave a cleaner product. Removed impurities that are larger than about half a millimeter can be trucked away and disposed of as solid waste.[4]

Unfortunately, beneficiation produces a second waste product that is much more difficult to handle. Crushing creates coal dust (called *fines* or *tailings*) at a rate of about 3 kilograms per metric ton of coal. These fines drain off as *slurry* and must be held in a basin known as an *impoundment*. Impoundments are often constructed up against embankments and look very similar to dams. A coal producer pumps the slurry into an impoundment, allows the fines to settle, and then recycles the water.

Needless to say, impoundments are environmental hazards. On October 11, 2000, an impoundment failure caused a flood of roughly 300 million gallons of slurry that contaminated some 80 miles of creeks and rivers and buried a part of Inez, Kentucky, under 7 feet of sludge. Twenty-eight years earlier, a similar failure in West Virginia left 125 people dead, 1,100 injured, and 4,000 homeless. For decades, the identification of more environmentally friendly ways for disposing of fines has been a priority of the coal industry and its regulators.

A concept dating back to the early 20th century involves mixing coal fines with asphalt (a binding agent) under intense pressure to create an end product very similar in appearance (but not content) to a charcoal briquette. These asphalt-bound briquettes were used for domestic heating through World War II, but they were never popular because the asphalt binder created a substantial amount of smoke when burned.

The Tax Credit

In 1994, the United States Congress set out to provide economic incentives for private firms to invest in technologies that would convert hazardous waste into alternative energy sources. An unproven idea was to reinvent coal briquetting by replacing the asphalt briquette binder with a clean-burning binder. If successfully developed, this new-style briquette could be sold to coal-burning public utilities as well as to steel plants as a replacement for mined coal.

Congress had two goals in mind here. The first was to encourage elimination of hazardous wastes (like coal fines). The second was to find alternative energy sources. Coal fines were particularly attractive on the second count, as experts estimate that the country's 700 active

---

[4] This process, called physical cleaning, can remove inorganic sulfur but not organic sulfur. Mining companies can remove the organic sulfur through chemical and biological processes.

impoundments contain over 1 billion tons of recoverable coal (which could generate as much electricity as the country's entire nuclear generating fleet does in five years).

To advance these goals, Congress enacted a tax code provision which would provide a bottom-line tax *credit* of $1.06 for every MMBtu (million British thermal units) of energy provided by the alternative fuel source. However, the credit would be available only between 1995 and 2004. Congress expressly approved briquetting of fines as a qualifying activity; a conforming briquette plant could operate after 2004, but no credit would be available beyond that point (regardless of when it was built). To get a rough idea of just how valuable this tax credit would be to a company that could successfully make the new-style briquettes, simply recognize that the market price of coal at the time was about $1.06 per MMBtu.

So *if* a company could successfully make the new-style coal briquettes from coal fines, and *if* the briquettes could be made to be perfect substitutes for coal, a briquette factory would be quite valuable. But in 1994 these were very big ifs, because the new clean-burning binder technology was not yet proven. In particular, no one was sure if the briquettes would be reasonable substitutes for coal in the furnaces of electric utilities and steel mills. If the end users were forced to adjust their operations to accommodate the physical properties of the briquettes, then the briquettes might end up selling at a very steep discount to coal.

Nevertheless, the tax credit was so enticing that the U.S. Internal Revenue Service (IRS) initially received over 200 applications for preliminary authorizations to develop conforming sites.

13.2   Koch's Investment Opportunity

Koch Industries received preliminary approval for a conforming site from the IRS and then finalized their investment analysis. Koch's engineers designed the plant to produce an estimated 17,588,000 MMBtu per year with a 30-year useful life. The plant would cost $150 million to build, and this cost could be depreciated over the plant's useful life using the straight-line method. Variable costs of operation were projected to be $0.25/MMBtu, and fixed costs were estimated at $5 million per year. Profits would be taxed at a 33% rate.

I'm going to work in real dollars here so that I don't have to keep track of the effects of inflation on operating costs and the cost to build the plant (if delayed). So we will assume that the numbers above are reals, and that Koch's real hurdle rate for the project was 8%. But working in reals creates one problem. Tax shields and tax credits are *nominal* amounts because they are fixed and not indexed to inflation.[5] Therefore, we'll have to adjust our tax offsets for the expected inflation rate of 3%. For example, if the plant is built immediately at a depreciable cost of $150 million, then the actual depreciation will be $150/30 = $5 million per year. But this is a nominal number, and its real value declines every year thereafter if there is any inflation. So after the plant is built, the first year's real value of the depreciation tax shield will be $5 million × 33% = $1.65 million, but the next year's real value will only be $5 million/(1.03) × 33% = $1.60 million. The same goes for the tax credit. It is $1.06 per MMBtu in calendar year 1995, but its real value drops every year after that. Just be careful.[6]

---

[5] For example, if you are depreciating an asset by $1,000 per year in an inflationary environment, the year-to-year *amount* of the depreciation tax shield remains at $1,000 × tax rate but the year-to-year *purchasing power* of that tax shield declines.

[6] Another way to approach this would be to work in nominals, which requires adjusting all numbers *except for* the depreciation tax shield and the tax credit for expected inflation. Inflation can create a convenience-yield effect, but it is not the driver of the exercise decision in this example.

Figure 13.1	Static NPV Analysis of Koch's 1994 Briquette Plant Opportunity (Including Tax Credit)						

Assumptions			1995	1996	...	2004	2005	...	2024
Starting year	1994								
Price/MMBtu	$0.75	Expected production (Bil.Btu)	17,588	17,588		17,588	17,588		17,588
Real appreciation	0.50%	Expected spot price/MMBtu	$0.75	$0.75		$0.78	$0.79		$0.87
Nominal credit/MMBtu	$1.06	Sales revenue (000)	$13,191	$13,257		$13,797	$13,866		$15,244
Real cost/MMBtu	$0.25	Variable cost (000)	$4,397	$4,397		$4,397	$4,397		$4,397
Real fixed cost (000)	$5,000	Operating margin (000)	$8,794	$8,860		$9,400	$9,469		$10,847
Real plant cost (000)	$150,000	Fixed costs (000)	$5,000	$5,000		$5,000	$5,000		$5,000
Expected inflation	3.00%	Real depreciation (000)	$5,000	$4,854		$3,832	$3,720		$2,122
Taxes	33%	Before tax income (000)	−$1,206	−$994		$568	$748		$3,725
Real WACC	8%	Taxes (000)	−$398	−$328		$187	$247		$1,229
		Net income (000)	−$808	−$666		$380	$501		$2,496
Results (000)		Add back: depreciation (000)	$5,000	$4,854		$3,832	$3,720		$2,122
PV FCF (credit yrs)	$140,087	Real tax credit (000)	$18,643	$18,100		$14,289	$0		$0
PV FCF (noncredit yrs)	$19,733	Net yearly cash flow (000)	$22,835	$22,288	...	$18,501	$4,222	...	$4,618
Total PV FCF	$159,820								
Less: cost of plant	$150,000								
NPV	$9,820								
At 12/31/1994									

These data give us just about enough information to produce a static discounted cash flow (DCF) analysis for the plant as of December 31, 1994. The greatest source of uncertainty, and the subject of much hand-wringing at Koch, was the price that end users would pay for the coal briquettes. Since there was no current market, there was no immediately available reference price. The price of coal was about $1.06/MMBtu at the time, and experts felt that utilities and industrial firms would demand a price discount for the briquettes for various operational reasons. For this reason, I have assumed that the best-guess in 1994 was that the briquettes would sell for $0.75 per MMBtu, and that this price was expected to appreciate in real terms by 0.5% per year. I'll also assume that Koch can sell forward each year's production at the spot price observed at the beginning of the year. My static net present value (NPV) analysis is in Figure 13.1.

Please note that I've shifted gears a bit here, in that I'm not pricing off a forward curve. Instead, I'm forecasting the expected spot price of briquettes. For this reason, it is appropriate that I discount the free cash flows at a risk-adjusted discount rate. Since I'm working in reals, the WACC must also be in reals.

In Figure 13.1, the first year's expected spot price of briquettes is $0.75/MMBtu; each subsequent year, the expected spot price rises at an annual rate of 0.50%; therefore, the expected spot price in 2024 (Year 30) is $0.75 \times (1.005)^{29} = $0.867 (which I round to $0.87 for presentation purposes). Nominal straight-line depreciation is $150mm/30 years = $5 million/year; on a real basis, the value of the depreciation tax shield falls at an annually compounded rate of 3%. So the depreciation deduction is $5 million in the first year, $5mm/(1.03) = $4.854 million in the second year, and so on. The real value of the tax credit falls annually in an identical way.

Given the initial assumptions, Figure 13.1 shows us that the project creates value: The static NPV of the coal briquetting facility is $9.82 million—a good opportunity for investing the

Koch family fortunes. And it is easy to see why it creates value: The 1995 tax credit ($18.6 million) is almost as valuable as the 1994 discounted value of all of the cash flows in the nontax credit years combined ($19.7 million)! This is a tax play, pure and simple: The present value of the tax credit itself is about $112 million, so the value of the plant without the tax credit is only about $47 million. At a market price of $0.75, the Koch family would lose money on the factory itself but make it back up (plus a little extra) with the tax credit.[7]

Nevertheless, Koch management expressed trepidation about this investment, for two reasons. First, the initial assumption about the market price of briquettes could be wrong. If briquette prices were to be only 7¢ below the projection ($0.68/MMBtu instead of $0.75/MMBtu), the project would be negative static NPV even with the tax credit—that is, the value of the tax credit would not justify construction of the costly plant. Second, briquette prices would most certainly be more volatile than coal prices. If the briquettes are not perfect substitutes for coal, then a small drop in coal prices could cause a large drop in briquette prices.[8] A bad resolution of either uncertainty could quickly turn this seemingly valuable project into a dog.

My students suggested that Koch look at this from a real options perspective. The intuition was as follows: A delay in building the plant by one year costs the company one year of tax credits (since the credits could only be taken yearly through the year 2004). But on the other hand, a delay of one year creates the benefit of learning more about the market price of briquettes before making an expensive investment. Specifically, if Koch waits a year, they get to see if coal prices rise or fall (and thus interpret a concomitant rise or fall in the value of briquettes), *and* they can observe the output prices of other companies that do go ahead and build briquette plants. Might this not be a good trade-off? Of course. Perhaps the company should wait two years, or even longer! The only way to figure this out properly is to look at the investment as an American option on a coal-briquetting facility and determine the optimal exercise boundary.

13.3 The Option Analysis

What we have is an American call on a new corporate asset. The investment cost is $150 million, so the strike price is $150 million. The act of exercising "purchases" a brand-new briquette plant, so the underlying asset itself is a new briquette plant.

The value of a new briquette plant was uncertain, for two reasons. First, as stated before, there was no way to fully know how receptive the end users would be to buying the briquettes at prices near the equivalent price of coal. The product is costly to transport over large distances, so its market would be somewhat regional, and thus the company faced a somewhat limited number of potential customers. Second, there is some variability in the price of coal itself. It is natural to think that the variability of price changes of briquettes would be greater than the variability of price changes of coal: If coal prices were to escalate, the briquettes might be seen as a viable alternative, and their price would go up as well; but if coal prices were to drop, the inferiority of the product would lead to a greater price drop for the briquettes.

---

[7] Without a tax credit, the 1994 spot price of briquettes would have to be above $1.49/MMBtu to make the new plant display positive static NPV.

[8] We see this in other markets. For example, the price of low-grade scrap steel is much more volatile than that of high-grade scrap steel.

Figure 13.2	Binomial Tree of Briquette Prices per MMBtu ($)									
Dec-94	Dec-95	Dec-96	Dec-97	Dec-98	Dec-99	Dec-00	Dec-01	Dec-02	Dec-03	Dec-04
0.75	0.92	1.12	1.37	1.67	2.04	2.49	3.04	3.71	4.54	5.54
	0.61	0.75	0.92	1.12	1.37	1.67	2.04	2.49	3.04	3.71
		0.50	0.61	0.75	0.92	1.12	1.37	1.67	2.04	2.49
			0.41	0.50	0.61	0.75	0.92	1.12	1.37	1.67
				0.34	0.41	0.50	0.61	0.75	0.92	1.12
					0.28	0.34	0.41	0.50	0.61	0.75
						0.23	0.28	0.34	0.41	0.50
							0.18	0.23	0.28	0.34
								0.15	0.18	0.23
									0.12	0.15
										0.10

Once again, we're in the position in which the underlying asset (a briquette factory) and the underlying uncertainty (briquette prices) are not exactly the same. Just as in the coal mine, fixed costs in the briquette factory will cause it to behave as a derivative on briquettes. However, the value of a factory is always a deterministic function of the market price of briquettes. So our approach will be to model the evolution of briquette prices in a binomial tree and then translate these into briquette plant values as we work backward in our option analysis. The annual standard deviation of log changes in coal prices was only about 10% per year, so for reasons just stated, I've assumed the annual standard deviation in price changes of briquettes to be 20%.

The binomial approach forces us to nominate a terminal point in the analysis where the decision must be made (if it has not already been made). This is usually somewhat intuitive, and there's a pretty good intuition for letting the option expire in December 2004 (i.e., 10 years from the date of analysis). Starting in 2005, a plant would be built only if it stood on its own merits (i.e., if the coal briquettes were very attractively priced). There would be no more erosion in the underlying beyond 2005 (since the tax credit would be exhausted), so this was a valid conclusion. In Figure 13.2, I've built a 10-year tree of briquette prices, with one step per year, given an annual return volatility of 20%, a starting value of $UND_0 = \$0.75$, $U = e^{0.20\sqrt{1}} = 1.2214$ and $D = 1/U = 0.8187$.

Remember what the tree gives us. We started with a December 1994 estimated briquette price of $0.75, and then used that price as our market price for all of 1995 production (see my DCF analysis earlier). So these numbers at each point in the tree give us the market price for briquettes in the *following* year, as if Koch can sell forward each year's production at the beginning-of-the-year spot price.

Our work plan is to take each spot price of briquettes from Figure 13.2, calculate the corresponding value of a new briquette plant in that very time *and at that very date*, calculate the optimal exercise decision and the value received for that decision, and work through the option analysis just like we did in Chapter 10. An important difference here is that we have to keep track of the year of potential investment in addition to the spot price. A new briquette plant built at December 1994 given a $0.75 spot price of briquettes will *not* have the same value as a new briquette plant built at December 1996 under the same spot price. The major reason for this is that an investment in 1994 purchases not only a new plant but also 10 full years of tax credit (1995 through 2004), whereas an investment in 1996 purchases a new plant but only eight years of tax credit.[9]

As always, we begin the analysis in the last year. Start by asking the following question: If the plant were not built by December 2004, would we build it then given the prices in the binomial lattice? To answer this question, we need a DCF model that begins in 2005 and has no tax credit (since the credit dies after 2004). If you use some thought in building your spreadsheet, you can make it handle the tax credit appropriately given the year the plant is built. This is yet another instance where Microsoft Excel's *DataTable* function comes in handy. In this case, we have a two-dimensional data table: Spot price and year begun.

Inspection of the binomial tree of briquette prices (Figure 13.2) reveals that the very top price-state in December 2004 is $5.54/MMBtu. Figure 13.3 presents the static DCF valuation of the free cash flows from a brand-new briquette plant in December 2004, if we reach that point without having built the plant yet and observe/estimate a spot price of briquettes of $5.54 at that time.

Do you see what I've done in Figure 13.3? I've redone the original static DCF valuation of the plant under the new assumptions that Koch builds it in December 2004 with a current

| Figure 13.3 | The Value of a New Plant in 2004 Given a Spot Briquette Price of $5.54 per MMBtu |

Binomial Tree of Briquette Prices per MMBtu ($)										
Dec-94	Dec-95	Dec-96	Dec-97	Dec-98	Dec-99	Dec-00	Dec-01	Dec-02	Dec-03	Dec-04
0.75	0.92	1.12	1.37	1.67	2.04	2.49	3.04	3.71	4.54	5.54
	0.61	0.75	0.92	1.12	1.37	1.67	2.04	2.49	3.04	3.71
		0.50	0.61	0.75	0.92	1.12	1.37	1.67	2.04	2.49
			0.41	0.50	0.61	0.75	0.92	1.12	1.37	1.67
				0.34	0.41	0.50	0.61	0.75	0.92	1.12
					0.28	0.34	0.41	0.50	0.61	0.75
						0.23	0.28	0.34	0.41	0.50
							0.18	0.23	0.28	0.34
								0.15	0.18	0.23
									0.12	0.15
										0.10

	Assumptions		Static DCF Analysis	2005	2006	⋯	2014	2015	⋯	2034
Starting year	2004		Expected production (Bil.Btu)	17,588	17,588		17,588	17,588		17,588
Price/MMBtu	$5.54		Expected spot price/MMBtu	$5.54	$5.57		$5.80	$5.83		$6.40
Real appreciation	0.50%		Sales revenue (000)	$97,469	$97,956		$101,944	$102,454		$112,637
Nominal credit/MMBtu	$1.06		Variable cost (000)	$4,397	$4,397		$4,397	$4,397		$4,397
Real cost/MMBtu	$0.25		Operating margin (000)	$93,072	$93,559		$97,547	$98,057		$108,240
Real fixed cost (000)	$5,000		Fixed costs (000)	$5,000	$5,000		$5,000	$5,000		$5,000
Real plant cost (000)	$150,000		Real depreciation (000)	$5,000	$4,854		$3,832	$3,720		$2,122
Expected inflation	3.00%		Before tax income (000)	$83,072	$83,705		$88,715	$89,336		$101,119
Taxes	33%		Taxes (000)	$27,414	$27,623		$29,276	$29,481		$33,369
Real WACC	8%		Net income (000)	$55,658	$56,082		$59,439	$59,855		$67,749
			Add back: depreciation (000)	$5,000	$4,854		$3,832	$3,720		$2,122
	Results (000)		Real tax credit (000)	$0	$0		$0	$0		$0
PV FCF (credit yrs)	$-		Net yearly cash flow (000)	$60,658	$60,937	⋯	$63,271	$63,576	⋯	$69,871
PV FCF (noncredit yrs)	$713,849									
Total PV FCF	$713,849									

[9] Moreover, the real value of every $1 of tax credit falls by the expected inflation rate for every year of delay.

Figure 13.4	Binomial Tree of Option Values (in $millions)									
Dec-94	Dec-95	Dec-96	Dec-97	Dec-98	Dec-99	Dec-00	Dec-01	Dec-02	Dec-03	Dec-04
										$563.85

briquette spot price of $5.54. I've maintained all of the other original assumptions. The spot price is expected to grow at 0.5% per year, real variable costs are $0.25/MMBtu, and real fixed costs are $5 million per year. Since we're working in reals, the construction cost does not change, and so annual depreciation is still $5 million. Moreover, the real value of the depreciation tax credit in the first year of this analysis (2005) is exactly the same as if Koch were to build the plant in December 2004 ($5 million). After that point, however, the real value of the depreciation tax shield drops at the expected inflation rate, just as before. A major thing you should notice about the valuation in Figure 13.3 is that it includes no tax credit. By statute, 2004 is the last year that the tax credit may be taken *regardless of when the plant is built.* Therefore, the plant must stand on its own merits in December 2004 in order to warrant construction at that time.

Would we exercise the option (i.e., build the plant) in this state? Absolutely. The strike price (or cost of building) is $150 million, so the payoff from exercising in this time-price state ($5.54 in December 2004) is $713.85 million − $150 million = $563.85 million. Our next task is to create a tree for the value of the American option on the briquette plant, write $563.85 million in as the top-state value in 2004, and highlight it to remind us that we exercise there. I've done this for you in Figure 13.4.

Let me do another one for you, all in one big step. If we move down to the second-highest spot price state at December 2004, we see a briquette spot price of $3.71. Given a spot price of briquettes of $3.71 at December 2004, the value of a brand-new briquette plant would be $459.92 million. Thus, the payoff to exercising the option and building the plant in that time-price state would be $459.92 million − $150 million = $309.92 million. Since the payoff to letting the option die is $0, the optimal decision if we reach that state without yet having made a commitment is to build the plant and take back the net value of $309.92 million. Figure 13.5 summarizes all of this.

When you complete all of the potential price states in December 2004, your tree of option values will look like Figure 13.6.

The next step is to work back to December 2003, remembering that we have an American option. To do this, we'll need our risk-free time value factor and our risk-neutral probabilities. Given a 2% real risk-free rate of return along with our earlier assumption of 20% volatility of returns in briquettes and 1 time step per year, we have $e^{r \times \Delta t} = 1.0202$ and

$$q = \frac{e^{r \times \Delta t} - D}{U - D} = \frac{1.0202 - 0.8187}{1.2214 - 0.8187} = 0.5003$$

and so $(1 - q) = 0.4997$.

It is easy to see from Figure 13.6 that if we reach the highest spot-price state in December 2003 ($4.54), *and we keep the option alive,* the subsequent year's payoff on the option will be $563.85 million if the spot price of briquettes rises and $309.92 million if the spot price of briquettes falls. The December 2003 value of the option *if left alive* is the expected present value of these two possibilities, with the expectation taken using the risk-neutral probabilities and discounting done at the

Figure 13.5 — The value of a New Plant in 2004 Given a Spot Briquette Price of $3.71 per MMBtu

Binomial Tree of Briquette Prices per MMBtu ($)

Dec-94	Dec-95	Dec-96	Dec-97	Dec-98	Dec-99	Dec-00	Dec-01	Dec-02	Dec-03	Dec-04
0.75	0.92	1.12	1.37	1.67	2.04	2.49	3.04	3.71	4.54	5.54
	0.61	0.75	0.92	1.12	1.37	1.67	2.04	2.49	3.04	3.71
		0.50	0.61	0.75	0.92	1.12	1.37	1.67	2.04	2.49
			0.41	0.50	0.61	0.75	0.92	1.12	1.37	1.67
				0.34	0.41	0.50	0.61	0.75	0.92	1.12
					0.28	0.34	0.41	0.50	0.61	0.75
						0.23	0.28	0.34	0.41	0.50
							0.18	0.23	0.28	0.34
								0.15	0.18	0.23
									0.12	0.15
										0.10

Assumptions

Starting year	2004	
Price/MMBtu	$3.71	
Real appreciation	0.50%	
Nominal credit/MMBtu	$1.06	
Real cost/MMBtu	$0.25	
Real fixed cost (000)	$5,000	
Real plant cost (000)	$150,000	
Expected inflation	3.00%	
Taxes	33%	
Real WACC	8%	

Results (000)

PV FCF (credit yrs)	$–
PV FCF (noncredit yrs)	$459,921
Total PV FCF	$459,921

Static DCF Analysis

	2005	2006	⋯	2014	2015	⋯	2034
Expected production (Bil.Btu)	17,588	17,588		17,588	17,588		17,588
Expected spot price/MMBtu	$3.71	$3.73		$3.89	$3.90		$4.29
Sales revenue (000)	$65,335	$65,662		$68,335	$68,677		$75,503
Variable cost (000)	$4,397	$4,397		$4,397	$4,397		$4,397
Operating margin (000)	$60,938	$61,265		$63,938	$64,280		$71,106
Fixed costs (000)	$5,000	$5,000		$5,000	$5,000		$5,000
Real depreciation (000)	$5,000	$4,854		$3,832	$3,720		$2,122
Before tax income (000)	$50,938	$51,411		$55,106	$55,559		$63,984
Taxes (000)	$16,810	$16,966		$18,185	$18,335		$21,115
Net income (000)	$34,129	$34,455		$36,921	$37,225		$42,870
Add back: depreciation (000)	$5,000	$4,854		$3,832	$3,720		$2,122
Real tax credit (000)	$0	$0		$0	$0		$0
Net yearly cash flow (000)	$39,129	$39,300	⋯	$40,753	$40,945	⋯	$44,991

Binomial Tree of Option Values (in $millions)

Dec-94	Dec-95	Dec-96	Dec-97	Dec-98	Dec-99	Dec-00	Dec-01	Dec-02	Dec-03	Dec-04

$max\,[\$459.92 - \$150, \$0] = \$309.92$ (invest)

Dec-04:
$563.85
$309.92

Figure 13.6 — Binomial Tree of Option Values (in $ millions)

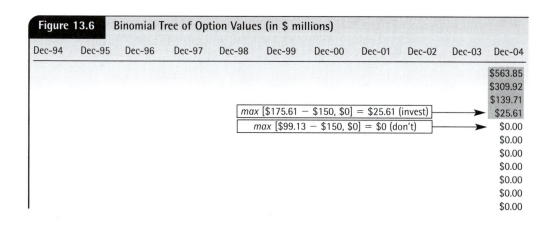

Dec-94	Dec-95	Dec-96	Dec-97	Dec-98	Dec-99	Dec-00	Dec-01	Dec-02	Dec-03	Dec-04

$max\,[\$175.61 - \$150, \$0] = \$25.61$ (invest) → $25.61

$max\,[\$99.13 - \$150, \$0] = \$0$ (don't) → $0.00

Dec-04:
$563.85
$309.92
$139.71
$25.61
$0.00
$0.00
$0.00
$0.00
$0.00
$0.00
$0.00

Figure 13.7	The Value of a New Plant in 2003 Given a Spot Briquette Price of $4.54 per MMBtu

Binomial Tree of Briquette Prices per MMBtu ($)

Dec-94	Dec-95	Dec-96	Dec-97	Dec-98	Dec-99	Dec-00	Dec-01	Dec-02	Dec-03	Dec-04
0.75	0.92	1.12	1.37	1.67	2.04	2.49	3.04	3.71	4.54	5.54
	0.61	0.75	0.92	1.12	1.37	1.67	2.04	2.49	3.04	3.71
		0.50	0.61	0.75	0.92	1.12	1.37	1.67	2.04	2.49
			0.41	0.50	0.61	0.75	0.92	1.12	1.37	1.67
				0.34	0.41	0.50	0.61	0.75	0.92	1.12
					0.28	0.34	0.41	0.50	0.61	0.75
						0.23	0.28	0.34	0.41	0.50
							0.18	0.23	0.28	0.34
								0.15	0.18	0.23
									0.12	0.15
										0.10

Assumptions

Starting year	2003	
Price/MMBtu	$4.54	
Real appreciation	0.50%	
Nominal credit/MMBtu	$1.06	
Real cost/MMBtu	$0.25	
Real fixed cost (000)	$5,000	
Real plant cost (000)	$150,000	
Expected inflation	3.00%	
Taxes	33%	
Real WACC	8%	

Results (000)

PV FCF (credit yrs)	$58,434
PV FCF (noncredit yrs)	$529,027
Total PV FCF	$587,461

Static DCF Analysis

	2004	2005	··· 2013	2014 ··· 2033
Expected production (Bil.Btu)	17,588	17,588	17,588	17,588 17,588
Expected spot price/MMBtu	$4.54	$4.56	$4.75	$4.77 $5.24
Sales revenue (000)	$79,801	$80,200	$83,465	$83,882 $92,220
Variable cost (000)	$4,397	$4,397	$4,397	$4,397 $4,397
Operating margin (000)	$75,404	$75,803	$79,068	$79,485 $87,823
Fixed costs (000)	$5,000	$5,000	$5,000	$5,000 $5,000
Real depreciation (000)	$5,000	$4,854	$3,832	$3,720 $2,122
Before tax income (000)	$65,404	$65,949	$70,236	$70,764 $80,701
Taxes (000)	$21,583	$21,763	$23,178	$23,352 $26,631
Net income (000)	$43,821	$44,186	$47,058	$47,412 $54,070
Add back: depreciation (000)	$5,000	$4,854	$3,832	$3,720 $2,122
Real tax credit (000)	$14,289	$0	$0	$0 $0
Net yearly cash flow (000)	$63,109	$49,040 ···	$50,890	$51,133···$56,191

risk-free rate of return. Therefore, given a spot price of $4.54 in December 2003, the value of leaving the option alive is $428.32 million:

$$\frac{q \times DERIV_{up} + (1 - q) \times DERIV_{dn}}{e^{r \times \Delta t}} = \frac{0.5003 \times \$563.85mm + 0.4997 \times \$309.92mm}{1.0202} = \$428.32mm$$

Since this is an American option on a briquette plant, we must compare the value of leaving the option alive in this time-price state ($428.32 million) with the value of exercising the option immediately. To determine the value of immediate exercise, we undertake the same procedure as I did in Figure 13.3: We reconstruct our static DCF valuation assuming construction of the brand-new plant in December 2003 at a spot briquette price of $4.46 (which I've done for you in Figure 13.7).

Before we go forward, note one important thing about Figure 13.7: The value of the tax credit in 2004 (the one year Koch gets it if they build the plant at December 2003) is $14.289 million, whereas the value of the first year of tax credit in our original static DCF valuation in Figure 13.1 (the first year Koch gets it if they build the plant at December 1994) was $18.643 million. Why are they different? Because the tax credit of $1.06/MMBtu is a nominal amount, and its purchasing power is $1.06 only in 1995. The real value must drop by 3% per year, and $18.643 million/(1.03)^9 = $14.289 million. Students often ask why I don't discount the depreciation tax credit the same way. The reason, quite simply, is that we've assumed that the

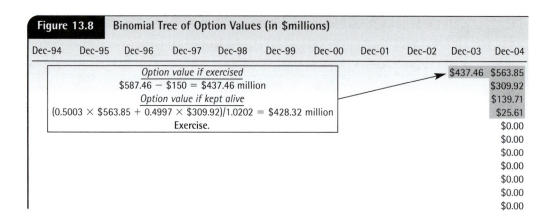

Figure 13.8 Binomial Tree of Option Values (in $millions)

Dec-94	Dec-95	Dec-96	Dec-97	Dec-98	Dec-99	Dec-00	Dec-01	Dec-02	Dec-03	Dec-04

Option value if exercised
$587.46 − $150 = $437.46 million
Option value if kept alive
(0.5003 × $563.85 + 0.4997 × $309.92)/1.0202 = $428.32 million
Exercise.

									$437.46	$563.85
										$309.92
										$139.71
										$25.61
										$0.00
										$0.00
										$0.00
										$0.00
										$0.00
										$0.00
										$0.00

real cost of building the plant is $150 million whenever you build it. Therefore, the first year's real value of the depreciation expense is $5 million regardless of when it occurs, but this amount then becomes a nominal number and must be discounted for inflation from that point forward.

Figure 13.7 shows us that the value of an immediately built briquette plant in December 2003 given a spot price of briquettes of $4.54 is $587.46 million. Therefore, the payoff to exercising the option immediately in this time-price state (and killing any future flexibility) is $587.46 million − $150 million = $437.46 million. Recalling that the value of leaving the option alive was only $428.32 million, we can conclude that the best strategy at this time-price state is to go ahead and build the plant and take back its net value ($437.46 million). Put this in the appropriate place in our tree of option values from Figure 13.6, and note that the optimal strategy is immediate exercise. I've done this for you, and documented the calculation, in Figure 13.8.

Let's remind ourselves about the intuition behind *why* we optimally exercise the option early and build the plant in this particular time-price state ($4.54 in December 2003) if we have not already done so. Figure 13.7 provides the critical clue. If we build the plant in December 2003, we get one year of tax credit which has an end-of-year value of $14,289 million (or a present value of roughly $14 million). If we wait and keep the option alive, we lose this $14 million tax credit in favor maintaining the benefit of waiting. But what are the benefits of waiting any longer? In this case, we *know* we'll be building the plant in December 2004 no matter which subsequent state occurs, so the *only* benefits to waiting are (1) holding out for a little higher expected spot price of briquettes (their expected appreciation is 0.5%, remember) and (2) saving the time value of the strike price, which in this case is only about $3 million. The cost of waiting far outweighs the benefits of waiting in this time-price state, and hence the best thing to do is to kill the option and build the plant.

I'll do another one for you, this time in one big step. Move down to the second-highest spot price state in December 2003, where the spot price of briquettes is $3.04. In this state, the value of the option if kept alive is $220.42 million:

$$\frac{0.5003 \times \$309.92\text{mm} + 0.4997 \times \$139.71\text{mm}}{1.0202} = \$220.42\text{mm}$$

At the same point in time, the value of a brand-new briquette plant would be $379.56 million, so the payoff to exercising the option on the plant immediately would be $379.56 million − $150 million = $229.56 million. The best decision is to exercise right away and have an asset worth $229.56 million; see Figure 13.9.

Figure 13.9   The Value of a New Plant in 2003 Given a Spot Briquette Price of $3.04 per MMBtu

Binomial Tree of Briquette Prices per MMBtu ($)

Dec-94	Dec-95	Dec-96	Dec-97	Dec-98	Dec-99	Dec-00	Dec-01	Dec-02	Dec-03	Dec-04
0.75	0.92	1.12	1.37	1.67	2.04	2.49	3.04	3.71	4.54	5.54
	0.61	0.75	0.92	1.12	1.37	1.67	2.04	2.49	3.04	3.71
		0.50	0.61	0.75	0.92	1.12	1.37	1.67	2.04	2.49
			0.41	0.50	0.61	0.75	0.92	1.12	1.37	1.67
				0.34	0.41	0.50	0.61	0.75	0.92	1.12
					0.28	0.34	0.41	0.50	0.61	0.75
						0.23	0.28	0.34	0.41	0.50
							0.18	0.23	0.28	0.34
								0.15	0.18	0.23
									0.12	0.15
										0.10

Assumptions

		Static DCF Analysis	2004	2005	⋯	2013	2014	⋯	2033
Starting year	2003	Expected production (Bil.Btu)	17,588	17,588		17,588	17,588		17,588
Price/MMBtu	$3.04	Expected spot price/MMBtu	$3.04	$3.06		$3.18	$3.20		$3.51
Real appreciation	0.50%	Sales revenue (000)	$53,492	$53,760		$55,948	$56,228		$61,817
Nominal credit/MMBtu	$1.06	Variable cost (000)	$4,397	$4,397		$4,397	$4,397		$4,397
Real cost/MMBtu	$0.25	Operating margin (000)	$49,095	$49,363		$51,551	$51,831		$57,420
Real fixed cost (000)	$5,000	Fixed costs (000)	$5,000	$5,000		$5,000	$5,000		$5,000
Real plant cost (000)	$150,000	Real depreciation (000)	$5,000	$4,854		$3,832	$3,720		$2,122
Expected inflation	3.00%	Before tax income (000)	$39,095	$39,508		$42,719	$43,110		$50,298
Taxes	33%	Taxes (000)	$12,901	$13,038		$14,097	$14,226		$16,598
Real WACC	8%	Net income (000)	$26,194	$26,471		$28,622	$28,884		$33,700
		Add back: depreciation (000)	$5,000	$4,854		$3,832	$3,720		$2,122
Results (000)		Real tax credit (000)	$14,289	$0		$0	$0		$0
PV FCF (credit yrs)	$42,113	Net yearly cash flow (000)	$45,482	$31,325	⋯	$32,454	$32,604	⋯	$35,821
PV FCF (noncredit yrs)	$337,449								
Total PV FCF	$379,562								

Binomial Tree of Option Values (in $millions)

Dec-94	Dec-95	Dec-96	Dec-97	Dec-98	Dec-99	Dec-00	Dec-01	Dec-02	Dec-03	Dec-04

Option value if exercised
$379.56 − $150 = $229.56 million
Option value if kept alive
(0.5003 × $309.92 + 0.4997 × $139.71)/1.0202 = $220.42 million
Exercise.

Dec-03: $437.46, $229.56 — Dec-04: $563.85, $309.92, $139.71, $25.61, $0.00, $0.00, $0.00, $0.00, $0.00, $0.00, $0.00

We then repeat this process for all of the other price states in 2003. Figure 13.10 shows my result.

In Figure 13.10, I've documented the calculation of the optimum strategy in one particularly interesting December 2003 state. If the spot price of briquettes is $1.37 in December 2003, then the American call on the new plant would be near-the-money and the early-exercise value would be −$3.21 million. Just as before, the cost of waiting is the loss of the one year of tax credit (about $14 million). In this particular state, however, the benefit of waiting actually exceeds the cost, and the option is worth more alive than dead. Why? Because waiting now generates something extra.

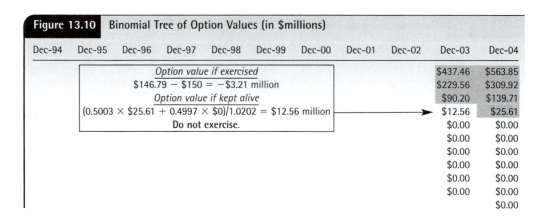

Figure 13.10   Binomial Tree of Option Values (in $millions)

Dec-94	Dec-95	Dec-96	Dec-97	Dec-98	Dec-99	Dec-00	Dec-01	Dec-02	Dec-03	Dec-04
									$437.46	$563.85
									$229.56	$309.92
									$90.20	$139.71
									$12.56	$25.61
									$0.00	$0.00
									$0.00	$0.00
									$0.00	$0.00
									$0.00	$0.00
									$0.00	$0.00
									$0.00	$0.00
										$0.00

Box contents:
Option value if exercised
$146.79 − $150 = −$3.21 million
Option value if kept alive
$(0.5003 \times \$25.61 + 0.4997 \times \$0)/1.0202 = \$12.56$ million
Do not exercise.

In this particular state, there is substantial flexibility value created by waiting because the optimal strategy in the subsequent year depends on what happens to briquette prices—if we wait and they go up, we'll build the plant, but if we wait and they go down, we won't. There's value to resolving some of the uncertainty about briquette prices, and in this particular time-price state the value of that flexibility (learn and respond) exceeds the cost of waiting (the lost tax shield).

If you follow what I did in Figure 13.9, then the rest is easy—just repeat that analysis over and over again, working backward through the tree all the way back to December 1994. In the end, you'll end up with a binomial tree of option values that looks like the one in Figure 13.11.

Figure 13.11 gives us a very important result. Even though the static NPV of the briquette plant is positive, and even though the tax credit that would be lost by waiting is quite large, the plant should not be built in December 1994. If Koch builds a briquette plant at that time, they create value for themselves of about $9.8 million (the static NPV of a now-or-never decision) but they miss an opportunity to hold an asset worth about $14.3 million (the option on a briquetting plant). The immediate investment and the option are mutually exclusive opportunities, and the value-maximizing course of action involves picking the one with the highest value.

What prices of briquettes would trigger exercise? We can find this out by laying the earliest optimal exercise points from Figure 13.11 onto our original binomial tree of briquette prices from Figure 13.2. I've done this for you in Figure 13.12.

Figure 13.11   Binomial Tree of Option Values (in $millions)

Dec-94	Dec-95	Dec-96	Dec-97	Dec-98	Dec-99	Dec-00	Dec-01	Dec-02	Dec-03	Dec-04
$14.31	$24	$41	$66	$97	$138	$189	$254	$336	$437	$564
	$5	$8	$15	$26	$44	$75	$115	$166	$230	$310
		$1	$2	$4	$8	$15	$28	$51	$90	$140
			$0	$0	$1	$1	$3	$6	$13	$26
				$0	$0	$0	$0	$0	$0	$0
					$0	$0	$0	$0	$0	$0
						$0	$0	$0	$0	$0
							$0	$0	$0	$0
								$0	$0	$0
									$0	$0
										$0

Figure 13.12 Binomial Tree of Briquette Prices per MMBtu ($)

Dec-94	Dec-95	Dec-96	Dec-97	Dec-98	Dec-99	Dec-00	Dec-01	Dec-02	Dec-03	Dec-04
0.75	0.92	1.12	1.37	1.67	2.04	2.49	3.04	3.71	4.54	5.54
	0.61	0.75	0.92	1.12	1.37	1.67	2.04	2.49	3.04	3.71
		0.50	0.61	0.75	0.92	1.12	1.37	1.67	2.04	2.49
			0.41	0.50	0.61	0.75	0.92	1.12	1.37	1.67
				0.34	0.41	0.50	0.61	0.75	0.92	1.12
					0.28	0.34	0.41	0.50	0.61	0.75
						0.23	0.28	0.34	0.41	0.50
							0.18	0.23	0.28	0.34
								0.15	0.18	0.23
									0.12	0.15
										0.10

Exercise.
Plant already open.

Figure 13.12 makes the story really clear. Remember that the static NPV from building right away is positive. But recognizing the value of the flexibility to wait on top of the uncertainty about briquette prices tells a different story: Don't invest now, give up the early tax credits, and wait until an appropriate time to invest. If the price of briquettes reaches $1.12/MMBtu by 1996, then we'll build the plant and capture the remaining tax credit. If we wait longer, we'll have to see an even higher briquette price to justify building a plant (since the tax shield will be a smaller and smaller portion of a new plant's total value as time goes by). Finally, in December 2004 we'll build the plant only if briquettes are sufficiently valuable on their own to justify a $150 million capital investment.[10]

Comparative Statics

Once again, we can learn something by playing with the assumptions. The most critical assumption in this case is actually the spot price of briquettes, as small changes here can lead to very different conclusions. Intuitively, if we increase the current spot price of briquettes, then the option on a briquette plant goes deeper into the money; this means that the value of waiting falls. Since the cost of waiting (the lost tax credit) does not change, we should expect an increase in the spot price of briquettes to cause exercise at earlier points. Indeed, if we raise the spot price of briquettes to only $0.85, the best strategy is to exercise immediately. Note that at $0.85/MMBtu, the briquette plant does not stand on its own merits. The investment is still at tax play, but the immediate tax credit outweighs the benefits of waiting.

Lowering the volatility has the same effect. As the volatility of changes in briquette prices drops, the value of waiting drops. If the volatility of returns on briquettes is only 14%, immediate exercise is the best policy. Remember that the volatility assumption does not affect the static NPV, so all that happens when you change it is that you change the value of the real option. Obviously, a higher volatility leads to a higher option value (more benefit to waiting) and hence later exercise.

It may surprise you to learn that the real cost of capital is important. This is because the cost of capital affects the value of the underlying asset (a brand-new briquette plant) at any point of

[10] Given our assumptions, the break-even price of briquettes (i.e., the price that gives a static NPV of $0), given no tax credit, is about $1.49. If you were to build a very large binomial tree with very small time steps, you would see the optimal exercise boundary start at a value somewhere near our $1.12 calculation in the early years and then rise period by period to the break-even price of $1.49 in December 2004.

the analysis. Since an increase in the discount rate makes the present value of any future cash flows drop, it decreases the moneyness of the real option and leads to longer waiting (though with less value). For example, at a real WACC of 10%, the static NPV of the project is $-\$7$ million, the real option is worth about $7.4 million, and the earliest optimal exercise point is December 1997 (as opposed to December 1996 in our original analysis). On the other hand, dropping the real WACC to 6% raises the static NPV so much (to about $31 million) that the best strategy is to exercise the option immediately.

With that intuition in mind, you can understand why changing the expected inflation rate will change the analysis. A higher expected inflation rate decreases the present value of the tax credit (and the depreciation tax shield) at any point in the analysis, which again reduces the moneyness of the real option and makes one wait longer to exercise. A drop in the expected inflation rate has the opposite effect; in our example, a 1.3% expected inflation rate is enough to trigger immediate exercise. Note that the *only* place in our analysis where inflation has an effect is in the tax shields.

13 PROBLEMS

1. Produce the Net Yearly Cash Flow for 1997 that corresponds to Figure 13.1.

2. Redo Problem 1 with a 1994 briquette price projection of $0.68/MMBtu instead of $0.75/MMBtu.

3. Value the remaining life of the tax credit, assuming the briquette plant is operational starting in 1995, 1996, 1997 . . . through 2004. Note, the value of the tax credit will decrease the later the plant becomes operational and should be discounted (in real terms) relative to one-year prior to the plant being operational. Use the following equation to evaluate the tax credit:

$$\frac{\$1.06 \times 17{,}588}{11.24\%} \left[1 - \frac{1}{(1 + 11.24\%)^N} \right] (1 + 3\%)^M$$

Year = One year prior to operations

N = 2004 − Year

M = 1995 − Year

11.24% = (1 + 8%) × *(1 + 3%) −1

4. Redo the binomial tree in Figure 13.2, using an initial price of $0.68/MMBtu instead of $0.75/MMBtu.

5. In Figure 13.5, produce the static DCF analysis when the briquette price is $2.49 in Dec-04. To perform this calculation, use $2.490088 as the price and the following algorithm developed from the work of Arnold and James (2000).

Static DCF (in $1000s) = Price × *138,985.233966 − 56,377.834196

(*Note:* The large number of decimal places are to prevent significant rounding error.)

Arnold, T. and J. James, 2000. "Finding Firm Value without a Pro Forma Analysis," *Financial Analysts Journal* (March/April), 77–84.

6. Using the algorithm in Problem 5 and the tax credit calculation for 1994 (i.e., 1995 is the first operational year) from Problem 3, produce the static DCF analysis for the $0.75 briquette price in 1994. Redo the static DCF analysis for a briquette price of $0.68.

7. Build the binomial tree in Figure 13.2, using an annual volatility of 25%. Use four-decimal place accuracy with the prices within the tree.

8. Using the algorithm in Problem 5, determine the value of the option for all of the states in Dec-04 for the binomial tree created in Problem 7.

9. Using the algorithm in Problem 5 and the tax credit calculations from Problem 3, determine the option value for all states in Dec-03 for the binomial tree created in Problem 7.

10. Redo Problems 7 through 9, assuming the expected briquette spot price in Dec-94 is $0.68.

DELAYED RESPONSE TO EXERCISE: FAB SHELLS AT INTEL[1]

Intel is the world's largest semiconductor maker. The company's core business involves design, manufacturing, and delivery of quality microprocessors for a wide range of computing needs.

The company originally produced chips for the complex computing and communications markets. But as Intel and its competitors developed ways to produce increasingly higher performance chips at continually decreasing costs, manufacturers of other consumer and industrial products (such as telephones and automobiles) found it valuable to introduce computing power into their offerings.

This growth in the range of applications for microchips presents both opportunities and challenges for Intel. Since the chips can be used to make virtually anything into an "intelligent" product, Intel management forecasts that by 2013 the world will be linked by over a billion connected computers (of varying types) through tens of millions of servers. But the exposure of chips to such a broad range of end markets creates a demand for chips that is highly sensitive to economic conditions. During a recession, businesses cut capital spending. This leads directly to a reduction in demand for semiconductor-rich applications like personal computers, and thus for chips. Similarly, demand for chips falls with the softening of demand for consumer products that have high semiconductor content (such as cellular phones, appliances, and video games). Industry utilization can range from 95% of capacity in boom times to below 75% in recessions.

Intel's Problem

Given management's long run forecasts, it is obvious that Intel will need additional production capacity at some time in the future. But when? This was the question that management pondered in January 2000, when the company was operating at only 80% capacity. There are substantial scale economies in microprocessor manufacturing, and an appropriately sized new fabrication facility would increase Intel's capacity for processors by about 50%. It would have

[1] The ideas and data for the Intel case study come from a term paper submitted by John Gilmore, Tom Lukawski, Brian MacNicol, and Karl Sandberg, all Kelley School of Business MBA Class of 2004. Thanks, guys—nice work.

been very naïve to spend $2 billion (the cost of a new fab facility) immediately, since the extra capacity was not needed at the time (and demand was expected to rise by only about 5% per year). But, as I mentioned before, demand for chips was known to be quite volatile. How long should Intel wait before building the new facility?

If this sounds to you like an American option problem, then give yourself a pat on the back. It is indeed a problem very similar to optimal coal mine development or Koch Industries' option on a tax shield. Intel management has the option to spend $2 billion at any time it likes, and in return receive back a new production facility. But this example has an interesting and important twist.

In everything we've done in this book up to now, we've assumed that the exercise of the option is instantaneous—that is, when management decides to spend the strike price, it gets back the underlying asset. In cases where there has been a delay between the exercise decision and the ultimate receipt of the underlying, we've simply accounted for it in our PV of free cash inflows given exercise. (Go back and look at how we did Wal-Mart Neighborhood Markets or Koch Industries, and see the appendix at the end of this chapter for an explanation of why this is a legitimate procedure.)

What makes the Intel case so unique is that construction of a new production facility (or *fab*, in industry jargon) takes two full years: One year for permitting, design, and construction of the *fab shell* (the exterior of the building), and a second full year for installation and testing of the production line. Hence, given the rather substantial volatility in the chip market, Intel faces two very significant problems with its American option on a new facility: If the company decides to build and chip demand drops unexpectedly, the company is stuck with an expensive investment in a plant that does not operate (and may never, since production technologies have limited lives); but if the company decides to delay building and chip demand spikes unexpectedly, the company will not have capacity to meet demand. In either case, the company faces serious "regrets" due to the time lag between deciding to exercise the option and the actual completion of the plant—and as I'll show next, this reduces the value of the American option on the plant considerably.

But Intel management did something very clever. In January 2000, even though the company was only at 80% capacity, management decided to spend $400 million on the *shell* for the new fab facility right away. At first blush, this seems like a rather foolish decision—you should either exercise an option completely or not at all, and it looks as though Intel actually killed some of their valuable flexibility by doing so.

While it is true that Intel did indeed kill some of their flexibility by spending the $400 million on the fab shell right away, it is not true that this decision was wrong. In fact, as we'll see in this chapter, this decision actually *created value* for the company. Why? Because by going ahead with the construction of the fab shell (*without* committing to the production line), Intel effectively converted their flexibility from an option on a full plant (shell and production line) with a strike price of $2 billion and a two-year delay into an option on a production line only with a strike price of $1.6 billion and a one-year delay. In other words, by spending the $400 million and killing some of the optionality, Intel management was able to reduce the potential regrets that they might experience due to the long time lag in building an entire plant.

The problem of time delay and regrets is really not all that difficult to handle, but I'd like to show you an example in simplified form so that I can highlight some important points and stress the intuition. We'll return to the Intel case momentarily.

14.1   A Very Simple Example

Let's consider a one-year European call option on a risky asset. The current value of the underlying is $100, its return volatility is 50% per year, the strike price on the option is $120, and the risk-free rate of return is 5% per year. If we build a binomial tree with four steps, each step will be one quarter year (or three months), and our parameters will be $U = 1.284$ and $D = 0.779$. In our recombinant binomial tree, there will be five terminal states of nature, and the tree looks like that in Figure 14.1.

It is easy to value this option. Given our parameters, the risk-free time value factor is $e^{r \times \Delta t} = 1.013$, our risk-neutral probability of an up-step is $q = 0.463$, and so the risk-neutral probability of a down-step is $(1 - q) = 0.537$. If we write in the values of the optimal exercise decision at the end of Q4 (Step 4), then work backward with our risk-neutral probabilities and our risk-free discount rate, we will find that the value of the option is $15.71. I've done this in Figure 14.2, and I've highlighted the last-period states in which we exercise the option in gray. I leave it to you to verify that it is correct.

For this illustration, I am going to reconstruct the binomial tree of underlying values by *ignoring* the recombination in the last period. This is not at all necessary for the analysis, and it does not change the mathematics of the tree at all, but it helps me demonstrate an important point. Please take a minute to look at the binomial tree in Figure 14.3 and understand why it is identical to the tree in Figure 14.1.

Valuing the American call on the underlying modeled by the tree in Figure 14.3 is *exactly* the same as valuing it in the completely recombining tree of Figure 14.1. You start at the exercise date and determine the payoffs from the optimal decision in each terminal state. Using these payoffs, work backward with the same risk-neutral probabilities and the same risk-free discount factor as before. As I show in Figure 14.4, you get exactly the same answer: $15.71. Again, I've

---

Figure 14.1

Binomial Tree of Underlying Values

	0	Q1	Q2	Q3	Q4
	$100.00	$128.40	$164.87	$211.70	$271.83
		$77.88	$100.00	$128.40	$164.87
			$60.65	$77.88	$100.00
				$47.24	$60.65
					$36.79

Figure 14.2

Binomial Tree of Option Values (No Delay)

	0	Q1	Q2	Q3	Q4
	$15.71	$29.40	$53.47	$93.19	$151.83
		$4.28	$9.37	$20.51	$44.87
			$0.00	$0.00	$0.00
				$0.00	$0.00
					$0.00

Figure 14.3 Binomial Tree of Underlying Values

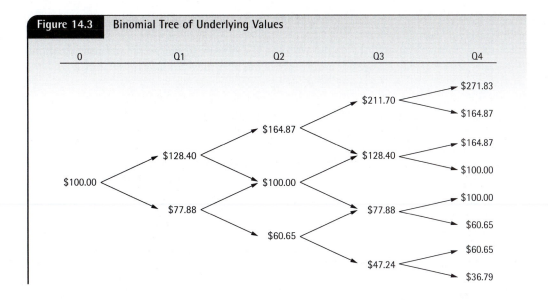

highlighted the states of nature when we optimally exercise in gray (and those where we let the option die in white boxes).

Once more, take a minute to make sure you follow what I've done here. In particular, notice three things. First of all, notice that the Q3 values of the option are the same in every state of nature in Figure 14.4 as they were in our "normal" recombining tree of Figure 14.2. Second, notice that all earlier values are the same as well, and that we get the same option value. Finally (and most important for this analysis), *notice that if we are in the second-highest state at Q3 (where the option is worth $20.51), we do not know yet whether or not we will exercise the option at the end of Q4.*

Now I want to ask a new question. Suppose that this is a very unique option, in that we must decide at Q3 whether we will exercise the option at Q4. In other words, we must commit to an

Figure 14.4 Binomial Tree of Option Values (Given No Delay in Exercise)

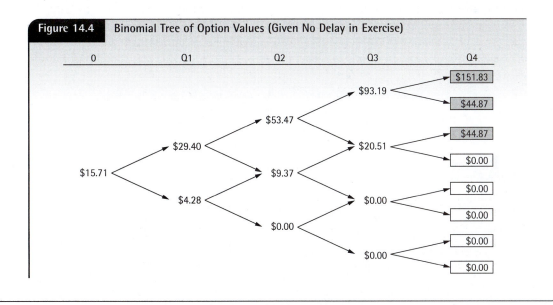

exercise decision before we see the actual state of nature that occurs at the option's maturity. We will still pay the same strike price, $120, and we will pay it at the same time (the end of the fourth step, or Q4). But we must tell the option writer at Q3 whether or not we will ultimately exercise the option, and we cannot change our minds or back out once the remaining uncertainty is resolved.

How do we value such an option? How do we make the exercise decision at Q3 even though there is still some uncertainty about the Q4 value of the underlying? Well, the only thing we can do is make the best decision at Q3 using what information we have at that time—we must calculate the *expected* value of exercising at Q4 and discount it back to Q3, and then only commit at Q3 to exercise at Q4 if the Q3 expected payoff of a commitment to exercise is positive. By taking expectations using risk-neutral probabilities and discounting at the risk-free rate, we will appropriately control for risk.

For example, suppose we are in the highest state at Q3—the state in which the underlying asset is worth $211.70 (Figure 14.3). From this state, the underlying can either go up to $271.83 or down to $164.87. So if we commit to Q4 exercise in this state at Q3, then we will get a net Q4 payoff of $271.83 − $120 = $151.83 *if the underlying goes up,* and a net Q4 payoff of $164.87 − $120 = $44.87 *if the underlying goes down.* The expected net payoff from committing to exercise (under the risk-neutral probabilities) is thus

$$q \times \text{net payoff if up} + (1 - q) \times \text{net payoff if down}$$
$$= 0.463 \times \$151.83 + 0.537 \times \$44.87$$
$$= \$94.39$$

and the Q3 present value of this (taken using the risk-free discount rate) is $94.39/1.013 = $93.19 (Figure 14.5). So, we can say that the Q3 expected present value of a commitment to exercise at Q4, conditional upon being in the highest state at Q3 (when the underlying is worth $211.70), is $93.19. Notice that this is exactly what the option was worth in the same state in our standard problem in Figure 14.4. This is simply because the forced early decision costs us nothing—if we are in this state at Q3, then we *know* that we will exercise the option at Q4 regardless of whether the underlying goes up or down—so the forced early decision does not lead to any potential regrets.

Now work down to the second-highest Q3 state in Figure 14.3, where the underlying asset is worth $128.40. From this Q3 state, the underlying can move up to $164.87 or down to $100. So if we commit in *this* Q3 state to exercise in Q4 (no matter what subsequently happens), our net payoff will be $164.87 − $120 = $44.87 *if the underlying goes up,* and $100 − $120 = −$20 *if the underlying goes down.* So in this Q3 state, the expected present value of a commitment to Q4 exercise is

$$(q \times \text{net payoff if up} + (1 - q) \times \text{net payoff if down})/e^{r \times \Delta t}$$
$$= (0.463 \times \$44.87 + 0.537 \times -\$20)/1.013$$
$$= \$9.89$$

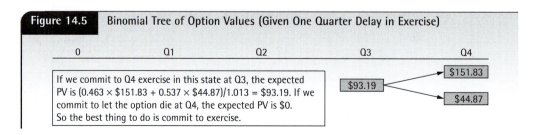

Figure 14.5   Binomial Tree of Option Values (Given One Quarter Delay in Exercise)

0	Q1	Q2	Q3	Q4

If we commit to Q4 exercise in this state at Q3, the expected PV is (0.463 × $151.83 + 0.537 × $44.87)/1.013 = $93.19. If we commit to let the option die at Q4, the expected PV is $0. So the best thing to do is commit to exercise.

$93.19

$151.83

$44.87

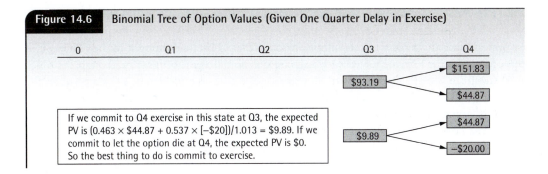

Figure 14.6 Binomial Tree of Option Values (Given One Quarter Delay in Exercise)

If we commit to Q4 exercise in this state at Q3, the expected PV is (0.463 × $44.87 + 0.537 × [−$20])/1.013 = $9.89. If we commit to let the option die at Q4, the expected PV is $0. So the best thing to do is commit to exercise.

Since this is positive, and we must make a decision immediately, we go ahead and commit to Q4 exercise and take the discounted expected value of $9.89, shown in Figure 14.6.

Notice that the forced early decision in this Q3 state *does* lead to potential regrets—if we commit and the underlying moves down over the last period, we end up paying $120 for an asset that is only worth $100. The forced early decision costs us here, in that we end up owning the underlying asset in a Q4 state in which we would rather not. This affects the Time-0 value of the option.

The rest of the binomial tree is easy, as it is obvious in the other two Q3 states that the appropriate thing to do is to commit to no exercise—since that is what we would do in Q4 regardless of what happens over the last step. Working backward from Q3 is the same as we've done all along. In the end, the value of this very different option, in which we must commit to a Q4 exercise decision one period in advance, is only $12.18 (see Figure 14.7 for the solution).

It is very important to understand exactly what happened here. The forced early decision caused the option value to drop by $3.53 (or by nearly 25%) from $15.71 (Figure 14.4) to $12.18 (Figure 14.7). Why? Because of regrets. The one difference between the binomial tree of option values given no delay in exercise (Figure 14.4), and the tree of option values given one quarter delay in exercise (Figure 14.7) is the fourth state down in Q4. In this Q4 state of nature, the underlying is worth $100, and in a normal option setting, the option expires worthless. But if we are forced to make our exercise decision in Q3, then we end up exercising the option in

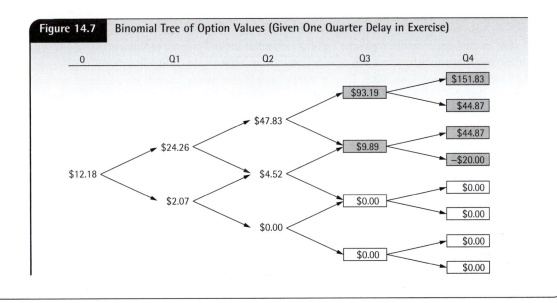

Figure 14.7 Binomial Tree of Option Values (Given One Quarter Delay in Exercise)

this state (because it was the ex-ante right decision at Q3) and paying $120 for an asset only worth $100. Thus, we suffer $20 in regrets.

We can trace this $20 in regrets in this one particular Q4 state right back to the reduction in option value caused by the forced early exercise decision. To get to this state though the binomial tree from time 0, the underlying must first get to the second-highest Q3 state (when the underlying is worth $128.40) and *then* move down. To get to the second-highest Q3 state from time 0, the underlying must make two up moves and one down move *in any particular order*. So, for us to end up with regrets in this particular example, the underlying asset must make two up moves in the first three steps, and then a down move in the last step. The risk-neutral probability of this occurring is

$$\binom{3}{2} q^2 (1 - q) \times (1 - q) = 3(0.463)^2(0.537) \times 0.537 = 0.1854$$

and so the Time-0 expected present value of the regrets, evaluated under the risk-neutral measure and discounted at the risk-free rate, is

$$\frac{0.1854 \times -\$20}{e^{.05}} = -\$3.53$$

which is exactly the change in the option value. I stress that *the reduction in the option value here is not due to time value of money.* I specifically set up this problem so that even though the exercise decision must be made at Q3, the strike price is not paid until Q4. (If you are forced to pay the strike price at Q3, then you will reduce the option value by a little bit more simply because the Time-0 expected present value of the strike price goes *up*.)

Regrets can work the other way as well—that is, a forced early decision can sometimes hurt you because it causes you to let an option die in states of nature that you would like to exercise. To see an example, simply take the problem above and either (1) change the volatility to 30%, or (2) change the strike price to $135 (I leave this as an exercise).

The ultimate point of all of this is that when there is a delay between the time that an exercise decision must be made and the time that payoffs are determined, *you must make the decision using expected present values.* One way to do this is to take expectations using subjective probabilities and discount at a risk-adjusted rate (which is what we implicitly did in our earlier examples such as the Boeing case and the Wal-Mart Neighborhood Markets case). A second approach, which we'll follow in the Intel example, is to take expectations using the risk-neutral probabilities and discount at the risk-free rate. The appendix extends this logic to show some further important points.

Not all problems look alike. In the Intel example (to which we will now return), we will assume that the strike price must be paid at the time the commitment decision is made (either one or two years prior to the receipt of the underlying asset). This is quite easy to handle. The Intel case is also unique in that it involves an option on a factory with a fixed production capacity—a feature that leads to some very unintuitive behavior of the underlying asset (a newly built factory). Nevertheless, we can agree on the following general three-step procedure for dealing with options where there is a delay between the date that the exercise decision must be made and the date that the underlying asset is actually received.

1. Create a binomial tree of your underlying asset values just as you would in a normal case with no "delayed response."
2. For a call option, calculate the *commitment date* payoff on the option in each state as the *commitment-date* present value of the expected *exercise date* payoffs, taking the expectation

using risk-neutral probabilities and discounting at the risk-free rate of return. Commit if the expected present value of committing to exercise is positive, do not commit if it is negative.

3. Work backward from the commitment date payoffs by calculating expected present values at the beginning of each binomial node using risk-neutral probabilities and the riskfree rate, just as you would in a normal case with no delayed response, to build a tree of option values. The calculation of the risk-neutral probabilities does not change. If your option is American, then at any node the value of leaving the option alive must be compared to the value of *early commitment to early exercise* (just use the same procedure as in Step 2) to find the optimal early commitment strategy and value.

14.2   The Fab Shell at Intel

Let's review the problem. Intel has two construction options: (1) The company can build an entire new production facility, both shell and fab, all at once at a cost of $2 billion and with a two-year delay between commitment and actual receipt of the plants, or (2) the company can spend $400 million immediately to build the shell only, and then maintain the option to complete the fab at a cost of $1.6 billion with a one-year delay. In both cases, the strike price will be paid at the time of the *commitment*. Should Intel management go ahead with the shell?

The decision date is December 31, 1999. Let's start with a static discounted cash flow (DCF) analysis that assumes the shell and fab can be built instantaneously. Although this is entirely unrealistic because of time delays from construction, it will be a fundamental piece of the option valuation process that we will get to later. We will need the DCF model with no delay in our option analysis, because we will account for the lag between commitment and actual receipt of the underlying using the method I described in Section 14.1.

Once built, the plant will have a 10-year useful life. It will cost a total of $2 billion to construct ($400 million for the shell and $1.6 billion for the fab) and will be depreciated straight-line over 10 years to a residual value of zero.

The total capacity of the plant will be 62.4 million chips per year. Currently, Intel has overall capacity (before the new plant) of 137.5 million chips per year, but Intel's total demand is only 110 million chips per year. Management expects chip demand to grow by 5% per year. Once built, the plant will not produce chips until Intel's overall demand exceeds its current capacity; moreover, total production from the new plant must be capped at 62.4 million chips regardless of the level of Intel's chip demand.

The plant will produce chips at a variable cost of $90 each; management's forecast for the average sales price of each chip is $160. The fixed costs of the plant (labor, power, etc.) are $600 million per year, whether or not the plant produces. Intel's marginal tax rate is 29%, and the company will have to maintain net working capital equal to 15% of sales revenue. The company assigns a 14% WACC to new production facilities.

The spreadsheet in Figure 14.8 provides the static DCF analysis of the new facility, assuming that both shell and fab can be built instantaneously. This is a standard analysis. I do wish to point out, however, that there is one feature in the spreadsheet that cannot be seen at this stage: The plant's maximum possible production level is 62.4 million chips. This will become important in the option analysis.

As you can see from the static DCF analysis of Figure 14.8, the static NPV of a brand new plant (assuming it could be put online immediately) is hugely negative. This simply reflects the fact that Intel's current capacity is well above its current requirements—the

Figure 14.8 Static DCF Valuation of Immediately Built New Chip Production Facility at Intel

Assumptions

Current annual chip capacity (millions)	137.50
Current annual chip demand (millions)	110.00
Expected yearly growth rate in chip demand	5%
Chip variable cost	$90
Chip price	$160
Shell cost (millions)	$400
Fab cost (millions)	$1,600
Complete facility cost (millions)	$2,000
New facility chip capacity (millions)	62.40
New facility fixed cost when operating (millions)	$600
New facility fixed cost when idle (millions)	$600
Tax rate	29%
WACC	14%
Net working capital (% revenues)	15%

All figures in millions	2000	2001	2002	2003	2004	2005	2006	2007	2008	2009
Total demand for Intel chips	110.00	115.50	121.28	127.34	133.71	140.39	147.41	154.78	162.52	170.65
Capacity before new plant	137.50	137.50	137.50	137.50	137.50	137.50	137.50	137.50	137.50	137.50
Capacity shortfall before new plant	0.00	0.00	0.00	0.00	0.00	2.89	9.91	17.28	25.02	33.15
Capacity of new plant	62.40	62.40	62.40	62.40	62.40	62.40	62.40	62.40	62.40	62.40
Production from new plant	0.00	0.00	0.00	0.00	0.00	2.89	9.91	17.28	25.02	33.15
Sales revenue	$0.00	$0.00	$0.00	$0.00	$0.00	$462.56	$1,585.68	$2,764.97	$4,003.22	$5,303.38
Variable costs	$0.00	$0.00	$0.00	$0.00	$0.00	$260.19	$891.95	$1,555.29	$2,251.81	$2,983.15
Operating margin	$0.00	$0.00	$0.00	$0.00	$0.00	$202.37	$693.74	$1,209.67	$1,751.41	$2,320.23
Fixed costs	$600.00	$600.00	$600.00	$600.00	$600.00	$600.00	$600.00	$600.00	$600.00	$600.00
Depreciation	$200.00	$200.00	$200.00	$200.00	$200.00	$200.00	$200.00	$200.00	$200.00	$200.00
EBT	−$800.00	−$800.00	−$800.00	−$800.00	−$800.00	−$597.63	−$106.26	$409.67	$951.41	$1,520.23
Taxes	−$232.00	−$232.00	−$232.00	−$232.00	−$232.00	−$173.31	−$30.82	$118.81	$275.91	$440.87
Unlevered net Income	−$568.00	−$568.00	−$568.00	−$568.00	−$568.00	−$424.32	−$75.45	$290.87	$675.50	$1,079.36
Add back: depreciation	$200.00	$200.00	$200.00	$200.00	$200.00	$200.00	$200.00	$200.00	$200.00	$200.00
Less: change in NWC	$0.00	$0.00	$0.00	$0.00	$0.00	$69.38	$168.47	$176.89	$185.74	$195.02
Free cash flow	−$368.00	−$368.00	−$368.00	−$368.00	−$368.00	−$293.70	−$43.92	$313.98	$689.76	$1,084.34

PV of free cash flows	−$800.06
(cash flow value of plant)	−$2,000.00
Capital expenditures	−$2,800.06
Static NPV	

present value of the operating free cash flows from the plant (i.e., the value of having a plant) is −$800 million.

Of course, the static NPV analysis gives Intel a now-or-never evaluation of the new plant. If the decision is indeed "build it now or never again," then the right thing for Intel to do is play the averages and commit to never building the plant. But we know that the decision is not now-or-never again, but rather "now or perhaps later, if appropriate."

So we turn to the option analysis. Our first order of business will be to calculate the value of a 10-year American option on a plant that can be constructed immediately for $2 billion. Why am I doing this, even though it is not the point of the example? Two reasons. First, I'd like to show the cost of "regrets" that come about by the forced two-year lag between the exercise decision and the opening of the plant. Second, doing this as an intermediate step will help me explain the procedure when there is delayed response.

We will assume that the key source of risk is Intel's total chip demand, and we will further assume that it is a lognormal random variable. We will model the random chip demand in a binomial tree, translate each possible chip demand at each point in time into the free cash flow value of a brand new plant using the DCF model above (just as we did in the earlier American option cases), and evaluate the optimal exercise strategy.

Intel's demand for chips was 110 million per year at the end of 1999. This will be the starting value of our underlying asset, and we will adopt the assumption that annual changes in chip demand have a volatility of 20%. In a tree with one time step per year ($\Delta t = 1$), the up step will be $U = e^{\sigma \sqrt{\Delta t}} = e^{0.20\sqrt{1}} = 1.22$, and the down step will be $D = 1/U = e^{-\sigma \sqrt{\Delta t}} = e^{-0.20\sqrt{1}} = 0.82$. These parameters give the binomial tree of chip demand at Intel as shown in Figure 14.9.

To begin the option analysis assuming no delayed response, we begin at the end of the tree (as always). Suppose Intel reaches 2009 without having yet built the plant. If they can build the plant instantaneously at that time, what will they do? Obviously, it depends on the total demand for the company's chips at that time. If the static NPV of building a new plant at that time is positive, they will build the new plant. Otherwise, they will not build it at all. This intuition tells us exactly what we have to do—we have to take each possible demand level (i.e., each state of nature at 2009), plug it into a static DCF model just like the one before, and calculate the present value of the plant's operating cash flows. We then compare this to the strike price (in this case, the $2 billion cost of building the shell and fab facility), create a tree for the value of the option on the plant, and write into the tree the value of the plant minus the strike if positive, or zero otherwise. I've done this for the very highest 2009 state—when Intel chip demand is 812.8 million—in Figure 14.10. Notice that even though chip demand exceeds current capacity by

Figure 14.9		Binomial Tree of Annual Intel Chip Demand (in millions)								
Current	2000	2001	2002	2003	2004	2005	2006	2007	2008	2009
110.00	134.35	164.10	200.43	244.81	299.01	365.21	446.07	544.83	665.46	812.80
	90.06	110.00	134.35	164.10	200.43	244.81	299.01	365.21	446.07	544.83
		73.74	90.06	110.00	134.35	164.10	200.43	244.81	299.01	365.21
			60.37	73.74	90.06	110.00	134.35	164.10	200.43	244.81
				49.43	60.37	73.74	90.06	110.00	134.35	164.10
					40.47	49.43	60.37	73.74	90.06	110.00
						33.13	40.47	49.43	60.37	73.74
							27.13	33.13	40.47	49.43
								22.21	27.13	33.13
									18.18	22.21
										14.89

Figure 14.10 Evaluating the Best Decision in 2009 Given Chip Demand of 812.80 Million and No Delay

Binomial Tree of Annual Intel Chip Demand (in millions)

Current	2000	2001	2002	2003	2004	2005	2006	2007	2008	2009
110.00	134.35	164.10	200.43	244.81	299.01	365.21	446.07	544.83	665.46	812.80
	90.06	110.00	134.35	164.10	200.43	244.81	299.01	365.21	446.07	544.83
		73.74	90.06	110.00	134.35	164.10	200.43	244.81	299.01	365.21
			60.37	73.74	90.06	110.00	134.35	164.10	200.43	244.81
				49.43	60.37	73.74	90.06	110.00	134.35	164.10
					40.47	49.43	60.37	73.74	90.06	110.00
						33.13	40.47	49.43	60.37	73.74
							27.13	33.13	40.47	49.43
								22.21	27.13	33.13
									18.18	22.21
										14.89

Assumptions

Current annual chip demand (millions): 812.80
Expected yearly growth rate in chip demand: 5%

Static DCF Valuation of Complete New Chip Facility at Intel

All figures in millions	Year 1	Year 2	Year 3	Year 4	Year 5	Year 6	Year 7	Year 8	Year 9	Year 10
Total demand for Intel chips	812.80	853.44	896.11	940.91	987.96	1,037.36	1,089.22	1,143.69	1,200.87	1,260.91
Capacity before new plant	137.50	137.50	137.50	137.50	137.50	137.50	137.50	137.50	137.50	137.50
Capacity shortfall before new plant	675.30	715.94	758.61	803.41	850.46	899.86	951.72	1,006.19	1,063.37	1,123.41
Capacity of new plant	62.40	62.40	62.40	62.40	62.40	62.40	62.40	62.40	62.40	62.40
Production from new plant	62.40	62.40	62.40	62.40	62.40	62.40	62.40	62.40	62.40	62.40
Sales revenue	$9,984.00	$9,984.00	$9,984.00	$9,984.00	$9,984.00	$9,984.00	$9,984.00	$9,984.00	$9,984.00	$9,984.00
Variable costs	$5,616.00	$5,616.00	$5,616.00	$5,616.00	$5,616.00	$5,616.00	$5,616.00	$5,616.00	$5,616.00	$5,616.00
Operating margin	$4,368.00	$4,368.00	$4,368.00	$4,368.00	$4,368.00	$4,368.00	$4,368.00	$4,368.00	$4,368.00	$4,368.00
Fixed costs	$600.00	$600.00	$600.00	$600.00	$600.00	$600.00	$600.00	$600.00	$600.00	$600.00
Depreciation	$200.00	$200.00	$200.00	$200.00	$200.00	$200.00	$200.00	$200.00	$200.00	$200.00
EBT	$3,568.00	$3,568.00	$3,568.00	$3,568.00	$3,568.00	$3,568.00	$3,568.00	$3,568.00	$3,568.00	$3,568.00
Taxes	$1,034.72	$1,034.72	$1,034.72	$1,034.72	$1,034.72	$1,034.72	$1,034.72	$1,034.72	$1,034.72	$1,034.72
Unlevered net Income	$2,533.28	$2,533.28	$2,533.28	$2,533.28	$2,533.28	$2,533.28	$2,533.28	$2,533.28	$2,533.28	$2,533.28
Add back: depreciation	$200.00	$200.00	$200.00	$200.00	$200.00	$200.00	$200.00	$200.00	$200.00	$200.00
Less: change in NWC	$1,497.60	$0.00	$0.00	$0.00	$0.00	$0.00	$0.00	$0.00	$0.00	$0.00
Free cash flow	$1,235.68	$2,733.28	$2,733.28	$2,733.28	$2,733.28	$2,733.28	$2,733.28	$2,733.28	$2,733.28	$2,733.28
PV of free cash flows										

PV of free cash flows: $12,943.42

Value of an American option on an Immediately Built new Plant, in millions

Current	2000	2001	2002	2003	2004	2005	2006	2007	2008	2009
										$10,943.42

max [$12,943.42 − $2,000, $0] = $10,943.42. Invest.

Production capped at 62.4 million chips

(812.8 − 137.5) = 675.3 million chips, the plant only produces its own capacity of 62.4 million. (Obviously, Intel will not get into this high-demand state without having already built the plant, but we have to start the analysis this way anyway.)

In this state of nature in 2009, the value of the plant is about $12.943 billion. Since it costs only $2 billion to build, Intel should exercise the option, spend the $2 billion, and get back a net payoff of about $10.943 billion.

You may have noticed that in this very high demand state, the plant produces its full capacity of 62.4 million chips per year. No matter how high demand goes, the plant can only produce 62.4 million chips. What this means, then, is that in any state in which demand exceeds Intel's existing capacity (137.5 million chips) by at least 62.4 million chips, the value of a just-finished plant will be the same amount: $12,943.42 billion before the capital expenditure, or $10,943.42 after it. That is, if total demand is greater than (137.5 + 62.4) = 199.9 million chips, the cash flow value of the plant is at its maximum of $12,943.42 billion. So in the highest four states of nature at 2009, the optimal decision will be to build the plant, and the payoff from exercising will be $10,943.42 billion.

To see a second example, move down to the fifth-highest state at 2009 where total demand is 164.10 million chips. I've calculated the present value of the free cash flows from a new plant in this state and the optimal exercise payoff in Figure 14.11.

When we complete the analysis for 2009, our results will look like Figure 14.12.

Our next task is to move backward in time, comparing the value of leaving the option alive (calculated as the discounted expected value of the payoff in 2009 using the risk-neutral probabilities and the risk-free rate of return) to the value of exercising immediately (calculated exactly as we did just now). Figure 14.13 exhibits the calculation for one example state of nature: the highest demand state in 2008 (where chip demand is 665.46 million units). Here we actually make two calculations, then take the highest value.

1. If Intel chooses to wait, it keeps the option alive. The value of the option if kept alive is just the discounted expectation of the two possible subsequent values in 2009: $10,943.42 million if the underlying goes up and $10,943.42 million if the underlying goes down (these are identical because of the fixed capacity of the plant). We take the expectation using the risk-neutral probabilities to adjust for risk, then discount at the risk-free rate of return. Since our risk-free rate of return is 5% per year and we're dealing with one time step,

$$e^{r \times \Delta t} = e^{0.05\sqrt{1}} = 1.051$$

and so the risk-neutral probabilities of the up and down steps are

$$q = \frac{e^{r \times \Delta t} - D}{U - D} = \frac{e^{0.05(1)} - e^{-0.2\sqrt{1}}}{e^{0.2\sqrt{1}} - e^{-0.2\sqrt{1}}} = 0.5775$$

$$1 - q = 0.4225$$

respectively. Therefore, the value of the option if left alive is

$$\frac{0.5775(\$10,943.42) + 0.4225(\$10,943.42)}{1.051} = \$10,412.39$$

2. If Intel chooses to build the plant immediately, it must pay the $2 billion strike price and receive, in return, the plant which will be worth $12,943.42 million in this state

Binomial Tree of Annual Intel Chip Demand (in millions)

	Current	2000	2001	2002	2003	2004	2005	2006	2007	2008	2009
	110.00	134.35	164.10	200.43	244.81	299.01	365.21	446.07	544.83	665.46	812.80
		90.06	110.00	134.35	164.10	200.43	244.81	299.01	365.21	446.07	544.83
			73.74	90.06	110.00	134.35	164.10	200.43	244.81	299.01	365.21
				60.37	73.74	90.06	110.00	134.35	164.10	200.43	244.81
					49.43	60.37	73.74	90.06	110.00	134.35	164.10
						40.47	49.43	60.37	73.74	90.06	110.00
							33.13	40.47	49.43	60.37	73.74
								27.13	33.13	40.47	49.43
									22.21	27.13	33.13
										18.18	22.21
											14.89

Assumptions

Current annual chip demand (millions) — 164.10
Expected yearly growth rate in chip demand — 5%

Static DCF Valuation of Complete New Chip Facility at Intel

All figures in millions	Year 1	Year 2	Year 3	Year 4	Year 5	Year 6	Year 7	Year 8	Year 9	Year 10
Total demand for Intel chips	164.10	172.31	180.92	189.97	199.46	209.44	219.91	230.91	242.45	254.57
Capacity before new plant	137.50	137.50	137.50	137.50	137.50	137.50	137.50	137.50	137.50	137.50
Capacity shortfall before new plant	26.60	34.81	43.42	52.47	61.96	71.94	82.41	93.41	104.95	117.07
Capacity of new plant	62.40	62.40	62.40	62.40	62.40	62.40	62.40	62.40	62.40	62.40
Production from new plant	26.60	34.81	43.42	52.47	61.96	62.40	62.40	62.40	62.40	62.40
Sales revenue	$4,256.00	$5,568.80	$6,947.24	$8,394.60	$9,914.33	$9,984.00	$9,984.00	$9,984.00	$9,984.00	$9,984.00
Variable costs	$2,394.00	$3,132.45	$3,907.82	$4,721.96	$5,576.81	$5,616.00	$5,616.00	$5,616.00	$5,616.00	$5,616.00
Operating margin	$1,862.00	$2,436.35	$3,039.42	$3,672.64	$4,337.52	$4,368.00	$4,368.00	$4,368.00	$4,368.00	$4,368.00
Fixed costs	$600.00	$600.00	$600.00	$600.00	$600.00	$600.00	$600.00	$600.00	$600.00	$600.00
Depreciation	$200.00	$200.00	$200.00	$200.00	$200.00	$200.00	$200.00	$200.00	$200.00	$200.00
EBT	$1,062.00	$1,636.35	$2,239.42	$2,872.64	$3,537.52	$3,568.00	$3,568.00	$3,568.00	$3,568.00	$3,568.00
Taxes	$307.98	$474.54	$649.43	$833.07	$1,025.88	$1,034.72	$1,034.72	$1,034.72	$1,034.72	$1,034.72
Unlevered net Income	$754.02	$1,161.81	$1,589.99	$2,039.57	$2,511.64	$2,533.28	$2,533.28	$2,533.28	$2,533.28	$2,533.28
Add back: depreciation	$200.00	$200.00	$200.00	$200.00	$200.00	$200.00	$200.00	$200.00	$200.00	$200.00
Less: change in NWC	$638.40	$196.92	$206.77	$217.10	$227.96	$10.45	$0.00	$0.00	$0.00	$0.00
Free cash flow	$315.62	$1,164.89	$1,583.22	$2,022.47	$2,483.68	$2,722.83	$2,733.28	$2,733.28	$2,733.28	$2,733.28
PV of free cash flows	$9,598.14									

Value of an American option on an Immediately Built new Plant, in millions

	2000	2001	2002	2003	2004	2005	2006	2007	2008	2009
Current $9,598.14										$10,943.42
										$10,943.42
										$10,943.42
										$7,598.14

max [$9,598.14 − $2,000, $0] = $7,598.14 Invest.

Figure 14.12	Value of an American Option on an Immediately Built New Plant (in millions)									
Current	2000	2001	2002	2003	2004	2005	2006	2007	2008	2009
										$10,943.42
										$10,943.42
										$10,943.42
										$10,943.42
										$7,598.14
										$0.00
										$0.00
										$0.00
										$0.00
										$0.00
										$0.00

(see Figure 14.13). So the payoff to exercising immediately is $12,943.42 million − $2,000 million = $10,943.42 million.

The maximum of these two values is $10,943.42, which Intel achieves by investing immediately. So we assert that Intel exercises in this state, and we write in the value of immediate exercise ($10.943.42) into our option value tree. Figure 14.13 illustrates.

The optimal decision, should Intel reach the high-demand state in 2008 without having already built the plant, is to exercise the American option and build it at that time. We can now see the really interesting (and somewhat bizarre) feature that the cap on the plant's production imposes on the option model. In the high-demand state in 2008, the plant operates at full capacity for 10 years—and the net value of investing immediately is $10,943.42. If Intel waits until 2009 to make the decision, the value of the optimal decision will be $10,943.42 for sure. This is because no matter what happens after the high-demand 2008 state, the plant will operate at full capacity and will have the same value. So the best thing to do is to go ahead and invest, because by investing immediately Intel gets a net payoff of $10,943.42 right away. If Intel waits, they get $10,943.42 one period in the future (which is only worth $10,412.39 in present value terms).

What this means, then, is that the cap on capacity actually imposes a *rate of return shortfall* (or *convenience yield*) on the value of the plant. In these very good states of nature, waiting produces little benefit (basically, it just saves the present value of the cost of construction), but it is costly (because it pushes all free cash flows out in time by one year, without any increase). So the cap on capacity can lead to optimal early exercise of the option.

The final value of the 10-year option on an *immediately built* full production facility is about $4.8 billion, which I show in Figure 14.14. The analysis also tells us that Intel should wait to construct the facility until total demand reaches at least about 200 million chips (see Figure 14.15). You should not interpret this literally, because I've set up the problem with a relatively small number of steps and rather large changes between each. If you look at the highest demand state at 2001 (164.1 million chips), you will see that after an up move, demand goes to about 200 million—which is full capacity for the plant, but after a down move, demand goes to about 134 million chips—which implies zero production for the plant. If we were to put finer time steps into the analysis, we would most likely see optimal exercise at some point where we expect the plant to operate at partial capacity.

Figure 14.13 Evaluating the Best Decision in 2008 Given Chip Demand of 665.46 Million and No Delay

Binomial Tree of Annual Intel Chip Demand (in millions)

Current	2000	2001	2002	2003	2004	2005	2006	2007	2008	2009
110.00	134.35	164.10	200.43	244.81	299.01	365.21	446.07	544.83	665.46	812.80
	90.06	110.00	134.35	164.10	200.43	244.81	299.01	365.21	446.07	544.83
		73.74	90.06	110.00	134.35	164.10	200.43	244.81	299.01	365.21
			60.37	73.74	90.06	110.00	134.35	164.10	200.43	244.81
				49.43	60.37	73.74	90.06	110.00	134.35	164.10
					40.47	49.43	60.37	73.74	90.06	110.00
						33.13	40.47	49.43	60.37	73.74
							27.13	33.13	40.47	49.43
								22.21	27.13	33.13
									18.18	22.21
										14.89

Assumptions

Current annual chip demand (millions)	665.46
Expected yearly growth rate in chip demand	5%

Static DCF Valuation of Complete New Chip Facility at Intel

All figures in millions

	Year-1	Year 2	Year 3	Year 4	Year 5	Year 6	Year 7	Year 8	Year 9	Year 10
Total demand for Intel chips	665.46	698.73	733.67	770.35	808.87	849.32	891.78	936.37	983.19	1,032.35
Capacity before new plant	137.50	137.50	137.50	137.50	137.50	137.50	137.50	137.50	137.50	137.50
Capacity shortfall before new plant	527.96	561.23	596.17	632.85	671.37	711.82	754.28	798.87	845.69	894.85
Capacity of new plant	62.40	62.40	62.40	62.40	62.40	62.40	62.40	62.40	62.40	62.40
Production from new plant	62.40	62.40	62.40	62.40	62.40	62.40	62.40	62.40	62.40	62.40
Sales revenue	$9,984.00	$9,984.00	$9,984.00	$9,984.00	$9,984.00	$9,984.00	$9,984.00	$9,984.00	$9,984.00	$9,984.00
Variable costs	$5,616.00	$5,616.00	$5,616.00	$5,616.00	$5,616.00	$5,616.00	$5,616.00	$5,616.00	$5,616.00	$5,616.00
Operating margin	$4,368.00	$4,368.00	$4,368.00	$4,368.00	$4,368.00	$4,368.00	$4,368.00	$4,368.00	$4,368.00	$4,368.00
Fixed costs	$600.00	$600.00	$600.00	$600.00	$600.00	$600.00	$600.00	$600.00	$600.00	$600.00
Depreciation	$200.00	$200.00	$200.00	$200.00	$200.00	$200.00	$200.00	$200.00	$200.00	$200.00
EBT	$3,568.00	$3,568.00	$3,568.00	$3,568.00	$3,568.00	$3,568.00	$3,568.00	$3,568.00	$3,568.00	$3,568.00
Taxes	$1,034.72	$1,034.72	$1,034.72	$1,034.72	$1,034.72	$1,034.72	$1,034.72	$1,034.72	$1,034.72	$1,034.72
Unlevered net Income	$2,533.28	$2,533.28	$2,533.28	$2,533.28	$2,533.28	$2,533.28	$2,533.28	$2,533.28	$2,533.28	$2,533.28
Add back: depreciation	$200.00	$200.00	$200.00	$200.00	$200.00	$200.00	$200.00	$200.00	$200.00	$200.00
Less: change in NWC	$1,497.60	$0.00	$0.00	$0.00	$0.00	$0.00	$0.00	$0.00	$0.00	$0.00
Free cash flow	$1,235.68	$2,733.28	$2,733.28	$2,733.28	$2,733.28	$2,733.28	$2,733.28	$2,733.28	$2,733.28	$2,733.28
PV of free cash flows	$12,943.42									

Value of an American option on an Immediately built new Plant (in millions)

Current	2000	2001	2002	2003	2004	2005	2006	2007	2008	2009
$12,943.42									$10,943.42	$10,943.42
										$10,943.42
										$10,943.42
										$10,943.42
										$7,598.14
										$0.00
										$0.00
										$0.00
										$0.00
										$0.00

Value of waiting:

$$[0.5775 \times \$10,943.42 + 0.4225 \times \$12,943.42]/1.051 = \$10,412.39$$

Value of investing immediately:

$$[\$12,943.42 - \$2,000, \$0] = \$10,943.42$$

Invest immediately.

Production capped at 62.4 million chips

Figure 14.14	Value of an American Option on an Immediately Built New Plant (in millions)									
Current	2000	2001	2002	2003	2004	2005	2006	2007	2008	2009
$4,848.17	$6,479.23	$8,500.93	$10,943.42	$10,943.42	$10,943.42	$10,943.42	$10,943.42	$10,943.42	$10,943.42	$10,943.42
	$3,207.11	$4,502.18	$6,194.06	$8,333.58	$10,943.42	$10,943.42	$10,943.42	$10,943.42	$10,943.42	$10,943.42
		$1,826.17	$2,736.01	$4,021.36	$5,777.66	$8,079.43	$10,943.42	$10,943.42	$10,943.42	$10,943.42
			$804.17	$1,311.17	$2,108.79	$3,332.65	$5,145.29	$7,689.02	$10,943.42	$10,943.42
				$208.79	$380.07	$691.89	$1,259.52	$2,292.83	$4,173.87	$7,598.14
					$0.00	$0.00	$0.00	$0.00	$0.00	$0.00
						$0.00	$0.00	$0.00	$0.00	$0.00
							$0.00	$0.00	$0.00	$0.00
								$0.00	$0.00	$0.00
									$0.00	$0.00
										$0.00

Figure 14.15	Binomial Tree of Annual Intel Chip Demand (in Millions), Showing Optimal Exercise Boundary for Immediately Built Plant									
Current	2000	2001	2002	2003	2004	2005	2006	2007	2008	2009
110.00	134.35	164.10	200.43	244.81	299.01	365.21	446.07	544.83	665.46	812.80
	90.06	110.00	134.35	164.10	200.43	244.81	299.01	365.21	446.07	544.83
		73.74	90.06	110.00	134.35	164.10	200.43	244.81	299.01	365.21
			60.37	73.74	90.06	110.00	134.35	164.10	200.43	244.81
				49.43	60.37	73.74	90.06	110.00	134.35	164.10
					40.47	49.43	60.37	73.74	90.06	110.00
						33.13	40.47	49.43	60.37	73.74
							27.13	33.13	40.47	49.43
								22.21	27.13	33.13
									18.18	22.21
										14.89

▨ Build plant.
══ Plant already built.

14.3   Valuation and Evaluation When There's Delay

We now turn to the more appropriate analysis—determination of the optimal exercise policy and option value when there is a delay between the exercise decision and the completion of the plant. We will first look at the situation where Intel has an American option on a full facility (shell and fab) that costs $2 billion and takes 2 years to build. We will assume that the $2 billion strike price is paid at the time the commitment decision is made.

A little intuition will help us learn how to do this analysis. Suppose Intel decides to commit to the plant in, say, a high demand state in 2007. What does Intel get back? Well, the company gets in return a fully operating plant *in 2009.* That is, it gets the free cash flows from the plant starting *two years later* in 2009, based on whatever the demand for chips will be in 2009 (which is not completely certain in 2007). So what is the 2007 value of that underlying asset? At any given state in 2007, the value of the underlying asset is the expected present value of the 2009 value of the plant, where the expectation is taken across all 2009 states that can be reached from the particular 2007 state, using the risk-neutral probabilities, and discounting at the risk-free rate of return. I show you with the diagram in Figure 14.16.

If we find ourselves in the state of nature at 2007 where demand is 244.81 million chips, there are only three possible states of nature we can reach by 2009: Either demand is 365.21 million,

Figure 14.16	Illustrating the Thought Process Given Two-Year Delay

Binomial Tree of Annual Intel Chip Demand (in millions)

Current	2000	2001	2002	2003	2004	2005	2006	2007	2008	2009
110.00	134.35	164.10	200.43	244.81	299.01	365.21	446.07	544.83	665.46	812.80
	90.06	110.00	134.35	164.10	200.43	244.81	299.01	365.21	446.07	544.83
		73.74	90.06	110.00	134.35	164.10	200.43	244.81	299.01	365.21
			60.37	73.74	90.06	110.00	134.35	164.10	200.43	244.81
				49.43	60.37	73.74	90.06	110.00	134.35	164.10
					40.47	49.43	60.37	73.74	90.06	110.00
						33.13	49.43	60.37	73.74	73.74
							27.13	40.47	49.43	49.43
								22.21	33.13	33.13
									27.13	22.21
									18.18	14.89

Binomial Tree of Value of Option on New Facility with Two-Year Delay

Current	2000	2001	2002	2003	2004	2005	2006	2007	2008	2009

The value of committing $2 billion to a new facility in the 244.81 million demand state at 2007 is the expected present value of what could possibly happen in 2009 subsequent to that 2007 state (demand is either 365.21, 244.81, or 164.10).

244.81 million, or 164.10 million. So if we commit to building a plant in 1997 in the 244.81 million chip demand state, we will get back either (1) a new plant in 2009 when Intel chip demand is 365.21 million, (2) a new plant in 2009 when Intel chip demand is 244.81 million, or (3) a new plant in 2009 when Intel chip demand is 164.10 million. So what we get back by committing $2 billion to the plant in this particular 2007 demand state is the *expected present value of the three 2009 possibilities,* calculated using the risk-neutral probabilities and our risk-free discount rate.

To get the appropriate risk-neutral probabilities for this calculation, we must remember a result from our review of derivatives pricing. We construct our binomial trees so that the risk-neutral probabilities of up (q) and down ($1 - q$) moves remain constant. So the risk-neutral probability that demand moves from 244.81 million in 2007 to 365.21 million in 2009 is the risk-neutral probability of two consecutive up moves, or q^2. The risk-neutral probability that demand moves from 244.81 million in 2007 down to 164.10 million in 2009 is the risk-neutral probability of two down moves, or $(1 - q)^2$. Finally, the risk-neutral probability that demand moves from 244.81 million units in 2007 to 244.81 million units in 2009 is $2q(1 - q)$, because this requires one up and one down move—and there are two possible paths with that pattern. Therefore, the payoff to commitment in 2007 when demand is currently 244.81 million units is

$$\text{(commitment payoff | demand } = 244.81 \text{ in 2007)} = \frac{q^2 \times (\text{value if demand} = 365.21 \text{ in 2009})}{e^{r \times 2}}$$

$$+ \frac{2q(1 - q)(\text{value if demand} = 244.81 \text{ in 2009})}{e^{r \times 2}}$$

$$+ \frac{(1 - q)^2(\text{value if demand} = 164.10 \text{ in 2009})}{e^{r \times 2}}$$

$$- \$2 \text{ billion}$$

We calculate the three possible 2009 values that follow this particular 2007 demand state using the DCF model spreadsheet just as before. We then take the expectation of the three possible values using $q^2 = (0.5775)^2 = 0.3335$, $2q(1 - q) = 2(0.5775)(0.4225) = 0.488$, and $(1 - q)^2 = (0.4225)^2 = 0.1785$, and we discount the expected value using $e^{r \times 2\Delta t} = e^{(.05)2} = 1.105$.

The 2009 free cash flow value of the new plant when demand is 365.21 million is \$12,943.42 million (shown in the spreadsheet in Figure 14.17). The 2009 value of the plant when demand is 244.81 million is also \$12,943.42 because of the production cap. The 2009 value of the plant when demand is 164.10 million units is \$9,598.14 billion. So, the expected present value of the payoff from committing to build the plant in 2007 when current demand is 244.81 million units, with a two-year delay, is

(commitment payoff|demand $=$ 244.81 in 2007)

$$= \frac{0.3335(\$12,943.42) + 0.488(\$12,943.42) + 0.1785(\$9,598.14)}{1.1052}$$

$$- \$2,000$$

$$= \$9,171.35$$

We complete the 2007 part of the tree of option values the exact same way, and I've done this for you in Figure 14.18. For each 2007 state, identify the three possible subsequent 2009 states. Use the DCF model to calculate the 2009 value of a brand-new plant in each of those demand states, then calculate the 2007 expected PV using the risk-neutral probabilities and the risk-free discount rate. This is what you get if you commit in 2007 to exercising the option (and getting the underlying back two years later); if you don't exercise the option at 2007, your payoff is zero (because the option expires worthless).

From Figure 14.18, we notice something interesting right away: When there's a two-year delay, we commit to building the facility in more 2007 states than we would when there is no delay. To see this, compare Figure 14.18 with the 2007 column of Figure 14.14.

The next step is the trickiest part of the analysis, because we have to make two calculations. If we are at any particular state at 2006, is it better to wait and keep the option alive until 2007, or is it better to commit \$2 billion immediately and accept the two-year delay in building the facility? The first calculation is just as we've always done in this course: the value of waiting is just

$$[q \times DERIV_{Up} + (1 - q) \times DERIV_{Dn}]/e^{r \times \Delta t}$$

The value of investing immediately in 2006, on the other hand, works just like the analysis of the best 2007 decision. At any 2006 demand state, do the following: (1) Identify the three possible subsequent 2008 demand states, (2) value the new plant in each of those states using the DCF model as before, (3) calculate the 2006 expected present value of the 2008 plant

Figure 14.17 — Evaluating the Best Decision in 2007 Given Chip Demand of 244.81 Million and Two Years Delay

Binomial Tree of Annual Intel Chip Demand (in millions)

Current	2000	2001	2002	2003	2004	2005	2006	2007	2008	2009
110.00	134.35	164.10	200.43	244.81	299.01	365.21	446.07	544.83	665.46	812.80
	90.06	110.00	134.35	164.10	200.43	244.81	299.01	365.21	446.07	544.83
		73.74	90.06	110.00	134.35	164.10	200.43	244.81	299.01	365.21
			60.37	73.74	90.06	110.00	134.35	164.10	200.43	244.81
				49.43	60.37	73.74	90.06	110.00	134.35	164.10
					40.47	49.43	60.37	73.74	90.06	110.00
						33.13	40.47	49.43	60.37	73.74
							27.13	33.13	40.47	49.43
								22.21	27.13	33.13
									18.18	22.21
										14.89

Assumptions

Current annual chip demand (millions)	365.21
Expected yearly growth rate in chip demand	5%

Static DCF Valuation of Complete New Chip Facility at Intel

All figures in millions	Year-1	Year 2	Year 3	Year 4	Year 5	Year 6	Year 7	Year 8	Year 9	Year 10
Total demand for Intel chips	365.21	383.47	402.64	422.78	443.92	466.11	489.42	513.89	539.58	566.56
Capacity before new plant	137.50	137.50	137.50	137.50	137.50	137.50	137.50	137.50	137.50	137.50
Capacity shortfall before new plant	227.71	245.97	265.14	285.28	306.42	328.61	351.92	376.39	402.08	429.06
Capacity of new plant	62.40	62.40	62.40	62.40	62.40	62.40	62.40	62.40	62.40	62.40
Production from new plant	62.40	62.40	62.40	62.40	62.40	62.40	62.40	62.40	62.40	62.40
Sales revenue	$9,984.00	$9,984.00	$9,984.00	$9,984.00	$9,984.00	$9,984.00	$9,984.00	$9,984.00	$9,984.00	$9,984.00
Variable costs	$5,616.00	$5,616.00	$5,616.00	$5,616.00	$5,616.00	$5,616.00	$5,616.00	$5,616.00	$5,616.00	$5,616.00
Operating margin	$4,368.00	$4,368.00	$4,368.00	$4,368.00	$4,368.00	$4,368.00	$4,368.00	$4,368.00	$4,368.00	$4,368.00
Fixed costs	$600.00	$600.00	$600.00	$600.00	$600.00	$600.00	$600.00	$600.00	$600.00	$600.00
Depreciation	$200.00	$200.00	$200.00	$200.00	$200.00	$200.00	$200.00	$200.00	$200.00	$200.00
EBT	$3,568.00	$3,568.00	$3,568.00	$3,568.00	$3,568.00	$3,568.00	$3,568.00	$3,568.00	$3,568.00	$3,568.00
Taxes	$1,034.72	$1,034.72	$1,034.72	$1,034.72	$1,034.72	$1,034.72	$1,034.72	$1,034.72	$1,034.72	$1,034.72
Unlevered net income	$2,533.28	$2,533.28	$2,533.28	$2,533.28	$2,533.28	$2,533.28	$2,533.28	$2,533.28	$2,533.28	$2,533.28
Add back: depreciation	$200.00	$200.00	$200.00	$200.00	$200.00	$200.00	$200.00	$200.00	$200.00	$200.00
NWC requirement	$1,497.60	$1,497.60	$1,497.60	$1,497.60	$1,497.60	$1,497.60	$1,497.60	$1,497.60	$1,497.60	$1,497.60
Less: change in NWC	$1,497.60	$0.00	$0.00	$0.00	$0.00	$0.00	$0.00	$0.00	$0.00	$0.00
Free cash flows	$1,235.68	$2,733.28	$2,733.28	$2,733.28	$2,733.28	$2,733.28	$2,733.28	$2,733.28	$2,733.28	$2,733.28
	1	2	3	4	5	6	7	8	9	10
PV factor	1	0.877193	0.7694675	0.674972	0.59208	0.5193687	0.4555865	0.3996373	0.3505591	0.3075079
PV	1083.93	2103.1702	1844.886	1618.321	1419.58	1245.2456	1092.3207	958.17605	840.50531	737.28536

PV of free cash flows: $12,943.42

Binomial Tree of Option Value, In Millions

Current	2000	2001	2002	2003	2004	2005	2006	2007	2008	2009
$12,943.42								$9,171.35		$12,943.42
										$12,943.42
										$9,598.14

$$\max[(0.3335 \times \$12{,}943.42 + 0.488 \times \$12{,}943.42 + 0.1785 \times \$9{,}598.14)/1.105 - \$2{,}000, \$0] = \$9{,}171.35 \text{ Invest.}$$

Production capped at 62.4 million chips

Figure 14.18		Binomial Tree of Value of Option on Full Facility with 2-Year Delay (in millions)								
Current	2000	2001	2002	2003	2004	2005	2006	2007	2008	2009
								$9,711.69		
								$9,711.69		
								$9,171.35		
								$6,014.67		
								$233.03		
								$0.00		
								$0.00		
								$0.00		
								$0.00		

using the appropriate risk-neutral probabilities (q^2, $2q(1-q)$ and $(1-q)^2$) and discount for two years at the risk-free rate, and (4) subtract the $2 billion strike price. If this is greater than the value of waiting, then commit immediately and take the value (net of the strike price) that you just calculated.

For example, suppose we are in the 2006 state of nature when demand is 134.35 million chips (the fourth state down from the top in Figure14.19). If we wait and leave the option alive, the 2007 value will be $6,014.67 after an up move in the underlying and $233.03 after a down move, so the value of the option if kept alive is

$$\frac{0.5775(\$6,014.67) + 0.4225(\$233.03)}{1.051} = \$3,397.69$$

On the other hand, we could invest immediately. The three possible subsequent 2008 demand states are (1) 200.43 million units (after two up steps), (2) 134.35 million units (after one up and one down), and (3) 90.06 million units (after two downs). The 2008 free cash flow values of a new plant in each of these possible demand states are (1) $12,943.42, (2) $3,343.19, and (3) −$1904.19, respectively. So the payoff from exercising early is

$$\frac{0.3335(\$12,943.42) + 0.488(\$3,343.19) + 0.1875(-\$1,904.19)}{1.1052} - \$2,000 = \$3,074.39$$

So in this particular state in 2006, the correct thing to do is to do nothing—wait until 2007 and see what happens to demand.

The rest of the analysis for the 2-year delay case works exactly the same way. I've presented the results in Figure 14.20.

We see two things here. First, the value of the option on the plant falls substantially when Intel must commit to the plant decision two years before the plant comes on line. The value of the option with no delay was $4,848.17 million, so the potential regrets from early commitment lower the option value by ($4,848.17 million−$3,445.47 million) = $1,402.70 million (or nearly 30%). Second, we see why regrets come about. With the two-year delayed response, Intel commits to the plant in some time-states that it would not under no delay. In 2007, for example, Intel will optimally commit to building the plant when total demand is only 110 million (the same as in 1999)—that is, when demand is less than current capacity. If demand makes two moves up from this state, the new plant will be worth $9.598 billion in 2009; if demand makes

Figure 14.19 — Evaluating the Best Decision in 2006 Given Chip Demand of 134.35 Million and Two Years Delay

Binomial Tree of Annual Intel Chip Demand (in millions)

	Current	2000	2001	2002	2003	2004	2005	2006	2007	2008	2009
	110.00	134.35	164.10	200.43	244.81	299.01	365.21	446.07	544.83	665.46	812.80
		90.06	110.00	134.35	164.10	200.43	244.81	299.01	365.21	446.07	544.83
			73.74	90.06	110.00	134.35	164.10	200.43	244.81	299.01	365.21
				60.37	73.74	90.06	110.00	134.35	164.10	200.43	244.81
					49.43	60.37	73.74	90.06	110.00	134.35	164.10
						40.47	49.43	60.37	73.74	90.06	110.00
							33.13	40.47	49.43	60.37	73.74
								27.13	33.13	40.47	49.43
									22.21	27.13	33.13
										18.18	22.21
											14.89

Assumptions

Current annual chip demand (millions): 200.43 — 5%
Expected yearly growth rate in chip demand

Static DCF Valuation of Complete New Chip Facility at Intel

All figures in millions	Year 1	Year 2	Year 3	Year 4	Year 5	Year 6	Year 7	Year 8	Year 9	Year 10
	2000	2001	2002	2003	2004	2005	2006	2007	2008	2009
Total demand for Intel chips	200.43	210.45	220.97	232.02	243.62	255.81	268.60	282.03	296.13	310.93
Capacity before new plant	137.50	137.50	137.50	137.50	137.50	137.50	137.50	137.50	137.50	137.50
Capacity shortfall before new plant	62.93	72.95	83.47	94.52	106.12	118.31	131.10	144.53	158.63	173.43
Capacity of new plant	62.40	62.40	62.40	62.40	62.40	62.40	62.40	62.40	62.40	62.40
Production from new plant	62.40	62.40	62.40	62.40	62.40	62.40	62.40	62.40	62.40	62.40
Sales revenue	$9,984.00	$9,984.00	$9,984.00	$9,984.00	$9,984.00	$9,984.00	$9,984.00	$9,984.00	$9,984.00	$9,984.00
Variable costs	$5,616.00	$5,616.00	$5,616.00	$5,616.00	$5,616.00	$5,616.00	$5,616.00	$5,616.00	$5,616.00	$5,616.00
Operating margin	$4,368.00	$4,368.00	$4,368.00	$4,368.00	$4,368.00	$4,368.00	$4,368.00	$4,368.00	$4,368.00	$4,368.00
Fixed costs	$600.00	$600.00	$600.00	$600.00	$600.00	$600.00	$600.00	$600.00	$600.00	$600.00
Depreciation	$200.00	$200.00	$200.00	$200.00	$200.00	$200.00	$200.00	$200.00	$200.00	$200.00
EBT	$3,568.00	$3,568.00	$3,568.00	$3,568.00	$3,568.00	$3,568.00	$3,568.00	$3,568.00	$3,568.00	$3,568.00
Taxes	$1,034.72	$1,034.72	$1,034.72	$1,034.72	$1,034.72	$1,034.72	$1,034.72	$1,034.72	$1,034.72	$1,034.72
Unlevered net Income	$2,533.28	$2,533.28	$2,533.28	$2,533.28	$2,533.28	$2,533.28	$2,533.28	$2,533.28	$2,533.28	$2,533.28
Add back: depreciation	$200.00	$200.00	$200.00	$200.00	$200.00	$200.00	$200.00	$200.00	$200.00	$200.00
Less: change in NWC	$1,497.60	$0.00	$0.00	$0.00	$0.00	$0.00	$0.00	$0.00	$0.00	$0.00
Free cash flow	$1,235.68	$2,733.28	$2,733.28	$2,733.28	$2,733.28	$2,733.28	$2,733.28	$2,733.28	$2,733.28	$2,733.28
PV of free cash flows	$1,235.68	$2,733.28	$2,733.28	$2,733.28	$2,733.28	$2,733.28	$2,733.28	$2,733.28	$2,733.28	$2,733.28

$12,943.42

Binomial Tree of Option Value (in millions)

	Current	2000	2001	2002	2003	2004	2005	2006	2007	2008	2009
	$12,943.42							$3,397.69	$9,711.69	$12,943.42	
									$9,711.69	$3,343.19	
									$9,171.35	−$1,904.19	
									$6,014.67	$0.00	
									$233.03	$0.00	
									$0.00	$0.00	
									$0.00		
									$0.00		

Payoff to immediate commitment:
[[0.3335 × $12,943.42 + 0.488 × $3,343.19 + 0.1785 × [−$1,904.19]]/1.1052 − $2,000]= $3,074.39
Payoff to Waiting:
(0.5775 × $6,014.67 + 0.4225 × $233.03)/1.051 = $3,397.69
Wait.

Production capped at 62.4 million chips

464

| Figure 14.20 | Binomial Tree of Option Value on Complete Plant with 2-Year Delay (in millions) | | | | | | | | | |

Current	2000	2001	2002	2003	2004	2005	2006	2007	2008	2009
$3,445.47	$4,698.48	$6,266.18	$8,181.02	$9,171.35	$9,711.69	$9,711.69	$9,711.69	$9,711.69		
	$2,150.92	$3,125.87	$4,436.67	$6,120.76	$8,161.02	$9,171.35	$9,711.69	$9,711.69		
		$1,079.36	$1,713.55	$2,673.20	$4,074.83	$6,014.67	$8,161.02	$9,171.35		
			$343.51	$609.80	$1,081.62	$1,917.89	$3,397.69	$6,014.67		
				$21.22	$38.63	$70.32	$128.01	$233.03		
					$0.00	$0.00	$0.00	$0.00		
						$0.00	$0.00	$0.00		
							$0.00	$0.00		
								$0.00		

Binomial Tree of Annual Intel Chip Demand In Millions, Showing Optimal Exercise Boundary

Current	2000	2001	2002	2003	2004	2005	2006	2007	2008	2009
110.00	134.35	164.10	200.43	244.81	299.01	365.21	446.07	544.83	665.46	812.80
	90.06	110.00	134.35	164.10	200.43	244.81	299.01	365.21	446.07	544.83
		73.74	90.06	110.00	134.35	164.10	200.43	244.81	299.01	365.21
			60.37	73.74	90.06	110.00	134.35	164.10	200.43	244.81
				49.43	60.37	73.74	90.06	110.00	134.35	164.10
					40.47	49.43	60.37	73.74	90.06	110.00
						33.13	40.47	49.43	60.37	73.74
							27.13	33.13	40.47	49.43
								22.21	27.13	33.13
									18.18	22.21
										14.89

Build plant.
Plant already built.

one up and one down move, the new plant will be worth −$800.06; and if demand makes two down moves, the new plant will be worth −$1,919. The expected present value of these, net of the $2 billion construction cost, is slightly positive. Several things are interacting here. First, the plant does not operate if demand is too low, so there's a bottom limit on the value of the plant. Second, demand is expected to grow at 5% per year.

Using what we've learned, we can now show that it makes sense for Intel to spend $400 million immediately in 1999 on the shell, kill some of its optionality, and maintain an option to complete the plant at a cost of $1.6 billion but with only a one-year delay. This analysis works exactly like the two-year delay case, except that we calculate the exercise commitment payoffs using expected values of the plant one year forward, and we use $1.6 billion as the strike price (instead of $2 billion). Of course, we have to subtract the $400 million cost of the shell (net of its depreciation tax shields) from the option value we get, because this is the price that is paid to receive this option and initiate this strategy.

Since the decision must be made by 2008 to have the plant operating by 2009, we start in 2008. Suppose, for example, we are in the fourth state down in 2008, where total demand is 200.43 million units (Figure 14.21). From this state, demand can either (1) go up in 2009 to 244.81 million units, in which case the free cash flow value of the new chip facility will be $12,882.91 million, or (2) demand can go down to 164.10 million units, in which case the free cash flow value of the new facility will be only $9,537.63 million. (The free cash flows values have changed slightly from the earlier numbers at the same levels of demand simply because in this case the act of spending $1.6 billion on the fab generates an incremental depreciation tax

Figure 14.21 Evaluating the Best Decision in 2008 Given Chip Demand of 200.43 Million and One-Year Delay

Binomial Tree of Annual Intel Chip Demand (in millions)

Current	2000	2001	2002	2003	2004	2005	2006	2007	2008	2009
110.00	134.35	164.10	200.43	244.81	299.01	365.21	446.07	544.83	665.46	812.80
	90.06	110.00	134.35	164.10	200.43	244.81	299.01	365.21	446.07	544.83
		73.74	90.06	110.00	134.35	164.10	200.43	244.81	299.01	365.21
			60.37	73.74	90.06	110.00	134.35	164.10	200.43	244.81
				49.43	60.37	73.74	90.06	110.00	134.35	164.10
					40.47	49.43	60.37	73.74	90.06	110.00
						33.13	40.47	49.43	60.37	73.74
							27.13	33.13	40.47	49.43
								22.21	27.13	33.13
									18.18	22.21
										14.89

Assumptions

Current annual chip demand (millions)	244.81
Expected yearly growth rate in chip demand	5%
Fab cost (millions)	$1,600

All figures in millions

	Year 1	Year 2	Year 3	Year 4	Year 5	Year 6	Year 7	Year 8	Year 9	Year 10
Total demand for Intel chips	244.81	257.05	269.90	283.40	297.57	312.45	328.07	344.47	361.70	379.78
Capacity before new plant	137.50	137.50	137.50	137.50	137.50	137.50	137.50	137.50	137.50	137.50
Capacity shortfall before new plant	107.31	119.55	132.40	145.90	160.07	174.95	190.57	206.97	224.20	242.28
Capacity of new plant	62.40	62.40	62.40	62.40	62.40	62.40	62.40	62.40	62.40	62.40
Production from new plant	62.40	62.40	62.40	62.40	62.40	62.40	62.40	62.40	62.40	62.40
Sales revenue	$9,984.00	$9,984.00	$9,984.00	$9,984.00	$9,984.00	$9,984.00	$9,984.00	$9,984.00	$9,984.00	$9,984.00
Variable costs	$5,616.00	$5,616.00	$5,616.00	$5,616.00	$5,616.00	$5,616.00	$5,616.00	$5,616.00	$5,616.00	$5,616.00
Operating margin	$4,368.00	$4,368.00	$4,368.00	$4,368.00	$4,368.00	$4,368.00	$4,368.00	$4,368.00	$4,368.00	$4,368.00
Fixed costs	$600.00	$600.00	$600.00	$600.00	$600.00	$600.00	$600.00	$600.00	$600.00	$600.00
Depreciation	$160.00	$160.00	$160.00	$160.00	$160.00	$160.00	$160.00	$160.00	$160.00	$160.00
EBT	$3,608.00	$3,608.00	$3,608.00	$3,608.00	$3,608.00	$3,608.00	$3,608.00	$3,608.00	$3,608.00	$3,608.00
Taxes	$1,046.32	$1,046.32	$1,046.32	$1,046.32	$1,046.32	$1,046.32	$1,046.32	$1,046.32	$1,046.32	$1,046.32
Unlevered net income	$2,561.68	$2,561.68	$2,561.68	$2,561.68	$2,561.68	$2,561.68	$2,561.68	$2,561.68	$2,561.68	$2,561.68
Add back: depreciation	$160.00	$160.00	$160.00	$160.00	$160.00	$160.00	$160.00	$160.00	$160.00	$160.00
NWC requirement	$1,497.60	$1,497.60	$1,497.60	$1,497.60	$1,497.60	$1,497.60	$1,497.60	$1,497.60	$1,497.60	$1,497.60
Less: change in NWC	$1,497.60	$0.00	$0.00	$0.00	$0.00	$0.00	$0.00	$0.00	$0.00	$0.00
Free cash flow	$1,224.08	$2,721.68	$2,721.68	$2,721.68	$2,721.68	$2,721.68	$2,721.68	$2,721.68	$2,721.68	$2,721.68
PV of free cash flows	$12,882.91									

Binomial Tree of Option Values on Fab only with One-Year Delay (in millions)

Current	2000	2001	2002	2003	2004	2005	2006	2007	2008	2009
$12,882.91									$9,310.13	$12,882.91
										$9,537.63

$$max\,[(0.5775 \times \$12{,}882.91 + 0.4225 \times \$9{,}537.63)/1.051 - \$1{,}600, \$0] = \$9{,}310.13 \text{ Invest.}$$

shield only on the $1.6 billion fab investment. The tax shield on the $400 million investment in the shell is already booked—and nearly gone by 2009—and we will account for it at the end to get the timing right.) So, in this state in 2008, the payoff to committing $1.6 billion to complete the fab with a one-year delay is

$$(\text{payoff}|\text{demand} = 200.43 \text{ in } 2008) = \frac{0.5775(\$12,882.91) + 0.4225(\$9,537.63)}{1.051} - \$1,600$$

$$= \$9,310.13$$

so the appropriate thing to do in this state is to spend $1.6 billion and commence installing the fab and thus receiving back a completed factory one year hence. I show this example calculation for you in Figure 14.21.

You should be able to follow this easily by now. The complete set of optimal 2008 exercise decisions and payoffs look like Figure 14.22.

Now we have to work backward as before, comparing the value of waiting and keeping the option alive with the value of investing $1.6 billion immediately and getting back a completed fab facility with one-year delay.

For example, let's suppose we are in the highest-demand state at 2007 (544.83 million units (Figure 14.21). If Intel commits at that time to investment of $1.6 billion, only two things can happen to demand during the one-year delay between the commitment and the completion of the plant: (1) Demand can go up to 665.46 million units (in which case the free cash flow value of a brand new plant would be $12,882.91 million), or (2) demand can go down to 446.07 million chips (in which case the value of a brand new facility would also be $12,882.91 because of the cap on production). So the expected present value of a decision to commit to exercise in this 2007 state, net of the $1.6 billion strike price, is

$$(\text{payoff}|\text{demand} = 544.83 \text{ in } 2007) = \frac{0.5775(\$12,882.91) + 0.4225(\$12,882.91)}{1.051} - \$1,600$$

$$= \$10,654.61$$

On the other hand, if Intel does not commit to exercise at this time but instead waits until 2008 to make a decision, the value of the option "kept alive" is only

$$\frac{0.5775(\$10,654.61) + 0.4225(\$10,654.61)}{1.051} = \$10,137.59$$

| Figure 14.22 | Binomial Tree of Option Values on Fab Only with One-Year Delay (in millions) |

Current	2000	2001	2002	2003	2004	2005	2006	2007	2008	2009
									$10,654.61	
									$10,654.61	
									$10,654.61	
									$9,310.13	
									$3,293.43	
									$0.00	
									$0.00	
									$0.00	
									$0.00	
									$0.00	

| Figure 14.23 | Binomial Tree of Option Values on Fab Only with One-Year Delay (in millions) |

Current	2000	2001	2002	2003	2004	2005	2006	2007	2008	2009
$4,126.92	$5,516.18	$7,235.87	$9,310.13	$10,654.61	$10,654.61	$10,654.61	$10,654.61	$10,654.61	$10,654.61	
	$2,728.85	$3,835.05	$5,278.78	$7,099.51	$9,310.13	$10,654.61	$10,654.61	$10,654.61	$10,654.61	
		$1,548.02	$2,327.09	$3,430.74	$4,939.51	$6,907.00	$9,310.13	$10,654.61	$10,654.61	
			$671.02	$1,100.99	$1,784.83	$2,849.70	$4,460.49	$6,796.27	$9,310.13	
				$164.74	$299.90	$545.94	$993.83	$1,809.17	$3,293.43	
					$0.00	$0.00	$0.00	$0.00	$0.00	
						$0.00	$0.00	$0.00	$0.00	
							$0.00	$0.00	$0.00	
								$0.00	$0.00	
									$0.00	

Binomial Tree of Annual Intel Chip Demand (in millions), Showing Optimal Exercise Boundary

Current	2000	2001	2002	2003	2004	2005	2006	2007	2008	2009
110.00	134.35	164.10	200.43	244.81	299.01	365.21	446.07	544.83	665.46	812.80
	90.06	110.00	134.35	164.10	200.43	244.81	299.01	365.21	446.07	544.83
		73.74	90.06	110.00	134.35	164.10	200.43	244.81	299.01	365.21
			60.37	73.74	90.06	110.00	134.35	164.10	200.43	244.81
				49.43	60.37	73.74	90.06	110.00	134.35	164.10
					40.47	49.43	60.37	73.74	90.06	110.00
						33.13	40.47	49.43	60.37	73.74
							27.13	33.13	40.47	49.43
								22.21	27.13	33.13
									18.18	22.21
										14.89

Build plant.
Plant already built.

So, the appropriate thing for Intel to do in this particular state of nature at 2007 is commit to installing the fab into the already built shell at a cost of $1.6 billion (with one-year delay). You repeat this procedure back, just as in any other American option, until you get the final results (shown in Figure 14.23).

The option on the fab, with a strike price of $1.6 billion and only one-year delay, is worth $4,126.92 million. But we have to be careful here. This represents an increase over the option value on the entire facility with a two-year delay ($3,445.47 million), but it comes at a cost—Intel must spend $400 million on the new shell in order to exchange/transform the less-valuable option on a full facility with strike price $2 billion and two-year delay into the option on the fab with strike price $1.6 billion and one-year delay. To ascertain whether or not an immediate investment in the shell creates value, we have to net out the cost of the shell (being careful to add back the present value of the depreciation tax shield Intel gets from the $400 million shell investment).

If Intel depreciates the $400 million shell straight-line over 10 years to a residual value of zero, then the yearly depreciation charge will be $40 million, so the yearly depreciation tax shield will be .29($40 million) = $11.60 million per year. The present value of a 10-year annuity of $11.60 million, taken using Intel's 14% WACC, is $60.51 million, which is the value of the depreciation tax shield.

So we can now see if Intel's management created or destroyed value by killing some of their flexibility in 1999 and building the shell at a cost of $400 million to reduce the delayed response between exercise of the option and final receipt of the plant.

Value of option on fab only with one-year delay = $4,126.92
Value of option on complete facility with two-year delay = $3,455.47
Net increase in option value due to lower regrets = $ 681.45
Less cost of building shell immediately = $ 400.00
Plus present value of depreciation tax shield = $ 60.51
Value creation = $ 341.96

That is, this action that seems to kill optionality actually creates about $340 million dollars in value for Intel's shareholders. Not bad at all.

Before we close, let's make absolutely sure that we understand *why* throwing away flexibility created value. You'll get the picture if you compare the optimal exercise boundary on a complete plant with two-year delay (Figure 14.20) with the optimal exercise boundary on a fab only with one-year delay (Figure 14.23). Notice when there's a two-year delay, Intel makes an optimal early commitment in more marginal 2005 and 2007 states than when there's only a one-year delay. In other words, the act of killing some optionality and spending $400 million on the shell reduces the potential for regrets. In this case, the eliminated regrets are worth more than the lost flexibility! Be careful—it always won't be this way.

What If Intel Bears a Cost of Undercapacity?

In the preceding analysis, I tacitly assumed that Intel faces no cost of having too little capacity. This may not be reflective of reality, as undercapacity could lead to lost future business because of competitive pressures.

Fortunately for us, it is very easy to build a penalty for undercapacity into the analysis. To see how, look back at the example calculation I showed in Figure 14.19. In that example, we were calculating the optimal exercise strategy of an option on a complete plant with a two-year delay, given a 2006 observed demand of 134.35 million chips; our result was that Intel should not commit to the plant in that state, but rather should wait at least another year to decide.

If you examine Figure 14.19 carefully, you'll notice that this strategy could lead to undercapacity in 2008. If actual demand is 134.35 million in 2006, then the three subsequent 2008 states have demand of 200.43 million (after two up steps), 134.35 million (after one up and one down), and 90.06 million (after two downs). Remembering that Intel's existing capacity is only 110 million, then not exercising the option in this state in 2006 leads to two possible states of undercapacity in 2008.

If this sort of undercapacity is costly, simply calculate the expected present value of the undercapacity costs (taking the expectation using the risk-neutral probability and discounting at the risk-free rate), and reduce the option value (the value of waiting) by this quantity. In this particular example, the value of waiting in the 2006 state when chip demand is 134.35 million should be reduced by [q^2 × the cost of undercapacity given demand of 200.43 million in 2008 *plus* $2q(1-q)$ × the cost of undercapacity given demand of 134.35 million in 2008]/$e^{r \times 2\Delta t}$.

Obviously, a cost of potential capacity shortfalls reduces the value of waiting. When you introduce it, you'll exercise earlier—which reduces the value of the option and the strategy.

14.4   Bibliography

Gilmore, John, Tom Lukawski, Brian MacNicol, and Karl Sandberg, 2004. "Creating Fabrication Shells at Intel—A Real Option Valuation," unpublished manuscript, Indiana University.

Appendix 14.1

Let's take one last look at our simplified problem from Section 14.1. Recall that we have an option that expires after four quarters, but we must commit to a final exercise decision at the end of the third quarter (i.e., three months early). In this problem, the strike price will not be paid until the actual date that the underlying asset is received (unlike the Intel example, where the strike price was paid on the early commitment date).

In mathematical terms, we only commit at Q3 to exercise the option at Q4 if the expected present value of exercise (taken using the risk-neutral probabilities and discounted at the risk-free rate) is positive. Commit to exercise if and only if

$$\frac{q \times (UND_{Up} - K) + (1 - q) \times (UND_{Dn} - K)}{e^{r \times \Delta t}} \geq 0$$

or commit to exercise if and only if

$$\frac{(q \times UND_{Up} + (1 - q) \times UND_{Dn}) - K}{e^{r \times \Delta t}} \geq 0$$

Now, if you were paying attention during the review of derivatives pricing, you will remember that the expected value of the underlying asset under the risk-neutral distribution—which is the term in parentheses in the numerator—is simply the forward price of the asset:

$$q \times UND_{Up} + (1 - q) \times UND_{Dn} = F_{\Delta t}$$

So we can evaluate the early commitment decision (i.e., the Q3 decision to exercise or not at Q4) using the theoretical forward price for delivery of the underlying asset at the time of actual exercise. Commit to exercise if and only if

$$\frac{F_{\Delta t} - K}{e^{r \times \Delta t}} \geq 0$$

But we know more. The relationship between the forward price of the underlying and the spot price is $F_{\Delta t} = UND_0 e^{(r - ncy)\Delta t}$ (where r and ncy are the continuously compounded annual risk-free rate and net convenience yield, respectively, and UND is the current price of the underlying asset), so our early-commitment decision reduces further to commit to exercise if and only if

$$\frac{UNDe^{(r - ncy)\Delta t} - K}{e^{r \times \Delta t}} \geq 0$$

or commit to exercise if and only if

$$UNDe^{-ncy \times \Delta t} - Ke^{-r \times \Delta t} \geq 0$$

Figure 14.24

Binomial Tree of Underlying Values

	0	Q1	Q2	Q3	Q4
	$100.00	$128.40	$164.87	$211.70	
		$77.88	$100.00	$128.40	
			$60.65	$77.88	
				$47.24	

That is, all we need is a simple adjustment to the current value of the underlying asset at the time the exercise decision is made—a reduction by its convenience yield—to analyze the early commitment decision.

Let's use this to go back and revalue our very unique option. First, we build our binomial tree exactly as before. However, since we will make the decision after Q3, and we really don't need the Q4 values any more, we will just stop construction of the tree at Q3. See Figure 14.24.

Notice that this tree is *exactly* the same as the first three time steps of our binomial trees of underlying asset values before (both the recombining tree in Figure 14.1 and the one that did not recombine after Q3 in Figure 14.3).

The next step is to write in the payoffs from the optimal decision at Q3. For a European call with early commitment but delayed payment of the strike price, the payoff function on the commitment date is

$$max[UNDe^{-ncy \times \Delta t} - Ke^{-r \times \Delta t}, 0]$$

and for a put, we have

$$max[Ke^{-r \times \Delta t} - UNDe^{-ncy \times \Delta t}, 0]$$

In this case, we have a call in which the exercise decision must be made at Q3, but the $120 strike price is paid at Q4. So $Ke^{-r \times \Delta t} = \$120e^{-0.05 \times 0.25} = \$118.51$ in all states. Moreover, we have no net convenience yield on our underlying asset (i.e., $ncy = 0$ in all states). The Q3 payoffs from the optimal commitment to exercise decision are shown in Figure 14.25.

Before we go any further with the analysis, let's notice something. The values from the optimal exercise decision that we've captured in Figure 14.25 are *exactly the same* as those in our earlier tree of option values where we analyzed the payoffs from early commitment using discounted expected values (see Figure 14.7). Make sure you see this. This method of analyzing the early commitment decision using the currently prevailing forward price of the underlying asset captures potential regrets! This is a very important point, because it tells us that even though the actual payoffs from exercise will not be received for three months (i.e., until Q4), we can value the early commitment (or delayed response) option using the properly adjusted Q3 values of the underlying asset *without any further discounting for the time*

Figure 14.25 **Binomial Tree of Option Values with Delay**

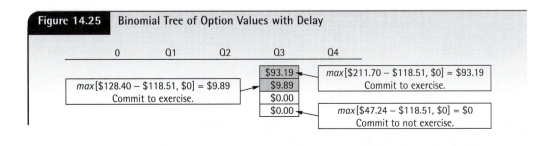

value of money. I stress this point, because there is a very strong temptation to adjust the Q3 payoffs for time value because the actual receipt of the underlying (and in this case payment of the strike price) will not occur until Q4. *Do not yield to this temptation*—the binomial tree takes care of the time value for you.

To understand why, it is necessary to revisit a result from Chapter 4. When we build binomial trees, the underlying asset's value increases (in expectation) by its required rate of return. This is true no matter where you are in the tree—if the required rate of return on the underlying is, say, 2% per time step in the tree, then the expected value of the underlying at the end of *any* binomial step in the tree is 2% higher than at the beginning of that step. In other words, the value of the underlying at any point in the tree is the *discounted* expected value of the underlying at a later point. When we look at the possible Q3 values of our underlying in our tree above, these are the *discounted* expected values of the underlying at Q4. When we use the Q3 values to evaluate our early commitment decision, we are properly discounting the value of the underlying to be received in the future.

We now finish the analysis by working backward using the same risk-neutral probabilities and the same risk-free rate as before. I've done the work for you in Figure 14.26; make sure you check it.

It should be no surprise that we get the right answer (i.e., the same answer as in Figure 14.7). We've used the exact same theory of valuation in this method that we used in the first method I showed you at the beginning of this section—the only change is that we've found a way to simplify the analysis. Once again, the cost of potential regrets is the difference between the option value when we can make the exercise decision right at Q4 ($15.71) and the value of the option when we must commit to a Q4 exercise policy three months early ($12.18), or $3.53.

We can generalize this result to the situation where the strike price is paid at any time—either when the commitment decision must be made, or when the underlying is actually received, or any time in between. For a call option, the commitment date payoff on the option in each state is given by

$$\text{Payoff on commitment date} = max[UNDe^{-ncy \times t(\text{receipt})} - Ke^{-r \times t(\text{payment})}, 0]$$

where *ncy* and *r* are the annual net convenience yield on the underlying and risk-free rate, respectively, *t(receipt)* is the amount of time in years between the commitment date and the actual receipt of the underlying asset, and *t(payment)* is the amount of time in years between the commitment date and the actual payment of the strike price.

For a put option, the commitment date payoff on the option is

$$\text{Payoff on commitment date} = max[Ke^{-r \times t(\text{payment})} - UNDe^{-ncy \times t(\text{receipt})}, 0]$$

Figure 14.26

	0	Q1	Q2	Q3	Q4
Binomial Tree of Option Values with Delay	$12.18	$24.26	$47.83	$93.19	
		$2.07	$4.52	$9.89	
			$0.00	$0.00	
				$0.00	

This seems really easy—why didn't we use this in the Intel example? Because in the Intel example, fixed costs of production and the upper bound on production capacity caused a situation where the underlying asset (a newly built production facility) behaves somewhat strangely: Its volatility and convenience yield are not constant (just as in our mining examples). Nevertheless, I show you this because we can learn something extremely important from the case when the convenience yield is always zero and the strike price is paid at the time of the early-commitment decision.

Look again at the commitment-date payoff function on a call where the commitment to exercise must be made early:

$$\text{Payoff on commitment date} = max\left[UND\, e^{-ncy \times t(\text{receipt})} - Ke^{-r \times t(\text{payment})}, 0\right]$$

Since corporate growth options are calls, this will be a very common payoff function for corporate investments with optionality. Now consider the case when the strike price is paid at the time of the commitment to exercise and when the net convenience yield on the underlying asset is always zero. In this very common case, $ncy = 0$ and $t(\text{payment}) = 0$, so the payoff function on the date that the commitment to exercise must be made reduces to

$$\text{Payoff on commitment date} = max\left[UND - K, 0\right]$$

That's right—it is just the standard payoff function for a call option. In other words, when there's no convenience yield on the underlying asset and the strike price is paid at the time of the commitment, then the problem of valuing an option when the exercise decision must be made prior to the actual expiration date (or receipt of the underlying) reduces to the valuation of the option as if it expires on the commitment date.

This looks somewhat strange, but it is actually quite intuitive. Just as I mentioned earlier, the value of the underlying at any node in the tree is the expected future value of the asset discounted at its required rate of return. So, when we use the values in the tree at a point before the exercise date (say, at Q3 in our example), we are making the decision by using the *expected* future value of the underlying and hence the *expected* future payoff on the option. Since there is still uncertainty as to what might happen between the commitment date and the actual exercise date of the option (i.e., between Q3 and Q4 in our example), then our decision may yield regrets, and the value of the option is lower than if we could wait until the actual exercise date to make the decision. The higher the volatility, the higher will be the potential regrets.

This leads to a larger point about real options—which is yet another issue that many armchair theorists are completely misinformed about. Some so-called experts claim that it is inappropriate to value an option on a corporate project because the corporate project is long-lived and its cash flows to be received after exercise are risky. For example, I've had several very intelligent people tell me that my Boeing example (Chapter 5) is nonsense, because Boeing does not completely resolve its uncertainty before exercising the option—if Boeing commits to building the super-jumbo jet, it still faces market risk in its free cash flows, and so the option payoffs are not certain. If you really understand what is going on in this chapter, then you will be able to explain why this logic is a non sequitur.

The explanation goes back to the heart of valuation. The value of any asset in an arbitrage-free world is the present value of its expected future cash flows (given the appropriate discount rate). In other words, the current value of the asset must be an unbiased predictor of its (discounted) expected future value. So, in the Boeing example, as long as the expiration-date payoffs on the option to build the super-jumbo jet are expected future cash flows on selling the jet discounted by the appropriate *risk-adjusted* rate of return, then the analysis is valid, and the option value is the value of the strategy. Boeing does not have to receive the cash from the strategy all at once in a lump sum at the date of exercise (as is the case with a financial option); rather, it only needs to receive a stream of risky future cash flows. The market value of that stream is the value of exercising in that particular state of nature. What would Boeing get if it exercises its option in a particular state, commits to a super-jumbo-jet project, and then immediately sells the business to someone else? It would get the present value of the free cash flows from the super-jumbo-jet product.[2]

In other words, we *could have* valued the Boeing option by considering the 2001 exercise date to be an *early commitment* date, and thus recognized that there is still risk in the cash flows (and hence the potential for regrets) if Boeing were to exercise in 2001. But we would get the exact same answer, because the 2001 exercise-date values of the underlying asset (the super-jumbo-jet product) are the discounted expected values of later-date values of the cash flows.

In almost all corporate real option settings, market risk in cash flows will remain after exercise of the option. Our valuation model recognizes this implicitly, and as long as we are careful in our cash flow forecasts (and how we build our trees), we can account for it appropriately. Exercise of a real option is equivalent to purchase of a risky asset.

---

[2] Once again, we see the power of the complete markets assumptions.

14   PROBLEMS

1. Redo Figure 14.7 using 30% annual volatility. *Note:* You will need to redo Figure 14.1.

2. Redo Figure 14.7 using a strike price of $135.00.

3. Calculate the present value of regrets from Problems 1 and 2.

The following three problems are based on the pro forma analysis illustrated in Figure 14.8.

4. Assume that the chip demand in 2000 is 90.00 million instead of 110.00, and determine the free cash flows for the new plant through 2009.

5. Assume that the chip demand in 2000 is 120.00 million instead of 110.00, and determine the free cash flows for the new plant through 2009.

6. At what maximum level of initial chip demand in 2000 will the new facility never be used? Why does this level not act as a lower bound within the binomial tree in Figure 14.15?

7. In the calculation of free cash flows based on the chip demand being 365.21 million (see Figure 14.17), calculate the effect the cost of the new facility being $1.7 billion instead of $2.0 billion will have on the sum of the discounted free cash flows. Redo the same calculation based on the cost of the new facility being $2.5 billion.

8. In Figure 14.20, reproduce the associated calculations for finding the value of the option for the top node in 2006.

9. In Figure 14.23, reproduce the associated calculations for finding the value of the option for the top node in 2007.

10. Suppose the fab shell costs $800 million, and Intel will still need to make a $1.6 billion investment to make the fab shell operational within a year. Also assume that a new facility without the fab shell would still cost $2.0 billion (i.e., the total commitment to production immediately is less expensive than building a shell facility and converting it later). Does the fab shell create or destroy value, and by how much?

In 1970, the U.S. Congress passed the Clean Air Act (42 U.S.C. 7401) to promote the nation's public health and welfare. The initiatives of the Act were (1) to create a national research and development program to achieve prevention and control of air pollution, and (2) to provide technical and financial assistance to state and local governments in connection with development of their own pollution prevention and control programs. Since 1970, Congress has amended the Act many times. One of the most significant amendments came in 1990.

Prior to 1990, the primary tool of air pollution (sulfur dioxide, nitrogen oxides, etc.) control was across-the-board limitations on the maximum yearly output of each particular pollutant at any industrial plant. Congress set an upper limit on pollutant production by any individual source, and it has periodically lowered the limit to achieve overall pollution reduction. While this seemed like a logical approach, it turned out to be very costly. Many of the largest air polluters were older, coal-fired electric-generation plants that would be decommissioned soon anyway, and the large costs of bringing these plants into compliance would bring only short-term benefits.

The 1990 Amendments—A Market-Based Approach

The 1990 Amendments to the Clean Air Act set minimum standards for air quality in the nation's cities and included many features designed to clean up air pollution as efficiently and inexpensively as possible by letting businesses make choices on the best way to reach pollution cleanup goals. The 1990 Amendments introduced new flexible programs called *market-based* approaches. Each pollution source would be endowed with a certain number of pollution *permits* (or *allowances*) every year that it could either use to legally produce pollution, sell to other pollution sources, or store for future use or sale. If a pollution source were to voluntarily reduce its pollution output, it could sell or bank its unused allowances.

The advantage of a market-based permit system is that it achieves the same reduction in pollutants as an across-the-board limitation at a lower cost. To limit the amount of sulfur dioxide (SO_2) pollution, for example, Congress can simply

[1] The data for this example, as well as the story itself, originally appeared in Edelson and Reinhart (1995). I've rewritten the case to make the presentation easier and to make some very minor changes to the analysis. Myriam Allendes (Kelley School of Business MBA class of 1999) provided excellent help with the spreadsheets.

limit the total number of SO_2 permits given out. Demand for (and supply of) allowances will determine their market value, and the market price of the allowances will certainly impinge on compliance strategy decisions. If the market price of permits is lower than the cost of modifying a particular pollution source, the owner of that source will buy permits on the open market. On the other hand, if actual modification of a plant is cheaper than buying permits, the owner of that plant will voluntarily modify the plant and then sell excess permits. The net effect is that cleanup occurs first where it is least costly, and in equilibrium, the marginal cost of cleanup becomes equal across all sources of SO_2 production. This minimizes the total cost of pollution abatement.

The 1990 Amendments created a two-phase process for the reduction of SO_2 emissions. In Phase I (January 1995 through December 1999), 110 very large, coal-burning electricity plants would each receive allowances to emit 2.5 million pounds of SO_2 per million Btu of coal burned. Since these 110 plants were currently producing around 1.75 times that much, the Phase I allowances would generate a 43% reduction in overall emissions from the targeted sources. In Phase II (beginning January 2000), permit allocations to the Phase I plants would drop to 1.2 million pounds SO_2 per mm Btu, leading to a 73% drop from their pre–Phase I levels; moreover, an additional 900 SO_2 sources would be added to the program. The map in Figure 15.1 shows the locations of the Phase I and II affected sources.

Figure 15.1   Phase I and Phase II Affected SO_2 Sources

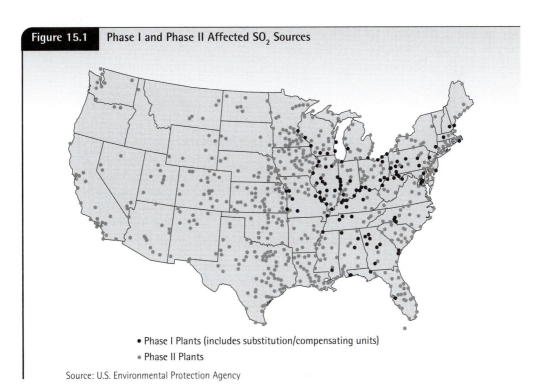

- Phase I Plants (includes substitution/compensating units)
- Phase II Plants

Source: U.S. Environmental Protection Agency

15.1   Georgia Power's Plant Bowen

One particular plant included in Phase I was Georgia Power's Plant Bowen, located in Bartow County, Georgia, near the community of Euharlee (about 50 miles northwest of Atlanta). Georgia Power, a subsidiary of Southern Company, constructed Bowen in 1975 to produce base-load electric power for industrial, commercial, and residential consumption. As of 1990, the plant generated about 21.5 billion kilowatt-hours of electricity annually by burning about 8.4 million tons of coal from Kentucky, and as a result, it produced about 267,000 tons of SO_2 per year.

Under the new market-based SO_2 program, the Bowen plant would receive allowances for 255,000 tons of SO_2 per year in Phase I but only 122,000 tons of SO_2 per year in Phase II. The Georgia Power managers had three alternatives for satisfying the 1990 Amendments:

1. They could operate Bowen without modification, and purchase the required allowances in the open market in both Phase I and II.
2. They could switch Bowen's inputs to a 1% sulfur coal. This lower-sulfur coal would be a more expensive fuel source, and experts expected its price to rise substantially at the begin-ning of Phase II (when the additional 900 facilities joined the program). This alternative would reduce Bowen's SO_2 emissions to 167,000 tons per year—a level below the Phase I requirement but not below the Phase II level, so Bowen would be able to sell excess allowances in Phase I but would have to purchase additional allowances in Phase II.
3. They could install expensive flue-gas desulphurization devices (FGDs), commonly known as *scrubbers,* which reduce SO_2 emissions to only 27,000 tons per year but also increase costs. The benefit to this alternative is that it would provide Bowen with many excess allowances which Georgia Power could either use elsewhere or sell on the open market in both Phase I and II.

The graph in Figure 15.2 shows Bowen's SO_2 production under each alternative, along with the allowances granted in each phase. Regardless of the alternative chosen, Georgia Power would decommission the Bowen plant on December 31, 2018.

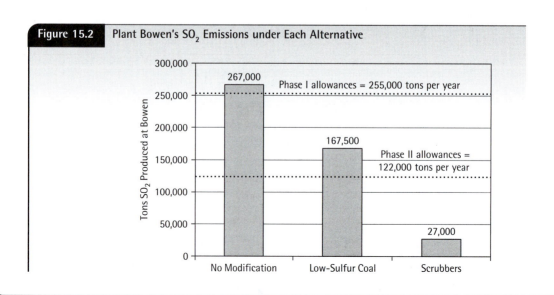

Figure 15.2   Plant Bowen's SO_2 Emissions under Each Alternative

15.2 Static Cost Minimization Analysis

The traditional approach to Georgia Power's decision was static DCF. It is important to remember that even though this was a mandated project, Georgia Power had a choice among several alternatives. Here, we will consider the problem a cost-minimization issue. Of course, the true base case for analysis is a do-nothing scenario in which Georgia Power would be heavily fined; as long as the cost of compliance is less than the fine, then the compliance efforts generate positive *incremental* cash flows.[2] We will assume that they are, and we will search for the lowest-cost alternative.

The one difficulty in the analysis was estimating the market price of allowances, as the market for them was nascent. On March 30, 1993, the Chicago Board of Trade (CBOT) sold a small number of allowances in an auction where winning bidders paid between $122 and $450 per ton. The Southern Company participated in some private trades in 1992 in the $250–$350 per ton range. Finally, there were rumors of private trades in the $200–$300 per ton range in 1993. Management, forced to make an approximation, used $250 per ton as the baseline 1995 estimate.

Since the permits are in limited supply, pay no dividends if stored, and cost nothing to store, they should theoretically behave like investment assets and earn a rate of return commensurate with their systematic risk.[3] A good approximation is that the expected return on permits will equal the expected return on electricity plants.[4] Georgia Power's required rate of return on an electricity plant such as Bowen was 10% at the time, and thus management assumed that permit prices would increase in value by 10% per year (and that the appropriate discount rate on cash flows from future permit purchases and sales was therefore 10%).

The first alternative we will consider is the *no modification* strategy, in which Georgia Power will buy permits on the open market to make up for its shortfall (which will be small in Phase I but large in Phase II). I present the static discounted cash flow (DCF) analysis as of January 1995 in Figure 15.3. The static DCF cost of compliance by doing no modification (and just purchasing permits) is about $471.5 million.

Several mechanical features of the DCF analysis are worth mention. First, the allowance price is growing at a *continuously compounded* 10% per year, and the free cash flows are then discounted assuming continuous discounting at 10% per year. I'll work in continuous compounding and discounting in the *scrubber* and *low-sulfur coal* alternatives as well, for a reason which you'll learn shortly. Second, in Figure 15.3 I've treated the free cash flows as occurring at the *beginning* of each year (i.e., we incur the 1995 costs immediately). While this represents a slight break from corporate finance orthodoxy, it has very little effect on the DCF value and *no* effect on the choice of optimal strategy. Why, then, do I work this way? It makes things easier later in the analysis. Finally, notice that each year's cash flow from compliance under the *no modification* alternative can be written very simply as

$$[(255,000 - 267,000) \times P](1 - 0.33)$$

Figure 15.3

No Modification Alternative 1995		1996	>>>	2000	2001	>>>	2018
Tons allowance	255,000	255,000		122,000	122,000		122,000
Tons created	267,000	267,000		267,000	267,000		267,000
Net	(12,000)	(12,000)		(145,000)	(145,000)		(145,000)
Allowance price/ton	$250.00	$276.29		$412.18	$455.53		$2,493.55
Allowance purch/sale	($3,000,000)	($3,315,513)		($59,766,146)	($66,051,807)		($361,564,114)
Lost revenue	0	0		0	0		0
Additional op. cost	0	0		0	0		0
Depreciation	0	0		0	0		0
Before tax income	(3,000,000)	(3,315,513)		(59,766,146)	(66,051,807)		(361,564,114)
Tax @ 33%	(990,000)	(1,094,119)		(19,722,828)	(21,797,096)		(119,316,158)
NOPAT	(2,010,000)	(2,221,394)		(40,043,318)	(44,254,710)		(242,247,956)
Add back depr.	0	0		0	0		0
Cash flows	($2,010,000)	($2,221,394)		($40,043,318)	($44,254,710)		($242,247,956)
PV of cost @ 10%	($471,512,500)						

in Phase I (1995–1999) and

$$[(122,000 - 267,000) \times P](1 - 0.33)$$

in Phase II (2000 and beyond), where P is the current market price of allowances. We'll use this later.

Scrubbers are costly. They require $700 million worth of capital expenditures (in 1995 present value) to install, and once installed, they increase plant operating cost by $28 million per year. In addition, they require electricity to work—and so they reduce plant revenue by $24 million per year (i.e., they use $24 million worth of the plant's output that could otherwise be sold to customers). On the plus side, scrubbers would reduce SO_2 output at Bowen to only 27,000 tons per year—and hence give Georgia Power the ability to sell permits on the open market. Scrubber costs would be offset partially by the depreciation tax credit; depreciation on the capital expenditure would be 14% for 5 years and then 2% for 15 years. Figure 15.4 gives my static DCF valuation and static *net present cost* analysis of the scrubber alternative.

The static net present cost of compliance via the scrubber alternative, about $520 million, had several components. The scrubbers would create a risky inflow of allowance-sale revenues in both Phase I and II, and the DCF value of these (after tax) was about $493 million. The discounted cost of operating the scrubbers, which was not related to the market price of allowances, was about $499 million. Therefore, the present value of the incremental operating cash flows from the scrubber alternative was only about −$6 million. However, the scrubbers themselves cost $700 million before the depreciation tax credit of $186 million (or $514 million net of the tax shield), leaving a net present cost of −$520 million.

Observe how I've broken things out here. I've assumed that allowances bear market risk, and I've discounted the future free cash flows associated with profit/loss on allowance sales (after tax) at the required rate of return of 10% (continuously compounded, as mentioned before). On the other hand, I've assumed that lost plant revenue and incremental operating costs due to the scrubbers are not subject to market risk, and therefore I've discounted them at the risk-free rate of 5% (again with continuous discounting). Finally, I've broken out the depreciation tax shield separately—this will make the option analysis a bit easier later—and I've discounted it at the risk-free rate as well.

Figure 15.4

Scrubber Alternative	1995	1996	>>>	2000	2001	>>>	2018
Tons allowance	255,000	255,000		122,000	122,000		122,000
Tons created	27,000	27,000		27,000	27,000		27,000
Net	228,000	228,000		95,000	95,000		95,000
Allowance price/ton	$250.00	$276.29		$412.18	$455.53		$2,493.55
Allowance purch/sale	$57,000,000	$62,994,742		$39,157,130	$43,275,322		$236,886,833
Tax @ 33%	18,810,000	20,788,265		12,921,853	14,280,856		78,172,655
	38,190,000	42,206,477		26,235,277	28,994,465		158,714,178
PV of risky flows @ 10%	$493,287,500						
Lost revenue	(24,000,000)	(24,000,000)		(24,000,000)	(24,000,000)		(24,000,000)
Additional op. cost	(28,000,000)	(28,000,000)		(28,000,000)	(28,000,000)		(28,000,000)
Before tax risk-free flows	(52,000,000)	(52,000,000)		(52,000,000)	(52,000,000)		(52,000,000)
Tax @ 33%	(17,160,000)	(17,160,000)		(17,160,000)	(17,160,000)		(17,160,000)
Net risk-free flows	(34,840,000)	(34,840,000)		(34,840,000)	(34,840,000)		(34,840,000)
PV of risk-free flows @ 5%	($499,202,509)						
Depreciation	(98,000,000)	(98,000,000)		(14,000,000)	(14,000,000)		—
Tax rate	33%	33%		33%	33%		33%
Depreciation tax shield	32,340,000	32,340,000		4,620,000	4,620,000		0
PV of depreciation tax shield @ 5%	$185,604,520						
PV of installation cost in 1995	($700,000,000)						
Net present cost	($520,310,489)						

On a yearly basis, the free cash flow from compliance under the scrubber alternative is

$$[(255,000 - 27,000) \times P - 24,000,000 - 28,000,000](1 - 0.33)$$

in Phase I (1995–1999) and

$$[(122,000 - 27,000) \times P - 24,000,000 - 28,000,000](1 - 0.33)$$

in Phase II (2000 and beyond), not including the yearly depreciation tax credit (which we'll fold into the capital expenditure), where once again P is the market price of allowances.

The final static alternative is *immediate conversion to low-sulfur coal.* Switching fuel sources would require a one-time investment of $22 million and would increase the price of fuel by $6 million per year in Phase I and by $44 million per year in Phase II.[5] A low-sulfur coal plant would produce 167,500 tons of SO_2 per year. Depreciation of the installation cost would be 14% for 5 years and 2% for 15 years. Figure 15.5 provides my static net present cost analysis of this third choice.

So, the static cost of compliance via immediate switching to low-sulfur coal is about $395 million. Again, I've discounted future permit transactions (sales in Phase I, purchases in Phase II) at their required rate of return of 10%, and all other items at the risk-free rate. Also, I've once again broken out the depreciation tax shield separately.

---

[5] In this instance, management was anticipating that the plants added in Phase II would switch to low-sulfur coal and drive up its price.

Figure 15.5

Low Sulfur Alternative	1995	1996	>>>	2000	2001	>>>	2018
Tons allowance	255,000	255,000		122,000	122,000		122,000
Tons created	167,500	167,500		167,500	167,500		167,500
Net	87,500	87,500		(45,500)	(45,500)		(45,500)
Allowance price/ton	$250.00	$276.29		$412.18	$455.53		$2,493.55
Allowance purch/sale	$21,875,000	$24,175,614		($18,754,204)	($20,726,601)		($113,456,325)
Tax @ 33%	7,218,750	7,977,953		(6,188,887)	(6,839,778)		(37,440,587)
Net of tax	14,656,250	16,197,661		(12,565,317)	(13,886,823)		(76,015,738)
PV of risky flows @ 10%	($71,522,500)						
Lost revenue	0	0		0	0		0
Additional op. cost	(6,000,000)	(6,000,000)		(44,000,000)	(44,000,000)		(44,000,000)
Before tax risk-free flows	(6,000,000)	(6,000,000)		(44,000,000)	(44,000,000)		(44,000,000)
Tax @ 33%	(1,980,000)	(1,980,000)		(14,520,000)	(14,520,000)		(14,520,000)
Risk-free flows	(4,020,000)	(4,020,000)		(29,480,000)	(29,480,000)		(29,480,000)
PV of risky-free flows @ 5%	($306,928,151)						
Depreciation	(3,080,000)	(3,080,000)		(440,000)	(440,000)		—
Tax rate	33%	33%		33%	33%		33%
Depreciation tax shield	1,016,400	1,016,400		145,200	145,200		0
PV of depreciation tax shield @ 5%	$5,833,285						
PV of installation cost in 1995	($22,000,000)						
Net present cost	($394,617,366)						

Look at what happens under the low-sulfur coal alternative. The discounted free cash flow from future permit market transactions is about −$72 million; that is, on net, Georgia Power would be buying allowances. The big nut in switching to low-sulfur coal is the future cost of coal—in present value terms, this accounts for about $307 million of the cost of compliance under this strategy. Net of the depreciation tax shield, the investment in switching is minimal: −$22 million + $6 million = −$16 million. The net present cost of compliance is thus −($72 mm + $307 mm + $16 mm) = −$395 mm. On a yearly basis, the free cash flow from compliance under the *low-sulfur coal* alternative is

$$[(255,000 - 167,500) \times P - 6,000,000](1 - 0.33)$$

in Phase I (1995–1999) and

$$[(122,000 - 167,500) \times P - 44,000,000](1 - 0.33)$$

in Phase II (2000 and beyond), not including the yearly depreciation tax credit (which we'll fold into the capital expenditure), where P is the spot price of allowances.

So to summarize, the static DCF model tells us that the lowest-cost alternative for achieving compliance with the 1990 Amendments at Bowen is an immediate switch to low-sulfur coal: The expected present value of its costs is only $395 million, as opposed to the $472 million cost of no modification and the $520 million cost of installing scrubbers. But, these results are highly sensitive to the assumed market price of allowances ($250 per ton in 1995), and if prices are lower or higher, then one of the other alternatives would actually be better from a static basis, as Figure 15.6 illustrates.

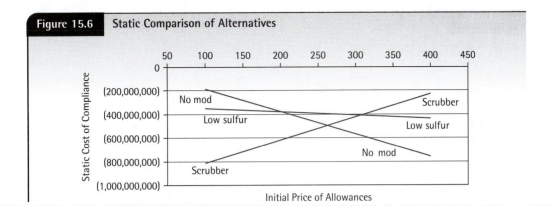

Figure 15.6   Static Comparison of Alternatives

What Figure 15.6 tells us is that from a purely static perspective, switching to low-sulfur coal is the cost-minimizing strategy only if allowance prices are in the $200–$300 range. If allowance prices are below $200, then the best static alternative is to do no modification and just buy cheap allowances in the open market, while if allowance prices are above $300, the best static alternative is to immediately install scrubbers and sell expensive allowances to other utilities.

There's an elegant intuition behind this result. The Bowen plant is naturally short a large number of SO_2 allowances. If Georgia Power does no modification, then they will have to buy a lot of allowances on the open market in the future. On the other hand, if Georgia Power installs scrubbers, then Bowen becomes long allowances, and Georgia Power will have to sell lots of allowances in the future. Finally, low-sulfur coal makes Bowen naturally long a small number of allowances in Phase I and naturally short a small number of allowances in Phase II. It doesn't take a Ph.D. in finance to recognize that Georgia Power would like to buy allowances if they are cheap and sell them if they are expensive.

This is why the static DCF analysis gives the results in Figure 15.6. If the decision is now-or-never-again (as the static NPV rule assumes), then Georgia Power is best off in expectation by immediately switching to low-sulfur coal (given their estimate that allowances are currently worth $250). But if the price of allowances is actually high, Georgia Power is best off by immediately creating a lot of excess allowances via the scrubber purchase and selling them in the future. On the other hand, if the current price of allowances is low, the best now-or-never strategy is to do no modification at all. The static NPV rule treats this as a now-or-never decision among three mutually exclusive alternatives.

15.3   Option Analysis

But the decision is *not* a now-or-never decision. There is tremendous uncertainty in our assumption that allowances will sell for $250 per ton, and Georgia Power management could be way off with this estimate. This is a classic example of a project competing with itself in time—if management waits, they bear the current year's cost of compliance via doing nothing, but they get the benefit of learning a more precise value for the market price of allowances. The question, then, concerns whether the value of waiting exceeds the cost. And if so, how long should Georgia Power wait before making a commitment?

Figure 15.7   Sketch of Georgia Power's Dynamic Compliance Opportunity

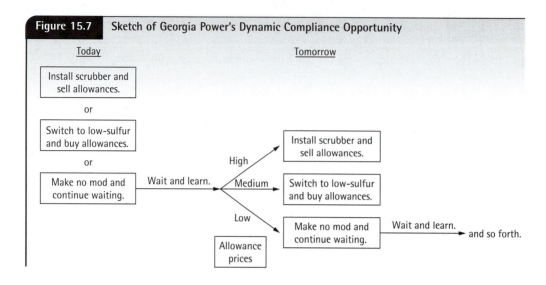

The first step is to get an idea of the problem. I always like to sketch something out, and I've done so in Figure 15.7. The key insight here is that the actions of *installing scrubbers* or *switching to low-sulfur* coal are *commitments*—once you do them, you can never go back and choose the other alternatives. But the act of *no modification* is *not* a commitment—if management chooses to make no modification in 1995, they maintain the ability to make the scrubber or low-sulfur decision in 1996 *or* do no modification and delay the decision further.

So, waiting to make a decision preserves optionality. What is somewhat unique about this problem is that the firm has two *mutually exclusive* American options: At any point, they can continue to wait, *or* they can exercise the option to install scrubbers, *or* they can exercise the option to switch to low-sulfur coal. But one kills the other: If you install scrubbers now, you kill the option to install scrubbers later, *and* you kill the option to switch to low-sulfur coal later.[6]

There are a couple of ways that we could approach this problem. If you think about it, you'll realize that the value of the option to wait to make a decision increases the value of the best compliance strategy (i.e., it reduces the cost of the compliance strategy):

$$\begin{array}{c} \textit{cost of compliance given best static strategy (now-or-never)} \\ - \textit{ cost of compliance given best dynamic strategy (wait)} \\ \hline = \textit{value of option to wait} \end{array}$$

So *one* way that we could approach this problem is to analyze the option to wait and calculate its value by figuring the payoffs from making the best decisions at the end and working backward as usual. This actually gets a bit tricky, because what happens if you install scrubbers, for example, is that you *give up* a strategy of waiting and *get back* a strategy with scrubbers, and the incremental payoff on installing scrubbers is the *difference between the two* minus the cost of installation.

---

[6] This is the way we'll treat the problem. If you allow switching back and forth, the option becomes path dependent. Path dependence would necessitate a more complex approach.

Another way to do the analysis, which turns out to be easier in this situation, is simply to calculate the value of the best dynamic strategy at every point. We'll start in the very last year and ask, "If we've waited until this point, what's the lowest-cost choice: do nothing, switch to low-sulfur coal, or install scrubbers?" We'll then work backwards, and at every earlier point ask the question, "If we've waited until this point, what's the lowest-cost strategy: Switch to low-sulfur coal, install scrubbers, or continue to wait?" When we work all the way back, we'll get the value of the best dynamic strategy (and the optimal exercise path), and we can calculate the value of the option to wait by the previous equation (if we really need the value of the option to wait). You'll see as we work through the problem.

I'll start things off by asking a relatively tough question: What is the underlying asset here? We've always said that the underlying asset is what you get if you exercise the option. Here we really have *two* options that are *mutually exclusive:* We can exercise one or the other, but not both. We have an option on a scrubber-based compliance strategy and an option on a low-sulfur based compliance strategy. If we exercise one, we kill the other. The key is that the payoff uncertainty on each option is driven by the same source of risk: the market price of allowances. If you think about it for a while, you realize that each compliance strategy is just an option on allowances themselves.

Look at it this way. As I said earlier, Georgia Power is naturally short allowances to the tune of 12,000 per year in Phase I and 145,000 per year in Phase II. If they do nothing, they just buy allowances on the open market each year. But if they "buy" either of the modification strategies, they are actually buying future allowances at a lump-sum price, and these allowances will be used to offset the company's short position and then sold on the open market if there is an excess. For example, if Georgia Power adopts the scrubber technology, they pay $700 million and suddenly have 228,000 excess allowances per year in Phase I and 95,000 excess allowances per year in Phase II which the company can sell on the open market. So the $700 million actually is equivalent to a one-time purchase of a printing press that generates $12,000 + 228,000 = 240,000$ allowances per year through the end of Phase I (if they exercise during phase one), then $145,000 + 95,000 = 240,000$ per year in Phase II through 2018. Similarly, the $22 million price of buying the low-sulfur strategy actually is a one-time purchase of 99,500 allowances per year for the remaining life of the plant.

So in our analysis, we can treat the underlying as *one* allowance (just like *one* share of stock in a stock-option problem), create a binomial lattice of allowance values, then attack the problem as an American option, where we will choose the one optimal policy at the optimal time. The initial value of one allowance is $250.

We will assume that annual volatility of log changes in allowance values is 20%, and that the risk-free rate is 5%. The plant will close in 2018, so that will be the expiration of our American-style option. Finally, I'll just do one step per year to keep the trees manageable.

Given these assumptions, the size of an up step in a binomial tree of allowance prices will be $U = e^{0.20\sqrt{1}} = 1.2214$ and $D = 1/U = 0.8187$, and the binomial tree of allowance prices will look like the one I present (in abbreviated form) in Figure 15.8. You can find the entire tree of allowance prices in the appendix at the end of this chapter.

The next thing we want to do is to translate this tree of allowance values into a tree of *current year compliance costs* for no modification, scrubbers, and low-sulfur coal using the equations we generated when we did the DCF. For example, the cost of compliance for each year and each allowance price state given *no modification* look like those in Figure 15.9. Again, I've put the complete tree of current year cost of compliance given no modification in the appendix. The *No Modification Cost Each Year* tree in Figure 15.9 is important for our analysis, because it gives us

Figure 15.8   Binomial Tree of Allowance Values ($)

1995	1996	>>>	2000	2001	>>>	2017	2018
250	305.4		680	830		20,363	24,871
	204.7		456	556		13,650	16,672
			305	373		9,150	11,175
			205	250		6,133	7,491
			137	168		4,111	5,021
			92	112		2,756	3,366
				75		1,847	2,256
						1,238	1,512
						830	1,014
						556	680
						373	456
						250	305
						168	205
						112	137
						75	92
						50	62
						34	41
						23	28
						15	19
						10	12
						7	8
						5	6
						3	4
							3

sigma = 20%/yr
Δt = 1 step/yr, so
U = 1.2214
D = 0.8187

Figure 15.9

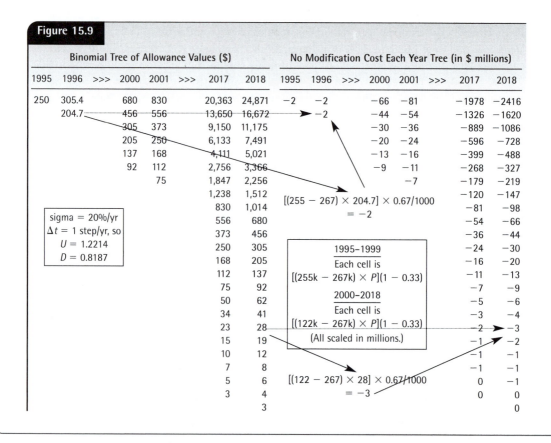

Binomial Tree of Allowance Values ($)

1995	1996	>>>	2000	2001	>>>	2017	2018
250	305.4		680	830		20,363	24,871
	204.7		456	556		13,650	16,672
			305	373		9,150	11,175
			205	250		6,133	7,491
			137	168		4,111	5,021
			92	112		2,756	3,366
				75		1,847	2,256
						1,238	1,512
						830	1,014
						556	680
						373	456
						250	305
						168	205
						112	137
						75	92
						50	62
						34	41
						23	28
						15	19
						10	12
						7	8
						5	6
						3	4
							3

sigma = 20%/yr
Δt = 1 step/yr, so
U = 1.2214
D = 0.8187

No Modification Cost Each Year Tree (in $ millions)

1995	1996	>>>	2000	2001	>>>	2017	2018
−2	−2		−66	−81		−1978	−2416
	−2		−44	−54		−1326	−1620
			−30	−36		−889	−1086
			−20	−24		−596	−728
			−13	−16		−399	−488
			−9	−11		−268	−327
				−7		−179	−219
						−120	−147
						−81	−98
						−54	−66
						−36	−44
						−24	−30
						−16	−20
						−11	−13
						−7	−9
						−5	−6
						−3	−4
						−2	−3
						−1	−2
						−1	−1
						−1	−1
						0	−1
						0	0
							0

$[(255 - 267) \times 204.7] \times 0.67/1000 = -2$

1995–1999
Each cell is
$[(255k - 267k) \times P](1 - 0.33)$

2000–2018
Each cell is
$[(122k - 267k) \times P](1 - 0.33)$
(All scaled in millions.)

$[(122 - 267) \times 28] \times 0.67/1000 = -3$

Figure 15.10

Binomial Tree of Allowance Values ($)								Scrubber Cost Each Year Tree (in $millions)							
1995	1996	>>>	2000	2001	>>>	2017	2018	1995	1996	>>>	2000	2001	>>>	2017	2018
250	305.4		680	830		20,363	24,871	3	12		8	18		1,261	1,548
	204.7		456	556		13,650	16,672		−4		−6	1		834	1,026
			305	373		9,150	11,175				−15	−11		548	676
			205	250		6,133	7,491				−22	−19		356	442
			137	168		4,111	5,021				−26	−24		227	285
			92	112		2,756	3,366				−29	−28		141	179
				75		1,847	2,256					−30		83	109
						1,238	1,512							44	61
						830	1,014							18	30
						556	680							1	8
						373	456							−11	−6
						250	305							−19	−15
						168	205							−24	−22
						112	137							−28	−26
						75	92							−30	−29
						50	62							−32	−31
						34	41							−33	−32
						23	28							−33	−33
						15	19							−34	−34
						10	12							−34	−34
						7	8							−34	−34
						5	6							−35	−34
						3	4							−35	−35
							3								−35

sigma = 20%/yr
Δt = 1 step/yr, so
U = 1.2214
D = 0.8187

$$[(0.255 − 0.027) \times 204.7 \\ -24-28] \times 0.67 \\ = −4$$

1995-1999

$$[(255k − 27k) \times P \\ -24 \text{ mm} − 28 \text{ mm}] \times (1 − 0.33)$$

2000-2018

$$[(122k − 27k) \times P \\ -24 \text{ mm} − 28 \text{ mm}] \times (1 − 0.33) \\ \text{All scaled in millions.}$$

$$[(0.122 − 0.027) \times 41 \\ -24 − 28] \times 0.67 \\ = −32$$

the cost of waiting an additional year to make a commitment given any time-price state. This is what will trigger early exercise in our American option.

The next step is to do the very same thing for the *scrubber* strategy. Figure 15.10 presents this step.

Before we do the same thing for the low-sulfur tree, we need to calculate the *cumulative remaining cost of compliance* under the scrubber strategy at every possible time-price state. This is easy. In the last year of the plant's life (2018), the cumulative remaining cost of compliance under the scrubber strategy is the 2018 scrubber cost (duh). In 2017, the cumulative remaining cost of compliance under the scrubber strategy at each allowance price is the 2017 scrubber cost plus the expected present value of the 2018 scrubber cost, using the risk-neutral probability and the risk-free rate. Given our 5% risk-free rate and one step per year, our risk-neutral probability of an up step is

$$q = \frac{e^{0.05 \times 1} − 0.8187}{1.2214 − 0.8187} = 0.577$$

So the risk-neutral probability of a down step is $1 − q = 0.423$. The risk-free time value factor is $e^{0.05 \times 1} = 1.051$, hence our tree of cumulative remaining cost of compliance under the scrubber strategy looks like that in Figure 15.11.

Figure 15.11

Scrubber Cost Each Year Tree (in $millions)						Cummulative Remaining Cost Using Scrubbers ($mm)					
1995	1996 >>>	2000	2001 >>>	2017	2018	1995	1996 >>>	2000	2001 >>>	2017	2018
3	12	8	18	1,261	1,548	−6	68	384	527	2524	1548
	−4	−6	1	834	1,026		−116	113	214	1670	1026
		−15	−11	548	676			−69	3	1097	676
		−22	−19	356	442			−191	−138	713	442
		−26	−24	227	285			−272	−232	455	285
		−29	−28	141	179			−327	−295	283	179
			−30	83	109				−338	167	109
				44	61					90	61
				18	30					38	30
				1	8					3	8
				−11	−6					−21	−6
				−19	−15					−36	−15
				−24	−22					−47	−22
				−28	−26					−54	−26
				−30	−29					−58	−29
				−32	−31					−62	−31
				−33	−32					−64	−32
				−33	−33					−65	−33
				−34	−34					−66	−34
				−34	−34					−67	−34
				−34	−34					−67	−34
				−35	−34					−67	−34
				−35	−35					−67	−35
					−35					−68	−35

Left inset box:

> **1995–1999**
>
> [(255k − 27k) × P − 24 mm − 28 mm] × (1 − 0.33)
>
> **2000–2018**
>
> [(122k − 27k) × P − 24 mm − 28 mm] × (1 − 0.33)
>
> All scaled in millions.

Middle formula (right panel):

$$[0.577 \times (-295) + 0.423 \times (-338)]/1.051 = -327$$

$$-29 +$$

Right inset box:

> Current cost
> + [q × next year cost if up
> + (1 − q) × next year cost if down]
> /exp (r × Δt)
>
> q = 0.577
> 1 − q = 0.423
> exp (r × Δt) = 1.051

The reason for constructing the cumulative remaining cost tree in Figure 15.11 is that it tells us the *benefit* of an immediate commitment to scrubber installation at any time-price state. That is, the right-hand panel of Figure 15.11 is the underlying asset for our American option on the scrubber strategy! Once again, you can find the full cumulative remaining cost of compliance tree for the scrubber strategy in the appendix.

At this point, I want to share an observation with you—an observation that amazes just about everyone who sees it. Given that the right-hand panel of Figure 15.11 is the underlying asset for our American option on a scrubber strategy, then it should tell us the value of making an immediate commitment to installing scrubbers in 1995. And it does. Notice that the cumulative remaining cost of compliance using scrubbers as of 1995 is −$6 million, which was *exactly* the discounted value of the operating cash flows from the scrubber strategy in our static DCF analysis of Figure 15.4 (+$493 million from selling allowances − $499 million from increased operating costs = −$6 million). If we subtract the $514 net capital investment required to install scrubbers ($700 million less the $186 million depreciation tax credit), we would get a net value of −$6 million − $514 million = −$520 million, which is *exactly the same as the static NPV calculated in Figure 15.4.*

What astonishes most people about this consistency between the valuation via static DCF and valuation via the binomial model is that the binomial model is invariant to the risk premium used in the static DCF, and the static DCF is invariant to the volatility used

Figure 15.12

Low Sulfur Cost Each Year Tree (in $millions)								Cummulative Remaining Cost Low-Sulfur Coal ($mm)							
1995	1996	>>>	2000	2001	>>>	2017	2018	1995	1996	>>>	2000	2001	>>>	2017	2018
11	14		−50	−55		−650	−788	−378	−424		−764	−814		−1299	−788
	8		−43	−46		−446	−538		−389		−635	−664		−890	−538
			−39	−41		−308	−370				−548	−563		−615	−370
			−36	−37		−216	−258				−489	−496		−431	−258
			−34	−35		−155	−183				−450	−451		−308	−183
			−32	−33		−113	−132				−424	−420		−226	−132
				−32		−86	−98					−400		−170	−98
						−67	−76							−133	−76
						−55	−60							−108	−60
						−46	−50							−91	−50
						−41	−43							−80	−43
						−37	−39							−73	−39
						−35	−36							−68	−36
						−33	−34							−64	−34
						−32	−32							−62	−32
						−31	−31							−61	−31
						−31	−31							−60	−31
						−30	−30							−59	−30
						−30	−30							−58	−30
						−30	−30							−58	−30
						−30	−30							−58	−30
						−30	−30							−58	−30
						−30	−30							−58	−30
							−30								−30

Box (left panel):

1995–1999

[(255k − 167.5k) × P −6 mm] × (1 − 0.33)

2000–2018

[(122k − 167.5k) × P −44 mm] × (1 − 0.33)

All scaled in millions.

Box (right panel):

Current cost
+ [q × next year cost if up
+ (1 − q) × next year cost if down]
/exp (r × Δt)

$q = 0.577$
$1 - q = 0.423$
exp (r × Δt) = 1.051

in the binomial model. As long as we are careful, we should get the exact same answer either way.[7]

The next step is to repeat the last two procedures (yearly cost of compliance and cumulative remaining cost of compliance) for the low-sulfur coal strategy. I've presented them in abbreviated form in Figure 15.12 and in complete form in the appendix.

Once again, we see the consistency between our static DCF approach and the binomial model. The right-hand panel of Figure 15.12 tells us that the cumulative cost of an immediate switch to low-sulfur coal in 1995 is $378 million, which is *exactly* the same as the discounted value of future allowance purchases (−$71 million) plus the discounted value of incremental operating costs (−$307 million) in our static DCF model of Figure 15.5. If we subtract the $16 million net capital cost of an immediate switch to low-sulfur coal ($22 million less the $6 million depreciation tax credit), we get a net present cost of −$394 million, exactly the same as in Figure 15.5.

Now let's think about how we will approach the American option problem. Each year, the benefit of waiting is that we get to observe more information about allowance values before making the costly and irreversible decision to adopt either strategy. The cost of waiting one more year is the current year's compliance cost under *no modification*. So our decision each year will look like this:

---

[7] It is not that easy to be careful, however. The single source of risk in both models is the market price of allowances. If you discount incremental operating costs and depreciation tax credits in the DCF model at anything other than the risk-free rate, you have to find a way to make them covary with allowance prices in the binomial analysis.

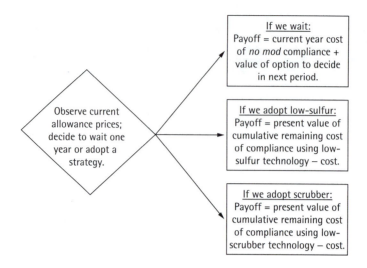

So in any year, the optimal decision is the one of the three that gives the maximum value (given current allowance prices), and the value of the option at that point in time will be the value of the maximum strategy, which is no different from what we've been doing all along.

Now to the fun part—from here on, the analysis is easy. We work backwards from the end, just as in our earlier American options tree, but now we choose the best among three alternatives: At any point, does it pay to wait further (do nothing), exercise the option by switching to low-sulfur at a net cost of −$22 million (the cost of switching) plus $6 million (the PV of the tax shield) = −$16 million, or switch to scrubbers at a net cost of −$700 million (the cost of the scrubbers) plus $186 million (the PV of the tax shield) = −$514 million?

Start with the very last period. In 2018, ask the following question: *If we have not switched to either low-sulfur or scrubbers by 2018, would we do so then, and if so which would we choose?* For each state in 2018, choose the maximum of the value in the *no modification* yearly cost of compliance tree (Figure 15.9), the corresponding value in the *low-sulfur* cumulative remaining cost tree (Figure 15.12) minus the net cost of switching to low sulfur coal ($16 million), or the corresponding value in the *scrubber* cumulative remaining cost tree (Figure 15.11) minus the net cost of installing scrubbers ($514 million). Keep track of which you do. I present the final result for 2018, and I document two example calculation, in Figure 15.13.

Now we work backwards. Starting in 2017, we compare three things:

1. The cumulative cost of continuing from this point on by immediately installing scrubbers (from the tree showing the cumulative remaining cost of compliance with scrubbers in Figure 15.11), minus the cost of installing scrubbers ($700 million), plus the depreciation tax shield on scrubbers ($186 million).

2. The cumulative cost of continuing from this point on by immediately switching to low-sulfur coal (from the cumulative remaining cost of compliance with low-sulfur coal tree in Figure 15.12), less the cost of switching ($22 million), plus the depreciation tax shield from switching ($6 million).

3. The cumulative cost of continuing from this point by making no immediate modification, but instead waiting to make the best decision in the next year. This is the current year's cost of compliance under no modification (from the current year cost of compliance

Figure 15.13

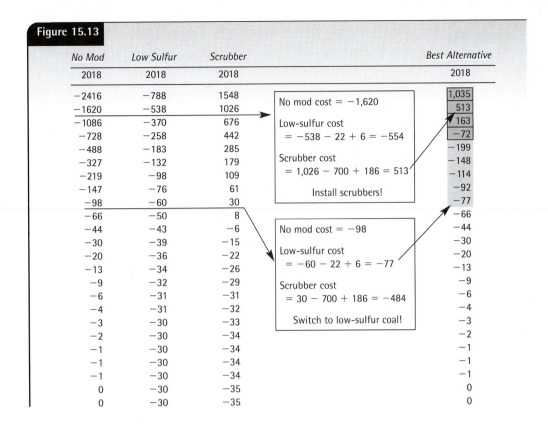

No Mod	Low Sulfur	Scrubber		Best Alternative
2018	2018	2018		2018
−2416	−788	1548	No mod cost = −1,620	1,035
−1620	−538	1026		513
−1086	−370	676	Low-sulfur cost	163
−728	−258	442	= −538 − 22 + 6 = −554	−72
−488	−183	285		−199
−327	−132	179	Scrubber cost	−148
−219	−98	109	= 1,026 − 700 + 186 = 513	−114
−147	−76	61		−92
−98	−60	30	Install scrubbers!	−77
−66	−50	8		−66
−44	−43	−6	No mod cost = −98	−44
−30	−39	−15		−30
−20	−36	−22	Low-sulfur cost	−20
−13	−34	−26	= −60 − 22 + 6 = −77	−13
−9	−32	−29		−9
−6	−31	−31	Scrubber cost	−6
−4	−31	−32	= 30 − 700 + 186 = −484	−4
−3	−30	−33		−3
−2	−30	−34	Switch to low-sulfur coal!	−2
−1	−30	−34		−1
−1	−30	−34		−1
−1	−30	−34		−1
0	−30	−35		0
0	−30	−35		0

under no modification tree in Figure 15.9) plus the expected present value of the best decision in the next period using the risk-neutral probabilities and the risk-free discount rate. I've completed the 2017 analysis for you and provided two documentary calculations in Figure 15.14.

Once you get this step, you've got it all—just repeat the procedure all the way back to 1995. You'll get a valuation tree and an optimal exercise boundary, like the ones shown in Figure 15.15 and Figure 15.16.

What Figure 15.16 shows us is that the optimal thing to do immediately is nothing—the best strategy is to wait (and perhaps quite a long time). Scrubbers should be installed if the price of allowances hits $556 per ton any time through 2006, or $680 per ton in 2007–2010. Switching to low-sulfur coal should not even be considered until 2011, and even then the switch to low-sulfur coal requires a market allowance price of $556. There's a significant likelihood that nothing will be done, ever.

Following the waiting strategy lowers the *dynamic* cost of compliance to about $277 million (see Figure 15.15). If you recall, the cost of compliance under the best *static* alternative (immediately switch to low-sulfur coal) was $395 million. So, the option to wait and make the best decision later is worth about $118 million, given the estimate that the current market price of allowances is $250 per ton.

The graph in Figure 15.17 provides some nice intuition about the value of this multiple-choice option.

Figure 15.14 Determination of the Best Dynamic Compliance Strategy in 2017

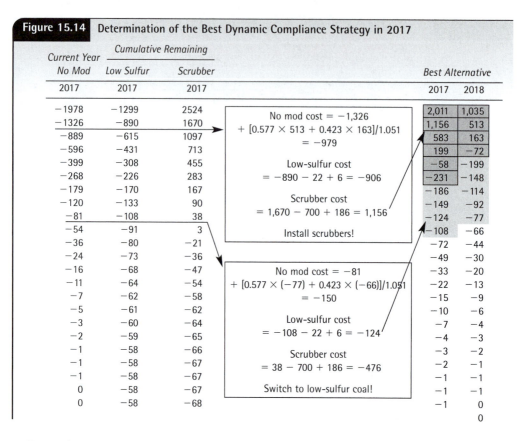

First, what we see in Figure 15.17 is that the waiting strategy looks like a portfolio that contains all three strategies. Indeed, it really is: Just as a call option is nothing more than a (dynamically changing) portfolio of the underlying and the risk-free bond, the American option on a compliance strategy is like a portfolio of plants under the three different alternatives plus some risk-free borrowing. Second, the value of the option to wait is the vertical distance between the *wait* curve and the line representing the cost of compliance under the next-best alternative. If allowance prices are really high, the option will not be worth much because we'll probably install scrubbers sooner than later. And if allowance prices are really low, there's little likelihood that they will increase enough to warrant any sort of modification. The option is most valuable in the gray area—exactly where Georgia Power management found themselves.

Another thing that this chart points out (subtly) is that the value of the option to wait and install scrubbers *or* low-sulfur coal is *not* equal to the value of the option to wait and install scrubbers *plus* the option to wait and install low-sulfur coal. Because the two strategies are mutually exclusive, they are not additive, and some of their values actually cancel out. If the only option available were the low-sulfur coal alternative, then under the parameters we've chosen, waiting lowers the cost of compliance by only about $25 million, and Georgia Power will optimally exercise if the price of allowances hits about $373 (which could occur rather quickly). But once we introduce the option to switch to scrubbers, we replace a large number of "switch to low-sulfur coal" states with "wait" or "install scrubbers" states.

The point is simple: When you have multiple options that are mutually exclusive, you cannot simply value each one individually and sum them up. They interact with each other, and you have to recognize this.

Figure 15.15   Option Value Tree: Switch to Scrubber or Low-Sulfur Coal (in $millions)

1995	1996	1997	1998	1999	2000	2001	2002	2003	2004	2005	2006	2007	2008	2009	2010	2011	2012	2013	2014	2015	2016	2017	2018
-277	-291	-291	-268	-208	-131	13	174	353	553	772	1,011	1,268	1,540	1,821	2,103	2,373	2,612	2,795	2,884	2,831	2,570	2,010	1,034
	-285	-321	-352	-373	-377	-301	-188	-62	77	229	396	574	763	959	1,155	1,343	1,512	1,643	1,712	1,686	1,520	1,155	512
		-268	-312	-359	-406	-416	-399	-341	-242	-134	-17	109	242	380	519	653	774	871	926	918	817	582	162
			-237	-282	-333	-368	-398	-417	-415	-378	-294	-203	-107	-7	93	191	280	353	399	403	345	198	-72
				-201	-242	-276	-311	-347	-380	-406	-417	-402	-341	-267	-193	-119	-52	6	46	58	29	-59	-199
					-168	-193	-221	-251	-284	-317	-349	-378	-399	-404	-384	-327	-274	-227	-191	-174	-183	-232	-148
						-131	-151	-173	-197	-223	-251	-279	-306	-329	-346	-351	-340	-325	-304	-277	-239	-186	-114
							-102	-117	-134	-152	-172	-193	-215	-236	-256	-272	-280	-275	-253	-227	-193	-149	-92
								-78	-90	-102	-116	-131	-146	-162	-178	-192	-204	-211	-209	-194	-163	-124	-77
									-60	-69	-78	-88	-98	-109	-120	-130	-139	-146	-148	-145	-132	-108	-66
										-46	-52	-59	-66	-73	-80	-87	-93	-98	-99	-97	-89	-72	-44
											-35	-39	-44	-49	-54	-59	-63	-65	-67	-65	-60	-49	-30
												-26	-30	-33	-36	-39	-42	-44	-45	-44	-40	-33	-20
													-20	-22	-24	-26	-28	-29	-30	-29	-27	-22	-13
														-15	-16	-18	-19	-20	-20	-20	-18	-15	-9
															-11	-12	-13	-13	-13	-13	-12	-10	-6
																-8	-8	-9	-9	-9	-8	-7	-4
																	-6	-6	-6	-6	-5	-4	-3
																		-4	-4	-4	-4	-3	-2
																			-3	-3	-3	-2	-1
																				-2	-2	-2	-1
																					-1	-1	-1
																						-1	0
																							0

Install scrubbers.
Switch to low-sulfur coal.

Figure 15.16 Optimal Exercise Strategy Given Spot Price of Allowances and Date

1995	1996	1997	1998	1999	2000	2001	2002	2003	2004	2005	2006	2007	2008	2009	2010	2011	2012	2013	2014	2015	2016	2017	2018
250	305	373	456	556	680	830	1014	1238	1512	1847	2256	2756	3366	4111	5021	6133	7491	9150	11175	13650	16672	20363	24871
	205	250	305	373	456	556	680	830	1014	1238	1512	1847	2256	2756	3366	4111	5021	6133	7491	9150	11175	13650	16672
		168	205	250	305	373	456	556	680	830	1014	1238	1512	1847	2256	2756	3366	4111	5021	6133	7491	9150	11175
			137	168	205	250	305	373	456	556	680	830	1014	1238	1512	1847	2256	2756	3366	4111	5021	6133	7491
				112	137	168	205	250	305	373	456	556	680	830	1014	1238	1512	1847	2256	2756	3366	4111	5021
					92	112	137	168	205	250	305	373	456	556	680	830	1014	1238	1512	1847	2256	2756	3366
						75	92	112	137	168	205	250	305	373	456	556	680	830	1014	1238	1512	1847	2256
							62	75	92	112	137	168	205	250	305	373	456	556	680	830	1014	1238	1512
								50	62	75	92	112	137	168	205	250	305	373	456	556	680	830	1014
									41	50	62	75	92	112	137	168	205	250	305	373	456	556	680
										34	41	50	62	75	92	112	137	168	205	250	305	373	456
											28	34	41	50	62	75	92	112	137	168	205	250	305
												23	28	34	41	50	62	75	92	112	137	168	205
													19	23	28	34	41	50	62	75	92	112	137
														15	19	23	28	34	41	50	62	75	92
															12	15	19	23	28	34	41	50	62
																10	12	15	19	23	28	34	41
																	8	10	12	15	19	23	28
																		7	8	10	12	15	19
																			6	7	8	10	12
																				5	6	7	8
																					4	5	6
																						3	4
																							3

Legend:

Install scrubbers.

Irrelevant—scrubbers already adopted.

Install low-sulfur coal.

Irrelevant—low-sulfur coal already adopted.

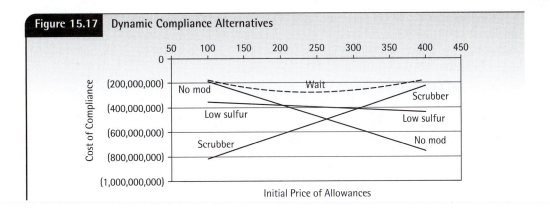

Figure 15.17   Dynamic Compliance Alternatives

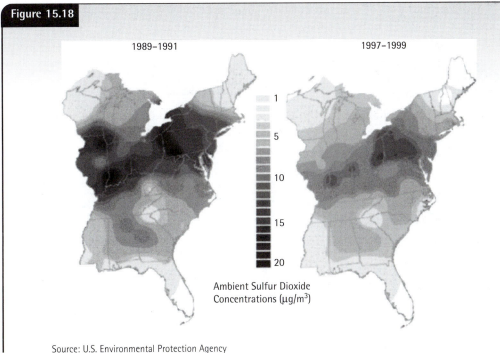

Figure 15.18

Source: U.S. Environmental Protection Agency

15.4   What Happened?

Georgia Power chose to immediately convert the Bowen plant to low-sulfur coal. Amazingly, many of the owners of Phase I plants chose to install scrubbers right away. This rush of scrubber installation flooded the allowance market and drove allowance prices down. By January 1997, the market price of one ton of SO_2 allowance was below $100. SO_2 allowance prices responded positively to the beginning of Phase II in January 2000, and bounced between $100 and $200 per ton through the end of 2004 with an annualized volatility of changes of around 20%.

Things changed in 2004, however, as the EPA issued the new Clean Air Interstate Rule, which would further reduce allowed SO_2 emissions (as well as other pollutants) starting in 2010. The market for allowances, which had been joined by speculative investors, including certain hedge funds, immediately incorporated the new regulation into spot prices—and the cost of an allowance rose to over $700 per ton by the end of the year.

The SO_2 program had an immediate effect on ambient SO_2 levels in the air and on wet sulfate deposition (acid rain), particularly in the Ohio River Valley area (as Figure 15.18 illustrates). At the beginning of Phase I, many critics feared that the market-based system would result in a shift of pollution from one region of the country to another. As it turned out, this did not occur. The vast majority of allowance transfers occurred *within individual companies,* and most inter-company transfers were between firms that operate in the same geographic region. According to observers, most firms initially chose to not rely on markets but rather assure that their entire portfolio of covered sources was brought into overall compliance through strategic pollution abatement investments at selected plants.

You can find a lot of great information about the market-based air pollution abatement system at the EPA's website: http://www.epa.gov/AIRMARKET.

15.5   Bibliography

Edelson, M., and F. Reinhart, 1995. "Investment in Pollution Compliance Options: The Case of Georgia Power," in *Real Options in Capital Investment: Models, Strategies, and Applications,* pp. 243–264. L. Trigeorgis, ed. Praeger, Westport, CT.

Appendix   15.1

Binomial Tree of Allowance Values ($)

1995	1996	1997	1998	1999	2000	2001	2002	2003	2004	2005	2006	2007	2008	2009	2010	2011	2012	2013	2014	2015	2016	2017	2018
250	305	373	456	556	680	830	1014	1238	1512	1847	2256	2756	3366	4111	5021	6133	7491	9150	11175	13650	16672	20363	24871
	205	250	305	373	456	556	680	830	1014	1238	1512	1847	2256	2756	3366	4111	5021	6133	7491	9150	11175	13650	16672
		168	205	250	305	373	456	556	680	830	1014	1238	1512	1847	2256	2756	3366	4111	5021	6133	7491	9150	11175
			137	168	205	250	305	373	456	556	680	830	1014	1238	1512	1847	2256	2756	3366	4111	5021	6133	7491
				112	137	168	205	250	305	373	456	556	680	830	1014	1238	1512	1847	2256	2756	3366	4111	5021
					92	112	137	168	205	250	305	373	456	556	680	830	1014	1238	1512	1847	2256	2756	3366
						75	92	112	137	168	205	250	305	373	456	556	680	830	1014	1238	1512	1847	2256
							62	75	92	112	137	168	205	250	305	373	456	556	680	830	1014	1238	1512
								50	62	75	92	112	137	168	205	250	305	373	456	556	680	830	1014
									41	50	62	75	92	112	137	168	205	250	305	373	456	556	680
										34	41	50	62	75	92	112	137	168	205	250	305	373	456
											28	34	41	50	62	75	92	112	137	168	205	250	305
												23	28	34	41	50	62	75	92	112	137	168	205
													19	23	28	34	41	50	62	75	92	112	137
														15	19	23	28	34	41	50	62	75	92
															12	15	19	23	28	34	41	50	62
																10	12	15	19	23	28	34	41
																	8	10	12	15	19	23	28
																		7	8	10	12	15	19
																			6	7	8	10	12
																				5	6	7	8
																					4	5	6
																						3	4
																							3

No Modification Cost Each Year Tree (in $millions)

1995	1996	1997	1998	1999	2000	2001	2002	2003	2004	2005	2006	2007	2008	2009	2010	2011	2012	2013	2014	2015	2016	2017	2018
-2	-2	-3	-4	-4	-66	-81	-98	-120	-147	-179	-219	-268	-327	-399	-488	-596	-728	-889	-1086	-1326	-1620	-1978	-2416
	-2	-2	-2	-3	-44	-54	-66	-81	-98	-120	-147	-179	-219	-268	-327	-399	-488	-596	-728	-889	-1086	-1326	-1620
		-1	-2	-2	-30	-36	-44	-54	-66	-81	-98	-120	-147	-179	-219	-268	-327	-399	-488	-596	-728	-889	-1086
			-1	-1	-20	-24	-30	-36	-44	-54	-66	-81	-98	-120	-147	-179	-219	-268	-327	-399	-488	-596	-728
				-1	-13	-16	-20	-24	-30	-36	-44	-54	-66	-81	-98	-120	-147	-179	-219	-268	-327	-399	-488
					-9	-11	-13	-16	-20	-24	-30	-36	-44	-54	-66	-81	-98	-120	-147	-179	-219	-268	-327
						-7	-9	-11	-13	-16	-20	-24	-30	-36	-44	-54	-66	-81	-98	-120	-147	-179	-219
							-6	-7	-9	-11	-13	-16	-20	-24	-30	-36	-44	-54	-66	-81	-98	-120	-147
								-5	-6	-7	-9	-11	-13	-16	-20	-24	-30	-36	-44	-54	-66	-81	-98
									-4	-5	-6	-7	-9	-11	-13	-16	-20	-24	-30	-36	-44	-54	-66
										-3	-4	-5	-6	-7	-9	-11	-13	-16	-20	-24	-30	-36	-44
											-3	-3	-4	-5	-6	-7	-9	-11	-13	-16	-20	-24	-30
												-2	-3	-3	-4	-5	-6	-7	-9	-11	-13	-16	-20
													-2	-2	-3	-3	-4	-5	-6	-7	-9	-11	-13
														-1	-2	-2	-3	-3	-4	-5	-6	-7	-9
															-1	-1	-2	-2	-3	-3	-4	-5	-6
																-1	-1	-1	-2	-2	-3	-3	-4
																	-1	-1	-1	-1	-2	-2	-3
																		-1	-1	-1	-1	-1	-2
																			-1	-1	-1	-1	-1
																				0	-1	-1	-1
																					0	0	-1
																						0	0
																							0

1995–1999

Each cell is

$$[(255k - 267k) \times P](1 - 0.33)$$

2000–2018

Each cell is

$$[(122k - 267k) \times P](1 - 0.33)$$

(All are scaled in millions.)

Scrubber Cost Each Year Tree (in $millions)

1995	1996	1997	1998	1999	2000	2001	2002	2003	2004	2005	2006	2007	2008	2009	2010	2011	2012	2013	2014	2015	2016	2017	2018
3	12	22	35	50	8	18	30	44	61	83	109	141	179	227	285	356	442	548	676	834	1026	1261	1548
	−4	3	12	22	−6	1	8	18	30	44	61	83	109	141	179	227	285	356	442	548	676	834	1026
		−9	−4	3	−15	−11	−6	1	8	18	30	44	61	83	109	141	179	227	285	356	442	548	676
			−14	−9	−22	−19	−15	−11	−6	1	8	18	30	44	61	83	109	141	179	227	285	356	442
				−18	−26	−24	−22	−19	−15	−11	−6	1	8	18	30	44	61	83	109	141	179	227	285
					−29	−28	−26	−24	−22	−19	−15	−11	−6	1	8	18	30	44	61	83	109	141	179
						−30	−29	−28	−26	−24	−22	−19	−15	−11	−6	1	8	18	30	44	61	83	109
							−31	−30	−29	−28	−26	−24	−22	−19	−15	−11	−6	1	8	18	30	44	61
								−32	−31	−30	−29	−28	−26	−24	−22	−19	−15	−11	−6	1	8	18	30
									−32	−32	−31	−30	−29	−28	−26	−24	−22	−19	−15	−11	−6	1	8
										−33	−32	−32	−31	−30	−29	−28	−26	−24	−22	−19	−15	−11	−6
											−33	−33	−32	−32	−31	−30	−29	−28	−26	−24	−22	−19	−15
												−33	−33	−33	−32	−32	−31	−30	−29	−28	−26	−24	−22
													−34	−33	−33	−33	−32	−32	−31	−30	−29	−28	−26
														−34	−33	−33	−33	−33	−32	−32	−31	−30	−29
															−34	−34	−33	−33	−33	−33	−32	−32	−31
																−34	−34	−34	−34	−33	−33	−33	−32
																	−34	−34	−34	−34	−34	−33	−33
																		−34	−34	−34	−34	−34	−34
																			−34	−34	−34	−34	−34
																				−35	−34	−34	−34
																					−35	−35	−34
																						−35	−35
																							−35

1995–1999

$$\frac{[255k - 27k] \times P}{-24\,mm - 28\,mm} \times (1 - 0.33)$$

2000–2018

$$\frac{[(122k - 27k] \times P}{-24\,mm - 28\,mm} \times (1 - 0.33)$$

All scaled in millions.

Cumulative Remaining Cost Using Scrubbers (in $millions)

1995	1996	1997	1998	1999	2000	2001	2002	2003	2004	2005	2006	2007	2008	2009	2010	2011	2012	2013	2014	2015	2016	2017	2018
-6	68	145	226	306	384	527	688	868	1067	1286	1526	1783	2054	2336	2618	2887	3127	3309	3399	3346	3084	2524	1548
	-116	-60	-2	56	113	214	326	452	591	744	910	1089	1278	1473	1669	1858	2026	2157	2226	2200	2034	1670	1026
		-197	-154	-111	-69	3	84	173	272	380	497	623	757	895	1034	1168	1289	1385	1440	1432	1331	1097	676
			-257	-223	-191	-138	-79	-14	58	136	221	312	408	507	608	705	794	867	913	917	859	713	442
				-299	-272	-232	-188	-139	-85	-27	35	103	174	247	322	395	463	520	560	572	543	455	285
					-327	-295	-261	-223	-182	-137	-89	-37	17	73	130	187	241	288	323	341	331	283	179
						-338	-310	-279	-246	-210	-172	-131	-88	-44	2	48	92	132	165	186	189	167	109
							-342	-317	-289	-260	-228	-194	-159	-122	-84	-46	-8	27	58	82	94	90	61
								-342	-318	-293	-265	-237	-206	-174	-142	-108	-75	-43	-13	12	30	38	30
									-337	-315	-290	-265	-238	-210	-180	-150	-120	-90	-61	-35	-13	3	8
										-329	-307	-284	-259	-233	-206	-178	-150	-121	-93	-66	-41	-21	-6
											-319	-296	-273	-249	-224	-197	-170	-142	-114	-87	-60	-36	-15
												-305	-283	-260	-235	-210	-183	-156	-129	-101	-73	-47	-22
													-289	-267	-243	-218	-193	-166	-138	-110	-82	-54	-26
														-271	-248	-224	-199	-172	-145	-117	-88	-58	-29
															-252	-228	-203	-176	-149	-121	-92	-62	-31
																-230	-205	-179	-152	-124	-94	-64	-32
																	-207	-181	-154	-126	-96	-65	-33
																		-183	-155	-127	-97	-66	-34
																			-156	-128	-98	-67	-34
																				-128	-98	-67	-34
																					-99	-67	-35
																						-68	-35
																							-35

Current cost +
[q × next year cost if up
+ (1 − q) × next year cost if down]
/exp (r × Δt)

q = 0.577
1 − q = 0.423
exp (r × Δt) = 1.051

Low Sulfur Cost Each Year Tree (in $millions)

1995	1996	1997	1998	1999	2000	2001	2002	2003	2004	2005	2006	2007	2008	2009	2010	2011	2012	2013	2014	2015	2016	2017	2018
11	14	18	23	29	−50	−55	−60	−67	−76	−86	−98	−113	−132	−155	−183	−216	−258	−308	−370	−446	−538	−650	−788
	8	11	14	18	−43	−46	−50	−55	−60	−67	−76	−86	−98	−113	−132	−155	−183	−216	−258	−308	−370	−446	−538
		6	8	11	−39	−41	−43	−46	−50	−55	−60	−67	−76	−86	−98	−113	−132	−155	−183	−216	−258	−308	−370
			4	6	−36	−37	−39	−41	−43	−46	−50	−55	−60	−67	−76	−86	−98	−113	−132	−155	−183	−216	−258
				3	−34	−35	−36	−37	−39	−41	−43	−46	−50	−55	−60	−67	−76	−86	−98	−113	−132	−155	−183
					−32	−33	−34	−35	−36	−37	−39	−41	−43	−46	−50	−55	−60	−67	−76	−86	−98	−113	−132
						−32	−32	−33	−34	−35	−36	−37	−39	−41	−43	−46	−50	−55	−60	−67	−76	−86	−98
							−31	−32	−32	−33	−34	−35	−36	−37	−39	−41	−43	−46	−50	−55	−60	−67	−76
								−31	−31	−32	−32	−33	−34	−35	−36	−37	−39	−41	−43	−46	−50	−55	−60
									−31	−31	−31	−32	−32	−33	−34	−35	−36	−37	−39	−41	−43	−46	−50
										−31	−31	−31	−31	−32	−32	−33	−34	−35	−36	−37	−39	−41	−43
											−30	−31	−31	−31	−31	−32	−32	−33	−34	−35	−36	−37	−39
												−30	−30	−31	−31	−31	−31	−32	−32	−33	−34	−35	−36
													−30	−30	−30	−31	−31	−31	−31	−32	−32	−33	−34
														−30	−30	−30	−30	−31	−31	−31	−31	−32	−32
															−30	−30	−30	−30	−30	−31	−31	−31	−31
																−30	−30	−30	−30	−30	−30	−31	−31
																	−30	−30	−30	−30	−30	−30	−30
																		−30	−30	−30	−30	−30	−30
																			−30	−30	−30	−30	−30
																				−30	−30	−30	−30
																					−30	−30	−30
																						−30	−30
																							−30

1995–1999

$$[(255k - 167.5k) \times P - 6\ mm] \times (1 - 0.33)$$

2000–2018

$$[(122k - 167.5k) \times P - 44\ mm] \times (1 - 0.33)$$

All scaled in millions.

Cumulative Remaining Cost Low-Sulfur Coal (in $millions)

1995	1996	1997	1998	1999	2000	2001	2002	2003	2004	2005	2006	2007	2008	2009	2010	2011	2012	2013	2014	2015	2016	2017	2018
−378	−424	−481	−554	−646	−764	−814	−872	−937	−1011	−1093	−1183	−1281	−1384	−1491	−1597	−1695	−1777	−1830	−1837	−1774	−1609	−1299	−788
	−389	−431	−484	−551	−635	−664	−698	−738	−783	−833	−888	−948	−1012	−1078	−1143	−1202	−1250	−1278	−1276	−1225	−1106	−890	−538
		−398	−438	−487	−548	−563	−582	−604	−630	−659	−691	−726	−763	−801	−838	−871	−897	−909	−899	−857	−769	−615	−370
			−407	−444	−489	−496	−504	−515	−527	−542	−558	−576	−596	−615	−634	−650	−660	−661	−647	−611	−543	−431	−258
				−415	−450	−451	−452	−455	−459	−463	−469	−476	−484	−491	−497	−501	−501	−495	−478	−446	−392	−308	−183
					−424	−420	−417	−415	−413	−411	−410	−409	−408	−407	−405	−402	−395	−383	−364	−335	−291	−226	−132
						−400	−394	−388	−382	−376	−370	−364	−358	−352	−344	−335	−324	−308	−288	−261	−223	−170	−98
							−378	−370	−361	−352	−343	−334	−324	−314	−303	−290	−276	−258	−237	−211	−177	−133	−76
								−357	−347	−336	−325	−314	−302	−289	−275	−260	−244	−225	−203	−177	−146	−108	−60
									−338	−326	−313	−300	−287	−272	−257	−240	−222	−202	−180	−155	−126	−91	−50
										−319	−305	−291	−276	−261	−244	−227	−208	−187	−165	−140	−112	−80	−43
											−300	−285	−270	−253	−236	−218	−198	−177	−155	−130	−103	−73	−39
												−281	−265	−248	−230	−212	−192	−170	−148	−123	−97	−68	−36
													−262	−245	−227	−208	−187	−166	−143	−119	−93	−64	−34
														−242	−224	−205	−184	−163	−140	−116	−90	−62	−32
															−222	−203	−182	−161	−138	−114	−88	−61	−31
																−202	−181	−159	−137	−112	−87	−60	−31
																	−180	−158	−136	−111	−86	−59	−30
																		−158	−135	−110	−85	−58	−30
																			−135	−110	−85	−58	−30
																				−110	−85	−58	−30
																					−85	−58	−30
																						−58	−30
																							−30

Current cost +
[q × next year cost if up
+ (1 − q) × next year cost if down]
/exp (r × Δt)

q = 0.577
1 − q = 0.423
exp (r × Δt) = 1.051

1. The equation below values the discounted revenue/cost stream associated with pollution permits/allowances. Prove the equation works with the revenue/cost streams associated with the permits in Figures 15.3, 15.4, and 15.5.

$$\{Q_1 \times \$250.00 \times 5 + Q_2 \times \$250.00 \times 19\} \times (1 - 0.33)$$

Q_1 = quantity of permits purchased or sold in Phase I
Q_2 = quantity of permits purchased or sold in Phase II

2. An analyst calculates the discounted value of the lost revenue section of Figure 15.4 in the following manner:

$$\frac{-\$34,840,000}{5.1271\%} \left[1 - \frac{1}{(1 + 5.1271\%)^{24}} \right] = -\$474,856,558$$

Correct the analysis to produce the appropriate number displayed in Figure 15.4. (*Hint:* The problem is not with the discount rate nor with the number of periods under consideration.) Rounding error within $700.00 may occur in correcting the problem.

3. Reproduce the calculation associated with the "No Modification Cost Each Year Tree" in Figure 15.9 for the following 2018 states: −2,416, −1,620, −1,086, and −728. Be certain to let your answers extend to two decimal places.

4. Reproduce the calculation with the "Scrubber Cost Each Year Tree" in Figure 15.10 for the following 2018 states: 1,548, 1,026, 676, and 442. Be certain to let your answers extend to two decimal places. Also, perform the same calculation for the following 2017 states: 1,261, 834, and 548.

5. Reproduce the calculation with the "Cumulative Remaining Cost Using Scrubbers Tree" in Figure 15.11 for the following 2017 states: 2,524, 1,670, and 1,097. Be certain to let your answers extend to two decimal places and to use the information calculated in Problem 4.

6. Reproduce the calculation with the "Low-Sulfur Cost Each Year Tree" in Figure 15.12 for the following 2018 states: −788, −538, −370, and −258. Be certain to let your answers extend to two decimal places. Also, perform the same calculation for the following 2017 states: −650, −446, and −308.

7. Reproduce the calculation with the "Cumulative Remaining Cost Low-Sulfur Coal Tree" in Figure 15.12 for the following 2017 states: −1,299, −890, and −615. Be certain to let your answers extend to two decimal places and to use the information calculated in Problem 6.

8. Using the information from Problems 3, 4, and 6, reproduce the calculation for the "Best Alternative" column in Figure 15.13 for the following 2018 states: 1,035, 513 (example displayed), 163, and −72. Be certain to let your answers extend to two decimal places.

9. Using the information from Problems 5, 7, and 8 (and Figure 15.14), reproduce the calculation for the "Best Alternative" column in Figure 15.14 for the following 2017 states: 2,011, 1,156 (example displayed), and 583. Be certain to let your answers extend to two decimal places.

16   What Else Can You Do?

When I wrote this text, my principle objective was to help corporate managers think about the world in a disciplined way so that they might make better investment decisions. Along the way, I faced a constant temptation to make things more technically sophisticated. I had to repeatedly remind myself to focus on the thought process as much as possible and on the method only as much as necessary.

To stay true to my purpose—helping managers—I've maintained one set of abstractions to simplify the world (the standard Black-Scholes assumptions) and used one solution technique to provide a valuation approximation (the binomial model).

My goal has never been to proffer a state-of-the-art presentation of option pricing; you'll have to go to another source for that material. The corporate manager's problem is very different from the option trader's problem, and my own experience tells me that corporate managers don't need the latest in mathematical sophistication. Rather, what they need is a better lens for viewing their situation—an eyepiece that highlights what's important and filters out everything else. I firmly believe that the Black-Scholes world provides a good first-order approximation for most situations that most corporate managers face.

Nevertheless, I think it is important to disclose to you that you *don't* have to approximate the world using the Black-Scholes assumptions, and you *don't* have to use the binomial approach as your solution technique. The aim of this short chapter is simply to point out to you some other ways to go about things. But, please take this one piece of advice: Before you go jumping off into a more esoteric model of the world or a more complex solution technique, *make sure you have a good reason for doing so.* Never put the methodology before the thought process.

16.1   The Binomial Solution Technique

Throughout this text, I've simplified the world with the following assumptions:

- There exists a single source of uncertainty (lets call it the *state variable*) which determines the value of our underlying asset.
- Any costs or benefits of holding the underlying asset are known in advance.
- Changes in the value of the state variable (i.e., its log returns) are described by a normal distribution (so future values are described by a lognormal distribution).
- The standard deviation of changes in the value of the state variable is constant per unit time and does not change over the life of the real option.
- The risk-free rate of return is constant.

To put it in lay terms, we've worked in a Black-Scholes world.[1] In Chapter 4, I presented the standard binomial model that first appeared in Cox, Ross, and Rubenstein (1979). I'll reiterate

---

[1] In addition, we've maintained the standard assumptions of corporate finance that I outlined in Chapter 3.

here that this formulation is not the only way to implement the Black-Scholes assumption in a binomial model. Several very popular derivatives texts present alternative (but equally valid) constructions, and I offered a couple of examples in the appendix to Chapter 4.

The history of the binomial model is quite interesting, in that its development did not take place until *after* the seminal work of Black and Scholes (1973) and Merton (1973). In the quest to relax the Black-Scholes assumptions, Cox and Ross (1976) came up with a continuous-time model in which, at any instant of time, the state variable (i.e., the underlying stock) could either make a discrete jump or not. Cox and Ross (1976) showed that under certain conditions, the Black-Scholes intuition would still hold: A derivative written on the stock could be hedged by an appropriate combination of the stock and the riskless bond.[2] The dispositive question then became *why* this general technique should work. The insight that led to the binomial model came when William Sharpe, attending a conference at the Dead Sea, said to some colleagues, "I wonder if it's really that there are only two states of the world, but three securities, so that any one of the securities can be replicated by the other two."[3] The idea that one can think of the world has having only two outcomes over a small, discrete time step led directly to what I showed in Chapter 4.[4]

Relaxing the Black–Scholes Assumptions

If you don't think that your underlying source of uncertainty can be adequately approximated with the Black-Scholes assumptions, the first thing I would suggest is that you apply an ad hoc adjustment. Cox and Rubenstein (1985, Chapter 6) worked through a host of issues numerically and provide some very good rules of thumb.

More formal adjustments to our binomial approach are sometimes (but not always) available. For example, you might have good reason to think that the volatility of changes in your underlying source of uncertainty is not constant, but rather is a function of time. Cox and Rubenstein (1985) showed that you can handle this by altering your binomial up- and down-step multipliers U and D as time marches on (based on your own assessment of *how* your volatility relates to time); however, the tree will no longer recombine. Clewlow and Strickland (1998) provided an alternative tree formulation that allows for time variation in volatility as well as the risk-free rate, and they achieved recombination by allowing the size of each time step to vary. Be that as it may, this is all easier in a trinomial model (see later).

If you truly think that the lognormality assumption is completely inappropriate to your situation, but you'd still like to use the binomial approach, you are not completely out of luck. There are many other distributional assumptions that the binomial model can handle. Ramaswamy and Nelson (1990) provided a general approach for constructing recombinant binomial lattices that converge to alternate distributions. You can't do this for any arbitrary stochastic process, but Ramaswamy and Nelson (1990) provided the requirements (which you must check) along with the procedure. For example, you might believe that the volatility of your underlying is a function of the level of the underlying. This is known as the *constant elasticity of*

---

[2] This in turn led Cox and Ross to the idea that they named *risk-neutral pricing*: If a derivative can be risklessly replicated, then its valuation must be consistent with elemental pricing that would occur in a world in which everyone is risk-neutral. In such a world, the price of any risky security equals its expected future value discounted at the risk-free rate of return; therefore, the value of any redundant real-world derivative must be equal to its discounted future expectation (under the risk-neutral measure) with no adjustment for risk.

[3] As quoted in Rubenstein (1992).

[4] The first published illustration of the binomial approach appeared in Sharpe (1978).

variance model. Or you might think your single source of uncertainty follows the basic *mean-reverting* process as in the interest rate model of Vasicek (1977), or that it is best described by the *square-root* process as in the interest rate model of Cox, Ingersoll, and Ross (1979). As examples of their general procedure, Ramaswamy and Nelson (1990) showed explicitly how to operationalize each of these in a recombinant binomial context.

One place where lognormality is clearly not an appropriate approximation is in the world of interest rates. Interest rate models are complex beasts, and they require a rather large investment in learning. While it is true that interest rates are random, I'm not convinced that explicit incorporation of this issue will materially alter decisions concerning real assets and options on real assets. When it comes to financing issues, however, explicit recognition of random interest rates is important. I recommend the books by Moore (2001) and Hull (2003) as good starting points. Clewlow and Strickland (1998) gave a general procedure for implementing certain types of interest rate models in a binomial framework.

16.2   Other Lattice Models

We call the binomial model a *lattice approach* because, well, because it looks like a lattice-work fence if you draw it out with arrows connecting each state. Other lattice models are available and sometimes are more helpful.

Maintaining the Black-Scholes Assumptions

A *trinomial* model is one in which any particular state can be followed by *three* possible future states (as opposed to two in the binomial model). Though the original purpose of trinomial models was to incorporate multiple uncertainties,[5] many practitioners use a trinomial lattice like the one described in Hull (2003) as a substitute for the binomial approach in a Black-Scholes world. This is perfectly justified, since in this context they are really doing the same thing.[6]

A common application in financial markets is to price *barrier* options (also called down-and-in/down-and-out or knock-in/knock-out), in which the option either becomes valueless or comes to life only if the underlying asset achieves a certain price (the barrier) over the life of the option. The trinomial model allows one to break apart the spacing of future state values from the size of the time step, and so you can always have one state at each time point where the underlying price equals the barrier value. I'm not aware of any real options examples that would look like a barrier option, but I can foresee certain licensing contracts or insurance deals as having this feature. See the excellent book by Clewlow and Strickland (1998) for the procedure for barriers as well as other path-dependent options.[7]

---

[5] See Boyle (1988).

[6] The trinomial approach is just a restatement of a numerical technique known as the *finite difference method*, which is frequently used to solve the Black-Scholes-Merton partial differential equation (PDE). Both the PDE and the binomial model are ways of describing the local behavior of a derivative's value relative to its underlying. Brennan and Schwartz (1978) tied this all together.

[7] Other applications of a trinomial model are for valuation of *lookback* options (where the final asset value or strike price is set equal to the minimum or maximum value attained by the underlying at certain dates through the option's life) and *Asian* options (where the final asset value or strike price is set equal to some average of the underlying's realized values during the option's life).

Relaxing the Black-Scholes Assumptions

A situation that I have not covered in this text but that you may encounter in practice is when your real option's payoff depends on the realization of two or more underlying variables. An option written on more than one underlying is often called a *rainbow option*. An example of a rainbow option is the flexibility that is embedded in an ammonia plant. The free cash flow from operating an ammonia plant is a function of both the market price of natural gas (the primary input) and the market price of ammonia (which is largely determined by the state of the global agriculture industry and is only loosely correlated with natural gas). In any period when the price of gas is so high and/or the price of ammonia is so low that the plant would lose money on production, you simply suspend production and wait for things to improve. The market value of a plant itself must reflect this flexibility.

One approach to valuation of rainbow options involves letting each underlying evolve in its own binomial tree and then correlating the variables through the risk-neutral probabilities.[8] Boyle, Evnine, and Gibbs (1989) derived this model under the assumption that the variables are jointly lognormal. A practical problem arises in that the calculated risk-neutral probabilities (or *transition probabilities* to be technically precise) may turn out to be negative. The only cure for this affliction is to make the time steps smaller in size, which brings about a nuisance problem of having to deal with a potentially large number of states in the latter time periods.

A very intriguing alternative was given to us by Chen, Yang, and Chung (2002), who consider a state of nature to be an $(N + 1)$ vector of N underlying asset values plus the value of the risk-free bond. The contribution of Chen, Yang, and Chung (2002) is to let the vector evolve through time as an $(N + 1)$-nomial lattice and to account for the correlations among the risky assets by the way the lattice evolves through a neat trick of spherical geometry. In the end you get an exact pricing model at every time-state: A delta (or hedge ratio) for each underlying as well as a position in the risk-free bond that together exactly hedge the derivative no matter what happens over the next period. I've used this model, and I like it.[9]

If that's not enough for you, I'll give you two more citations for lattice models that can handle multiple uncertainties: The original trinomial model presented in Boyle (1988) for two state variables, and the more complex lattice model of Kamrad and Ritchken (1991), which, for k sources of uncertainty, has $2k + 1$ branches leading out of each node.

The biggest benefit of trinomial trees is that they give the analyst/modeler some additional flexibility in solving problems (which is something I hinted at a couple of paragraphs ago). There are several ways to harness this additional flexibility when you're faced with a situation that doesn't jibe with the Black-Scholes assumptions. For example, Hull (2003, Chapter 28) showed how you can build a trinomial tree that matches up with observed futures prices under the assumption that the underlying's value exhibits a certain type of mean reversion. This is a nice

---

[8] In the ammonia plant example, there would be one binomial tree for ammonia prices and another for natural gas prices, so after one time step there would be *four* potential states of nature (gas up and ammonia up, gas up and ammonia down, etc.). At first blush, this would appear to be an intractable problem as the model only has three assets available (ammonia, natural gas, and the risk-free bond) to hedge four outcomes. But there's a solution: Cox, Ingersoll, and Ross (1985) derived the partial differential equation that describes the behavior of any derivative written on N assets and showed that it can always be replicated by the N risky assets plus the risk-free bond. Boyle, Evnine, and Gibbs (1986) used this result—essentially that the market is complete over an infinitesimal time step—and derived the multinomial lattice parameters so that the probability distribution matches up correctly as the time steps get small. This is a classic example of taking a solution that already exists and finding a new way to reach it.

[9] Don't get frustrated when working through the numerical example in Chen, Yang, and Chung—there's a typographical error at one critical point.

solution technique to use when there are traded futures contracts written on your underlying, and you think that its price tends to revert to a long-run mean.

Taking this one step further, a host of thinkers have used the flexibility provided by trinomial approach to generate what are called *implied* trees. The idea here is to use the information that is reflected by observed market prices of traded options to build a lattice that is consistent with those prices. See Clewlow and Strickland (1998).

The flexibility of the trinomial model makes it very useful for modeling interest rates. Again, I refer the reader to Hull (2003) and Clewlow and Strickland (1998) for details and examples.

16.3   Monte Carlo Simulation

The development of cheap desktop computing power combined with some really good software has made Monte Carlo simulation a popular managerial tool in a variety of situations. With care, you can use this technique to price options (both real and financial) as well.

Maintaining the Black-Scholes Assumptions

Simulating the future value of a lognormal random variable is really easy—all you have to do is make random draws from a standard normal probability distribution (that is, a normal distribution with mean 0 and standard deviation 1), and then perform a little arithmetic. The key is that to price options (real or financial) via simulation, *you have to draw from the risk-neutral distribution.* You *cannot* use a physical/subjective/ "real world" distribution for the reasons we covered in Chapter 2: Every draw will be associated with a certain state of the macroeconomy in some way, and thus different possible payoffs on the option may require different risk-adjusted discount rates. We get around this by risk-neutral pricing. Here's a quick rundown of the general procedure.

- Start with the current value of your underlying, UND_0.
- Decide how long your time increment Δt will be. This is in fractions of a year. For example, if you are going to simulate the value of the underlying at the end of every day from now until the time your flexibility expires, then $\Delta t = 1/365$.
- Estimate the other parameters you need: The annual volatility of log returns on the underlying σ, the annual risk-free rate of return r, and the annual net convenience yield on your underlying *ncy*.
- Each trial is one *price path*, which is a simulated price at the end of each time increment from now until the expiration. A trial looks like this:
  - For the first time increment (say, Day 1), make a random draw from a normal random variable with mean 0 and standard deviation 1, and call this quantity ε_1.
  - The log of the value of your underlying at the end of the first time increment will be

$$\ln UND_1 = \ln UND_0 + (r - ncy - 0.5\sigma^2)\Delta t + \sigma\varepsilon_1 \sqrt{\Delta t}$$

  - Exponentiate to get the simulated value of your underlying at the end of the first time increment:

$$UND_1 = \exp\{\ln UND_0 + (r - ncy - 0.5\sigma^2)\Delta t + \sigma\varepsilon_1 \sqrt{\Delta t}\}$$

- Now repeat: To get the simulated value of the underlying at the end of the second day, draw ε_2 from an $N(0,1)$ distribution, use it along with $\ln UND_1$ and your other parameters to get $\ln UND_2$, and then exponentiate to get UND_2. Continue repeating until you have the full price path.
- Repeat for as many trials as you desire.

To value a derivative, calculate the derivative's payoff based on each price path, and discount back to the present at the risk-free rate of return. You'll have one simulated derivative value for each trial you've run; take the average as your approximation of the derivative's value.

For standard European options, this is all very easy. For American options, however, simulation poses a problem. At any early exercise date, the payoff to immediate exercise is easy to calculate, but the payoff to leaving the option alive is not. You'll need a shortcut, and a very popular one appears in Longstaff and Schwartz (2001).

Monte Carlo simulation is a great tool when your option (real or financial) has a *path-dependent* payoff. The term *path-dependent* means that you can't calculate the payoff on the derivative by simply looking at the value of the underlying at expiration; rather, you must know the underlying's price history.

Path dependent real options are everywhere, and they appear quite frequently in real estate management contracts as well as in custom-tailored risk management arrangements. An example would be an electricity supply contract between a utility and an industrial user that allows the utility to interrupt the user's power supply for a day with one day's notice up to a maximum of, say, four times in a summer; on any day the utility chooses to do so, the utility must make a fixed payment to the industrial user. In this very typical arrangement, the utility is actually buying a portfolio of call options on power (with strike equal to the fixed payment), one expiring each day of the summer. How much should the industrial user demand up front? You can't simply value each day's option independently and add them all up, because the utility's exercise decision early in the summer affects its ability to exercise later in the summer (there are a maximum number of calls—remember?). The only way to value this contract is via simulation.[10]

The downside to Monte Carlo simulation is that you need to run many, many trails in order to get accurate results, and you simply may not have the computing power to do so. Hull (2003) and Clewlow and Strickland (1998) provided good explanations of *variance reduction techniques* that help the accuracy of your procedure.

Relaxing the Black–Scholes Assumptions

If you've got multiple sources of uncertainty, Monte Carlo simulation may be the way to go. Clewlow and Strickland (1998) provided the basics for European-style options; Raymar and Zwecher (1997) offered a nice technique for valuing American rainbow options via simulation.

Commodity prices really don't behave as the Black–Scholes assumptions would suggest, and we now have some very nice alternative models that can be used to simulate future prices, assuming things like stochastic convenience yields. Schwartz (1997) provided an excellent survey of

---

[10] A couple of issues make this a particularly thorny problem. First, electricity prices are not at all lognormal, so the standard Black-Scholes assumptions won't be appropriate. Second, the volatility of power prices is much higher in August than in June, so it is *not* optimal for the utility to exercise every time the market price of power exceeds the fixed fee. Rather, the utility maximizes the value of its options by treating the early-summer dates as if the strike price (fixed fee) were very high, then gradually reduces this trigger point as the summer passes.

three alternative models and used observed futures market prices for several commodities to estimate the parameters in each model. If you understand how to implement the standard lognormal model and price derivatives in a simulation, you should have little trouble using these more complex models.

You may at some point find yourself in a situation where you want to run a simulation that draws its trials from observed past data. Why? Well, there are some assets in the world whose price processes can't be described by existing formulations,[11] and so the past may be the best model you have. The problem with this approach is that if you want to simulate by drawing trials from past observed prices, then calculate the payoff on an option (financial or real) based on that draw, you have to find some way to handle risk. The only real way out is to somehow find the risk-neutral counterpart to your historically observed distribution, and Stutzer (1996) proffered a very intriguing approach (called *canonical valuation*), which borrows a technique from the physical sciences known as the *maximum entropy principle* to transform the observed historical distribution into its risk-neutral sibling.

16.4 A Few Final Words

Broadly speaking, the field of microeconomics is all about trade-offs. The paradigm that microeconomists have developed is a worldview that serves to simplify things, through a carefully chosen set of abstractions, so that we can arrive at some useful understanding about how people (or groups) make decisions that involve sacrificing one thing for another. These abstractions (which economists call models) often lead to technical equations and mathematical formulae (e.g., the Slutsky equation, the envelope theorem, etc.). Unfortunately, many students miss the boat by focusing on rote memorization and slavish application of the equations/formulae. The power (and beauty) of microeconomics is that it provides a disciplined way to think about the world—a way to disregard things that are unimportant and concentrate on things that are. Once a student learns to think about the world this way, the technical analytics serve to summarize what has been learned and to communicate it to others.

Finance is a subdiscipline of microeconomics that studies one particular trade-off: The exchange of money today for risky money in the future. The future is an incredibly difficult thing to talk about or even to comprehend, and the goal of academic research in finance is to provide abstractions (models) that give the decision maker a way of handling the chaos. The field of finance is itself a worldview, and the models we use to simplify the world lead to technical equations and formulae (the DCF formula, the CAPM, the Black-Scholes equation, etc.), which yield seemingly precise results. But just as in microeconomics, many students miss the forest for the trees. The calculations are not ends in themselves but rather are summaries: Once you've thought about the world in a certain way, you can use your conclusions as inputs for a technical model that just tidies things up. The outputs of the equations/formulae are not absolutes, but are only as good as the thinking process that goes into construction of the inputs. The good practitioner is one who understands the worldview and its limitations, and can thus interpret any calculations in a sophisticated and critical way. In terms of activity, finance is something that is done in the head—not on a calculator.

---

[11] One example is peak-time electric power: Because of production and capacity constraints, the price of peak-time electricity in the summer can suddenly spike to extremely high levels.

.   I couldn't possibly begin to provide examples of every possible managerial situation that you might encounter. My hope is that the cases I've presented will act as canonical examples of the important thinking processes. If I've done my job, you should be able to tailor your analysis to the specifics of the problems that you must face while remaining true to first principles. I honestly would like to hear about your successes and failures.

16.5   Bibliography

Black, Fischer, and Myron Scholes, 1973. "The Pricing of Options and Corporate Liabilities," *Journal of Political Economy* 81, 637–659.

Boyle, Phelim P., 1988. "A Lattice Framework for Option Pricing with Two State Variables," *Journal of Financial and Quantitative Analysis* 23, 1–12.

Boyle, Phelim P., Jeremy Evnine, and Stephen Gibbs, 1989. "Numerical Evaluation of Multivariate Contingent Claims," *Review of Financial Studies* 2, 241–250.

Brennan, Michael J., and Eduardo S. Schwartz, 1978. "Finite Difference Methods and Jump Processes Arising in the Pricing of Contingent Claims: A Synthesis," *Journal of Financial and Quantitative Analysis* 13, 461–474.

Chen, Ren-Raw, Tyler Yang, and S. L. Chung, 2002. "Option Pricing in a Multi-Asset, Complete Market Economy," *Journal of Financial and Quantitative Analysis* 37, 117–136.

Clewlow, Les, and Chris Strickland, 1998. *Implementing Derivatives Models,* Wiley, New York.

Cox, John C., Jonathan E. Ingersoll, and Stephen A. Ross, 1979. "Duration and the Measurement of Basis Risk," *Journal of Business* 52, 51–61.

Cox, John C., Jonathan E. Ingersoll, and Stephen A. Ross, 1985. "An Intertemporal General Equilibrium Model of Asset Prices," *Econometrica* 53, 363–384.

Cox, John C., and Mark Rubenstein, 1985. *Options Markets,* Prentice-Hall, Englewood Cliffs, New Jersey.

Cox, John C., and Stephen A. Ross, 1976. "The Valuation of Options for Alternative Stochastic Processes," *Journal of Financial Economics* 3, 145–166.

Cox, John C., Stephen A. Ross, and Mark Rubenstein, 1979. "Options Pricing: A Simplified Approach," *Journal of Financial Economics* 7, 229–263.

Hull, John C., 2003. *Options, Futures and Other Derivatives* (5th edition), Prentice-Hall, Upper Saddle River, New Jersey.

Kamrad, Bardia, and Peter Ritchken, 1991. "Multinomial Approximating Models for Options with k State Variables," *Management Science* 37, 1640–1652.

Longstaff, Francis A., and Eduardo S. Schwartz, 2001. "Valuing American Options by Simulation: A Simple Least-Squares Approach," *Review of Financial Studies* 14, 113–147.

Merton, Robert C., 1973. "Theory of Rational Option Pricing," *Bell Journal of Economics and Management Science,* 4, 141–183.

Moore, William T., 2001. *Real Options and Option-Embedded Securities,* John Wiley & Sons, New York.

Ramaswamy, Krishna, and Daniel B. Nelson, 1990. "Simple Binomial Processes as Diffusion Approximations in Financial Models," *Review of Financial Studies* 3, 393–430.

Raymar, Steven B., and Michael Zwecher, 1997. "Monte Carlo Estimation of American Call Options on the Maximum of Several Stocks," *Journal of Derivatives* 5, 7–23.

Rubenstein, Mark, 1992. "Guiding Force," *From Black-Scholes to Black Holes: New Frontiers in Options,* Risk Magazine Ltd.

Schwartz, Eduardo S., 1997. "The Stochastic Behavior of Commodity Prices: Implications for Valuation and Hedging," *Journal of Finance* 52, 923–973.

Sharpe, William F., 1978. *Investments* (2nd edition), Prentice-Hall, Englewood Cliffs, New Jersey.

Stutzer, Michael, 1996. "A Simple Nonparametric Approach to Derivative Security Valuation," *Journal of Finance* 51, 1633–1652.

Vasicek, Oldrich, 1977. "An Equilibrium Characterization of the Term Structure," *Journal of Financial Economics* 5, 177–188.

INDEX